MERCIA
The Anglo-Saxon
Kingdom of
Central England

To
John Zaluckyj, Stanley and Pauline Coleman,
Helen and Fali Mistry

with much love as always, Sarah

and in loving memory of
Percy & Tristan
who died in 2002

MERCIA

The Anglo-Saxon Kingdom of Central England

by

Sarah Zaluckyj

with a chapter on Offa's Dyke by
Marge Feryok
and other contributions by
John Zaluckyj

Logaston Press

LOGASTON PRESS
Little Logaston, Logaston,
Woonton, Almeley, Herefordshire HR3 6QH

First published by Logaston Press 2001
reprinted in 2002
Copyright © Author(s) of each chapter as stated 2001

ISBN
1 873827 62 8

Set in Times by Logaston Press
and printed in Great Britain by
the Bath Press Group

Contents

Please Note

I have used Dorothy Whitelock's main chronology for the *Anglo-Saxon Chronicle* as shown in her translation in *English Historical Documents c.500-1042*. A variance of several years can exist for the same event in the different versions of the *Chronicle*.

The reader should assume all dates are A.D. dates unless bearing the suffix B.C.

There are often several ways of spelling Anglo-Saxon personal names. For the sake of clarity I have used those spellings used in *A biographical dictionary of Dark Age Britain - England, Scotland & Wales, c.500 - c.1050* by A. Williams, A.P. Smyth & D.P. Kirby, (Seaby, 1991), but the reader should be aware there can be quite significant variations on how a name is spelt depending on the source, ancient or modern.

Sarah Zaluckyj, July 2001

Illustrations

All the photographs used in this book have been provided by Sarah Zaluckyj and remain her copyright, with the exceptions as noted below. In addition, thanks are due to a number of individuals and organizations for some of the illustrations as follows (where not credited in the caption) and with whom copyright remains: Cover figure: Regia Angolorum; Chap.1, Fig.2 & Chap.9 Fig.4: English Heritage; Chap.2, Fig.1 & Chap.4, Fig.2: Phaidon Press for permission to base the map on that in J. Campbell's *The Anglo-Saxons*; Chap.2, Fig.2: Cyril Hart (for whom also thanks to base Chap.8, Fig.2 on his work); Chap.3, Figs.2 & 3 and p.254 (bottom) and p.255 (top right and bottom) : Jane Potts; Chap.3, Fig.4 & Chap.5, Fig.16 & Chapter 6, Figs.15, 16 & Chap.8, Figs.15, 16, 17, 18: Logaston Press; Chap.5, Fig.6: Bruce Coplestone-Crow (and for basing Chap.6, Fig.2 on his work); Chap.5, Fig.19: Dean and Chapter of Lichfield Cathedral; Chap.6, Fig.10: Joe Hillaby; Chap.6, Fig.13 & Chap.9, Figs.9, 10: Ron Shoesmith; Chap.6, Figs.17-19, 21: County Archaeological Service, Worcestershire County Council; Chap.6, Figs.20 & 23: John Chaluk; Chap.6, Fig.37 & Chap.7, Fig.6: photos by Chris Guy, Cathedral Archaeologist, Worcester, reproduced by permission of the Dean and Chapter of Worcester; Chap.7, Fig.3: Martin Biddle, © The Repton Project; Chap.8 Fig.3: The Radnorshire Society and David Allen; Chap.8, Figs.6 & 7: The National Library of Wales, Aberystwyth; Chap.8, Figs: 9, 10, 11, 13, 14 & 23: Marge Feryok; Chap.8, Fig.12: Chris Musson; Chap.9, Fig.2: Alan Vince & Nick Griffiths; Chap.9, Figs.5, 8: English Partnerships; Chap.9, Fig.7: The Royal Archeological Institute and *Archaeological Journal*; Chap.9, Figs.12, 13: The Field Archaeology Unit of the University of Birmingham; Chap.9, Fig.14: Dr. John Cole.

Acknowledgments

I would like to express my deep gratitude to my husband, John, for his unwavering interest and support throughout the writing of this book, especially for his help in the groundwork for chapters 7, 10 and 11. My very warm thanks to my parents, Stanley and Pauline Coleman, and friends for their interest shown throughout this project, and a particular mention to Bob Jenkins of Arrow Books, Kington for his generous loan of books and unstinted help.

I owe a particular debt of gratitude to Andy Johnson and Ron Shoesmith of Logaston Press for their extraordinary patience and help, and also their consistent kindness and consideration. Their commitment to this book has been greatly appreciated.

I am indebted to Jane Potts for her help, not least in taking me to many places in the east midlands and Derbyshire and helping me to photograph various Anglo-Saxon sites.

To John Charuk who very kindly photographed Droitwich and Hanbury, my sincere thanks too.

I have been very fortunate in having the help of several archaeological departments and individuals: Andy Chapman, Senior Project Officer, Northamptonshire Archaeology, Northampton; John Clark, Medieval Curator, Early London History and Collections, Museum of London; Margaret Gelling for comments on early draft of parts of the text; Chris Guy, Cathedral Archaeologist, Worcester; Bob Meeson, Historic Buildings Consultant, of Tamworth; David Wilkinson, Borough Archaeologist, Stafford Borough Council, all of whom read through my drafts on their areas of expertize and corrected my errors and gave invaluable suggestions for improvements. My very sincere thanks are extended to them. Any mistakes and/or misinterpretations that exist are, of course, entirely my responsibility.

I would also like to thank most sincerely the staff of the Worcestershire Archaeological Service, Worcester: Malcolm Atkin, Victoria Buteux, Derek Hurst and Hal Dalwood, and James Dinn, Worcester City Council Archaeology Officer, for their invaluable help in answering several pages of questions. Again any misinterpretation falls squarely at my door. I am very grateful to the Reverend Canon Iain MacKenzie, Worcester Cathedral, and the Dean and Chapter of Worcester for making my visit to the cathedral library such an interesting and rewarding experience and for their subsequent assistance.

I would also like to thank Roger White of the Birmingham Field Archaeological Unit for sending information concerning Wroxeter; and my warm thanks to Judy Stevenson, Collections Officer for Human History of Hereford Museums, for making available Anglo-Saxon finds for me to photograph.

To Dr. Keith Ray, Dr. Rebecca Roseff, Tim Hoverd and Julian Cotton my thanks for their help on my visits to the Herefordshire Archaeological Unit at Leominster, and to Dr. Ray for checking through the section on Offa's Palace.

I am particularly grateful to Rev. John Woods of Much Wenlock for his generosity in allowing me to use his thesis 'Through the Needle's Eye: Cornovian Place-Names in Shropshire'.

I must also thank the Sisters of the Society of the Precious Blood in Peakirk, Lincolnshire for a fascinating visit in May 1999; and Norman Reeves B.A. for a fascinating correspondence concerning Holy Wells, especially that of Saints Cosmas and Damian at Stretford in Herefordshire.

My special thanks are also due to Irene and Steve White of Printex, Kington for their help over the years, and to John Wilson for his help in preparing the index. I am also most grateful to David Swinscoe for his help in tracking down books on Anglo-Saxon history.

To Don Mackreth, Cathedral Archaeologist at Peterborough, sincere thanks for checking my photographs and captions on Peterborough Cathedral and the Monk's Stone and for providing extra information.

I would also like to express my special gratitude to Margaret Bowdler and Peter Holliday, of Kington and Leominster libraries for their help over the last five years in providing a host of books concerning Anglo-Saxon England from a wide variety of sources.

Special thanks to Peter Freeman of Woodbridge for sending Norman Scarfe's article on Iken and St. Botolph—it was much appreciated!

Finally I must thank Percy, Tristan, Benjy, Kay and Jacob for keeping me firmly grounded in reality!

Sarah Zaluckyj, August 2001

I would like to acknowledge first and mainly the help and support of my writing partner Sarah Zaluckyj throughout the creation of this book, and also Bob Jenkins for many useful conversations and loan of many books, especially the long loan of Sir Cyril Fox's *Offa's Dyke*, a book that is not easy to come by. I thank Andy Johnson and Ron Shoesmith for entrusting and guiding me through the writing of my chapter, a process that is new to me.

I deeply appreciate the knowledge and guidance of Margaret Worthington, David Hill and others of the Offa's Dyke Project. It was while participating in their excavation of the Dyke at Chepstow that I began to realize some of the difficulties involved in the study of the monument.

Ian Bapty of the Offa's Dyke Initiative was very helpful for the interest he took and for information he gave me, some of it timely. I am grateful to the other staff at Clwyd-Powys Archaeological Trust as well for allowing me the facilities to study Early Medieval Wales, Offa's Dyke and the many short dykes in Wales. Rebecca Roseff of Herefordshire Archaeology assisted by sending me an archaeological report on the section of Offa's Dyke on Garnon's Hill, Herefordshire. Several other archaeologists from county departments have also contributed key information: Hugh Hannaford of Shropshire County Council on his excavation of Wat's Dyke; Roy Canham, Wiltshire County Archaeologist for some advice about Wan's Dyke; and Jon Hoyle of Gloucestershire County Council for kindly sending me his survey of Offa's Dyke in the lower Wye valley. I am also indebted to all those who sent their work to me which in the end was not used.

I would like to thank Steve Clarke of Monmouth Archaeology for listening to my ideas about Offa's Dyke in the lower Wye valley, as well as three other residents of the lower Wye area: Rosamund Skelton of Ross, Ron Whittle of Walford, and Roz Lowe of Goodrich, all of whom gave me key bits of local knowledge. Others whose contributions were helpful include Roger White for information about King Offa and Wroxeter and Chris Dyer for some advice on parish boundaries, both from the University of Birmingham. Beryl Lewis kindly gave me the use of her unpublished manuscript 'Boundary Landscapes'; Geoff Ridyard allowed me to use the facilities of the library of the Radnorshire Society in Llandrindod Wells as well as copying many articles for me.

Finally I owe a debt of gratitude to my daughter Laura for her patience and support and for putting up with my lack of attention throughout the writing of this chapter.

Marge Feryok, August 2001

A Note on the Written Sources

Mercia is in the unenviable position of having no primary written sources for its history, apart from the brief *Mercian Register* covering the years *c*.902-924. There was no Mercian chronicle and no ecclesiastic to leave a history or a collection of letters as there was for Northumbria and Wessex. There is not even a reference, however indirect, in the extant sources of other kingdoms to a written Mercian chronicle or annals—such a source may never even have existed. Even if Mercia had possessed a written history, it may well have been destroyed when the Danes plundered much of its territory in the late 9th and early 10th centuries. What do exist are the 159 charters issued by Mercian kings, the majority being grants to religious houses in Kent and in the kingdom of the *Hwicce*—a territory which equates with Worcestershire, Gloucestershire and the south-western part of Warwickshire—a province of Mercia with its own sub-kings and these seem to have been written 'by local ecclesiastics rather than by Mercians'.[1] Yet even here caution has to be exercised—some charters are forgeries made by the unscrupulous in later years when trying to lay claim to certain lands, and even those that do remain are likely to be but a fraction of the original complement and so give a biased view of charter activity. The surviving authentic charters were written by members of the Church, the most literate sector of society, who also composed the *Lives* of various saints.

The early laws, which include those of the Kentish king, Aethelberht, and the West Saxon king, Ine, provide insights into secular society, but their main concern was with the rate of *wergild* (literally the 'man-price' or 'payment'—compensation paid by a lawbreaker and/or his kin to that of the victim) for each strata of society. It is necessary to be wary of viewing Mercian society through the patchy accounts of the aristocracy, the judiciary and the Church. Whereas the voices of the wealthiest and most influential in society are heard in the earliest documents (and there is little doubt that along with the Anglo-Saxon nobility, the Church by the late 7th century was very wealthy and very powerful, being virtually hand-in-glove with royalty), for the majority of the people there is silence.

One of the reasons why there may be no early 'History of Mercia' is in the number of small tribal groups from which the kingdom was formed. With no overall dominant unit or dynasty in the late 5th and early 6th centuries, it is not surprising that there was no feeling of a shared identity and, consequently, little, if any, reason to write down a general record of events.[2] Regrettably, there are also no surviving records from the tribal groups that eventually made up Mercia.

Of the more 'general' sources, the most reliable for early Anglo-Saxon history is Bede's best-known work *A History of the English Church and People* which he completed in 731. Bede was a monk and eventually a priest and scholar at the monastic community of Jarrow which lay in the Northumbrian kingdom. Bede's work, apart from being the main source for the history of the English conversion to Christianity, also contains general information and, as such, is invaluable to the historian. He had scant sources for the 5th century, comprising mainly of Gildas (see below) and Constantius of Lyon. The latter mentioned Britain in his *Life* of St. Germanus of Auxerre who visited the island in the first half of the 5th century. Constantius was writing in southern or central Gaul in 480-90 and, as the *Life* is a hagiography, its aim was 'to promote [the] spiritual edification and moral improvement' of his readers (an observation which can also be made of Gildas' work)—and not accurate historical fact.[3] The closer Bede comes to his own period the more records, even personal memories, he can call upon. It is within this work that Mercia has its first written reference under the year 627 when mention is made of Coenburg, 'daughter of Cearl, King of the Mercians'.[4] The indifference of the entry is not surprising as, during most of the 7th century, Northumbria and Mercia had been fighting one another bitterly for domination over southern Britain. As Bede was a Northumbrian, his cool treatment of the Mercians is understandable and demonstrates that he was not necessarily an impartial observer. For instance, when preparing the history, he gained direct contact with the religious houses of each kingdom, with the notable exception of Mercia. Indeed, his main source for information of the rival kingdom was the Deiran monastery of Lastingham, which had supplied an early

Mercian bishop, St. Chad, and also various communities in Lindsey. Deira was in Northumbria, and Lindsey had passed into permanent Mercian control after the battle of the Trent in 679 and, therefore, would have had a Mercian identity for only about 50 years when Bede finished his manuscript in 731.

Where some facts did not appeal to Bede's Northumbrian sensibilities he became reticent, a typical example being his lack of definition concerning the extent of Mercia's control over southern England in the late 7th century. And yet, for all this, Bede is still widely respected as being the most conscientious and accurate historian of his time. His native sympathies might colour his views, and although he may remain silent, or at least understate, certain events favourable to Mercia, he never resorted to the sort of fevered tirade which the 6th century historian Gildas used against the Britons in his *On the Ruin of Britain*.

Gildas was an ecclesiastic writing in the mid-6th century, probably in south Wales, although it has been suggested he may have lived at the monastery at Bangor-on-Dee (Bangor-is-y-Coed),[5] 5 miles south-east of Wrexham. Gildas' main concern was to rail at the then present-day society and to show them the error of their apparently slovenly and ungodly ways by criticizing their leaders and warn them, by Old Testament example, of what might befall them if they carried on regardless. He believed the Romans were a noble and civilizing force among the Britons and saw their departure as a terrible blow which was partly a result of the ingratitude of the British who had had their hand in several usurpations of western emperors in the late Roman period. In his eyes the Britons had brought about the 'invasion' of the Anglo-Saxons whom Gildas regarded with a contempt that descends into undiluted loathing. He refers to them in bestial terms, as predators upon the Britons who, by their own doing, had become weak and decadent. In Gildas' view the Britons had reaped what they had sown. With this type of prejudice, his use as an historian is understandably more limited. Generally, when he recounts events, they are used to make a moralistic point in favour of his argument. But there is a genuine passion to his work as if he genuinely regrets the fall from grace of the Britons. Gildas' worth is also in that he was closest to the events that brought about the first Anglo-Saxon settlement and is eye-witness to some of the history of the 6th century. For example, it has been argued by Berresford Ellis that on the subject of the migration of the British Celts in the face of Anglo-Saxon aggression, Gildas' account should not be discounted.[6]

There also exists a collection of historical documents which is commonly called after Nennius, the person whom it is believed collected them. It was Nennius' intention to put together pieces of information dealing with British history which had been written by others, and in Wade-Evans' view was 'impelled to do [so] by what seemed to him the stupidity of his countrymen, who neglected such memoranda'.[7] Nennius did not try to work a coherent history from these different documents but on his own admission 'made a heap of all I found'. Apart from collating them into what he believed to be their historical order,[8] Nennius did not, it appears, intervene any further, and it might be argued there is no guiding principle to the work. However, as the collection is deemed to have been written down in about 800 and Nennius was an established writer by 820, his work is an extremely important source of history for the sub-Roman and early Anglo-Saxon period. As the last mentioned person is Offa of Mercia's son, Ecgfrith, who reigned from July 796 until his death in December of that year, Wade-Evans contends that this was the year when Nennius finished his work and its first appearance may be limited to between 796-801. It is possible that the book was reissued in 830 and certainly later editions followed as it became a popular work; inevitably though there were various changes by different hands.[9]

As well as giving an outline of the history of Britain from the earliest times, Nennius' work gives a particular emphasis on the Anglo-Saxon 'take-over' and wars with the British. There is a section on Arthur which lists his 12 victorious battles, as well as an account of St. Patrick and Anglian genealogies. Nennius also lists the 28 cities in the British language 'which are in the whole of Britain' and describes the Marvels of Britain which range from Loch Lomond, the river Trent, the salt springs at Droitwich, and an apple-bearing ash tree by the river Wye, together with various marvels in the Gower, Gwent, Builth, Archenfield and Cardiganshire. As each document is independent of each other, Morris argues that each should be considered separately. Although some are considered little more than 'fanciful legend', Morris postulates that there are two which are of great importance for the history of the 5th century: a *Kentish Chronicle* covering events between 425-60, and the work of a chronographer who sought 'to find exact dates for early fifth-century British events'. Both, he deems, to have been first written down 'not much later than the sixth century'.[10]

Another source of information, the *Anglo-Saxon Chronicle*, has problems of reliability. The *Chronicle* itself is not one continuous annal but up to the early 890s is a compilation of mainly yearly records brought together by King Alfred of Wessex. This archetype was copied and sent out to various monasteries around the country and supplemented thereafter by 'new bulletins from Wessex'[11] which are referred to as the 'Wessex continuations'. The *Chronicle* was continued at various monasteries, sometimes with different and independent information additional to that supplied from Wessex. There are seven surviving manuscript copies: five principal versions, commonly given letters 'A' to 'E', and two fragments. Of the former, Chronicle 'A', known as the *Parker Chronicle* after Archbishop Parker (1504-75) who owned the manuscript and then left it to Corpus Christi College, Cambridge, is the oldest surviving manuscript with all the entries up to 891 written in one hand of the late 9th or very early 10th century.[12] The *Parker Chronicle* originally belonged to the Old Minster (St. Swithin's) at Winchester. Manuscripts 'B' and 'C' are called The *Abingdon Chronicles* and both are 11th century copies of an exemplar held at Abingdon, which Garmonsway considers was 'ultimately derived from another copy of the original Alfredian chronicle to 891'.[13] Manuscript 'D' was copied in about 1050 from a lost original and was continued up to 1079 somewhere in the western midlands, probably at Worcester. The original from which 'D' was copied was a north country chronicle and Garmonsway suggests it was probably compiled at Ripon.[14] 'D's knowledge of 11th century events in the diocese of Worcester has led to it often being being described as the *Worcester Chronicle* but Whitelock doubts whether that version left the north before the end of the 11th century.[15] As the sees of York and Worcester were held together in plurality between 972 and 1016, knowledge of affairs in each see would have been known to the other. Garmonsway states that Florence of Worcester was indebted to 'a West Midland version of the *Chronicle* which resembled D, the Worcester Chronicle'[16] in the writing of his own work. Chronicle 'E' known as the *Laud Chronicle* after Archbishop Laud (1573-1645) but also known as the *Peterborough Chronicle*, is now in the Bodleian Library and was copied at Peterborough between 1121-1154 from a chronicle borrowed from St. Augustine's at Canterbury. The first scribe copied it out up to 1121 and added versions of what Garmonsway regards as spurious charters, as well as brief notes of local events and Latin passages concerning religious or foreign affairs. After 1023 'E' develops its own originality and the shift of its focus moves from the north to the south. Henry of Huntingdon appears to have used 'C' and 'E' chronicles in his work.[17] When dealing with areas further afield than Wessex, Sussex and Kent (remembering that up to the 890s it was a West Saxon compilation), the *Anglo-Saxon Chronicle*'s political motivation is suspect.

Further early sources may be inferred in the post-Conquest chronicles of Henry of Huntingdon, Roger of Wendover and Matthew Paris, the first of whom wrote in the first half of the 12th century and the latter two in the first half of the 13th century.[18] These medieval chroniclers apparently had access to early annals, now lost, and incorporated them into their own histories. However, the Anglo-Saxons were illiterate until at least the late 6th century when the introduction of Christianity and its associated learning into pagan England meant a select few were able to record events in writing. Davies states that it is 'conventionally supposed' that any English annals detailing the 5th and 6th centuries cannot have come from a contemporary written record, but must have been written at a later date from stories handed down by word of mouth, with all the inevitable inaccuracies, but considers that 'it is by no means impossible that some of the earliest English annals were originally recorded by British sources ...'.[19]

Davies has proposed that although these medieval chronicles are not interdependent, in part they all draw upon a common but lost source for the 6th century and that, since the source's interest is midland and eastern England, it is likely that it originated from a mid- or East Anglian archive which was not available to the West Saxon compilers of the *Anglo-Saxon Chronicle* in the 9th century as East Anglia was then under Danish control. It appears that these medieval chroniclers were dependent neither upon each other nor on the *Anglo-Saxon Chronicle* for all of their early material but were utlizing a collection of annals of mid-9th century or earlier date which are now lost.[20] However, Brooks cautions that 'it cannot be said that it is yet clear that what lies behind these scattered entries ... is anything more important than some inventive conjectures by an English monk, perhaps as late as the early twelfth century, on the basis of the names available in Bede, the Mercian royal genealogy and the Anglo-Saxon Chronicle'.[21] And yet some fragments of annals which tell of the foundation of the Mercian kingdom which are used by the medieval chroniclers do appear to have been of East Anglian origin, although Brooks notes that 'the date of their composition remains to be determined'.[22]

Of the medieval chronicles used in this book, Florence of Worcester's is the earliest post-Conquest source. He was a member of the monastic community of St. Mary's at Worcester during the episcopate of Bishop Samson (1096-1112). A contemporary at this community, John of Worcester, is believed, however, to be responsible for the 'production of the chronicle in its receieved form', although Florence was probably responsible for gathering the earlier material, especially that relating to the 9th, 10th and 11th centuries. Bishop Wulfstan (II) of Worcester, whose episcopate ran from 1062-95, had already set one monk, Hemming, to work 'on the muniments of the church' and he may well have employed another to work on a wider history, possibly Florence. If so, Florence would have been a bridge between the Anglo-Saxon and Norman eras. On 7 July 1118 John of Worcester records: '... Florence (Florentius) of Worcester died, through whose acute understanding and through the industry of whose assiduous labour this Chronicle of Chronicles pervails over all others'.[23] The edition used in this book is *The Chronicle of Florence of Worcester - with the two continuations*, translated by Thomas Forester in 1854, and reprinted by AMS Press in 1968.

William of Malmesbury's *Chronicle of the Kings of England*, also known as the *Gesta regum Anglorum* was completed in its first form in 1125/6 and revised at least twice between 1135 and 1143. William was born in the late 11th century and died in about 1143 and is described as 'one of the most distinguished English historians'.[24] Of Anglo-Norman parentage, he was brought up as a child oblate at Malmesbury Abbey where he later became librarian. It appears he travelled widely around England and used a variety of sources, ranging from monastic archives, local historical tradition, monuments and anecdotal sources, as well as memories, from community to individual level. His other works include the *Deeds of the Bishops of the English* (*Gesta pontificum Anglorum*); a *Life* of St. Dunstan, the famous 10th-century monastic reformer; a *Life* of St. Wulfstan (Wulfstan II, bishop of Worcester) adapted from a lost *Life* by a local monk called Coleman) and an account of the origin of Glastonbury Abbey, *De Antiquitate Glastoniensis Ecclesiae*.[25] The edition of William of Malmesbury's *Chronicle of the Kings of England* used in this book is that translated by J.A. Giles in 1847 and reprinted by AMS Press in 1968.

Henry of Huntingdon was also of Anglo-Norman parentage. His father was a Norman clerk to whose position of archdeacon of Huntingdon Henry succeeded in 1110.[26] Henry lived between about 1088 and 1155 and wrote his chronicle between 1129 and 1154 'in a number of volumes and editions which he constantly expanded and revised'.[27] He used Bede's work and the *Anglo-Saxon Chronicle* as models for his work. In the 12th and 13th centuries his chronicle was very popular and widely used by other historians, partly no doubt because of his 'good stories and dramatic accounts of fighting' but it is conceded that Henry was 'scrupulous in his work, ranging widely for his sources, and copying documents into his text'.[28] It was Henry who first thought up the idea of the Heptarchy—the seven Anglo-Saxon kingdoms. The edition used in this text is *The Chronicle of Henry of Huntingdon* with the addition of the *The Acts of Stephen* translated and edited by Thomas Forester in 1853, and reprinted in 1968 by AMS Press.

The Flowers of History or the *Flores Historium* was allegedly written by one Matthew of Westminster but the latter was an imaginary name given to a chronicle originally written in about the early 14th century at Merton but which was apparently added to and collated by various authors at the monasteries of St. Alban's and Westminster.[29] The edition used in this book is that translated by C.D. Yonge in 1853 and reprinted by AMS Press in 1968. For ease of reference the tag 'Matthew of Westminster' is used but with the undertsanding this chronicle is a composite work.

CHAPTER 1
Roman Departure and Anglo-Saxon Arrival

What is commonly called the 'Dark Ages' is a period in Britain which runs from the end of Roman rule to around the end of the 7th century. In relation to all other historical periods it is a period that is lacking in contemporary written sources, but it is 'dark' too in the imagined sense of lawlessness which pervades this post-Roman era when an imperial rule had gone and the old society turned in on itself and crumbled. In the intervening period that led up to the Norman Conquest of 1066, the identity that was forged—'Englishness'—was derived chiefly from the Angles and Saxons who migrated primarily from what is now southern Denmark and Germany. The very name 'England' is derived from 'Angle-land'. The native Britons, themselves the result of prehistoric migrations, were either assimilated into the new culture or were gradually confined to the more inhospitable upland areas of Wales, Cornwall and Cumbria, or migrated to other parts of Europe, notably Brittany.

Our most commonplace features—our place-names, the shire system, parishes, indeed much of our eventual language—were all set down between the 5th and 11th centuries. Why is it that so much of the Anglo-Saxon period remains in our everyday lives when so little of the Roman era survives? It is a question which becomes even more poignant when one realizes that for nearly 400 years England was Romanized and, with the exception of a few early episodes of resistance, there were no revolutionary uprisings to rid the country of the government. Roman rule was gradually accepted, but within 30 years or so of Rome's break with Britain, the first Anglo-Saxon settlements appeared. During this time the collapse of Roman life had been swift and total; the Anglo-Saxon incomers did not find a Romanized culture to assimilate or destroy, there was simply little or nothing left.

Dr. Esmonde Cleary has suggested that the seeds of this collapse should be sought not just in the fall of the western part of the Roman empire and the rise of barbarian successor states, but also in the removal of the economy which was peculiar to late Roman Britain. The economy had sustained what was Roman about Britain—the 'buildings, goods, coins, clothes, languages, laws, religions, [and] cultural values used and shared by the people'.[1] The towns and countryside villas, the taxation system and state-directed industries were all linked to the state-generated supply and demand system which was the hub of Roman life. None of these things had existed prior to 'Roman Britain' when life had been rural and largely self-sufficient, although there had been some trading networks extending to the Continent.

It was towns above all else that distinguished Roman Britain from its predecessor and in part from its early and middle Anglo-Saxon successor, and Roman towns essentially came in two sizes—small and large, although with some overlap between the two. Small towns were those that developed along main roads and at road junctions or other nodes of communication (rather like medieval towns) and as a consequence lacked any formal planning, possessing neither the large or prestigious public buildings nor the street grids of the large towns. They were somewhat similar to later villages with their local, market-based economy, and lay within a territory controlled by a larger town. At best they had very limited administrative functions. Buildings were often built on long narrow plots, with artisan-style goods manufactured at the rear of the plot and sold from the street frontage. Living quarters lay above the commercial premises. Small towns also had few, if any, large houses used simply for domestic purposes.[2]

The large towns were constructed on a Mediterranean-derived plan and had a street grid, a forum/basilica complex (the commercial and often religious heart of the town), a water supply and public baths, and often an amphitheatre, and functioned as an administrative centre for the area. They were also centres of distribution of finished goods imported from the Continent or those manufactured in the town or its hinterland. From the mid-2nd century there was also an increasing number of landowners who lived in these large towns for at least part of the year, in houses set in spacious grounds which became 'an increasingly important component of the late [Roman] urban landscape'.[3] By the 4th century these town houses were numerous and a major part of such large settlements. However, by the 4th century archaeological evidence indicates that the more extravagant displays of wealth were largely to be found in the countryside villas rather than in the town houses. Esmonde Cleary suggests that a 'picture of a country-based aristocracy, resident on occasion in the towns, may ... be appropriate for fourth-century Britain' as it appears to have been in contemporary Gaul.[4]

Large towns were places where the rural population (which comprised about 90% of the whole) could bring their goods to sell and thereby pay their taxes, for, with an end to expansion, the Roman empire needed to raise money from inside its boundaries to finance the army, administration and, as it transpired, the landowners (see below). Indeed, the most important role of the town was its function in converting agricultural surplus into coin and in acting as a centre where the state gathered the vast supplies needed to feed its own employees, notably the army and the administrators—including those of the tax system itself. It was imperative to raise their equivalent incomes in coin and kind from the productive population and this was imposed as a priority. Therefore the State's needs and expenditure and associated taxation dominated the economy, with the need to obtain coin stimulating trade and explaining why towns in their marketing role were crucial in preserving all that was Roman.[5]

In the 3rd century the Roman empire underwent a crisis. Between 235 and 285 there were some 20 recognized emperors, along with many usurpers and individuals who ruled over part of the empire.[6] The empire became unstable and fragmentary and the security of her borders became imperilled. Around the 250s and 260s there came a succession of invasions by barbarian forces, of greatest impact to Britain being the destruction of northern Gaul for this area had previously supplied the armies of the Rhine, supplies which afterwards had to be sought from Britain,[7] so tying her economy more tightly into that of the empire.

The Roman military system began to disintegrate. The empire's defensive strategy, developed from the late 1st and 2nd centuries, had geared itself to one major military operation in one place at any one time and was not suited to facing simultaneous threats on different fronts. In the 4th century the empire found a new form of stable government in dynastic succession under the line founded by the emperor Constantine. Even when this dynasty died out with the death of the emperor Julian (360-3), the last male heir, a smooth transfer of power took place to the linked dynasties of the Houses of Valentinian and Theodosius.[8]

Morris observes that the 3rd century crisis also led to a change in the army, forcing the empire to keep large mobile reserves. These cost more to supply than the former more static army which had been spread thinly along the empire's frontiers and could be supplied locally. The new government had to levy taxes on the landowners, but they were reluctant to pay and a bureaucratic machine had to be created to extract the revenue, and this turned out to be costly, corrupt and inefficient. The powerful land magnates in turn leant on the rural population and passed the burden of taxation downwards. From the beginning of the 4th century countryside villas make a sudden appearance in Britain and Morris suggests that their proliferation was a symptom of a general trend in the concentration of wealth into the hands of fewer and increasingly more powerful magnates 'at the expense of the poor and middling freeholders'.[9] It is estimated that between 25% and 33% of gross yields might have been levied in tax, but for peasants also paying rent it would have meant that 'half or more of their produce might have been forfeit'.[10] This was not unique to Britain. Indeed, in many of the empire's provinces up to five-sixths of the peasant's produce was taken, which led to severe hardship, even starvation and dwindling populations as those affected could not afford to raise children. The archaeological record suggests that their British counterparts fared a little better—in some farmsteads 4th-century window-glass and doorkeys have been recovered indicating that there was something worth stealing inside, and several other sites provide evidence that some of this class lived way above mere subsistence level. One explanation may be that the increased wealth of 4th-century lowland Britain, now supplying some of the food requirements of the armies on the Rhine, may have compensated for increases in rent and tax. In Britain most of those who actually owned countryside villas and estates appear to have lived in them, unlike their Continental counterparts, suggesting that in Britain property was less concentrated in the hands of the few than in Continental Europe where there were many cases of absentee landlords.[11] If a landowner was resident he would be far more motivated into making his estates productive. Yet even in Britain it is undeniably true that the peasantry were forced to produce significantly more than for their historic self-sufficiency, whilst still living in farmsteads that were not appreciably Roman in character.

By the late 4th century there were changes in town-life, with evidence for a lack of enthusiasm to build any new public works. Archaeological excavation has shown that in some large towns, such as Wroxeter in Shropshire and Silchester in Hampshire, the forum/basilica complexes—the heart of Roman civic pride and status—were being used for industrial purposes in the 3rd and 4th centuries. In other towns, such as Caerwent, there is no evidence for change of use of the basilica before the end of the Roman period, whereas at Leicester, Gloucester and Cirencester the forum/basilica complexes appear to have stayed in use throughout the 4th century. The overall impression, however, is that the aristocratic classes preferred to spend their money on their own private town houses or countryside villas. Civic pride had given way to personal glorification, in line with other areas of the Roman empire.[12] When a society turns away from a community orientation and becomes inward-looking and individualistic it is often on a gradient of decline. However, the construction of defensive works in the aftermath of the barbarian revolution of 367 (see below) showed there was still sufficient co-ordination for communal building when a major threat was posed.

It is possible that, as Britain was Rome's furthermost province and was only marginally affected by the 3rd-century crises on the Continent, its defences had not been adapted in the same way, which stood it in poor stead for the troubles of the early 5th century. The increasing threat of raiding and piracy from the peoples of the North Sea littoral who were outside the Roman empire had occasioned the building of the Saxon Shore forts from the early 3rd century,[13] which ran from Brancaster on the north Norfolk coast to Porchester on the Hampshire coast near Portsmouth harbour.

However, the barbarian conspiracy of 367 shook Britain into some sort of defensive response that led to the increase in town defences. The Picts—'the painted men' from north of the Forth and the Clyde in Scotland, the Attacotti from the Western Isles, whose ferocity was well known to the Romans, the Scotti from Ireland and the Franks and Saxons from the Low Countries, combined forces and led an attack on Britain and the coastal regions of northern Gaul. Britain was in chaos with bands of raiders moving around the countryside unchecked. Deserters from the Roman army joined these gangs. Fortunately for Britain this confederation was not firmly bound together and whatever central control that might have existed soon evaporated as the raiders enjoyed their pickings. To restore order, Rome sent over four first-rate units from their field army under the able command of Count Theodosius. Peace was restored and the country rid of barbarian bands. Theodosius also shrewdly recalled the deserters back to the Roman army, in effect giving them a pardon.[14] He then directed a period of reconstruction which took two years to complete.

Even before the barbarian conspiracy there had been two failed attempts by army commanders stationed in Britain and Gaul to seize control from the western emperors, the first in 286-96, the second in 350-353 by Magnentius, who was of probable British birth. A third occurred between 383-88, and in 406 troops in Britain once more proclaimed their own emperor, Marcus, in defiance to Rome, which, in effect, meant that the country was in revolt. When the Emperor of the West, Honorius, said that he could supply no more troops to aid Britain in 410, Britain had to make do with what forces were left in the country, a further British emperor-in-revolt, Constantine III, having taken a large part of the British-based forces to Gaul to fight barbarian raiders who had launched a massive raid from north of the Rhine. Indeed, for decades Roman troops had been drained away from Britain to cope with barbarian threats on the Continent, and Britain now lay open to raids which escalated in frequency and ferocity.

Factual details are hard to come by. A reference in the Gallic Chronicle of 452 to the devastation of Britain by the Saxons in 410 or 411 may be suspicious as the Chronicle is not recording events at first-hand and may be extrapolating actions that happened later back into the early part of the 5th century.[15] The Chronicle may be more reliable in its statement that Britain fell under Saxon control in 441 as it is much closer to the date of writing of 452; yet it was composed in relatively distant Provence which begs the question of how much the chronicler would have known about events in Britain for the information to be wholly accurate.[16]

Bede's narrative of the early 5th century is very sketchy and his sources unreliable, yet he does add several pieces of valuable information: he dates the invitation of the Germanic mercenaries to Britain to about 449 and, most importantly, provides information on the origins of the eventual invaders:

> These new-comers were from the three most formidable races of Germany, the Saxons, Angles, and Jutes. From the Jutes are descended the people of Kent and the Isle of Wight and those in the province of the West Saxons opposite the the Isle of Wight who are called Jutes to this day. From the Saxons - that is, the country now known as the land of the Old Saxons - came the East, South and West Saxons. And from the Angles - that is, the country known as Angulus, which lies between the provinces of the Jutes and Saxons and is said to remain unpopulated to this day - are descended the East and Middle Angles, the Mercians, all the Northumbrian stock (that is, those peoples living north of the river Humber), and the other English peoples.[17]

The Angles' homeland centred around Schleswig-Holstein in northern Germany. Today there is still a rural area north of Schleswig called Angeln which runs approximately south-eastwards from the harbour town of Flensburg close to the Danish border to north of Kappeln, a small coastal town facing eastwards onto the Baltic sea. Deteriorating climatic changes and rises in sea levels may have had a profound effect on agricultural production, so triggering emigration to Britain in the early 5th century, for in 731 this area, which Bede calls 'Angulus', was described as being unpopulated.

However inaccurate or thin the information given by historical sources at this time, an outline of events and figures emerge from the gloom. One of the latter is Vortigern. Vortigern was not a personal name but a description meaning 'overking' or 'overlord'—Morris suggests he may have been an emperor and that his real name was Vitalinus.[18] He probably had political authority over an extensive part of the British Isles, especially the southern half, in the immediate post-Roman period, between *c*.425 to *c*.455.

It is likely Vortigern came from the landed aristocracy of late Roman society and genealogists identify him as a 'notable of Gloucester' from an area which was rich in countryside villas.[19] In the centuries after Roman rule ceased in Britain, Kate Pretty suggests that the British population may have been relatively stable and gave their allegiance to the old ruling hereditary families whose status had been recognized but which had been veiled during the Roman occupation.[20] As the Roman way of life disintegrated after the 430s these families may have produced leaders or kings within their own tribal territories. It is possible that Vortigern was descended from such a native ruling family and traditionally he is said to have married Magnus Maximus' daughter, Severa, although this claim should be treated with caution.[21] Magnus is synonymous with Maxen (or Macsen) Wledig of Welsh fame whose wife was Elen, allegedly the finder of the True Cross. He is remembered in medieval Welsh tradition as the ancestor of a number of princely British dynasties.[22] (see also p.121).

 Vortigern appears to have been a very able leader and retained his authority for over a generation. The naming of two of his three sons with native British names—Vortimer and Categirn—suggests he wanted to appeal to British sympathies.[23] The Pillar of Eliseg in the Vale of Llangollen remembers 'Britu son of Vortigern, whom Germanus blessed, and whom Sevira bore to him, daughter of Maximus the king, who killed the king of the Romans'.[24] This pillar, once a tall cross, was set up by Cyngen ap Cadell, king of Powys, who died in Rome in 854, and shows that British dynasties, such as the kings of Powys and of Gwrtheyrnion (approximating to Radnorshire) were not afraid to claim descent from Vortigern.[25] This near hero status contrasts with the vilification Vortigern receives in the accounts of Gildas and Nennius (see below) and indicates there were other accounts, now lost, upon which the unstated eulogy of the Pillar of Eliseg were based.[26]

When the incursions from the Picts and Scots became too severe to withstand, Vortigern made a decision which was to radically change the course of British history: he invited mercenaries from north-western Europe to settle in eastern England to help defend the country against raiders. Gildas wrote scathingly of Vortigern's decision, but this is ironic for the Romans, whom Gildas so admired, had been using barbarian 'mercenaries' since the 2nd century! In the early Roman empire this system operated in the form of client rulers governing areas held by the Romans, but in the later years, as the pressures of barbarian tribes on the frontier increased, they allowed selected groups of such peoples to settle in their frontier territories as long as they acted as defenders and stopped other barbarians invading Roman lands. Significantly, Bede states that the British 'all agreed with the advice of their king, Vortigern, to call on the assistance of the Saxon peoples across the sea' in order to 'avoid or repel the frequent fierce attacks of their northern neighbours'.[27] He further adds that the Germanic mercenaries sent word back to their homeland that the 'country was fertile and the Britons cowardly', inspiring others to come over.[28] As their numbers grew, so the balance of power shifted.

Nennius records that 'Hengist [their leader], inasmuch as he was a shrewd man and crafty and cunning, when he had found that he had to do with an indolent king and his people, who were wont to live without arms, took counsel and said to the British king, "A few we are; if thou art willing, we will send to our country and invite soldiers from the soldiers of our region, that there may be a larger number to fight on thy behalf and on behalf of thy people."'[29] Nennius indicates that Vortigern agreed with Hengist, ambassadors were despatched 'And they returned with sixteen keels, and picked soldiers came in them ...'.[30] Morris' translation renders this number as 19 keels and he rates the new forces in the thousands rather than the hundreds.[31] Vortigern's move essentially led to civil war between himself and the Saxons on one side, and the British who now wished to see the Saxons expelled on the other.

Nennius reports Vortigern as being beset 'with fear of the Picts and Scots, and by Roman aggression, and also by dread of Ambrosius'.[32] Morris suggests that, considering the time span involved in which a leader named Ambrosius is mentioned, there were two players by that name, the one the father of Ambrosius Aurelianus who was the resistance leader of the British in the 460s.[33] The older Ambrosius may, therefore, have been a rival emperor to Vortigern once civil war had broken out; in 437 there is a record in Nennius that Ambrosius fought with one Vitalinus (Vortigern's possible personal name) at *Guoloph*, identified with Wallop in Hampshire.[34]

Vortigern became ever more dependent upon the Saxons. Tradition has it that he had already married Hengist's daughter and, as a marriage gift, the district of Kent was ceded to Hengist and his men. Nennius suggests that Hengist continued to invite more of his race to Kent, especially Canterbury.[35] Whereas the earliest Saxon pottery has been found at Canterbury and reinforces the idea that Germanic people were occupying the town at a very early date, Hengist's mercenaries were not the first settlers of Germanic origin in Britain. Other archaeological finds have shown that in the coastal areas of Lincolnshire and Yorkshire there were already settlements of Angles and Saxons, and at Abingdon, south of Oxford, and Dunstable, 5 miles west of Luton in Bedfordshire, there is archaeological evidence of small merchant communities, as well as Anglian settlement in what was to become East Anglia.[36]

With the benefit of hindsight, Hengist's eventual putsch seems inevitable. Gildas writes:

> For the fire of just vengeance on account of preceding crimes [Gildas saw this uprising as retribution on the British for their lax and immoral ways] blazed from sea to sea, heaped up by the eastern band of sacrilegists, and, devastating all the nearest cities and lands, ceased not, being kindled until, consuming almost the whole surface of the island, it licked the western ocean with its red and savage tongue ... So that all the *coloniae* [here meaning all inhabited centres] by frequent strokes of battering rams and all the *coloni* [inhabitants] along with bishops of the church, with priests and people, swords on every side gleaming and flames crackling, were together mown to the ground, and, lamentable to behold, in the midst of streets were seen the bottom stones of towers erased with lofty door and of high walls, sacred altars, fragments of bodies covered with clots as if congealing of purple-coloured blood, mixed as in a sort of fearful winepress, and burial of any kind there was none except the ruins of houses. The bellies of beasts and birds, in the open ...[37]

Bede, very likely following Gildas' account, gives a similar picture.[38] John Morris dates this, the first Saxon revolt to about 442. Berresford Ellis, however, dates it to 450 and states that Hengist did not simply rely on the mercenary soldiers, but gave out a call to the Angles and Saxons already settled in Britain. The centre of the rising appears to have been in the east, where the Saxons and Angles had settled, and where most of the physical damage was wrought. Elsewhere the rising seems to have been largely 'contained at a local level'.[39] It was a revolt that ultimately saw the end of Roman life in Britain as it destroyed the economy upon which the towns and countryside villas depended.[40] Britain did indeed plead for help from Rome in about 446, complaining to the Consul Flavius Aetius, Supreme Commander of the Army of the Western Empire of Rome, that the 'barbarians drive us into the sea, and the sea drives us back to the barbarians. Between these, two deadly alternatives confront us, drowning or slaughter.'[41] But no help came or, indeed, ever came again from Rome.

The attempted putsch united the British factions against a common enemy, and by 452 Vortigern and his son, Vortiper, had taken back Kent, some of the Germanic settlers returning 'home'. Morris suggests that if a strong central government had been instituted at this stage, the previous economy and civilization of Romanized Britain may have been restored. However, the wealthy south and west of Britain seem not to have contributed to Vortigern's victories or to have continued to acknowledge his authority.[42]

It appears that in mid-5th-century Britain, no-one in a sufficient position of power wanted to co-ordinate paying for an army or raising men to expel the Germanic incomers. Instead a peace treaty was suggested by the Saxons. Vortigern and his council agreed to meet with Hengist and his men unarmed, but at the meeting 300 British elders, probably comprising 'most of the great men of the island', were massacred by the Saxons on Hengist's orders.[43] Vortigern was taken prisoner and forced to cede Essex and Sussex to the Saxons, territory which would subsequently be used for further Saxon assault.

In defence of Vortigern, Morris notes that he was faced with a 'leaderless nobility too proud to condone a government that hired Germans, but too tight-fisted to free it from the need, too divided and inept to construct an alternative, [who] drifted to disaster, and stood amazed when catastrophe destroyed them, blaming their own futility upon the will of God.'[44]

In the aftermath of the massacre and the return or arrival of more Germanic peoples, a sizeable number of Britons moved to Gaul and elsewhere on the Continent. Morris notes that it was an emigration of Roman provincials of Britain headed by the upper echelons of Romano-British society and included a fighting force of about 12,000 men. They were given estates north of the Loire by the ruler of northern Gaul, Aegidius, in return for the services of the fighting men which he needed desperately to protect his borders[45]—just when they would have served a similar purpose in Britain. Settlements by the name of Bretteville in Gaul indicate where the Britons settled.[46] Gildas himself migrated from Britain in about 555 and died in Brittany (renamed from Amorica after the number of Britons) in about 570, and is the earliest authority on this migration'.[47]

Whatever the precise details, the Britons would have been in straitened circumstances following the massacre or emigration of sizeable numbers of their people. Those that stayed were, according to Gildas, harried mercilessly by the Anglo-Saxons. Then came a respite, for with 'some time intervening, when the most cruel plunderers had returned home, the remnants, to whom most wretched citizens fled together on every side from divers places, as eagerly as the bees of a hive, a storm threatening. ... [took] up arms, challenging their victors to battle, lest they should be destroyed even unto extermination, Ambrosius Aurelianus being leader, a modest man, who alone by chance of the Roman nation had survived in the collision of so great a storm, his parents, no doubt clad in the purple, having been killed in the same, whose progeny now in our times [mid-6th century] have greatly degenerated from their ancestral excellence, to whom, the Lord assenting, victory fell.'[48]

Ambrosius Aurelianus was at least a military leader, a general (*dux*), of the Britons and it appears his father, probably Ambrosius senior, was an emperor, for 'wearing the purple' denoted a royal position. It appears that it was Ambrosius Aurelianus who began the long war of independence against the Anglo-Saxon raiders but that he died in the conflict, for Nennius ascribes the culminating victory of the British at Badon Hill to a figure called Arthur. It is not the intention of this book to enter into the area of shadowy debate concerning Ambrosius and Arthur. Suffice it to say that Badon Hill (probably one of a couple of contending sites in northern Wiltshire and Somerset) resulted in a peace which lasted for about two generations, the period in which Gildas lived.

So much for the sparse written accounts—what can archaeology tell us? One of the strangest features of the post-Roman, pre-Anglo-Saxon period is that, in terms of artefactual material, it is one of the most impoverished periods in Britain of all time. It might be imagined that after the collapse of Roman rule a material culture similar to that of the Iron Age might re-establish itself, but this was not the case. Roman Britain was by comparison awash with artefacts, but after the break with Rome the artefactual evidence drops to virtually nothing. It could be that enduring materials such as pottery, metal and glass were replaced with perishable media, for instance wood and leather, and the level of skill that can be used on these materials would be unavailable to the archaeological record. What pottery has been found from this period was hand-made and, by comparison to the wares produced on the Roman fast wheel, is crude, indicating that there had been a technological recession, perhaps indicating profound stress in society, both economic and social.[49] Some late Roman belt fixings, such as buckles, buckle plates and strap ends, that have been found used to be interpreted as belonging to a 'class' in the Roman army called the *foederati*. These were groups of barbarians who had joined the empire by way of a treaty (*foedus*) but who retained 'their ethnic identities, methods of fighting and leaders'[50] and were increasingly used in the Roman army during the 4th century. As similar belt fittings were found in Germanic burial grounds elsewhere in the Roman empire, it was erroneously thought that such articles were made as specific issue for Germanic soldiers, and would have indicated the presence of these 'mercenaries' even before Britain was left to fend for herself. However, more recent research has shown that in the late empire the belt was seen as a symbol of office, and 'to put on and take off the belt' were phrases which came to signify joining and leaving the civil service.[51] Such finds may, therefore, indicate no more than the presence of officials.

Archaeological excavation has so far produced no evidence to show that the Romanized landowners of the countryside tried to carry on with the old way of life, unlike their counterparts on the Continent.

As for the Roman towns, some, such as Wroxeter, Canterbury and Lincoln, obligingly provide an extended sequence of habitation into the 6th century, but the majority do not. Even where continuity has been demonstrated in part of the town, excavation often reveals that most of the other buildings were abandoned. At *Viroconium*, Wroxeter, on the western extreme of what was to become Mercia, a large area of excavation has revealed that, after the split with Rome, the baths basilica area was remodelled through three successive phases. At the end of the 5th century the baths basilica and perhaps part of the baths were still in use but in a dilapidated state. The basilica was then closed to the public but a number of small, flimsy structures were built within it, with metal-working apparently taking place in the south-eastern corner. Evidence that a maintenance team used part of the basilica after first using a nearby annexe suggests that attempts were being made to keep the baths in operation. The roof was then taken off the basilica, the internal columns removed and the area once again used by the general public, quite possibly as a local market conducted through barter as the money economy had collapsed by the early 6th century. The indications are that some central authority was still in control of the former public build-ings—but whom? The Anglo-Saxons only penetrated this far west around a century later, so the authority was likely to have been of Romano-British origins. As White and Barker suggest, it may have been 'one of the leading families of the community [who] had seized power and, taking on

Figs.1 & 2 Wroxeter as it today (top) and a reconstruction of the baths basilica site as it may have appeared in the 6th century. The site of the latter is behind the tall wall called the 'Old Work' in the top illustration

the trappings of a military warlord, ruled Wroxeter as his domain'.[52] Perhaps he was one of the *tyranni* to whom Gildas refers. The famous Cunorix stone, which was ploughed up in 1968 in the city's eastern rampart, celebrates Cunorix, a possible later military commander of Irish origins as the Latin text has Irish spelling. The funerary inscription is dated on linguistic grounds to A.D. 460-475, but in whose employ Cunorix was, or if he was acting as an independent ruler is not known.[53]

White and Barker suggest that town dwellers, who would have become used to a level of self-government, would probably not have taken to authoritarian rule under a petty tyrant.[54] Indeed, archaeological and documentary evidence shows that such rulers established their bases in the deserted hill forts like Dinas Emrys in Snowdonia. White and Barker further postulate that Wroxeter may have had a bishop in control. The Roman emperors had established bishoprics in every major town in the 4th century and it is suggested that, once established, the office became self-perpetuating with appointments being made among the bishops themselves. In 5th- and 6th-century Gaul these clerics were very likely chosen from the local aristocracy, and it is possible that in England a bishop ruling a Romano-British town would have come from a similar lineage and now had vested interests in keeping the fabric of the town intact.[55] However Gelling suggests that the absence of Christian symbols or artefacts from Wroxeter 'tells against the bishop and church hypothesis'.[56]

Yet, the possibility of such an entity should be borne in mind when considering the final stage of Wroxeter's baths basilica complex which probably began around 530-570 and lasted about 75 years. This was the most radical phase for it involved the demolition of most of the basilica's shell and its replacement with buildings of which many were of substantial construction. Platforms were built carefully from heaps of demolished material, and the largest appears to have been used for a 'massively-constructed timber-framed building'.[57] Whereas these buildings were constructed using Roman measurements and in a Roman style, they were unlike the timber-framed or masonry buildings of the early Roman city.[58] White and Barker suggest that the *frigidarium* (the room of the former Roman bath house which one entered first and which was probably used for undressing) may have found a new use as a chapel or church as it is orientated east-west and would have been appropriately grand for use as a religious building if the decoration had survived; such a re-use has been observed at Leicester where St. Nicholas' church was built above the unheated room of the public bath house and reused one if its walls which today survives as the Jewry Wall.[59] The bath house pools would have also been useful for baptismal purposes.

The changes to former public space indicates a more inward-looking community. Even the massive timber-framed house faced onto the blank southern wall of the former baths basilica, rather than over a newly made street. This may have been the result of 'the Great Death', probably bubonic plague, that swept Britain in the mid-6th century. Whereas the results at Wroxeter may not have been necessarily catastrophic in physical terms if the plague had hit this town, White and Barker suggest the emotional effect may have been to leave the survivors more wary of close and free association with their fellow townsfolk.[60]

Thirty-three buildings have been identified in this phase from the baths basilica site which, coupled with new buildings elsewhere on the site of the Roman city,[61] does not suggest a community in excessive decline, nor one in total social chaos. Nevertheless, it seems that the towns that survived into the sub-Roman period became increasingly more isolated and inward-looking.

With the ending of central Roman-style rule in Britain, it appears that the collection of tax revenues plummeted, the need for surplus agricultural production declined, and consequently the role of the towns was drastically reduced. The economy would have gone into sharp decline, which the archaeological evidence supports. The countryside villas were either abandoned or were taken over in parts for subsistence living. There is some evidence that more marginal land was taken out of cultivation, although the pollen record indicates that agricultural activity was still fairly high in the post-Roman period as there is 'no evidence for significant regeneration of woodland at the expense of agricultural land' until the 6th century,[62] indicating that there was still a sufficiently high level of population to cultivate the land already cleared. The idea that the Anglo-Saxons came into a country that was thick with ancient and/or regenerated woodland through which they had to hack their way is not true. It was a productive countryside, for the majority of the British population had always lived on the land, and continued to do so. The land offered a very attractive prospect to settlers.

Fig 3: Roystone Grange, Derbyshire. Here a Romano-British settlement appears to have been 'planted' by the Roman administration and was based partly on lead mining and wool production up to the 4th century

Indeed some peripheral areas were taken into cultivation in the earlier Roman period, an example of which can be seen along the Roystone Grange trail, 6½ miles west of Matlock in Derbyshire. Farming communities of this date have been found at about 2 mile intervals along most of the Peakland valleys as well as around Roystone. However when the economy on the Continent and in Britain went into recession, marginal land in the 4th century was no longer viable, and in the case of Roystone Grange which had been artificially settled, it emptied 'almost as swiftly as it had been colonised,'[64] a situation doubtless repeated on similar sites.

There is evidence that several Iron Age hill forts, for example Dinas Powys in south Wales and Cadbury Congresbury in Somerset, were refortified and reinhabited during the late 5th and early 6th centuries. In the case of Dinas Powys and South Cadbury, which was re-used in the 5th century, these were large sites with widespread trading contacts that extended abroad. Such sites have been interpreted as the residences of local leaders such as has been suggested for the huge 6th-century timber-framed building at Wroxeter. At South Cadbury the presence of a large 'hall' has been revealed through excavation and this, along with the substantial labour force thought necessary to rebuild the ¾-mile length of ramparts, indicates this was a high-status settlement of 'more than local significance and resources',[65] even of a high-ranking leader. But none of these sites survived into the Anglo-Saxon period—they were either stop-gaps or settlements that failed to bridge the gap.

Indeed, the post-Romano-British and early Anglo-Saxon societies are likely to have had many basic aspects in common. As Esmonde Cleary explains, both had 'subsistence agricultural economies' with social organizations based on family and kin; both had 'relatively undeveloped social hierarchies' probably comprising 'local rulers and the occasional paramount war-leader', and although there were cultural differences, finds from settlements and cemeteries show that both ethnic groups had similar technological expertise.[66] It might have led to an ease of integration for, as shall be shown, Anglo-Saxon society was largely agricultural. When obviously Germanic artefacts such as disc- and square-headed brooches are found on known British sites, such as South Cadbury in the west and Saffron Waldon in the east, it does not necessarily mean there was a sudden Germanic occupation, but perhaps that the indigenous British

Fig.4 The short wooden stakes outline the site of a two-period building which was the living accommodation of a Roman farm at Roystone Grange. The earliest building was 'a large, sub-rectangular, aisled farmhouse'. Better known from the midlands, this type of structure is usually regarded as a prototype for a villa. A smaller but similar aisled structure was found a short distance to the south of this building with a further two dwellings nearby which suggests that this settlement was a fairly prosperous one in Roman times[63]

population found such articles acceptable and that a process of trade and assimilation had begun.

However, although many scholars champion the assimilation theory between the English and Britons, Berresford Ellis makes a good case for non-assimilation. Concerning language he states that 'nothing survives in pre-Norman Conquest English of a Celtic language apart from a few place-names and a few words pertaining to religion.' If there had been constructive interaction between the two groups he argues that there would have been a situation like that in France where the Franks, the conquerors of Gaul and cousins to the Anglo-Saxons, soon accepted Christianity and absorbed 'a significant Gaulish vocabulary' into a language that became French.[67] The Anglo-Saxons did accept Christianity at the very end of the 6th century and into the 7th, but this was through the auspices of Rome and not through the British, and they remained illiterate until this time. It seems that most of the British were driven out in areas of early Anglo-Saxon settlement for, as Berresford Ellis states, archaeologically nothing Celtic (British) survives in terms of burials or agricultural systems which are 'distinct from the Saxon open field system, indeed, nothing at all to show the existence of "the survival of a native British population carrying on its arts undisturbed by political changes."'[68] It is his premise that in the face of Anglo-Saxon attacks large sections of the Celtic (British) population were either killed or moved away to the west or to Gaul, Brittany and Ireland. Some, surprisingly, even appear to have settled on the Rhine for the town of Brittenburg means 'town of the Britons', yet others moved to north-east Spain.[69] An 8th-century Frankish monk, Ermald Le Noir, states that the people of Armorica had pitied the British refugees from humanitarian reasons and because they, too, were Christians, unfortunately the Britons showed no gratitude and as Ermald puts it 'had made themselves supreme throughout the country.'[70] The British migration to Armorica appears to have comprised three distinct migrations according to Morris, the first occurring during the time of Magnus Maximus, in the 380s, the second in the late 5th century following the massacre of the British nobility at the supposed peace conference, and the third and final mass migration in the mid-6th century following the death of the leader called Arthur.[71] But the evidence also indicates that many Britons stayed, either to fight or, at least in the west, to eventually be assimilated.

One aspect of 'Britain' that definitely survived was the Church, most notably in the west (as is detailed in chapter 5). Gildas, the earliest post-Roman British commentator, wrote in Latin and also used a well-known Roman style of construction and methods of argument, which shows he was possibly conversant with the great Roman works. This suggests there must have been a schooling system in operation, even if it was for the more privileged members of society. The fact that he was also able to refer to earlier documents indicates there was a place of learning at hand, almost certainly under the auspices of the British Church. As Esmonde Cleary states 'That there should have been education available in early sixth-century western Britain is interesting enough; that it should have preserved the forms of late Roman secular education is totally unexpected.' The earlier of the Llandaff charters, which record the transfer of land-holdings in south-eastern Wales, also use Latin unlike the vernacular used in the early Anglo-Saxon laws, and use a general legal structure, concepts and a 'specific legal terminology' which is derived from the late Roman period.[72]

Whatever the precise details, by the 7th century it can be surmised that much of central England was under Anglo-Saxon control. To what degree they lived side by side with the remaining Britons and in what numbers will probably remain a subject of debate.

In the centre of what became England, the kingdom of Mercia was soon to emerge.

CHAPTER 2
Mercia: The Beginnings

The name Mercia is derived from the Anglo-Saxon word *Mierce* — 'boundary', thus making Mercia 'the land of the boundary people' and the Mercians 'the boundary folk' or 'dwellers on the March'. Stenton argues that in the 7th century the Mercians occupied the area from the forests of the western midlands to the lower Trent and that this people, who comprised some 12,000 households, came to 'adopt a name which originally described the portion of the race in contact with its British enemies', suggesting that the boundary referred to may have been 'the belt of high land connecting the hills of Cannock Chase with the forest of Arden',[1] roughly that between today's southern Staffordshire and north-western Warwickshire. It was not until the 8th century that the area west of this zone was occupied by Anglo-Saxon settlers. Stafford, following Hunter Blair, considers that the border in question was with the Northumbrians and that the name applies particularly to the lower Trent valley.[2] However, Yorke notes that, although Mercia and Northumbria shared a common border in the 8th century, in the 7th they were separated by groups who included the *Elmetsaete* and *Pecsaete*, peoples listed, significantly, in the Tribal Hidage as distinct from the main Mercia province (see pp.17-19).[3] Stenton's view is probably the correct one.

The early annals recorded in the medieval chronicles suggest that there was an invasion into the midlands from East Anglia in the early 6th century, a date which accords with the known archaeological evidence from pagan cemeteries. In Roger of Wendover's and Matthew Paris' *Flores Historiarum* under the year 527 it is reported that '... pagans came from Germany and occupied East Anglia ... some of whom invaded Mercia and fought many battles with the British; but, since their leaders were many, their names are missing'.[4] (From detailed consideration of many sources, Davies concludes that the date for the invasion was more probably 515 and not 527.)[5] A similar sentiment is expressed in a work from St. Albans called the *Lives of the Two Offas* (those of Angeln in what is now southern Denmark, and Offa of Mercia). This states that an ancestor of the Mercian kings, Wermund, was associated with the Western Angles and implies that 'the Angles formed two groups—Eastern and Western', and, as such, there was a possible connection between the earliest Mercians and East Anglians.[6]

Archaeological research and place-name study can be of help either where written history is absent, or in its qualification and bolster the view that the Angles came into the midland region from the east, probably with a small number of Saxons, travelling up the river valleys, such as the Nene and Trent. Research has suggested that the earliest settlements in what was to become the Mercian region were relatively poor, small and of 6th rather than 5th century date.[7] Generally, if a settlement includes pagan cemeteries or burials it can be fairly confidently ascribed to a pre-7th century date which, in Anglo-Saxon settlement terms, is early. Although Christianity had become a feature of Roman life in Britain, albeit mainly among town dwellers and the rural élite, the Christian church only became firmly established

*Fig.1 Map showing the main kingdoms and provinces
of England and Wales in c.600*

among Anglo-Saxon settlers after 597, following a mission from Rome led by St. Augustine. After an initial slow start this mission was subsequently successful, and at the time of the Synod of Whitby in 664, when rivalry between the established British and the new English churches was settled in favour of the latter, the conversion to Christianity was virtually complete, even if an undertone of pagan belief persisted (see chapters 4 & 5). In the middle Trent valley, where the core of Mercia was eventually to be formed, there are many pagan cemeteries including both cremation and inhumation burials, contrasting greatly with their virtual absence on the westerly fringes in what is now the Welsh borders. (Pagan burials are usually identified through the accompanying finds of grave goods such as weapons, jewellery and domestic artefacts. After the conversion to Christianity, it was common practice to bury a body without any artefacts other than the clothing in which the body was wrapped and which often had accoutrements such as cloak clasps. In the *Hwiccian* region— Worcestershire, Gloucestershire and south-west Warwickshire— the preference for 6th-century pagan grave orientation was on a north/south axis which is unusual,[8] and hence a changeover to the east/west orientation can usually be taken as a Christian burial.)

In the western midlands only Worcestershire has pagan cemeteries and these are located solely in the east of the county, with two possible exceptions. One is a single adult cremation found in 1992 south of Hoarstone Farm (SO 794 767) between Bewdley and Kidderminster, buried in a small hollow next to a large pit for which radiocarbon dating suggests a date between 663 and 773;[9] whether this was of an Anglo-Saxon or native Briton is not known. The second is located at Bromfield, 3 miles north-west of Ludlow where an Anglo-Saxon cemetery was excavated in 1978 within an Iron Age farmstead enclosure. Traces of about 31 graves were found which were orientated approximately east-west but three of these had grave goods.[10] This might suggest the cemetery represented a population that had recently converted to Christianity but where there was an overlap of some pagan Anglo-Saxon practices. Stanford suggests that the cemetery 'should date to the period 650-750 when similar sites were in use over much of Saxon England'[11] and would tie in with the first movements of Anglo-Saxons into this region at a time when Christianity was being widely accepted among the English race. It also suggests how long-lived pagan practices were (see chapter 4). These two examples do not add up to much in terms of pagan funeral practice but the lack of cemeteries, Christian or pagan, in the region are noteworthy. Indeed, no clear pagan cemeteries have been found in Shropshire, Herefordshire or western Worcestershire, although this does not mean that the Anglo-Saxons only reached this western area of England after the influence of Augustine's mission. The British Church was active along the current Welsh border and this may have resulted in the conversion of the majority of Anglo-Saxons as they arrived, if they had not been converted already. However, if it is accepted that some would have probably died before adopting the new religion, then their graves may well await discovery. The evidence suggests that the early Anglo-Saxon settlers were pagan, the later ones Christian, suggesting that the move westwards took place over many years.

One might expect that the survival of British names along the Welsh border would be stronger than elsewhere in Mercia but in Shropshire, for example, British place-names are surprisingly rare.[12] Gelling suggests that in this part of England in the post-Roman period there would have not been enough Germanic settlers to have swamped the population, yet that the new arrivals were the dominant group and gave their own names to the settlements many of which had probably existed in Roman times, if not before[13]—rather as happened centuries later when subsequent English people settled in East Africa. It is probable that this is what occurred in other areas along the Welsh border.

Although a case has been made in chapter 1 for the mass emigration of British people in the face of Anglo-Saxon aggression in the 5th century, place-name evidence in Central Mercia indicates there was a certain mingling of the remaining British and new Anglo-Saxon peoples. For example, Walsall, which in 1163 is recorded as *Waleshale*, is interpreted as *Walh*'s valley, *Walh* probably standing for a Celtic (British) or Latin speaking foreigner, in this case probably representing a Celtic presence.[14] However, some authorities suggest that the element *Walh* meant 'serf' with no significance attached to the racial origins of those living in many of the settlements with names like Walton, though it is likely they would have been Celts.[15] There are several Waltons and Walcots scattered throughout Mercia which presumably refer to places where Welsh speech was noticeably present in an area that was English-speaking. There are some interesting survivals of British names such as Penkridge in Staffordshire which is a Romano-British name derived from *Pennocrucium*, a Roman station, 2 miles south of Penkridge. In 985 it was recorded in Old English as *Pencric* and 'faithfully reproduces the Primitive Welsh form of the earlier British name'. The Roman name is made up from *penn*, which is often used to describe hills and head-lands, and *crug* which is 'sometimes used for a tumulus' (a burial mound), the latter now a virtually ploughed-out feature 1,200 yards north of Watling Street at SJ 9025 1180, near Rowley Hill Farm. Nearby Lichfield appears to have derived its name from Wall, 2 miles to the south-west, which, in Romano-British times, was called *Letocetum*, 'a British name meaning grey wood'.[16]

The swamping of areas with English place-names, and later in the east midlands with Danish ones, might suggest a cataclysmic event, it is important to stress that Old English was the language of the ruling nobility and to some degree the Church, and it was they who first recorded such names. As has been suggested earlier, conquerors of territory often re-name geographical features and settle-ments, sometimes adapting existing names which makes it difficult to derive firm evidence for either assimilation or displacement of the British population by the Anglo-Saxons simply on place-name analysis.

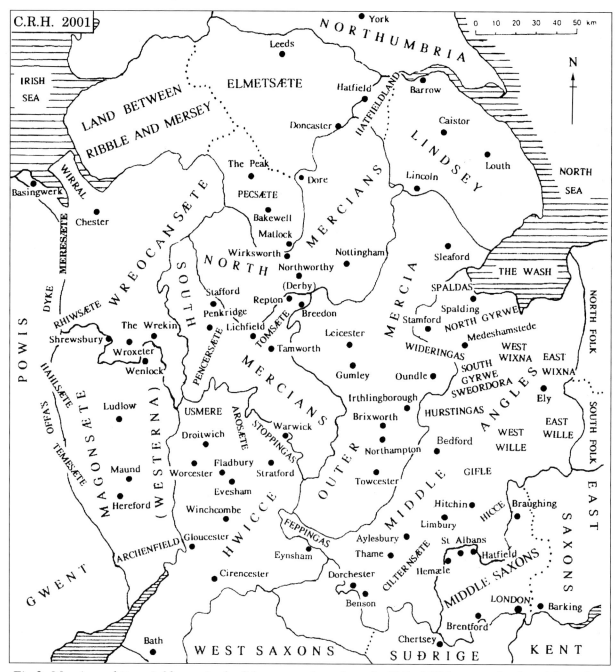

Fig.2 Mercia and its neighbours in the 8th century, based on the Tribal Hidage, early chronicles, charters and place-names (Cyril Hart)

As the Anglo-Saxons gradually penetrated westwards, small groups would have settled in areas which possessed a certain number of necessary attributes: access to a water supply and building materials, dry sites for housing, fertile soils, grazing land and a defensible position. Such requirements explain why many ancient land boundaries have such a variety of shapes and sizes. In these new settlements the tribal name was almost certainly taken from the leader of the group who was responsible for the initial settlement. For example, a small land unit has been identified around Wootton Wawen about 7 miles south-east of Redditch. In the early 8th century, between 716 and 737, land was granted by 'Aethelbald, king of Mercia, and of the South Angles' in '*regione ...* [of the] *Stoppingas*' at Wootton (Wawen) to 'Aethelric *comes*'. By the 8th century the *Stoppingas* are considered to have existed only in name, but this folk group may have begun as an extended family unit 'perhaps with Stoppa as their founder or the earliest remembered common ancestor'. Subsequently other settlers who were not blood relatives would have identified themselves with the group, by then dominant in the area, and thus a tribal identity was born. As the tribe grew, so the idea of land being owned by a tribe but controlled by a leader developed.[17] Thus, while a family unit might have had free use of an area of land it was under the leader's overall control. This concept eventually developed to the point where a king would have rights over all of his kingdom, and in return for holding even a portion of land, an individual had to pay a variety of dues and services. In the case of the *Stoppingas,* a family who could claim descent from Stoppa would probably achieve some sort of patriachal control, for in early Anglo-Saxon society, great store was set upon descent from the founder of the folk group or dynasty. Several other folk groups are known from this early period such as the *Husmerae* based around Kidderminster, the *Pencesaete* near Penkridge, the *Tomsaete* based around the river Tame, a tributary of the Trent, in a territory that later included the settlements of Tamworth and Lichfield but which spread as far as Breedon-on-the-Hill in Leicestershire, and the *Arosaete* (or *Arosaetna*) roughly between Stratford and Fladbury. There were probably many others of which all trace is lost.

Within the kingdom there gradually formed Central Mercia, its own tribal unit, and Outer Mercia,* a series of smaller tribes of varying sizes, who eventually owed allegiance to the former. Many of these smaller units had their own leaders or kings who were often left in place and deployed by the Mercian king to govern on his behalf. Over time many became absorbed into the Mercian core. Two of these peoples, the *Hwicce* and *Magonsaete*, are examined in detail in chapter 6. The hierarchy of kingdoms went beyond Mercia itself with the concept of the *bretwalda* or *brytenwalda*, the 'Britain ruler' or 'wide ruler', who ruled as overlord over most of the other Anglo-Saxon kings and their kingdoms. This superior position was achieved through conquest and statecraft. In the 7th century, for example, the king of Northumbria might claim control over the largest kingdoms such as Mercia, Wessex and East Anglia, whose rulers were then regarded as sub-kings. The subordinate kingdoms would be expected to pay tribute in money or goods, and defer to the overlord the right to decide legal matters, especially the area and the recipients of grants of land.

There exists a remarkable document called the Tribal Hidage. This document is believed to be either a list of tribute assessments which one of the major kingdoms was able to extract from its subordinate territories, or a general register of hidage. There is much disagreement about whether the list originated in Mercia or Northumbria. Dumville, in terms of an overkingship which is set out territorially in the Tribal Hidage, considers it to date to the early 670s or 'just possibly the late 660s',[18] during Wulfhere's reign in Mercia for Wulfhere appears to have been overlord of the English south of the Humber, at least in the latter part of his reign. Hart, however, suggests that the Tribal Hidage was drawn up as a tribute list in the second half of the 8th century, and probably for the great Mercian king, Offa who reigned between 757-796,[19] when Mercia was at the height of its power. On the Northumbrian side, Brooks believes that Northumbrian provenance should be considered because, if the Tribal Hidage is a tribute list, a kingdom

* To ease understanding when considering Mercia's territory the following terms are used: 'Mercia' describes the whole kingdom. 'Central Mercia' comprises the original early kingdom—based around the Trent valley in Staffordshire and southern Derbyshire; whereas 'Outer Mercia' refers to the subordinate territories taken over by 'Central Mercia'—the modern counties of Worcestershire, Herefordshire, Gloucestershire, Shropshire, Cheshire, Northamptonshire, Leicestershire, Lincolnshire, as well as Oxfordshire and Berkshire, of which the latter, being on the border of Wessex, was a hotly disputed area between the West Saxons and Mercians. Mercia's territory was never static and it continually expanded and contracted as its fortunes changed during its 300 to 400 years' existence.

would be unlikely to take tribute from itself—and the very first name on the list is Mercia! Moreover, as the Deirans and Bernicians (the constituent parts of the Northumbrian kingdom) are left out of the document, then, as a tribute list, these omissions add further weight to the Tribal Hidage being of Northumbrian origin.[20] However, if the document is seen merely as a general assessment of hidage, which may have had a variety of uses, then a Mercian origin is possible. The absence of Northumbria may be explained in that, as a rival kingdom, it was outside of Mercia's remit for everyday affairs and would not come under a general register.

If it is accepted as a Northumbrian tax assessment, the most likely case, then the hidage probably dates to the 7th century as this accords with this kingdom's overlordship of southern England. Only a *bretwalda* would be able to extract such wide-ranging tribute, and Northumbria's greatest years were within the reigns of Edwin (616-633), Oswald (634-642) and Oswiu (642-670). Higham contends that the Tribal Hidage comprises two lists of tributaries which were both written at Edwin's court, but at two distinct times: the main list in the late summer or autumn of 625 and secondary additions about a year later. The first list enumerates 19 kingships and is headed by 'the lands anciently called Mercian' and represents 'original Mercia'. He further suggests that the first 16 entries of the primary list may represent those tributaries which Aethelfrith, king of

Myrcna landes is þrittig þusend hyda þær mon ærest Myrcna hæt.	30,000
Þocen sætna is syfan þusend hida.	7,000
Þestema eac spa.	7,000
Pecsætna twelf hund hyda.	1,200
Elmed sætna syx hund hyda.	600
Lindesfarona syfan þusend hyda mid Hæþ feldlande.	7,000
Suþ gyrpa syx hund hyda.	600
Norþ gyrpa syx hund hyda.	600
East pixna þryu hund hyda.	300
Þest pixna syx hund hyda.	600
Spalda syx hund hyda.	600
Þigesta nygan hund hyda.	900
Herefinna twelf 'hund' hyda.	1,200
Speord ora þryu hun'd' hyda.	300
Gifla þryu hund hyda.	300
Hicca þry 'h'und hyda.	300
Þiht gara syx hund hyda.	600
Noxgaga fíf þusend hyda.	5,000
Ohtgaga twa þusend hyda.	2,000
þæt is syx 7 syxtig þusend hyda 7 an hund hyda.	66,100
Hpinca syfan þusend hyda.	7,000
Ciltern sætna feoper þusend hyda.	4,000
Hendrica þryu þusend hyda 7 fíf hund hyda.	3,500
Unecu'n'g[a]ga twelf hund hyda.	1,200
Arosætna syx hund hyda.	600
Færpinga þreo hund hyda.	300
'[i]s in Middelenglum Færpinga' (left-hand margin)	
Bilmiga syx hund hyda.	600
Þiderigga eac spa.	600
Eastpilla syx hund hyda.	600
Þestpilla syx hund hyda.	600
East engle þrittig þusend hida.	30,000
Eastsexena syofon þusend hyda.	7,000
Cantparena fiftene þusend hyda.	15,000
Suþsexena syufan þusend hyda.	7,000
Þestsexena hund þusend hida.	100,000
	[178,000]
Dis ealles twa 'hund' þusend 7 twa 7 feopertig þusend hyda 7 syuan hund hyda.	
	242,700
	[recte 244,100]

Fig.3 The Tribal Hidage

The list as set out in the Old English with the hidage figures added in numbers. (After Dumville)

Northumbria, seized after possibly defeating Cearl, king of Mercia, at the battle of Chester in late 615/early 616. These tributaries are likely to have passed to the East Anglian king, Raedwald, after his victory over Northumbria in 616, and thence by gift to Edwin, Aethelfrith's Northumbrian rival. Higham further contends that Wight and the two other, probable, southern peoples were perhaps added to the primary list following 'Edwin's marriage alliance with Kent', and that the addition of the whole of southern England in the secondary list was probably a result of Edwin's victory over Wessex. The two

The Tribal Hidage

Name	Hidage	Suggested Location
Myrcna landes	30,000	Mercia: Trent valley and land to the south-east
Wreocensaete	7,000	Wrekin Dwellers, Wroxeter region northward to river Mersey
Westerna	7,000	Between river Severn and Offa's Dyke
Pecsaete	1,200	Peak dwellers, Peak District
Elmed saete	600	Elmet dwellers, Leeds and Elmet
Lindes farona and Heath feld land	7,000	Lindsey-folk, Lindsey and Hatfield Chase
South Gyrwa	600	Fenland east of Peterborough
North Gyrwa	600	Fenland east of Peterborough
East Wixna	300	Fenland around the Cambridgeshire Ouse
West Wixna	600	Fenland around the Cambridgeshire Ouse
Spalda	600	Spalding region, Lincolnshire
Wigesta	900	Wiggenhall parishes in Norfolk marshland
Herefinna	1,200	Wooded territory of Huntingdonshire and Northamptonshire
Sweordora	300	Whittlesey Mere, Huntingdonshire
Gifla	300	R. Ivel valley, Bedfordshire
Hicca	300	Hitchin region, Hertfordshire
Wihtgara	600	Wight spear(men), Isle of Wight
Noxgaga	5,000	Region of Wokingham, Berkshire, and Woking, Surrey
Ohtgaga	2,000	The eastern half of Surrey
- -		
Hwicce (or Hwinca)	7,000	Worcestershire, Gloucestershire and part of Warwickshire
Ciltern saetna	4,000	The Chilterns
Hendrica	3,500	North Oxfordshire
Unecung-ga	1,200	Buckinghamshire
Arosaetna	600	Region about river Arrow, Warwickshire
Faerpinga	300	Region about Charlbury, Oxfordshire
Bilmigga	600	Region about Belmesthorpe, Rutland
Widerigga	600	Wittering and Werrington, Soke of Peterborough
East Willa	600	East of river Cam, Cambridgeshire
West Willa	600	West of river Cam, Cambridgeshire
East Engle	30,000	East Angles, East Anglia
East Sexena	7,000	East Saxons, Essex, Middlesex and most of Hertfordshire
Cantwarena	15,000	Kent
Suth Sexena	7,000	South Saxons, Sussex
West Sexena	100,000	West Saxons, Wessex

Fig.4 The Tribal Hidage
Locations for the peoples mentioned in the hidage as suggested by Hart, 1971, most names from Hart (1977).
The dotted line marks the break between Higham's primary list (above)
and secondary additions (below) made a year later (in 626)

lists were then merged and the resulting document could show Edwin's rise to power over all of Britain, as recorded by Bede: 'King Edwin received wide additions to his earthly realm, and brought under his

The Homeland of a Tribal Grouping

Figs.5-7 Wootton Wawen, near Redditch, Worcestershire, identified as the homeland of the small tribal grouping of the Stoppingas. *The current church dates largely from the 13th to 15th centuries, but evidence of Anglo-Saxon work of c.10th-century date is contained in the tower's southern archway (lower left) and the northern archway (lower right). The tower has four arches, one in each wall, which opened into the arms of what would have been a small cruciform church*

sway all the territories inhabited either by English or by Britons, an achievement unmatched by any previous English king.' The fact that the hidation shown for the 'original Mercia' entry exceeds any other group by a factor of four in this first list has been interpreted by Higham as perhaps containing 'a penal element' of tribute.[21]

Whatever the list's provenance, it provides a picture of the tribal groupings just before many smaller units were absorbed. Were it not for this document there would be no record of such delightfully-named peoples as the *Unecung-ga*, *Noxgaga* and *Ohtgaga*. These small groups, with several others, have not been definitely placed and, although Figure 2 shows Hart's interpretation.

Figure 2 shows something of a snap-shot of kingdom development. In the years before the Tribal Hidage's compilation, it is most likely that there were many more smaller units such as those shown on the eastern edges of the midlands. Dumville states the 'relative rapidity' with which the Tribal Hidage crosses the western midlands may 'suggest that this area had already been brought securely under Mercian domination'. (The peoples shown in the territory of the Middle Angles [see fig.2] were apparently only incorporated under Penda of Mercia's son Peada in the mid-7th century.) The *Anglo-Saxon Chronicle* states that Penda had 'come to terms' with the West Saxon kings at Cirencester and that in the mid-640s he was able to drive the West Saxon king into exile in East Anglia. Dumville suggests that the 'first major and successful phase of Mercian expansion ... was that directed south-westwards' at the expense of the West Saxons.[22] If this was before Edwin's reign (616-633) it shows that this expansion was early, even belonging to the 6th century. Place-name evidence in an area somewhat further north also tends to support this early activity (see pp.22-3).

Quite why the Tribal Hidage shows such a concentration of small kingdoms in the eastern midlands, which was to become Middle Anglia, is uncertain. Only once this region had been dominated could the kingdom of Mercia really begin to expand, an event which probably occurred under Penda in the first half of the 7th century. As these small east midland 'kingdoms' are included it is surprising that the tribal groupings around Tamworth and Lichfield are not shown. The *Tomsaete* ('the dwellers by the River Tame') are missing, as are the *Pencesaete*, the group around Penkridge in Staffordshire. In fact, many of the west midland tribes are omitted, including the *Stoppingas* and the *Husmerae*, the latter whose name still lingers in one of Kidderminster's outer localities: Ismere. Either these units were just too small to be shown or they had, by the time of the Tribal Hidage, already been incorporated into Central Mercia.

The early annals apparently contained in the work of Roger of Wendover, Henry of Huntingdon and Matthew Paris indicate that the kingdom of Mercia began in 585 with a king/leader called Crida or Creod(d)a, and that he was succeeded by Wibba/Pipba/Pypba who possibly reigned between 593 and 597. Cearl reigned for 10 years between 597-607[23] (although it is possible he reigned until 616, see chapter 3), and is the first Mercian king mentioned in Bede. He was followed by Penda, the most famous of the early Mercian kings, but whose date of accession is uncertain. Only his death in 655 is recorded when he was killed at the battle of the river *Winwaed* near Leeds. Penda's achievements, which were decisive in the development of Mercia, are described in the next chapter.

The three medieval chronicles seem to agree in placing the accession of Creoda in 584, as a result of the battle of *Fethan leag* between the West Saxons and the Britons. Seven years earlier, in 577, Ceawlin, the West Saxon king and overlord, had fought alongside his apparent co-king of Wessex, Cuthwine, against the Britons at Dyrham in Somerset, a decisive battle which opened up the lower Severn valley to Anglo-Saxon penetration. *Fethan leag* seems a less clear cut battle. The *Anglo-Saxon Chronicle* for 584 records that 'In this year Ceawlin and Cutha fought against the Britons at the place which is called *Fethan leag*, and Cutha was killed there; and Ceawlin captured many villages and countless spoils, and in anger returned to his own land'.[24]

The site of the battle is usually associated with a wood in Stoke Lyne, about 11 miles south-east of Banbury in Oxfordshire, which was called *Fethelee* in 1198, although an alternative site has been suggested near Stratford-upon-Avon.[25] Wherever its location, the battle ended the West Saxon expansion into what became southern (Outer) Mercia, with both West Saxons and Britons suffering heavy casualties. Henry of Huntingdon states: 'Ceaulin [Ceawlin] and Cuthwine again fought with the Britons at *Fedhanlea* ... with great loss and fury on both sides. Cuthwine, overcome by numbers, was struck down and slain; and the English were routed and put to flight. But the king Ceaulin succeeded in rallying his troops, and snatched the victory from those who had been at first victors, and, pursuing the vanquished, gained much land and great booty'.[26] The battle perhaps created a power vacuum that allowed Creoda, to the north, to emerge as dominant. All extant Mercian regnal lists start with Creoda, and it seems plausible that he can be attributed with founding the Mercian kingdom and dynasty.

The dynasty to which Creoda, Pypba and Penda belonged claimed descent in the 8th century from Icel, and became known as the *Iclingas*. The '-ing' ending suggests that Icel may well have been a leader during or just after the migration of the Anglian people from north-western Europe, and may even indicate that Icel was considered to be the founder of the line in Britain, certainly members of the Mercian genealogy who came before Icel are only mentioned in Continental contexts. It appears from Mercian royal genealogies that there were four generations between Icel and the brothers Penda and Eowa, with the line being: Icel, Cnebba, Cynewald, Crida (Creoda), Pypba and Penda/Eowa. This may put the period in which Icel was involved in the migration from the Continent at about 510-35 .[27] The omission of Cearl may be explained in that he belonged to a different dynasty (see chapter 3).

Most dynasties claimed mythological/heroic lineage and the *Iclingas* claimed descent from Offa, king of Angeln in Slesvig, southern Denmark, whose own lineage was traced back to the pagan war-god, Woden. King Offa of Angeln was one of the main heroes of Germanic legend and was remembered as 'the best of all mankind between the seas', and Stenton suggests that Icel was his great-grandson.[28] The claimed descent from Woden was probably no more than propaganda to emphasize the war-like qualities of the Mercian dynasty, as it was in other kingdoms.[29] If the rest of the lineage is essentially true, it may explain why the dynasty remained so powerful and long-lived, for the family spanned the period from the migration from the Continent to the historically recorded Mercian kings, some eight generations. The perception of this exceptional lineage could also help to explain why the Mercian kings held such a powerful position in central England, and why they were able to forge such a successful single political unit from so many disparate midland peoples.[30]

However, genealogies could be lengthened or dove-tailed at will to suit the needs of a dynasty; if two kingdoms merged, their separate genealogies could be combined, providing the new kingdom with a false credence and longevity. Image was crucial. Yet it is equally true that however strong a descent, the success of a dynasty depended on the emergence of strong and charismatic leaders, and Mercia was soon blessed in Penda who, more than any other early king, expanded the boundaries of the kingdom and laid the cornerstones for its enormous success in the 8th century. If such a leader had not emerged, it is possible that the *Iclingas* may have dropped into obscurity and become no more or less royal or powerful than any of the other neighbouring dynasties.[31]

The concentration of place-names, notably in the south-west midlands, containing the personal names of some of the kings in this dynasty has excited interest. In 1927 Stenton remarked that the place-names which apparently preserved the unusual personal names Pypba and Penda were concentrated in Worcestershire and Warwickshire. Such a regional concentration is considered unlikely to be accidental. Although it is not suggested that these places have a direct, personal relationship with these early Mercian kings, Brooks, following Stenton, suggests that these personal names became 'popular among Anglian settlers and lords in the West Midlands' because of the success of the *Iclinga* dynasty and, at one remove, such place-names probably reflect the early activities of this dynasty.[32] The naming of a child after a king by his subject population also suggests the high regard with which his subjects viewed him. The following has been mainly sourced from Brooks[33] and uses only the examples of Creoda, Pypba and Penda, with additional place-name examples taken from the *Place-Names of Worcestershire* volume:

For Creoda there are Credenhill—'*Creoda*'s hill', 4 miles north-west of Hereford; Curbridge—'*Creoda*'s bridge', a village 2 miles south-west of Whitney in Oxfordshire; Curdworth—'*Creoda*'s *worp*', 3 miles north-west of Coleshill, Warwickshire (*worp* means an enclosure or fence, and subsequently 'enclosure round a homestead' or simply 'homestead'); Kersoe—'*Criddi*'s *hoh* or spur of land' with *Criddi* being related to the name *Creoda*.[34] Kersoe is in Elmley Castle, 4 miles south-west of Evesham in Worcestershire, as is the unidentified *Creodan ac*.

For Pypba, we have Pedmore—'Pybba's moor', a south-east district of Stourbridge;[35] Pepwell—'*Pyppa*'s spring' a farm near Hartlebury in Worcestershire;[36] Pepper Wood—'Pypba's clearing' near Belbroughton in Worcestershire and part of an old forest area;[37] and possibly Peopleton—'Pyppel's farm', a village 3 miles north of Evesham;[38] and also perhaps Peplow, a hamlet 3 miles south-east of Hodnet in north Shropshire, which would have a meaning akin to '*Pyppa*'s hill'.

Regarding Penda, there is Pinbury (now Pinbury Park) in Gloucestershire (SO 956049), about 4 miles north-west of Cirencester; Peddimore and possibly Pinley west of Warwick; *Pendiford* in King's Norton; Pendeford—'*Penda*'s ford'[39] now Upper and Lower Pendeford Farms, east and north-east of Codsall, Staffordshire; and Pinvin—'fen or marsh of *Penda*',[40] a village 2 miles north of Pershore.

As Brooks remarks, the place-names formed from the personal names of Creoda, Pypba and Penda, concentrated as they are in the west midlands and especially in, or on the fringes of, the later sub-kingdom of the *Hwicce*, are to be found nowhere else. As they appear to have gained such a local 'unique popularity' in this area, unlike those of other early members of the dynasty, these place-names may 'commemorate a particular and early phase of Anglian colonization'.[41]

So what was life like for these early Anglo-Saxon kings? They were essentially itinerant, moving from one royal vill to another and presenting themselves and their vast retinue to the nobility who were expected to provide food rent (*feorm*)—food and shelter fit for a king and his court. It was considered an honour to be chosen to host the royal entourage, but the food and drink needed for one night's stay in the late 7th century was breath-taking: '10 vats of honey, 300 loaves, 12 "ambers" [casks] of Welsh ale, 30 of clear ale, 2 full-grown cows, or 10 wethers [castrated sheep], 10 geese, 20 hens, 10 cheeses, an "amber" full of butter, 5 salmon, 20 pounds of fodder and 100 eels' was the food rent expected from 10 hides'.[42]*

There was a common sense logic to the Anglo-Saxon king's itinerant arrangements as it meant that he could keep in touch with what was happening in his territory since at each stop he would hold court and listen to the needs of the local community. Visits could be in terms of weeks or even months.

As smaller territories were engulfed by larger kingdoms and became little more than provinces, so the struggle for overall power, the *bretwaldaship*, was reduced to the few—at most seven. The word 'heptarchy' has often been used to refer to the larger kingdoms of Anglo-Saxon England, but the expression was coined by the 12th-century archdeacon and historian, Henry of Huntingdon and was never used by the Anglo-Saxons themselves. As given by Henry, the seven included Northumbria, Mercia, Wessex, East Anglia, Kent, Sussex and Essex. Over the centuries the three greatest kingdoms can be recognized as Northumbria, Mercia and Wessex, with East Anglia and Kent in a supporting role.

---

* A hide was a unit of assessment originally considered to be the amount of land required to support one free family with its dependents and was defined as the area which could be tilled with one plough in one year. Nominally 120 acres, a hide could vary enormously depending on soil productivity. Thus the hide was not strictly a measure of land area but rather a unit of assessment for calculating tribute, taxation and military service, used as late as the 13th century. The measure is first noted in the laws of King Ine of Wessex drawn up between 688 and 694 where 'the hide appears as a unit of assessment enabling the king to collect his dues'.[43]

At its height in the 8th century, Mercia controlled an area which extended from Kent in the southeast, through London and the midlands as far north as the Derbyshire Peak District. The Welsh Marches formed its western flanks and the Cambridgeshire fens its eastern fringes. Within its heart were the rich agricultural lands of the central and eastern midlands. Here, the topography and the soils were well-suited to the growing of crops, there were no extensive areas of marshland or heath except in the extreme eastern midlands, and over these rolling lowlands flow the broad rivers of the Trent, the Welland and the Ouse. It is not surprising that it is within these richer agricultural areas that the earliest settlements within Mercia have been detected. The Trent along its course through the eastern midlands has superb communication potential; it is broad, reliable and gives rise to considerable areas of rich agricultural land and easy settlement along its banks. Further west the same can be said of the river Severn. If the remnants of the Roman road system retained a semblance of their original state most of the Mercian lands would have been provided with some form of reasonable access.

Mercia was not only blessed with abundant tracts of arable land, but its more peripheral provinces contained large areas of woodland, pasture and meadowlands of varying quality. Shropshire, Herefordshire and Derbyshire are still predominantly pastoral, supporting meat and dairy production. But areas of good grazing in counties such as Gloucestershire and Worcestershire would have also, no doubt, supported the flocks of sheep that supplied Mercia's subsequent trade in textile manufacture, an industry for which it was known in the 8th century.

There was more extensive woodland in the western part of the kingdom of which Wyre Forest, the Forest of Dean and Wychwood in Oxfordshire are but small remnants. In the more inhospitable moorland areas of Staffordshire, Shropshire and Derbyshire there were valuable sources of lead and stone. The former had been worked since Roman times and created much local wealth, as demonstrated by the high status pagan burials in Derbyshire. There were also stone quarries in the Cotswolds and east midlands, such as Barnack in Cambridgeshire, and highly valuable salt workings in Cheshire and at Droitwich in Worcestershire. It is little wonder that Central Mercia expanded to include the peripheral extensive areas of woodland, lead mines, salt workings and stone. A king had an eye on tribute, for without it, his power, based on wealth, was untenable.

CHAPTER 3
Cearl, Penda and Wulfhere

Cearl

The first king of Mercia mentioned in written sources is Cearl. He preceded Penda as king but it is suggested that later attempts to link him to the same dynasty as Penda are spurious[1] or at best unproven. The only mention in Bede of Cearl is that his daughter married Edwin, later king of Northumbria. Northumbria was made up of two constituent parts: Deira, the southerly region, centred on York, and Bernicia to the north and east which was centred around Bamburgh; there was rivalry between the two for overall control of the kingdom. Aethelfrith, king of Northumbria between 604-617, hailed from Bernicia and banished Edwin, one of the heirs to the royal dynasty in Deira in about 604, Edwin finding refuge in Mercia under Cearl's protection.

Cearl, who may have exercised control over the territories bordering Deira to its south including Elmet, could well have felt threatened by Aethelfrith in which case, by marrying his daughter to Edwin, Cearl would then have backed Edwin's claim to the Deiran throne, intending to use him to destabilize Aethelfrith's kingship and extend his own influence through a presumably 'grateful and dependent son-in-law'.[2]

It is likely that Edwin spent some years, perhaps even a decade, under Mercian protection and that his elder sons, Osfrith and Eadfrith, were born in Mercia. This span suggests strongly that Cearl was Aethelfrith's equal[3]—a subordinate, or even an independent but weaker king, would not have countenanced harbouring Aethelfrith's enemy for so long or, presumably, have been left alone to do so for so many years.

Edwin became king of Northumbria after Aethelfrith's death at the battle of the river Idle in 617 (see below). If the Tribal Hidage is of Northumbrian origin and shows the territories subsequently paying tribute to Edwin, then its first 16 entries could be a long list of dependencies that originally belonged to Cearl. If this theory is correct, then this implies that the Mercian kings were dominant in the midlands and even Wales before Penda rose to power in the mid-7th century. Indeed, Higham suggests that Cearl was in control of this area from about 604 to about 615/6, even that 'Mercia's regional supremacy ... stretched back one or more generations from Cearl, [and] so into the prehistory of Anglo-Saxon England'.[4]

There is the possibility that there was an alliance, albeit unequal, between Mercia and several 'powerful but tribute-paying' British kingdoms, headed by that of Gwynedd of north Wales, which predated the known alliance between Gwynedd and Mercia in Penda's reign (*c.*633-655). The mid-6th century historian, Gildas, appears to have believed that there was an English war-leader, a *dux*, who was of superior power to the 'overking' of Wales: Maglocunus of Anglesey in the kingdom of Gwynedd. Higham suggests that only an English king who was all powerful in the midlands 'would have been in a position to exert pressure on Gwynedd'.[5] In addition, there is a tradition that Edwin spent some time in north Wales during his exile presumably, therefore, with Cearl's approval. That the Mercian dynasty retained its name, 'the borderers', when it could have changed it to the 'West Angles', for example, to bolster its position in England by advertising the Germanic credentials of its kings, Higham suggests it implies that held a certain confidence in its own regional identity and power which was not shared by other dynasties who changed the names of their kingdoms, and may even 'imply a degree of sensitivity towards its British client-kings'.[6]

By the early 600s, Higham observes that Mercian supremacy over the centre of England (and possibly central Wales) was apparently more secure than the equivalent 'overkingships' centred in Bernicia and in Kent, which are the two mentioned by Bede. The tributaries of Aethelberht, king of Kent, stretched as far as East Anglia and the *Hwicce* to the west by about the 600s. Aethelberht is known to have pursued the conversion of the English and their kings, and actively supported the Augustinian mission in London, East Anglia and even in the far west. But Bede makes no reference to any attempt to convert the Mercian king, indicating that Cearl was independent of Aethelberht, or, at the very least, more powerful than Raedwald, king of East Anglia, who was baptized at Aethelberht's court, and was presumably under his jurisdiction. Writing under the protection of Northumbria, Bede gave short shrift to Cearl, probably on account that he was both a pagan and a Mercian. Yet it would appear that Cearl was head of a third 'English-led overkingship' of which there is, alas, no historical record. If the primary list of the Tribal Hidage shows Cearl's former tribute-paying territories, Higham suggests it appears he was 'overking' and protector of most of central Britain, stretching from Pembroke to the valley of the Great Ouse in Bedfordshire and Cambridgeshire, and up to the river Warfe in Yorkshire, as well as the possible ultimate overlord in Wales.[7]

This Mercian 'overkingship' may well have suffered temporary dissolution after the battle of Chester (see below). It is noted by Higham that the attempts by successive kings of Northumbria to take over the region were ultimately frustrated by the determination of Penda's dynasty to restore the supremacy of the Mercian kingship, a determination supported by the subordinate leaders and kings of Wales and the midlands who apparently preferred Mercian to Northumbrian overlordship.[8]

The battle of Chester and the implications for Cearl and Mercia

There is a certain inevitability in the eventual confrontation between Cearl and Aethelfrith of Northumbria, if it is accepted that both held political and military parity, and that Mercia was protecting Aethelfrith's arch rival, Edwin. Higham has identified the battle of Chester as being the decisive event; indeed this battle is the only one 'known to have been fought by Aethelfrith against his southern neighbours'. It is contended by Higham that unless Bede failed to mention another battle of equal importance, Cearl was likely to have been a victim of this campaign because evidence of his kingship disappears by 616 at the latest.[9] Bede records the battle (and in so doing demonstrating his antipathy to British Christianity):

> ... the powerful king Ethelfrid [Aethelfrith] .... raised a great army at the City of the Legions - which the English call Legacestir, [Chester] but which the Britons more correctly name Carlegion - and made a great slaughter of the faithless Britons.[10]

According to this account, the Britons alone seem to be Aethelfrith's opponents, although their actual identity is not clearly stated by Bede. As Chester was chosen for the venue of the British synod in about 601, it implies that the town was under the control of a British and Christian king,[12] probably that of Powys.

As Higham observes, Aethelfrith's near obsession with getting Edwin out of Raedwald of East Anglia's protection later in 616 might imply that capturing or killing Edwin was one of Aethelfrith's main objectives in the Chester campaign; indeed, that Aethelfrith fought this far west does not make it less likely that the campaign was aimed mainly against Cearl and Edwin.[13] Chester would be a convenient, central mustering point for troops gathering from north Wales and the west midlands, and Aethelfrith may have decided on a pre-emptive strike.

That Cearl fell at the battle of Chester and Aethelfrith took control of Mercia seems the most plausible explanation for Edwin's flight from Mercia at a date which Higham states to be no later than the spring of 616, when he sought protection with King Raedwald of East Anglia; to have stayed would have been suicidal. The fact that Aethelfrith sent three emissaries to Raedwald to threaten him with war unless he gave Edwin up also suggests that Cearl was dead, because Aethelfrith would have needed a safe passage through the core region of Mercia along the Trent valley.[14]

Aethelfrith held something of a reputation. Bede describes him as 'a very powerful and ambitious king ... He ravaged the Britons more cruelly than all other English leaders, so that he might well be compared to Saul the King of Israel, except of course that he was ignorant of true religion. He overran a greater area than any other king or ealdorman, exterminating or enslaving the inhabitants, making their lands either tributary to the English or ready for English settlement.'[15] To the British writer Nennius, Aethelfrith was known by the name Aedlfred/Eadfered Flesaurs, the latter word meaning 'dodger' or 'doubler'.[16] His death was recorded in the Welsh Triad as among the 'Three Fortunate Assassinations of the Island of Britain'.[17] The Welsh clearly had no love for the king.

Raedwald, king of the East Anglians, who reigned between *c*.599-*c*.625, was also no friend of Aethelfrith's. Aelthelfrith cajoled, threatened and tried to bribe Raedwald to have Edwin either murdered or handed over, but it seems that Raedwald's queen stiffened his resolve not to betray Edwin, fearing that 'his betrayal of the obligations of a host towards his guest would shame him'.[18] In 616 or 617 Raedwald raised an army and marched on Aethelfrith and met him on the east bank of the river Idle on the northern borders of Mercia. Henry of Huntingdon gives a singularly colourful account of the battle and Aethelfrith's death who '... charging among the enemy's squadrons, became separated from his own troops and was struck down on a heap of bodies he had slain'. Raedwald, who had made a '... brilliant and formidable display, marching in three bodies, with fluttering standards and bristling spears and helmets' won the day but lost his son in the battle 'from whence it is said "the river Idle was stained with English blood".'[19] Whether Henry was embellishing events somewhat is probable, but it must have retained a 'folk memory' of being a ferocious battle.

It has been suggested that the battle of the Idle was fought near the point where the Roman road from Lincoln to Doncaster crosses the river, with a further suggestion that the kings battled at or in the area of the Roman fort of Scaftworth 'where the Roman road from the south-east crosses the Idle into Yorkshire at Bawtry'.[20] This area was to provide the setting for several decisive battles between Northumbria and Mercia, the Roman road system often bringing armies face to face as they tried to avoid the surrounding marshes and swamps. Marsden however, places this battle near Retford, some 8 miles south-south-east of Bawtry.[21]

With Aethelfrith's death his own Bernician-led supremacy fell in tatters.

Fig.1 The land of the river Idle

27

Penda

The first recorded military action of Penda is occurred in 628, the *Anglo-Saxon Chronicle* stating that 'In this year Cynegils and Cwichelm [the joint kings of Wessex who were father and son] fought against Penda at Cirencester, and afterwards came to terms'.[22] Henry of Huntingdon fleshes out the incident, recording that the Saxon kings and Penda 'Both having vowed not to turn their backs on their enemies, each firmly maintained [their] ground until they were happily separated by the setting sun. In the morning, as they were sensible that, if they renewed the conflict, the destruction of both armies must ensue, they listened to moderate counsels, and concluded a treaty of peace'.[23] One suspects this may be another piece of elaboration on Henry's part for, if Bede's accession date of 633 for Penda is accepted, then Henry is suggesting that the uncrowned Penda was already sufficiently powerful to fight against other leaders in the most south-westerly parts of what was to become the Mercian sub-kingdom of the *Hwicce*, but that he was also able to come to terms with kings. The terms agreed may have simply involved the transfer of land in the area from West Saxon domination to Mercian control, but may also have included a marriage arrangement between Penda and one Cynewise, a name that indicates she was a Saxon, even the sister of Cynegils.[24]

If Penda was not king by then, to act in such a way suggests either he had considerable audacity in acting on his own terms—indeed William of Malmesbury states that Penda assumed the title of King of the Mercians in 626 'after he had already fostered his presumption by frequent incursions on his neighbours'.[25] It is possible that it was Penda who made the sub-kingdom of the *Hwicce* a subordinate province to Mercia at this time in which case he was presumably acting with the agreement of the Mercian dynasty. Interestingly, Bede refers to Penda as 'a warrior' of this house, which Stenton qualifies by suggesting he may have 'been merely a landless noble of the Mercian royal house fighting for his own hand',[26] in which case he might have carved out the sub-kingdom for himself.

When king, Penda fought on the southern, eastern and northern frontiers of Mercia, constantly pushing out the boundaries and consolidating many of the smaller tribes under the unity of Mercia. It is believed that he was on good terms with the British on the westerly boundaries, and his support, or even his creation of the kingdoms of the *Hwicce,* and possibly the *Magonsaete*, was probably achieved through co-operation and agreement with the Welsh than through conquest. It is even possible that Penda may have fought the Cirencester engagement with Welsh assistance, supported by Cadwallon of Gwynedd or the exiled prince Cynfeddw of Gwent.[27] Certainly Penda and Cadwallon were in alliance when they marched on Edwin of Northumbria at the battle of Heathfield in 633.

Henry of Huntingdon, with reference to this battle, significantly remarks that Cadwallon 'was a most powerful king, was at the head of an immense army; and Penda the Strong was truly the strongest'. If the tradition is true that Edwin had for a while been fostered by Cadwallon's father, Cadfan of Gwynedd, Cadwallon's later personal hatred of the Northumbrian king is understandable when one reads that Cadwallon had been besieged off Anglesey and forced into exile in Ireland, probably at Edwin's instigation. It is little wonder that the Welsh termed Edwin 'the deceitful'. Higham, however, suggests that the sense of betrayal felt in Gwynedd may have been a reflection of Edwin's change in attitude towards this Welsh dynasty since his conversion to the Roman form of Christianity, even though they had stood against Aethelfrith.[28]

Penda was bent on increasing his political power through invasion to gain more territory and/or tribute, and Northumbria was one direction in which he could strike. As it is possible that Aethelfrith installed Penda's dynasty after Cearl's demise, the fact that Edwin (Aethelfrith's arch rival) was related to Cearl's family may have encouraged Penda to try to annihilate the line. Thus personal revenge mixed with desire for land and booty provided the reasons for the conflict with Northumbria.

According to Bede, the battle of Heathfield took place on 12 October 633 'on the field called *Haethfelth*' when Edwin was 48 years old. Bede reports that Edwin's entire army was slain or scattered and that one of his sons, Osfrith, was killed in front of him, while the other, Eadfrith, was forced to surrender to Penda.[29] Edwin, too, was killed. It is feasible that Penda took Eadfrith hostage with the idea of installing him as a puppet ruler in Northumbria at a later stage,[30] but if this was so, he clearly had a dramatic change of heart, for he subsequently had him murdered during Oswald's reign (634-42).[31] The killing of Edwin's sons, Cearl's grandsons, might suggest that Penda was not related to Cearl, yet there is some evidence that he later fought his own brother, Eowa, suggesting that blood ties may not have meant a great deal to him.

Although the battle's precise location is unknown, there are at least two contenders—one in the region of Hatfield in south Yorkshire, the other around Cuckney, near Mansfield in Nottinghamshire. The *Anglo-Saxon Chronicle* refers only to Hatfield and, like Bede, is no more specific, but dates the battle to 14 October.[32] In more recent times historians have made the link between Hatfield and Hatfield Chase, respectively 7 miles and *c.*12 miles north-east of Doncaster, a trend that appears to have stemmed from Camden's *Britannia* of 1586 in which Camden links the present day place-names, the fact that Hatfield Chase was still a royal forest and that there had also reputedly been an Anglo-Saxon palace in the vicinity.[33] It is significant that Leland, although he described a journey over Hatfield Moor some 40 to 50 years earlier, made no mention of the battle of 633, suggesting there was no tradition for the battle being fought there.[34] Aerial survey has shown crop-marks of field systems to the west and south of Hatfield and, although 'characteristic of Iron Age/Roman period activity', there are parallels from East Anglia and Kent which suggest continuity of use into the early middle ages. As Higham observes, fieldwork in the Fens and areas of western Lindsey has revealed 'ceramic evidence of early to mid-Anglo-Saxon occupation in very similar terrain',[35] thus habitation of the Hatfield area in Edwin's time is possible. And if it was this Hatfield (rather than the Hatfield in Hertfordshire) that was used for the important religious synod of 680, a palace in Edwin's time is quite likely as high-status ecclesiastical and secular sites were often part of the same complex in the 7th century.

It is suggested by Higham that Edwin might have been breaking his journey at this putative palace, with only his household thegns accompanying him, on his way back from 'Lindsey to Yorkshire for the annual tribute-taking ceremony'. If so, his enemies could well have predicted his movements through this area.[36] The area is low-lying and, nearly 1,500 years ago, it would have been surrounded by marshes and mosses to the north, east and south, and by the river Don to the west. Any fords offering means of escape were miles away around Doncaster. Half a mile east of Hatfield lie Slay Pits and Slayborough Hill and it is possible that their names recall this battle. However, it is suggested by Revill that these evocative names may relate to the earlier defeat of Aethelfrith by Raedwald at the battle of the Idle, likewise fought in this area.[37]

More recently, however, the site of the battle of Heathfield has been suggested in the neighbourhood of Edwinstowe and Cuckney, respectively about 7 miles north-east and north of Mansfield in Nottinghamshire. The place-name Edwinstowe has been inter-

Fig.2 St. Mary's Church, Edwinstowe

preted as 'Edwin's holy place', the most likely 'Edwin' being the 7th-century Northumbrian king. Traditionally, the church at Edwinstowe is believed to have been the place where Edwin's headless body lay after the battle. After Edwin's elevation to a saint (he was, after all, slaughtered by the pagan, Penda) the spot where his body had lain became a hallowed place. A church was founded on the site and probably became associated with a local cult of St. Edwin which would account for an unusually large church in what was, for a long time, little more than 'an obscure forest hamlet'. Even in the late 11th century the church was a chapelry of Mansfield, and it was not until the 12th century that Edwinstowe ranked as a manor in its own right.[38]

A few miles west of Edwinstowe is St. Edwin's Cross, which was set up in 1912 on the alleged site of St. Edwin's Chapel. The origin of this chapel is unknown, but it appears to have been a chantry chapel. During King John's reign (1199-1216) a yearly payment of 40 shillings was made to the chaplain by the king, and bequests were occasionally made by other rulers later on,[39] suggesting that this little chapel had some much wider and lasting significance—the cult of St. Edwin perhaps? Why the chapel was located exactly at this spot is unknown, but it may have been one of the places where those carrying Edwin's body rested *en route* to Edwinstowe.[40] Wherever it rested temporarily, Edwin was later buried at Whitby Abbey and his head, which had been taken to York just after the battle, was subsequently buried at St. Peter's, York.

Several other local place-names support the theory that this area was in fact the *Haethfelth* to which Bede refers. Between the site of St. Edwin's chapel and Cuckney lie Hatfield Farm and Hatfield Grange.[41] But some of the fighting may have occurred at Cuckney itself for, during strengthening measures to the church by the National Coal Board in 1950-1, a mass burial was discovered under the nave. Skeletons were found under the north wall of the present church and under the footings of an earlier Norman church, and these burials extended outside the church for at least 2m (7ft). The vicar at the time counted 200 skulls and there were numerous other skeletal parts; workmen on the site suggested that, in places, the bodies had been piled on one another to a depth of 2m (7ft). All the skeletons appeared to be of males. As the nave was only trenched in sections, it is likely that the unexposed areas would have their own share of burials and, although there is no way of knowing how far these went beyond the north wall of the church or beyond the south wall, the remains noted are likely to represent but a small proportion of the total number of people buried. The most likely explanation is that the burials constitute a battle pit. But from when? Unfortunately nothing was found that gave any dating evidence—apart from the fact that they predated the church and its Norman predecessor. The only known conflict which might fit the facts is that of Heathfield. As Revill states, a mound heaped over the bodies of the long dead would also have made a 'convenient starting point for the hasty construction of a motte' made necessary during the Anarchy in the reign of King Stephen and built to the west of the present church by Thomas de Cuckney at some time between 1138-54.[42] If the

Fig.3 St Mary's at Cuckney lies down a village lane with a small knoll running parallel behind it, which might have formed part of the battlefield of Heathfield

motte to the west and the nave to the east do stand over the dead of the battle of Heathfield, then the scale of this confrontation becomes all too horribly apparent.

Whether the battle was indeed fought in and around the quiet village of Cuckney and its environs, or in the flat plains around Hatfield by the river Idle, Penda and Cadwallon were victorious and Bede describes with apparently genuine horror what ensued: 'At this time a terrible slaughter took place among the Northumbrian church and nation, the more horrible because it was carried out by two commanders, one of whom was a pagan and the other a barbarian more savage than any pagan. For Penda and all his Mercians were idol-worshippers ignorant of the name of Christ; but Cadwalla [Cadwallon], although he professed to call himself a Christian, was utterly barbarous in temperament and behaviour. He was set upon exterminating the entire English race in Britain, and spared neither women nor innocent children, putting them all to horrible deaths with ruthless savagery, and continuously ravaging their whole country'.[43] It has been suggested by Hunter Blair that Bede's grandparents, possibly even his parents, may have recalled this time vividly and 'may have seen the valley of the Tweed aflame with burning straw on harvested fields'.[44]

With such a decisive defeat the affairs of Northumbria were thrown into disarray. The Northumbrian bishop Paulinus fled with Edwin's queen Athelburh (his second wife, the daughter of the late king Aethelberht of Kent) and her children and grandson, Yffi, to Kent. From there Edwin's young son Wuscfrea, together with Yffi, were sent to King Dagobert of Gaul for safety but the two boys died, presumably of natural causes, in infancy, so ending Edwin's immediate male line. Meanwhile, Aethelfrith's son Eanfrith took over the kingship of Bernicia whilst Osric, Edwin's cousin, succeeded to Deira. Osric led an attack against Cadwallon but died in the process. It appears that Eanfrith sought a peace treaty but, within 18 months of *Haethfelth,* Cadwallon had killed him, a move which was to turn Aethelfrith's surviving successors against one of Edwin's conquerors. On Aethelfrith's death in 616/7, the three brothers, Eanfrith, Oswald and Oswiu, had fled north. Oswald was to stay under the protection of the Scottish kingdom of Dal Riata until he was about 24,[45] but now returned to do battle with Cadwallon, defeating and killing him near Hexham in 634 and going on to reunite the Northumbrian kingdom. Although later reviled by the Northumbrians, Cadwallon was highly regarded in Wales. In an early poem *Marwnad Cadwallon* ('Lament for Cadwallon') he is described as 'a fierce affliction to his foe, a lion of hosts over the Saxons'. His 'camp on the uplands of Mount Digoll' is believed to have been at Long Mountain, near Welshpool in Powys 'in the centre of a district called Meigen'.[46]

It is probable that after the battle Penda returned to Mercia, leaving Cadwallon active in Northumbria, to establish himself as king. He next appears in the *Anglo-Saxon Chronicle,* as well as in Bede's narrative for the year 642, at the battle of *Maserfield.* This battle, also called *Maserfelth,* and *Cocboy*/*Maes Cogwy* in Welsh poetry, presents several problems to the historian, not least in its location. It is generally assumed that the battle was fought at Old Oswestry in Shropshire in the province of the *Wreocensaete,* one of the extreme western sub-kingdoms of Mercia. Gelling states that the name Oswestry means 'Oswald's Tree' and, although probably pre-Conquest in origin, it was not recorded as a place-name until *c.*1180. It may be that an already existing place-name, after some long-forgotten Oswald, both fuelled the association with the saintly Oswald of Northumbria and even the dedication of the church. This latter link would no doubt have been enthusiastically fostered by the priests. At some stage 'Oswestry' was misinterpreted as meaning the 'cross of St. Oswald' and, then, in the Welsh form *Croes Oswald*' by the 13th century.[47] Thus the association with the St. Oswald of Northumbria seems to have been assured by a process of overt encouragement and covert misinterpretation.

Gelling suggests that the original 'Oswald's tree' was merely a reference to 'a boundary-marker on the northern edge of Maesbury', 2 miles south of Oswestry, and which itself means 'manor of the boundary'. Oswald in this case might have been just another Anglo-Saxon who had some proprietorial right over that particular tree. Maesbury was recorded in the late 13th and 14th centuries as one settlement in a large estate and it appears that the administrative centre moved from Maesbury to Oswestry when the Normans built their castle at the latter in the northern part of the estate. It may have been the superficial resemblance between Bede's *Maserfelth* and *Meresbyrig* (Maesbury), which encouraged both the Welsh and English traditions to believe that this was the site of the battle of 642 between Penda and Oswald. (An alternative location for the battle has been made at Wigan, the Roman *Coccium*, in Makerfield in Lancashire by D. Kenyon.)[48]

The battle of Chester had been fought in the same region of the Welsh borders in which Oswestry lies some 25-26 years earlier, and its location in the then boundary area between the Welsh and Northumbrian kingdoms is understandable. But Oswestry was then deep in the territory controlled by Powys into which Oswald would have had to penetrate. The ruler of Powys in the mid-7th century was Cynddylan who figures in early Welsh bardic fragments. In a stanza of the *Canu Llywarch Hen* Cynddylan is represented as being present at the battle of *Cocboy (Maserfelth)* as an ally of Penda. In another poem, the *Marwynad Cynddylan* or 'Lament for Cynddylan', is the statement 'When the son of Pyb [Penda or his brother Eowa] desired, how ready he [Cynddylan] was!' which is among the earliest written evidence for the alliance between the Welsh and Mercians, if the poem was indeed written shortly after Cynddylan's death as has been suggested.[49] If Oswald was trying to annexe Powys, Cynddylan would clearly be in opposition and Penda, as an ally of the Welsh with an eye for future territorial gain, would be present.

The importance of the Welsh alliances should not be under-estimated. The fact that Penda was a life-long pagan does not appear to have stopped this bond developing with the Christian British kings. It must have been a mutually beneficial arrangement for there does not seem to be any evidence in the early to mid-7th century of one kingdom being subordinated by the other, with the exception of an account by Matthew of Westminster.[50] For the leaders, perhaps with different agendas, there was a common goal: to rid themselves of the Northumbrian threat.

The battle of *Maserfelth* took place on 5 August 642. Not a great deal is known about the course of the battle other than that Oswald was slain and had his arms and head cut off and displayed on the battlefield by Penda, perhaps following a pagan war-god ritual. It took a year for Oswald's body to be recovered by his brother Oswiu. Oswald was 38 years old when he died and Bede wrote about him in the most glowing terms, advancing the memory of Oswald as a fine example of what a good Christian king should be, perhaps as a covert criticism at the less than saintly kings of his own time. That he had been killed by a pagan also gave Oswald a martyr status which was further encouraged when miracles occurred at the spot where he died on the battlefield.

These miraculous stories began when a horse, which was going through the throes of colic, rolled on the ground where Oswald was slain and immediately recovered. The rider, convinced that the place must

Fig.4 Oswestry hillfort

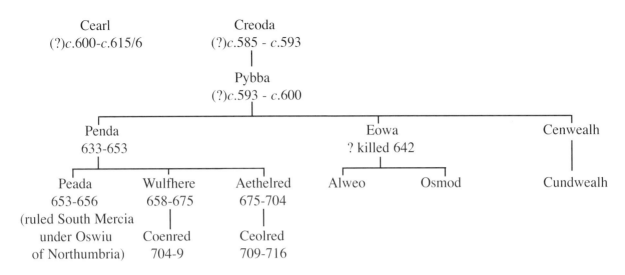

Fig.5 The early Mercian Royal Family Tree

have some special sanctity, marked the spot and eventually reached an inn where he met with the land-lord's niece who had long suffered from paralysis. She was taken to the place in a cart and slept for a short while on the marked spot. On waking she was completely cured of her affliction, and walked back to the inn. These and other stories were reported far and wide and soon many people visited the site and took away the earth until 'a pit was left in which a man could stand'. The soil was mixed with water and given to ailing humans and beasts who 'received great benefit' from the concoction.[51] Thus Oswald's cult began, promoted partly by Wilfrid, bishop of Northumbria, and also by Oswiu, Oswald's brother and successor, and his daughter Osthryth. It was in their interests to foster such a cult, as a royal saint added consider-able prestige to a dynasty.

Eowa, Penda's brother, was also present at the battle, where he too was killed, but the relationship between the two brothers is unclear. One theory suggests that Penda's political power was then in eclipse and that Eowa was the leading Mercian ruler, but was subject to the northern Angles from the mid-630s until his death at *Maserfelth*.[52] Penda and his brother may even have been rivals for the Mercian throne and it is possible that, when Eowa died in battle, he was fighting alongside the Northumbrian king, Oswald, in order to keep his own possession of the throne against Penda.[53] On the other hand Kirby makes the suggestion that Penda and Eowa were ruling Mercia jointly with Eowa as king over northern Mercia and Penda as king over the southern part. Eowa's death at *Maserfelth* would then have made Penda sole Mercian king. It should be borne in mind that the Mercians may have always been ruled by joint kings before the mid-7th century,[54] as shared kingship was common in the 7th and 8th centuries in Anglo-Saxon kingdoms. Contradictory as these theories are, there is room to suggest that Penda might have lost control of Mercia to his brother sometime after the battle of Heathfield in 633 and before *Maserfelth* in 642, which could explain Bede's statement that after Heathfield Penda 'ruled that nation [Mercia] with varying success for twenty-two years'.[55]

Whatever was the actual course of events, the deaths of Eowa and Oswald at *Maserfelth* left Penda undisputed ruler of Mercia—both Nennius' *History of the Britons* and the *Annales Cambriae* consider that Penda's reign ran from his victory in this battle to his death at the battle 'of the field of *Gai*', which we know, through Bede, as being *Winwaed*, near Leeds, in 655.[56]

Penda was now a formidable presence for the battle left him with a much weakened Northumbria on his northern border and strong ties with the Welsh kingdoms to his west. By the end of his reign he had succeeded in uniting under the Mercian title many smaller kingdoms which had, for the most part, been won through his policy of aggression. A good example of this is his treatment of the East Anglians. After the assassination of King Eorpwald, Raedwald's son, his step-brother, Sigeberht, succeeded to the East Anglian kingdom, but, being a devout Christian, he resigned the kingdom to his cousin Ecgric in order to become a monk in the monastery which he founded—possibly that at Bury St. Edmunds, Suffolk. When Penda invaded East Anglia, Sigeberht was literally dragged out of the monastery against his will so that his presence might instill confidence in the troops—Bede writes that he 'had once been a gallant and distinguished commander'.[57] The plan did not work, as Sigeberht insisted on carrying only his staff of office into the battle and, not surprisingly, he was slaughtered along with Ecgric, the reigning king, and the army scattered. The date of this battle is not known—636/7 is the generally accepted date—but Anna, Raedwald's nephew, succeeded to the East Anglian throne probably in that year,[58] but certainly before 644, when Cenwealh, king of Wessex, temporarily fled to Anna's court.

Cenwealh was yet another victim of Penda's apparent boundless hostility which had this time been caused by Cenwealh spurning his wife, who unfortunately just happened to be Penda's sister! That Penda could force the king of Wessex into exile for three years is significant for it demonstrates the power he now wielded.

King Anna seems to have been involved in opposition to the Mercians throughout his reign and it was only a matter of time before Penda confronted him too. An attack in about 651 duly resulted in Anna being expelled. Scarfe suggests that Anna may have lived in exile among the *Magonsaete* between c.651-654, either near Ludlow or Shrewsbury, and there is a story recounted by Osbert of Clare in the 12th century of a canon of Bromfield near Ludlow 'who had spoken with people who had seen a vision of Anna's daughter, St. Etheldreda, "at a church dedicated to her on the Welsh borders".' Osbert claims this small wooden church was built by Anna. Although this story has been dismissed by some scholars, Scarfe points out that landed endowments were exchanged between the monastery at *Icanho* (probably Iken) in Suffolk and the double monastery at Much Wenlock in Shropshire, indicating some link between the two parts of England. Furthermore there does seem to be a family link between Anna and the *Magonsaete* because another of Anna's daughters, Seaxburg, queen of Kent, was closely related (probably as an aunt) to the wife of Merewalh, ruler of the *Magonsaete*.[59] If Anna needed to get as far away from East Anglia as possible then exile among kin on the other side of the country seems a sensible idea. However, as Penda was the ultimate ruler over the *Magonsaete*, it seems a very strange choice.

Anna's unexpected return to East Anglia temporarily checked further Mercian advance. Yet by c.654 he became another of Penda's victims, possibly killed at Blythburgh near the Suffolk coast where his remains were apparently enshrined and venerated in the 12th century.[60] Henry of Huntingdon records that 'King Anna and his army fell quickly at the edge of the sword, and there was scarcely one who survived. Ethelhere succeeded his brother Anna, and was slain in his turn by Penda, Ethelwulf succeeding. The kingdom of East Anglia having been plundered, Penda the Strong withdrew his army into Northumbria'. For Penda it appears that 'destruction eager burns',[61] and Northumbria remained the main threat to Mercian power.

On Oswald's death, Oswiu had become ruler of Bernicia, the northerly component of Northumbria, and conciliated the Deirans by marrying Edwin's daughter and allowing Oswine, the son of Edwin's cousin, to rule over Deira from 644 until c.651 at which date Oswiu had him murdered. In his place he installed his nephew, Aethelwold. Although Bede lists Oswiu as seventh overlord, or *Bretwalda*, of England and states that for a while he ruled the same territory as Edwin and Oswald before him, namely 'all the peoples of Britain, both Angles and Britons, with the exception of the Kentish folk' together with 'the British Mevanian Isles'—the Isle of Man and Anglesey—and 'to a large extent conquered and made tributary the Picts and Scots in the northern parts of Britain',[62] it would appear that Penda was not Oswiu's subordinate.

That Northumbria was a target for Penda's aggression is shown by Bede's account of how Penda and 'his enemy army of Mercians' had reached the gates of the royal city of Bamburgh when Aidan was bishop (635-51), in about 651, after spreading 'ruin far and wide throughout the lands of the Northumbrians'. Bede then recounts Penda's determination and resourcefulness: 'Unable to enter it [Bamburgh] either by force or after a siege. Penda attempted to set fire to it. Pulling down all the neighbouring villages, he carried to Bamburgh a vast quantity of beams, rafters, wattled walls, and thatched roofs, piling it high around the city wall on the landward side. Directly the wind became favourable, he set fire to this mass, intending to destroy the city'.[63] On seeing the column of smoke and fire above the city from his hermitage on Farne Island nearby, Bishop Aidan, raising his eyes and hands to heaven, as so many had undoubtedly done before him, uttered 'Lord, see what evil Penda does!' Miraculously the wind changed direction and turned the flames back on the Mercians, who fled.

From such accounts one would be justified in seeing the relations between Northumbria and Mercia based purely on conflict, yet history can confound us at every turn. In the early 650s Oswiu's son, Alhfrith, married Penda's daughter, Cyneburh, and Penda's son, Peada—recently raised by Penda as the ruler of the Middle Angles, the core of which territory is today's Leicestershire and Northamptonshire—married Oswiu's daughter, Alhflaed, and was duly urged to accept Christianity by his newly acquired brother-in-law, Alhfrith.[64] What was going on? Both kings must have been in agreement about the marriages taking place and one can surmise at the underlying motives. Marriages between kingdoms regularly took place to secure alliances, or at least neutrality. These marriages between the royal families of Northumbria and Mercia must have meant that, for a time, relations were perhaps equable between Oswiu and Penda. It may be that the spread of Christianity into Middle Anglia also played its part. Peada was converted in about 653, two years before Penda's death, and was baptized by Finan, bishop of Lindisfarne, returning to Middle Anglia with four Northumbrian priests: Cedd, Adda, Betti and Diuma. It is noteworthy that Peada turned to Northumbria for his religious advice and instruction instead of south to Canterbury, which suggests that his 'political and cultural orientation was still northwards, his world essentially that of the [North]Humbrians'. Kirby also suggests that if Bede is correct in saying that Diuma was consecrated bishop of the Middle Angles and the Mercians while Penda remained a heathen, it was as if Oswiu was 'treating Penda's territory as a northern Anglian sphere of influence'.[65]

If there was a truce or understanding, it did not last long for after 'savage and intolerable attacks'[66] by Penda, Oswiu was reduced to handing over his ten year-old son, Ecgfrith, as a hostage to the Mercian court under the keeping of Penda's wife, Cynewise. Oswiu also tried to bribe him to stop his devastation of Northumbria and to return home. An 'incalculable quantity of regalia and presents [were offered] as the price of peace' but Penda refused to consider the offer and declared that he would wipe out the entire nation 'from the highest to the humblest'.[67] This pay-off may have actually occurred, possibly at Stirling, called *Iudea* in Nennius. Perhaps it was a step too far for Bede to give the accolade of overlord to the pagan and Mercian Penda, but it is possible that the overlordship of southern England passed backwards and forwards between Penda and Oswiu depending upon the fortunes of each kingdom, and more likely that it was only with Penda's death in late 655 that Oswiu was acknowledged, briefly, as overlord in Mercia.

What precipitated the final act of violence, which culminated in the battle of the river *Winwaed* on 15 November 655, is not known, but it is fairly certain that Penda was the instigator and central figure of a wide-ranging coalition. His power at this time is evidenced by the fact he was able to take with him 'thirty battle-hardened legions under famous commanders'.[68] Aethelhere, the king of the East Anglians was there, as was Cadafael, king of Gwynedd and possibly Cynddylan.

From all accounts the battle of the river *Winwaed* should have been an easy victory for Penda as Oswiu was vastly outnumbered—Bede says that Penda's armies were 30 times greater.[69] Indeed, Oswiu's nephew and the ruler of Deira, Aethelwold, had deserted to the Mercian side and acted as a guide to the army, which was another blow for the beleaguered Oswiu. There was another desertion, this time from the Mercian force, when Cadafael, king of Gwynedd, withdrew on the eve of the battle to north Wales. His name means 'Battle Chief' or 'Battle Seizer', but after *Winwaed* he gained the unfortunate epithet 'Battle Shirker'.

If the British kings had been rewarded at *Iudeu* and if, as Kirby suggests, Penda and his army were homeward bound and Oswiu surprised them, then it is possible that Penda's forces were disinclined to fight, which might explain Cadafael's departure and Aethelwold's further shift in allegiance. The river *Winwaed* has been identified with the Went, a tributary of the Don, and the battle site in an area just southeast of Leeds. There may have also been 'some dissatisfaction among Penda's allies with what had been achieved at *Iudeu*',[70] thus a sense of demoralization may partly explain the surprising outcome of this battle. During the conflict Aethelwold withdrew and viewed events from the sidelines.

Torrential rain had caused the *Winwaed* to flood, and the battlefield must have soon become a sea of mud, Bede recording that as many lives were lost in the flood-waters as were killed in battle. Henry of Huntingdon gives a typically gripping and probably imaginative account of Penda's death: '... for the God of battles was with his [Oswiu's] faithful people, and broke the might of King Penda, and unnerved the boasted strength of his arm, and caused his proud heart to fail ... He was struck with amazement at finding that his foes were now become to him what he had formerly been to them ... He who had shed the blood of others now suffered what he had inflicted on them, while the earth was watered with his blood, and the ground was sprinkled with his brains ...'.[71] The battle was a crushing defeat for the Mercian alliance. Almost all of the 30 leaders were slain, including Aethelhere of the East Angles and all his men. As a final defiant gesture Oswiu had Penda's body decapitated, perhaps in revenge for the deplorable way his own brother's body had been mutilated and displayed after the battle of *Maserfelth*.[72] Penda was dead, and with him went the independence of Mercia for the next three years.

Penda's Legacy

One thing about Penda is certain: one cannot be indifferent to him. Whether he inspires admiration or revulsion he stands out like a giant in the history of early Anglo-Saxon England and rightly so, because his achievements in expanding and consolidating the midlands into a mighty kingdom, whatever Cearl's achievements had been, was the foundation from which sprang its successes in the 8th century. It is unlikely that Mercia would have emerged into one of the most important kingdoms of the Anglo-Saxon era unless there had been a leader with the personal strength and military prowess that Penda had in abundance. Even the chroniclers, who were clearly not Penda's champions, had to accede that he was personally brave. But being an excellent warrior alone would not be enough to have reached the position of power he held. There must have been more than the chroniclers are telling us. At times Penda might appear to be something of a megalomaniac, slaughtering those who opposed him and yet there is no evidence that he killed anyone treacherously or by cunning as so many kings did in this period. with the possible exception of Edwin's son, Eadfrith, whom he murdered after promising to keep him alive. His savagery in battle might be no more or less than any of the other kings of his time. Certainly he comes across as an aggressor but it must be remembered who wrote the chronicles and why. One source which clearly had a great influence on later writers is Bede—a Christian and a Northumbrian; Penda as a pagan and a Mercian was certainly *persona non grata* in his eyes! Bede's indifference and at times hostility is particularly understandable when it is realized that the then current king of Northumbria and later saint, Ceolwulf, had commissioned Bede to write his history, to whom it was also dedicated.

Nennius, whilst decrying Penda for his paganism and stating he was 'victorious by diabolical agency', does credit him with separating Mercia from 'from the kingdom of the *Nordi*, (Northerners)'.[73]

If Stenton is right in believing that Penda was merely a 'landless warrior' at the start of his career then this may explain his motivation. There have been many people throughout history who have come from relatively modest backgrounds, but who have achieved positions of great power, and perhaps Penda belongs in this group. Aware of his background, he may have driven himself that much harder to achieve what he desired most: recognition and influence. And maybe it was those very qualities of audacity, determination and tenacity which he displayed throughout his adult life that gave him the edge over others.

However, Bede mentions one aspect of Penda which so far has not been explored—his toleration. Although he was a life-long pagan, he nonetheless allowed his son, Peada, to accept Christianity and also nurtured several saintly daughters. He did not object to the spread of Christianity within Mercia, even saying what angered him most were those people who professed a belief in the religion but did not live up to it. This suggests a fair and rather moral individual, the sort of person to whom the epitaph 'loyal to his friends but terrible to his enemies' might well apply. It has been suggested by Brooks that if the later demise of Mercia and Penda's paganism had 'not combined to prevent his memory from being cultivated', his memory might have been be passed down to us in the lines of English poetry 'like some early El Cid, as a great war leader who had made nonsense of the ethnic and religious divisions of his day'.[74] In short it is a question of what we would today call 'good press and bad press'. Unfortunately for Penda, he suffered from the latter.

Following his death Mercia fell under direct Northumbrian control. Oswiu had won the day and Penda's son Peada had been married into the Northumbrian dynasty. Bede states that, as Oswiu's kinsman, Peada was granted 'the Kingdom of the South Mercians, which consists of five thousand hides of land and is divided by the River Trent from the land of the North Mercians, which consists of seven thousand hides'.[75] Northern Mercia was presumably retained under Oswiu's direct control. Bede's account suggests that there was a recognized division between southern and northern Mercia; perhaps once ruled separately by the brothers Eowa and Penda and those before them. That Oswiu entrusted such a large amount of the kingdom to Peada suggests that the two were on good terms; indeed it is said that together they founded the monastery at *Medeshamstede* (Peterborough). However, Peada did not survive long, for in the following spring during the festival of Easter he 'was foully assassinated through the treachery, it is said, of his own wife'.[76] It is a bleak statement, but unfortunately nothing else is recorded. It has been suggested that there may have been some Mercian hand in the murder, of 'sinister undercurrents' and 'intrigues'.[77] If Peada had 'gone Northumbrian'—and he certainly seems to have been compliant with Oswiu—he might well have built up hostility among a group of Mercians who were to bid for independence only a few years later. If Peada's murder was a precursor to an immediate Mercian bid for freedom, it back-fired because Oswiu at once took effective control over the whole Mercian kingdom.

When the Mercian coup finally came in late 657/658 it was dramatic. The revolt was led by three ealdormen or thegns—Immin, Eafa and Eadbert—who brought Wulfhere, Penda's younger son, then aged between 16 and 18, out of hiding and proclaimed him king of the Mercians. Bede adds that the three Mercian leaders drove out 'the representatives of a king whom they refused to acknowledge, [and] they boldly recovered their liberty and lands'.[78] By expelling Oswiu's governors, the Mercians effectively threw off the Northumbrian domination which had succeeded in extending northern Anglian control over most of Britain and had reduced Mercia to the status of a dependent province. Wulfhere's survival under the nose of Northumbrian domination suggests his whereabouts was a well-kept secret. For Mercia it was doubly fortunate, for he was soon to show that he had the strengths of his father.

Oswiu's overlordship over southern England was broken by the Mercian revolt.[79]

Wulfhere

There is some uncertainty about the date for the beginning of Wulfhere's reign: the different versions of the *Anglo-Saxon Chronicle* put it at 656 or 657, Bede at 658, while recent historians have suggested the end of 657[80] and 659[81]. What is certain is that his reign lasted until 675 and during this time, like his father before him, he expanded and consolidated Mercia, bringing it once again to the forefront of the English kingdoms. But one significant difference between Penda and Wulfhere is that while Penda was a pagan to the end, his son reigned as a Christian king. The date of his conversion is not known, but he married a Christian Kentish princess, Eormenhild, in about 660, at a time when much of Mercia was being Christianized. Kirby remarks that the marriage was probably sought so as to increase Mercian contact with 'the Anglo-Frankish world of the Kentish court'[82] and through that with the Christianized world of the Continent. Most of the English rulers were attracted by the prospect of contact with the Continent, particularly in the re-establishment or strengthening of trade-links and the status which contact with the Romanized, and apparently sophisticated, Frankish culture would offer. While not wishing to appear overly cynical, it has to be said that the Anglo-Saxons had a very pragmatic attitude to most aspects of life and a sound political and economic alliance through Wulfhere's marriage would be high on the agenda.

Ashley states that his marriage to the Kentish princess meant that he was able to seek the help of the church of Canterbury in subjugating Essex, undoubtedly giving him ready access to the port of London which was becoming increasingly important.[83] Indeed, Wulfhere seems to have expanded his authority throughout southern England through alliances and agreement with the southern kings rather than by warfare,[84] for example establishing his brother-in-law, Frithuwold as king of Surrey in about 670. Frithuwold was apparently the father, or at least the kinsman of the Frithuric who appears in the reign of Aethelred, Wulfhere's successor, with his gift of *Bredun* (Breedon-on-the-Hill, Leicestershire) to the monastery of *Medeshamstede* (Peterborough). Under Wulfhere, Frithuwold seems to have been responsible for territory stretching across the Thames into north Buckinghamshire and around Thame in southern Oxfordshire where Wulfhere had a royal residence.[85]

In 673, after the death of Wulfhere's other brother-in-law, Ecgberht, he effectively ruled Kent through Ecgberht's sons, Eadric and Wihtred, who were probably only 2 or 3 years old, by standing as guardian to them.[86]

Although Wulfhere's power in southern England eventually eclipsed Oswiu's influence, a statement in the *Anglo-Saxon Chronicle* in relation to *Medeshamstede* Abbey strongly suggests that any animosity between the two kings had disappeared. Wulfhere is at his most pious when, under the year 656, the *Laud Chronicle* states 'In his [Wulfhere's] time the abbey of *Medeshamstede*, which his brother Peada had begun, grew very wealthy. The king loved it much for love of his brother Peada, and for love of his sworn brother, Oswy [Oswiu] ...'. Later, Wulfhere is reported as referring to his 'dear friend Oswy'.[87] However, caution must be exercised here as the *Laud Chronicle* was written up in the 12th century and the initial scribe added details of various spurious charters.[88] Florence of Worcester records that, in 669, Wulfhere 'with the concurrence of king Oswy' requested of Archbishop Theodore that 'Ceadda [Chad] ... take charge of the united sees of Mercia and Lindisfarne'.[89] But it appears that either Oswiu had declined to become Wulfhere's equal or even that he had became his subordinate, indicating just how much the balance of power had shifted. Oswiu died after an illness in mid-February 670/1 aged 58, the first Northumbrian king to die of natural causes rather than in battle.

By 665, Wulfhere, as well as being king of Mercia, was overlord of Essex. In this capacity he sold the bishopric of London to Bishop Wine who had recently been expelled from his position at Winchester, an act of simony (the trafficking in ecclesiastical benefices) for which the latter was shunned by his more principled clerical contemporaries. Wulfhere then attempted, and must have succeeded, in detaching Lindsey from Northumbrian control because by the early 670s episcopal authority was exercised over Lindsey from Lichfield, the see of which was founded in 669. By the first half of the 670s his power extended south of the Thames to Surrey, and it is possible that the northern territory of the West Saxons from Berkshire to Somerset was also under pressure from Mercia which, as Kirby notes, could have created the precedent for further Mercian involvement in these regions at a later date. Wulfhere took control of the Isle of Wight, an act which suggests a near total breakdown of previous military and political order south of the Thames, and took over the Meon valley in Hampshire. There is even an indication that the people of these territories were allies of Wulfhere's and the latter's gift of the lands to Aethlwealh, king of the South Saxons, on the occasion of his baptism was received favourably by the ruling dynasty of the Isle of Wight who may well have 'welcomed the conjunction of Mercian and southern Saxon interests'. Kirby also observes that 'a new hierarchy of power' was apparently being built in southern England which, if Wulfhere had been able to consolidate it, might have seriously curtailed or even destroyed the growing power of the West Saxons.[90] But events intervened and it was ironically from Northumbria, and from Oswiu's son, Ecgfrith who had been held hostage at the Mercian court by Penda in 655, that the challenge came when he vied for control of Lindsey.

Wulfhere decided to invade Northumbria in 674 to counter this threat. The early 8th-century Northumbrian writer, Eddius Stephanus, records that Wulfhere, 'a man of proud mind and insatiable will, stirred up all the southern nations against our own, intent not merely on war but meaning even to enslave us to him as tributaries'.[91] Indeed, it seems that Wulfhere rode against Ecgfrith with an army drawn from all the southern kingdoms, in the same way that Penda had done at *Winwaed* 19 years before. For all this, Wulfhere was defeated by Ecgfrith and was forced to pay tribute. In addition Mercia temporarily lost control of Lindsey to Northumbria.

This defeat was soon followed by Wulfhere's authority in Kent being overthrown, when Hlothere, the late Ecgberht's, king of Kent's, brother, rose against him. Then, in late 674 or 675 Wulfhere was challenged by one of the kings of Wessex, Escwin or Aescwine at a battle in an unidentified place called *Biedanheafde* or *Biedanheafod*. The outcome of the battle is unclear, but Henry of Huntingdon provides a typically colourful, though perceptive, account: 'Inheriting the valour of his father and grandfather, the Mercian king had rather the better of it in the conflict, though both armies were severely handled, and on either side many thousand soldiers were sent to the shades below. We are led to reflect how worthless are human achievements, how perishable the warlike triumphs of kings and nobles, when we find that, of the two kings, who, for the sake of vain pomp and empty glory, inflicted such grievous sufferings on their country, the one, Wulf[h]ere, died from disease the same year, the other the year following'.[92] This account is also significant in that it appears to be the only chronicle that records Wulfhere's death from disease in 675; he was still a relatively young man in his mid-30s.

During his life Wulfhere gave much land for the founding of monasteries and often saw to it that they were richly endowed. When, during the plague which ravaged the country in 665 (Matthew of Westminster records that the outbreak was such 'that men came in crowds to the precipices which overhang the sea, and threw themselves headlong down, preferring to perish by a speedy death rather than by the slow torture of disease'),[93] Wulfhere found that the East Saxons had lapsed into idolatory, he sent his own bishop, Jaruman, 'to correct their error and recall the province to the true Faith' which he did successfully.[94] Bede speaks of his deeds matter-of-factly (after all Wulfhere was a Mercian!) but does not use any harsh, critical terms in relation to him. Florence of Worcester speaks kindly of him, stating that he was the first of the Mercian kings to receive Christianity 'and abolishing, and utterly rooting out the worship of idols among all his people, he caused the name of Christ to be published throughout his dominions, and built churches in many places'.[95] Add to this that Wulfhere was the father of a saintly daughter, St. Waerburh, and it is not surprising that Florence has only good words to say about the king.

It was also under Wulfhere that the English Church's first general synod was organized under Archbishop Theodore of Canterbury, which took place on 24 September 672 at Hertford. It was here that it was decided that the Church should be organised into smaller dioceses which would be less tribally-based, these new diocesan centres subsequently also becoming administrative ones.[96]

William of Malmesbury, who only had bad words for Penda, is much better disposed towards his son, stating at the beginning of his reign 'that he might not disappoint the hopes of the nation, [Wulfhere] began to act with energy, to show himself an efficient prince by great exertions both mental and personal', adding that he gave 'every possible assistance' to Christianity. William reports how he led the Isle of Wight, which had 'yet [been] panting after heathen rites', into 'the proper path'. It is only Wulfhere's economic dealings over the bishopric of London that caused William obvious difficulties: 'But these and all his other good qualities are stained and deteriorated by the dreadful brand of simony; because he, first of the kings of the Angles, sold the sacred bishopric of London to one Wini, an ambitious man'.[97]

Peterborough Abbey (Medeshamstede)

Fig.6 The much later medieval remains of the cathedral which replaced the pre-Conquest monastery. Bede claims that Seaxwulf (later bishop of the Mercians) founded the first abbey. However, Hugh Candidus, who compiled the local chronicle of Peterborough in the 12th century, claims Peada (Penda's son) and Oswiu began the monastery 'with the aid of a man of great power named Saxwulf'.[98] The building stone came from one of the main pre-Conquest quarries, that at Barnack (9 miles to the north-west of the abbey) with the abbot of Peterborough owning these quarries from, at least, the late Anglo-Saxon period. Peterborough became a centre from which a number of other monasteries were founded

Fig. 7 (Left) This carving, re-set in the west wall of the south transept, dates from the late 8th-early 9th century. It is thought to depict two bishops. They are sometimes referred to as 'the two dancing bishops' but they are not dancing, rather the depiction of their feet and robes is typical of the style of middle Anglo-Saxon art that emanated from Mercia and Northumbria at this time[99]

Fig.8 (Right) The 'Monks' Stone', also known more commonly as the 'Headda Stone', is now displayed in the apse of the present cathedral. See Figs.9 & 10 for detail

Figs.9 & 10 The name 'Headda Stone' derives from a forgery from the later Middle Ages which tried to 'prove' the unbroken history of Crowland Abbey by claiming Peterborough Abbey had been destroyed by the Danes in the late 9th century, which sound documentary evidence refutes. The stone dates to the late 8th-early 9th century. It is believed that there was almost certainly a figure at either end, indicating that the stone has been cut back. With these extra two figures, there would have been a total of 14, comprising the 12 Apostles, the Virgin Mary and Christ. These two latter form the two central figures in the top drawing: the Virgin Mary, with veiled head and holding the lily of the Annunciation, centre-left, and Christ to the right. St. Peter stands to the right of Christ, holding the keys and St. Paul is probably depicted to the left of the Virgin Mary.[100] The stone is approximately 3¹/₂feet (1m) long and is carved on the 'roof' of the stone, which is rare for this period. Its sheer size suggests it may have formed the top of a shrine containing relics

Matthew of Westminster's appraisal of Wulfhere is interesting in the back-door compliment he gives to Penda, whom he described as 'a most atrocious pagan' and the 'perfidious head' of Mercia:

> But he [Wulfhere] displayed all his father's valour, and enjoyed his father's fortune, and so prevailed and put the king of the West Saxons to flight, and ravaged his territories.[101]

It is clear from his military exploits that Wulfhere was a warrior king of considerable stature, otherwise he would not have been able to re-establish Mercian domination south of the Humber and extend Mercian rule as far as Essex and the Isle of Wight. Indeed at the height of his power, in the early 670s, he held authority over most of southern England, with the exception of Wessex (perhaps excluding its northern territory), East Anglia and the kingdom of Dumnonia in south-west England,[102] holding authority over more of England than any Mercian king before him. Yet he does appear to be an odd mixture of warrior and convert as compared to his father, ruling with both piety and power. Even his gift of the Isle of Wight and the Meon valley to Aethelwalh of Sussex as a sign of adoption as his godson (which significantly took place at the Mercian court) suggests the behaviour of a king who is asserting his control over another. But once his overlordship began to falter after the battle with Ecgfrith in 674, it appears as if cracks were appearing in his support which may have then prompted the challenge by the king of Wessex, Aescwine. One can conjecture what might have happened to Wulfhere if he had not died of illness in 675. Would his support have dropped away, to be ousted by a more successful man? Once a king became old, poor, weak or unwell, he could well find himself passed over by his followers for the next man.

The secular poem *Beowulf* provides a fascinating insight into these times. Campbell points out that 'In the political world of the poem four things stand out: the importance of the king's noble retinue, ... an indissoluble connection between success and gifts of gold; the store set by good weapons [which were in themselves status symbols and were thereby regarded as treasure]; and the endless insecurity associated with feud'. The king's noble warriors were always with him, they feasted with him, slept in the same hall, fought for him and were 'ready, or anyway sincerely hoped to be ready, to die for him'. For a warrior to have survived his lord in battle was seen as a disgrace. Campbell asserts that the number and loyalty of these warriors were critical to royal power, without them the king would be unable to reign in a world where power was largely achieved through warfare. But this loyalty had to be bought; it was a case of everything having a price, even friendship! In *Beowulf* there is much talk of the giving of rings and other treasures, and kings were described as 'gold-friends' and 'ring-givers'. In short, a successful king gave; a bad king hoarded. Yet it was not merely a case of naked materialism on the part of the king's retinue, as the receiving and wearing of gold and armour or a sword, for example, was a symbol of honour and pride, a reminder that one had been rewarded by one's leader for bravery and loyalty. Only a king who was successful in battle would have ongoing access to booty and could carry on being a treasure-giver. War became a necessity, and for success in battle he needed his warriors—it was a cycle which fed upon itself. There were many young noblemen who were attracted by the prospect of reward, and a treasure-giving king could even attract them to his court from other kingdoms. But as soon as the king began to falter then there were always enemies waiting in the wings to 'seize their advantage ... [to take] the treasure, the men, and the glory'.[103]

It was a harsh reality that the early Mercian kings must have known, and for men such as Penda and Wulfhere it was a reality they could not ignore. Their great success as kings in creating such a powerful kingdom and leading so many people suggests that they heeded these warnings well.

CHAPTER 4
Pagan Mercia

In 597 occurred one of the most dramatic events to affect the social fabric of Anglo-Saxon England: the re-establishment of Christianity from Rome to England with the mission of Augustine.

The British Isles already had a flourishing Church based in Wales, Scotland and Ireland and it is highly probable that there were some British Christians in Mercia, Northumbria and Wessex prior to 597. It is believed that Britain was first Christianized in the early 3rd century when still a part of the Roman empire, with the religion initially being introduced by migrants and missionaries. What became known as the British Church in the sub-Roman period was a natural successor to this form of Christianity. By 597 this Church was separated from Rome by geography, as well as by certain differences in observance which created serious divisions. Although British Christians could be found throughout England, when Augustine wanted to meet the official leaders of the British Church he had to travel as far west as the river Severn, which suggests that their power-base had receded into these westerly regions.

When the missionaries came from Rome there would have been the scattered remnants of British Christian communities living among the pagan Anglo-Saxons. However, their numbers are unlikely to have been high, for paganism had revived in Roman Britain during the 4th century; indeed, archaeologists have uncovered a substantial amount of pagan cult objects from this period.[1] The very fact the Anglo-Saxons also commemorated the Britons' churches in place-names also suggests that by this time they were unusual enough to be noteworthy!

History is full of examples of the religion of an area being that of the conqueror. In this case the Anglo-Saxons were the conquerors and they already had a religion that worked, that helped to explain their world and their daily lives. By the time they reached Britain their paganism was 'rich and highly developed in content and mythology' but was fairly simple in purpose: 'to make supernatural provision for the whole gamut of social needs'.[2]

Unlike Christianity, which had a definite structure and belief system, paganism was an amorphous collection of beliefs, 'a cobweb of superstitions, tendencies, customs and relatively simple propitiatory rituals' which existed, at least in rural areas, 'more as a system of relationships than as a system of theology'. It was this very fluidity and amorphousness which may well have been the key to its survival long after Augustine and his successors. Even after the 7th century, the clergy and the king lived in a world where superstition, magical practice and the observance of pagan beliefs existed in parallel with Christianity and the secular establishment. Indeed Christianity, during the 7th to the mid-9th centuries, has been described 'as a kind of crust upon the surface of popular culture' with its thriving undercurrent of heathen beliefs. Moreover, the very existence in the 11th century of religious and royal prohibitions against pagan practice is surely evidence enough of its survival. Early prohibitions range from the third canon passed at the Council of *Clofesho* (possibly Brixworth, central Northamptonshire, or some other Mercian location) in 747, through the laws issued by Edmund in the mid-10th century, to the 'Canons of Edgar' and the 'Northumbrian Priests' Law' which were both passed in the early 11th century. Even as late as 1284 a guild regulation of the Palmers of Ludlow suggests 'that dark games involving corpses during the night preceding a funeral were still being played in the thirteenth century'.[3]

Paganism persisted longer in rural regions than in towns because it had developed in a pre-urban society to meet the needs of country dwellers. Indeed, the very name 'pagan' is derived from the Latin word *paganus*—'rustic or country dweller'. The worship of deities associated with the earth and sky was clearly important to people who were dependent on those very things for their livelihoods and, ultimately, their survival. Christianity in the Roman era was associated with towns. At the beginning of the Anglo-Saxon period, Christianity would still have offered a formularized religion for urban dwellers to cling to when their structured life was disintegrating around them; town dwellers were used to living by rules, and a religion which offered a comparable system would be more attractive than a nebulous array of beliefs which only interpreted the rural world. It was only in the late 9th and early 10th centuries, as towns once again developed, that paganism was severely threatened.[4]

It is probable that the 'intellectual shapelessness of paganism helped it to persist'; if it had possessed a clear structure it would have been easier for the Christian Church to stamp it out. As it was, the Church could only attack its specifics, but not get at its roots which were multi-stranded and deep-seated. Yet for a religion that had such widespread and long-lived appeal, it is surprising that so little from the sub-Roman and Anglo-Saxon pagan era apparently survives, even though Roman pagan relics exist in some numbers in Britain. Bede refers to pagan temples and images carved out of stone and wood but, to date, no stone image has been found that can be definitely ascribed to Anglo-Saxon pagan manufacture. As the English do not have a record as carvers in stone until the later 7th century, the stone idols mentioned by Bede are more likely to be of Roman origin.[5] The Roman altar that has been re-sited in St. Michael's church at Michaelchurch, a tiny settlement west of Ross-on-Wye, Herefordshire, is an example of later re-use; it is now used a stoup cut from an altar which might have formerly stood at a road junction. There is also a Roman altar in St. Swithin's church in Lincoln, this time dedicated to the Fates—who determined the span of a person's life—perhaps made by an official of a guild, suggesting 'that the altar may have belonged to a burial club, which maintained a communal tomb, or a cemetery, where the memory of its members was kept green by ritual ceremonies'.[6] Wooden objects of either Roman or Anglo-Saxon period would have disintegrated unless they were preserved in water-logged, anaerobic conditions. Even in these contexts no Anglo-Saxon pagan idols have been unequivocally identified.

Old English authors used the words *hearg*, *weoh*, and *wih* in a variety of meanings, for example

Fig.1 Roman altar re-used as a stoup, Michaelchurch, near Ross-on-Wye, Herefordshire

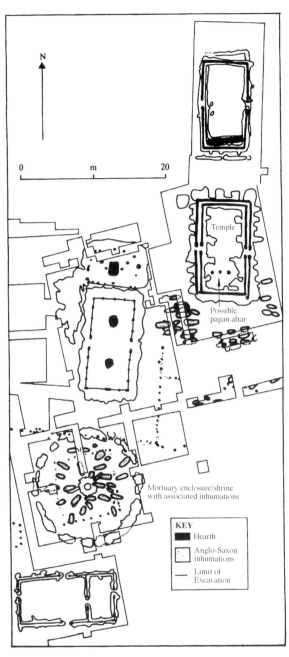

Fig.2 Plan of Yeavering showing the pagan temple erected on the earlier Roman site

as as an 'idol', 'shrine', or 'temple', making it difficult to appreciate how a pagan religious site would have appeared.[7] Were they small or large? Open or enclosed? Bede's account of Edwin of Northumbria's conversion provides a feel for one of these sites. In this, a senior pagan priest, Coifi, attacks his heathen temple as a way of breaking with paganism. Coifi sets out on a stallion bearing a spear (pagan priests were only permitted to ride a mare and go unarmed) and rides up to where the idols are lodged, then casts his spear into the temple to profane it and instructs his companions 'to set fire to the temple and its enclosures and destroy them'.[8] The account both indicates a professional priesthood with its own rules of conduct and that there were temples made, partially at least, from wood which were big enough to have their own enclosures.[9] Although this story relates to a male priest, graves of a few rich females, buried with gold beaded headwear and perforated spoons and other symbolic objects, suggest that women might also have had some religious function.

If archaeologists do not know exactly what they are looking for in terms of pagan Anglo-Saxon structures, especially as there appears to be no diagnostic features or finds, then it is quite possible that they have misinterpreted some structures on church sites as belonging to the Christian period when they might legitimately belong to a pagan precursor. In this respect the work done at Yeavering in Northumberland is critical.

Yeavering was an early Bernician royal residence from Aethelfrith's time where excavations have revealed what is believed to be a heathen temple, the Anglo-Saxons re-using a site which had had religious importance from the Bronze Age. The continuity was even maintained in the Christian era when a Bronze Age barrow, which had carried a tall post, was enclosed within the churchyard. The temple 'was a rectangular wooden structure, orientated north-south', with internal dimensions of approximately 10.5m (35ft) by 5.1m (17ft) and had doors in both of its long sides. When the building was enhanced by being encased in an outer close set ring of large timbers, these doors became double entrances. The outer walls were rendered and buttressed, while 'the inner walls were lined with wattle and daub'.[10] At the southern end three post-holes marked the position of a possible pagan altar which was removed when the temple became a church after the visit of Paulinus, a colleague of the Roman missionary Mellitus, in 627. The roof was supported by posts at the middle of each end wall. Beyond the temple enclosure was an inhumation cemetery and to the north-west of the temple building a massive post, almost 0.6m (2ft) square, was sunk 1.2m (4ft) into the ground, which Owen suggests perhaps symbolically represented 'the sacred tree of more primitive Germanic heathenism' as well as 'continuing the tradition of sacred pillars already established on the site'. The presence of a pit within the temple building containing animal bones, mainly of oxen—especially their skulls—suggests a ritual use. Indeed, so many bones had been placed there (probably as offerings) that they had 'overflowed the pit and had been stacked against the wall'.[11]

Bede records that *Blodmonath* (equivalent to November) was 'the month of sacrifices because in it they [pagans] dedicated to their gods the cattle which they were on the point of slaughtering'.[12] This annual slaughter, undertaken because of the difficulty of over-wintering stock, created a sudden excess of food which occasioned a time of feasting and probably developed into a religious ritual that included offering ox-heads to the gods. It may be that 'the magnificent head of the beast, with the brain which had controlled the powerful shoulders and strong limbs, was an awesome object containing heathen magic'. The discovery of ox-skulls in ritual contexts have been made throughout England: at Harrow Hill in Sussex over 1,000 were discovered and, in the early 14th century, ox-heads were discovered on the south side of London's St. Paul's Cathedral. In Mercia a single ox-head was found among human burials and cremations in a pagan cemetery at Soham, 5 miles south-east of Ely, and, at Sutton Courtenay, 8 miles south of Oxford, part of an ox skull, complete with horns, 'was found at the centre of the floor of an Anglo-Saxon building'. Such offerings were probably made to the gods to thank them for their benefice during the last year and to ensure the fertility of the remaining stock in the next.[13]

But the most important source of information regarding Anglo-Saxon paganism lies in the place-names of their early settlements,[14] even though they are very rare. There are only about 20 existing or locatable place-names which incorporate the names of Old English gods, and about 27 names in England as a whole which incorporate the words *hearg*, *weoh* and *wih* that denote a heathen sanctuary.[15] Yet these few survivals are remarkable when it is considered that the Church might have been expected to eliminate all traces of paganism. Almost certainly, other places with pagan names were subsequently renamed and any trace of an earlier name has vanished. East-central Mercia has a relatively high percentage of pagan place-names with an almost even spread between *hearg* and *weoh* names, and a few places celebrating a specific English pagan god (see Fig.2). Their virtual absence in the westerly and northerly regions of Mercia may be because these areas retained a strong British Church and/or that they were among the later areas reached by the heathen Anglo-Saxons—Roman Christianity was following hard on their heels by this time. For example there is no record of the conversion to Christianity of the *Hwicce* who formed a sub-province of Mercia and included what is now Worcestershire, Gloucestershire and the south-western part of Warwickshire, which indicates they were already Christian. Gelling suggests that the British Christian element of the *Hwicce* may have been numerous enough to cause incoming Anglo-Saxon settlers to abandon their paganism. She also remarks that there 'may only have been one generation of English paganism' among the *Magonsaete*, who occupied what is now northern Herefordshire and southern Shropshire, which might not have allowed 'for the growth of noteworthy centres of pagan worship'. However, the idea that place-names that indicate sites of pagan Germanic worship date from the earliest stages of Anglo-Saxon settlement has been questioned by Gelling, as such place-names are not generally in the earliest areas settled by the Anglo-Saxons:[16] certainly Wednesbury and Wednesfield, near Birmingham, are not.

Yeavering has shown that Anglo-Saxon pagan temples were not all built on greenfield sites. In Mercia, Great Harrowden, 2 miles north of Wellingborough in Northamptonshire, contains the element *hearg* and means 'hill with heathen temples'[17] and is close to a Roman settlement; a Roman coin hoard discovered at Harrow Farm near Hinkley in Leicestershire may have possibly been 'a votive offering at a rural shrine'.[18] The lost name of *Harowdonehull* in the parish of Woodeaton in Oxfordshire probably incorporates *hearg* and, as such, may refer to a stone-built 'Romano-Celtic temple which stood on the main hill in the parish', in which case it would be a significant example of an older structure being re-used by the pagan Anglo-Saxons.[19] *Hearg* may also be present in the first element of Arrowfield Top, about 5 miles north-north-west of Redditch in Worcestershire, although this has been disputed; the *Place-Names of Worcestershire* states it was first recorded in about 1300 as *Harewemede*, suggesting a heathen temple/sanctuary was worshipped in an open field or mead. Interestingly, Arrowfield Top lies only about 5 miles south of the pagan site at Weoley (Castle).[20]

Some pagan temples developed into permanent features which, at least in the case of Yeavering, were wooden-framed, ridge-roofed, rectangular structures, which could be set within forest clearings associated with sacred groves, a holy well or special tree. Inside the temple there 'was a sanctum with an altar' and the likeness of perhaps several gods.[21]

Probably the best known names containing the *weoh* or *wih* elements in Mercia are Weedon Bec and Upper Weedon, south-east of Daventry in Northamptonshire, and Weedon Lois, north-east of Banbury. The 'Bec' and 'Lois' suffixes are post-Conquest additions from Continental religious houses and do not concern us here. Tradition has it that Mercian kings had a royal residence at Weedon and that King Wulfhere's daughter, St. Waerburh, (also known as Werburgh and Werburga) founded a monastery at a place called Weedon in about 680.[22] While a nun at Ely her uncle, King Aethelred of Mercia, recalled her to found several monasteries in Mercia, including those at Weedon, Hanbury in Staffordshire and Threckingham in Lincolnshire.[23] While much of what is said about Waerburh is legendary, Morris notes that her association with Weedon seems to be quite secure.[24] The actual site of Waerburh's monastery is not known but it may have been superimposed on the site of the *Weoh*, a pagan temple or shrine, as part of the policy of Christianizing pagan sites encouraged by the Augustine mission to Britain. As the second part of the name Weedon is from *dun* or 'hill', (Weedon, therefore, meaning the 'hill with a heathen temple'), the most likely spot for the temple is considered to be Weedon Hill, the highest place in the parish and about a mile south-west of the present church of Saints Peter and Paul at Weedon Bec.[25] An alternative suggested by Morris is a site in the neighbouring parish of Stowe-Nine-Churches where the parish church of St. Michael stands on the brow of a hill. Its elevated position again makes it a candidate for the site of the pagan *weoh* and indeed the church is said to be built on a site associated with Neolithic worship.[26] The first element of Stowe-Nine-Churches derives from *stow* which can be interpreted as 'a holy place, hermitage or monastery' and its church has fragments of architectural sculpture which appear to have been taken from a large and impres-

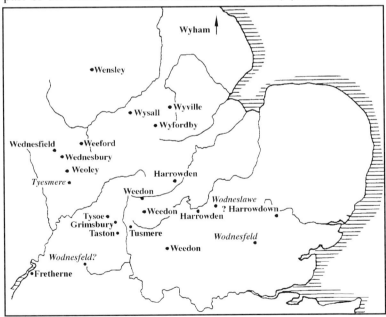

Fig.3 Some place-names in Central Mercia that refer to heathen places of worship, denoted by the weoh, wih *or* hearg *place-name elements, and to pagan Anglo-Saxon gods.*
Lost names are in italics

sive Roman building.[27] Built into the north-west corner of the tower, which itself dates to the late Anglo-Saxon or Saxo-Norman period, is a fragment of an earlier carved stone, possibly part of an early cross-shaft. In about 1860 parts of the foundations of a narrow Saxon church were found during restorations.[28] St. Michael's church and its immediate environs still possess an unusual, almost hermetical atmosphere, in spite of being so close to the A5 and the old Watling Street—a memory of a pagan and then a monastic past maybe?

There are several other *weoh* examples in Mercia, including Weeford in Staffordshire—'ford by a heathen temple';[30] Wyham, a parish in Lincolnshire, 7 miles north-north-west of Louth—'(at the) heathen temple'; Wyville, south-west of Grantham—'a holy place, heathen temple' associated with a spring or stream[31] or 'heathen-temple spring';[32] possibly Wyfold Grange, (SU 687817), about 5 miles north-north-west of Reading; Wysall—'heathen temple on the spur of a hill'[33]/'?hill-spur of the heathen temple';[34] and Wyfordby, east of Melton Mowbray in Leicestershire, which may derive from Wigford 'ford by a *wig*, or *weoh* or temple'[35] with the 'by' being a later Norse addition. There is also a suggestion that 'an alternative native form, *weo*', may occur in the first element of the Wellingtons in Herefordshire and Shropshire.[36] (Wellington has been interpreted as 'estate associated with Weola' but it is conceded that, as there is no other trace of this personal name, 'it is unlikely that it would be found only in four *-ingtun* formations'—two in Herefordshire (the other is Wellington Heath, 2 miles north of Ledbury), one in Shropshire and the fourth in Somerset.[37]

Pagan Deities

Perhaps the most important Anglo-Saxon deity was Woden, also worshiped in Germany and Scandinavia as Odin. It appears that the English thought of Woden as a god of the dead and a god of wisdom.[38]

Woden became associated with the 'Wild Hunt', a recurring feature of northern mythologies. In Norse mythology Woden (Odin) was the leader of the Hunt 'who careered across the stormy night sky followed by his pack of hounds in full cry'. Woden's role in the Wild Hunt may be taken as a deified development of the ancient German storm giant, Wode, who led his '"wild army", ... his procession of the homeless dead across the sky'. The Celts had their own version in the 'Dogs of Hell' who behaved in the same

Fig.4 The church at Stowe-Nine-Churches, one of the sites where St. Waerburh is suggested to have founded a 7th-century monastery in the area. A legend grew up that while living at Weedon she was troubled by a flock of geese which were grazing young crops and causing damage. She commanded the birds to go and it was later believed that wild geese would never land to graze in the locality. This is but one legend which associates an abbess with wildfowl, but it may conceivably be interpreted as an attack on ornithomancy (divination from the flight patterns and cries of birds) which was part of the pagan religion, or that the story disguises an account of the ritual cleansing of a pagan site by a Christian abbess[29]

way. Christianity duly modified the story by interpreting the Wild Hunt as being 'howling demons' led by the Devil. Woden's airborne activities are also associated with Santa Claus, since it was originally Woden 'who careered across the night sky in his chariot, bearing gifts at the time of the winter solstice'.[39] In Norway, Woden's associates were the Valkyries—battle maidens who chose the slain by reading the omens in bloody entrails and determined who would be killed in a forthcoming battle. In this, however, they acted as agents for Woden. The slain were then taken to Valhalla, one of the god's halls, and were feasted nightly. From here Woden would lead these chosen warriors out into the final battle against the giants, the pagan gods' mortal enemies who represented the forces of evil. It is through his role of leading the souls of the dead that Woden came to be identified with the Roman god Mercury—'the leader of souls', a link still apparent in the names for the middle day of the week: Wednesday is derived from the Old English *Wodens-daeg*, while the French *Mercredi* comes from the Roman *Mercurii dies*.[40]

However, Woden is probably best known for his identification as the god of war or the promoter of strife; it is said that he had first caused war amongst the gods by flinging his spear amongst them. Coifi's action of throwing a spear into his pagan temple as a sign of desecration shows that he must have been aware of such a mythology for, by using the god's own gesture, he was demonstrating that he was an enemy of the old heathenism.[41]

Woden's cult may be behind the practice of cremation used by some pagan Anglo-Saxons. In Icelandic literature it is recorded that Odin established cremation, and those who were burnt after death with their possessions went to join him,[42] which is perhaps one of the reasons why the early Christian church was so vehemently against cremation. However, it was as god of war that the Anglo-Saxon kings invoked him in their ancestry, first the earliest Anglian kings, then Penda and even the Christian Offa of Mercia.

Woden's name is found in several Mercian place-names. The most well-known is Wednesbury—'Woden's *burg* or fortress' in Staffordshire. To the north-west is Wednesfield—'Woden's field' (first mentioned as *Wodensfeld* in 996)[43] which suggests an open area of land named after the god. It is possible that, being only 4½ miles apart, these two names indicate part of the same sacred area dedicated to Woden.[44] St. Bartholomew's church at Wednesbury is in an elevated position and the 'bury' element could refer to an earlier defended site within which the Anglo-Saxons established 'a cult-place dedicated to Woden',[45] a place that was in turn 'supplanted by, or transformed into, a Christian church in the second half of the seventh century ...'.[46] Intriguingly, it is suggested that St. Chad placed the centre of the Mercian see at nearby Lichfield partly because 'unregenerate worshippers of Woden seemed an inducement to this particular saint'.[47]

The lost place-name of *Wodnesfeld* in Gloucestershire shares the same meaning with Wednesfield—and also Wensley, 2 miles west of Matlock in Derbyshire, and Wensley in Bedfordshire—of 'Woden's field', and denotes a wood or glade dedicated to Woden.[48] A lost place-name *Wodneslawe* in Bedfordshire may remember a burial mound connected with Woden.[49]

The Anglo-Saxons often named large landscape features after Woden, and he seems particularly associated with man-made mounds and earthworks. It appears that the earliest Anglo-Saxon settlers presumed that such landscape features formed before their arrival were the work of the gods. But this does not mean that a pagan temple or sanctuary was necessarily associated with these places.[50] Dykes often bear Woden's name and the fact that Woden's nickname, Grim, is used for many of them in England suggests the popular nature of his cult. Grim's Ditch, a possible Iron Age territorial marker, impinges on Mercia near Charlbury, in Oxfordshire and a Grim's Ditch is also found in Hertfordshire and Middlesex. In Hampshire there is Grims Dyke and also Woden's Dyke—indeed a now obsolete name *Grimesdich* was recorded in the 13th century for the latter.[51] Woden's name is also found in Wansdyke which runs partly through Hampshire. While Woden's name is most commonly linked with linear earthworks, this god's name can be related to other prehistoric landscape features. Gelling notes that Grimsbury, an eastern suburb of Banbury in Oxfordshire, is interpreted as 'Grim's burg/fortification' and probably records a lost fortification; however a 'Grim's Hill', recorded in the Anglo-Saxon charter bounds of Hawling, east of Cheltenham, in Gloucestershire, does mark a hill still topped by a fort, and a hill-fort exists at Grimsbury Castle in Hampstead Norris, 6 miles north-east of Newbury in Berkshire. Yet not all such names containing Grim may have been coined by pagan Anglo-Saxons, as it is likely that the name survived the Christian conversion of the 6th and 7th centuries and became synonymous with the devil, hence the number of 'Devil's' dykes, ditches and highways still in existence which refer to earthworks and Roman roads.[52]

Fig.5 *A Grimsditch in north-west Herefordshire, marked on Isaac Taylor's map of the county drawn in the mid-18th century, is no longer marked on current Ordnance Survey maps*

Thunor or Thor, sometimes represented as the son of Woden, was another important Anglo-Saxon deity—his name, which means 'thunder', is reflected in our Thursday, *Thunres-daeg*. He had been associated with the Roman god Jove or Jupiter, the father of the gods, on the Continent. In Anglo-Saxon England Thunor is portrayed as 'driving over the storm-clouds in his chariot drawn by two goats' and flinging 'his thunderbolt from mountain-peak to mountain-peak'.[53] It was believed that the rumble of the chariot wheels as they passed overhead created the noise of thunder and the hammer he carried acted as a thunderbolt. Unlike Woden, who made use of resourcefulness and cunning, Thunor was decidedly more brutal, using his short-handled hammer to mete out his revenge, sometimes hurling it as a missile.[54]

Thunor's name is generally associated with the *leah*—'clearing'—element of place-names, which suggests that he was worshiped in sacred groves or meadows, possibly associated with a pole or pillar, as in the one found at Yeavering.[55] Through his connection with pillars and also oak trees, he became the protector of men's homes, as the pillars in buildings, especially in aristocratic halls, were often made of oak.[56] Thunor also ruled 'the fair weather and the fruits of the earth' and therefore appears to have had a role as a fertility god,[57] another reason, perhaps, for his association with pillars and posts. Coupled with his position as the god of men's homes, Thunor may be interpreted as the friend of the farmer, and would clearly be of importance to an agriculturally-based community. He has also been linked with the practice of cremation, and his swastika emblem indicating, among other virtues, good luck, fecundity, long-life and health, has been found on cremation urns.[58] There are, however, no certain place-names in the

Fig.6 Upper, Middle and Lower Tysoe in Warwickshire, about 7¹/₂ miles north-west of Banbury, are at the edge of an enscarpment called the Vale of the Red Horse. Tysoe is interpreted as meaning 'Tiw's hoh or hill spur', and it is believed that the district derives its name from the now lost figure of a great galloping horse cut into the reddish soil of the hillside and which was the emblem of the war-god Tiw.[64] It is possible that Tiw was associated with horses at Tysoe for sacred horses were significant in northern religions and were believed to be the confidants of the gods and were used to forecast the future—certainly a useful attribute in war.[65] The horse figure may have had an even older Celtic connection. In the Celtic religion horses were linked with the 'cults of war-gods and red was a colour associated with death', so a red horse really was an omen of disaster.[66] If Tysoe's horse was originally a British cult-symbol carved on the hill it would have been a potent warning to aggressors approaching across the southern Warwickshire plain to stay away, or suffer the consequences! In Mayr-Harting's scenario the pagan Anglo-Saxons would have taken on the symbolism and substituted their own war-god Tiw in place of the earlier British/Celtic gods. The figure was scoured annually at least into the mid-17th century when the Warwickshire antiquarian, Sir William Dugdale, mentions it, but it has since disappeared. The horse figure is believed to have been near the 'Sunrising Inn', a mile north of Old Lodge Hill,[67] where the arrow above indicates.

Mercian kingdom which can testify to his cult—although Taston, just north of Grim's Ditch 2 miles north of Charlbury, and Tusmore, some 5¹/₂ miles north-north-west of Bicester in Oxfordshire, may mean 'Thor/Thunor's stone' and 'Thunor's Pool' respectively. However, with both place-names there are 'etymological problems' which render them dubious cases.[59] Thundridge, about 4¹/₂ miles north-east of Hertford, does, however, link Thunor with a ridge. There is a record of *on thunres lea* in Hampshire which connects the god with a sacred grove or meadow. The location of the majority of Thunor names, extant and lost, suggests that the god was more commonly worshipped in Saxon areas, especially Essex and Wessex, than in the Anglian areas of settlement.[60]

The god Tiw, who has given his name to our Tuesday, *Tiwes-daeg,* was essentially a god both of battle, and law and order. He is probably of greater antiquity than Woden and Thunor, and may once have been the supreme deity, for his name is related to the Romans' Jupiter and the Greeks' Zeus, as well as being equated with the Roman war-god Mars.[61] It has been suggested that Tiw was but one later name of the deity that had originally been the old Sky Father, Tiwaz, and chief of the gods among north-western Europeans.[62] Through time Tiw's position was relegated to the position of solely a war god. The runic symbol ↑ represented Tiw's name and was 'traditionally carved on weapons to ensure victory'; such symbols have been found on sword-pommels and spears in Kent. The ↑ sign is also the most common of all runes and rune-like symbols found on English cremation urns.[63]

Tiw is represented in three place-names in Mercia. The now obsolete *Tyesmere* in Worcestershire celebrates a lake that was sacred to Tiw and suggests the pagan Anglo-Saxon worship of pools, wells and springs, and the lost *Tislea* in Hampshire which links him with a sacred grove or meadow. The other is Tysoe (see Fig.6).

The other pagan deity worshiped in Anglo-Saxon England, who makes a fleeting place-name appearance in Mercia, is the goddess Friga/Frigg. She has given her name to Friday, *Frig-daeg*, and is represented in old English and Norse sources as Woden's wife and the mother of the gods.[68] Not surprisingly she is therefore the goddess of childbirth and marriage.[69] Our modern day slang of 'frig/frigging' is very likely derived from the old English word 'frig' which means sexual passion, itself possibly derived from Friga/Frigg's name—a long way from the goddess' former association with her Roman equivalent Venus! Although Friga/Frigg may have originally been the goddess of married love, it is possible that this 'pagan matriarch degenerated to become synonymous with lust' when the Christian church provided the newly converted Anglo-Saxons with the 'pure Mother-figure' of Mary.[70]

As a matriach, Friga/Frig can be identified with the 'Earth Mother' who is older than the worship of personalized gods. Like most pagan people, the Anglo-Saxons acknowledged such a figure for her favour was essential for their survival.[71] In southern Denmark and northern Germany this deity was known as 'Nerthus' and one of the tribes who worshiped her in the 1st century A.D. were the Angli, ancestors of the Anglian complement of the Anglo-Saxons which included the Mercians. Friga may have also been one of the Mother Goddesses mentioned by Bede in his *De Temporum Ratione*. In northern mythology Friga is accredited with foreknowledge and magical skills: Germanic people, it seems, believed in women's ability to look into the future.[72] There are few traces of the cult of the goddess Friga in Mercia—Fretherne—'Friga's thorn-bush'—on the Severn Estuary 8 miles west of Stroud in Gloucestershire is one, although the significance of the thorn bush has not been explained; Froyle (*c.*6 miles south-west of Farnham) and Frobury (*c.*9 miles north-west of Basingstoke), which are both in Hampshire but about 19 miles apart, apparently shared the identical name of *Freohyll* which may mean 'the hill of the goddess Frig'. Freefolk also in Hampshire, east of Andover, was recorded as *Frigefolc* in 1086 and possibly means 'Friga's people'.[73]

The veneration of trees was also part of Anglo-Saxon paganism. As mentioned, oaks were associated with Thunor, whereas ash was held in esteem for the shafts of spears, which were so important to the war-conscious Anglo-Saxons. Yew was also of some importance, although it has been suggested that the Germanic peoples may have learnt superstitions about the yew from the neighbouring Celts. It is probable that any surviving British paganism would have influenced that of the incoming Anglo-Saxons—notably in head cults—for no culture remains untouched by others into which it comes into contact. The Celts cut ogham characters into wands made from yew and it is possible that this wood came to have especial associations with runes, the magic letters by which evil could be repelled.[74] Like the Celts, it is possible the Germanic peoples saw the yew as a symbol of protection, and excavations in Frisia revealed two possible amulets made from yew with runic inscriptions,[75] worn to protect their wearers. A circle of yews was believed to give protection: in a burial site it supposedly protected the dead from evil spirits and in early Anglo-Saxon England 'clusters of yews were used as stockades' within which the local inhabitants could store their possessions and gain sanctuary.[76] However, the traditional belief that large yews in churchyards point to a pre-Christian origin and that churches were built on sacred pagan sites 'has received disappointingly little support from excavation'. Indeed, it has been pointed out that if yews were such a feature of early church sites then there should be several place-names in the nature of 'Yewchurch'.[77] Having said that, there are yews over 2,000 years old standing in some churchyards, and Richard Mabey notes that 'yews of great ages are rarely found outside churchyards and conversely that 'no other type of ancient tree occurs so frequently inside', going on to say 'I do not know of any similarly

Tissington Wells

Figs.7 to 12 The wells at Tissington, north of Ashbourne in Derbyshire. Clockwise from top left: Town Well, Yew Tree Well, Coffin Well, Hall Well, Children's Well and Hands Well. The number of wells and the fact that St. Mary's church is set on a raised mound suggests a pre-Christian origin to the settlement. The wells are still dressed on Ascension Day each year, a ceremony which may have its antecedence in the Christianization of a pagan ritual honouring each well's deity

exclusive relationship between places of worship and a single tree species existing anywhere else in the Western world'.[78] Perhaps the connection between yews, pagan sites and churchyards will never be satisfactorily resolved.

Springs, streams and pools were also worshiped by the heathen Anglo-Saxons, a practice with strong links to the Celtic pagan past. The term 'well' is often used for a spring and will be so used in this chapter; in fact it is unusual for a holy well to be a shaft well. It is notoriously difficult to determine the date of a holy well as there is often little structure or remnants of offerings to date. The continuity of the Celtic pagan head cult into the Christian period may be seen in wells which possess the representation of a saint's head as part of its structure, such as St.

Fig.13 St. Peter's Well near Peterchurch, Herefordshire. The head allegedly represents St. Peter, but is reminiscent of the pagan head cults in the use of a representation of a head alone. The water issued from the head's mouth which supplied a bathing pool, the water of which apparently cured rheumatism. Two apertures at the back of the head supplied water which was believed to cure eye troubles

Peter's Well near Peterchurch, 5 miles west of Hereford (Fig.13). Depictions of heads are sometimes found carved onto church fonts, showing how the pagan past has found its way through the church door.[79]

One of the major prerequisites for habitation is the availability of water. When a hermit chose a site in a remote area he/she would look for a reliable, clean supply of water and such a practical need is in danger of being overlooked in today's quest for a more spiritual or ritual explanation. Only when a hermitage had fallen into disuse might the well/spring take on a religious aura and become a site of pilgrimage. Similarly the existence of a spring might be one of the defining reasons for a particular siting of a later church; water would be needed for religious purposes such as baptism and for the domestic needs of the priest.[80] As geology favours the creation of springs in western and northern England, their scarcity elsewhere should not automatically be taken as evidence of difference in religious belief.

In pre-Christian times wells were used in the art of divination. This connection with the future explains why so many wells are now called wishing wells, but divination and augury (the art of predicting future events from signs and omens) were seen as pagan practices and were condemned by the Church council of *Clofesho* in 747.[81] The curious assemblages of prehistoric to medieval objects that have been found in wells may be explained as 'gifts' given to propitiate the wells' gods or spirits.

There are several place-names in Mercia which suggest pagan divination and augury rites. The combination of the elements 'holy' and 'well' may suggest purely Christian use but this should not be assumed. There is an Old English word *hael* which means 'omen' and some 'holy-well' place-names are, in fact, derived from the meaning 'Omen-well' where the pagan art of divination was practised. The meaning of 'Omen/wishing well' is fairly secure in Holywell (Hall) in Lincolnshire, about 6½ miles north-north-west of Stamford; it was first recorded in 1190 as *Helewelle*, the first element deriving from *hael*. Fritwell, some 8 miles south-east of Banbury, also means 'Augury or wishing well' as the first element *freht* or *firht* means 'augury': its earliest spelling, in 1086, was *Fert(e)welle*.[82]

Seawell in Blakesley, 4 miles west of Towcester; Sywell, 5 miles west of Wellingborough in Northamptonshire; Sewell in Bedfordshire and Showell, a small hamlet 3½ miles north-north-east of

Chipping Norton, Oxfordshire, may also have springs associated with religious or superstitious beliefs as they contain, as their first element, the number 'seven'.[83] This is believed to have been the most mystical and magical of numbers. There is also a place called Seven Springs, 4 miles south of Cheltenham, Gloucestershire, and it is suggested that Sevenhampton, 5 miles east of Cheltenham, may have been named from *Seofenwyllas* (seven wells) which was a locality mentioned in an Anglo-Saxon charter for a village called Aston Blank, several miles to the east.[84]

If wells are known to have been used for divination and/or for healing purposes, the likelihood is that they have a pagan past; where votive objects have been recovered, the case is stronger still.

Another category of object which was worshiped in pagan religions were stones. Unfortunately there are no pre-Norman sources which tell us anything about the appearance, or use, of stones which were part of heathen sites but a stone might have been chosen for veneration because of its unusual shape or properties.[85] It is clear that the pagan Anglo-Saxons respected and often re-used prehistoric sacred sites.[86] It is possible that stones were incorporated into pagan temples because of their past veneration. The carvers of high crosses in the 8th and 9th centuries may have made use of the tall, prehistoric standing stones as blanks for the shafts.[87] The practice of using such crosses may hark back to the pagan use of tall posts in sacred areas, demonstrating yet another possible pagan to Christian transition. Radstone, about 8 miles east of Banbury, is derived from the Old English *rode-stan* ('rood-stone') and means something akin to 'stone with a cross'[88] which may indicate it was recut from a prehistoric monolith, or was a pagan stone that was re-dedicated for Christian use.

A recent study has shown that the pagan Anglo-Saxons also re-used a variety of monuments, dating from the Neolithic to the Romano-British era, as foci for their burial sites, in a deliberate act which made use of the visual impact of the monuments and their ritual significance. Such activity continued until the 8th century, and overlapped with the conversion of the heathen English through missionaries from Rome.[89] In Mercia round barrows were most frequently used as a focal point for Anglo-Saxon pagan burial with 19 being reused in the Peak District, whereas in the midlands 17 round barrows and 14 Roman structures were re-used, along with three hill forts. In the Upper Thames region 11 Roman structures were re-used, along with 10 hill forts and 27 round barrows. A few long barrows and henges/enclosures were also used in each area.[90] Unlike the Christian Church, Anglo-Saxon heathenism did not actively suppress other forms of religion. As mentioned earlier, at Bromfield, Shropshire, an Iron Age enclosure was re-used for what appears to have been an early (650-750) Anglo-Saxon cemetery as traces of up to 31 burials were found orientated roughly east/west, with three possessing grave goods,[91] suggesting a continuance of pagan practice in what was apparently a transitional period.

As well as the beneficial gods and spirits, the pagan Anglo-Saxons lived in a world inhabited by malevolent spirits which included goblins, sprites, elves and ghosts, and Mercia had its fair share of places associated with such demons or evil spirits: Shucknall—'Hill of the demons' or 'Goblin hill/haunted hill', east of Hereford; Shuckburgh, 5 miles west of Daventry in Warwickshire, Shugborough, 5 miles east-south-east of Stafford and Shuckborough also in Staffordshire,—'Demon fort or hill'.[92] Shocklach in Cheshire, 7 miles east of Wrexham, is interpreted variously as 'Demon stream'[93] or a demon linked with 'a trap' or 'water channel'.[94] (Shocklach and Shugborough Hall reputedly have modern ghosts!) Shuckton Manor in Derbyshire suggests a demon is linked with a thorn[95] (compare with *Fretherne* which is linked to the goddess Friga) although it has also been interpreted as 'Demon's farmstead',[96] while Shacklow in Derbyshire and Shucklow Warren in Buckinghamshire mean 'Demon mound or hill'.[97] The first elements of these names derives from the Old English *scucca*—demon', 'evil-spirit' or 'goblin'. Interestingly, the majority of such surviving names lie in the Mercian region. It is noteworthy that evil spirits were thought to haunt ordinary features such as a hill, a watercourse, a thorn or a farmstead. But what was it about the hill at Shucknall or the stream at

Shocklach, for example, that worried these pagan settlers? Unpleasant and/or frightening places must have gained a reputation and were named accordingly.

Our Mercian ancestors were also menaced by other supernatural creatures that populated the dark world outdoors. We know that giants were the enemies of the gods and the monster in *Beowulf* is depicted as a man-eating giant. Giants or demons were referred to as *entas*, *thyrs*, *pyrs* or *eoten* and it appears that, once again, Mercia had more than its fair share. An *eoten* apparently lurked by a ford in Shropshire and is possibly remembered in the obsolete name *eotanford* (although this name may relate to a personal name, Eota), and a *pyrs* was connected with a pit in Warwickshire which is recorded in the lost place-name *pyrs pyt*—'giant's pit'. A *pyrs* inhabited a thicket in Northamptonshire, recorded in an obsolete name *Thirsqueche*—'giant's thicket', and gave its name to Thyrspittes in Lincolnshire. Interestingly, Tusmore in Oxfordshire may mean *pyrs*-mere—'giant's pool' (see also p.51).[98]

Elves and dwarfs were also deemed as being wicked, unlike their modern-day benevolent counterparts. Elves were held responsible for diseases in man and beast by shooting arrows at their victims, thus man or animal could be 'elf-shot' and need a magical charm to recover. There are a number of Anglo-Saxon herbal remedies against elves who could also bring nightmares to the unfortunate.[99] Not surprisingly, the obsolete *Elvenfen* in Lincolnshire refers to an 'elves' fen' which is evidence again of the fear these desolate places held. Other Mercian examples include Eldon Hill (a hill linked with elves) in Derbyshire and Elvendon—'elf hill'—at Goring, 9 miles north-west of Reading. Gelling notes that some of the 'elf' and 'dwarf' names may indicate that echoes were generated there.[100]

Dwarves, *dwerg*, were also hostile creatures against whose evil influence the Anglo-Saxons invoked ritual actions and charms. A Mercian example is Dwarfholes in Warwickshire, which associates dwarves with a valley. Various terms for goblins, similarly evil creatures, are found in a variety of forms. The term 'hob' as in hobgoblin is found in Hob Hill in Derbyshire which is interpreted as 'hill of the goblin' and it is particularly common in minor names in this county.[101] Another term for a goblin, *Puca*, may be found in Pucklechurch, Gloucestershire, where the first element, the personal name Pucela, appears to be a familiar form of the Old English word *Puca*.[102] Puckeridge, about 8 miles north-north-east of Hertford, is identified as meaning 'the stream of the goblin or watersprite' from the elements *puca*—'goblin'—and *ric*—'stream'.[103] Indeed, there is an association of pucks with pits, in minor names and field-names, especially in the south-west midlands, which has never been explained. This is most noticeable in Gloucestershire, where names such as Puck Pit, Puckpits, Pugpit and Pucksholf occur widely.[104] A north-westerly suburb of Kidderminster, Worcestershire, called Puxton, may have the element *Pucel*—'goblin'—and may mean 'Goblin's farm', although it probably contains a personal name.[105] Today there still exists a remnant of what would have been a sizeable marsh and it is possible to imagine the will'o'the wisp, which rises occasionally from marshlands in the right atmospheric conditions, may have given Puxton the alternative meaning of 'Puck's or goblin's farm'.

It has been suggested that 'puck' and 'hob' names may occasionally be associated with earthworks. Hobditch Causeway, which runs south of Birmingham, is a Roman or pre-Roman linear earthwork which has been traced for up to 4 miles, and was clearly ascribed to a goblin, rather than the usual pagan god, Woden/Grim. At its eastern end lies Harborough Banks in Warwickshire where, in the 16th century, the field-names *Pouke Ditch* and *Grymshill* were recorded.[106]

The Old English word *haetse* has the same meaning as the modern word 'witch' and a possible Mercian example is Hassop, 2 miles north of Bakewell. In 1086 it was recorded as *Hetesope* where the first element may be *haeste*,[107] giving the sense of 'witches' valley'. This is a wide, flat valley contained between striking hills in the Peak District and is within a wider area of lead mining which is known to have been worked from Roman times. One wonders if, during the production of lead, an unusual atmosphere was created in the environs of Hassop suggestive of magic and witches?

The last major category in these supernatural names are those containing the word 'dragon' or 'reptile/snake' which is a potent symbol in the religious beliefs and literary work of the pagan Anglo-Saxons. In Germanic mythology dragons were believed to guard treasure in burial mounds. In the poem *Beowulf*, a work of probable 8th- or early 9th-century date, and possibly of Mercian origin (an Anglian origin is suggested linguistically), the dragon is described as 'the primeval enemy that haunts the dusk: the scaly, malicious Worm which seeks out funeral mounds and flies burning through the night, wrapped about with flame, to the terror of the country folk. Its habit is to seek out treasure hidden in the earth and mount guard over the pagan gold ...'.[108] In this poem the hero meets his death in confrontation with a dragon, who was guarding a burial mound, which Beowulf's subjects had had the impudence (or stupidity) to plunder. It is significant that here the dragon only posed a threat to the community after he had been disturbed by the thief. The appearance of flying dragons was considered an evil and dangerous portent; in the *Anglo-Saxon Chronicle* for 793, for example, dragons were seen flying over Northumbria, a spectacle which was followed by famine and the destruction of the church at Lindisfarne by the Vikings—their first devastating raid on Britain. And if dragons were not flying through the air, then their usual abode seemed to be in a barrow guarding treasure.[109]

From place-name evidence it is clear that the image of a dragon guarding treasure in a tumulus was known and understood, not only to the poets, but also among the people of the countryside.[110] In Mercia dragons apparently guarded mounds at Drakelow 'the dragon's mound'—3 miles north of Kidderminster, one just south of Burton-upon-Trent in Derbyshire and another in Bedfordshire. At Drakenage—'dragon's edge'—a minor name in Kingsbury, Warwickshire, a dragon was associated with a slight topographical slope, and at Drakeholes—'dragon's valley'—some 4 miles south-east of Bawtry, Nottinghamshire, with a valley.[111]

The same meaning, of a threat when disturbed, is found in the Old English term *wyrm*, meaning 'reptile, snake' and also 'dragon'. This derivation is found in Mercia at Wormwood Hill in Stapleford, just south-east of Cambridge, and was earlier recorded as *Wyrmelawe* suggesting 'that the tumulus here was considered to have a resident dragon'.[112] Care should be taken with seemingly identical 'Worm(e)low' place-names, for example Wormelow Tump, 6 miles south of Hereford, where the 'Worme' element refers to the Worm Brook, whose name is derived from a Celtic river-name meaning 'dusky, dun'.[113] The 'low' *hlaw* element probably referred to a prehistoric burial mound, which was obliterated during 19th-century road-widening—there was clearly no dragon guarding this one! However, Wormhill and Wormsley, respectively about 5 miles west and 6 miles north-west of Hereford may derive from *wyrm*.[114]

The connection of a dragon guarding a mound may also be implied where the words *hord* 'hoard' and *hlaw*—'low'—are found in combination, in Mercia one example is Hurdlow Town in Hartington, 9 miles north of Ashbourne in Derbyshire. When the word *hord* occurs in place-names Gelling observes reference is probably being made to 'finds of coins or other metal objects' and place-names 'containing *hord* will mostly indicate that the treasure was found and removed in pre-Conquest times, but they may sometimes be a clue to burial-mounds, even if these have been robbed'.[115] Hordley, about 7 miles east of Oswestry in Shropshire, and formerly in the province of the *Wreocensaete*, may be interpreted as a 'hoard found in a woodland clearing', although Ekwall suggests '*Leah* with a storehouse'.[116] However, in 1950 a Roman coin-hoard was found and 'it is possible that the *hord* of the place-name refers to earlier finds of this kind'.[117] Medieval field-names which contain the compound of *hord* and *draca* (another name for a dragon) are also indicative of treasure guarded by a dragon, an example of which occurs at Garsington, 5 miles south-east of Oxford, with the name *Brokenebereue*[118]—'broken barrow'—which probably refers to a robbed-out tumulus. It would be an effective form of social control, reiterated through place-names, to suggest dragons guarded tumuli and that these creatures could wreak havoc on a community because of one person's misdemeanours; it would stop anyone, save the most criminally-minded, from looting what was, in essence, a status symbol of those in power.

Conclusion

It is clear that the pagan Anglo-Saxons had a complex religion which had evolved to interpret and support their agrarian way of life. Their paganism was clearly deeply-rooted, for it continued to exist, albeit in a suppressed form, for many centuries after St. Augustine re-introduced Christianity into England. The pagan world was ruled by a variety of gods who had to be propitiated for continued favour and protection. In Mercia protection was not only sought from practical troubles but also from the malevolent spooks, goblins, dragons and elves who lived in the dark world beyond the safety of their halls, who lurked in pits and fens, on hill-sides and in streams. It was a multi-faceted and intricate set of beliefs which the Christian church struggled so hard and for so long to control.

CHAPTER 5
Christian Mercia

The well-known story of the introduction of Christianity from Rome through Augustine in 597 recounts that an Italian abbot, Gregory, later Pope Gregory the Great, was struck by the beauty of young Deiran slaves on sale in the market-place in Rome and learnt that they were heathen. He approached the then pope for permission to preach the Gospel in England but was turned down. On becoming pope, Gregory duly sent Augustine, the prior of his monastery. Two years earlier Gregory had written to the 'ruler of the papal estates in southern Gaul, instructing him to use surplus funds to clothe the poor and to buy from captivity English youths of about 17 or 18 to be given to monasteries'. It is possible that some of these youths may have joined Augustine in 597 or been part of a second wave of clergy in 601.[1]

By the time Augustine reached the Anglo-Saxons he had been elevated first to abbot and then to bishop in order to bolster his determination—it is clear that Augustine, and particularly his companions, had serious misgivings about going through with a mission 'to a barbarous, fierce, and pagan nation, of whose very language they were ignorant'.[2] Augustine duly reached Kent in May 597, and he and his mission were received hospitably by Kent's pagan king, Aethelberht, whose Frankish queen, Bertha, was already a Christian and had brought with her Bishop Liudhard, her chaplain from Frankia.

The account of Augustine's mission suggests that English Christianity began in the year 597, but the English had been exposed to Christianity from more than one direction throughout the 6th century. There is archaeological and literary evidence that some Germanic settlers who came from the Rhineland and other areas of western Germany, had had long associations with the Franks. Some of these Saxons settled in Gaul and some, ultimately, may have come to Britain, thus cementing links with the Rhineland and Gaul. There must have been some cultural contact and it is likely that, even before Augustine's mission, there were already Germanic Christians in England. Indeed, Kent may have resembled the Continent more closely than it did most of the rest of England at this time because of its contacts with Gaul and, as such, provided the suitable base for Augustine's mission. There was also the influence of the Celtic Church which was strong in the north and west of the British Isles with, no doubt some British Christians living, albeit in a minority, among the pagan Anglo-Saxons. In Adomnan's *Life of Columba*, two Christian Englishmen—Pilu and Genereus (the latter the community's baker) are recorded at the monastery at Iona before Columba's death in 597.[3]

The existence of Christians in Anglo-Saxon England prior to Augustine's mission is attested in part by the survival in place-names of the element *ecles*, which derives from the British word *egles*—a church or Christian centre. About 20 such names have been identified, many of them lying on or near Roman roads, and although not all are in areas of early Germanic settlement, the presence of such a name is taken to mean that the Anglo-Saxons 'noted the existence of a British church and called a place after it'.[4] In the Mercian region there are notable examples, such as Eccleshall—'nook at a Celtic Christian centre'[5]—7 miles north-west of Stafford in Staffordshire; Eccles—simply 'church'—4 miles west of Manchester and

Fig.1 Eccleshall church, Staffordshire. The place-name suggests a British church flourished here in central England at least since the 7th century

Eccleston—'church farmstead'[6]—3 miles south of Chester in Cheshire. There are two Exhalls in Warwickshire—one near Alcester, the other north of Coventry. Here, as with Eccleshall, the second element, *halh*, which normally means 'a sheltered place' Gelling suggests refers to 'land not included in the general administrative arrangements of a region' and that 'eccles' may have referred to a Christian community rather than a church building as such.[7] The name of the river Ecclesbourne in Derbyshire perhaps derives its name from a now lost settlement of *Eccles*.[8] In Herefordshire, Eccles Green, today a scattering of houses by Norton Canon on the A480, is interpreted tentatively as the Old English term for 'a Celtic Christian centre' and Eccleswall Court, south-east of Ross-on-Wye, may mean a 'Spring at a Celtic Christian Centre'.[9] However, caution needs to be exercised—some places may contain the personal name Eccel, a derivative of Ecca.[10] A third Herefordshire example of Eccles Alley (SO 344520), a minor place-name near Almeley, is so derived; the earliest recorded reference is in 1369-70 to *Eckeley*—'Ecca's wood or clearing'.[11]

It is often said that King Aethelberht of Kent was baptized in 597, but this is not certain. However, in a letter from Pope Gregory to the Patriarch of Alexandria, Gregory states that he had heard that 10,000 Anglo-Saxons had been baptized. This is probably a huge exaggeration.[12] Yet the missionaries from Rome were astute and would appreciate that the best way to convert the people was to convert their king—the rest would surely follow. So when King Edwin of Northumbria was baptized on Easter Day in 627, it is not surprising that he was joined by 'all the nobility of his kingdom and a large number of humbler folk'.[13] However, a king could not decide that he was going to become a convert on his own whim; he needed the support of his thegns. Bede records some of the discussions that occurred before Edwin's conversion, one of the most moving being contained in the council of chief men called by Edwin to discuss the matter. One of his chief advisers states:

Your Majesty, when we compare the present life of man on earth with that time of which we have no knowledge, it seems to me like the swift flight of a single sparrow through the banqueting-hall where you are sitting at dinner on a winter's day with your thanes and counsellors. In the midst there is a comforting fire to warm the hall; outside, the storms of winter rain or snow are raging. This sparrow flies swiftly in through one door of the hall, and out through another. While he is inside, he is safe from the winter storms; but after a few moments of comfort, he vanishes from sight into the wintry world from which he came. Even so, man appears on earth for a little while; but of what went before this life or of what follows, we know nothing. Therefore, if this new teaching has brought any more certain knowledge, it seems only right that we should follow it.[14]

This speech clearly illustrates, in the most human and most immediate terms, the fear that still concerns many today: the fear of the unknown and of what is to come. It is likely that a message, put over in such effective imagery, would have made even the most dyed-in-the-wool pagan listen.

But what else persuaded the kings to become converts? The missionaries were sufficiently shrewd to also appeal to the human weaknesses of greed and the desire for status. When Pope Gregory wrote to Aethelberht of Kent he stressed that God could make the king's 'glorious name still more glorious even to posterity' while, at the same time, drawing attention to indications that the end of the world was imminent.[15] Which king would not be attracted by this appeal of glory and long-lasting fame when mixed with fear, especially when he would also have increased access to the world of the Continent with its trade, its cultural opportunities and its perceived sophistication? The tactics used by the early missionaries may be gauged from the advice given by Bishop Daniel of Winchester to St. Boniface, at that time working as a missionary on the Continent among pagan Germans, in a letter of 723 or 724. Daniel suggests two lines of attack, firstly by tying the pagans in 'dialectical knots "calmly and with great moderation"' so making the heathens 'ashamed of the illogicalities and follies of paganism "more out of confusion than exasperation"', and, secondly, by arguing that their gods had treated them badly by leaving them in "the frozen lands of the north" while Christians enjoyed possession of lands which were "rich in wine and oil"'.[16] The arrival of Christian priests might have also added a certain amount of prestige and entertainment value to a royal court. The presence of 'important strangers, equipped with luxurious objects and performing unusual ceremonies' gave the impression of contact with distant powers,[17] with the sophisticated and the exotic. In the rather rough-and-tumble confines of a hall in the cold, damp Anglo-Saxon island this cannot have failed to impress the king's guests.

Bishop Daniel also states that, although the pagans believed in the importance of making sacrifices to gods, they did not know which was the most powerful of them, so they might be offending the one who needed most propitiation by paying him the least attention. A religion which had just one God could be proffered as a much safer bet. However, the Christian church's refusal to allow for the existence of any but their own god meant they may have underestimated the anxiety of many of their converts about what would happen if their old gods were left unpropitiated and decided to take revenge.[18] Not surprisingly then, in early Anglo-Saxon England Christian conversion was often transitory, as can be seen in the reversion to paganism in times of hardship or fear. And an outbreak of plague was just such an occasion. It hit Britain in about 664 and might have confirmed the belief of some that they should be more holy in Christian terms, whereas for others it may have meant a reversion to the paganism which had served them so well in the past and had the security of familiarity. This plague was the first major epidemic recorded in England and coincided with a total eclipse of the sun, a bad portent in itself. It ravaged nearly all of England from the south coast to Northumbria. Some have identified it with small-pox, some with bubonic plague, while others believe it may have been a recurrence of the Irish yellow plague of the 540s. Whatever its source, it lasted for about 20 to 25 years and contemporary accounts indicate it caused widespread death, social disruption and abandonment of religion.[19] The East Saxons under their king, Sighere,

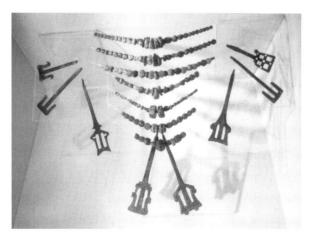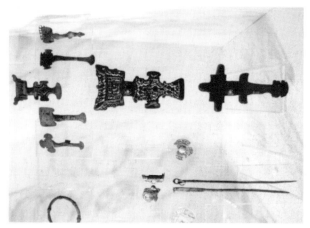

*Figs.2 and 3 Grave goods from pagan Anglo-Saxon graves from the midlands,
on the right they include a variety of square-headed and cruciform brooches*

reverted to paganism and it was the Mercian king, Wulfhere, who sent his own bishop, Jaruman, to bring them back to the faith. Bede recorded that Sighere and many of his people 'loved this life and sought no other, or even disbelieved in its existence. Hoping for protection against the plague by this means, they therefore began to rebuild the ruined temples and restore the worship of idols'.[20] This indicates a profound move away from Christian doctrine—and this around 665, nearly 70 years after Augustine had arrived. The conversion of England was clearly a long, hard process.

Duality of worship can be seen in the graves of this period. Generally it is considered that if a grave does not have an east-west alignment but contains grave goods, then it is a pagan burial. However, if it is aligned east-west and has only the body and perhaps a few clothing accessories, then it is Christian. Yet many 7th-century graves showing Christian orientation contain grave goods, indicating a possible fear of letting go of the old religion. It is only by the 8th century, when artefacts disappear from graves, that one can be fairly sure paganism, at least in terms of burial rites, had been abandoned.

Perhaps it is this ambivalence that can be seen in Penda's life-long paganism while at the same time allowing Christian missionaries to enter his kingdom to preach. It is likely that as a young man Penda would not have wanted to leave the gods who had served him so well, through a sense of loyalty and fear of reprisals, and, as an older man who saw the pagan context of his kingdom shrinking, it might seem more important than ever for him to keep the pagan gods appeased. His son, Peada, had become Christianized through the Northumbrian connection, and Penda's daughters included several future saints: Cyneburh, founder and abbess of Castor in Northamptonshire, Edith of Bicester and Eadburga who was a nun and possibly abbess of Aylesbury. Thus, with an eye on the past, as well as an eye to the future and on the benefits which could accrue to his kingdom through the new religion, Penda became the pagan tolerant of Christianity and critical of those who did not live up to the standards of the new religion they professed to believe in.[21]

For a *bretwalda* there might have been another reason to convert, as often the overlord became the Christian godfather to a client sub-king, giving an additional avenue of control to the *bretwalda*. It is thought likely that Oswiu of Northumbria stood as godfather to Peada at his conversion, implying a degree of subordination on Peada's part to Oswiu. Similarly, when Wulfhere, one of Penda's other sons and Peada's eventual successor, was probably overlord of the southern English, Aethelwalh of Sussex was baptized at the Mercian court in Wulfhere's presence and at his suggestion. When Aethelwalh stepped forward from the font, Wulfhere 'accepted him as a son' and, as a token of his adoption, gave Aethelwalh the provinces of the Isle of Wight and the Meon valley. It was clearly a ceremony of adoption that also

Fig.4 The churchyard at Llansantffraed-in-Elvel in eastern Powys. Although not in Mercia,
it is a classic example of a round churchyard and a ring of yews, perhaps
indicating at least an early Christian site, if not a pre-Christian one (see p.52)

succeeded in keeping the lesser kings in inferior positions, but which also 'provided means of uniting dignified subordination with mutual obligation'.[22]

Kent was the first kingdom to convert in the late 590s/early 600s, East Anglia followed in the early 7th century and Wessex set up a bishopric at Dorchester-on-Thames in 634. Northumbria had felt the influence of the British Church for many years through the monastery at Iona which had been founded by St. Columba in 563. Christianity as espoused by Augustine was brought into Northumbria by Paulinus, a member of the second Roman mission in 601, and who subsequently became the first bishop of the Roman tradition in Northumbria and established his see at York. With strong British and Romanized churches, there was bound to be a clash and it culminated in 664 at the Synod of Whitby (see box on p.64).

The Mercians held out against outright conversion for most of Penda's reign. It was under Wulfhere that official sanction was given to Christianity with an episcopal see founded at Lichfield in 669 under Chad and, in the late 7th century, the foundation of the important double monastery at Repton in Derbyshire, which had very close associations with the Mercian royal house.

Monasticism

Western Mercia in particular would have had extensive contact with British monasticism and the British Church. The concept of monasticism originated in late 3rd century Egypt among what are now called the 'Desert Fathers'. As a young man St. Antony of Egypt had sold all of his possessions and went to live in isolation in the desert. Soon others joined him, living in remote places in caves, or on hill tops, in huts or abandoned buildings, which included temples and tombs, and sought God through prayer and meditation, austere living conditions and manual work. The aim was that by self-denial and living a hard but simple life one would be free of worldly distractions and more able to spend time in religious contemplation and in closer communication with God. At its best it produced men and women of deep integrity and wisdom.[25] There soon developed two sorts of monasticism: solitary or 'eremitical', and collective or 'coenobitcal' where like-minded people lived in tightly ruled communities. Hermits generally started in coenobitic monasteries as preparation for the solitary life—monasteries were considered a vital training

The Synod of Whitby and its implications

This synod, held in 664, under the auspices of the Northumbrian king, Oswiu, and the abbess of Whitby, Hild (also known as Hilda), was arguably the most important synod held in the Anglo-Saxon period, seeing the 'victory' of the Roman over the British Church. At the heart of the debate was the date on which Easter should be observed, as each Church followed different traditions, but there were other differences too, such as the form of tonsure worn by monks and the style of baptism. It is possible that the synod had been prompted by the political tension that existed between Oswiu and his son Alhfrith, the sub-king of Deira. Alhfrith was a friend and patron of the Roman Church's exponent, Wilfrid. In c.658 he had given Wilfrid the monastery of Ripon which had entailed the expulsion of the British monastic community,[23] and had adopted the Roman form of Christianity himself. Oswiu, however, was a British Christian and followed Irish customs which came from Iona and Lindisfarne, although his wife, the Kentish princess Eanflaed, was converted in the Roman form with the result that husband and wife would sometimes be observing Easter at different times.[24] At the synod, after hearing both sides of the debate, Oswiu decided to accept the Roman over the British form of Christianity, partly perhaps through political expediency, both to diffuse the tense situation with his son and to gain the approval of the pope and thereby strengthen his political position within England. This decision was a severe blow to the British Church. St. Colman, bishop of Lindisfarne, resigned his see and returned to Ireland with other dissenters. It was several decades before the British Church accepted the decision reached at Whitby and, indeed, it was not until 768 that the bishop of Gwynned persuaded the church in Wales to adopt the Roman way of calculating Easter. However, the Synod of Whitby put a virtual end to the controversy surrounding Easter in the West and paved the way for the unification of the English Church under Theodore of Tarsus who became archbishop of Canterbury in 668.

ground and would-be hermits had to obtain permission from their superiors before embarking on such hermetical careers.

It was this style of monasticism which created the likes of Gildas, educated future saints such as Illtud, Dubricius and Samson, and produced a literary élite that made St. Patrick feel self-conscious about the lack in his own education. As early as the 400s Britain had produced some outstanding intellectuals, including Pelagius[26] who preached the importance of free will and the efforts that should be exerted by the individual to avoid sin and to attain salvation through living an austere life of Christian integrity, all of which questioned the idea of Original Sin. Pelagius had been deeply disappointed by the lax moral standards he had found in Rome and had tried to address the deficiency. Yet, in return for his free-thinking and well-argued philosophy, he was twice excommunicated and described by the Roman monk and writer, Jerome, as a 'fat hound weighed down by Scotch porridge'.

As some of the first monasteries in Gaul originated through the transformation by their aristocratic owners of country houses into religious communities comprising family, retainers and servants, there is no reason why such domestic monasteries should not also have been founded in Britain.[27] Initially holy men tended to come from landed families and some chose to live on the marginal land within or just beyond the boundaries of the family's estate.[28] Indeed, in Britain there is a correlation between centres of early monasticism and high status Roman buildings, and Morris suggests 'that British monasticism had roots in the behaviour of late Roman landowners and noblemen'. The precise position of the important monastery at Llantwit Major, Glamorgan, (originally called Llanilltud Fawr after its founder St. Illtud), is not known, but the settlement is the site of the largest Romano-British villa yet found in Glamorgan. That the 'most celebrated monastic centre in early post-Roman southern Wales' is somewhere in the vicinity of this large villa does resemble the circumstances in Gaul. Other monastic sites in south-east Wales are located near to villa sites, such as Llandough and Llancarfen,[29] both south-west of Cardiff.

Whereas the earliest monasteries were often built within the outer boundaries of villa estates, later ones were often founded in isolated, inhospitable areas following the ascetic margin-seeking behaviour of the original Desert Fathers. Areas which were shunned by the general populace, because the land was poor or were considered to be haunted by ghosts or evil spirits, were actively sought by these early ascetics. These monks undertook increasingly austere ways of living and early penitentials suggest some of this degraded into competitive self-abuse which had to be regulated: the Irish canons, for example, listed the penance for the sins of drinking blood or urine as $7^{1}/_{2}$ years on bread and water. There were also problems at the other end of the scale as over-indulgence was another problem; for example, drunkenness and gluttony were behaviours which had to be addressed. St. Samson (c.490-c.565) left the monastic community on Caldey Island because of the 'persistent drunkenness of its abbot'; bearing in mind the latter was regarded as a saint, this does not show the monasteries in a particularly good light! Sexual behaviour also had to be legislated against by penance and occupies a good deal of space in the penitentials with a range of penalties. Whereas the *Lives* of the saints, written by their disciples or later followers, portray a supremely holy vision of monastic society, the reality appears quite bleak. As Morris puts it so succinctly: 'In a society where filth, buggery, incest, sodomy and pederasty seem to have been taken for granted, a monk who kept himself fairly clean, avoided fornication, did not engage in the seduction of small boys, watched his diet and masturbated only occasionally might have the makings of a minor saint'. The penitentials of the 6th and 7th centuries derive from Ireland and Wales, but Morris states there is no reason to

Fig.5 At St. Andrew's (above), which stands just within the southern end of the original enclosure of the Roman town of Wroxeter, large blocks of stone re-used from Roman buildings are present in the north wall of the nave. Forty feet of its eastern length represents the early Anglo-Saxon nave and, with the exception of the insertion of two later windows and the blocking of its original window, this section remains unchanged.[30] The lower parts of the nave walls of St. Eata's at Atcham, a few miles north-west of Wroxeter, are constructed from very large stones, some over 2ft in height which also presumably came from the Roman town. H.M. and J. Taylor also suggest that, since neither church shows any late Saxon features, they can both be tentatively placed in the early period of Anglo-Saxon building, with the approximate date range of 600-800[31]

Archenfield - British Christianity on the edge of Mercia

The strength of the British church in western England is exemplified by Archenfield, formed out of the small British kingdom of Ergyng (now part of Herefordshire and Gloucestershire). Sometime after 750 political control of Ergyng passed to the English, some of the territory being taken into English hands, part remaining as the reduced kingdom of Archenfield. Welsh law was allowed to continue and, as Mercian power increased, Archenfield acted as a buffer state between the Welsh and English. This was a unique circumstance along the Welsh borders, indeed even between Anglo-Saxon kingdoms with the possible exception of the British kingdom of Elmet which eventually, unlike Archenfield, was engulfed by its Anglian neighbour, Northumbria, in about 616.

Fig.6 No-one is quite sure of Ergyng's maximum extent. The Book of Llandaff *suggests that in the 6th and early 7th centuries the kingdom covered all of what is today called Archenfield and the area north of it as far as the river Wye and land in the upper Dore valley. However, a good case has been made for the territory extending eastwards to Gloucester and the Malvern Hills.[33] The putative boundary above uses land west of the river Dore, the river Monnow and the southerly extent of the Wye on the Welsh borders as its western limit. The boundary may then have run north-eastwards along the Severn to Gloucester, northwards up the river Leadon to Dymock in Gloucestershire and then struck out slightly north-eastwards to take in the Malvern Hills. Its northern boundary may have followed what later became the boundary of the hundreds of Greytree, Radlow and Winstree*

St. Dubricius was the principal saint and prime missionary in Archenfield. He was a man of great influence within the early British Church and was the first bishop recorded as holding episcopal power in the district which was to become the see of Llandaff, although he was not the see's founder.[34] Dubricius' adult life and work is in two parts: the first spent as a missionary and teacher, and the second as a bishop.[35] It is the first part, when his activities were centred upon Archenfield, which provides a clear example of how the Church developed along the western borders of Mercia.

The Llandaff Charters record grants of land given to him by the reigning kings of Ergyng to enable him to found *llans* (monastic enclosures). Dubricius' earliest foundation was at *Ariconium*, near Weston-under-Penyard in southern Herefordshire, which strengthens the case for this former Roman town being the original centre of the British kingdom and as the possible source of the Welsh Christian movement of the 5th and 6th

*Figs.7 & 8 Top: Hentland church
Bottom: Llanfrother Farm*

centuries (and after which both Ergyng and Archenfield derive their names).[36] As a teacher Dubricius attracted many students and followers from all over Britain who wanted to study at the schools and colleges connected with his monasteries. His most famous foundation is said to be at Hentland in south-east Herefordshire. The very place-name is indicative of antiquity for it is derived from the Welsh *hen* and *llan* meaning 'Old Church'. There is a tradition that a church was founded here by Dubricius' alleged great-grandfather, Brychan, king of Brycheiniog, in the 5th century. This might explain why Hentland and neighbouring Llanfrother do not appear in any ecclesiastical charters—if it was Dubricius' by hereditary right then it did not need to be granted to him.[37]

There is, however, another contender for Dubricius' monastery: Llanfrother Farm, about 1 mile north of Hentland. Local tradition has it that it was here, rather than at Hentland, that Dubricius' famous seminary stood in the 6th century. A spelling of 1334 for Llanfrother—*Hendresroudre*—possibly translates as the 'old place of the brethren',[38] even its modern name suggests the 'old sacred enclosure/church of the monks'. The foundations of this putative monastery were allegedly still visible at Llanfrother as late as 1633, and in 1810 it was said 'traces of extensive buildings can sometimes be seen at the top of a hill on the west part of the River Wye', although modern field investigations in the area reported 'nothing of interest'.[39] Whether these features were anything to do with the possible monastery is questionable because, as early British monasteries were usually timber-framed with wattle and daub infilling, it would be virtually impossible for anything to survive, other than post-holes.

Wherever its precise location, the monastery was sizeable. Some writers reported it housed 1,000 monks in training for the priesthood, although an earlier authority quotes only 100.[40] However, numbers running into thousands were known at major monasteries: according to Bede, at Bangor-is-Coed, south-east of Wrexham, 'there are said to have been so many monks that although it was divided into seven sections ... none of these sections contained less than three hundred monks, all of whom supported themselves by manual work'.[41] Other British and Irish communities are 'said to have contained upwards of 2,000 devotees'.[42]

After seven years Dubricius moved from his monastery at Hentland and founded another at Moccas, approximately 19 miles to the north-west. The reason for the move is not known, but it has been suggested that Hentland was found to be too near to the Anglo-Saxon border for safety and a more remote site was required.[43] Dubricius died at Bardsey Island or *Ynys Enlli*—'Island of the Currents' where he was buried. However, in 1120 his remains were translated to Llandaff Cathedral.

It is probable that Dubricius exerted considerable influence on part of the western fringe of Mercia, for the lack of pagan burials in the area may be explained by the fact that incoming Anglo-Saxons were soon converted under the auspices of the British Church of which Dubricius was one of its leading lights. Church dedications to him in south Wales and Somerset suggest that he or missionaries trained by him also worked further afield.

believe that English monastic communities were any better behaved.[32] Yet even if standards were low, this should not detract from the fact that there were clearly some—perhaps even many—who did strive for spiritual and personal perfection. And by acknowledging that there were problems, it is clear that the Church was striving to control or even root out the negative aspects of monastic life: inactivity would suggest denial or condonance.

In the 7th and 8th centuries there were close links between double monasteries (monasteries catering for men and women on the same site, with the sexes segregated, and ruled over by an abbess) and the ruling royal dynasty. These monasteries were often connected with royal administrative centres or dwellings, sometimes serving as meeting places for a royal family's councils and even becoming power bases for the royal families who supported and indeed founded them. Such monasteries would add to the prestige of a dynasty, as well as acting as burial centres where their memorial cults could be tended. Double monasteries also acted as retreats, both permanent and temporary, from the world for the daughters and widows of royal dynasties, enabling them to use the 'power traditionally exercised by women in Germanic societies', with the dynastic character of double monasteries in Anglo-Saxon England considered similar to their counterparts in Gaul.[44] Many monasteries were indeed ruled by members of ruling dynasties as abbot or abbess, so that royal families were both actively involved in the cult of saints as well as in providing most of them. England, it seems, produced more royal saints than its neighbours, although royal involvement in the Church was apparently no greater. It has been suggested that this was one way that the Church countered the strength of English paganism. As pagan kings exercised priestly functions and were considered to have religious, supernatural powers, it is quite possible that the Church encouraged royal saints—and especially saint-kings—as their Christianized equivalent.[45] It was one way of enticing the rest of the population into the new religion. Through the celebration of a saint's feast day the ideal of Christian kingship could be disseminated widely. It was propaganda at its finest and the Church could not lose—a live king meant royal patronage of Christianity; a murdered 'martyred' king generated a 'saint's' feast day, when their sanctity and 'goodness' could be emphasized, along with the guilt and wickedness of the murderer.[46] In Mercia where saints were buried, venerated or in some way remembered, there are signs that they were linked with royal administrative centres and with ancient minsters founded at such centres.[47] Royal cult centres were also reminders of the ruling dynasty's power; in the east midlands, for example, some of these foundations were on the fringes of Mercian power as if

Fig.9 Sculptural crosses, which seem so quintessentially British, became a feature of Mercia too. Above are those at Sandbach in Cheshire. Such crosses were initially set up instead of churches as a point at which the faithful would know to congregate

Fig.10 Breedon-on-the-Hill. A monastery was founded in the late 7th century as a probable missionary centre

the royal family were asserting its claim to the area: notably at Peterborough on Mercia's border with East Anglia, and in Lindsey which, in the 7th century, was a disputed territory between Mercia and Northumbria.[48]

However, the monasteries were also refuges for those who were in some way unemployable, either physically or mentally. Although these people were denied admittance into the priesthood by canon law, they were looked after by the brethren. Indeed, many monasteries played a prominent role in the care of the sick, and some, for example Ely, included men who were described as doctors or physicians. Monasteries were also used as a repository for surplus daughters 'who could be much more cheaply wedded to Christ than to man' and were safe havens for widows and for those who sought to escape unhappy marriages, as entry into the religious life appears to have been recognized as grounds for dissolving a marriage.[49]

Relics were a useful way of securing a monastery's importance and provided a constant source of revenue from pilgrims, which may explain why so many dramatic 'discoveries' were made of saints' remains. Prestige could also be translated into political control as in the case of Bardney Abbey in Lindsey which had been recently conquered from Northumbria. A niece of St. Oswald, Osthryth, removed the headless and armless torso of her uncle, which had just been 'discovered', to the abbey where his cult was established. Initially Bede reports that the monks at Bardney would not accept the saint's remains as he had been a king of Northumbria and

> had ruled over them as an alien king. So it came about that the king's bones remained outside the gates all night, with only a large awning spread over the waggon in which they lay. But a sign from heaven showed them that the bones should be welcomed with respect by all the faithful: for throughout the night a pillar of light shone skywards from the waggon, and was seen by nearly all the inhabitants of the province of Lindsey. Early next morning, therefore, the monks who had previously refused to admit it, began to pray earnestly that the relics so dear to God should find a resting-place in their midst. Accordingly the bones were washed and laid in a casket made for the purpose, which was placed in the church with fitting honour. And to furnish a lasting memorial of the royal saint, they hung the king's banner of purple and gold over his tomb.[50]

At first view, establishing the cult of a Northumbrian king and saint in Mercia seems odd, but Oswald was from Bernicia, the northern part of Northumbria, and by establishing Oswald's cult, it may have helped Mercia challenge Lindsey's affinity with Deira.[51]

An aspect of early monasticism is the existence of double monasteries already referred to. Where a community was headed by an abbess in early Anglo-Saxon England, whenever sufficient evidence is available, it invariably proves to be a double monastery rather than a nunnery. In Bede's time (in the early 8th century) nunneries were rare, even unheard of. Repton monastery almost certainly began as a double monastery for it is said that in *c.*700 St. Guthlac received his monastic tonsure from Abbess Aelfthryth

Repton - Burial place of Mercian Royalty

Fig.11 The crypt at Repton, drawn in c.1896. The crypt, the mausoleum of the 8th- and 9th-century Mercian kings, is one of the supreme Anglo-Saxon survivals in Mercia. Aethelbald was the first king to be buried here after he was murdered at Seckington in 757, some 12 miles away. The crypt is very small. It was begun in the 8th century and started out as a simple square room with a recess in the middle of each wall, with access from the chancel by a short flight of steps in what is now the western recess. Over time stairs, whose rough walls contrast with the carefully dressed stone of the crypt, were provided on either side of the nave to provide access

Fig.12 (Top left) Repton church showing the stepped plinth around the crypt on the right

Fig.13 (Top right) H.M. Taylor describes this piece of Anglo-Saxon cross-shaft being 'of special merit with delicate human figures and foliage'. It is now kept on the west bench of the porch at St. Wystan's church, Repton, but is said to have come from Ingleby, about 2 miles to the east

Fig.14 (Left) One of the stone staircases to the crypt One can imagine pilgrims entering by one flight and leaving by the other; the lower treads are very worn and irregular, the most tangible evidence of the large numbers of people who visited the shrine. However, it was not Aethelbald's remains that the pilgrims visited, but another Mercian royal, Wystan, who is the titular saint of Repton church. St. Wystan was murdered in 849 and thereby became a royal martyr.

There is an immediacy in the crypt's compactness and a simple beauty in its design with its barleytwist decorated pillars, buff-coloured stone and vaulted stone ceiling. In the candled or lamp-lit gloom of the past it would have been perfect for instilling a sense of awe and of reverence into any pilgrim. Even now there is a dignified wonder about the place which is quite unforgettable

who was of royal descent. It is thought that double monasteries originated in Gaul and in the late 7th century were established in Britain. Some were still flourishing in the 9th century, including Much Wenlock in Shropshire and Winchcombe in Gloucestershire. Other examples of monasteries ruled by abbesses in Mercia—and which by implication were double monasteries—include Gloucester, possibly Inkberrow in Worcestershire, Bath, and Withington, south-east of Cheltenham. Leominster Priory might be added because in 1046 and 1086 there is reference to an abbess and in 1086 provision was made for the maintenance of nuns, making it possible that Leominster had been ruled by abbesses for centuries as its history between the 7th and 10th centuries is obscure.[52]

As time passed the founding of monasteries became increasingly attractive to laypeople. By 734 Bede was concerned that the proliferation of monasteries was out of control, with many lay people founding one to house their own family and retainers. These monasteries came to be populated 'by whomsoever they may perchance find wandering anywhere, expelled from true monasteries for the fault of disobedience, or whom they can allure out of monasteries, or, indeed, those of their own followers whom they can persuade to promise them the obedience of a monk and receive the tonsure. With the unseemly companies of these persons they fill the monasteries which they have built ...'.[53] It was clearly not that people were becoming more holy but that the founding of a monastery was seen as a sort of 'tax dodge' by the rich. By turning a family home into a monastic establishment, the land would be free of most secular taxes and duties, such as the requirement to provide men for military service, and in Morris' words Bede feared this 'would sap the strength of the kingdom, leaving it open to physical attack from without and corruption within'. Laymen were even bribing kings to provide lands, allegedly for monastic foundations which were then permanently alienated to the Church. Such alienation led to a situation about which Bede complained that there was a 'complete lack of places where the sons of nobles or of veteran thegns can receive an estate'.[54] Bede saw these foundations as having nothing to do with the monastic way of life, for he observed that no regular life was being observed and standards were lax with wanton living, vanity and gluttony being the norm.

In spite of Bede's worries, kings often had a way of ensuring a secular balance. They might expect large-scale expenditure and duties on the part of a monastery, such as providing men for work on fortresses and bridges or payment in lieu. King Aethelbald of Mercia was heavily criticized by St. Boniface for violating the privileges of churches and monasteries: taking their revenues, forcing monks to join work parties in the construction of royal residences and allowing his reeves and *gesiths* (noblemen) to impose 'greater violence and servitude on monks and priests than any other Christian kings before', which suggests Aethelbald was only being more extreme in his dealings with the Church. It was only after the Synod of Gumley in 749 that Aethelbald granted monks immunity from royal works, except bridge-building and the defence of fortifications (see chapter 9); it is not clear whether this applied outside Central Mercia, but it is probable that similar privileges were issued in the Mercian sub-kingdoms.[55] It appears that Aethelbald's successor, Offa, regarded army-service, work on bridges and defence of fortresses as an obligation on all of his people, monks included.

Early Anglo-Saxon monasteries performed two main roles: as a base for missionary work from which to evangelize the inhabitants of the surrounding area, and as a centre for devotional and contemplative life for the monks. There is no evidence that these early monastics saw these roles as in any way incongruous. In most areas the first monasteries were probably built as mission stations where the local populace were first converted, with monks providing pastoral care thereafter;[56] indeed, the word 'minster' derives from the Latin *monasterium*. In its broadest, and perhaps 7th- and 8th-century sense, the word describes a range of religious communities which were self-supporting from their own lands; were often royally founded; were free from most royal taxes and obligations; lived by a common rule headed by an abbot or abbess; worshiped in a common church within the monastic precinct and often provided the local people with a priest or priests.[57] As a rule minsters were of superior standing to other churches to which people paid their ecclessiastical taxes such as plough-alms (a penny paid annually to the parish priest within a fortnight of Easter by each plough team) and church-scot (a church-tribute paid as a custom of corn collected on St. Martin's Day, 11 November) and were usually long-established with much more extensive '*parochiae*' than the local parishes which took shape in the 11th and 12th centuries.[58]

Some monasteries may have been founded close to centres of population with the purpose of converting the populace to Christianity. The foundation charter of Breedon-on-the-Hill in Leicestershire, which is admittedly of dubious authenticity, suggests a missionary role. Twenty *manentes* (hides) of land at Breedon were given by a powerful patron called Frithuric (also known as Friduric) in the last quarter of the 7th century to *Medeshamstede* (Peterborough) 'so that they should found a monastery at Bredun and appoint a priest of good repute to minister baptism and teaching to the people assigned to him. The brethren of Medeshamstede chose one of their number, a priest named He[a]dda, and appointed him abbot on condition that he should acknowledge himself to be one of their fraternity'.[59] Frithuric, 'when he knew abbot He[a]dda to be diligent in preaching to the people committed to him, gave him the land of thirty-one *manentes* called Hrepingas'. This last place may be Repton and could therefore be the endowment of land for the monastery. Of particular interest is how this transaction was undertaken: 'For the confirmation of this gift, at Friduric's request, king Ædilred [Aethelred] and bishop Saxulf [or Seaxwulf, bishop of the Mercians] joining their hands placed a turf from the land on a gospel-book before a multitude of people...'. Abbot Headda also received 15 *manentes* (hides) of land called *Cedenan ác* in return for money and 'King Ædilred in his chamber in his own *vicus* called Tomtun, joining hands with the queen and bishop Saxulf, placed a turf from the land on a gospel-book before many witnesses in confirmation'.[60] This appears to be the earliest reference to Tamworth. One also wonders if our modern turf-cutting ceremony has its origin in this early practice.

Other monasteries were probably founded specifically for the contemplative life. But, in rather the same way as the first hermetical Desert Fathers attracted followers, these monasteries attracted people to visit or even to settle within the vicinity, and the monastery would then be obliged to provide for the spiritual welfare of these people and so take on a pastoral role by default.[61]

St. Chad - Anglian by birth, Celtic by nature
St. Chad or Ceadda was installed as bishop of Mercia by Archbishop Theodore in 669. Chad, an Angle, was born in Northumbria around 638 and was possibly the youngest of four brothers, the others being Cedd, who like Chad became a saint and a bishop (in Cedd's case of the East Saxons), Cynibil and Caelin. As Bede observes 'all became famous priests, and two became bishops, which is a rare occurrence in one family.'[62] The brothers entered the monastic school established at Lindisfarne.

The monastery at Lindisfarne had been founded in 635 with King Oswald's help. Oswald had appealed to the monastery at Iona for a priest to help him with the Christianization of Northumbria. The first monk proved unsuitable and returned, but the second, Aidan, was acceptable. Oswald duly offered him any site within his realm on which to found his see, Aidan choosing the island of Lindisfarne to found a monastery in the British tradition and of which he became the first abbot and bishop. The site was close to the Northumbrian royal citadel at Bamburgh and the royal residence at Yeavering, but retained the sense of isolation which was so important to these early monks.[63] The monastery had only been established for a few years when Chad and his brothers joined. Here they learnt to read and write in English and Latin and were trained to become Christian priests and missionaries. Bishop Aidan then sent Chad to Ireland for further study, a common practice at the time, for Bede says that scholars 'went round from cell to cell of the Masters, and they all were most willingly welcomed by the Scots [the original name of the Irish] who supplied them with their daily sustenance without charge, as well as books for their reading, and free tuition.'[64] Here Chad would have also mixed with like-minded men from the Continent who had fled the ravages of the hordes sweeping across Europe, but the teaching would still have been of the tenets of British, as opposed to Roman, Christianity. In Ireland Chad was remembered by a contemporary called Ecgberht, later abbot of Iona, as being 'constantly occupied in prayer, fasting, and meditation on the sacred scriptures'.[65]

Chad was recalled to Britain in 664 by his brother Cedd, then dying of the plague that was sweeping the country, to take charge of the monastery which Cedd had founded in 658 at Lastingham in a wild and solitary spot on the Yorkshire moors, about 25 miles north-east of York. There is a tradition that on his return from Ireland Chad worked in the midlands, for Chad's brother, Cedd, was one of the four Northumbrian missionaries who came to evangelize the Middle Angles under Peada in 653, but Chad's role in this can only be guessed at.[66]

The year 664 saw the Synod of Whitby when the observances of the Roman Church were chosen in favour of that of the British Church (see box p.64). The Roman Church's key advocate was Wilfrid, abbot of Ripon, who was then appointed bishop of Northumbria with his see at York and promptly left for Paris to be consecrated amidst great pomp, for he considered there were not enough non-British bishops in

Britain to consecrate him in the Roman tradition. Wilfrid then lingered in Gaul for two years, during which time King Oswiu grew tired of waiting and chose Chad to be bishop of York in Wilfrid's place. Chad was duly dispatched to Canterbury to be consecrated but, on arrival, found that the archbishop had died of plague. His successor then died on his journey to be consecrated at Rome. The nearby bishop of Rochester was also dying, which left Bishop Wine of London (the bishop who had been involved in simony) the task of organizing Chad's consecration. Chad was duly consecrated at Winchester, largely in the presence of British bishops, and returned to Lastingham which he used as his base.[67]

The outbreak of plague had left Mercia, Wessex and East Anglia without bishops and gave Theodore, archbishop of Canterbury, the opportunity to reorganize the dioceses into manageable units, as well as appointing bishops of the Roman tradition. When Theodore visited Northumbria he found Chad's position problematical. Believing Chad's ordination to be irregular as it had been partly performed by British bishops, he reinstated Wilfrid as bishop of York, consecrating Chad as a bishop in accordance with the Roman Church, but Chad nevertheless retired to Lastingham. In the meantime, Theodore was approached by Wulfhere who asked him to provide someone for the vacant Mercian bishopric caused by the death of Bishop Jaruman. Wilfrid, apparently a friend of Wulfhere's, suggested Chad, who was duly brought out of retirement and, with Oswiu's permission, was appointed bishop of Mercia, with Wilfrid even assisting Theodore at Chad's installation.[68]

Chad followed Aidan's example and undertook his missionary work on foot, so enabling him to approach people more easily than if he had been on horseback. This reaction went back to Martin of Tours, a 4th-century bishop in Gaul. According to his biographer, Sulpicius Severus, Martin chose to ride a donkey and often dressed in ragged clothes; for him even the keeping of a horse was a sign of 'the worst vainglory'.[69] The British bishops often looked to Martin's life for inspiration. One of Theodore's first actions was, therefore, to provide

Fig.15 The carving in Eccleshall's Holy Trinity church that may represent St. Chad. However, the spear seems inexplicable, especially when the gentle nature of St. Chad is considered, unless it is a symbol of the fight of Christianity against paganism. It is possibly of 10th- or 11th-century date and is part of a cross shaft

Chad with a horse, which he thought became a bishop's dignity. When it was clear Chad was demurring, Theodore bodily placed him in the saddle. Realizing he had little choice, Chad accepted the gift,[70] which may be seen as a metaphor for the 'victory' of the Roman over the British Church. The fragment of an Anglo-Saxon cross-shaft, found on the right-hand side of the choir vestry window in Eccleshall church in Staffordshire, depicts a horseman with a spear which has been tentatively identified with St. Chad[71] and may possibly commemorate this event (see Fig.15).

Chad's see was considerable, comprising 17 modern counties.[72] It is possible that the Mercian bishopric had no fixed seat until, at Wilfrid's suggestion, a site was chosen at Lichfield. Lichfield had been given to Wilfrid by King Wulfhere in the 660s as 'a place made ready as an episcopal see for himself or for another'. Its position near to the junction of two major Roman roads, one of which, Ryknield Street, led to Wilfrid's diocese, may explain his suggestion.[73] Indeed, Wilfrid, with his passion for building monasteries, may have already built one on the Lichfield estate.[74] Eddius Stephanus, Wilfrid's contemporary biographer notes that Wilfrid took over church sites in Northumbria that had been deserted by British clergy, and Lichfield may have been acquired on a similar basis.[75] It was relatively close to the *Pecsaete* of the Peak District, with their economically important lead and silver mines, and was also easily accessible to the inhabitants of the Mercian heartlands and the Trent valley. Lichfield would also have been close to the principal royal residence at Tamworth, assuming it had been constructed by then.[76]

A few miles to the south lay the Roman town of *Letocetum*, or Wall, which may have conceivably had a British bishop and monks in Penda's reign.[77] However, the Welsh poem *Marwnad Cynddylan* refers to a great Welsh victory at *Caer Luitcoed*, believed to be *Letocetum*, where cattle and horses were captured in the presence of 'book-clutching monks'. Whether this was a Welsh raid into Mercia, or the by-product of actions in support of an alliance with Penda against Northumbrian invasion, is not clear.[78] It may have been that the monks were there to serve 'the religious needs of a Northumbrian army' and would have therefore been the enemies of the Welsh.[79]

But Lichfield had been neither a Roman town nor an Anglo-Saxon one;[80] indeed the 12th-century historian William of Malmesbury described it as a 'mean place', which seems at odds with the choice of a site for a Roman Christian see which generally favoured pre-existing towns. If the choice of site was Chad's, as opposed to Wilfrid's, having been brought up in the British tradition with its predilection for founding monasteries amidst difficult terrain, the choice of Lichfield makes more sense, as it was surrounded by forest and marsh—it may have been the nearest Chad could find to an inland Lindisfarne. However, the good access by road would then have been something of a compromise. The proximity to the intransigent heathens, suggested in the names of Weeford, Wednesbury and Wednesfield, implies Lichfield may have also been a suitable base for primary missionary work.[81]

Fig.16 The Roman town of Letocetum *(Wall), a few miles south of Lichfield, may have had a role in the development of Christianity in the region. It is possible that Penda of Mercia allowed British clergy to stay on at Wall to minister to the needs of a putative Christian British population and, as such, it would have been the 'prototype' for the later Anglo-Saxon see at nearby Lichfield*

The cathedral established by St. Chad is thought to have been dedicated to St. Mary next to which Bede says Chad was subsequently buried.[82]

A church dedicated to St. Chad stands about a third of a mile north-east of the present cathedral at the north end of Stowe Pool, and traditions that St. Chad preached there date to the 13th century. To the west of the church (Fig.18) is St. Chad's Well, associated with him since at least the mid-16th century when Leland described it as 'a thinge of pure watar, where is sene a stone in the botom of it, on whiche some say that Cedde was wont nakyd to stond on in the watar, and pray'. Leland adds that 'At this stone Cedd had his oratorie in the tyme of Wulphere Kynge of the Merchis'.[83]

Leland's mention of the oratory in Wulfhere's time links this Mercian king with one of the best known legends associated with St. Chad. The story describes how, after succeeding to the kingdom, the Christian Wulfhere reverted to paganism, being so persuaded by an evil counsellor named Werbode, who was a chief supporter of paganism in the kingdom. Two of Wulfhere's sons, Wulfhad and Ruffin, consequently grew up as pagans. One day Wulfhad left his father's stronghold near Stone (in Staffordshire) to go hunting, in the course of which he pursued a stag which fled to St. Chad's retreat at Stowe and plunged into the spring. On seeing the animal's distress Chad soothed and fed the stag before sending it back into the woodland. Wulfhad then appeared and asked him where the stag had gone, to which Chad replied that the stag was the 'means of his salvation'. Wulfhad challenged him to bring it back and, after Chad had prayed, the stag reappeared and Wulfhad, clearly impressed, begged to be baptized. After instructing the young prince, Chad baptised him at the spring. On returning home Wulfhad persuaded his brother, Ruffin, to meet with the saint and, on their way, the stag magically appeared and guided them to Chad's oratory. Ruffin was then baptized. The brothers persuaded Chad to build a cell and oratory nearer to their home so that, on the pretence of hunting, they could go and hear Mass. Wulfhere's counsellor, who is said to have been rebuked by the princes for having the audacity of seeking the hand of their sister Waerburh, spied on them. He reported to Wulfhere what the brothers were doing and, inciting the king to rage, led him to Chad's oratory. On finding his sons in prayer, Wulfhere threatened them with violence if they did not renounce their faith. Wulfhad refused and was beheaded by his father. Ruffin tried to escape but was also killed by Wulfhere. The brothers were then surreptitiously buried. On returning home Werbode went mad and died in agony, whereas Wulfhere, broken with guilt, became dangerously ill. Eventually, at his wife's instigation, the king went in search of Chad and was led to the original oratory by the stag. As penance Chad ordered that Wulfhere should 'replace paganism with Christianity throughout his kingdom, ... found churches and monasteries and ... lead a Christian life'. Wulfhere took Chad back with him and carried out his penance.[84]

Fig.17 Engraving of Lichfield Cathedral at the end of the 18th century

This legend has been handed down at the monastery at Peterborough and also at Stone Priory, the origins of which reputedly lie in a church built by Wulfhere's wife to take the bodies of her murdered sons. The story is unlikely to be true as it suggests that Chad lived as a hermit rather than a missionary, and presents Wulfhere as an apostate after Chad had arrived in Lichfield, which he was not. If there is any historical foundation, it may relate to a time when Chad worked in the midlands before going into Northumbria (on his return from Ireland), when Wulfhere might have been a pagan. However, there is no other evidence of the existence of the princes Wulfhad and Ruffin, and the story may be an invention of Chad's cult. Bede, indeed, makes no mention of the story but does refer to a similar incident where two young princes fled to mainland England from the Isle of Wight in the face of a West Saxon invasion in the mid-680s. Here they were betrayed and beheaded after first being allowed to convert to Christianity.[85] Why then, does Bede not mention Wulfhad and Ruffin which would have capitalized on the goodness and virtue of these two martyred Christian princes? Yet Wulfhere was recorded as among the generous founders of the monastery at Peterborough, where it is said that the legend was once depicted in the cloister windows, beneath which were couplets telling the story. Tantalizingly Wulfhere's generous patronage of Peterborough Abbey was said to have been an act of penitence.[86]

Another story attached to Chad is significant for its nuance of pagan belief. Bede tells us that one of Chad's monks, Trumbert, who had been trained under Chad's direction, reported that if a gale arose Chad would call upon God for mercy and if the wind increased in violence he would prostrate himself on the ground and pray even more earnestly. 'But if there was a violent storm of wind and rain, or thunder and lightning startled earth and air, he would go to the church and devote all his thoughts to prayers and psalms continuously until the tempest had passed. When his monks asked him why he did this, Chad replied: "Have you not read, '*The Lord thundered in the heavens, and the Highest gave His voice. He sent out His arrows and scattered them; He shot out lightnings and discomforted them?*' For God stirs the air and raises the winds; He makes the lightning flash and thunders out of heaven, to move the inhabitants of the earth to fear Him, and to remind them of judgement to come.'"[87] How easily the pagan god Thunor, who was the god associated with thunder and lightning, could be substituted in this passage.

Chad had served the Mercian diocese for only 2½ years before he died of plague at Lichfield on 2 March 672. When the new cathedral to St. Peter was consecrated in December 700 Chad's remains were moved there from the original St. Mary's Cathedral—one of the earliest known translations for an English saint.[88]

*Fig.18 An engraving dated 1785 of Stowe Pool. St. Chad's Well is
between the church and the house on the hill to the left*

Many miracles were credited at both burial places, and the cult of St. Chad was born. Bede reports that 'Chad's burial place is covered by a wooden tomb made in the form of a little house with an aperture in the wall through which those who visit it out of devotion may insert their hand and take out some of the dust. They mix this in water and give it to sick men or beasts to drink, by which means their ailment is quickly relieved and they are restored to the longed for joys of health'.[90] Chad's cult flourished and when Offa made Lichfield an archbishopric, albeit for only 15 years (787-803), it is likely that St. Chad was given a new and grander shrine. It is possible that the cathedral was robbed or even laid waste in the late 9th century during the Danish wars, but Chad's cult survived and his name still appeared in litanies of the late 10th and 11th centuries.[91] In the 12th century a bigger church was built upon the previous Anglo-Saxon structure to cater for the increased number of pilgrims and in the 13th century the present Gothic cathedral was constructed with an enlarged east end and a Lady Chapel, again to cater for pilgrims.[92] Gelling observes this focus upon St. Chad and the presence of a cathedral at Lichfield may partly explain why Tamworth, only six miles away and the royal capital of Mercia in the 8th and 9th centuries, if not earlier, did not reach its full commercial potential which it might have done if it had been the ecclesiastical centre with its attendant gatherings. Pilgrimage to the tombs of saints and their relics was a lucrative business and yet, in Lichfield's case, the cathedral and St. Chad's relics did not lead to the growth of an urban centre as one might have expected. The bishopric was transferred to Chester in 1075, and thence to Coventry in 1102.[93]

Several of St. Chad's bones were sent as relics to other religious centres: tradition has it that in the mid-11th century, one of St. Chad's teeth was among the relics held at the New Minster at Winchester which, by 1066, bore his dedication. By the mid-15th century the saint's head and right arm were kept with other relics at Lichfield Cathedral in a room above the chapel built to St. Peter in the 13th century. A gallery was added to this in the early 14th century in order to display the relics to people standing below. By 1445 the head was kept in a gilded reliquary which weighed 16lbs and was adorned with gold and jewels; made in two parts it could be opened to display the skull. Chad's right arm was held in a silver gilt reliquary weighing nearly 5lbs, while other of his bones were kept in a portable shrine and the rest in the main shrine.[94] In the Middle Ages some of these bones were taken into

Fig.19 The gospel-book, known as the Lichfield Gospels or the Gospel of St. Chad, is still held at Lichfield Cathedral. However, its nomenclature is misleading as the book was not written at Lichfield, nor does it have any direct link with St. Chad. It dates to the early 8th century and some pages bear a striking resemblance to their equivalents in the Lindisfarne Gospels. Farmer, however, believes it was written in south-west Mercia and refers to it as a 'fine Mercian illuminated Gospel Book'. It reached Lichfield during the 10th century, but before that it was in Wales, for a note added in Latin states that in the early 9th century a man called Gelhi gave his best horse in exchange for the book and 'offered it to God at the altar of St. Teilo', probably referring to St. Teilo's church at Llandeilo Fawr in Carmarthenshire. The true origin of the gospel book may remain something of a mystery[89]

the diocese on fund-raising exercises, as were most relics of the time. By convoluted means some of these bones ended up at the Catholic cathedral in central Birmingham, which was consecrated in 1841 and dedicated to St. Chad.[95] In 1995 six of the bones reputed to belong to the saint were radiocarbon tested. Part of a leg bone, which had been held separately in a glass and bone reliquary, was dated to the 8th century or possibly the 9th, which takes Chad out of the picture as he was dead by the late 7th century. Five others, which were held in a wooden box, could have belonged to the 7th century but the bones represented at least two people and anything up to five. The very most that can be said is that one of the bones *may* be from St. Chad.[96]

Chad is credited with founding several monasteries besides that at Lichfield. Wulfhere gave him 50 hides of land at *Adbearw* in the province of Lindsey (Barrow-upon-Humber, Lincolnshire), sometime between 669 and 672 to build a monastery.[97] Bardney Abbey, 10 miles east of Lincoln, apparently owes its foundation to St. Chad.[98] There are also 33 ancient churches dedicated to him, the majority being in the present Lichfield diocese, and especially Shropshire and Cheshire. A few of these churches may have started out as preaching crosses where Chad was said to have preached, with a church later being built on the site: indeed a stone was discovered in 1919 at Middlesmoor, North Yorkshire with the inscription *CROS SCE CEADA*—'St. Chad's Cross'.[99]

Of all the early saints it is St. Chad who should be remembered for his part in the development of Christianity in Mercia. As a man, he was renowned for his modesty, conscientiousness and magnanimity. From a child he was brought up to a religious calling, in a background firmly rooted in the British Church with its emphasis on missionary work and simple living, a calling which he undertook, as far as can be ascertained, faultlessly.

St. Guthlac - A royal Mercian freebooter and hermit of the Fens

Guthlac's origins and early years were quite different from Chad's. The earliest and main source concerning Guthlac is his biography or *Life* which was written by a near contemporary, an East Anglian monk called Felix. Felix was in the fortunate position of writing within a generation of Guthlac's death and was able to use information from people who actually knew Guthlac personally. This contemporane-ousness has a distinct advantage—there was not enough time for accretions of legend and myth to build up, a problem that much later hagiographies suffered from. Nevertheless, Felix was influenced by earlier writings, especially the *Life* of St. Cuthbert by Bede and the *Life* of the first Desert Father, St. Antony, written in the late 4th century by Bishop Athanasius of Alexandria. In Rollason's words, like Antony, Guthlac 'turned from the world to a monastic or quasi-monastic community, learned virtues from those around him and then sought solitude, overcame demonic temptations, notably those of despair and lust, and was besieged by demonic hosts; and, as with Antony, powers of prophecy and miraculous healing flowed from victory over them'.[100]

Felix wrote his work at the request of Aelfwald, king of the East Anglians between 713-749, which means the biography can be no later than 749 and was probably composed in its Latin original between 730 and 740.[101] One might ask why an East Anglian king would be so interested in a Mercian warrior-turned-saint but it is suggested that, as Crowland, the site of Guthlac's hermitage, was on the border of Mercia and East Anglia, St. Guthlac was of interest to both kingdoms. The fact that Aethelbald (see also chapter 7) figures so largely and so favourably in the *Life* suggests that relations between this Mercian king and Aelfwald were good when the work was written.[102]

Felix wrote that Guthlac's father was 'of distinguished Mercian stock named Penwalh, whose dwelling, furnished with an abundance of goods of various kinds, was in the district of the Middle Angles. Moreover the descent of this man was traced ... through the most noble names of famous kings, back to Icel in whom it began in days of old.'[103] As mentioned in chapter 2, Icel was the first generation of the future Mercian royal family to have been mentioned as living in England, but Icel's father, Eomer, is mentioned in the poem *Beowulf*, and thus myth and reality become entwined. Indeed, there are many similarities between Felix's *Life* and *Beowulf*. As for Penwalh, Colgrave suggests that he might have been an ealdorman (an under-king, prince or local ruler) who wielded power over part of the territory of the Middle Angles.[104] Guthlac was named after his mother's tribal name, the *Guthlacingas*.

At the age of 15 'when his youthful strength had increased, and a noble desire for command burned in his young breast, he remembered the valiant deeds of heroes of old, and as though awaking from sleep, ... [he] gather[ed] bands of followers [and] took up arms'. But his rampages were rather different to the norm for 'when he had devastated the towns and residences of his foes, their villages and fortresses with fire and sword, and, gathering together companions from various races and from all directions, had amassed immense booty, then as if instructed by divine counsel, he would return to the owners a third part of the treasure collected'.[105]

Some of this warfare was presumably against the Britons and some, but not all, of the fighting may have taken place on the Welsh Marches, at a time before Offa's Dyke was built and raids were frequent; the politics of earlier alliance with the Welsh had changed. It was also a time when the western border tribes, such as the *Hwicce* and possibly the *Wreocensaete* and the *Magonsaete*, were being brought more effectively under Mercian control.[106]

Guthlac clearly had a good deal of experience of the Britons and Felix records that at one time he was an exile among them, possibly as a result of the reigning Mercian house considering him a potential rival as he was of royal descent, and had learned their language. Rather than being in exile it has been suggested that Guthlac was their hostage, perhaps captured in his early youth during the warfare he is believed to have conducted.[107]

Guthlac spent nine years engaged in 'pillage, slaughter, and rapine' before, at the age of 24, he had a life-changing spiritual experience, his own 'light on the road to Damascus'. Guthlac told his companions to choose another leader and entered the monastery at Repton, initially incurring the hatred of his fellow monks for his abstinence from alcohol and his desire for austere living. After two years at Repton, Guthlac sought to establish his own hermitage; his personal desert was to lie in the Fenlands. Felix states: 'There is in the midland district of Britain a most dismal fen of immense size, which begins at the banks of the river Granta not far from the camp which is called Cambridge, and stretches from the south as far north as the sea. It is a very long tract, now consisting of marshes, now of bogs, sometimes of black waters overhung by fog, sometimes studded with wooded islands and traversed by the windings of tortuous streams'.[108]

After talking to the locals regarding a suitable spot, he chose 'Crowland, an island in the middle of the marsh which on account of the wildness of this very remote desert had hitherto remained untilled and known to a very few'.[109] Several times Felix refers to Crowland as an island and talks of the landing-place for boats coming to the hermitage. In

Fig.20 St. Guthlac as depicted in stained glass in Crowland Abbey, Lincolnshire

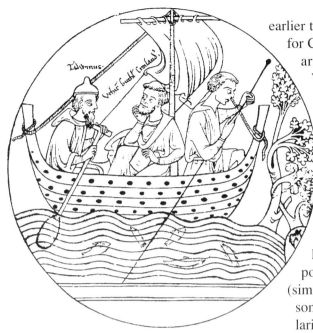

Fig.21 An illustration in the Guthlac Roll showing St. Guthlac arriving on Crowland island, with Tatwin, his guide, at the tiller, and his servant, Beccelm, in the prow of the boat

earlier times there is evidence that this area was not so desolate, for Crowland was the meeting point of three possible Roman artificial watercourses which incorporated the river Welland, (the Roman Car Dyke still runs past Peakirk, about 5½ miles to the south-west), and a probable Roman road also passed through Crowland linking it with Spalding which was virtually on the coast in Anglo-Saxon times.[110] Research has shown that during Romano-British times parts of the Fens were comparatively thickly settled and the 'irregularly shaped and small rectangular fields' associated with British agriculture existed throughout the area.[111] Indeed, between the 1st and 3rd centuries, the Fenlands had 'been open to a relatively intense British settlement, possibly under direct Imperial [Roman] stimulus'[112] (similar to that at Roystone Grange noted in chapter 1), with some evidence of planning by a central authority in the regularity of the Lincolnshire settlements. But if Crowland was linked to other settlements in Roman times, by the early 8th century it had reverted to a wilderness, a nightmarish area of desolation and imagined demons.

Felix tells us that Guthlac stayed at Crowland for some days during which he 'investigated every part of that place with diligent search' and then left for Repton to bid farewell to his fellow monks, which for some reason took 90 days, before returning to Crowland accompanied by two boys. He reached the island on 25 August 698/699, then celebrated as the feast of St. Bartholomew. With the help of the two boys he apparently made himself a hermitage in a robbed-out burial mound, which Felix describes as 'a mound built of clods of earth which greedy comers to the waste had dug open, in the hope of finding treasure there; in the side of this there seemed to be a sort of cistern, and in this Guthlac ... began to dwell, after building a hut over it'.[113] The stone from a cist would have been reasonably easy to shape into the walls of a hut. As an aside, this incidence of barrow-robbing by the previous treasure-hunters is the 'first historically attested grave-robbing in England'.[114]

Bishop Headda (or Headde, Hedde, Hedda), who was consecrated as the bishop of Lichfield in 691 and who had been the first abbot of Breedon-on-the-Hill, ordained Guthlac at Crowland, probably having consecrated the church on the island on the same day, as a church had to be consecrated before a priest could be ordained in it. Guthlac's church evidently had an altar and, as a priest, he could then take Mass.

The site of Guthlac's hermitage is traditionally thought to be within an area called Anchorite or Anchor Church hill, a quarter of a mile north-east of the present abbey at Crowland. In 1708 the antiquarian Stukeley saw the remains of a chapel which had been turned into a cottage, called Anchorage House, but associated it with Guthlac's sister, the anchorite Pega. In 1866 the cottage was demolished, but two antiquarians made a record of the building before it disappeared. The foundations 'consisted of two parallel walls running east and west, about 14 feet apart and 84 feet in length. On either side, towards the western end, was a room, making the whole width of the western end 42 feet'. At intervals along the foundations were 'substantial bases of unhewn stone, more than 8 feet square ...'. The precise nature of this building is unknown but it is suggested the plan is like a medieval chapel with the unhewn stones of the access passages giving it a prehistoric air. Colgrave suggests that the foundations may represent Guthlac's

7th-century adaptation of the prehistoric or Roman barrow with later medieval additions.[115] Alas, there is nothing to see above ground today; Anchor Church Hill is a field next to the busy A1073 which by-passes Crowland, but the outlines of a building are sometimes seen as crop marks.

On his island Guthlac lived as frugally as possible, wearing clothes made from skins, eating only a scrap of barley bread and drinking a small cup of water after sunset each day. Felix's account relates many encounters with devils. Some of the incidents might be seen as an explicit warning to monks tempted to take up the hermetical life without training and permission from their superiors in the monastery—awareness, for example, that near starvation could cause hallucinations.[116] These episodes recall the archetypal battle of good and evil, the sort that was fought in the poem *Beowulf*. However, in this poem there lurks an underlying mood of despair which stalks the victories and surrounds Beowulf's death at the claws of the dragon; in Guthlac's battles the hermit is armed with the confidence that goodness and the Christian faith will prevail. Other similarities have been drawn between *Beowulf* and Felix's *Life of St. Guthlac*: the landscape of the demons and monsters, of the black marshes, the mist-sodden moorlands and evil-haunted fens; the fiends that attack at night in both, provoked by Guthlac's singing of psalms and canticles, and the festivity in the magnificent hall of 'Heorot' in *Beowulf*. Guthlac lived over a robbed-out tumulus, possibly a chamber-tomb, and it was a chamber-tomb that Beowulf's killer, the dragon, had guarded.[117] Although *Beowulf* may be a Mercian work it is not known if the poem had been written down in Guthlac's or his biographer's lifetime in the first half of the 8th century.[118] If it had not been available to Guthlac, then the sentiments of heroic deeds and the imagery of the struggle between good and evil must have been in wide currency in the 7th and early 8th centuries for there to be such a similarity.

Guthlac was to die of a wasting sickness after 15 years in this watery solitude on 11 April 714.

When Aethelbald of Mercia had sought refuge in East Anglia from King Ceolred he was a frequent visitor to Guthlac's hermitage. Ceolred was Penda's grandson and Aethelbald the grandson of Penda's brother Eowa; such dynastic rivalry was common and Ceolred could have gone much further than merely exiling his relative. When Aethelbald heard of Guthlac's death, 'he spent the night in a certain hut in which he used to stay when Guthlac was alive, his sorrowing mind tossing hither and thither'. He awoke at one point 'and saw the whole cell in which he was resting lit up with the splendour of a mighty light' and standing before him was Guthlac who prophezied that within a year he would

Figs.22 Crowland Abbey. The existing Norman and later remains of the abbey. A 12th-century chronicler, Orderic Vitalis, apparently began the idea that the Mercian king, Aethelbald, founded a monastery at Crowland after Guthlac's death in the 8th century, but there is no evidence for this. As Felix does not mention the foundation of a monastery in his lifetime it suggests that a late Anglo-Saxon or early post-Conquest date for Crowland Abbey is more likely. On 11April 1999 a commemorative stone was set near Anchor Church Hill to celebrate Guthlac's arrival at Crowland 1,300 years previously

be king of Mercia.[119] His prophecy proved correct. After Ceolred died in 716, Aethelbald succeeded peaceably to the throne of Mercia.

Twelve months after his death, Guthlac's body was moved by his sister, Pega, and placed inside 'a certain monument; and now, built around it, we [Felix] behold wonderful structures and ornamentations put up by King Aethelbald in honour of the divine power'. As Rollason observes, Felix's 'terminology is maddeningly vague' and the translation may have been into a type of consecrated chapel, 'perhaps even a royal minster'.[120] Yet, if this is so, then it is odd that Felix makes no reference to it. When moved, Guthlac's body was found to be undecayed—possibly the result of being buried in a lead coffin which an abbess, Ecgburh, had presented to him before his death. Medieval burials of important people were sometimes made in lead coffins as it was known this would preserve the body for a time; excavations still uncover bodies buried in such coffins which retain soft tissue. However, Felix records that Guthlac looked as if he were sleeping and that the 'garments in which he had been wrapped were not only undefiled but shone with all their former newness and original brightness'.[121]

Fig.23 Pega, Guthlac's sister, founded a hermitage seven miles upstream at Peakirk ('Pega's church'). The present Hermitage, home to the nuns of the Society of the Precious Blood, is reputed to be on the site of Pega's hermitage and the small artificial platform on which it stands might be of early origin. This fragment of a cross-shaft, which is decorated with interlaced foliage carving, is displayed in the hermitage's chapel and is the only tangible evidence for an Anglo-Saxon religious house on this site. Pega travelled to Rome on a pilgrimage and died in about 717

Guthlac's cult may have started immediately after his death, indicated as much by Felix's early commission to write the *Life* and may have reached the western extremities of Mercia by the 8th century. Given Aethelbald's close friendship with the saint, his campaigns against the Welsh and Guthlac's own putative history of warfare with the Welsh, it would not have been surprising that some of Guthlac's relics reached Hereford so early.[122] But it is uncertain which relics reached the city. In the 12th century, Crowland claimed to possess the saint's remains, but in the 13th century it was believed that Hereford had the saint's body, yet there is no record of such a translation.[124] Thacker describes the situation poignantly. 'By then [the 12th century], however, relics of St. Guthlac seem to have been multiplying: Henry of Blois, for example, was believed to have given "a great part" of the saint's body to Glastonbury. The relics at Hereford were presumably always important, but the 13th-century tradition is probably confused as to their nature'.[125] However, Whitehead

Fig.24 On Pega's death, her heart was brought back to Peakirk and St. Pega's Heart Stone (above) in the parish church is suggested to have been its resting place[123]

suggests that St. Guthlac's church, which was situated on the present Castle Green in Hereford, eventually obtained Guthlac's remains, based on a chance reference to a fire at Hereford Castle which accidentally destroyed 'the wooden shrine which covered the saint's remains' and adds that Hereford clearly had a 'special place in the development of the cult of St. Guthlac'.[126]

An analysis of Guthlac in the religious and secular politics of the day

It was only by the 8th century that land could be left by will from one generation to the next and Guthlac would have therefore grown up in a culture where a young man could not presume to inherit his father's lands.[127] Although land was granted by the king as a reward for his companions in war, usually the aristocracy, this normally came late in a warrior's career—they would have to prove themselves worthy first. And of course this relied on being part of a king's retinue of warriors. The picture of an aristocratic or royal young man without property was therefore not unusual: Penda for example is believed by some historians to originally have been a 'landless noble of the Mercian royal house'. When royal succession became more assured, it generally bought about more peaceful conditions and, similarly, when the institution of thegnage* became more formal in the 10th and 11th centuries a curb was 'placed on the violent and dissatisfied men' such as the youthful Guthlac may have been.[128]

In Guthlac's time, the leading of a warband which raided neighbouring kingdoms was, for some, the way to kingship: Penda apparently achieved royal power in this way and so did Caedwalla, king of the West Saxons. It is suggested that Guthlac tried this and failed and consequently turned to living as a hermit, and that his bid for kingship was symptomatic of the times when dynastic uncertainty gave the chance for rival dynasties or members of collateral lines to bid for power. His father's, Penwalh's, land lay in the kingdom of the Middle Angles, and Penwalh flourished during Aethelred's reign (675-704), which was the 'crucial period of Mercian expansion' to the south-east. As Penwalh was descended from the royal *Iclingas*, and was also a Middle Anglian magnate, he must have played some part in the expansion, perhaps even having some overall authority in the area. Guthlac's ambition, perhaps, did not lie in being a sub-king of Middle Anglia, which his father's position would have fitted him for, but rather he aimed at being king of the Mercians.[130] If Guthlac really did make a bid for kingly power, it seems his was one of several that failed, and perhaps it was then that he spent some time in exile among the Britons.

It will probably never be known whether Guthlac did choose the hermetical life as a reaction to a failed attempt at worldly success, or whether he did undergo some life-changing religious conversion. But what is certain is that within his lifetime he became an exemplary hermit saint of great standing.

Felix's *Life* can, in one sense, be seen as presenting the saint as the model of how an ideal monk or hermit should live.[131] In this light, the friendship between Guthlac and Aethelbald is understandable: both strove for the highest attainment—sainthood or kingship, and both came from royal lines. The specialness of a saint accorded in many ways with his social background. Such hermit saints as Guthlac were regarded as being closer to God, precisely because they had stripped away as much of the worldliness from their lives as was humanly possible, and having done so, it was thought they were able to see things which were hidden from the ordinary man and were able to influence the course of events. As kings could pardon and grant land, so their near kin, the saints, could hand out religious privileges: it went with the social territory. Believing these men to be in touch with God and impartial to human life, people approached them to arbitrate with God in their affairs[132]—they were advocates to God. And how reminiscent this is of the way in which subjects approached their king for secular favours.

---

*A thegn was the title given to a man in late Anglo-Saxon times who held at least five hides of land and who was obligated to serve the king in battle. Their closest predecessor was the *gesith*, and successor the knight of post-1066. The rank of thegn was hereditary but a *ceorl* who came to own five hides could obtain the rank.[129]

CHAPTER 6
The Sub-Kingdoms of the *Magonsaete* and the *Hwicce*

Mercia is unusual in relation to the other large Anglo-Saxon kingdoms in that its core was surrounded by large subordinate sub-kingdoms which retained their own identity to varying degrees throughout most of Mercia's existence. These sub-kingdoms were important to the central heartland, both in terms of the resources they provided and as buffer zones against Mercia's enemies. In the latter role the sub-kingdoms of the *Wreocensaete* and the *Magonsaete* acted against the Welsh, relations with whom had deteriorated throughout the 8th century; the *Pecsaete* of the Peak District of Derbyshire was a buffer against the Northumbrians whilst the more north-easterly British kingdom of Elmet may have had a similar role for a short time before it was subjugated by Edwin of Northumbria (who reigned 616-633) according to Nennius.[1] The eastern province of Lindsey, which covered the area south of the Humber estuary and north of Lincoln, was bitterly contested between the Northumbrians and Mercians throughout the 6th and 7th centuries. Assessed at 7,000 hides in the Tribal Hidage, Lindsey was a kingdom on a par with the East and South Saxons and in the 7th century its port at Barton-on-Humber, close to the present Humber Bridge, 'may have been an important point of entry for Frankish Trade'.[2] Access to the Severn Estuary was gained via the sub-kingdom of the *Hwicce*, whereas control of the estuaries of the rivers Dee and Mersey must have been gained by control of the *Magonsaetan* and *Wreocensaetan* sub-kingdoms and the area later known as Cheshire (and possibly the *Westerna* of the Tribal Hidage). It may be no coincidence that Offa's Dyke separated these estuaries from the Welsh. During Wulfhere's reign Mercian control extended into Essex and even London and Kent, kingdoms that had strong maritime links with the Continent and especially with the Merovingian and Carolingian courts in Gaul. Through trade a kingdom's economic and political power expanded and, unlike Northumbria which had natural eastern and western boundaries with the North and Irish seas, Mercia had to create such links and then protected them jealously. In terms of defence, economics and social-standing, the sub-kingdoms which survived, and which subsumed the many nameless smaller tribal areas in the process of agglomeration in the 6th century, were anything but peripheral to the Central Mercian kingdom: they were vital.

Two of these Mercian sub-kingdoms are explored in some detail: the *Magonsaete* and the *Hwicce*.

The *Magonsaete*
The *Magonsaete* inhabited Herefordshire north of the river Wye and southern Shropshire, at least as far east as Much Wenlock. Bede, writing in the early 8th century, does not appear to know the name of this people and refers to them as 'the folk who dwell west of the river Severn'; neither does he refer to Merewalh, the kingdom's first recorded leader. The origin of the *Magonsaete* is certainly obscure. The earliest surviving record of their name is in a charter dated 811 when Yarkhill, a hamlet 5 miles east of Hereford, is referred to as being '*on Magonsetum*'.[3] There is no reference to the *Magonsaete* in the Tribal Hidage.

Gelling comments that St. Mildburg's post-conquest biographer terms Merewalh (or Merewald) as *'rex Westehanorum'*, a theme which is followed in the appendix of Florence of Worcester's Chronicle, in which he is called *'Westan-Hecanorum rex'* — king of the West *Hecanas*. The list of Hereford's bishops is headed *'Hecana'* in the same work, with the subtitle 'The Names of the Bishops of the *Magesaetas*, or people of Herefordshire'.[4] It has been suggested by Hart that the Western *Hecani* may have originally been the 'West *Hwicce*' who crossed the river Severn in order to establish colonies in the west. However, if the *Magonsaete* are thought to be a branch of the *Hwicce*, it would be unlikely that two separate dioceses would have been formed in the 7th century, one in Worcester, and one in Hereford.[5]

But Pretty has postulated that if this movement occurred before Penda's time, then the possibility of the *Hwicce* having a western settlement in what is now Herefordshire, before the establishment of the sees of Hereford and Worcester, is less problematic. She suggests that these early Anglo-Saxon settlers are likely to have moved into Herefordshire from the Worcester region, an area of westerly pagan Anglo-Saxon burials at Upton Snodsbury and Wyre Piddle. Any such movement is likely to post-date 577, (when Gloucester, Cirencester and Bath were taken by the Anglo-Saxons after their victory at the battle of Dyrham), and before 628 when Penda is first recorded in this region. The intervening 50 years would have given ample time for Merewalh's putative Anglo-Saxon predecessors to have gained possession of estates in the Lugg valley and possibly even further north in southern Shropshire around Much Wenlock where Merewalh's daughter, Mildburg, was later given land. Penda's success at the battle of *Maserfelth*, if Oswestry is the site of the battle, would, in any event, have given him the ability to augment Merewalh's kingdom with additional territory in southern Shropshire if Merewalh had been put in power by Penda. Pretty also notes that the presence of more than one folk name in the area might indicate the existence of several small kingdoms, and the possibility that the Western *Hecani* and the *Magonsaete* were, in fact, separate until the see of Hereford was established. As the *Magonsaete* are only mentioned from the early 9th century onwards, and then in terms of land grants for three places in Herefordshire: Yarkhill near Hereford, Staunton-on-Arrow to the west of Leominster and possibly in Archenfield, she suggests that the *Magonsaete*, in the strictest sense, should be identified 'only with the Lugg valley and Leominster'. This implies that the *Hecani* should be sought elsewhere, perhaps around Corve Dale and Clee Hill in southern Shropshire, although if they were actually the West *Hwicce* this would be unlikely.[6]

Another theory, put forward by Margaret Gelling, is that southern Shropshire and possibly northern Herefordshire might have been part of *Wreocensaetan* territory before the *Magonsaete* became a separate unit. This would make more sense of the *Wreocensaete* taking their name from the Wrekin, as it would then have been more central on a north-south axis of this larger area.[7]

The name, *Magonsaete*, or *Magonsaetan*, may have been derived from the place-name Maund, the name borne by three hamlets some 5-6 miles south-east of Leominster: Maund Bryan, Rosemaund and Whitechurch Maund. The element 'Maund' is sometimes believed to derive from the Romano-British town name of *Magnis*, 3 miles west of Hereford. *Magnis* itself is considered to be a probable British name meaning 'the rocks', possibly the original name of nearby Credenhill fort. However, Gelling states that the theory that this is the root for the name *Magonsaete* has been rejected on etymological grounds as the 'British name would not have had -g-' when the Anglo-Saxons arrived in the area in the later 7th century; the *gn* of *Magnis*, if left to a solely British etymological development, would have ended up as the modern Welsh *maen* — 'stone' or 'rock'. Whether or not *Magnis* had a role in providing the name of Maund, Maund in any event appears to have been derived from the same British word meaning 'rock' or 'stone' as *Magnis*.[8]

Gelling presents the theory that the name *Magnis* may have become 'known to English speakers before A.D. 550, and that their knowledge of the name was preserved without influence from British speakers after that date', i.e. perhaps by German federate soldiers who may have remained in the area at the end of the Roman period. Such a Germanic presence is implied at Caerwent and Cirencester from

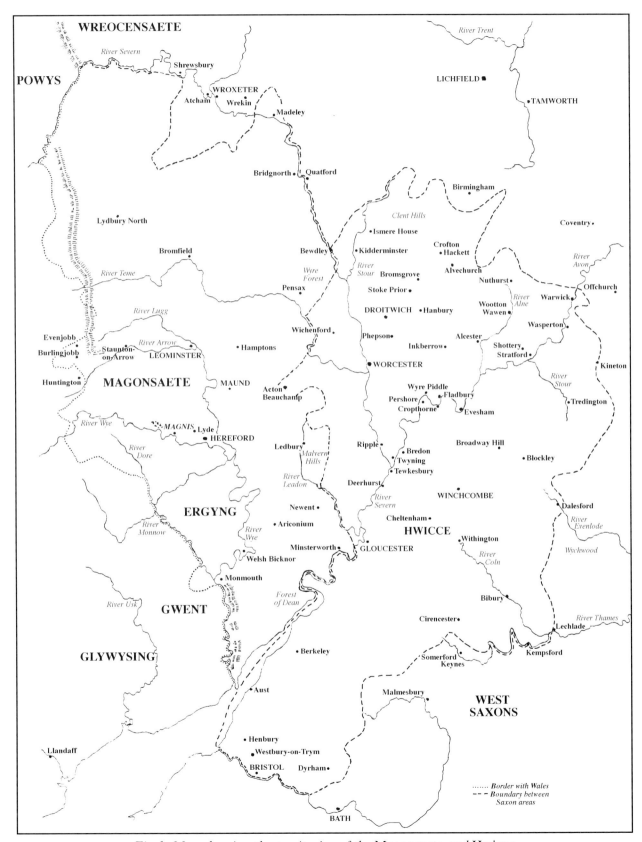

Fig.1 Map showing the territories of the Magonsaete *and* Hwicce

certain types of decorated metalwork. If *Magnis* was known as a district name by these mid-6th century Germanic soldiers, then it is just possible that it was re-used as such when Anglo-Saxon settlers took control of the area in the later 7th century.[9]

Certainly some archaeological evidence indicates that *Magnis* was occupied into the 5th century. The west gate was narrowed and the ditch was re-cut, suggesting a requirement for increased security. *Magnis* must have remained fairly intact throughout the Anglo-Saxon period for as late as the mid-16th century Leland states that the site of the Roman town 'ys al over growen with brambles, hasylles and lyke shrubbes. Nevertheless here and there yet appere ruines of buyldinges'.[10] Stukeley confirms that standing ruins still existed in the 18th century. One can therefore be fairly confident that substantial remains of buildings would have been present in the 6th century, and that such a walled site would have been an obvious choice for a re-emerging British dynasty and for it to become the focus of a small 'kingdom'. The inhabitants of this putative kingdom, or their immediate forebears, had lived in the Roman era—were, indeed, Romano-Britons—and thus such a site would not have been alien to them.

There is less trouble with the *-saete* suffix, which means 'settlers, inhabitants' (or 'dwellers in'). Gelling comments that it is a typical element in the province names to the west and north of Birmingham.[11] Hence, also the *Wreocensaete*, the *Tomsaete* (Birmingham/Breedon-on-the-Hill area) and the *Pecsaete* (the Derbyshire Peak District).

The majority of the kingdom's early population would have been British, unless there had been a massive exodus when the Anglo-Saxons first arrived, and the two groups may have co-existed largely peacefully. The fact that there are no surviving records of Mercian/Welsh hostilities until the early 8th century when Welsh victories are recorded[12] may suggest accommodation and assimilation. However, Brooks observes that this absence of recorded conflict may well have more to do with the sparse record of the Welsh chronicle, the *Annales Cambriae,* for that period, and the complete lack of Mercian sources, or, indeed, the understandable reluctance on the part of the Welsh to record defeats. Brooks further remarks that one should not presume that Penda's brother, Eowa, shared his brother's apparent cordiality with the Welsh; Eowa's putative reign (up to 642) (see p.33) may in fact provide a context for the Welsh raid led by one Morfael on Wall, near Lichfield in Staffordshire (see p.75). If the Welsh poem, the *Marwynad Cynddylan*, in which this raid is recorded, was composed as early as the mid-7th century, and if the bishop and clergy at Wall were British and their continued presence countenanced by Penda to serve the needs of any British subjects, it is unlikely that the raid on what would then have been Penda's Mercia, and therefore friendly territory, would have been reported so enthusiastically in the *Marwynad Cynddylan*.[13] If there really were peaceful relations between the 7th-century Welsh and Mercians, and if, as Gelling postulates, it can be accepted that both the annexation of eastern Powys occurred and the kingdoms of the *Magonsaete* and the *Hwicce* were created

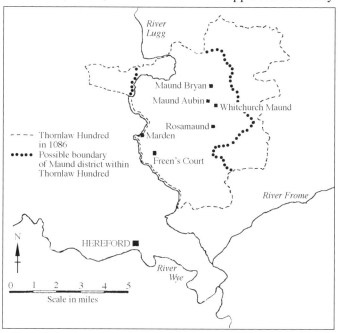

Fig.2 Map of Maund area of Herefordshire (after Coplestone-Crow)

during Penda's time, she suggests that it is 'reasonable to suppose that the administrative arrangements in those territories continued undisturbed until the end of the seventh century'.[14]

However, recent research suggests that these western sub-kingdoms may have been based on earlier British kingdoms.[15] The antiquity of land units and a British past is exemplified for example in a study of the manor of Marden (north-west of Hereford) where it is considered by Sheppard that Thornlaw Hundred, which included the Marden estate, 'may be regarded tentatively as indicating the approximate extent of the territory controlled from Sutton Walls [a large hillfort] in Iron Age times'. Sheppard interprets the name '*Magonsaete*' as 'the dwellers in *Magene*', a possible district-name for the area 'extending north-east of Hereford', with Marden appearing to mean '*Maund* or *Magene* enclosure'. Sheppard suggests that this sub-kingdom may have had a 'special association with the smaller *Magene* district' and speculates whether 'a place called *Magene* enclosure might not have had some particularly significant role within the early Anglo-Saxon principality'.[16] If Marden is the '*Magene* enclosure' in question, it lies south-west of the Maund settlements and north-east of *Magnis* and is thus relatively central to the district. It may be significant that in the 8th century King Offa of Mercia is said to have had a palace in the area of Sutton and Marden, perhaps choosing this location because of some established primacy within the region (see also p.150).

Indeed, Coplestone-Crow suggests that it may be possible, on place-name evidence, to define the original extent of the district of Maund (see Fig.2 opposite) as 'Maund' names are known to survive, or to have formerly existed, only in an area covered by the six central modern day Herefordshire parishes of Thornlaw Hundred: Bodenham, Marden, Sutton, Felton, Preston Wynne and Withington. These parishes appear to make up nearly 50 hides, a half-hundred territorial unit which is based on the Welsh 50-trefi multiple estate or commote, and it is perhaps in this possible early British territorial unit, based on Sutton Walls' hillfort, that the origin of the district of Maund may exist, suggesting a British ancestry which was taken over as a unit by the incoming Anglo-Saxons. In 1086 a district of 46½ hides existed around Lyde, two miles north of Hereford city centre, which again might have its origins in this British territorial unit which the English named *Lydas*.[17]

Hillaby suggests that Leominster and the 'land of the Lene' may have been part of a northern counterpart to the kingdom of Archenfield/Ergyng mentioned in chapter 5. Such small kingdoms were a feature of south-east Wales and this border region in the 6th and early 7th centuries, with Archenfield and Gwent being the two best known examples. The 'land of the Lene' may well have been at the heart of this putative unnamed kingdom bounded by the river Severn on the north and by the Wye to the south. Hillaby further speculates that the ruling family of the Lene folk accommodated Mercia's rising power and accepted a state of dependency, and were, in time, assimilated with the incoming Anglo-Saxons to become the *Magonsaete*.[18]

It appears, therefore, that in its embryonic stages the *Magonsaetan* kingdom comprised several earlier British territorial units with some form of primacy accorded to the area around Maund and Marden. With the extension of Anglo-Saxon rule in this region, these small units appear to have been subsumed into a larger whole under the overall rule of one Merewalh.

Fig.3 Anglo-Saxon spearhead found in Hereford. Notice the pattern welding in the centre

Merewalh

Merewalh, *c.*625-*c.*685, was the earliest recorded ruler of the sub-kingdom that was later known as the *Magonsaete*. He is remembered largely because of an 11th-century *Life* of his daughter, St. Mildburg, written in about 1080, probably by a hagiographer and Flemish monk called Goscelin. According to this Merewalh had three saintly daughters: Mildburg (Mildburh/Mildburga), who was the second abbess of the monastery at Much Wenlock in the late 7th century; Mildrith (Milthyryth) who became abbess of Minster-on-Thanet in Kent after the death of her mother who was the foundress; and Mildgith who, according to tradition, was either a nun in Northumbria or at Eastry, 3 miles south-west of Sandwich in Kent. These daughters were the progeny of Merewalh's second marriage to a Kentish princess known as Eafe (or Domneva), who was the niece of Eorcenberht, king of Kent from 640-664. There was also a son, Merefin, who died in infancy but whose burial site was allegedly the site of miracles. Merewalh also had two sons from his first marriage, Merchelm and Mildfrith, who survived into adulthood and are noted in the history of the *Magonsaete* (and which is given later on this chapter), but what happened to Merewalh's first wife is unknown.

Merewalh's racial identity has been a matter of debate among Anglo-Saxon historians. The *Life* states that Merewalh was Penda's third son and thus an Anglo-Saxon. This tradition is also recorded in the later versions of the legend of the Kentish royal family, where Merewalh is mentioned in relation to his daughter Mildrith, the abbess of Minster-in-Thanet. In Garmonsway's translation of the *Anglo-Saxon Chronicle* (Laud 'E' version) under the year 653, it is stated that King Wulfhere wished to honour and revere the abbey of *Medehamstede* (Peterborough) 'according to the advice of his brothers Aethelred and Merewala'.[19] This is a seemingly early reference but it must be borne in mind that the *Anglo-Saxon Chronicle* was compiled in the kingdom of Wessex in the 9th century, and although it undoubtedly used older sources their accuracy is suspect. Possibly the most convincing evidence for Merewalh being of Anglo-Saxon extraction is found in a charter of 748 which states that Aethelbald, king of Mercia, 'granted to the church of Minster-in-Thanet half the toll due on one ship "for love of his blood relationship with the abbess Mildred [Mildrith]"'. The charter is considered authentic,[20] and suggests that Merewalh was part of the Mercian dynasty. But the evidence is confused and insubstantial for the literal meaning of Merewalh is 'famous [illustrious] Welshman'.[21]

If Merewalh was Penda's son, one might ask why should an Anglian king give his son such a name unless it was some honorary title adopted by Merewalh himself to help in his relations with the Welsh. As it is known from Bede that Penda made his eldest son, Peada, sub-king over the Middle Angles in eastern Mercia, it is quite possible that he placed another son in control of the Welsh borders, 'possibly by agreement with his Welsh allies'.[22]

Yet, a more obvious explanation of the name is that Merewalh was indeed Welsh. If the incoming Anglo-Saxons in western England took over existing British land units and administration, they may have worked through ruling British dynasties which had re-formed after the cessation of Roman rule, and Merewalh may have been one of them. As Penda wanted to retain good relations with the Welsh it would seem more politic to adopt an existing British ruler as sub-king when the territory of the *Magonsaete* became a dependent Mercian sub-kingdom. A British leader/king would know the 'lie of the land' politically, economically and socially in his own region and, if such a man could be adopted by an overlord, the smooth running of the kingdom would then be that much more assured. In return, Merewalh's territory would have benefited by having the protection of Mercia against attack by Northumbria, Wessex and even rival British kingdoms. It is a pity that no information exists about the rulers of the *Wreocensaete* for comparative purposes.

Penda's apparently good relations with the Welsh, and especially with Cadwallon of Gynwnedd, (see chapter 3) would have made dealings with a British ruler that much easier and would have eased the Anglian settlement of the lands west of the Severn. Nora Chadwick has even suggested that the name

Penda 'has a Welsh look' to it;[23] if there was any British ancestory in Penda's lineage this might also explain why he was able to form such a strong alliance with the Welsh against their shared enemy the Northumbrians, especially under the rule of the voracious Aethelfrith (see chapter 3). Although it has been argued that a Welshman would never have been so Anglicized as to leave no trace of a Welsh personal name among his children,[24] it may be that Merewalh's success in retaining an independent kingdom is exemplified in his choice of Anglo-Saxon names for his offspring. In naming his eldest son Merchelm — 'helmet of the Mercians' — he was paying more than a hollow compliment, he was becoming one of the Anglo-Saxons and making sure his children were best suited to the political situation.

However, supporters of British origins for Merewalh's name have one other conundrum to answer. Merewalh was converted to Christianity in c.660 by a Northumbrian priest, Eadfrith. But Christianity had been flourishing to the west since the 6th century under the auspices of St. Dubricius and his followers, and there is also the possibility that Leominster was already a Christian centre under British rule (see below). With such a strong British Christian influence it would be surprising if a British leader had remained completely untouched by it.

It is reported in St. Mildburg's *Life* that Merewalh retired to and was later buried in the monastery at Repton in c.685. This poses chronological problems as it is not certain that the monastery was even founded by that time (700 is the earliest recorded date, although it is unclear whether this reference is to Repton or elsewhere) and even if it was, there is no evidence that it was used that early for royal burials. The first historically attested burial of a Mercian king is that of Aethelbald in 757. It might be more prudent to view the *Life's* story of Merewalh's burial at Repton as a later assumption, and one which saw him in an entirely Anglo-Saxon light. If it was an early tradition that was later written down in the *Life* of 1080, it was a tradition that would have helped to strengthen the Mercian claim over the *Magonsaetan* territory.

There is another legend concerning Merewalh's burial place, one recorded by the 16th-century antiquary, John Leland. After mentioning that Merewalh, 'kynge of the Marches' built Leominster monastery, he goes on to say that he heard that the skulls of Merewalh and Ethelmund (supposedly another king of the Marches) were there, but that Thomas Hackluyt, a clerk to the Council in the Marches of Wales, told him that Merewalh's body was found 'in a wall in the old church of Wenlok'.[25] Certainly burial within his own kingdom would be more fitting to a leader of British extraction, especially in a monastery that he had founded.

Merewalh's daughters chose a conventual life and thus remained childless and so dynastic continuity has to be sought through St. Mildburg's half-brothers from Merewalh's first marriage — Merchelm and Mildfrith. The two brothers apparently ruled the kingdom jointly for a time after Merewalh's death, for together they gave land in Shropshire to Mildburg between the years 674-704. However, it seems that Merchelm died before his brother, and as Mildfrith and his queen, Cyneburh, are mentioned among the names inscribed upon a now lost 8th-century cross at Hereford Cathedral, it appears that by the 8th century Mildfrith was acknowledged as the sole ruler. It may have been he who presided over the putative political and ecclesiastical move from Leominster to Hereford (see below). If we accept that the *Magonsaetan* kingdom was the creation of Penda, from the available evidence it appears the dynasty lasted for merely two generations, for neither Merchelm nor Mildfrith appear to have had any children. However, if it was a development from a British kingdom, Merewalh and his sons could be seen as the last of an old line. There is no record that anyone succeeded as king of the *Magonsaete* after Mildfrith's death from either a rival dynasty or a scion of Merewalh's family.

The Magonsaetan capital — Maund, Leominster or Hereford?
The centre of the kingdom is variously thought to be be Maund (discussed above), Leominster or Hereford. Leominster's claim is mainly centred on Merewalh's connection with the town's priory, although there is reason to consider Leominster as the early 'capital' of the kingdom.

In 1538 Leland records that people 'about Leonminstar [believed] ... that Kynge Merewalde, and some of his successors, had a castle or palace on an hill syde by the towne of Leominstre half a mile of by est. The place is now caullyd Comfort-castle, where now be some tokens of dyches where buildings hathe bene'.[26] This site is thought by some to have stood either at the northern end of the spur of Eaton Hill overlooking Hay Lane and the A49 (SO 506598), 1/2 mile north-east of the priory, while others favour a site nearer to the hamlet of Stockton, also to the north-east. It was 'probably a timber structure protected by earthworks and stockades' and was 'still a place of considerable strength in 1055'.[27] Medieval ruins are known to have existed overlooking Hay Lane but, as yet, there is no archaeological evidence of any Anglo-Saxon structure(s). However, Eaton Hill would have made a most suitable defensive position as the ridge rises abruptly from the river Lugg to the west, overlooks Leominster and is the westerly spur of a wider area of higher land to the east. In an area prone to heavy and sudden flooding this would have surely been a consideration.

Leland also records that 'There was a Castle at Kyngsland a 2. miles northe west from Leonminster, the diches whereof and a parte of the kepe be yet sene by the west parte of Kyngsland churche. Constant fame saythe Kynge Merwald sometymne lay in this place'.[28] Any palace or defensive structure, if it existed, is likely to have stood on the tump later occupied by the Norman castle and earthworks immediately west of St. Michael's church.[29] Coplestone-Crow notes that the name, Kingsland, means 'Royal estate in Leen', but, as it was first recorded as *Lene* in 1086 (Domesday) and *Kingeslen(a)* in 1137-9 in the *Herefordshire Domesday Book*,[30] one cannot reasonably make any connection of the royal element in the name in relation to Merewalh nearly 400 years earlier. In the 19th century the meadow next to the castle was called 'Merwold Croft'[31] but one wonders if this was so named because of the tradition.

But it is Leominster Priory that is more important. As Hillaby observes, if early sources can be trusted and the minster at Leominster was in fact (re)founded in *c*.660, it is 'the earliest documented site of Mercian Christianity', predating Chad's church at Lichfield by nine years, the traditional foundation date of Worcester Cathedral by 19 years, St. Peter's Abbey at Gloucester by about 20 and the cathedral at Hereford by nearly 30.[32]

The *Life of St. Mildburg* relates that Merewalh was converted to Christianity by Eadfrith, a Northumbrian monk.[33] A spot was chosen to build a church dedicated to St. Peter which Merewalh royally endowed and richly decorated, of which Eadfrith was placed in charge. Merewalh's choice of Leominster for his first and most important religious foundation may indicate an existing site of religious significance. There is a passage in the *Life of St. David* written in about 1090 by Rhygyfarch, (1057-1099), which suggests that this 6th-century Welsh saint actually founded a monastery at Leominster. In the original of St. David's *Life* the Welsh name for Leominster is used: Llanllieni, which means the same as its English counterpart: the 'Church in the district of the streams'. However, a good case can be made for Leominster being an early British monastery, even without St. David's involvement. Leominster's monastic precinct, demarcated by the rivers Kenwater and Lugg and a bank which is still defined in parts on its western and southern sides, measures roughly 360m by 330m (1,200ft by 1,100ft) which marked the

Fig.4 Looking towards Eaton Hill to the east of Leominster where 'Comfort Castle' is said to have stood

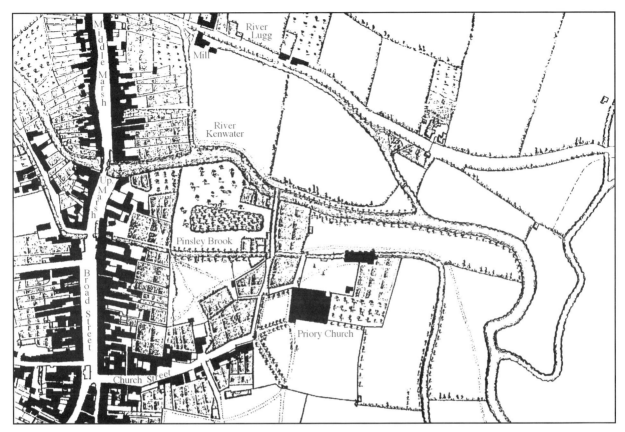

Fig.5 Map based on Gallier's map of 1832 showing part of the precinct of Leominster Priory. Hillaby observes that there is further evidence of a secondary embankment extending east, and then north-east, 'behind the properties within the precinct on the south side of Church Street' which has been emphasized by the making of the cricket ground where the embankment makes its northern boundary; the question has been raised by Hillaby whether this 'may represent part of a later division of the precinct, either between monks and nuns or between nuns and minster-priests'.[38] This would certainly be later than the 7th century when the idea of double monasteries were brought over from Gaul

ecclesiastical area off from the secular world. This is similar in size to early monastic sites in Ireland, Iona and at Glastonbury.[34] In addition, such marshy areas as Leominster once stood in, were often used when headland or island sites were not available.

The possibility of an early British monastic site at Leominster pushes the date for a Christian community on the site back to the mid-6th century, a hundred years or so before Merewalh's foundation. If this was a community organized on the strict rules of St. David's *Aquaticus,* the monks would not have been allowed to use animals in farming, or to eat meat or drink alcohol, or own land.[35]

However, for all Merewalh's connections with Leominster, Hereford was eventually chosen as the see of the *Magonsaetan* kingdom, indicating that this was then (or possibly always had been) considered the 'capital' of the area.

In 668, Theodore of Tarsus, archbishop of Canterbury from 668-90, was at Rome 'when the archbishop-elect' of Canterbury, Wigheard, inconveniently died at the papal court. The pope appointed Theodore, who was of Greek extraction, to take his place but it was a year before Theodore reached his destination. He arrived in Canterbury in May 669 to find the English church in disarray: insufficiently staffed (the plague of 664/5 had wreaked havoc), suffering from conflicting customs and usages and 'with a chaotic diocesan structure'.[36] England had only seven bishops and in Mercia there was no bishop at all, which Theodore soon remedied by bringing St. Chad out of retirement from Lastingham and sending him to Mercia to create the see of Lichfield in 669. But Theodore saw this latter as a makeshift arrangement and determined to break up the vast area of Mercia into smaller and more manageable religious units.[37] The division of Mercia into five sees: Hereford, Worcester, Leicester, Lincoln and, of course, Lichfield is thus generally ascribed to the late 670s.

Fig.6 Leominster Priory today

It has been suggested that Mildfrith moved the ecclesiastical centre from Leominster to Hereford after 690. As Merewalh (re)founded a minster at Leominster, it has been assumed that this was the original religious focus of the kingdom, but there must have been a very good reason to relocate the religious centre to a frontier town, however good relations were with the Welsh. Yet, if there was already an important church at Hereford then this is a somewhat different matter. Indeed, Whitehead states that apart from the information recorded in St. Mildburg's *Life* that Merewalh was converted to Christianity by Eadfrith who was then put in charge of a new monastery, 'there is no other evidence to suggest that Leominster was ever Merewalh's capital or that it was the main centre of ecclesiastical activity in the borderland'.[39] If Hereford was already a religious focus, what evidence is there for a church which pre-dates the establishment of the see in the late 690s? An answer may be sought below the public park at Castle Green.

Hereford

'It was not large but it showed itself, by the remains of steep ditches, to have been something great'.
William of Malmesbury *c*.1125.[40]

Castle Green in Hereford is situated on a terrace which drops down steeply to the river Wye on its south-western side. Below the cliff (which was revetted by the City Council in 1973) there was an important thoroughfare in medieval times. Leland refers to an old ford 'by the castle, by the whiche many passyd over, or evar the great bridge on Wy at Herford were made' in *c*.1100.[41] Indeed, the place-name, Hereford, derives from the Old English for 'army ford'. Whitehead remarks that the 'palace ford' is believed to have run in front of the Bishop's Palace on a continuation of a line running from Broad Street and the northern part of Gwynne Street, and the alleged 'castle ford' may have been a continuation of the line of Mill Street, originally called Britons' or Bruton Street, just below the present Victoria suspension bridge.[42] At the very beginning Hereford seems to have comprised merely one street which ran southwards, perhaps on the line of Broad Street, to the 'palace' ford, and this road may date back to the Roman period when the river crossing is thought to have formed part of the Roman military road running from Chester to Caerleon along the Welsh border.[43]

Numerous human remains have been recovered from the Castle Green site, and in the adjoining bank of the Wye over the past couple of centuries and in 1973 archaeological excavation established that Castle Green was, indeed, an early medieval cemetery, with a few burials possibly dating back to the 7th or early

94

8th century. Evidence of a timber building of no later date than the start of the 9th century and built on an artificial platform at least 1m (3¹⁄₄ft) high was uncovered in excavations in 1960. This was replaced by a stone structure in about the mid-11th century, both of which were interpreted as churches. As the timber church did not have any burials either within it or disturbing its layout, and as the platform was built before burials commenced in the immediate vicinity, it suggests that the church was erected before the site was used as a cemetery and could, therefore, be of 7th century date or earlier. Tantalizingly there is a reference in the Iolo manuscripts to one Geraint, the son of Erbin (who flourished in the mid-6th century), who founded the church of *Caerfawydd* (Hereford) indicating that the latter half of the 6th century could be the approximate date at which Hereford became an ecclesiastical centre.[44] This predates the establishment of the see by at least 100 years. Such a date would be in line with the archaeological evidence found for early British churches at Much Wenlock and the documentary evidence for Leominster. This British church may have had a *clas* ('mother') status, akin to an English minster.

Another building lay about 50m (*c.*160ft) south-east of the timber church and it, too, seems to have pre-dated the cemetery as it had burials from the 7th-early 8th centuries 'in close proximity but not within or disturbed by it'; this could have been a second church or more likely a mortuary chapel or *porticus*;[45] the existence of two churches on one site is not uncommon in Anglo-Saxon contexts. Initially Castle Green lay outside the town to the east, which looked back to the pagan Anglo-Saxon tradition of burying the dead in open ground away from settlement. The Romans also forbade burials within a town. The site was eventually enclosed within Hereford's defences in the late 9th century or early 10th, implying that by then the monastery had achieved collegiate status, and, with the possession of some of St. Guthlac's relics (see chapter 5), was clearly a religious site sufficiently important to be included within the fortifications.[46]

The cemetery at Castle Green was Hereford's principal burial ground for the monks and also the local community in the Anglo-Saxon period. It is estimated that it contains about 15,000 burials, representing about 50 burials a year for the cemetery's 300 year existence, indicating that Hereford's population in the pre-Conquest period was less than 1,000.[47]

St. Guthlac's, as it became known, may have been founded by the Mercian king, Aethelbald (reigned 716-57), in honour of his friend and mentor. However, the possible 7th century date of the earliest burials and the timber church undermines any notion that Aethelbald founded a completely new church on the site. (The dedication to St. Guthlac is indeed likely to have originated in the 10th century when Guthlac's cult became more widespread.)[52]

Fig.7 The river Kenwater to the north-west of the priory complex in Leominster

If this site did house Hereford's original church, a head minster, why was a presumably new site chosen for the cathedral, the first documentary reference to which occurs in 803, and St. Guthlac's not 'upgraded'? As there is no evidence for a 7th-century or earlier church on the cathedral site, it appears that a new cathedral church was built on a 'virgin' site a short distance to the north-west of St. Guthlac's. The reason for this may remain unresolved, although it may simply have been to keep one church in operation whilst the next was built.

In about 1125 William of Malmesbury recorded two verse

Much Wenlock Priory - A Magonsaetan Royal Foundation

Fig.8 (Right) Much Wenlock Priory looking parallel to the nave towards the abbot's lodgings.

In 1101 a lay brother allegedly found a box containing a parchment written in Old English above the high altar of the then derelict Holy Trinity at Much Wenlock when he was repairing the church.

This document was a certificate drawn up by a priest called Aelfstan stating that the body of St. Mildburg was buried near another altar in the same church. This prompted the monks to look for her remains and excavations proceeded. However, it was not the monks who found her grave but two boys who were playing in the ruined church and fell into a hole that revealed a burial, which through a 'series of miraculous occurrences' was identified as St. Mildburg's body.[48] One is reminded of the later 'discovery' by monks of the reputed bodies of Arthur and Guinevere at Glastonbury in 1191; it was not uncommon that when a cult needed a boost, the body of the saint in question was invariably found.

One of the most surprising aspects of the original Anglo-Saxon monastery at Much Wenlock is that it was a daughter-house to St. Botolph's monastery at Icanho, believed to be Iken in Suffolk. There is a suggestion that Iken was built in commemoration of King Anna who had been slain by Penda. Under 654 the Anglo-Saxon Chronicle *records 'In this year King Anna was slain, and Botwulf began to build the minster at Icanho'; some have linked the meaning of these two sentences together, the first causing the second, and Iken is certainly close to the heart of King Anna's kingdom. In chapter 3 Anna's possible exile among the* Magonsaete *was discussed. It seems that Saexburg, one of Anna's daughters, was closely related, probably as an aunt, to Merewalh's wife, and Anna might quite naturally have found refuge with his kinsmen. Hence one reason for the possible link between the two monastic settlements.[49]*

Fig.9 (Left) The tower of Holy Trinity Church, Much Wenlock

inscriptions in the cathedral written by Bishop Cuthbert, who left Hereford in 740 after four years as bishop to become the archbishop of Canterbury. Cuthbert is the only bishop of Hereford for which there is any detail before the Norman Conquest; the others are little more than names on charters or in episcopal lists. Whether William actually recorded the inscriptions first-hand, or transcribed them from other works held in Malmesbury Abbey's library, is unclear. The first verse was inscribed upon a magnificent cross, decorated with gold and silver which was begun by his predecessor Wealhstod who died in 736. The second verse was on a tomb or tombs which Cuthbert had built for three previous bishops: Tryhthel, Torhthere and Wealhstod, and for Mildfrith, the last recorded *Magonsaetan* king, his wife Cyneburh (or Cwenburg), and 'Osfrith son of Oshelm' whose identity is unknown[53] but who must have been of some standing to have been buried in such an important place:

> Here overshadowing marble holds the six bodies of these people who once lived, famous far through the world, and the present tomb, made with marvellous elegance, covered with a carved roof above, confines (them). I, Cuthbert, successor to holy honour, have enclosed them in tombs and adorned them with sepulchres. Of these, the sacred stole(?) encircled three bishops. Torhthere, Walhstod and Tyrhtil are their names; the fourth of them was the sub-king Milfrith, with his worthy wife Cwenburg; she lived fifth in order of the six. The sixth besides is Osfrith son of Oshelm. Behold, a tomb shuts up six bodies here.[54]

Sims-Williams suggests that Mildfrith and his wife may have been dead for some time when the epitaph was composed and also remarks that in the *Life* of Aethelberht, the East Anglian king whom Offa beheaded, it is alleged, in Sims-Williams' words, that 'the minster at Hereford was built by a certain Milfrith, a far off king (meaning one based in the north of the sub-kingdom?)'. Does this minster refer to the one at Castle Green or the cathedral church? However, the fact that Cuthbert honours Mildfrith in the inscription may indeed suggest that it was he who was remembered as the founder of Hereford's cathedral church early in the 8th century.[55] And this implies that the see was already fixed at Hereford in Mildfrith's day.

The tomb(s) Cuthbert built for his predecessors is described as being held together 'from above, from on high, with a ridged or gabled roof', probably a *porticus*, which was a square or rectangular building usually attached to the north or south side of the church with access only from inside the latter. Hillaby speculates that it is more likely, however, that Cuthbert built this *porticus* or burial chapel on a site to the east of the cathedral, a so-called 'axial' chapel which gave rise to a linear pattern, with the cathedral standing on the same line with this new building. It is thought that building to the east of the cathedral church would have enhanced rather than diminished the latter; conversely a large building standing parallel to the old minster would have reduced the minster's visual impact.[56] Such a *porticus* probably originated from the desire of those with enough wealth and/or status to be buried as near to the tombs of saints as possible, but who were forbidden, until the late 10th century, from being interred in the main body of the church as this was retained strictly for ceremonial purposes. A *porticus* was therefore a way of underlining the power and 'specialness' of the interred and, in so doing, underpinning the struc-

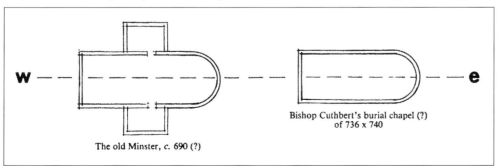

The old Minster, *c.* 690 (?)

Bishop Cuthbert's burial chapel (?) of 736 x 740

Fig.10 The possible arrangement of the cathedral and Cuthbert's tomb

Barrow Church, near Much Wenlock

Figs. 11 and 12
The church of St. Giles, Barrow, (SJ 657000), sits upon a raised circular graveyard. Cameron and Ekwall give the meaning of '(at the) grove or wood' from the Old English word bearu. *St. Giles possesses a superb chancel, which has been dated, tentatively, to the 8th century. If this is so, it makes it one of the oldest in the country. The Taylors record that the chancel is small—internally just under 6m (19ft) long and about 4m (12³/₄ft) wide—and outside has the typically Anglo-Saxon features of a small double-splayed, round-headed window near the eastern end of the north chancel wall and the remains of a pilaster strip about 7in wide which rests on a square corbel-like base.[50]*

An unusual stone has been recognized by Rev. John Woods of Much Wenlock. This stands outside and is 'still set upon a sandstone stipes [stem-like structure] *which in turn is still set into a pedestal. The* stipes *in particular has the appearance of a British* cromlegh *and thus may be pre-Saxon. The whole assembly is some 30 inches too high for an altar ... [and] gives the impression that it may have originally been a memorial dolmen.' This, with the circular walled graveyard may suggest a British, pre-Anglo-Saxon origin for Barrow church. Rev. Woods believes that, while Barrow is an English name, it*

is more likely to derive from beorg—*'burial mound', ('the equivalent Cornish word "runen" is found in the name for the path leading to the mound—runenwey'), and postulates that if Barrow is a burial mound then it might be the burial place of St. Owen, who may have given his name to Much Wenlock. If the chancel is of early 8th century date and if St. Mildburg was responsible for ordering its building, her interest may be explained by the saint's burial site. On the north side of the nave is a small chapel of probable 19th century date but Woods suggests that it might replace an earlier shrine, St. Owen's grave maybe?[51]*

Inside the church the late Anglo-Saxon chancel arch is an excellent example of its type, but the Anglo-Saxon style architecture is now thought to be of transitional Anglo-Norman date.

ture of this very heirachical society. It was also a lasting reminder to those who were ruled, that their king had been sanctioned by those who were the intermediaries of God, and by implication by God.

Alternatively, it is possible that the cross and new tomb described by William of Malmesbury could have celebrated the removal of the ecclesiastical centre of the *Magonsaete* from Leominster to Hereford and the subsequent transference of the bodies. This putative move may have occurred in King Aethelred's reign (675-704),[57] one of relative stability as relations with Northumbria and Kent had been settled (at least temporarily). The stable atmosphere fostered religious and political growth throughout Mercia.

Hillaby observes that the 'establishment of a tribal diocese with a fixed seat at Hereford represented another triumphant victory' of Theodore's policy.[58] Leominster may have represented the British version of Christianity where there was no permanent seat or fixed administrative centre—the British bishops moved from place to place and were more akin to missionaries than modern day bishops. Hereford was the antithesis with its permanent fixed seat where the bishop's stool or *cathedra* could be established in a fixed Roman diocese. The early cathedral, which held the bishop's stool, the *cathedra*, which was on or near to the present cathedral site, is first referred to in writing in 803, although it had probably existed since as early as 690. It was almost a century before the diocese took on the name of the town, until then the bishop was known as the bishop of the *Magonsaete*. The first reference to a bishop of Hereford occurred in 800-1 when Bishop Wulfheard professed his faith and his obedience to the archbishop of Canterbury.[59]

Fig.13 Archaeological excavations on Castle Green in Hereford in 1973 exposed remains of St. Guthlac's monastery and an extensive collection of burials from the Saxon cemetery

Hillaby considers that the change from British to Roman ways appears to have taken longer among the *Magonsaete* than it did among the *Hwicce* or the Middle Angles, for example, as the area south of the *Magonsaete* 'had been the cradle of Celtic Christianity' and Merewalh was converted to the British form of Christianity via the Northumbrian priest Eadfrith.[60] As Merewalh was clearly an effective king of this borderland, which could have been so troublesome, it is possible that his Mercian overlord chose not to interfere. The apparent break from the British form came after Merewalh's death in about 685 and probably under the auspices of his son, Mildfrith. We may further speculate that if St. Guthlac's on Castle Green did indeed have a British past, then when the Roman diocese of Hereford was created in the 690s, a clean break was made by establishing a cathedral church on a new spot.

There is a strong tradition that King Offa of Mercia became a lavish benefactor of the cathedral after 794 out of remorse for having ordered the cold-blooded murder of Aethelberht, king of the East Angles (see chapter 7, p.153). Aethelberht became a patron saint of the cathedral but the first mention of this dedication occurs in the mid-10th century. This leaves the question as to whether Aethelberht was first buried in the cathedral or, as Whitehead suggests, 'within the graveyard on Castle Green, in the area which was eventually to receive relics of St. Guthlac'.[61]

A 10th century the will of a man called Wulfgeat, a Shropshire thegn, together with an early 11th-century legal document imply that St. Guthlac's was considered to be of equal standing to the cathedral church and that it was still 'an important church, the equal of many of the most ancient foundations in Britain'.[62] St. Guthlac's was untouched by the monastic reforms of the 10th century, when monasticism was regularized under the Benedictine Rule, but by 1086 most of its property had passed into lay hands. The cathedral estates had gone likewise but, unlike those of St. Guthlac's, they were returned at the time of the Norman Conquest. St. Guthlac's demise began when it became enveloped in the castle bailey, and it was probably finally abandoned during the civil war between Stephen (1139-1153) and Matilda. In 1140 the castle was savagely attacked, the attackers forming a rampart from corpses dragged out from the graves. Oddly, it appears that the wooden shrine containing St. Guthlac's relics was left after the community reset-tled at Bye Street, to be accidentally destroyed during a fire during Edward I's reign (1239-1307).[63]

The tombs of Cuthbert's forbears do not now exist, nor is there any archaeological evidence of the first cathedral church; even its site is a matter of speculation. Hillaby believes that the last vestiges of the minster built prior to Bishop Cuthbert's rule, must have been incorporated into a new cathedral built by bishop Athelstan between 1020-1040. This was destroyed by the attack on Hereford in 1055 when the cathedral was 'stripped and robbed [by the Welsh] ... of relics and vestments and everything'.[64] A third cathedral church was built after 1066.

When Mercia was divided into shires, the old tribal units were gradually subsumed and, as a conse-quence, the secular and religious parted company on the map for ever.[65] It is only necessary to look at the diocesan map to see the ghost of the *Magonsaetan* kingdom.

The *Magonsaete* in the later Anglo-Saxon period

The last reference to the *Magonsaete* occurs in 1016, and it is a rather unfortunate parting shot. On 18 October of that year a decisive battle was fought, after a series of inconclusive engagements, at a place called *Assundan,* between the Danish invader Cnut and Edmund Ironside who was king of the English for six months between April and November 1016. *Assundan* has been identified with either Ashington in south-east Essex or Ashdon, north-east of Saffron Waldon on the Cambridgeshire/Essex border; Ashington is the preferred location. *The Anglo-Saxon Chronicle* (versions 'C', 'D' & 'E') for 1016 record that:

> [Cnut's invading army] went again inland into Essex, and proceeded into Mercia and destroyed every-thing in its path. When the king [Edmund Ironside] learnt that the army had gone inland, for the fifth time he collected all the English nation; and pursued them and overtook them in Essex at the hill which is called Ashingdon, and they stoutly joined battle there. Then Ealdorman Eadric did as he had often done before; he was the first to start the flight with the *Magonsaete*, and thus betrayed his liege lord and all the people of England. There Cnut had the victory and won for himself all the English people.[66]

In Garmonsway's translation from manuscript 'D' the account of the battle ends poignantly with the statement that among the slain were 'all the flower of the English nation'.[67]

The account demonstrates that the *Magonsaete* were still a clearly recognizable and understood unit. Quite what the link was between the turncoat Eadric Streona and this Mercian sub-kingdom, beyond that Eadric was a Shropshire magnate, is unclear. It is a pity that the *Magonsaete* exit from history on such an inglorious note.

The *Hwicce*

Unlike for many of the peoples of Mercia, many charters have survived concerning the *Hwicce*, principally for the area that became Worcestershire. The church in Worcester was one of the largest landowners for which there are many charters either in original form or in early copies—Worcester Cathedral was not ransacked in the way that many other Mercian *scriptoria* were in pre-Conquest times.

The name '*Hwicce*' is believed to be an ancient folk-name which may have originated in the pre-migration period[1] before the late 5th century. However, Gelling believes that the most likely derivation is from the Anglo-Saxon word *hwicce* meaning 'ark' or 'chest'; looking out from the Cotswold heights near Cheltenham across the flat plain of the Severn valley to the Malverns, she notes the landscape somewhat resembles 'a flat-bottomed, steep-sided vessel' rather like an ark.[2]

The extent of the pre-1541 diocese of Worcester is considered to be about the same as *Hwiccian* territory and included Worcestershire, Gloucestershire (east of the river Severn) and the south-western part of Warwickshire. The diocese lost Gloucestershire when the see of Gloucester was established in 1541 (see Fig.2 p.87).

There are also clues as to the boundaries of *Hwiccian* territory on the ground. In Radway parish, north-west of Edge Hill, there is a field-name 'Martimow' which has been traced back through earlier forms to *Mercna mere* or 'boundary of the Mercians'.[3] This field name is a remarkable survival, and pinpoints exactly where the *Hwiccian* and the earliest Mercian kingdoms met; the boundary between the dioceses of Worcester and Coventry (formerly Lichfield) still follows this line.[4] Whichford in Warwickshire (5 miles north of Chipping Norton) has been interpreted by Ekwall as 'the ford of the *Hwicce*' and may have been a 'gateway' between the *Hwiccian* kingdom and original Mercian territory. After running south-eastwards through Warwickshire, the *Hwiccian* boundary ran south to Daylesford in the Cotswolds. The south-eastern extent is indicated by several *Hwiccian* references, such as the high land near Cutsdean (4 miles east of Winchcombe), which was known as *mons ... Huuicciorum* in a charter of 780, and a wider area encompassing estates in Blockley, Evenlode, Daylesford and Icomb (which are all east of Winchcombe) were referred to as *monte Wiccisca* in a charter of 964.[5] In 811 Winchcombe itself was said to be '*in provincia Wictionum*' and, in 775, Bredon, south of Worcester, is described as '*in provincia Hwicciorum*'.[6] Kempsford (a village some 8 miles north of Swindon town centre)—the site of a battle in 802 when Aethelmund, ealdorman of the *Hwicce*, was killed by West Saxon forces—was then described as on the boundary of these two kingdoms. In the late 9th century Asser described Cirencester as being in the southern part of the *Hwiccian* kingdom. Westbury-on-Trym, today a north-westerly suburb of Bristol, was also said in the late 8th century to be within the *Hwiccian* province.[7] The western boundary is known from an 11th century manuscript which described the eastern boundary of the neighbouring *Magonsaete*. The dividing line between the two kingdoms followed the river Severn from the Severn estuary as far as Minsterworth, and then turned west up the river Leadon, followed the ridge-top of the Malverns as far as the river Teme, then ran north to Stanford Bridge (about 5 miles north-west of Wichenford) in Worcestershire. The boundary then took a line across a ridge of rocks which forms the Abberley Hills, rejoined the Severn and ran up to Quatford south of Bridgnorth.[8]

The *Hwiccian* kingdom was thus a long thin territory, approximately 75 miles at its longest extent, but only some 40 miles at its maximum width and only 15 miles at its narrowest—near Berkeley in Gloucestershire.

It appears that Bath, which lies beyond the southern tip of the medieval diocese, was once part of the *Hwiccian* kingdom, as Osric, a 7th-century king of the *Hwicce*, is claimed as the founder of its monastic house of St. Peter's. In addition the work ascribed to the 9th century historian Nennius, there is a reference among the wonders of Britain to 'the Hot Lake where the Baths of Badon are, in the country of the Hwicce', believed to be a reference to the baths and springs at Bath.[9]

In the late 7th century, and throughout the 8th, there was constant dispute with the kings of Wessex over these southern Mercian territories in the upper Thames valley, and the battle of Kempsford in 802 shows that the struggle continued into the early 9th century.

In contrast to this later southerly contraction of *Hwiccian* territory, the kingdom appears to have expanded on its northern boundary and took in the little developed zone on the margins of the Birmingham plateau. Significantly, the Worcester diocesan boundary runs north of land which had been claimed by two Staffordshire folk groups, the *Tomsaete* and the *Pencersaete* who made up part of Mercia proper. Hooke notes that the boundaries of these two folk groups 'are said to have met upon the boundary of the estate at *Coftune* [Cofton Hackett], at the north-eastern end of the Lickey Hills'. This boundary meeting-place lay some miles within the diocese of Worcester and probably represented the furthest territorial claim by the *Tomsaete* to the south-west. The *Pencersaetan* heartland seems to have 'been in the basin of the river Penk near the Roman centre of *Pennocrucium*' and extended southwards to include the Birmingham plateau's northern spurs. Hooke suggests that the northern part of Worcestershire, which included the southern fringe of this plateau, might have been 'a region of inter-commoning [sharing of natural resources within the border zone] between folk-groups'.[10] From charter and place-name evidence it appears the area was heavily-wooded and under-developed during the earlier Anglo-Saxon period, and in such regions a spirit of co-operation, or at least tolerance, is perhaps to be expected. The Clent and Lickey Hills created a natural eastern boundary in the same way that the Wyre Forest to the west and the forests of Kinver and Morfe to the north created northern and western boundaries. Wychwood Forest in Oxfordshire also created a barrier to the Saxons in what was to become Wessex.[11]

The influence of the *Hwicce* outside their own territory can be gauged from place-name study. As *Hwiccian* names are found many miles from the kingdom this suggests that individuals or families migrated, and were identified by their origins. Thus Whiston—'*tun* (farmstead or estate) of *Hwicca*' (a personal name), is about 6 miles east of Northampton, over 40 miles from the *Hwiccian* border, and Wychnor—'the slope or bank of the *Hwicce*', a hamlet some 4 miles north-west of the centre of Lichfield, is over 17 miles from the boundary of the *Hwicce*.[12]

One of the most interesting distant *Hwiccian* place-names is that of Wychwood—'the woodland of the *Hwicce*', in Oxfordshire. This is remembered in today's names of Milton-under-Wychwood, Shipton-under-Wychwood and Ascot-under-Wychwood which lie some 16-18 miles north-west of Oxford. It is first recorded in a charter supposedly of 862 as *Hwicca wudu*. Wychwood appears to have been 'part of the diocese attached to Dorchester on Thames' but in the 9th century was listed among the endowments of Gloucester Abbey in the kingdom of the *Hwicce*. In 841 the Mercian king, Beorhtwulf, apparently granted rights to the woodland at Wychwood to Heahberht, bishop of Worcester, and these rights may imply some prior claim to territory by the *Hwicce* in this area.[13]

The origins of the kingdom of the *Hwicce*

As with the *Magonsaete*, there are a variety of theories concerning the origin of the *Hwicce*.

The first, that the kingdom was a creation of an original Saxon conquest, is favoured amongst others by Stenton. The entries in the *Anglo-Saxon Chronicle* for 577 and 584 provide the basis for this theory. The battle of Dyrham in 577, in which three British kings were defeated by the West Saxon king, Ceawlin, enabled the West Saxons to settle in the lower Severn valley until after the battle of Cirencester in 628 in which Penda appears to have had the upper hand as he 'came to terms' with the West Saxon kings Cynegils and his son Cwichelm (see chapter 3). This would have given groups of West Saxons just over 50 years in which to settle territory that became the *Hwiccian* kingdom. However, it may be that the battle of *Fethan leag* in 584, the location of which is uncertain, but thought to have occurred in Oxfordshire, largely halted any such influx much earlier. Another theory, advanced by A.H. Smith, mainly on the basis of a study of place-names, is that the kingdom was a result of Anglian conquest and states 'it is in the Midlands rather than the south that the origins of the Hwicce should be sought'. A third option is that the kingdom was the creation of a mixed group of Angles and Saxons; E.T. Leeds showed that the 'distribution of several types of brooch in graves' indicated there was a strong element of both peoples. A fourth suggestion is that the kingdom was conquered by a branch of the Bernician royal family. This theory, proposed by Stubbs, and supported by Finberg who used charter evidence, centres on the possible different origin of the royal family to that the rest of the *Hwiccian* people. Stubbs suggested that the west midlands was a refuge for some of the Bernician royalty who were forced into exile, noting the same names occurred frequently in the royal families of both kingdoms. Yet another possibility is that the area was settled by invited Germanic merce-nary troops—as the size of the *Hwiccian* assessment in the Tribal Hidage (7,000 hides) is so markedly larger than the numerous small units of the east midlands, it is suggested that the *Hwicce* was a 'united group rather than the haphazard settlement of the overspill population from Wessex and/or Mercia'. A similar theory (proposed by J.C. Russell) is that, after the Romans had moved German *foederati* into these frontier areas, the latter stayed on after the withdrawal of Roman rule from Britain. The examination of 'animal-ornamented buckles and other military belt-fittings', and the discovery of British-made versions of this mili-tary metalwork near towns, implies there was such a force in the midlands in the 5th century 'which may have been maintained by Germanic recruits' after the Roman withdrawal,[14] although these burials could simply be those of a few high-status Britons who took on the accoutrements of the incomers. This theory does, however, link with Gelling's idea of the way the Roman town of *Magnis* may have been preserved in the name *Magonsaete* via Germanic *foederati* stationed at Gloucester and elsewhere (see p.86).

The theory of a Bernician royal 'transplant' and the idea of Germanic *foederati* staying behind and creating the kingdom are thought to be the least likely, especially as it is probable that the majority of the population were still native Britons who, one would expect, would not have tolerated a small minority ruling them for long. Possibly the truth lies in an amalgam of the other theories, with the kingdom formed from a mixed population with no predominating racial or tribal element—groups of West Saxons, Angles, and Britons who were all brought into some political unity by Penda of Mercia.[15]

There is some circumstantial evidence to suggest that the kingdom may have been based upon some pre-existing territory, for there is a striking similarity between the boundaries of the territory of the *Hwicce* and that controlled by the Dobunni of the late Iron Age. Hooke records that Cirencester had been the tribal centre of the Dobunni and the distribution of their coinage reveals that they had been active in what became the *Hwiccian* kingdom as well as around Whichford and Wychwood where *Hwiccian* influ-ence is evidenced by place-names. Dobunnic coinage has also been found deep in the territory of their westerly neighbours, the Cornovii, who, interestingly, inhabited the area that was, in part, to become the kingdom of the *Magonsaete*. The Dobunnic heartland appears to have centred on Gloucestershire and included nearly all of Somerset and parts of Oxfordshire, Worcestershire, Herefordshire and Wiltshire. How far such a region remained intact throughout the intervening 400 years of Roman rule is uncertain, but it may be no coincidence that the three British kings at the Battle of Dyrham were kings of Cirencester, Bath and Gloucester—the affluent belt of Dobunnic territory.[16]

Study of decorative metalwork and certain types of jewellery found in pagan cemeteries especially in the middle Avon valley suggest that such goods were being imported into the area from the east of England, although whether initially through trade or more long term contact with settlers from the east midlands can only be surmised. Cemeteries with such finds are found close to Roman roads implying that they were used to gain access into the *Hwiccian* region, along with the river Avon, whereas other evidence suggests that penetration via the Cotswolds met with some resistance. As the cemeteries occupy good agricultural land in the more prosperous regions it indicates the Anglo-Saxons were in a dominant posi-tion[17] and being dominant may not, therefore, have been popular with the indigenous population.

After this early settlement of the eastern *Hwiccian* territory, it apparently took the Anglo-Saxons a long time to settle the more westerly regions, presumably due to a strong British presence, which might have allowed time for assimilation.

The idea that the kingdom was forged from an amalgamation of peoples is given added weight by the number of smaller Anglo-Saxon folk groups that it included: the *Husmerae* based around Kidderminster, the *Stoppingas* centred around Wootton Wawen, the *Pencersaete* around the south-west of the Birmingham area, the *Weogoran*, based around Worcester, and the *Arosaete* (who at 600 hides were the only local minor tribal group to be mentioned in the Tribal Hidage) were possibly centred around the river Arrow in Warwickshire. As some of the minor groups used the '-saete' suffix, it suggests they took their name from the landscape they settled in, and indicates they did not have a united, recognizable identity as a folk group before reaching the area.[18] In other cases it is likely that some groups brought an identity with them into the *Hwiccian* territory. Thus, near Bredon Hill in south Worcestershire there is the place-name Conderton, spelt *Cantuaretun* in 875 and probably derived from the Old English *Cantwaratun* — 'farm of the men of Kent'.[19] The Whitsun brook, which runs between Bishampton and Fladbury, was originally spelt *Wixenabroc* and the settlers there may have been derived from an offshoot of the *Wixan*, a folk group who appear to have lived in the Fenlands. Phepson in Worcestershire was called *Fepsetnatun* in 956. Mawer *et al.* suggest that migrants known as the *Fepsaete* came into this area of Worcestershire from the *Feppingas* district of Middle Anglia and 'their new home [was called] *Fepsetenatum*, "farm of the *Fepsaete*"' — the folk group called the *Feppingas* in the Tribal Hidage.[20] There is place-name evidence for a possible Irish (then called *Scotti*) settlement on the Shottery Brook near Stratford as it was called *Scotta rith* between 699-709 and *Scotbroc* in 1016.[21]

It is possible that the area around Winchcombe was the heartland of the *Hwiccian* royal family,[22] and indeed that both King Offa and King Coenwulf of Mercia came from this line (see p.143 onwards for Offa, p.228 for Coenwulf).

The rulers of the *Hwicce*

The first mention of *Hwiccian* rulers or princes is found in Bede's *Ecclesiastical History*. During his description of St. Wilfrid's missionary work amongst the subjects of Aethelwalh, king of Sussex (whom Wulfhere had adopted as godson) Bede mentions that Aethelwalh's queen was Eabae 'who had already received baptism in her own province of the Hwiccas, [and who] was the daughter of Eanfrid [Eanfrith], brother of Aenheri [Eanhere], both of whom were Christians, as were their people'.[23] The date of Eabae's birth is unknown, but it is thought likely to have been between 630 and 650 and that her father and uncle would have belonged to the 2nd and 3rd quarters of the 7th century.[24] This suggests that the *Hwicce* were Christian possibly from the mid-7th century and that their Christianity predates the foundation of the *Hwiccian* see by several decades.

Bede does not say anything about the political status of Eanfrith and Eanhere and certainly does not style them kings or princes. However, the implication is that they were joint rulers of the *Hwicce* who are called 'their people'. The marriage of Eabae to the king of Sussex suggests cordial relations between Mercia and the *Hwicce*, for Wulfhere could have stopped his godson from marrying the *Hwiccian* princess if he so wished.

There is no charter evidence for Eanhere and Eanfrith's putative reigns. One of the first recorded charters issued to a *Hwiccian* ruler is that allegedly by King Aethelred of Mercia in the later 670s. The charter, which apparently records two separate events, records that Aethelred granted 'to Osric, his nobly-born thegn in the province of the Hwicce ... the land of 300 "tributarii" [hides] at Gloucester [and that] the king later sells to Osric the city and its territory, so that he may found a minster [St. Peter's] there'.[25] From the available evidence from Bede and the charters, Finberg suggests that very early in Aethelred's reign (675-704), or possibly during that of his predecessor, Osric had received a grant of land in Gloucestershire and by 675/6, if the Bath charter is trustworthy (see below), 'Osric had assumed the kingly title' and may even

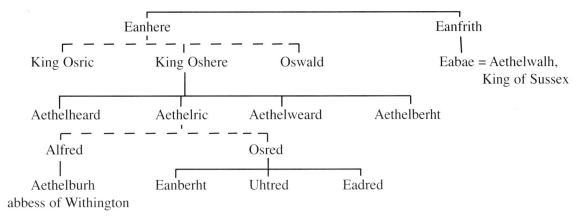

Fig.14 The family tree of the rulers of the Hwicce
(after The Princes of the Hwicce *in Finberg (1972))*

have had some part in the negotiations for the creation of the bishopric at Worcester.[26] At around the same time Aethelred also granted to Oswald, 'his nobly-born thegn in the province of the Hwicce, brother of Osric, 300 "cassati" [hides] at Pershore'.[27] It appears, therefore, that the brothers Osric and Oswald were of equal political status. St. Peter's at Gloucester became closely associated with the *Hwiccian* royal dynasty when it was at the height of its power, and this church, presided over by some of the dynasty's most powerful women, 'probably served as a focus and symbol of Hwiccian independence'.[28] St. Peter's may have originally been established 'as a home for royal and noble widows and a place of education for their children', all of whom were ministered to by resident priests. After the death in 757 of the third abbess, Eafe, who had apparently ruled for 33 years, it ceased to run on these lines, but remained as 'a college of secular priests'.[29]

The elevation of Osric from thegn to king of the *Hwicce* is also implied in the granting of land in 676 to an abbess for a nunnery at Bath, where Osric refers to himself as 'king', but there are reservations as to the charter's authenticity, especially as, wherever the evidence is available, an abbess ruled over a double-monastery (for men and women) and not a nunnery alone.[30]

It seems that Osric shared at least part of his rule (his recorded activity falls between 675-685) with Oshere, possibly his younger brother, whose activity is recorded between 679-693. Both are termed kings.[31]

Osric died in about 685 and, as he left no sons, the *Hwicce* then appear to have been ruled solely by Oshere who became the 'progenitor of all the later Hwiccian princes'.[32] Florence of Worcester reports that it was Oshere's ambition that his principality should have its own bishop which brought about the establishment of the *Hwiccian* see in *c*.679.[33] It would also appear that Oshere may have founded monasteries at Ripple and Inkberrow (Worcestershire), and Withington in the Cotswolds.

It is not clear when Oshere died, or how, but as he was the last ruler styled 'king', it is possible that relations with central Mercia soured during his reign. It is even possible that he was suspected of trying, with the Northumbrian wife of King Aethelred of Mercia, to 'detach the kingdom of the Hwicce from Mercian overlordship, just as they had already detached it from the episcopal jurisdiction of Lichfield'.[34] Oshere's four sons survived him, boasting the potentially confusing names of Aethelheard, Aethelweard, Aethelberht and Aethelric, which all appear in charters from 692. By 709 they are attesting charters without Oshere whom, it must be assumed, was then dead. Aethelweard's own attestations stop after 717, by which time it appears that he too had died. Charter evidence suggests that Aethelric survived the longest, even attesting a charter of King Aethelbald of Mercia as late as 736.[35] Here Aethelric signs as 'I, Aethelric, subking and companion of the most glorious prince Aethelbald ...' and is third on a list of 13 witnesses after Aethelbald (who styles himself 'king of Britain') and the bishops of Lichfield and Worcester.[36]

The titles of *subregulus* (sub-king) and even *rex* (king) given to Aethelheard and Aethelweard are questioned by Sim-Williams who observes that they are only recorded in what are generally held to be spurious Evesham charters and are not supported by evidence elsewhere.[37] In another charter, given the date range of 717-736 by Sawyer, Aethelbald, who calls himself king 'not only of the Mercians but also of all the provinces generally called the Southern Angles', grants land in the region of the *Stoppingas* to Aethelric who is referred to as 'my most esteemed and beloved thegn, son of the former king of the Hwicce, Oshere'.[38] The phrasing speaks for itself: Aethelric's father was a king, but he is relegated to a thegn.

It is not clear whether Oshere's four sons governed individually, together or in different combinations for different periods of time but, as Oshere was active from about 679 and Aethelric to at least 736, this branch of the *Hwiccian* royal family ruled for a relatively substantial amount of time: roughly 60 years.

Another member of the *Hwiccian* royal family, Osred, appears in the charters but, again as a subordinate to Aethelbald. He may be the Osred who appears on the witness list in one of Aethelbald's charters in 718, as he appears alongside Aethelric. Sometime between 737 and 743 Aethelbald granted 20 hides at Notgrove and Aston Blank (formerly known as Cold Ashton) east of Cheltenham to Osred, in which Osred is referred to as 'my most faithful servant who is of the not ignoble royal stock of the Hwiccian people'. It is not known whether Osred was a ruler of the *Hwicce*[39] or what relation he bore with the Oshere's four sons, but Finberg suggests he might have been Aethelric's son (see Fig.14) and also the brother of Alfred who is mentioned as having held Fladbury in succession to Aethelheard, and leaving Twyning minster (near Tewkesbury) to his daughter, Aethelburh.[40]

It is just possible that Alfred ruled the *Hwicce* between Osred and the three brothers Eanberht, Uthred and Ealdred who appear from 757. The latter are all called *regulus* in the charters, with indisputable evidence for joint rulership among the *Hwicce*.[46] This shared control of the *Hwiccian* kingdom is evidenced by an authentic charter of 759 where the three brothers, who are termed under-kings, grant 10 *cassati* at Andoversford, a village 4½ miles south-east of Cheltenham, to Abbot Headda 'by leave of King Offa'.[47] Another charter of 757 finds the brothers granting '24 "cassati" in one place and 6 in another, by the River Stour, called *Tredingctun* [Tredington, now in Warwickshire]' to 'Bishop Milred and St. Peter's, Worcester, where the bodies of their [our] ancestors lie buried' which was 'to be held in return for daily prayers and masses'.[48] Finberg regards this charter as authentic but other scholars, such as Sims-Williams, find it suspicious. If this charter is genuine, the statement that the brothers' ancestors are buried at St. Peter's in Worcester is significant for it marks a change in custom, as the first recorded *Hwiccian* king, Osric, is said to have been buried at Gloucester, although he may have died before the see at Worcester was founded. The change of location for royal burials from the royal proprietary monastery at Gloucester to the episcopal see in Worcester may be symptomatic of the declining importance of the *Hwiccian* royal dynasty, which is also reflected contemporaneously among the *Magonsaetan* dynasty who changed from burying their rulers at Wenlock Abbey to Hereford Cathedral.[49]

Eanberht had probably died by 770, but Uthred and Ealdred appear in charters until between 777-779. Uthred may have had the senior role in the later years, as he is generally the only one listed as grantor in charters from the 760s onwards. But his titles diminish in prestige throughout the third quarter of the 8th century: 'ruler of the Hwicce', '*regulus* of the Hwicce' and latterly '*subregulus* of the Hwicce',[50] and after 779 Ealdred appears on his own[51] by which time Uthred was probably dead. In a grant of land at Sedgeberrow, Worcestershire of 778, Offa refers to Ealdred as 'my under-king, ealdorman, that is, of his own people of the Hwicce'.[52] Ealdred's last appearance is in 789 or 790 when he attests Offa's grant of Broadwas to the church of Worcester where he describes himself as 'under-king of Worcester'.[53] He probably died shortly afterwards.

As no children are mentioned from any of the three brothers, they may be viewed as the last of the royal *Hwiccian* dynasty. Certainly after 800 the *Hwicce* were governed by ealdormen who did not claim

St. Oswald's, Gloucester

Fig.15 Looking across the ruins of St. Oswald's towards the tower of Gloucester Cathedral

St. Oswald's was founded by Aethelflaed in the late 9th/early 10th century when she restored Gloucester as a fortified centre, and it was she who brought St. Oswald's relics from Bardney Abbey in Lincolnshire in 909.[41] Oswald was the 7th-century Northumbrian king whom Penda had killed at the battle of *Maserfelth* in 642 and whose cult was made famous in Bede's *Ecclesiastical History*. At the time of its foundation, the new minster was dedicated to St. Peter but was soon identified with St. Oswald. Oswald's shrine at Bardney Abbey had been under Mercian control for nearly 200 years from the late 7th century, and the shrine had been honoured by none less than King Offa of Mercia. In the early 10th century Bardney was under Danish authority, and in 909 a joint army of Mercians and West Saxons attacked the Danelaw, returning with St. Oswald's remains. Similar translations occurred at other of Aethelflaed and Aethelred's *burhs*, for example St. Waerburh's relics were taken from Hanbury in Staffordshire to Chester because of the danger posed by the Danish armies. (Waerburh, also known as Werburg or Werburga, an abbess, was traditionally Wulfhere's daughter who died in about 700.) These translations, as well as being acts of piety and undertaken for reasons of security, probably had a political undertone — a translation of a well-known saint gave a ruler and a place added status.[42]

It has been asked why a new foundation at Gloucester was necessary, and it is thought that St. Oswald's had an educational role with the learning at the pre-existing minster, St. Peter's being in decline. St. Oswald's was built out of re-used Roman stone, probably from a nearby temple, to a standard plan with two notable exceptions: firstly, there was a western apse which was a feature of contemporary and much larger Carolingian churches on the Continent; and, secondly, an eastern crypt was added which may have been Aethelflead's mausoleum. The importance of St. Oswald's to Aethelflaed and Aethelred is evidenced in that they were both buried there, even though Aethelflaed died at Tamworth.[43]

In the 10th century a tower seems to have been added and the western apse was then taken down. Archaeological finds from the site include an early 10th-century bell-pit, bell metal and an inscribed bell

Fig.16 Part of the standing remains of St. Oswald's

mould. Sculptural finds include '9th-century cross shafts, and 10th century decorated grave covers'. Both St. Oswald's and St. Mary's at Deerhurst to the north of Gloucester were 'extensively decorated with sculptured carving' and it appears that these were painted. Indeed, some pieces at St. Oswald's show traces of colour and at Deerhurst the beast-head sculpture on the chancel arch also shows evidence of original paint. The walls of both churches were also embellished with paintings.[44]

Like any church which was heavily visited by pilgrims and which received such handsome donations, St. Oswald's would have been 'full of reliquaries, candlesticks, and other gold and silver ornaments, of all kinds, as well as gold and silver embroidered hangings', which, together with the painted sculpture and wall paintings, would have created highly decorative interiors. In about 1000 both St. Oswald's and St. Mary's at Deerhurst would probably have been composed of buildings with 'small spaces, many altars, brightly painted carvings of animals, birds, pattern and foliage, dimly seen by candlelight, everything enhanced by the gleam of gold and silver.'[45] It is little wonder then that St. Oswald's was once termed 'the golden monastery'.

royal power. The first known of these was Aethelmund. In Uthred's charters of 767 and 770 there is reference to an Aethelmund 'his faithful *minister*'; in the latter Aethelmund is described as 'son of the Ingeld who was [an] ealdorman of Aethelbald king of the Mercians', although it is unlikely that Aethelmund was of the *Hwiccian* royal family himself. In one of Offa's charters, given sometime between 793 and 796, there is an Aethelmund who is referred to as 'his *minister*' to whom Offa grants land at Westbury-on-Trym in Gloucestershire, and a man of the same name was killed at the battle of Kempsford in 802 by the people of Wiltshire. It appears he was trying to take 'advantage of, or [was] reacting to, a change of king in Wessex'.[54] By now, however, the *Hwiccian* kingdom was virtually extinct as a political entity, but its identity remained. In a charter of 855 there is reference to the province of the *Hwicce*, and in the early 11th century the *Hwiccian* territory was still regarded as a province distinct from Mercia.

The Economy and Trade of the *Hwicce*

The *Hwiccian* kingdom was blessed with valuable agricultural lands, as well as several main rivers including the Severn, Teme and Avon which were not only useful for communications but also valuable for fisheries. The territory also included the salt works at Droitwich.

Much of the northern part of the *Hwiccian* kingdom would have been wooded. Designated areas of these woodlands were often used by people in the more intensively developed arable land south and south-east of the kingdom to collect timber, fuel and pasture pigs. As the population increased and agriculture developed, so areas of woodland were cleared to make fields. In the later Anglo-Saxon period such development had spread into the woodland known as *Weorgorena leage,* west of Worcester and the river Severn. For example, at Oddingley and at Libbery in Grafton Flyford in mid-Worcestershire there is charter evidence dating from 963 and 972 respectively suggesting that some hedges had been planted to stop woodland animals from grazing crops, for example, a 'roe-deer hedge' exists in both estates' charter boundaries.[55] This implies that fairly sizeable woodland still existed. It is likely that hedges would also have been used to keep domestic grazing animals away from crops in an area of mixed farming, but charters only mention the edges of an estate; what was happening in the core is not recorded.

Some of the most westerly parts of the kingdom stayed under- or undeveloped throughout the whole era, for instance the Malvern foothills on the very western edge of the kingdom were not developed until the medieval period.

The woodlands in the Cotswolds may have regenerated on land once farmed under the wealthy Roman villa estates, but woodland there must have been, for the very name 'Cotswolds' is derived from an Anglo-Saxon personal name *Cod* and the Old English word *wald* meaning 'woodland'. It was only later that *wald*, still present in the word 'weald', changed its meaning and its spelling locally to 'wold' to denote 'open, high land'. On the higher ground to the north, charter and place-name evidence suggests 'that much of the woodland had gone by the middle and late Anglo-Saxon period', and the Domesday Survey of 1086 shows there was little woodland remaining in the north Cotswolds. Arable cultivation is evidenced from the charters for the eastern and south-eastern region of the northern Cotswolds, and sheep-rearing was being practised on the escarpment by the middle Anglo-Saxon period—an abbess of St. Peter's in Gloucester had acquired land by the 8th century to the south-east of Cheltenham 'for bringing in her flocks'.[56]

Arable farming was focussed on north-east Gloucestershire, the Vale of Evesham and the central Avon valley. The 'Gloucestershire Cotswolds formed one of the richest areas of Roman Britain' with Cirencester (*Corinium*) being 'the second largest town in the province'. Roman settlements are found in quantity in the Vale of Evesham and Warwickshire's central Avon valley [57] and it is no surprise that these regions continued to stand out as prime agricultural areas in the Anglo-Saxon period. A measure of the Vale's prosperity may be gauged from its ability to support wealthy ecclesiastical estates, including Pershore, Fladbury, Evesham and Cropthorne. This area continued to have a high proportion of slaves among its population, particularly on the church of Worcester's estates, estates that actively exploited and developed the area. Watermills for grinding corn are especially numerous in the Vale of Evesham, and meadow land and fisheries are also recorded on estates in the Anglo-Saxon period.[58] The active exploitation of the Vale is also implied by the numerous references to routes and fords in the charter boundaries;[59] clearly a reliable network of roads and tracks were needed if trade was to flourish between town and country, as well as between regions.

Charters also indicate that in the south and south-eastern areas of the west midlands the peripheries of estates were being cultivated, implying intensive practice; they also show that the open field system of agriculture was being established in these regions by the end of the Anglo-Saxon period.[60] This seems to have first appeared in parts of eastern and north-eastern England, and involved the replacement 'of scattered hamlets and farmsteads by larger nucleated settlements'. At the risk of seriously oversimplifying the process, once people began settling in the core of an estate, then the fields would have to be 're-designed' and were often laid out in huge strip divisions which radiated outwards from the core. The earliest reference to communal farming in the *Hwiccian* kingdom occurs in 849 in a charter for Cofton Hackett where mention is made of 'the common land', but more obvious references to open field systems and hence partitioned land occur later, for example in a lease by Bishop Oswald of Worcester dated to 966 where land held with an estate at Alveston, Warwickshire, is mentioned as lying 'in the divided hide' at Upper Stratford (-upon-Avon) 'where the lease is of "every other acre" here and of "every third acre" of ..."open land" at *Fachanleage*'.[61]

The Salt Industry of Droitwich

'The fourth marvel consists of wells of salt, which are found in the same [the region of the *Hwicce*], from which wells salt is refined. Thence divers kinds of food are salted, and [the wells] are not near the sea, but spring from the earth.'[88] So it is written in the work attributed to Nennius, the 9th-century historian, implying the inland salt works at Droitwich were the fourth of his marvels of Britain. (The first three were: 'the Lake of Lumonoy'—possibly Loch Lomond; 'the estuary of the river Trahannon'—possibly the Trent—'because in one wave like a mountain it covers its shores at a rush and recedes as other seas'; and a 'hot pool, which is in the region of the Huich [*Hwicce*], and is surrounded by a wall made of brick and stone' in which the water could become hot or cold according to the bather's wish—this is thought to be Bath.)[89]

The colloquy ascribed to the 10th-century writer, Aelfric, describes salt's everyday importance. 'What man enjoys pleasant foods to the full without the flavour of salt? Who fills his pantry or storeroom without my [salter's] craft? Indeed you will lose all butter and cheese-curd unless I am present with you as a preservative; you couldn't even use your herbs without me.'[90]

Salt was indeed essential for the preservation of meat and other produce over winter, and had been a vital commodity since the prehistoric period which, because of its limited availability, became an important object of trade and, in some areas, was even used as a form of currency. Salt was usually extracted

Fig.17 Anglo-Saxon hearth at Droitwich

from sea water or coastal salt-encrusted silts, an activity probably carried out since at least the Neolithic period as inland salt springs were comparatively rare,[91] although less so in the west midlands. As vast quantities of wood had to be burnt in the process of extracting the salt, it was important that the brine was of sufficiently high salt content to make the work economically viable. Outer Mercia was blessed indeed with saline springs at both Droitwich and in Cheshire that had been worked in the Roman period, but in Cheshire most archaeological evidence has been recovered from the Roman and then the medieval to modern periods, unlike at Droitwich which has virtually continuous sequences revealed by excavations at the Upwich site.[92] The purity of the Droitwich brine made it pre-eminent.

There is evidence for Iron Age salt production at the Old Bowling Green site and Friar Street in Droitwich, but excavations in 1983/4 at the site of the main brine well—Upwich, first mentioned by name in 962—indicated that salt was being produced in the sub-Roman/early Anglo-Saxon era. Upwich was apparently the largest well, the

The Anglo-Saxon Social Order

Slaves were the lowest rank in society and included a variety of people, for example those who had had to sell themselves into slavery through an inability to pay a fine for a crime; those who sold themselves or their family, including children, through desperate domestic hardship; or those who were the captives of war. Slaves had few rights but—theoretically—did have some protection under law. There were penalties for raping a slave-woman but the fine was in accordance to her owner's rank: a fine of 12 shillings was set for any man raping a nobleman's slavewoman, but at only 6 shillings for a commoner's slave.[62] It appears that the crime was considered an abuse against the master, not the victim.

On one estate in the 10th or very early 11th century a female slave could expect to have 'eight pounds of corn for food, one sheep or threepence for winter supplies, one sester of beans for Lenten supplies, whey in summer or one penny. All serfs ought to have Christmas supplies and Easter supplies, an acre for the plough and a "handful of the harvest", in addition to their necessary rights.'[63]

Female slaves could be employed as domestic servants, called *birele*—'cup-bearers', or on farms, with one of their duties being to grind corn. To distinguish them from their freeborn counterparts, female slaves had their hair cropped.[64] Male slaves were termed *theow*. The difference between a slave and a serf appears to have been that a serf had a household and a plot of land by which to support himself—a slave had nothing. The serf class may have included a category called the *esne* who could apparently marry and, therefore, presumably had a household; an *esne*'s master provided him with a home and the means to support himself but still owned the man and his property.[65] Finberg tentatively identifies the *esne* with the Continental class of *servus casatus* whose master provided them with a hut dwelling, but had the right to call on them for agricultural services. If the Anglo-Saxon *esne* was such a counterpart, Finberg suggests he would have spent 'much of his time working on his master's land' in return for money or food; when not so employed he would probably be working on his own plot of land or hiring himself out to work for his wealthier neighbours.[66]

Intermediate between slaves and freemen is another class called the *laet*. In common with slaves the *laet* had three levels within the class depending on the rank of the master. Whitelock suggests that a *laet* may have been a manumitted slave (one who had bought his or her way out of slavery or been bought out) or 'perhaps a member of a subject (pre-English) population'.[67]

The term *ceorl* may be viewed as a generic term covering all types of commoners. The *ceorl* was liable for military service but in the commissariat (going on campaign to bring provisions to the troops) and was not 'in the fighting line'.[68] The word *ceorl* translates most closely to 'husbandman' and he may have had dependents such as farm-hands and domestic slaves whom he had to feed and would therefore have had a certain amount of economic standing. However, it is not clear to what degree the *ceorl* was free or unfree nor is there any clue to his racial origin.[69] Although he had a *wergild* (what a person was worth in relation to injury or death, in effect 'blood-money'), the amount is not stated,[70] but Finberg suggests that an 11th century compiler of older laws, possibly Wulfstan, archbishop of York, states the *wergild* for a Mercian husbandman was 200 shillings while that of a thegn was 1,200 shillings; in brutal terms the life of a Mercian nobleman was deemed to be six times the value of a Mercian husbandman, and the same proportions probably held true for Wessex.[71] The *ceorl* appears to have occupied a farm and had a share in the ploughland and meadowland with other *ceorls*.[72] Yet the fact that he had on occasion to hire oxen from his neighbour for ploughing indicates that he could be of humble means. As Finberg states, 'a succession of bad harvests, an enemy raid, a cattle plague could soon reduce him to such poverty' that he would be forced to sell himself and his children into slavery, merely to survive.[73] There was no caste system and people could rise and fall within the classes according to their economic circumstances.

The next class up from the *ceorl* appears to have been the freeman but, confusingly, this category may have included some types of *ceorl*. King Aethelberht of Kent's early 7th-century laws speak of freemen and in some clauses it appears that the freeman stood in some form of 'special relationship with the king'.[74] It seems then that the freeman had more rights and was financially more secure than the *ceorl*.

It is uncertain if these actual terms were used in Mercia because no Mercian law code has survived as they have done for the 7th-century codes of Kent and Wessex from whence these terms derive. Indeed, the term *laet*, and their status between that of a slave and *ceorl* is only mentioned in the earliest of the Kentish laws, those of King Aethelberht, written *c*.602-3, and appear nowhere else.

Other classes mentioned included the *gebur*, 'a free, but economically dependent peasant'[75] who received his land and stock from his lord and gave back agricultural services and other dues.[76] The duties of each party varied from estate to estate—on some estates he was expected to work 'two week-days each week for every week throughout the year, and three week-days at harvest-time, and three from Candlemas to Easter' for his lord.[77] A cottager's duties depended '... upon what is determined for the estate. In some he must work for his lord each Monday throughout the year, or three days each week at harvest-time. He need not pay ground rent. He ought to have five acres; more, if it be the custom on the estate; and if it ever be less, it will be too little, because his labour must always be available. He is to pay his hearth-penny [a tax called 'Peter's pence' that was levied on every house and was introduced by Offa of Mercia probably in expiation of his murder of the East Anglian king Aethelberht, see also p.154] on Ascension day, just as every freeman ought, and serve on his lord's estate, if he is ordered, by guarding the coast, and (work) at the king's deer-fence, and at similar things according to what his rank is; and he is to pay his church dues at Martinmas [11th November]'.[78]

A *geneat* was a term which originally denoted 'a member of a household' and may have been used in a quite general sense in early Anglo-Saxon laws.[79] A *geneat* did not necessarily have the king as their master.[80] By the 11th century the term was used of men who held land from a lord, who paid rent and performed 'certain honourable services', particularly riding duties, and seems to correspond with the class termed *radcnihts* in the *Domesday Book*. Noble members of the household were generally termed *gesiths*, meaning 'companions of the king'. Whitelock notes that the term was applied in 'poetry and elsewhere to the members of a king's *comitatus*' (bodyguard). In the Laws of Wihtred *c*.695 (a Kentish king who ruled 690-725) the term *gesith-cund*—'born a *gesith*' suggests the term had 'come to denote a member of a class'. In the West Saxon King Ine's Laws (688-694) *gesiths* had a *wergild* of 600 or 1,200 shillings, but after King Alfred the Great's time the 600 *wergild* class disappears and men of the 1,200 *wergild* class become known as thegns. A man of *gesith* status was usually in charge of his own house-hold and was likely to be a lord over other men.[81] A *gesith* could be a landowner and several texts depict him as being the landlord of a village, although he could be under another's lordship, and laws imposed responsibility upon him for his 'men's good behaviour'.[82]

But the vast majority of the Anglo-Saxons were agricultural labourers and Aelfric, a monk, priest and possible schoolmaster at Cerne Abbas monastery from about 987 to 1002, gives an indication of their life in the colloquy ascribed to him. However, such colloquies were designed to teach pupils 'grammar, vocabulary and correct pronunciation of Latin',[83] it may be a rather sanitized version of farming life.

When the ploughman is asked how he carries out his work, he answers: 'I go out at daybreak driving the oxen to the field, and yoke them to the plough; for fear of my lord, there is no winter so severe that I dare hide at home; but the oxen, having been yoked and the share and coulter fastened to the plough, I must plough a full acre or more every day ... I have a lad driving the oxen with a goad, who is now also hoarse because of the cold and shouting ... I have to fill the oxen's bins with hay, and water them, and carry their muck outside ... It's hard work, sir, because I am not free'.[84]

When the shepherd is asked about his work, he replies: 'In the early morning I drive my sheep to their pasture, and in the heat and in cold, stand over them with dogs, lest wolves devour them; and I lead them back to their folds and milk them twice a day, and move their folds; and in addition I make cheese and butter; and I am loyal to my lord'.[85]

When asked about his work, the oxherd replies: 'When the ploughman unyokes the oxen, I lead them to pasture, and I stand over them all night watching for thieves; and then in the early morning I hand them over to the ploughman well fed and watered'.[86] This last reply suggests cattle-rustling was a particular problem.

It is clear that Anglo-Saxon society, and Mercia's by implication, was very hierachical with everyone appearing to know what was expected of them and what rights they had. From the surviving evidence, Finberg suggests that: 'The English countryside in the seventh century was largely dominated by an aristocratic slave-owning class, with demesnes [home farms] cultivated for them partly by slaves, partly by tenants with servile antecedents. For positive evidence of independent and self-governing village communities we search in vain'.[87]

source of the greatest volume of brine and the longest 'lived' of all the brine wells. In the 17th century it was said to have contained three separate springs. It appears that in the 5th to early 7th centuries salt production was heavily concentrated at the Upwich site, as the lack of pollen and seeds in the soil samples taken at this level suggest repeated dumping of sterile waste from salt extraction.[93]

From this earliest Anglo-Saxon phase, ten stone-built, brine-boiling hearths were discovered (see Fig.17). The hearths were set in elongated trenches and in most cases found to have been lined with stone. Radiocarbon dates were taken from the charcoal fills of seven of the hearths and showed them to have been in use between the 4th and 7th centuries, although the excavations showed that the principal phase of activity occurred in the second half of the 6th century. The presence of numerous globules of melted lead from the hearth fills suggested that the brine was boiled in lead pans which began to melt when the temperatures rose too high.[94]

The excavations discovered evidence for over 400 stakes, the regular spacing of some of them on a north-south alignment suggesting the use of wattle fences to provide some shelter for the hearth, built on a similar alignment, from the prevailing wind (see Fig.18) To the north of the site there seems to have been an area where rough stone blocks were collected for use in the construction of the hearths (the occasional dressed stone, if not freshly quarried, may have come from the Bays Meadow Roman villa about 1/4 mile north-west of Upwich), and on the west was a large pit which may have been used for making or storing charcoal.[95]

This process of salt production may have changed little between the Roman period and the 16th and 17th centuries, although specialized wooden salt-making tools gradually make their appearance from

Fig.18 Reconstruction of Anglo-Saxon salt-making operation (S.Whitby)

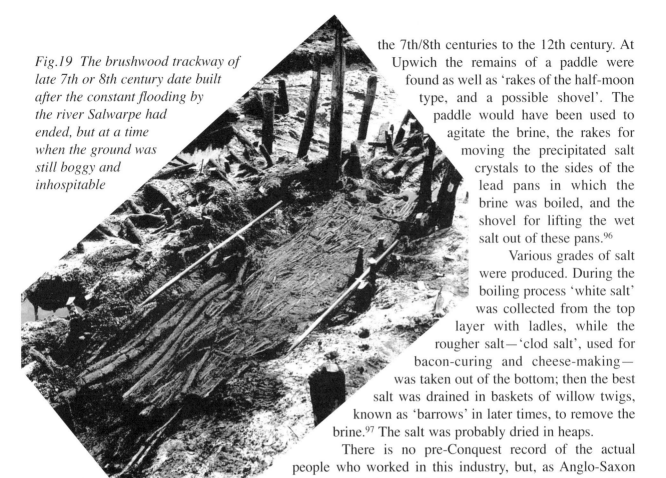

Fig.19 The brushwood trackway of late 7th or 8th century date built after the constant flooding by the river Salwarpe had ended, but at a time when the ground was still boggy and inhospitable

the 7th/8th centuries to the 12th century. At Upwich the remains of a paddle were found as well as 'rakes of the half-moon type, and a possible shovel'. The paddle would have been used to agitate the brine, the rakes for moving the precipitated salt crystals to the sides of the lead pans in which the brine was boiled, and the shovel for lifting the wet salt out of these pans.[96]

Various grades of salt were produced. During the boiling process 'white salt' was collected from the top layer with ladles, while the rougher salt—'clod salt', used for bacon-curing and cheese-making— was taken out of the bottom; then the best salt was drained in baskets of willow twigs, known as 'barrows' in later times, to remove the brine.[97] The salt was probably dried in heaps.

There is no pre-Conquest record of the actual people who worked in this industry, but, as Anglo-Saxon society was tightly stratified, the likelihood is that the hard physical graft in the salt-houses was done by those at the poorest end of the social scale. It may well have been carried out by slaves, for there were a higher proportion in the *Hwiccian* kingdom than elsewhere, or a Mercian equivalent of a *laet*, the second level in the hierarchy. Indeed, in the 16th century Leland commented of Droitwich that the 'people that be about the fornacis be very ille colorid' and that 'The great avauncement of the towne is by makynge of salt; and yet thoughe the commoditie thereof be syngular great, yet the burgesses be poore for the most parte; bycawse gentlemen (have) for the moast parte the great gayne of it, and the burgesses have all the labowre'.[98] It is unlikely that the division of work would have been much different in earlier periods.

The earliest Anglo-Saxon phase of salt-production at Upwich was brought to an end by a major period of flooding by the river Salwarpe. The thick layer of alluvium (up to about 0.5m thick) found on the site comprised many thin layers of silts and clays, indicating slow-moving water and frequent and regular episodes of inundation that would have rendered the site too wet for any industrial activity or habitation. Significantly, the name 'Salwarpe' (first recorded in 716-717) is Anglo-Saxon (nearly all river-names are British) and comes from the Old English *salu weorpan* meaning the 'thrower of yellow-brown material' or 'alluvium thrower'—a most apposite name. This period of flooding began between the years 600 to 660 and ended sometime between 686-788 when a brushwood trackway was built at the site along the original north bank of the Salwarpe.[99] The river was straightened and moved to its present position, just north of the Upwich site, in the 18th century but the canal follows the old line of the Salwarpe in the Vines Park vicinity.

The brushwood trackway (Fig.19) was built from tree trunks laid side to side to form a base 1.6m (5¼ft) wide which was then covered with brushwood, with stakes being used at intervals to hold the trackway in place. A post and wattle revetment was built along the edge of the Salwarpe and backfilled with ash and charcoal which is thought to be waste from the salt-making process, presumably to try to contain the river and strengthen the bank.[100] There is no evidence of the Upwich site being extensively and regularly flooded after the 8th century, indicating the success of these and other remedial works.

The earliest written reference to brine wells in Droitwich is perhaps implied in a charter dated to between 657-74 when King Wulfhere of Mercia granted 50 *manentes* (hides) at Hanbury (*Heanburg*) 'with all the meadows, woods, and brine-pits belonging thereto' to Abbot Colman. An early, although by no means certain, reference to the Upwich brine well is in a lost charter of 691 when Aethelred, king of Mercia, granted to Oftfor, bishop of Worcester, a 'shed and two furnaces belonging to the great brine-pit at *Wic* [Droitwich]'.[101] However, any traces of a mid- to late Anglo-Saxon structure would probably have been removed in the 13th century when the brine well at Upwich was reconstructed. The layers of alluvium fortunately protected the earlier remains, hence the survival of the hearths. However, other documentary evidence confirms that Droitwich was intensively developed throughout the Anglo-Saxon period.[102]

The earliest surviving charter by the Mercian king Aethelbald, dated 716-717, provides evidence for the expansion of the salt industry in Droitwich in the early 8th century:

> I, Aethelbald, by divine dispensation king of the Mercians, having been asked by the holy community of Christ dwelling in the place whose name is Worcester, will concede and grant into their free liberty of possession for the redemption of my soul a certain portion of ground on which salt is wont to be made, at the south side of the river which is called Salwarp, in the place which is called *Lootwic* and *Coolbeorg*, for the construction of three salthouses and six furnaces; receiving in exchange from the afore-mentioned community of Christ six other furnaces in two salthouses in which likewise salt is made, namely on the north side of the said river whose name is Salwarp. And we agreed to make this mutual exchange because it seemed more convenient to us both.[103]

Unfortunately, *Lootwic* and *Coolbeorg* have not been identified, although Finberg suggests a possible location at Stoke Prior, 2¹/₂ miles to the north-east of Droitwich.[104] However, one wonders if they were earlier names for Netherwich and Middlewich, the approximate locations of which are shown on Fig.21. Although there is, as yet, no archaeological evidence for salt-making in the Anglo-Saxon period

at these two latter locations, it is thought likely that they were operating simultaneously with the Upwich pit, given that all three appear to be named in relation to one another.[105] Leland records that the 'othar 2. salt

Fig.20 Hanbury Church stands about ¹/₂ mile west of the rather dispersed village of Hanbury, the Heanburg *of Wulfhere's charter, itself about 5 miles east of Droitwich. The present church is thought to stand on or near the same site as the minster which, in the mid-7th century, is said to have been granted the brine pits belonging to land nearby, presumably referring to those at Droitwich*

springs [presumably Middlewich and Netherwich] be on the lefte ripe of the river, lower a praty [pretty?] way then the othar great springe and at the very townes end'. He also comments that 'the profit and plenty of these 2. springs be nothinge comparable to the great springe', the latter almost certainly refers to the Upwich site.[106] Again one wonders if this was the situation in the Anglo-Saxon period. All three pits were recorded by the later 10th century: Upwich in 962 as *Upwic*, Middlewich as *Middelwic* in 972, and Netherwich in the same year as *neodemestan wic* and *Neopomaest wic*.[107]

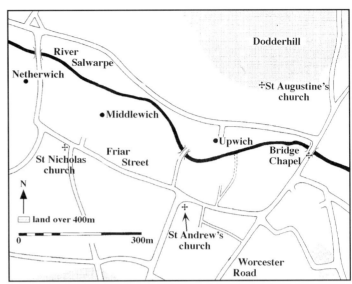

Fig.21 *Medieval street plan of Droitwich showing the locations where brine was extracted*

The charter's reference to salthouses implies that the furnaces used in the salt manufacturing process stood within buildings and that they might have been similar to those described in 1694 as 'essentially simple structures, the sides being made of timber with rafters placed on top to support a roof of straw thatch'.[108] Gone are the wattle fences and open working areas of the 6th- and 7th-century hearths.

Another charter of 716-717 records a grant by King Aethelbald to the monastery of St. Mary's, Evesham of 'a share of a house in (Droit)Wich, place of trade (mart), for salt'[109] and demonstrates that Droitwich was trading in salt in the early 8th century. In the Anglo-Saxon period Droitwich passed under a variety of names, including *Wiccium emptorium* in 716, *Saltwich* in 717 and *Saltwic* in 888. It was only by 1347 that it was being called *Drihtwych* or *Dryghtwych* which appears to mean 'foul or dirty wic'[110] — being low-lying and with much industrial activity would doubtless have rendered it so.

Fig.22 *A late 19th-century photograph of the salt works in the Upwich area with St. Augustine's church on the hill in the background*

Before the Domesday Survey of 1086 an Earl Edwin owned the manor of Bromsgrove to which belonged '13 salt-houses in Droitwich, and 3 salt-workers who pay 300 measures of salt from these salthouses'. Hooke observes that Earl Edwin's rights to Droitwich's salt wells were shared only with the king of England and that these 'may represent an inheritance from the original sub-kings of the *Hwicce*'.[111]

One of the taxes levied in Mercia were tolls

Fig.23 Today's view of the Upwich site, with St. Augustine's church on the hill to the left

on salt and this is mentioned in several charters. In 884 Aethelred 'lord of the Mercians' granted five *manentes* in *Hymeltun* (Himbleton, 4 miles southeast of Droitwich) 'free of all taxes, and with liberty to make six boilings of salt without paying any toll on cart-loads to the ruler of Mercia, to any public officer, or to any one else but the lord of Himbleton'.[112] This charter, albeit in reverse, implies that tolls on cart-loads of salt were common practice.

In a charter written sometime between 884 and 901 Aethelred, now termed 'ealdorman' and his wife, Aethelflaed, (King Alfred of Wessex's eldest child) in a grant of rights to St. Peter's and the bishop at Worcester, reserve 'to the king the toll of a shilling on cart-loads and of a penny on pack-loads at *Saltwic*'.[113] In Harmer's translation it is stated '... but the *waegnscilling* [wagon-shilling] and the *seampending* [load-penny] are to go to the king as they always have done at Droitwich.' The 'wagon-shilling' was a toll on the wagons as they stood at the salt-pans in Droitwich, and the 'load-penny' a toll upon each load placed them.[114] In 1066 Droitwich's tax yield was second only to that of London, and Domesday Survey records that Droitwich had about 250 buildings in which salt was produced and five brine wells.[115]

Given that the Droitwich salt industry was an important source of revenue for the king of Mercia and was in royal control by the late 7th century,[116] and that settlements described as a *wic* (i.e. a commercial centre) in Anglo-Saxon charters often have a nearby settlement at which royal, ecclesiastical and ceremonial duties could be performed,[117] it would not be surprising if there was a royal palace or administrative centre close by. Charter evidence that Mercian councils were held at Droitwich includes a charter of 888 from Ealdorman Aethelred to a *minister*, Wulfgar, that was signed 'in a public meeting gathered at *Saltwic*', (though this charter is considered not to be wholly reliable),[118] and one which Harmer tentatively dates to 903-4, concerning a disagreement between Bishop Waerferth of Worcester and the family of a layman, which was settled when Ealdorman Aethelred 'summoned the Mercian council to Droitwich to deal with many necessary matters, both spiritual and temporal'.[119] Against this evidence for Droitwich being the royal centre, charters of 815 and 831, which are considered generally to be both contemporary and genuine, suggest that council meetings were in fact held at Wychbold.[120] They record grants made 'in the royal vill' of Wychbold, indicating the presence of a royal palace.[121] This location would make sense as the archaeological and post-Conquest place-name evidence suggests Droitwich would have been an industrialized and unpleasant place; what better than to build a royal palace a mile or so away to the north-east on a spur of land which rises above the river Salwarpe. To date no archaeological evidence has been found for any Anglo-Saxon settlement, let alone a royal hall, at Wychbold.[122] The settlement is first recorded as *Uuicbold* in an 11th-century manuscript for the year 692, as *Wicbold* in 831, and *Wicelbold* in 1086, and probably means 'buildings by the *wic*'.[123] Yet there is the possibility that the place-name element of the Old English word *bool* or *bold*, was used on occasion, and possibly at Wychbold, to signify 'a superior hall'.[124]

Droitwich lay at the centre of a network of trade routes, or salt-ways—routes often mentioned as lying at and marking the boundaries of estates as mentioned in charters. It is clear that these salt-ways were major roadways. The word *here-paed*—'highway', or *straet*—'street' are often used in their connection, indicating that a Roman road is probably referred to, or, at the very least, a paved and maintained roadway. *Straet* roads were in fact some of the best maintained in the area. *Here-paed* routes were at least as important as *straets*, possibly even more so, as the word *here* ('army') implies that these were roads used by soldiers wishing to move easily and swiftly. The word *weg*—'way' was used to describe routes which were of lesser importance, and it is noticeable that there are very few *weg* routes referred to in conjunction with the salt industry.[125]

The evidence of tax revenues, salt ways and links with places holding salt rights in Droitwich, which in 1086 stretched as far as Princes Risborough in Buckinghamshire, coupled with archaeological work on the sites, indicate that Droitwich was an important settlement in Mercia.

The Worcester Diocese

Between the 4th and 6th centuries, Worcester and the river Severn lay on something of a cultural boundary between the British Christian culture and the pagan Anglo-Saxons, evidenced by the fact that no pagan burials of the latter have been found west of Worcester.[129]

In 1970 two 7th-century burials were found barely 2in. (5cm) below the level of the Norman undercroft floor of the present College Hall of Worcester Cathedral.[130] Both burials were orientated east-west. There were no grave-goods and nothing closely datable with the skeletons, other than a few sherds of Roman pottery, which were probably residual. However, around the left-hand side of the neck of one skeleton, that of a man aged between 25 and 30 years, were fragments of very fine spun gold which may have formed part of a braid. A 9th or 10th century date was considered when the spun gold was compared with similar gold threads found in a 9th-century grave at Winchester, but a 6th or 7th century date was thought possible as such spun-gold strips have been found in Continental graves of that period; indeed such fragments have been found from Roman tunics of the 3rd and 4th centuries.[131] Two samples of bone from the skeleton of the man were radiocarbon dated, providing information which has been recently recalibrated to give a date centring on the mid-7th century.[132] The east-west orientation suggests Christian burial, as does the absence of grave goods, and the date indicates a period around the time when the *Hwicce* were converted, suggesting that the fragments of spun gold could be part of a stole of one of the first priests of the Anglo-Saxon minster at Worcester, or even of an earlier British church.[133]

The Anglo-Saxons are known to have come across British churches—hence the *ecles* derived place-names (see p.59). Eddius Stephanus, St. Wilfrid's foremost biographer who died in *c*.720, described how, in the 7th century, Wilfrid 'went on to enumerate holy places in various parts of the country which the British clergy, fleeing from our own hostile sword, had deserted'.[134]

Even if it is impossible to be too precise about dates, there is further evidence of a possible British Christian presence in Worcester. One tenuous link hangs on the discovery of a coin found beneath the castle mound that stood in the cathedral precinct until it was levelled in 1830. The coin's inscription reads: 'from Augustus to Phocas AD 602,'[135] implying some form of trading in Worcester after the Romans left. In addition, a possible late Roman copper alloy chi-rho (symbol of Christianity) was discovered during the building of the Lychgate centre, just north of the present cathedral.[136] This find again tentatively suggests some sort of late/sub-Roman Christian presence.

There is also some circumstantial evidence that St. Helen's church in Fish Street, off Deansway, may be an early British foundation. The dedication of this church is usually associated with Helen, the mother of emperor Constantine the Great who was proclaimed Emperor at York in 306. Helen (*c*.250-330) was

Mining in Mercia

Lead vats at Droitwich are referred to in several charters, as well as leaden furnaces in a charter of 836 by King Wiglaf of Mercia to Hanbury minster.[126] Archaeological evidence confirms the use of lead in Droitwich. Where the lead came from is not revealed, but the bounds of a charter of 833 relating to land in the far south-west of the *Hwiccian* kingdom at Stoke Bishop (now a north-western district of Bristol) delineates land 'from the lead-mine to the mill-pool, from the mill-pool to the river Avon'.[127] It is also possible that lead was brought in from the *Pecsaete* of the Peak District where it had been mined extensively in the Roman period, and for which there is some documentary evidence for lead mines in the 8th century. Some of the Wirksworth mines were in the possession of Repton monastery in pre-Conquest times and in 835 Cyneuuara, abbess of Repton, conveyed land here to a Prince Humbert (of the *Tomsaete*) 'on condition that he shall pay annually a rent of lead worth 300 *solidi* [shillings]', to the archbishop of Canterbury and his successors.[128] This suggests lead was being exported from Derbyshire over considerable distances.

Figs.24 and 25 (Left) Odin's mine near Castleton in Derbyshire. The name Odin (also known as Woden) may suggest an Anglo-Saxon origin, but later lead extraction has obliterated any possible archaeological evidence

Fig.26 (Below right) A figure set in the north wall of the south transept of Wirksworth Church. Its date is unknown, but the simplicity of carving suggests it is pre-Conquest. The figure appears to represent a lead miner complete with his pick and kibble (bucket). It was found at Bonsall (2½ miles north-west of

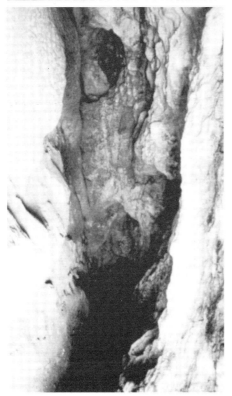

Wirksworth) and given to St. Mary the Virgin's church in 1876. In 714 the abbess of Repton is recorded as sending a coffin made from Wirksworth lead to St. Guthlac in the Fenlands of Lincolnshire

converted to Christianity when she was over 60, and was renowned for the being the mother of the first Christian emperor. She is also known for her part in the Finding of the True Cross (a tradition that began to crystallize 70 years after her death) which is the subject of the (probable) Mercian poet, Cynewulf's, best work *Elene*.[137] A dedication to St. Helen is unusual, especially in Mercia; most are found in Yorkshire and Lincolnshire, probably because of her son's connection with York, and the dedication has strong pre-Anglo-Saxon associations. St. Helen's-on-the-Walls church in York dates to the 10th century but lies over a single-celled Roman structure, and the chapel of St. Helen in Colchester, Essex, is believed to be a rebuilt Roman structure.[138] Worcester's St. Helen's lies within the late Roman and post-Roman defences, again implying the existence of a late Roman Christian community.[139]

St. Helen's is unusual in that it had jurisdiction over 11 rural chapels in a wide area around the city before the Norman Conquest. This influence must date from a time before the division of Worcester's estates in the 10th century,[145] and 'may be based upon territorial links of some antiquity'.[146] The question has been raised by Baker as to why these chapels owed allegiance to St. Helen's rather than the cathedral, and why this church was 'thus able to establish rights over a wide area'.[147] Work by Steven Bassett has confirmed St. Helen's 'leading rôle in the early Church of the region' and it is likely it 'pre-dated the foundation of the see in 680'.[148] This is certainly suggested in a record of the outcome of a synod held in 1092 in Bishop Wulfstan's newly-built cathedral crypt to settle a dispute between the presbyter of St. Helen's and that of neighbouring St. Alban's about the rights of their respective churches. The synod decided that St. Alban's had no rights over St. Helen's and 'the church of St. Helen, in fact, had been a vicarage of this Mother Church [the cathedral] from the days of King Ethelred, and Archbishop Theodore, who founded the See at that time and placed Bosel there as first bishop in the year of our Lord's Incarnation 680 [or 679] ...'. This record could simply be based on tradition, but St. Helen's must have certainly been in existence in 960 when its priest gave the church to the priory on his becoming a monk.[149]

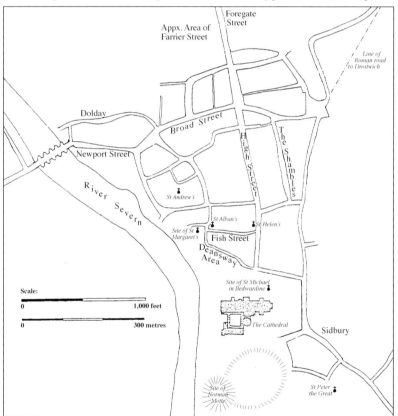

Fig.27 Medieval Street Plan of Worcester
It is evident that three possible British churches—St Helen's, St. Alban's and St. Margaret's—together with the late 7th century cathedral church of St. Peter's, stood within the enclosure of the Roman defences of Worcester, demonstrating that the focal centre of Anglo-Saxon settlement was in the southern part of today's city

Other early churches also flourished. St. Alban's is an early dedication and stands very close to St. Helen's just over the modern Deansway road; there is a tradition that it is second only to St. Helen's in antiquity.[150] The lost church of St. Margaret's—again such a dedication is generally regarded as early—stood immediately west of St. Alban's. The

120

The Poet Cynewulf

It is uncertain whether Cynewulf came from Mercia, Northumbria or Wessex, but the four poems ascribed to him are generally held to be written in a Mercian dialect.[140] He appears to have lived in the earlier part of the 9th century but there are no biographical details available. *Elene* is the longest, by far, of the four poems which are 'signed' by Cynewulf, in that his name is written in runes interwoven in the text. The others are *Christ II (The Ascension)*, *Juliana* about a martyr in the emperor Diocletian's time, and *The Fates of the Apostles* which tells the story of the missionary journeys of Jesus' disciples.[141] It is suggested by Bradley that in working his name so carefully into the poems Cynewulf intended that these works should keep their precise form rather than undergoing the mutations which one would expect in the solely oral transmission of poetry. It is therefore possible that Cynewulf was the first poet using the English language to compose in the written rather than the oral form.[142] Judging by the religious nature of these poems, it is likely that Cynewulf was in religious orders.

The historical setting of *Elene* (of which a small part is quoted below) is the 4th century wars between the Romans, Huns and the Germanic nations which signalled the end of the Roman empire. Bradley notes that the character of 'the formidable Helen' places her in the sizeable gallery of women, both literary and historical, whom the Anglo-Saxons recognized 'as being in virtue, intellectual strength, vision, purpose and practical efficacy the peers or superiors of men'.[143]

> Constantine commanded the envoys furthermore to bid her to build a church there on the hillside for the benefit of them both, a temple of the Lord on Calvary as a pleasure to Christ and a succour to men, where the holy Cross was found, the most celebrated of the trees of which earth's inhabitants have ever heard on their way through the world. She acted accordingly when her kindred friends brought from the west across the watery fastness many a loving message.
>
> The queen then ordered men trained in their crafts to be severally sought, the best ones, those who knew how to build most exquisitely in stone-bondings, in order to prepare God's temple upon that spot, according as the Keeper of souls directed her from the skies. Then she commanded that the Cross be encased in gold and intricately set with gems, with the noblest precious stones, and then enclosed with locks in a silver casket. There the tree of life, the most excellent tree of victory, has ever since remained, unimpeachable as to its origin. There, ever ready, is a support to the infirm in every torment, trial and sorrow. There, through that holy artefact, they shall at once find aid and grace divine.[144]

Chronicon Abbatiae de Evesham (Evesham Abbey's chronicle) records that King Aethelbald of Mercia (716-57) 'gave the chapels of St. Alban and St. Margaret in Worcester ... to Evesham'[151] in 721, but this evidence for an early foundation must be treated with caution as it is otherwise unsupported. All these churches stood within the northern boundary of the old Roman defences and it is suggested that possibly as early as 721, but certainly by the late 9th century, St. Helen's, St. Alban's and St. Margaret's stood within Worcester's old defended enclosure along with the cathedral, which had itself been founded in the 690s. The cathedral and its precinct occupied about two-thirds of the old Roman defended area and the cathedral's expansion to the north may have been restricted by these three early churches.[152] St. Andrew's, along with the church of St. Peter the Great which used to stand in the vicinity of the present Royal Worcester Porcelain factory, may also have Anglo-Saxon origins.

The siting of Worcester and the See

The siting of the settlement at Worcester may indicate why it was chosen as the site of the episcopal see. It lay on an easily defended site and on a river that was navigable as far as Bewdley in the first half of the 15th century,[153] and quite possibly in Anglo-Saxon times too. Two fords may have existed: one near Newport Gate, which is just north of the modern bridge, and another south of the cathedral—'the Diglis ford'. It is suggested that Worcester was the first place upstream from the sea where the river Severn could be forded beyond undue effect of the tides, and the town probably owes its origin to this.[154]

The derivation of the city's name from *Uueogorna civitas* (in 692) and *Uueogorna ceastre* in 889— 'The Roman fort of the tribe called *Wigoran* or *Weogoran*',[155] indicates a Roman fort, the exact location of which is unknown, although it probably lay within the later medieval walled city.[156] There is evidence of Roman activity throughout Worcester from the cathedral area northwards into the Tything. Pottery and artefacts from the 1st to 4th centuries have been found in a variety of locations, as well as evidence of iron working from Pitchcroft, Sidbury and Broad Street. The core of the Roman settlement was probably around and north of the cathedral where pottery has been found in the admittedly restricted archaeological excavations.

The settlement seems to have shrunk in size in the sub-Roman and early Anglo-Saxon period. Certainly it appears that the southern Farrier Street area was abandoned, to the extent that soil accumulated sufficient to allow for the possibility of subsequent cultivation,[157] and that the northern part of Deansway was no longer used for domestic or industrial use after A.D. 300.[158]

Yet there is some evidence that a settlement of sorts existed, albeit much reduced. The remaining network of Roman roads, the bridging point and a navigable river would have almost certainly been important deciding factors in its subsequent choice as an Anglo-Saxon episcopal centre. It seems that the establishment of the see and cathedral at Worcester led to the development of the Anglo-Saxon town, and not *vice versa*.

The Anglo-Saxon bishops of Worcester

Tatfrith, according to Bede, 'an energetic and very learned man of great ability ... had been elected bishop [of Worcester] while a monk at [St.] Hilda's monastery, but met an untimely death before he could be consecrated'.[159] Bosel, another monk from St. Hilda's monastery at Whitby, was consecrated by Archbishop Theodore in 679. Yet another Whitby monk, Oftfor, succeeded Bosel in 691, when the latter had to retire due to ill health.[160] Oftfor was residing in the *Hwiccian* kingdom from before 680 (Osric was then king) and may well have given 'quasi-episcopal leadership' in the kingdom between Tatfrith's death and Bosel's consecration (675-679).[161] Oftfor was a gifted and well-learned man who had studied under Archbishop Theodore in Kent and then decided to visit Rome 'which in those days was considered an act

Fig.28 St. Alban's Church, Worcester

of great merit'.[162] Oftfor is supposed to have been the author of many books which the Danes destroyed in their raids.[163]

Ecgwine succeeded Oftfor in 693 and was bishop of Worcester until 711. The first *Life* of Ecgwine, written in about 1039 but which claimed to incorporate older elements, stated that he was related to King Aethelred of Mercia (reigned 675-704).[164] A native of Worcestershire, Ecgwine had an outstanding reputation as a preacher and bishop, obtaining from Pope Constantine the privilege of sanctuary—which comprised a hallowed circle around the cathedral where people could take refuge.[165] In about 709 he founded Evesham Abbey after he had seen a vision of the Virgin Mary and angels on the site, having been led there by a swineherd by the name of Eoves who had first seen this vision. Ecgwine became Evesham Abbey's first abbot where his cult as a saint developed. By the late 11th century, 'when some of the Anglo-Saxon saints' cults were questioned by [Archbishop] Lanfranc and the Normans', Ecgwine's sanctity was assured 'by an ordeal through fire by miracles' and led to a very successful fundraising tour in 1077 of southern England when the Evesham monks carried his relics.[166]

Figs.29 & 30 One thegn-abbot, Buca, received 3 hides of land from Aethelbald at Acton Beauchamp on the Herefordshire border. A piece of (possible) early 9th-century sculpture survives as a lintel over the doorway to the tower of the present church of St. Giles, which suggests the continuing existence of the monastery at this time. Although Acton Beauchamp was in the Hereford diocese at an early stage it was actually on a tongue of Worcestershire which projected into Herefordshire, and it is suggested that it was already a possession of a Worcestershire religious house when the shire boundary was established in the 11th century; indeed there is a close similarity between the Acton Beauchamp stone carving and the cross-shaft at Cropthorne (south of Worcester) which may indicate such a link[172]

Ecgwine was succeeded by Wilfrith, previously his chaplain, who held the episcopate from 718 until 743 or 745. King Aethelbald had returned from exile to take the Mercian kingship in 716, by which time at least 10 monasteries had been established in the *Hwiccian* kingdom: Hanbury, Evesham, Fladbury, Tetbury, Bath, Gloucester, Pershore, Ripple, *Penintanham* (?)Inkberrow, and Withington.[167]

Bishop Wilfrith's rule coincided with the rise in the number of 'family monasteries' and thegn-abbots—those thegns which Aethelbald appears to have pensioned off with land for monastic use. Bede complained in 734 that 'numberless people have been found who call themselves abbots and at the same time reeves (*praefecti*) or thegns (*ministri*) or servants (*famuli*) of the king ... Such persons suddenly receive the tonsure at their pleasure, and at their own judgement are made from layman not into monks, but abbots.'[168] In effect the thegns were rewarded with a secular pension.

One of the best examples is Aethelbald's charter of 736 in favour of a laymen, Cyneberht, a charter witnessed by Bishop Wilfrith and consented to by the then sub-king of the *Hwicce*, Aethelric. Ten hides were granted (*c*.1,200 acres) to Aethelbald's 'venerable companion' Cyneberht, to establish a monastery 'in the province to which was applied by the men of old the name Ismere, by the river called Stour'. The land in question is in the very north-

The Monastery at Bibury, Oxfordshire

Figs.31 & 32 St. Mary's, Bibury. The lower illustration shows the chancel arch, a medieval addition which has cut into the Anglo-Saxon string-course. The Taylors suggest that the string-course may originally have supported a Rood (a representation of the Crucifixion) of stone or plaster. The two blocked square-headed window recesses may be of Anglo-Saxon origin— they are widely splayed facing into the nave, but with shallow splaying into the chancel[175]

Bibury, in the extreme south-east of the *Hwiccian* kingdom, is recorded as *Beaganbyrig* in 721-743. This may be an instance where the *byrig* element refers to a monastery, for when this element is used in conjunction with a female name, it can indicate a monastic site. The abbess in question was probably Beage, the daughter of a thegn called Leppa to whom Bishop Wilfrid had leased five acres of land at Ablington in Bibury for the duration of Leppa's life and that of Beage 'on account of the old friendship between us'. The church of Worcester owned 15 hides of land by the river Coln here and thus Wilfrid was able to lease five of these to his friend; Aethelbald attested the charter but does not appear to have been involved in any other way.[173] There is no definite evidence that an 8th-century monastery existed here, but there are certain features which suggest it might have been an important foundation. The 'greater parts of the walls of an Anglo-Saxon church are incorporated' into the present building of St. Mary, which the Taylors date to 950-1100, and there are several architectural and sculptural features of the same date.[174] The size of the surviving Anglo-Saxon nave and chancel suggest St. Mary's was an important church and a lease of 899 which ensured that church-scot (literally 'church tribute', a custom whereby corn was collected on St. Martin's day, 11th November) and

soul-scot (a due on behalf of a dead person paid to the church of the parish to which the deceased belonged) went to Bibury, implies that the church was a major one with ancient rights, in other words an 'old minster'.[176] It may be reasonable to extrapolate this back to the 8th century and suggest St. Mary's later importance was a consequence of it being a monastic foundation.

Fig.33 (Left) This late Anglo-Saxon carved stone, located on the north wall of the chancel at Bibury, was found near the church in 1913 and was reset on top of an original pilaster strip base

Figs.34 and 35 (Above) Casts of late Anglo-Saxon stones found in 1913 near the church; the originals were presented to the British Museum. These and other casts are kept inside the church

western part of the *Hwiccian* kingdom, its name surviving in Ismere House, 2 miles north-east of Kidderminster, although whether the monastery was sited at Ismere, or on the site of the present parish church of St. Mary's in Kidderminster is open to debate.[169] In the charter Aethelbald states that Cyneberht 'as long as he shall live, he is to have the power of holding and possessing it [the estate], and, whether during his lifetime or indeed after his death, of leaving it to whom he shall wish'.[170] Cyneberht appears to have left it to his son, Ceolfrith, who then granted his inheritance to Bishop Wilfrith's successor, Milred, during Offa's reign. After 816 the monastery disappears from the record, possibly a casualty of the Danish invasions.

Bishop Milred (or Mildred) probably succeeded Wilfrith during the latter's lifetime sometime between 743 and 745 when Wilfrith was apparently incapacitated through old age or illness. As well as his episcopal duties, Milred travelled to Germany in 753 and his correspondence with Lull, a West Saxon who joined his kinsman Boniface as a missionary in Germany and succeeded him as archbishop of Mainz in 754, demonstrates that Milred was a well-educated and literary man.[171]

Mercia seems to have been particularly connected with the evangelization of Germany, and especially of their 'Saxon brothers' during Milred's episcopacy. Yet this mission does not seem to have had official backing from the Anglo-Saxon Church. The Mercian connection may owe its origins to the appreciation that in the 8th century, Mercia had access to the best education in southern England, notably that offered at Malmesbury Abbey, and also by the eminence in the English Church of Mercian ecclesiastics at this time.[177]

Mildred also corresponded with the former bishop of the *Magonsaete*, Cuthbert, who had been elevated to the archbishopric of Canterbury in *c*.740. Like Cuthbert, Milred collected and composed epigrams and poems. His collection, which is thought to have been extensive and varied in content, probably drew, in part, upon the notebooks of Anglo-Saxon pilgrims who had returned from Rome and had copied inscriptions or acquired works of their own.[178] Milred was instrumental in the cultivation of literary appreciation and lent and borrowed books from other bishops, including Archbishop Cuthbert. The books he owned show the breadth

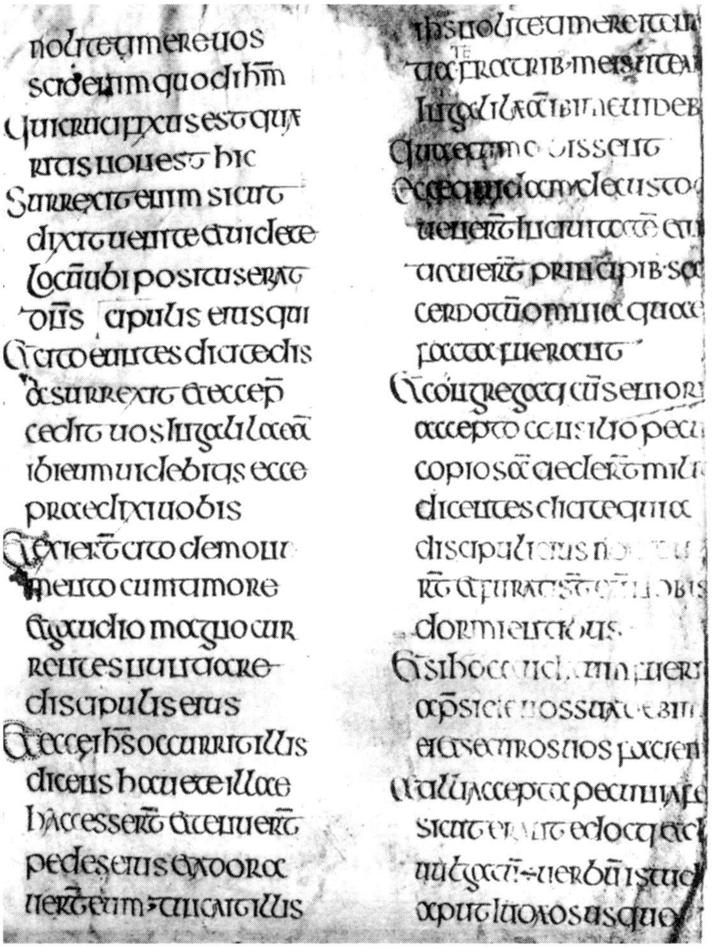

Fig.37 Tilhere, who had been abbot of Berkeley monastery from at least 759, was bishop of Worcester between c.777-c.780/1 and it is during his episcopate that King Offa presented the cathedral with a gospel book (of which this is a page) which was the custom when a deed for land was granted

of poetry that was available: from the Roman inscriptional verses that had come back from the Continent to the 'new Anglo-Latin poetry which had been founded upon Christian Latin models by Theodore, Aldhelm and Bede', and from poets closer to Worcester. Milred's own collections were made at a time when there was a great interest and expansion in the fields of education, architecture and the decorative arts.[179] Bishops Tilhere and Deneberht followed and it was during Tilhere's episcopy that Offa presented Worcester Cathedral with a gospel book (see Fig.37).

Waerferth was bishop of Worcester between 872-914/5 and was a native of Mercia. Asser states that he translated Pope Gregory the Great's *Dialogues* from Latin into English, and he may also have had a part in translating Bede's *Ecclesiastical History* as the Old English version is in the Mercian dialect and was translated at that time.[180] Indeed, he was one of the scholars whom Alfred the Great of Wessex brought into his court, with two other Mercians, to help in his campaign to raise educational standards in England, which had fallen to a deplorably low level. Alfred's choice says a great deal about the standard of learning in the Mercian kingdom. Waerferth ruled as bishop through the Danish invasions, receiving in 874 'an important grant of privileges' from Ceolwulf whom the Danes had set up as a puppet ruler in English Mercia.[181] However, Waerferth seems to have allied himself with King Alfred and was instrumental in having Worcester fortified by Alfred's daughter, Aethelflaed and her husband Aethelred who was the Mercian ealdorman. At Bishop Waerferth's request 'Ealdorman Ethelred and Aethelflaed ordered the borough at Worcester to be built for the protection of all the people'. The charter later states:

> land-rent, the fine for fighting, or theft, or dishonest trading, and contribution to the borough-wall, and all the (fines for) offences which admit of compensation, are to belong half to the lord of the church, for the sake of God and St. Peter, exactly as it has been laid down as regards the market-place and the streets. And outside the market-place, the bishop is to be entitled to his land and all his rights, just as our predecessors established and privileged it.[182]

The charter was issued with the cognisance of Alfred as well as that of 'all the councillors of the Mercians'. The lasting impression that this charter presents is that Worcester was a thriving and sophis-

Fig.38 An engraving of 1778 showing the west end of Worcester Cathedral, the walls along the river bank and the Norman castle mound, since removed

ticated town by the late 9th century.

The Danish invasions had clearly left their pyschological mark as a lease of Nuthurst in Warwickshire demonstrates. Two hides at Nuthurst were leased by Waerferth (still termed 'bishop of the *Hwicce*') to a king's thegn, Eanwulf, in return 'for his friendship and acceptable money - 20 mancuses of tested gold', continuing that 'This, however, the above-mentioned bishop agreed to chiefly because of the very pressing affliction and immense tribute of the barbarians, in that same year when the pagans stayed in London'.[183] As Whitelock observes, this lease shows the far-reaching effects of the taxation raised 'to buy off the Danes' in 872.[184]

Waerferth's episcopate lasted for over 40 years and has been viewed as a force for both stability and continuity during this very troubled time; his contact with King Alfred was probably instrumental in drawing together Mercia and Wessex, so helping with their greater integration in the 10th century.[185]

Recent finds[186]

During the late 1990s a curved sandstone foundation was uncovered at Worcester Cathedral which stands about 3m (*c.*10ft) from the wall of the chapter house. Three suggestions have been made as to the purpose of the foundation. One is that the remains may post-date the building of the Norman chapter house and could represent some kind of buttressing or are the foundations of an ambulatory (a covered walkway around the building). A second possibility is that the foundation was contemporary with the building of the chapter house and represents a first attempt at a larger building. The third, and most exciting, is that the foundation pre-dates the chapter house and are part of one of the Anglo-Saxon churches on the site.[187]

The latter possibility, although entirely speculative at present, is considered the most plausible. In this scenario, the foundation is either of an Anglo-Saxon rotunda or a free-standing circular church, possibly with an attached apse and with a single-storey ambulatory running around it. It is possible that this may be St. Mary's church which Oswald built in the 10th century. It is likely that if this was a rotunda or a circular free-standing church, it was re-used in the Norman chapter house design and, perhaps, even in the structure. The Norman chapter house was originally circular and there is no precedent for this in England but, if the builders incorporated this putative free-standing structure into their design, then its shape would make sense. The main, two-storeyed 'drum' of this Anglo-Saxon rotunda would probably have had a series of arcades which the Normans might have blocked in and used as part of their building. The ambulatory would not then have had any function as there would have been no access to it, and would have been demolished, leaving the curving foundation wall.

Round churches and circular monuments were the fashion on the Continent in the 10th century. Such a copy in Worcester would show the city to have had a high status. Future excavations hope to determine whether the present chapter house incorporates the plan of this postulated rotunda/circular church and

Figs.39 & 40 Worcester Cathedral chapter house (top) with part of the wall of the earlier foundations discovered during excavations in October 1999 (lower). The 10-sided exterior of the chapter house was a 14th-century addition

whether it re-used the fabric. One of the questions archaeologists hope to answer is whether the present chapter house is on the exact site of the rotunda/circular church or, if not, determine the spatial relationship of the two.

As suggested, the building could date to Oswald's construction of the church of St. Mary. Oswald, bishop of Worcester from 961 to 992, created St. Mary's as a monastic church and absorbed the secular priests of St. Peter's, the old cathedral church, into the new monastery,[188] but this transformation happened slowly. There was evidently a need for another church in the cathedral precinct because it is reported that Oswald had to preach from a stone cross in the cathedral churchyard, as St. Peter's was too small for the crowds of people who wanted to hear him. Presumably this was the same cross as that mentioned in 781 which stood over the graves of an Anglo-Saxon called Wigferth and his wife Alta. This cross was taken down during Edward the Confessor's reign (1042-1066) for church repairs and, alas, has never been rediscovered.[189] It appears that work began on St. Mary's in 966 and was completed in 983. Although St. Mary's may have been considered of greater importance than St. Peter's, in 991 Oswald was forced to admit that St. Peter's held his episcopal throne. By this time there were three churches in the cathedral precinct: St. Mary's was clearly the monks' church, St. Peter's was possibly enlarged in the 1030s, and a chapel or church dedicated to St. Michael, which was probably much smaller, was 'endowed with the specific function of being used for prayer for the dead'. It is likely that it was under Bishop Oswald's episcopate that the cathedral enclosure was altered in that its northern boundary was moved further south. This took St. Helen's and St. Alban's out of the precinct and meant streets were built around them. The southern end of High Street believed to have 'been lined by houses and workshops belonging to lay people' was demolished, resulting in a 'more narrowly defined precinct'.[190]

CHAPTER 7
The Age of Mercian Supremacy

The reigns of Aethelbald (716-757) and Offa (757-796) herald an era of change in the status of Mercia in relation to its neighbouring provinces—an era known as the 'Age of Mercian Supremacy'. Both kings were regarded as *bretwaldas* during their terms of power. Even Bede with his known antipathy to Mercia states that nearly all the provinces 'south of the river Humber and their kings, are subject to Ethelbald, King of the Mercians'.[1] He could not comment on Offa as he died in about 735, decades before Offa came to power. The 8th century was the first and only time when Mercian power lasted for a sustained period, although, because of political upheavals and warfare, it was not completely stable even during this period.

Some writers have assumed that the aim of the major Anglo-Saxon kingdoms was to unify England under their rule and judge Aethelbald and Offa accordingly. But unification may not have been the objective of the early or middle Anglo-Saxon kings for multiple small kingdoms or states were the expected norm in the past—consider the Greek city states, the various British tribes and even subsequent German princedoms. Indeed, Kirby has suggested that Mercia's rise in the 8th century may have represented a serious upset in the equilibrium of power south of the Humber that had only been recently reached between the three kingdoms of Mercia, Wessex and Kent.[2] The frequent battles necessary to enable Mercia to continue its domination, lends support to this theory.

Although the three kings preceding Aethelbald and Offa did not hold the same scale of power, or the same determination with regard to expansionist policies, their reigns paved the way for this increase in authority. Of these three rulers—Aethelred, Coenred and Ceolred—Aethelred is the most significant and reigned the longest: nearly 30 years.

Aethelred (reigned 675-704)

'More famed for his pious disposition than his skill in war'. William of Malmesbury[3]

It is probable that Aethelred did not expect to succeed his brother Wulfhere, who died suddenly in his mid-30s.[4] Certainly Aethelred was not next in line for the throne but as Wulfhere's son, Coenred, was still an infant, he was obliged to take over. Aethelred was probably in his early 30s and faced an unstable outlook. Mercia was under threat from Northumbria and Kent, whilst Middle Anglia still lacked a secure government and administration following Peada's murder in 656. It was perhaps for this reason that Aethelred married Oswiu of Northumbria's daughter, Osthryth. Osthryth was sister to the then reigning Northumbrian king, Ecgfrith (670-685), and Aelfwine, Oswiu's youngest son, was king of Deira. In addition, Sighere, the king of Essex, was married to Osyth, Wulfhere's niece. If the intention was to create a web of family connections that helped ensure peace between the kingdoms, it failed.

As the kings of Kent were attempting to take control of Surrey and Essex, one of Aethelred's first major actions was to attack the Kentish forces in 676 and push them back into their own territory. Bede reports that Aethelred 'with his wicked soldiery, profaning churches and monasteries without fear of God or respect to religion ... destroyed the city of Rochester'.[5] Aethelred and his forces caused so much destruction in the Rochester diocese that the see had to be temporarily abandoned.[6] Dutton suggests this raid was undertaken at the East Saxon kings' request, as the Kentish kings had sought to establish domination over them. Certainly, after the defeat of their army, the Kentish kings Hlothere and Eadric were only allowed to stay on as rulers under Mercian overlordship.[7]

However, it appears that only 10 years later Mercian control of Kent faltered. In 686 King Caedwalla of Wessex and his brother Mul raided Kent, and Mul apparently took the kingship not long after, with the possibility that the two brothers joined forces with the East Saxons.[8] This control of Kent by Wessex came to an end in 687 when Mul was burnt to death by Kentishmen. A year later, after wreaking revenge on Kent, Caedwalla abdicated in order to go on a pilgrimage to Rome, where he died soon afterwards, an act which caused further political trouble in the kingdom. Sighere, who ruled Essex with his cousin Sebbi and who, it seems, had supported Caedwalla and Mul in spite of his beneficial associations with Mercia, filled the power vacuum and for the final year of his life (687-8) ruled both Kent (albeit probably only the western part) and Essex. It is thought he secured the accession of his second cousin Swaefheard to rule in Kent.[9] Kirby relates that a prince of the native Kentish house, Oswine, had also emerged to claim the throne, and probably took the crown soon after Caedwalla's abdication, ruling with Aethelred's support as he sought to re-establish Mercian influence. Swaefheard appears in Oswine's circle as a witness to two charters, but by January 690 Oswine's power may have been in decline as the second of the two charters refers only to 'those Kentish nobles who were able to be with him'. The supposition must be that Kent remained divided in support between Oswine, backed by Aethelred, and Swaefheard now backed by the East Saxons. It could be that Aethelred 'was not entirely master of the situation' in Kent and that there had been a resurgence of East Saxon power, Aethelred perhaps requiring their assistance.[10]

The lack of support for Oswine among his own people weakened his position still further and he was toppled by Wihtred, the son of a previous Kentish king, Ecgberht. Wihtred was viewed as the legitimate heir by the church in Canterbury and by Bede who states that Wihtred, Kent's 'rightful king ... freed the nation [Kent] from foreign invasion by his devotion and diligence'. Wihtred may have briefly had to accept the co-rule of Swaefheard until 694, but in 695 he was able to issue a law code in his own name. He reigned until 725 without acknowledging the overlordship of any other king or kingdom, possibly exercising power even north of the Thames (which, over the centuries, was constantly in dispute between Mercia and Wessex) as he issued one charter at Berkhamsted, 40 miles north-west of London.[11]

Although Mercian power in Kent faltered, Mercian overlordship of the East Saxons was soon consolidated. Aethelred granted land to the bishop of London between 693 and 704, and consented to a grant by Swaefred (Sebbi's son), co-king of Essex, to land in Middlesex in 704, which was later confirmed by Aethelred's successors Coenred and Ceolred.[12]

Following Penda's death in 655 at the battle of *Winwaed*, near Leeds, and Wulfhere's defeat in 675, Mercia had remained in a subordinate position to the Northumbrians, and was still paying tribute. However, in 679 Aethelred attacked Northumbrian forces who had entered Mercian territory, defeating them at the battle of the river Trent. It was during this battle that Aethelred's Northumbrian brother-in-law Aelfwine was killed. Bede records:

> In the ninth year of his reign, King Egfrid fought a great battle near the river Trent against King Ethelred of the Mercians, in which Egfrid's brother Elfwin was killed. The latter was a young man of about eighteen, who was much loved in both provinces since Ethelred had married his sister Osthryd. This gave

every indication of causing fiercer strife and more lasting hatred between the two warlike kings and peoples, until Archbishop Theodore, the beloved of God, enlisting God's help, smothered the flames of this awful peril by his wholesome advice. As a result, peace was restored between the kings and peoples.

Henry of Huntingdon adds, echoing Bede: 'For a long time afterwards the treaty of peace concluded between the two kings and their respective kingdoms continued unbroken'.[13]

The battle of the Trent, as well as permanently returning Lindsey to Mercian rule, has been described by Stenton as 'one of the decisive incidents in early English history' because Ecgfrith never again tried to gain control over any part of southern England, and the attention of his Northumbrian successors was turned towards new dangers on their northern borders. The battle established a northern frontier for Mercia on the river Humber, and tribute was no longer paid.[14]

Having gained control of the northern boundary of Mercia, and reached an accommodation in the south-east, Aethelred began a period of consolidation in which the Church was closely involved.

Aethelred and the Church

At the synod of Hertford, which was summoned by Archbishop Theodore in 673, the proposal to create more manageable units through increasing the number of dioceses was put forward. As it stood, each kingdom was ruled over by one bishop in a single diocese, often of immense size. No agreement on the number of dioceses was reached at the Synod as the move was unpopular with those bishops who felt such a re-organization would reduce their authority. Indeed, Bishop Wilfred of York appealed to the synod of Rome in 679, who stipulated an increase to only 12 dioceses.

The co-operation of the ruler of a province was also important in the establishment of a new diocese. Aethelred was well-disposed towards the Church, and of the 12 new sees, three were set up in the areas under Aethelred's auspices: the *Hwiccian* see at Worcester, that of the *Magonsaete* at Hereford and, between 675-685, a Mercian bishopric was established at Dorchester-on-Thames in what is now Oxfordshire. This latter see had originally been established by the West Saxon king Cynegils in about 635 after his conversion to Christianity. As Stenton observes, although its Mercian successor was short-lived, it demonstrates that Mercian power was recognized in this area to the north of the river Thames during Aethelred's reign. There is even evidence that the lands south of the Thames, which had been in the control of the West Saxon kingdom, had passed under Mercian control at this time. Local tradition associates the name of Aethelred with the foundation of Abingdon Abbey (in southern Oxfordshire) which has led to the suggestion that he was wielding power in the surrounding area shortly after Cenwealh of Wessex's death in 672. Aethelred also gave land in Tetbury in southern Gloucestershire and Long Newton in north Wiltshire to Aldhelm, abbot of Malmesbury Abbey, in 681, and in 685 Aldhelm received a large estate at Somerford Keynes, 4 miles south of Cirencester, from Aethelred's nephew, which were all places that had at some time been in West Saxon control.[15]

After Bishop Wilfrid was expelled from Northumbria in 691, following a failed attempt to claim the whole of the Northumbrian diocese, Aethelred offered him protection even though the Northumbrian see had been divided in line with Archbishop Theodore's changes, with bishops at York, Lindisfarne and Hexham established in 678. Eddius Stephanus, Wilfrid's contemporary biographer, in recording this event refers to Aethelred as Wilfrid's friend and that he welcomed the bishop 'with great honour' and that Wilfrid was 'held in high respect'. For a time, Wilfred administered the whole of the Mercian diocese and subsequently Bede describes him as 'acting as Bishop of the Middle Angles, since Theodore had died and as yet no bishop had been appointed to succeed him'.[16] This bishopric was probably based at Leicester.

Aethelred's reasons for taking Wilfrid's side are not known for certain, but politics were probably involved: by supporting Wilfrid, Aethelred was engaging in a drawn-out dispute which must have proven an embarrassment to the Northumbrian king and the archbishop of Canterbury. Wilfred had been causing trouble in Northumbria under its king, Ecgfrith, for some years, at least since 678, and had appealed to Rome on at least two occasions against the decision of the Northumbrian synod. He was imprisoned and then expelled from Northumbria in 680. Then in 685 Theodore reached an agreement with the new king of Northumbria, Aldfrith, to install Wilfrid as bishop of Ripon. After Theodore's death in 690 Wilfrid made his failed attempt to become bishop of all Northumbria and was exiled for the second time in 691. He continued to agitate for a unified Northumbrian see from his exile in Mercia, an aggravation to Northumbria that Aethelred was no doubt happy to support. Kirby suggests it is also possible that Aethelred would have much preferred Wilfrid as archbishop of Canterbury to Beorhtwald, the existing archbishop whom he might well have associated with the eclipse of Mercian power in Kent in the 690s.[17] Wilfrid has the reputation of being a pedantic, difficult, even a self-serving man, but he was certainly a man of discernment and great intelligence, and his friendship with Aethelred says much for the latter's qualities. Aethelred must have been an intellectual equal to Wilfrid.

In true character, Wilfrid did not let go of the idea of the Northumbrian diocese and returning as bishop of York, and in c.699/700 took his case by proxy to the pope in Rome, who referred it back to an English synod. This led to the council of Austerfield (near Bawtry, south-east of Doncaster and very near to the site of the battle of the river Idle in 617) which ruled against Wilfrid. Eddius Stephanus relates that one of the motives of the Austerfield synod was to 'strip Wilfrid of all he possessed so that he would not be able to call the smallest cottage his own in either Northumbria or Mercia'. A well-wisher of Wilfrid's at the synod had secretly warned that the archbishop and bishops would try to force Wilfrid, among other things, 'to surrender to the archbishop everything you have gained in Mercia from King Aethilred. [Archbishop] Berthwald will then give it to whom he pleases'. Wilfrid refused to accept any ruling and, entrusting his interests to the Mercian king, set off for Rome to appeal against the decision. The case was eventually 'solved' by compromise after King Aldfrith's death in 704 and Wilfrid was restored to the churches of Hexham and Ripon. Wilfrid's last journey took him back into Mercia. Eddius records how he went 'round the abbeys ... sharing out his property [as if] among his heirs ... Every community was provided for according to its needs; some got grants of land to increase their revenues, the rest were left a legacy ... At the end of the round his company came to the monastery at Oundle where Wilfrid had once dedicated a church to St. Andrew, and here he was twice overcome by sudden illness'. Wilfrid died at Oundle in 709 aged 76, and was buried in the basilica he had built at Ripon.[18] For the pious Aethelred, Wilfrid was a wise choice of friend and between them they were clearly great benefactors to the Church in Mercia.

In 697, Aethelred's wife, Queen Osthryth, was murdered. Opinions differ as to the reason. Finberg considers that Oshere, the sub-king of the *Hwicce*, and Osthryth may have have been working on a plot to separate his kingdom from Mercia, for he believes the *Hwiccian* rulers were possibly of the Northumbrian royal family. The failed plot then provides an explanation for the later rulers of the *Hwicce* not being considered as kings, with tighter central Mercian control being exercised. However, Oshere was dead before 680, more than 17 years before Osthryth's murder. Another possibility suggested by Kirby is that she was killed in vengeance for the murder of Aethelred's brother, Peada, allegedly through the treachery of his wife, Ealhflaed, who was Osthryth's sister.[19] As Peada was murdered in 656 one might ask, if a revenge killing was the reason, why did the murderers wait for over 40 years? Nevertheless, Northumbrian princesses were disliked and viewed with suspicion in Mercia, and so it is at least likely that Osthryth was murdered for political reasons.

Bede records the event thus in his synopsis: 'In the year 697, Queen Osthryd was killed by her own people, the Mercian chieftains'. Henry of Huntingdon puts it more dramatically: 'the Mercians, who are also called South-Humbrians, perpetrated a scandalous crime, for they barbarously murdered Ostrythe, the wife of their King Ethelred, and sister of King Egfrid'.[20]

While the motive for the murder remains a mystery, so does Aethelred's apparent unwillingness to seek justice for it. No-one seems to have been brought to book for the crime, and no *wergild* (blood price) was claimed for Osthryth. It is possible that any relevant records have been lost, or that, at the time of her murder, Osthryth had become a nun and their marriage had thereby been annulled, as was the custom, for there is a suggestion that Aethelred may have taken a second wife.[21]

Osthryth was buried at Bardney Abbey to which Aethelred retired in 704 to become its abbot, after abdicating from the kingship of Mercia. This was seven years after Osthryth's death and it is perhaps significant that he chose to retire to a monastery in Lindsey, the province which he had won (permanently as it turned out) from the Northumbrians in 679. Was his choice purely political in that this move would help to keep this area in Mercian control? Or did the fact that his former wife was buried there persuade him?

Fig.1 A see had been founded at Dorchester-on-Thames, (Oxons.) by the West Saxons in the 630s. Under King Aethelred of Mercia's reign it became a Mercian bishopric but was short-lived. Religious life continued at Dorchester thereafter, and in the 9th century it was again a bishopric which was subsequently moved to Lincoln in 1072.[22] The present church is of medieval date

After Aethelred's death both he and Osthryth were worshipped as saints at Bardney. Indeed, Mercian royal saint cults were encouraged beyond the core of Mercia and into its sub-kingdoms as part of the kingdom's policy of control.[23]

Although Aethelred may not be considered a dynamic ruler in comparison to Penda, Aethelbald and Offa, he was certainly effective. He was a strong enough king to make the political position between kingdoms work well and forceful enough to turn the turbulent position of Mercia at the beginning of his reign into a secure one. He set the stage for subsequent Mercian expansion by creating a stable environment within the sub-kingdoms. For any later monarch to have attempted such an expansion with the possibility of internal rebellion would have been disastrous. Indeed, Aethelred's successors were able to build upon his legacy of strong, cohesive administration and secure boundaries.

Coenred 704-709

'... equally celebrated for piety to God and uprightness towards his subjects, ran his mortal race with great purity of manners ...'. William of Malmesbury[24]

Coenred was Wulfhere's son but, at the time of his father's death, was still an infant. When Aethelred abdicated he nominated Coenred, then aged about 25, as successor and the changeover seems to have passed smoothly. However, information on Coenred's reign is scant, for he only reigned for five years.

Bede's first mention of Coenred provides a significant insight into his character when he comments on '... the case of a man living in the province of the Mercians, whose visions and words - although not his way of life - benefited many others, but not himself. For in the reign of Coenred, Ethelred's successor, there was a layman who held a military command, and pleased the king as greatly by his public diligence as he displeased him by the carelessness of his private life. The king repeatedly warned him to confess

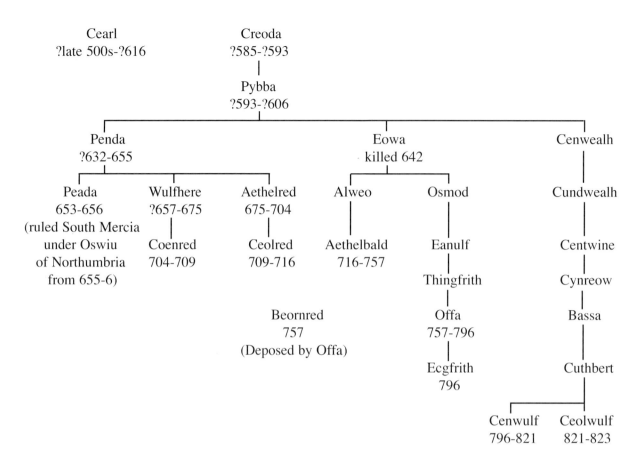

Fig.2 The Mercian family tree, based on Cyril Hart (1977),
with dates amended in line with current theories

and amend, and to abandon his wicked ways before a sudden death deprived him of any time for repentance and amendment. But, although frequently warned, he rejected his salutary advice, and promised that he would do penance at some future date. Meanwhile he fell ill and, taking to his bed, began to suffer severe pains. The king, who was fond of him, visited him and urged him even then to repent of his sins before he died'.[25] The man does not, succumbs to hallucinations, dies and ends up in hell, the moral of the story being that one should repent of one's sins before it is too late. Coenred is portrayed here as a caring and spiritual man, more a monk/confessor than king.

Coenred's reign appears to have been uneventful, with the exception of some serious raids into Mercia by the Welsh, perhaps taking advantage of the fact that he was a new and inexperienced monarch. Stenton suggests that such raids, which took place between 704 and 709, prompted the construction of Wat's Dyke, which runs from Basingwerk on the Dee estuary to the Morda Brook, south of Oswestry, during Aethelbald's reign (716-57) to protect this vulnerable part of the Mercian border.[26] However, a recent radiocarbon date from charcoal found beneath the bank has suggested a much earlier date of construction. For more on this earthwork see chapter 8.

Charter evidence provides an idea of Coenred's authority at this time, although it must be stressed that they can only give a partial picture as it is not known how many charters are missing. In addition the charter evidence for grants, or confirmation of grants, of land to Evesham Abbey in Worcestershire for 708 and 709 are considered spurious.[27] Evesham Abbey fabricated a good deal of its earliest charter evidence, a common phenomenon in the late Anglo-Saxon and early post-Conquest periods where a claim to land was needed but original sources did not oblige. A record of a charter dated between 704-9, however, significantly states that Coenred 'renews the *sanctio* of Aethelberht, king (of Kent), in favour of St. Paul's, London' which implies he had control in that city.[28] Another, authenticated charter shows that Coenred granted land at *Liya* to a nun Feleburg.[29] *Liya* is usually identified with Lingen or Lye in Herefordshire, although a case has been made for it being in the vicinity of Much Wenlock Abbey 'at Hughley, where St. Witburga [probably St. Milburg] is said by *Domesday Book* to be associated with the settlement'.[30] All the sites lie within the *Magonsaetan* kingdom and demonstrates Coenred was exercising authority there. An authentic grant of land by Tyrhtil, bishop of Hereford, to Wealdhere, bishop of London, for 50 hides at Fulham is given with 'the consent and permission' of Coenred and Sigeheard of the East Saxons and confirms Coenred's authority in both areas. (Mercian dealings with land in Middlesex is attested in Aethelred's reign when, between 693-704, he granted '10 hides [in Middlesex] for the increase of the monastery in the city of London' to the same bishop.) It is suggested that Bishop Tyrhtil may have originated from this region which could explain why he had property so far away from Herefordshire.[31]

Coenred seems to have had a good relationship with the East Saxons. When, like his uncle, he abdicated in 709—in his case to go to Rome and become a monk—he was joined by his cousin and close friend Offa, one of the junior kings of the East Saxons, whom Bede describes as 'a very handsome and lovable young man'. However, whether they went willingly to find a monastic life or under pressure as political exiles is not known.[32]

As there is little evidence of military activity during his years in power, it could be inferred that Coenred had little impact upon Mercia, making no advances politically or militarily, but it should be acknowledged that he did not lose any land, power or property either, and appears to have kept a secure hold on his satellite provinces, whilst the charter evidence suggests he was wielding control as far away as Essex.

He apparently passed the kingdom on to Ceolred in much the same condition as it had been upon his own succession. Certainly Bede remarks he 'had ruled the kingdom of Mercia with great renown for some while', and Bede was not a natural champion of the Mercian monarchs.[33] Unfortunately his successor, his cousin, was no match.

Ceolred - reigned 709-716

'Ceolred succeeded these kings in the kingdom of Mercia, which he governed with honour ... inheriting his father's and grandfather's virtues'. Henry of Huntingdon[34]

'Ceolred ... the debaucher of nuns, the infringer of ecclesiastical privileges'. Boniface quoted in William of Malmesbury's *Chronicle of the Kings of England*[35]

Ceolred was probably the son of Aethelred's putative second wife, for his first wife, Osthryth, had remained childless. If this is so he would have only been 10 or 11 when he became king. It is possible that he was a spoilt child as years later he was remembered for his dissolute behaviour and sinfulness, at least in William of Malmesbury's Chronicle. Boniface groups Ceolred with his contemporary Osred of Northumbria as an abuser of the Church, with Osred being described as 'driven by the spirit of wantonness, fornicating, and in his frenzy debauching throughout the nunneries virgins consecrated to God'.[36]

Ceolred's reign was quite unlike that of either Aethelred or Coenred, and appears to have been one of friction, with both neighbouring kingdoms and the Church; one wonders why Henry of Huntingdon described him in such glowing terms. He employed an expansionist policy that brought to an end the era of peace enjoyed between Mercia and King Ine of Wessex, for in 715 he attacked Ine at a battle recorded at a place called *Wodnesbeorg*, the outcome of which is unknown, but which Kirby states shows Ceolred was 'unquestionably the invader' as this was deep in West Saxon territory. (*Wodnesbeorg*—'Woden's fortification' has sometimes been identified with Wanborough, a village 4 miles east of Swindon on the Wiltshire downs, and, more usually, as Adam's Grave in Alton Priors, about 7 miles east of Devizes in Wiltshire.) Henry of Huntingdon records that '... the slaughter was so great on both sides, that it is difficult to say who sustained the severest loss'. The attack appears to have been planned for the time when Ine's resources were stretched, following a campaign against British forces in the west country. The battle set the scene for future unnecessary hostilities between Mercia and Wessex, which could have been so easily avoided.[37]

Aethelbald, a rival for the Mercian kingship who was descended from Penda's brother Eowa, was sent into exile in the Fenland by Ceolred, where he formed his friendship with Guthlac (see chapter 5).

The charter evidence for Ceolred's reign is slight. He apparently confirmed an earlier grant of land at Ombersley to St. Mary's church in Evesham;[38] and confirmed a grant of land of questionable authenticity at Twickenham in Middlesex to the bishop of London.[39] In a charter of between 709-716, Ceolred granted land at *Peandan Wrye* to Mildburg, the abbess of Much Wenlock Abbey.[40] *Peandan Wrye* is traditionally identified with Wyre Piddle in southern Worcestershire, although a place near Much Wenlock has also been suggested.[41] In common with Coenred's grant to Feleburg, this charter shows Ceolred was exercising authority in the *Magonsaetan* kingdom.

Ceolred died in 716 and was buried at Lichfield. Boniface describes his demise as he was '... feasting in splendour amid his companions [when] - as those who were present have testified - suddenly in his sin sent mad by a malign spirit, who had enticed him by his persuasion to the audacity of breaking the law of God; so that without repentance and confession, raging and distracted, conversing with devils and cursing the priests of God, he departed from this light without a doubt to the torments of hell'.[42]

It may be that Ceolred died of some sort of seizure or possibly that he was epileptic, but the fact that Osred died in the same year has led to the suggestion that they may have been murdered, in Ceolred's case through poisoning, which allowed new branches of each kingdom's royal families to take the throne. Indeed, a monk at Much Wenlock Abbey had experienced a vision of the terrible punishments that awaited Ceolred on his death. It is possible that Abbess Mildburg, who may have been Ceolred's cousin if Merewalh was Penda's son, was responsible for spreading this story, which suggests there was a rumbling discontent with Ceolred's rule even in the most saintly quarters of Mercia. If Ceolred had been only 10 or 11 on his accession, then he would have been only 17 or 18 when he died and supposedly in the peak of health, so foul-play cannot be discounted.[43]

For all of Ceolred's alleged profligacy the political position of Mercia remained largely unchanged, with the exception of the broken peace with Wessex, and the kingdom was left intact at the time of Aethelbald's accession.

There is a slight suggestion that Ceolred was initially succeeded by a man called Ceolwald who may have been his brother. Anglo-Saxon dynasties appear to have had the first elements of their names in common, in this case 'Ceol'. Three 9th-century Mercian kings have names starting simply with a 'B' — Beornwulf (823-26), Beorthwulf (840-52) and Burgred (852-74) — who may represent a rival dynasty, and also the ill-fated Beornred, who reigned briefly between Aethelbald and Offa in 757, may also have belonged to the same branch of the family. Another 9th-century king, Wiglaf, belonged to a branch of the royal family with a 'Wig' prefix who contested for, and in Wiglaf's case, gained the Mercian throne. Familial links can thus be suggested where certain name elements are common. Nothing else is known about Ceolwald or his fate and he appears in only one version of the Worcester regnal list. But with his and Ceolred's demise, a new branch of the Mercian royal family comes to the fore, this time descended from Penda's brother Eowa.[44]

Fig.3 King Aethelbald depicted on a 'bird and branch' coin discovered at Dorchester-on-Thames, Oxfordshire

Aethelbald (reigned 716-757)

'Ethelbald ... became king, as St. Guthlac, inspired by a prophetical spirit, had predicted to him'. Florence of Worcester[45]

'... a brave and active prince, who reigned victoriously 41 years'. Henry of Huntingdon[46]

For nearly 30 years Aethelbald was the dominant figure in southern England, Bede stating that all of the provinces and kings south of the Humber were subject to him. In a charter of 736, concerning a grant of land to a monastery at Ismere/Kidderminster, drawn up at Worcester, Aethelbald refers to himself as king of all the 'provinces which are called by the general name South English' and attests the grant as *'rex Britanniae'* — 'King of Britain'. Whitelock suggests this title corresponds to the term *Bretwalda*.[47]

At the beginning of Aethelbald's reign Wessex had fallen into turmoil. Between 710 and 715 it had been in a state of internal rebellion, and in 721 the *Anglo-Saxon Chronicle* records that King Ine slew the aetheling, Cynewulf, which implies a failed insurrection on the part of the latter. In 722 another rebellion broke out. Henry of Huntingdon records '... Eadbert, the Etheling, who was the king's enemy, had got possession of [Taunton] castle [only built by Ine in 710], but Ina's Queen Ethelburga stormed and razed it to the ground, compelling Eadbert to escape into Surrey'. Kirby observed that Ealdberht (Henry's Eadbert) may have been Ine's son or nephew seeking recognition as his heir.[48]

Ine dealt with any problems in the south-east of the kingdom, before fighting the South Saxons in 725, even slaying Ealdberht. As Ealdberht had found refuge in Surrey and among the South Saxons, this suggests that the area was attempting to break away from Wessex, perhaps either under renewed Kentish influence, or in reaction to the growth of Aethelbald's power.[49]

The following year Ine abdicated. Although a powerful king for much of his reign, Ine's control over his lands had been reduced during the previous 15 years. He travelled to Rome to seek a religious life in the company of his wife Aethelburh (Henry of Huntingdon's Ethelburga) who is said to have been instrumental in persuading him to retire there. Ine's succession was disputed between his kinsman Aethelheard, and a rival, Oswald, who may have been a descendent of Ceawlin, king of Wessex. A civil war resulted in which Aethelheard gained the advantage and subsequently became king of Wessex which, according to the *Anglo-Saxon Chronicle* he held for 14 years, Oswald dying in 730. It is thought that Aethelbald may have had a part in the outcome, and because of his support that Aethelheard, and his brother and successor, Cuthred, were established as Aethelbald's dependents, or were at least obliged to concede territory. However, in 733 Aethelbald moved across Wessex, attacked Aethelheard's forces, occupied Somerton, and subsequently ruled a large part of Wessex directly until 752. Indeed, Stenton observes that for most of the period between 726 and 802, Wessex was 'little more than a large, outlying province of the Mercian kingdom' and a good deal of what had been West Saxon territory was annexed to Mercia. Concerning the Somerton attack, Henry of Huntingdon records that '... Ethelbald, the very powerful king of Mercia, assembling a formidable army, besieged Sumerton, investing it with camps formed all around, and as there was no force to throw in succours to the besieged, and it was impossible to hold out against the besiegers, the place was surrendered to the king'.[50]

After Aethelheard died in 740, fighting broke out between Cuthred and Aethelbald. For in 741 Henry writes '... the proud king Ethelbald continually harassed him [Cuthred], sometimes by insurrections, sometimes by wars. Fortune was changeable; the events of hostilities were, with various results, now favourable to the one, then to the other. At one time peace was declared between them, but it lasted but for a short interval, when war broke out afresh'.[51]

On occasion they joined forces, but even then they were in competition with one another as Henry observes. 'In the fourth year of his reign [743], Cuthred joined his forces with those of Ethelbald, king of Mercia, with whom he was then at peace, against the Britons, who were assembled in immense multitudes. But these warlike kings, with their splendid army, falling on the enemy's ranks on different points, in a sort of rivalry and contest which should be foremost, the Britons, unable to sustain the brunt of such an attack, betook themselves to flight, offering their backs to the swords of the enemy, and the spoils to those who pursued them. The victorious kings, returning to their own States, were received with triumphant rejoicings'.[52]

Aethelbald clearly remained in control of parts of Wessex, as both he

Fig.4
This piece of sculpture was unearthed at Repton in 1979 and is believed to represent Aethelbald. If so, it it is 'the oldest known large-scale representation of an English king'. The stone would originally have formed part of the shaft of a cross or other memorial

and Cuthred witnessed the sale of land to Glastonbury Abbey with the former's consent in 744, a charter in which Aethelbald is referred to as 'monarch of Britain'. In 746 Aethelbald sold 4 hides of land at unidentified places to the Abbot of Glastonbury. In an agreement of 798 it states that Athelbald gave Cookham monastery in Berkshire to Christ Church at Canterbury, which shows he had authority in this much disputed area between the two kingdoms. After his reign, control of Cookham, and by implication this part of Berkshire, passed back to Wessex, only to be taken back by Offa of Mercia probably after the battle of Bensington in 779.[53]

In 752 Cuthred made a bid for independence, as Henry of Huntingdon, Florence of Worcester and the *Anglo-Saxon Chronicle* record that he fought against Aethelbald at *Beorhford*, presumably Burford in western Oxfordshire. As usual Henry gives the most vivid account:

> Cuthred, in the thirteenth year of his reign, being unable to submit any longer to the insolent exactions and the arrogance of King Ethelbald, and preferring liberty to the hope of life, encountered him at *Bereford* with bannered legions. ... Ethelbald, who was king of kings, had in his army the Kentish men, the East Saxons, and the Angles, with a numerous host ... There was no thought of flight, confidence

in victory was equal on both sides, The arrogance of their pride sustained the Mercians, the fear of slavery kindled the courage of the men of Wessex ... wherever the brave King Ethelbald turned, the enemy was slaughtered, for his invincible sword rent armour as if it were a vestment, and bones as if they were flesh ... But the God who resists the proud, and from whom all might, courage, and valour proceed, made an end of his favour to King Ethelbald, and caused his wonted confidence to fail. Since then he no longer felt courage or strength, Almighty God inspiring him with terror, he was the first to flee while yet his troops continued to fight. Nor from that day to the day of his death was anything prosperous permitted by divine Providence to happen to him.[54]

Florence of Worcester, however, merely records under the year 752 that: 'Cuthred, king of Wessex, in the twelfth year of his reign, fought a severe battle with Ethelbald, king of the Mercians, near *Beorhford*'.[55]

The battle apparently left Wessex to some degree independent of Mercia, at least until Cuthred's death four years later in 756. Indeed, Yorke suggests Cuthred regained control over northern Wiltshire and northern Somerset even before this battle. The subsequent position is unclear; Cuthred's successor, Sigeberht was deposed by his own people within 12 months, and another Cynewulf, for whom no precise genealogical information has survived, took the throne. It would seem that Cynewulf was instrumental in encouraging the Witan (council) of Wessex to vote Sigeberht out of office and in this he may have had the support of Aethelbald, for one of his first recorded acts was to appear at Aethelbald's court to attest a charter granting 10 hides of land to a West-Saxon abbot in Wiltshire. This charter describes Aethelbald as 'king of the Mercians and of the surrounding peoples', which implies a lesser kingdom than the one recorded in his title of 744 as 'monarch of Britain'. It is just such a putative diminishment of power that Kirby postulated may have played a part in exposing him to the danger of assassination. Nevertheless, it

is probable that Wessex was once again a Mercian dependency when Aethelbald was murdered only a few months later in 757, his death allowing Cynewulf to regain lands in Wiltshire and Berkshire.[56]

The border between Mercia and Wessex was clearly a source of trouble over many years and in the 8th century the Mercian kings endeavoured to push forward their claim to the more northerly areas of the West Saxon kingdom. As both sides were evenly matched, and each recorded victories, it is no surprise that the lands in the upper Thames valley, northern Wiltshire and Somerset appear to have changed hands between these kingdoms quite frequently.[57]

Fig.5 A coin from Aethelbald's reign showing the king holding up a bowl or a chalice on the one side. Probable date c.735-40

Stenton remarks that there is some evidence to suppose that London and Middlesex finally became detached from the East Saxon kingdom and became part of Mercia's territory in Aethelbald's reign. His predecessors had power to give grants of land here, but Aethelbald appears to have been free to deal with the area as he wished, even if indirectly.[58] It is said that Aethelbald had a good relationship with the East Saxon ruler, Saelred (also spelt Selred and Selered), through whom he gained increasing power over London and 'the commercial trade along the Thames'.[59] London was the prize and was an important mint for Aethelbald and Offa. Through commerce came wealth, and through wealth, power. That Aethelbald's control of this area was undisturbed is supported by charter evidence: in 734 is a grant of the toll due on one ship in the port of London to St. Andrew's church at Rochester,[60] similar grants exist to the abbess and monastic communities at Minster-in-Thanet in *c*.733[61] and 748,[62] and the remission of tolls for two ships for the benefit of Worcester Cathedral in 746 or 747.[63]

Keeping control over, or even peace with Kent had been difficult for Aethelbald's predecessors. Under Aethelbald the position seems to have changed and eventually stabilized, which, it might be argued, was a contributing factor to historians' willingness to accord him the title of *bretwalda*, although Bede and the *Anglo-Saxon Chronicle* never conceded him this title, probably due to political bias. After the death of Wihtred of Kent in 725, his sons Aethelberht, Eadberht and Ealric were left as heirs and his kingdom was partitioned between them. A charter of 738 refers to land being given to the church by Eadberht and the necessity of the grant being confirmed by Aethelberht, who is acknowledged by the former as his superior. In this grant the authority of Aethelbald is not sought,[64] suggesting that a degree of autonomy on the part of the Kentish kings existed. The grants of remission of tolls to the churches of Rochester and Minster-in-Thanet, together with a charter for confirmation of privileges to the Kentish churches by Aethelbald in 742, do, however, demonstrate his authority and the rapport that existed with Kent, which continued throughout his reign.[65] As some degree of autonomy and discretion on the part of the Kentish kings still existed, this probably eased any feelings of resentment that might have occurred towards Aethelbald as overlord, resulting in more co-operation between the kingdoms than had ever occurred during the reigns of his predecessors. Thus, Henry of Huntingdon states that Kentish soldiers fought with Aethelbald at the battle of *Beorhford* (Burford) in 752. A stability had finally been established.

Aethelbald did not hold any authority in Northumbria. In common with Penda and Wulfhere, Aethelbald's style of rule was aggressive so it is no surprise that in 740 (Henry of Huntingdon records 737) he devastated part of Northumbria while its king, Eadberht, was occupied with attacking the Picts. A note from the 'Continuation' of Bede states: 'Aethelbald, king of the Mercians ... laid waste the region of the Northumbrians'. Henry of Huntingdon naturally gives a more colourful account, observing that: 'Ethelbald, the haughty king of the Mercians, a prince of a different character in this royal fellowship, [Henry had just been discussing the decision of the former king of Northumbria, Ceolwulf's, decision to become a monk in line with six previous kings of his own and other kingdoms, including Aethelred and Coenred of Mercia] ... despising holiness, and setting might above right, invaded Northumbria, where, meeting with no resistance, he swept away as much booty as he could transport with him to his own country'. But this attack achieved no long term gain, for in 758, the year in which King Eadberht abdicated to live as a clerk in his brother's minster at York, Stenton observes that the 'Northumbrian kingdom was stronger and its boundaries were wider' than at any time during the previous 73 years. In fact Northumbria was enjoying its own 'golden age'.[66]

Aethelbald was on good terms with the East Angles for it was on the borders of their territory that he had spent his exiled years when Ceolred, who viewed him as a rival to the Mercian throne, had driven him out of Mercia. Aethelbald spent much of this time in the company of the Fenland hermit and saint, Guthlac. Aethelbald's succession would have been welcomed in East Anglia, for, as Kirby remarks, it broke the monopoly held by Penda's direct descendants on royal Mercian power which had lasted for over 70 years. Penda had been no friend of the East Angles—he had killed several of their kings, including Anna and the saintly King Sigeberht. It is clear that a good relationship existed between Aelfwald, the king of the East Anglians (713-49), and Aethelbald as it 'would be difficult to explain the dedication of the *Life* of a Mercian saint', Guthlac, to an East Anglian king in any other way. Indeed Kirby postulates that an alliance between Aethelbald and East Anglia may have been 'the cornerstone of Aethelbald's ascendancy'.[67]

Mercia's position with East Anglia at the end of Aethelbald's reign is unclear but we know nothing to its detriment. Aelfwald ruled East Anglia until his death in 749. One of his successors, Beonna, was minting his own coins in the late 750s or early 760s which implies that he had broken free from Mercian domination for a while, but it may equally well be associated with the disintegration of Mercian overlordship following Aethelbald's murder in 757.[68]

Aethelbald's character and his rule

Middle Anglia, Lindsey, the *Hwicce*, the *Wreocensaete* and the *Magonsaete* were all under Mercian authority by Aethelbald's reign and were ruled either by sub-kings, or directly with the assistance of ealdormen. With the establishment of the new episcopal sees in the territories of the *Hwicce*, the *Magonsaete*, Middle Anglia and Lindsey prior to Aethelbald's reign, Mercian influence increased.

Charter evidence shows Aethelbald to have been constantly active. The usual purpose of the charters was to give grants of land for religious establishments; however one of the earliest, possibly dated to 716/717, is a charter for the exchange of land at the Droitwich salt-works (see p.115). This charter is almost industrial in nature, although the Church was one of the parties involved.

Other charters, evenly spread throughout the period of his reign, deal with grants of land to the Church for its own purposes, or for the building of monasteries. They exist for the modern counties of Gloucestershire, Herefordshire, Worcestershire, Warwickshire, Oxfordshire, Berkshire, Middlesex, Kent and Wiltshire, and cover the Anglo-Saxon kingdoms of the *Magonsaete*, the *Hwicce* and the East and West Saxons.[69]

Views of his personality as a strong ruler vary in different appraisals. He is sometimes portrayed as a rather unpleasant individual (see Henry of Huntingdon's remarks on the previous page) and in character Stenton considers him a 'barbarian master of a military household'.[70] There is also a contemporary account of Aethelbald in a letter written to him by Boniface, the Anglo-Saxon missionary, archbishop of Mainz and then a papal legate, in about 746-7 which gives another view. Two versions of the letter exist, a Continental version and a much briefer one given by William of Malmesbury. The longer version was edited and amended by Egbert, archbishop of York, before being delivered to Aethelbald, and William of Malmesbury's version could either be a copy of this, or his own arrangement of the longer text.[71]

The purpose of the letter was to upbraid Aethelbald for his transgressions. The Malmesbury version states: 'Moreover, we have heard that almost all the nobles of the Mercian kingdom, following your example, desert their lawful wives and live in guilty intercourse with adultresses and nuns'. Such information would surely have triggered an ecclesiastical reaction! However, we learn much more about Aethelbald from the beginning of both texts. In some ways his character shines: he is acknowledged for his generosity in giving alms and in his strong prohibition of theft 'and iniquities, perjury and rapine'. He is also recognized as a defender of widows and the poor and a maintainer of 'firm peace' in his kingdom. Then follow the criticisms: '... you have, as many say, neither taken a lawful wife nor maintained chaste absti-

Fig.6 Two types of 'bird and branch' sceattas depicting Aethelbald holding two crosses, produced c.730-5, three times actual size. On the left is depicted a western style, on the right an eastern, probably London style. A sceatta was a small silver coin minted between c.690 to c.790 in southern England. They were made from pellets of metal hammered between two dies, unlike later coinage which was made from flattened metal

nence for God's sake, but governed by lust, have stained the fame of your glory before God and men by the sin of lasciviousness and adultery ... And yet, what is worse, those who tell us this, add that this shameful crime is especially committed in the monasteries with holy nuns and virgins consecrated to God. For there is no doubt that this is doubly a sin'. Boniface goes on to point out that Aethelbald has been appointed as king and ruler over many, not through his own merit, but by 'the abundant goodness of God' and seems to be concerned that the English might get the reputation of 'spurning lawful marriage' and living 'foul' lives 'in adultery and lasciviousness after the pattern of the people of Sodom, it is to be expected that from such intercourse with harlots there will be born a degenerate people, ignoble, raging with lust; and in the end the whole people, sinking to lower and baser things, will finally neither be strong in secular warfare nor stable in faith ...'[72] There's more:

> Moreover, it has been told us that you have violated many privileges of churches and monasteries, and have stolen from them certain revenues. And this, if it is true, is regarded as a heavy sin ... Therefore he who steals or plunders the possessions of Christ and the Church, will be adjudged to be a homicide in the sight of the just Judge ... And it is said that your ealdormen and companions offer greater violence and oppression to monks and priests, than other Christian kings have done before. Now, ever since the apostolic pope, St. Gregory, sending preachers of the catholic faith from the apostolic see, converted the race of the English to the true God, the privileges of the churches in the kingdom of the English remained untouched and unviolated until the times of Ceolred, king of the Mercians, and Osred, king of the Deirans and Bernicians.[73]

Clearly the Church wanted its wealth and objected to anyone pilfering its coffers. After more religious lecturing Boniface finishes the letter with an entreaty to Aethelbald to amend his ways. That an ecclesiastic, even of Boniface's stature, felt able to write in such a way to an Anglo-Saxon king, is testimony to the immense power and social control the Church had at the time.

It is difficult to say whether Aethelbald did moderate his personal behaviour, but he was present at a synod at *Clofesho* in 747 which was attended by bishops from the areas under his control. The synod, among other matters, dealt with the problems of the lay control of monasteries, the excesses of dress of many of the churchmen and 'the immorality and drunkenness of Anglo-Saxon clergy'. At the Council of Gumley in Leicestershire, held two years later, Aethelbald, probably in response to Boniface's criticisms, issued decrees that all churches in Mercia should be free from the impositions of royal food rents and all works and burdens except work on building bridges and the defence of fortresses in times of need. As Kirby observes, that Aethelbald was involved with these councils might suggest that he was not quite so beyond 'contemporary convention' as Boniface's letter implies,[74] or, indeed, that he was a much reformed man.

The Legacy of Aethelbald

That Aethelbald was a stronger ruler than his immediate predecessors is beyond doubt. That he was the dominant king in southern England for nearly 30 years and kept a wider and longer ascendancy than any king before him is also certain. Through the work of Aethelred and to some extent Coenred, he had inherited a stable and well-established kingdom. That Aethelbald left a larger kingdom than Aethelred (or his successor Offa) and was able to rule with little more, or possibly even less, fighting than either Aethelred or Offa were obliged to use to govern a lesser area says much about his effectiveness as a monarch; witness his rule of Kent.

Aethelbald may have been the first Mercian king to mint coins, possibly at London after he took control of the city in 731/2 and at a mint in the Oxford region or elsewhere in southern Mercia where the *sceattas* depicted in Fig.6 were produced. However, it appears that Offa was the first to mint a Mercian coinage to include the king's name and royal title. The acquisition of mints and the production of coins depicting the king led to 'new opportunities for the aggrandizement of royalty'. In a charter dated to the 740s Aethelbald identifies himself as of the '*gens Anglorum*', and it was from this time that his subjects began to call themselves *Aenglisc*—'English'—testimony perhaps to Aethelbald's widespread authority in 'that the English became English and not Saxons'.[75]

In the middle of Aethelbald's reign coinage was circulating more widely in to the midlands than it did at the end of Offa's reign in the late 8th century. But Aethelbald's issue was affected by a silver shortage at the end of the 730s, and the coinage was accordingly rapidly debased in the 740s. There is even reason to think that, in the light of 'a multiplicity of distinctive *sceatta* coinages in eastern and southern England', that Aethelbald did not impose his authority over the minting of coins by others[76] which may bring into question the degree of his overlordship in these areas.

Overall Aethelbald gives the appearance of being a very effective king, well in control, whose power only declined towards the very end of his 41 year reign. He was murdered at night by his own bodyguard at Seckington, a village 4 miles north-east of Tamworth, in 757. The reason is unknown, but, as a contemporary writer had described him as a 'royal tyrant', and a Mercian abbess received lands from Aethelbald 'because he had stabbed - or smitten - her kinsman' (which, as Stenton points out, are hardly the words that would be used to describe an ordinary killing in war), it is quite possible this was a revenge killing. Henry of Huntingdon, however, has another, not widely accepted version, for he records that four years after the battle at Burford with Cuthred '... in another battle at *Secandune*, in which the carnage was wonderful, disdaining to flee, he [Aethelbald] was slain on the field ...'.[77]

It is possible that his murder was part of a dynastic coup, for his immediate successor was one Beornred, who belonged to a rival dynasty. The details of the murder are, indeed, similar to the coups that were occurring in Northumbria at this time.[78] That his own bodyguard murdered Aethelbald was an act of extreme treachery, for they were supposed to protect him with their lives if called upon, and it suggests that his popularity in Mercia had diminished, or even vanished. Aethelbald was buried in the crypt at Repton's monastic church, a somehow fitting resting place, for it was at this monastery that Guthlac had begun his religious life, and it was Guthlac who had given Aethelbald support when he had most needed it as a young, dispossessed exile.

Offa

'He was a man of great mind, and one who endeavoured to bring to effect whatever he had preconceived. ... At one time, in the same character, vices were so palliated by virtues, and at another virtues came in such quick succession upon vices that it is difficult to determine how to characterize the changing Proteus'. William of Malmesbury[79]

'... a youth of the noblest extraction. ... Offa proved a most warlike king, for he was victorious in successive battles over the men of Kent, and the men of Wessex, and the Northumbrians. He was also a very religious man ...'. Henry of Huntingdon[80]

It is claimed in the Anglian genealogies contained in Nennius' work that Offa was the son of Duminfert (Thingfrith), who was the son of Eandulf (Eanwulf), son of Ossulf, son of Eua (Eowa) son of Pubba [Penda?]. This would make Eanwulf the cousin of Aethelbald and means that Offa and Aethelbald were cousins twice removed. If so, the two kings may be regarded as coming from the same broad family group and there is evidence of mutual co-operation between them. A familial link between these two kings may also be suggested by the large grants of land Aethelbald made to Eanwulf, Offa's grandfather, some of which Eanwulf used to found the proprietary monastery at Bredon, south of Worcester, and of which Offa was subsequently a patron.[81] Further grants included land at Westbury-on-Trym and Henbury, each now part of northern Bristol, and places them in the kingdom of the *Hwicce*, implying a *Hwiccian* connection

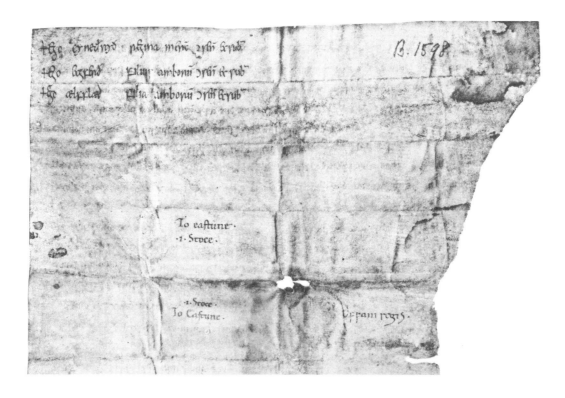

In the name of our Lord Jesus Christ.

It is most certainly evident and thus free from doubt that all things which are seen are temporal, and the things which are not seen are eternal.

Therefore I, Uhtred, by the gift of God sub-king of the Hwicce, have meditated that, out of the portion of the earthly kingdom which I have received from the Giver of all good things, I should expend something, however unworthy, for the profit of ecclesiastical liberty, for the relief of my soul. Hence [I will grant] most willingly for the sake of the Lord Almighty to my faithful thegn, namely Aethelmund, son of Ingild, who was ealdorman and 'prefect' of Aethelbald, king of the Mercians, with the advice and permission of Offa, king of the Mercians, and also of his bishops and leading men, land of five hides, *i.e.* the village which is called [Aston], by the river which is called Salwarp, on its eastern side, to possess by ecclesiastical right; that as long as he lives he may possess it, and leave it to two heirs after him, whomsoever he shall wish. And when these have departed from the world, the land with the deeds is to be given back to the church of Worcester, for their table, without any contradiction, as alms for me and for us all, [for the love of the celestial] country and for their intercession to the living and true God. Moreover, as a fitting price has been received from the aforesaid Aethelmund, [let everyone know] that this land is free from every tribute, small or great, of public matters, and from all services whether of king or ealdorman, except the building of bridges, or the necessary defences of fortresses against enemies. Also in every way [we forbid] in the name of God Almighty, [that, if] anyone in this aforenamed land steals anything outside it, anything [be paid] to anyone except specifically 'price for price' [as a settlement, nothing outside as a fine].

May the Almighty God not cease to increase the benefits in eternity of him who increases this my injunction; may he who diminishes it—which [we hope no one will—let him know that he] must render account [before] the judgment-seat of Christ, unless he has previously made sufficient amends to God and men.

[This donation] was drawn up [in the year] of the incarnation of our Lord Jesus Christ 770, the ninth indiction, the eleventh decenoval, the eighth of the lunar cycle.

> [I, Offa by the gift of God king] of the Mercians, have consented to this, my sub-king's, donation and have placed on it the sign of the Holy Cross.
>
> [I, Mildred, the grace of Christ] conceding, humble bishop of the Hwicce, have consented and subscribed.
>
> [I, Uhtred], by the grant of the dispensation of [the merciful God], sub-king of my own people, corroborating this my donation of privilege conceded for the sake of the Lord, have written the sign of salvation.
>
> [I, Ealdred, sub-king] of the Hwicce, subscribe consenting to this donation conceded by my brother.
>
> [I, Eata, have consented and] subscribed.
>
> [I, Brorda have consented and subscribed.
>
> I, Eadbald, have consented and subscribed.
>
> I, Cynethryth, queen of the Mercians, have consented and subscribed
>
> I, Ecgfrith, son of them both, have consented and subscribed.
>
> I, Aelfflaed, daughter of them both, have consented and subscribed.

Fig.7 Left: A charter recording a grant of land at Aston Fields in Stoke Prior (now part of Bromsgrove) in north-west Worcestershire, dated 770, given by the Hwiccian *sub-king, Uhtred, to one Aethelmund. The latter may have been the ealdorman killed at the battle of Kempsford fought with Wessex in 802. The charter is in Latin and might be a 9th-century copy of the 8th-century original. The order of signatures and their wording makes it clear that Uhtred of the* Hwicce *is subordinate to Offa of Mercia. Although this copy is incomplete, a translation (above) is possible due to a version of another, lost, charter making the same grant in 767, though the latter's wording is slightly briefer it is 'couched in identical terms'. This charter would appear to be the earliest 'undoubtedly genuine' document to mention the public duties of building bridges and erecting fortresses when required. The list of signatories is not reproduced in the original on the left, but is included above. The translation is found in Whitelock no.74, pp.462-64*

for Offa. Indeed, Sims-Williams records that there seems to have been a tradition at Worcester Cathedral, reflected in a forgery contained in an 11th-century cartulary, that Offa lived in the *Hwiccian* kingdom

145

before he became king of Mercia in 757. There is even a theory that this was Offa's power base and, by Bassett, a suggestion that Eanwulf was a member of the *Hwiccian* royal family, presumably on his mother's side, or that Eanwulf had married into the royal dynasty, although there is no direct evidence for this.[82] Intriguingly, in a charter of about 757 between the *Hwiccian* rulers, the brothers Eanberht, Uhtred and Ealdred, land is granted at Tredington, Warwickshire, to the bishop of Worcester, Milred, and Offa attests the charter immediately after the three brothers and the bishop and he is qualified by the phrase *indolis puer*, thought to be the equivalent of aetheling,[83] so presumably pre-dating his rise to the Mercian kingship which occurred in the same year.

The co-operation between Aethelbald's and Offa's lines is further evidenced by the fact that the former's brother, Headbert, an important noble in Aethelbald's reign, retained a leading role in the early years of Offa's rule. Additionally, in a record of an agreement made in 781 at a synod at Brentford, Offa tried to reclaim lands in the *Hwiccian* kingdom from the church of Worcester which he stated were 'the inheritance of his kinsman, to wit King Aethelbald'. Kirby observes that, like Aethelbald, none of Offa's immediate predecessors had been kings of Mercia and he is described as another example of 'an aetheling competing successfully for the kingship from outside the innermost core of royal power'.[84]

Offa did not succeed immediately to the crown following Aethelbald's murder for, as mentioned, this had been taken by Beornred. Beornred's genealogy is obscure but Yorke suggests he may have been connected with the Mercian kings with names which alliterate with 'B' who came to power in the 9th century. Florence of Worcester records that Aethelbald's kingdom was 'usurped by the tyrant Beornred, who held it for a short time with little joy or comfort, and then lost his crown and his life together'. The 'Continuation' of Bede states that 'Offa put Beornred to flight and strove for the kingdom of the Mercians with a bloody sword' (in which Scharer suggests he received *Hwiccian* help), while the *Anglo-Saxon Chronicle* simply notes that Beornred had 'succeeded to the kingdom and held it for but a little space and unhappily'.[85]

Matthew of Westminster provides rather more detail:

> A tribe of the kingdom of Mercia rose in insurrection against their king, Beornred, because he was ruling the people, not according to just laws, but tyrannically. And accordingly, all men, both noble and ignoble, met together, and, under the leadership of Offa, a most gallant youth, expelled him from the kingdom. And when this had been done, by the unanimous consent of all men, both clergy and people, crowned the aforesaid Offa as king. For Offa was descended from the royal family...[86]

Matthew also records under the year 769: 'The city Cataracta [?] was burnt with fire, by Beornred, the tyrannical king of Mercia, who had been deposed. But Boernred himself perished miserably by fire, the same year.'[87] From this it seems that Beornred was at large for at least 11 years after his deposition and was causing havoc until his death.

Fig.8 Obverse of a penny of Offa with a bust of the king

Aethelbald apparently made no preparation for the handover of power to a successor. Even without the civil war that followed his death, Offa would still have come to the crown raw, unprepared and inexperienced. This contrasts with the planned and organized way in which Aethelred had been able to hand over a politically stable regime to his nephew Coenred.

Offa started his reign with the disadvantage of the recent instability, and Mercia suffered as a result. Stenton postulates that the confederacy which Aethelbald had built disintegrated after his death and for the first seven years of his reign Offa appears to have possessed 'little, if any, power outside Mercia and its dependencies in the southern midlands'. Indeed, the archbishop of Canterbury wrote to his Continental colleague, Lull, explaining that he had been unable to send a letter during this period because of the disturbances in Britain and Gaul. Yet, Offa's re-establishment of Mercian power is, as Stenton notes, 'the central fact in English history in the second half of the eighth century'.[88]

Because of the lack of a Mercian 'history', Offa's reign has often to be followed through the records and charters of the adjoining kingdoms. The main evidence for Offa's influence in Kent comes from charters. King Wihtred's sons, Aethelberht and Eadberht, were still reigning in Kent and had been since 725. Eadberht's son, Eardwulf, had since joined them, but they are last mentioned in 762 and there is no evidence that they survived this date. Thus this Kentish dynasty, which was supposedly founded by Oisc, son of Hengist, ended. In 762 Sigered, whose name suggests he may be of East Saxon origin, calls himself 'Rex Cantie' — 'King of Kent' — and is seen granting land at Rochester to its bishop with King Eadberht's consent.[89] He appears again in a grant of land at Islingham in Kent dated between 761-765 where this time he is called 'king of half Kent', presumably of West Kent, but this time with confirmation by a King Eanmund, who was probably a co-ruler, possibly of East Kent.[90] In 764 Offa appears in person at Canterbury with members of the Mercian nobility, in the company of a third king, Heahberht, who had witnessed Sigered's 762 charter, and Offa regranted this Islingham estate in his own name.[91] This is the first time a Mercian king is known to have granted land in Kent in his own name and suggests that Heahberht may have been established and supported in his rule by Offa.[92] By 765 another Kentish king is named, Ecgberht, 'king of Kent' in a grant of land at Rochester to the bishop, which was confirmed by Heahberht 'king of Kent' and Offa 'king of Mercia'.[93]

Two further charters provide evidence of Offa's power. In 774 he granted land in his own right to the archbishop of Canterbury, Jaenberht, at Higham Upshire and again at Lydd in Kent.[94] But the charters have some 9th and 10th century anachronisms in the language and terms used.[95] For example, Offa terms himself 'rex Anglorum' — 'king of the English', which was the normal regnal style by the mid-10th century to which it is thought the script of the first charter belongs, but that it was copied from an earlier charter.[96]

Change was in the air, however, for in 776 the Mercians and the Kentish men fought at Otford, 3 miles north of Sevenoaks in Kent. The *Anglo-Saxon Chronicle* records a rather peculiar medley of facts: 'In this year a red cross appeared in the sky after sunset. And that year the Mercians and the people of Kent fought at Otford. And marvellous adders were seen in Sussex'. Henry of Huntingdon reports that the battle occurred in 773 and that 'after a dreadful slaughter on both sides, Offa gained the honour of victory'. Neither Florence of Worcester nor William of Malmesbury comment on the outcome.[97] According to Stenton, the Mercians were probably defeated for Offa's domination in Kent appears to have been broken until he was able to re-establish it in 785 when he is, again, recorded as granting land in this kingdom in his own name. If it is uncertain whether Offa was able to reassert his authority in Kent after 776, there is some evidence that he had lost political control as early as 765: in, or just after that year, Heahberht witnessed a charter in which one of the Kentish kings, Ecgberht, granted land to the bishop of Rochester 'without any reference to Offa'.[98] In fact Kirby suggests that Offa may have only exerted real control over Kent in the early years of his reign between 764-5. As there were four kings apparently ruling Kent at this time Offa would almost certainly have tried to take advantage of potential rivalries. What prompted the battle of Otford is not known, but Heahberht died in about 771 and Ecgberht became the sole king. Offa initially acknowledged him as such, but gradually started to act, according to Ashley, as if he were the only ruler. This would have bred resentment amongst the Kentish people and Ecgberht, and possibly led to the battle. Otford does seem to have allowed the people of Kent to regain their independence until Ecgberht's death in 784/5. Offa clearly resented the reactions of Kent, and Stenton suggests that the antipathy born in these years was one of the primary motives for his subsequent move to create a separate archbishopric for Mercia.[99]

On Ecgberht's death, Ealhmund emerged briefly as king before Offa staged a complete take over. Offa's behaviour can be ascertained from charter evidence. He cancelled donations of land by Ecgberht and his reeve, Ealdhun, to Canterbury and Rochester. In 811 the archbishop of Canterbury declared that Offa had negated one of Ecgberht's charters because the latter had 'no right to grant land by charter in perpetuity', indicating Offa's intention to annexe the Kentish kingdom and suppress the native royal line.[100] In both these objectives he apparently succeeded.

Charter evidence suggests that from this resumption of control until his death in 796, Offa's control of Kent remained uninterrupted. In 785 there is a grant to Ealdbeorht, *minister,* and the latter's sister Selethryth, of land at Ickham and Palmstead in Kent, woodland in the Weald and elsewhere, and grazing and fishing rights in different locations in Kent.[101] In 786 there is another grant of land to these same individuals in four locations in Kent, with swine pasture, fishing and wood-gathering rights elsewhere.[102] In 788 he granted land in the Eastry district of Kent to Osberht, his *minister.*[103] It is possible that these *ministers* were assisting Offa in controlling the area, and the grants were their reward.

Offa also stamped his authority on the Church. Between 765 and 792 he granted land at Beauxfield in Kent to the abbot of the church of Saints Peter and Paul,[104] and in 787 he confirmed privileges to the abbot and community of St. Peter's church at Chertsey.[105] There are grants of land in Kent to the bishopric and church at Rochester—one in 788 and two in 789.[106] Land in Hayes, Twickenham and *Geddingas* in Middlesex was also granted to the archbishop of Canterbury in *c*.790.[107] Much the same land that was granted to Ealdbeorht (*minister*) and his sister in 785,[108] was granted by Offa to Christ Church, Canterbury in 791.[109] In 792 Offa gave a confirmation and grant of privileges to the churches of Kent.[110]

Offa's position with Wessex was quite different to that with Kent. It has been mentioned how his predecessor Aethelbald had ruled over much of Wessex for the greater part of his reign, and that after Cuthred's death, he had backed Cynewulf against Sigeberht in his struggle for the throne to such an extent that, after Cynewulf gained the throne, he was obliged to appear in Aethelbald's court in 757 to witness a grant of land to Eanberht, a West Saxon abbot.[111]

Cynewulf had become such a strong monarch that he not only ruled Wessex effectively, but also, for a while at least, gained territory from the Mercians north of the Thames, territory which had been under the latter's control for many years. However, in 779 at a battle at Bensington or Benson, 2 miles north of Wallingford, in Oxfordshire; the *Anglo-Saxon Chronicle* records that Cynewulf and Offa 'fought ... and Offa captured the town.'[112]

Yet Offa's authority in parts of Wessex is evidenced in the charters, possibly even before his victory at Bensington. Finberg mentions a lost charter of the grant of the important manor of Potterne in Wiltshire (2 miles south of Devizes) to the church of Sherborne; another charter concerns land at Pyrton, about 5 miles north-east of Benson, and could be regarded as part of the southern Outer Mercian kingdom. Here land was granted by Offa to the church of St. Peter's, Worcester but, alas, the charter is considered a 10th-century forgery.[113] Doubt has also been cast on a charter of 775-777 where Offa granted land at Eisey in Latton in Wiltshire, as well as Doughton in Tetbury in Gloucestershire to St. Mary's minster at Worcester—in a charter of Offa's reign the grant would have had to have been to St. Peter's as the dedication to St. Mary's belongs to the 10th century. Nevertheless, Finberg considers the charter may refer to a genuine transaction.[114] Another charter of 794 in a lost/incomplete text finds Offa granting 10 hides of land near to Huntspill (ST 2945), Somerset, to the church of Glastonbury. It is suggested that Offa granted this estate to an individual who then passed it on to Glastonbury.[115] The land is presumably in the flat coastal area 10 miles south of Weston-super-Mare, on the extreme western borders of Wessex. Finberg refers to another, lost, charter where Offa granted 1 hide to his thegn Aethelmund at Huntspill who then passed it on to the abbot of Glastonbury. He also notes a grant of land in Downton (6 miles south of Salisbury) of a West Saxon king 'Cynevalc' to the church of SS Peter and Paul in Winchester in which all the witnesses, with the exception of the archbishop of Canterbury, are Mercian. This has led Finberg to suggest this is a doctored text in which lies an authentic Mercian grant dating to the last three years of Offa's reign. Like Potterne, Downton was another extensive Wiltshire manor.[116]

In another charter of 796 and belonging to the reign of Ecgfrith (Offa's son), it is said that Ecgfrith restored land at Purton (5 miles north-west of Swindon in Wiltshire) to the abbot and his bretheren at Malmesbury 'which his father Offa took away from them'. While Finberg considers this an authentic charter, others have raised doubts.[117] However, in a charter possibly dating to 758, Cynewulf grants land to the 'brethren of St. Peter's, Bath in North Stoke', (presumably the North Stoke 4 miles north-west of Bath), which is confirmed by Offa and implies he was in control of this area and the West Saxon king.[118]

By contrast there are about 16 charters of Cynewulf concerning land in Wessex, and in those that survive between 758 and 778 no reference is made to Offa or an overlord, and similarly with several charters of his successor, suggesting that until Bensington Offa had no authority in this area.[119] With the exception of one appearance at Offa's court there is no evidence in Stenton's words that Cynewulf 'ever became Offa's man', and he appears to have recovered most of the West Saxon provinces that Aethelbald had taken,[120] even holding land in Berkshire and Oxfordshire.

Indeed, so strong was Cynewulf's reign and so forceful the loyalty of his subjects that an outstanding series of events unfolded at his death in 784. Whilst making arrangements to expel Cyneheard, the brother of his old rival Sigeberht, who was laying claim to the crown, Cynewulf visited his mistress' house at Merton (presumably that 3 miles south of Bicester). Staying there overnight, he was discovered by Cyneheard, who, with his men, burst into the house and murdered Cynewulf. The crux of this story is that both Cynewulf's bodyguard, and his main force under his thegn and ealdorman, were separately offered bribes and riches if they allowed Cyneheard to secure the crown. Such was Cynewulf's popularity, and so enraged were Cynewulf's men by his murder, that the bodyguard refused and were killed in the ensuing fight, before the main force killed Cyneheard and his followers. As Whitelock points out, the loyalty of Cynewulf's followers must have seemed all the more impressive when set against the murders of Aethelbald of Mercia and Oswulf of Northumbria by their own households in 757 and 759 respectively.[121] With such loyalty it is perhaps not surprising that Offa was unable to take control of Wessex.

After the death of Cynewulf, the West Saxon crown passed to Beorhtric. The view of succeeding events is contradictory. It is generally portrayed that Beorhtric was Offa's protégé and was strongly supported by the Mercian king, and although Beorhtric was styled king of Wessex, he was not able to act independently. It has been suggested by Stenton and others that Offa sided with Beorhtric and helped him drive a young aetheling, Ecgberht, a possible claimant to the crown and grand-nephew to King Ine, from the country; Ecgberht was the son of the deposed king of Kent, Ealhmund, and Offa was determined he should not return.[122]

However, William of Malmesbury presents a quite different account of Offa's involvement in Wessex after Cynewulf's demise. After describing Ecgberht's noble ancestry, his good education, and that he 'had been conspicuous among the West Saxons from his childhood', William states that his 'uninterrupted course of valour begat envy' and that Beorhtric, 'jealous of his rising character, was meditating how to destroy him. Egbert, apprised of this, escaped to Offa, king of the Mercians. While Offa concealed him with anxious care, the messengers of Bertric [Beorhtric] arrived, demanding the fugitive for punishment, and offering money for his surrender. In addition to this they solicited his [Offa's] daughter in marriage for their king, in order that the nuptial tie might bind them in perpetual amity. In consequence Offa, who would not give way to hostile threats, yielded to flattering allurements, and Egbert, passing the sea, went into France'. As William of Malmesbury was based in territory that once belonged to Wessex, he may have wished to portray Beorhtric as a powerful king, a monarch who would not be cowed by another. Yet, Beorhtric is not portrayed in a favourable light: he is jealous and stoops to bribery. If William wanted

Offa of Mercia and Aethelberht of East Anglia

Fig.9 (Above). Marden church is built over the spring that, tradition relates, burst forth at the spot where Aethelberht's body was flung into the marshes by the Lugg

Fig.10 (Top left) The site of St. Aethelberht's Well in Hereford, which appeared where the cortège carrying his body into the city rested

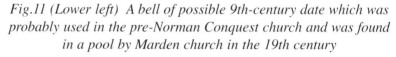

Fig.11 (Lower left) A bell of possible 9th-century date which was probably used in the pre-Norman Conquest church and was found in a pool by Marden church in the 19th century

Offa's Palace near Hereford?

The accounts of Aethelberht's murder infer that Offa had a palace at Sutton at a time when Hereford was just emerging as a town. One putative site near Freen's Court, below Sutton Walls, has recently been ruled out as a result of archaeological investigation. To the north-east of this site, at Downfield Knoll, a flat-bottomed, vertical-sided ditch was partly revealed which had an unusual double lobed end which may have held posts side by side. This would have formed a palisade that may have continued towards the river.[123] To the east, at St. Michael's church, a rectangular ditched enclosure was found, in 2000, to be an embanked area through which a massive ditch was later cut, probably in the 16th century. The embanked area was originally enclosed by another palisade like that at Downfield Knoll. The presence of 11th-century pottery in the area of both palisades suggests that they may be of Anglo-Saxon date. A vertical wheel watermill has also been found just north of Marden church, at Wellington Quarry. Dedrochronology indicates that this mill was constructed in the early years of the 8th century. The massive palisades and the mill indicate the likely presence of a royal centre in the near vicinity, possibly at Marden itself.

to embellish Ecgberht's reputation, it is odd that he should depict this future great West Saxon monarch as having to run to a king of a rival kingdom. Just maybe then there is a strong element of accuracy in this account as it cannot be adduced as mere West Saxon propaganda. It is significant that Offa is portrayed as a man who can be won over by flattery and inducements, particularly as it is set against the recent example of Cynewulf's men who would not be bought at any price to betray their king, even in death, and one is reminded too of the early 7th-century East Anglian king, Raedwald, who refused to give up the Northumbrian exile Edwin to Aethefrith, the king of Northumbria, in similar circumstances. As no-one comes out of William's account favourably, one may ask why was it written, unless it was, indeed, recounting the truth.

Even if Offa was the master of Beorhtric, it is likely that Offa did not have the degree of power as that held by Aethelbald in Wessex.

Offa's firm control of the central areas of Mercia and the lands of the *Magonsaete*, *Hwicce* and Middle Anglia has never been in any doubt. Likewise he had control over the Middle and East Saxons. Offa treated London as his own town, as had Aethelbald[124] and it emerged as an important minting centre, if not the main one, during his reign. Silver pennies were being produced here from the 760s in response to Frankish currency reforms for trading abroad, and there is no indication of any friction between the East Saxons and Mercia; the important trading links were clearly mutually beneficial for both kingdoms.

In some of his earlier extant charters Offa granted land in the Middle and East Saxon kingdoms. In either 764 or 767 he granted land between Harrow and Wealdstone Brook, and elsewhere in Middlesex, to an abbot, in exchange for land which may have been in the Chilterns at High Wycombe in Buckinghamshire.[125] Land at Harmondsworth in Middlesex was granted by Offa in 781 to his *minister* Aeldred,[126] and a charter of *c*.790 apparently finds Offa making further grants of land at Hayes, *Geddingas* and Twickenham in Middlesex to the archbishop of Canterbury.[127] To the south-west of London he grants land at Woking in Surrey to its church.[128] Although Offa was treating these provinces as his own, the East Saxon dynasty survived into the 9th century.[129] As there is no evidence of conflict, and no evidence, indeed, to suggest that Offa did not retain full control in Essex as his predecessors had done, this indicates the native East Saxon dynasty accepted his overlordship.

Mercia's relationship with Sussex was not as stable in Offa's reign as it had been in that of Aethelbald's. The South Saxon lands had never been governed as one unit, but had been split into smaller territories. For example the area around Hastings was regarded as distinct from the rest of Sussex even in the early 11th century.[130] Kirby observes that a man called Osmund appears to have been king of the South Saxons until about 770, but he ruled in association with three other kings. In an admittedly doubtful charter of 770 Offa is said to have consented to Osmund's grant of land at Henfield, about 10 miles north-west of Brighton in West Sussex, to Henfield's St. Peter's church.[131] If this was a reliable charter it would indicate that West Sussex and its king were under Offa's authority and further charter evidence suggests that Offa did have some authority in this disparate kingdom. Again in a somewhat doubtful charter given between 733-754, Offa, presumably at a later date, confirmed a grant of land given by Aethelberht 'king of Sussex', at Wittering in West Sussex.[132] In a similarly suspicious charter of 772 Offa 'king of the English' grants a lease for life of land at Bexhill, East Sussex, to bishop Oswald with reversion to the bishopric of Selsey (West Sussex).[133] A grant of land in London to the Abbey of St. Denis in 790 refers to Offa's confirmation of land in East Sussex at Rotherfield, Hastings and Pevensey to the abbey but here again there is some thought that this charter may be spurious, even a French forgery.[134] Although some of these charters are of questionable authenticity, Kirby suggests that they 'hint at a sequence of events similar to those in Kent', with Offa using a multiple native kingship to play one off against the other in an attempt to increase his own power. In a much more reliable charter of *c*.791 Offa consents to a grant of an unidentified woodland by Aldwulf '*dux* of the South Saxons' to 'Wihthun, bishop, for St. Andrew's church' at Ferring in West Sussex.[135] Offa also consents to another grant presumably by the same *dux*, Aldwulf, for land at two unidentified locations to the church of St. Peter at Selsey;[136] and confirms a grant of land at Earnley in West Sussex and an unidentified place by one Oslac '*dux* of the South Saxons' to the church of St. Paul.[137] These last three Sussex grantors are not called rulers but *dux*, a lesser title comparable with a military leader or duke. Stenton records that while Offa seems to have had some authority in western and central Sussex, it appears that he did not have any power east of Pevensey until after 771 when he fought and subdued the men of Hastings.[138]

Simeon of Durham records this battle under 771, together with another event which was to have a far-reaching affect on Offa: 'In these days Offa, king of the Mercians, subdued the people of Hastings [i.e. the district of East Sussex] by force of arms. Also in the same year Carloman, the most famous king of the Franks, died, cut off by a sudden illness. Moreover, his brother Charles, who had previously held half the dominion of his father, hereupon obtained the sovereignty of the whole kingdom and the supreme dignity of the Frankish peoples with unconquered strength'.[139] Charles is the man better known as Charlemagne and he was to have a great influence on Offa.

It has been suggested by Kirby that Offa intervened in East Sussex in 771 perhaps as a response to the political instability among the South Saxons, as he had done in Kent between 764-5 in similar circumstances. Any kingdom that had up to four kings ruling at one time was presumably ripe for intrigue. In the Bexhill lease of 772 Offa leased the land at a court attended by King Ecgberht of Kent, King Cynewulf of Wessex and, significantly, four South Saxon magnates entitled *dux*, one of whom, Osmund, at least had been called 'king' in 770. Similarly Aldwulf (or Ealdwulf) was once titled 'king' in a charter of *c*.765 whereas, in the two above-named charters, he is referred to simply as *dux*. Power in Sussex had shifted to Offa and Stenton observes that from 771 until his death Offa was overlord of the whole area between Hampshire and Kent. However, an alternative theory put forward by Kirby postulates that Offa's involvement may have been short-lived and limited. Indeed, Stenton described the lease of 772 as a 'patent forgery' in an article in 1918 before taking a less severe view in later years. If it is false, there is actually no evidence for Offa being a 'dominant factor in South Saxon affairs until the late 780s'. Before the late 780s, Sussex may have been within King Ecgberht of Kent's sphere of influence, and a Kentish hegemony in the south-east possibly spurred Offa's intervention in Kent in 784-5 and thereafter to gain control of it.[140]

East Anglia had been a Mercian ally during Aethelbald's reign and the two kingdoms were closely connected. After the death of the East Anglian king, Aelfwald, the province probably enjoyed a degree of autonomy under Mercian overlordship, a fact demonstrated by one of Aelfwald's successors, Beonna, who ruled from *c*.749 to *c*.761, and set up his own mint. Coins were also minted by a later East Anglian king, Aethelberht, who ruled from 790-4. That good relations continued between these two kingdoms is suggested by the inclusion of the two East Anglian bishoprics of *Dommoc* or *Domnoc* (?Dunwich) and Elmham in the temporary archdiocese of Lichfield created in 787, which put them under the jurisdiction of a Mercian archbishop. Secure in his relationship with East Anglia, Offa was able to concentrate his energies in the south-east of England.[141]

Why then did Offa find it necessary to cold-bloodedly murder the youthful king of East Anglia in 794? Aethelberht had apparently been invited to Offa's palace at Sutton near Hereford to sue for the hand of Offa's daughter in marriage. Several post-Conquest *Lives* exist for Aethelberht, including one by Osbert of Clare who was a Suffolk man and a monk at the Priory of Stoke near Clare and from whose version the following is essentially derived. Osbert had become prior of Westminster in 1138 where the head of Aethelberht ended up after Hereford Cathedral was sacked in 1055. It was here that Osbert wrote a *Life* of Aethelberht which he dedicated to Bishop Foliot of Hereford. However, an early 12th-century manuscript exists in Corpus Christi College, Cambridge which originates from Hereford and seems to form the basis for Osbert's work. M.R. James has argued that this was the work of a native Herefordian as it reveals a local knowledge of Herefordshire, and is presumably, therefore, a more accurate account. This version also lacks the eulogies, the elaborations and interpretations of the visions and the speech from Offa's queen that the later *Lives* of Aethelberht contain. It is possible that both Osbert, and later Giraldus Cambrensis, who wrote a very accessible and colourful account of Aethelberht's murder, used this source. Unfortunately, there is no trace of the author's name or its dedication, but Brooks considers it depended on sources and traditions that were older than the early 12th century and which were preserved in Hereford Cathedral's monastic *Scriptorium*.[142]

The main characters in the Aethelberht story are Offa, who is depicted as a suffering from 'vacillation and paranoiac suspicion, feeding on malicious rumour'; his wife 'a strong-willed queen, jealous, protective and over-reactionary'; the mother of Aethelberht; obviously Aethelberht—who is innocent and trusting; and Offa's daughter who is enamoured of the young East Anglian king but is dangerously politically tactless.[143]

The basic story is that the young and virtuous king, Aethelberht, is invited by Offa to his palace to marry his daughter. Aethelberht's mother is reluctant to let her son go as she mistrusts Offa and the Mercians, but Aethelberht is persuaded by one of his foremost advisers, Oswald, who thought it was about time Aethelberht married and produced an heir, and, as Mercia was the most powerful kingdom in the country, this is where he should seek an alliance. After several bad omens, which suggest the reverse, Aethelberht travels to Herefordshire and before reaching Sutton, sends on gifts and greetings to Offa. As he approaches the palace he is seen by Offa's daughter who ineptly comments on how fine the young king looks and how fitted to being a ruler he is. She urges her father to acknowledge his superiority. Not surprisingly, this arouses the suspicion of Offa's queen, Cynethryth, who succeeds in poisoning Offa's mind against the young visitor by making him believe Aethelberht is a dangerous rival. They cordially receive the youth into the palace, where he was then killed by beheading. In most versions Offa is cajoled to kill the youth by his wife, but in a version by Matthew Paris, Cynethryth herself organizes the murder when she fails to persuade Offa against Aethelberht.[144] As Offa was the founder or benefactor of St. Alban's monastery, and Matthew Paris was a monk there, the monastery would, understandably, be reluctant to blacken Offa's name by ascribing the murder directly to him. This is also the account given in Matthew of Westminster, where Offa's wife points out that by killing Aethelberht, Offa will take control of the East Anglian kingdom, not only for himself but his successors 'for ever'. She is rebuffed by Offa but goes on to organize Aethelberht's murder. On finding out, Offa

> mourned, and shut himself up in a chamber, and for three days would not taste food. But, although he was quite innocent of all participation in the king's death, he nevertheless sent a powerful expedition, and annexed the kingdom of the East Angles to his own dominions.[145]

Aethelberht's body was dishonourably thrown into the middle of marshes close to the river Lugg at Marden but a column of light revealed it and a miraculous spring appeared, now enclosed inside Marden church. A vision of Aethelberht appeared to a nobleman on the third night after the burial, and commanded the man to take his body to Hereford, but unfortunately, during the journey, Aethelberht's head fell off the cart. This was found by a blind man, who was miraculously restored to sight. At one point the cortège stopped to rest and another spring appeared where Aethelberht's body had lain. This is now known as St. Ethelbert's well in Hereford.

Aethelberht was buried at Hereford and his name was added to the dedication of the cathedral church which, for a time, became second only to Canterbury as a pilgrimage centre.[146] A rich and important shrine to this young king and martyr was housed in the pre-Conquest cathedral.

The story continued. After taking the opportunity to invade East Anglia, Offa suffered great remorse for the murder, built a number of churches and monasteries in recompense and is said to have travelled to

Rome in expiation where he gave many gifts to the churches there and promised the see of Rome a yearly payment of 365 *mancuses* (1 *mancus* equated to 30 silver pennies) for the poor and for lights in the church of St. Peter's, which may be the precedent, or even the origin of, Peter's Pence.*[147]

But does jealousy alone explain why Offa would commit such an act of unnecessary violence against a young king of a long standing friendly kingdom who wanted to marry his daughter? The answer may well be political. Whether his queen did succeed in poisoning Offa's mind or that of his advisers, or whether Offa himself instigated the killing is in some ways immaterial. There must have been some pressing reason to get rid of the young East Anglian king. As Aethelberht was a respected and clearly able young ruler, it may have been perceived that his existence posed a threat to the ageing Offa and his dynasty. Wood has observed that at first Aethelberht minted coins in East Anglia which bore Offa's name as overlord, but subsequently issued coins solely in his own name, suggesting he asserted the independence of East Anglia and rejected Offa's overlordship.[148] If Aethelberht were to bid for the Mercian crown against Ecgfrith (Offa's son) on the latter's death this would have meant all of Offa's murderous purging to allow his son to remain rival-free would have been for nothing. And yet Offa had allowed his other two daughters to marry the kings of Wessex and Northumbria, who were presumably more powerful than the king of East Anglia. In addition Offa's own son had already been anointed into a formal association with his father in kingship, the first time this is believed to have happened in England, and thus it would seem that the succession issue had already been settled.[149] There seems no real sense to the murder, if sense there can ever be. So was Aethelberht's murder actually committed out of some personal paranoid fear of, and malevolence towards, the young and happy that only absolute power and ageing bitterness can breed? It is said that his daughter turned her back on the secular world and her family and became a nun.

But what of the kingdom of Northumbria? Stenton suggests that Aethelred, king of Northumbria may have joined 'the confederation of which Offa was the head' to strengthen his own position. In 774, Offa styles himself '*rex totius Anglorum patriae*' — 'king of all England'[150] —and it is possible that his use of this title was connected with the deposition of the previous king of Northumbria, Alhred, at Easter 774, which first brought Aethelred to power. Alhred was deposed at a Council called by Archbishop Athelberht of York, for reasons that are not clear, but Aethelred probably neded Offa's support to feel secure on the throne. Aethelred was driven out of Northumbria in a revolt of 779, and with him went Offa's primary source of influence.

Nevertheless, the consolidation of Offa's power in southern England did give him some influence in Northumbria. Aethelred staged a come back in 790 when Osred II was expelled and from then, until his murder in March 796, Aethelred seems to have been in full control of his kingdom. In 792 he married Offa's daughter, Aelfflaed, and this marriage was perhaps an attempt on Aethelred's part to 'secure outside help for his regime'.[151]

Offa's Fame, Reputation and Statesmanship

There are three reasons why the name of Offa has resounded down the centuries to the present day, the first is the building of the dyke which is attributed to him by Asser, the second is his influence with the Church and Papacy, and the third his role as a European statesman. Offa's Dyke is discussed in detail in chapter 8, so it is with the other two aspects that this section deals.

The nature and emphasis of Offa's relationship with the Church changed throughout his reign, in line with other apparent alterations in his character. As a wise king and an able diplomat and statesman, he generally maintained a close connection with the Church, regardless of any personal devotion he may

---

*(St.) Peter's Pence was a tribute exacted in England of one penny for 'every hearth or house' which was paid on Lammas Day, 1 August, annually to the Papal see in Rome. However, it is said that this was instituted in *c*.787, which would pre-date Offa's putative pilgrimage to Rome by about seven years. In a letter of 797/8 from Coenwulf to the pope, the gift appears to have been made by Offa in gratitude for the 'victories granted to his kingdom'.

have had, as this institution continued to be a most powerful political and social tool. Charter records show that he made grants of land and property, as well as confirming and granting privileges to the Church throughout his area of overlordship.[152] However, after the battle of Otford in 776 and his loss of power in Kent, the position with the Church changed. His earlier endorsement of the appointment of Archbishop Jaenberht in 765 led to satisfactory relations with him, as shown by grants of land to the Church in Kent. But during the nine years of Kentish independence, prior to Ecgberht's death and Ealhmund's removal in 786, the relationship between Offa and Jaenberht deteriorated to the point of hatred for the archbishop on Offa's part. This is confirmed by Offa's successor, Coenwulf's letter to Pope Leo in 798: '... King Offa tried to remove and to disperse [the archbishopric] into two provinces, on account of the enmity he had formed against the venerable Jaenberht and the people of Kent ...'.[153]

At the same time rumours spread in Europe that Offa had suggested that Charlemagne depose Pope Hadrian I and substitute a Frankish pope, which caused understandable anxieties in Rome. Offa sent envoys to Charlemagne, then on to the pope to explain that this had not been his intention at all, but a slur campaign started by enemies of both Offa and Charlemagne in order to blacken their characters. It is suggested by Brooks that such a campaign may have been orchestrated by Jaenberht and his Kentish kinsmen in order to sow discord between Offa, Charlemagne and the pope in order to protect Jaenberht and his see from Offa's attacks. As an alternative theory, Brooks postulates that 'there may have been those in the Mercian and Frankish courts who wished to threaten a pope who seemed to be protecting the awkwardly independent archbishop'.[154]

The pope's probable fear of the alienation and loss of control of England, coupled with a grumbling mistrust of Offa, resulted in the despatch of papal legates to England in 786, the first since St. Augustine's time. Ostensibly this trip was concerned with putting forward 20 or more ecclesiastical canons, half of which related to devotional and ecclesiastical matters within the structure of the Church, the other half bearing upon secular matters and the behaviour of lay persons, particularly those of prominence. The covert reason for the visit may well have been for the legates to gauge the political position in England with relation to the Church and the Papacy, and to assess the attitudes of English kings and leaders. The fact that the legates, George, bishop of Ostia, and Theophylact, bishop of Todi, were so experienced, and in the case of George so aged and of such great stature in papal business, emphasizes the significance of the mission to Pope Hadrian I. They were met by Jaenberht at Canterbury, and 'Journeying from there, we arrived at the court of Offa, king of the Mercians. And he received both us and the sacred letters sent from the highest see with immense joy and honour on account of his reverence for the blessed Peter and your apostolate. Then Offa ... and Cynewulf, king of the West Saxons, met together in a council; and to him also we delivered your holy writings; and they promised forthwith that they would reform these vices'. Thereafter Theophylact toured Mercia and Wales, and George toured Northumbria, where the province was known to be unstable. The resultant report to Hadrian laid some importance upon the nature and mood of their reception by the English kings and their willingness to conform to the canons and leads one to suspect that Rome was keen to receive good news and comfort itself that it still had significant influence in England. Offa's desire to create a second archdiocese at Lichfield was not mentioned by the legates but was discussed at the council held at Chelsea in 787, where Offa was given permission for the division.[155]

By creating an archdiocese at Lichfield Offa hoped to gain more power over the Church, cut links with his enemy Jaenberht and distance himself from the antagonistic attitude of Kent. Offa's move to create this second archdiocese, whilst ground-breaking in England, was a copy of Charlemagne's policy of reducing the size of archdiocesan units. Offa maintained that the change was necessary because of the large area under Mercian control. Hygeberht was made the first archbishop of Lichfield and by the end of 788 he had received an archbishop's pallium (a white woollen vestment) from the pope.

According to William of Malmesbury, the bishops of Worcester, Leicester, *Sidnacester*, Hereford, Elmham (in Norfolk) and Dunwich (on the Suffolk coast) came under the archbishopric of Lichfield, while those of London, Winchester, Rochester and Selsey (West Sussex) stayed under Jaenberht.[156]

In 787 another unusual step was taken by Offa. His personal need for the security of dynastic succession as well as recognition abroad, probably prompted him to have his only son, Ecgfrith, anointed king of the Mercians by the new archbishop in recognition of Ecgfrith's future claim to the throne. This is the first recorded consecration of a king in England, at least where a Christian ceremony was used, but it copied contemporary Frankish practice—in 781 Charlemagne's sons, Pippin and Louis, had been anointed into kingship by Pope Hadrian. Matthew of Westminster records (erroneously under the year 789) that this took place at the council of Chelsea (*Chalthuthe*) and that Ecgfrith 'reigned in conjunction with his father to the end of his life'.[157] The consecration took place at a time when Offa's power was growing in England, as was his importance abroad. But this also seems to be the time when his own greed for power and wealth was burgeoning, as well as a malignant paranoia which saw its murderous expression in Aethelberht's death seven years later.

In his early years as king, Offa's position towards the Church appears to have been fairly conventional but by the end of his reign it could be said that his treatment of it was politic—at times honourable, and at others manipulative. Two examples illustrate the latter. His cancellation of a gift of land by the king of Kent, Ecgberht and his reeve, Ealdhun, to Canterbury has already been mentioned. Offa redistributed these lands to his thegns, but they were returned to Christ Church by Coenwulf in 799, implying that Offa had acted incorrectly. Coenwulf, however, returned it not only for his own 'everlasting salvation and the peace and victory of the most loyal race of the Mercians', but also 'because of the payment of money, whose estimation amounts to 100 mancuses ...' which shows that Coenwulf, in common with most, had an eye not only on his soul, but also on his coffers.[158]

The second instance concerns the protracted case of the monastery and land at Cookham in Berkshire which came before the synod at *Clofesho* a year earlier in 798. Cookham, 3 miles north of Maidenhead on the Thames, then lay in the long-disputed southern territories of Mercia. In the 7th century the monastery was in West Saxon hands but Aethelbald had taken it into Mercian control in the early 8th century. The proceedings of the synod at *Clofesho* take up the story:

> This monastery, namely with all the lands belonging to it, Aethelbald, the famous king of the Mercians, gave to the church of the Saviour which is situated in Canterbury, and in order that his donation might be the more enduring, he sent a sod from the same land and all the deeds of the aforementioned monastery by the venerable man Archbishop Cuthbert, and ordered them to be laid upon the altar of the Saviour for his everlasting salvation. But after the death of the aforesaid pontiff, Daegheah and Osbert, whom the same pontiff had brought up as pupils, impelled by the evil spirit, stole these same documents, and delivered them to Cynewulf, king of the West Saxons. And he, receiving immediately the evidence of documents, took over for his own uses the aforesaid monastery with all things duly belonging to it, disregarding the words and actions of the aforenamed Archbishop Cuthbert. Again, archbishops Bregowine and Jaenberht complained through their various synods concerning the injury sustained by the church of the Saviour, both to Cynewulf, king of the West Saxons, and to Offa, king of the Mercians, who seized from King Cynewulf the oft-mentioned monastery, Cookham, and many other towns, and brought them under Mercian rule.
>
> At length, King Cynewulf, led by a tardy penitence, sent back to the church of Christ in Canterbury the charters, that is to say, the deeds which he had wrongfully received from the above-mentioned men Daegheah and Osbert, with a great sum of money, humbly asking that he might not be imperilled under an anathema of so great authority. Truly, King Offa as long as he lived retained the afore-mentioned monastery, Cookham, without documents, just as he had received it, and left it to his heirs after him without the evidence of documents.[159]

It has been shown how Aethelbald had sought to make the possession of the monastery more secure by sending a turf from the land and the deeds to the then archbishop, Cuthbert, and ordered that they should be placed upon the altar, which was the way such a transaction was effected in pre-Conquest times. Cynewulf's fear of eventual damnation shows how strong was the power of the Church, but having lost the monastery to Offa, it might be argued that not having any particular use for the documents, he was making the best personal mileage out of the situation. Offa, however, flouted every convention by wrongfully taking possession of the monastery without the title deeds. This did not stop him leaving it to his heirs as if it were his own and shows he did not respect religious conventions any more than he did secular ones. The outcome at the synod at *Clofesho* was that:

> ... Abbess Cynethryth, [Offa's widow] who at the time was in charge of the oft-mentioned monastery, and the elders assembled for this purpose from both sides, Kent, namely and *Bedeford*, [?Bedford] that the same Cynethryth should give to me [the present archbishop, Aethelheard of Canterbury] in exchange for the oft-mentioned monastery land of 110 hides in the region of Kent: 60 hides, namely in the place which is called Fleet, and 30 in the place which is called Tenham, and 20 in a third place which is called the source of the Cray. These lands, truly, King Offa formerly caused to be assigned to himself while he was alive and to his heirs after him, and after the course of their life, he ordered them to be consigned to the church which is situated at *Bedeford*. This also we decided in the presence of the whole synod that the abbess should receive from me the oft-mentioned monastery with its documents, and I should receive from her the lands and the deeds of the lands which she gave to me in Kent, to the end that no controversy may arise in the future between us and our heirs and those of King Offa, but that what was confirmed between us with the testimony of so noble a synod may be kept for ever by an unbroken covenant. I, Archbishop Aethelheard, also concede to the possession of Abbess Cynethryth the monastery which is situated in the place which is called *Pectanege* [probably, Patney 5 miles south-east of Devizes, in Wiltshire], which the good King Ecgfrith gave and granted by charter for me to possess with hereditary right.[160]

The 'King Ecgfrith' mentioned here is very likely Offa's son who ruled Mercia between July and December 796. Aethelheard was probably Offa's candidate for the see of Canterbury, yet it is significant that it was only after Offa's death that Aethelheard was able to recover the estates which the Mercian king had confiscated. It is suggested by Brooks that Offa's mistrust of the community of Christ Church at Canterbury, and the Kentish see overall, must have outweighed his regard for Aethelheard.[161] It is also interesting that Offa's queen, Cynethryth, became the abbess of Cookham and of another monastery at *Pectanege*. This is the queen who, according to Matthew Paris and Matthew of Westminster, poisoned her husband's mind against the youthful King Aethelberht of East Anglia and had him murdered.

William of Malmesbury demonstrates Offa's very ambivalent attitude towards the Church:

> The relics of St. Alban, at that time obscurely buried, he [Offa] ordered to be reverently taken up and placed in a shrine, decorated to the fullest extent of royal munificence, with gold and jewels; a church of most beautiful workmanship was there erected, and a society of monks assembled. Yet rebellious against God, he endeavoured to remove the archepiscopal see formerly settled at Canterbury, to Lichfield ... Nor did Offa's rapacity stop here, for he showed himself a downright public pilferer, by converting to his own use the lands of many churches, of which Malmesbury was one.[162]

William, a monk of Malmesbury Abbey, would clearly have had an axe to grind, but his description does convey something of Offa's complex attitude to the institution of the Church—generous on the one hand, grasping and hard-nosed on the other.

His turbulent relations with the Church were repeated with Charlemagne, but there is little doubting his acute statesmanship abroad. He vied with other major leaders as an international figure on the

European stage, which sets him apart from his predecessors. Under his rule, Mercia became an internationally recognized power of some consequence.

Offa's correspondence was principally with the Frankish king, Charlemagne and his adviser Alcuin of Northumbria, who had been residing at the Frankish court since 782, and was conducted during the later years of Offa's reign.

In a letter dated between 787-796, which is one of introduction for a tutor sent by Alcuin to Offa at the latter's request, Alcuin states:

> ... it greatly pleases me that you are so intent on education, that the light of wisdom, which is now extinguished in many places, may shine in your kingdom. You are the glory of Britain, the trumpet of proclamation, the sword against foes, the shield against enemies ...[163]

Charlemagne always showed Offa the highest respect with regard to his station and his person, and 'wished to be regarded as Offa's friend'. Matthew of Westminster provides a credible reason for Offa wishing to be associated with Charlemagne, from earlier in his reign in 775:

> Offa, king of Mercia, being eager to gain over all the neighbouring kings to be his friends, that he might be free from foreign enemies, in spite of all the damage which he had done to his neighbours, endeavoured, by many presents, to make a friend of Charlemagne.[164]

Some friction did occur which demonstrates that Offa demanded to be treated as an equal. Charlemagne wrote to him in, or shortly before, 789 and requested that Offa's daughter (probably Aelfflaed who ended up marrying the Northumbrian king, Aethelred, in 792) marry his eldest son. This may have been to patch up bad relations,[165] and even some embarrassment that may have existed on both sides, as many exiles from Offa's kingdom seemed to have used Frankish territory as a sanctuary. The suggested marriage may also have been a way of cementing a stronger alliance between the two kingdoms. But Offa reacted in a belligerent fashion, stating that such a marriage would be quite acceptable if his son, Ecgfrith, also married one of Charlemagne's daughters. The result was a diplomatic breakdown as Charlemagne was offended by being told what to do. In retaliation he closed down all Frankish ports to English merchants.

Early in 790 Alcuin wrote to an old associate and mentor, Colcu, about the embargo:

> But I do not know what is going to happen to us. For a certain dissension, fomented by the devil, has lately arisen between King Charles and King Offa, so that on both sides the passage of ships has been forbidden to merchants and is ceasing. There are some who say that we are to be sent to those parts to make peace. But I implore you that we may be protected by your holy prayers, whether we stay or come.[166]

Whether Alcuin did go to England to mediate is unclear, but it is interesting to note that Offa also shut down the English ports to Frankish trade. That Charlemagne considered this an effective act of hostility shows there must have been a regular, perhaps even a sizeable trade, between England and the Frankish kingdom.[167]

However, the bulk of overseas trade in the 7th and 8th centuries appears to have been with Frisia and many English coins of this date have been found on sites of early Frisian settlements.[168] Loyn points out that the centre of Frisian commercial activity was the *emporium* at Dorestad (now Wijk bij Duurstede) on the river Kromme Rijn, a small branch of the Rhine. Equally important for England was the port of Quentovic, now a deserted site in the flood plain south of the river Canche some 6 miles from the Channel coast in north-

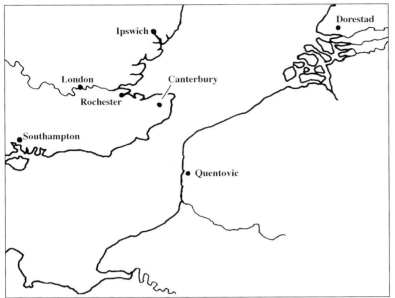

Fig.12 The main ports of England and the Continental coast in the 9th century

west France, but then readily accessible by river and 'at the head of a network of Roman roads'. In the 5th and 6th centuries Quentovic replaced Boulogne as the point of departure for Britain and, in the 7th century, its importance as the principal 'Christian point of entry rivalled that of heathen Dorestad'. Like Dorestad, Quentovic was one of the chief centres for tolls and had an extremely important mint. In England, foreign merchants were welcome as long as sureties could be found for them. Trade developed such that 8th-century English kings considered the remission of tolls on ships in London an appropriate gift to a favoured monastic house or bishop's see. Dorestad was destroyed by Vikings in 863 and its importance as a port dwindled by the end of the 10th century. Quentovic was able to maintain its position in spite of severe Viking attacks in 842 and 900 until the mid-10th century when Wissant became the main port in the area, possibly because Quentovic's harbour had silted up.[169]

At one stage during Charlemagne's trade embargo with England two intermediaries were used. One was Grippo, the reeve of Quentovic's *emporium*, and another was Gervaldus, abbot of St. Wandrille, who had supervised royal rights in a variety of markets and cities, but principally in Quentovic, and was a good friend of Offa's.[170] However, despite their efforts, the ports remained closed until at least late 790. A few years later friendly relations had finally been re-established and in 796 Offa and Charlemagne drew up the 'first commercial treaty in English history'.[171]

The letter which not only records details of the agreement between the two men, but is also of such importance to our knowledge of the relationship of these two kings and of English trade, is worth quoting in some length. It was written by Charlemagne who refers to Offa as a 'most beloved brother', 'most longed-for brother', 'a most strong protector of your earthly country, but also a most devout defender of the holy faith' and then goes on to air his grievances and expectation of the conduct of each country with regard to merchants. Charlemagne writes:

> Concerning pilgrims, who for the love of God and the salvation of their souls desire to reach the thresholds of the blessed Apostles, as we granted formerly, they may go in peace free from all molestation, bearing with them the necessities for their journey. But we have discovered that certain persons fraudulently mingle with them for the sake of commerce, seeking gain, not serving religion. If such are found among them, they are to pay the established toll at the proper places; the others may go in peace, immune from toll. ...
>
> You have written to us also about merchants, and by our mandate we allow that they shall have protection and support in our kingdom, lawfully, according to the ancient custom of trading. And if in any place they are afflicted by wrongful oppression, they may appeal to us or to our judges, and we will then order true justice to be done. Similarly our men, if they suffer any injustice in your dominion, are to appeal to the judgement of your equity, lest any disturbance should arise anywhere between our men.[172]

Charlemagne goes on to discuss his displeasure at the recent inadequate size of English cloaks, a slightly later account describing his indignation at what Loyn describes as the 'new-fangled custom of rounding cloaks at the knees'. Apparently the Frisians had been selling the 'miserable little cloaks' at the same price as the previous longer ones, even though they did not contain as much cloth. But what really seems to have affronted Charlemagne was the fact that 'I cannot cover myself up with them in bed, when riding I cannot defend myself against the wind and rain, and getting down *ad necessaria naturae tibiarum congelatione deficio*'[173] — literally 'I am without the bone structure for the requirements of nature'.

Loyn states that the 'mention of cloaks from England is the first indication of the importance of English sheep and English wool', and that the letter implies there was a significant trade. Although Hinton suggests that, while the letter demonstrates that English cloth did reach the Continent, it may have been that of the highest quality which was fit for kings, indicating 'diplomatic gift exchange' rather than regular trade.[174] However, mention has already been made of sheep farming in the Cotswolds from the 7th and 8th centuries, and as the wool trade was to become so important in the later Middle Ages, it would not be surprising if England was well known for it in the Anglo-Saxon period.

Moreover, there is other evidence which hints at the importance of the export of textiles from England at this time, for example the abbot of Wearmouth stated in 764 that he had sent two pallia of 'the most ingenious workmanship' with other goods to the bishop of Mainz, and in 800 the abbey of St. Bertin (in France) kept back part of its revenue to purchase English cloth. Even 9th- to 11th-century Arabic sources refer to the fame of English cloth.[175]

In spite of his irritation concerning the cloaks, that Offa and Charlemagne were once again on good terms is shown, for Charlemagne continues:

> Moreover, we make known to your love that we have sent a gift from our dalmatics [loose-fitting, wide-sleeved ecclesiastical robes] and palls [rich cloth coverings] to the various episcopal sees of your kingdom and of Ethelred's [Aethelred of Northumbria], in alms for the apostolic lord, Hadrian, our father and your friend ... Also from the treasure of earthly riches ... we have sent something to each of the metropolitan cities; also to your love, for joy and thanksgiving to Almighty God, we have sent a belt, and a Hunnish sword and two silk palls.[176]

The fact that both Offa and Charlemagne were personally concerned in trading matters demonstrates how important, critical even, foreign trade was to their countries. This is also shown by Offa's enhancement of his coinage to a specification acceptable to the Franks. Offa's was the most developed Mercian coinage system to date, and the upgraded version of his coins from the later years of his reign were minted from better quality silver and were slightly heavier. They were not so artistically designed as his earlier coins which Stenton remarks show 'a delicacy of execution which is unique in the whole history of the Anglo-Saxon coinage', and the upgraded coins lost his portrait and instead emphasized his name. These developments paralleled similar changes in the Frankish currency which is significant in terms of the trading links between England and Gaul. The changes to the English currency persisted and the basic design of a silver penny, which showed the king's name on the obverse and the moneyer's name on the reverse, lasted from Offa's reign to that of Henry III's in the 13th century. The extent of foreign trade is also demonstrated by a gold coin, which imitates an Arabic dinar struck in 774 by the Caliph Al-Mansur, but which carries the

Fig.13 Copy of the Arabic dinar of Caliph Al Mansur, dated 157 in the Arabic Calendar (A.D. 774), with 'Offa Rex' added on the obverse (1.5 times actual size)

words '*Offa Rex*' in Roman capitals across the reverse (see Fig.13). This coin suggests very strongly that, during Offa's reign, there was enough trade between England and the Caliphate in Arabia to justify manu-facturing a gold currency which Arab traders might find acceptable.[177]

Offa's correspondence with Charlemagne covered many aspects of kingship and Charlemagne was conscientious in keeping Offa informed of any problems on the Continent. He deals with the subject of one Eadberht Praen, who was trying to claim the Kentish crown even though it was said he was ordained as a priest, with considerable tact and common-sense when he writes to Offa:

> Regarding the priest Odberht, [the Continental form of Eadberht's name] ... I inform you, dear brother, that we have sent him to Rome with the other exiles who in fear of death have taken refuge under the wings of our protection; so that in the presence of the apostolic lord [the pope] and your archbishop - since, as your letters have informed us, they had bound themselves by a vow - their cause may be heard and judged, that equitable judgement may be effective where pious intercession failed. What could be safer for us than that the opinion of the apostolic authority should determine a case in which the views of others disagree?[178]

Sometimes the letters are cautious and occasionally appear to be an exercise in damage limitation, but that is the nature of statesmanship. Indeed, only a few months before Offa's death, Alcuin wrote to him that '... Charles, has often spoken to me of you in a most loving and loyal way, and in him you certainly have a most faithful friend'.[179]

Offa died on 29 July 796. Curiously no-one is sure of his burial place. A site near or in Lichfield has been suggested, and this would follow the example set by Ceolred who was buried there. Yet no good evidence has emerged to support the claims of any one of a range of sites, for example Offlow in Staffordshire, Offchurch near Leamington Spa in Warwickshire or even the most likely royal burial site at Repton. Wood, for one, favours the opinion of the monks of St. Alban's who maintain that Offa was buried in a small chapel at Bedford because they had good reason to remember: to their bitter disap-pointment they were unable to secure Offa's body for burial, and it was Offa who was their great bene-factor.[180] Matthew of Westminster gives a particularly vivid account of the putative resting place at Bedford and its eventual fate, which has a reassuring air of authenticity:

> ... Offa, the magnificent king of Mercia, having built a most truly noble monastery, after the discovery of the body of the blessed Alban, in the town which is called Offaeleia, died, and his body was borne to the town of Bedford, and is said to have been buried with royal magnificence in a chapel outside the town, built on the banks of the river Usk. [Bedford is actually on the banks of the Ouse.] And to this day [in the 14th century] the report of nearly all the people of that district affirms, that the afore-said chapel was destroyed by length of time and by the violence of the river, and was, together with the royal sepulchre, by the rapidity of the stream thrown down into the water; and in consequence, even to the present day, that sepulchre is at times clearly seen in the deep water by men who bathe in the river there in the summer, while at other times, as if there were some fate about it, if you seek for it ever so carefully, you cannot find it.[181]

If Bedford was Offa's last resting place, it begs the question as to why a location on the fringes of Mercia was chosen for such a powerful Mercian king?

The Legacy of Offa

Offa was obviously a substantial statesman who had the confidence to write to Charlemagne as an equal, which sets him apart from his predecessors. In addition to ruling a large area of England, Offa was also receptive to matters abroad. That he was able to rule with his attention directed towards the Continent, as well as at home, is a sign of his gift of kingship. Charlemagne was the most powerful ruler that Europe had seen for 400 years and his military and political achievements were enormous. He was very closely associated with the Roman Church and increasingly viewed himself as the defender of the faith in western Europe.[182] It is thus no surprise that he was made Holy Roman Emperor in 803. In gradually adopting this stance in relation to the Church, Charlemagne put himself in an unusual position because the political, moral and religious well-being of countries became his personal concern. He was well aware of his own importance, of his power over the centre of Europe and, from his letters, he seems aware of his ability to deal with other leaders with tact, diplomacy and subtlety. He also corresponded with Northumbria, which was in turmoil at this time, and it is quite possible that if Aethelred or Aethelbald of Mercia had been in power Charlemagne would have written to them in similar terms.

It is interesting that the bulk of Charlemagne's correspondence with Offa occurs at the time when Mercia must have been causing Charlemagne and Rome some anxiety: there were rumours that Offa wanted Charlemagne to depose the pope, and the very real fact that Offa had fallen out with the arch-bishop of Canterbury and wanted to set up his own archbishopric at Lichfield. It was good political sense on Charlemagne's part to view Mercia with some degree of caution and observe further developments closely.

Offa was not the only notable Mercian monarch of the 8th century. Great and powerful leader he certainly was, but so too were Aethelbald and Aethelred. In terms of Offa's military conquests in England and the amount of territory he ruled as overlord, he actually falls between his two predecessors. Both Offa and Aethelred had severe problems in controlling Kent, and lost control of that kingdom for a proportion of their reigns. Aethelred seems to have struggled more, but the province was hostile to Mercia at his accession, whereas at Offa's it was compliant. Offa had control of East Anglia, a huge area, but this was partly a political choice of East Anglia's. Aethelred was in the position of having to subdue Northumbria, and did so successfully, but having secured Mercia's borders, he did not evidently pursue this province; rather he concentrated on consolidating the territory under his command and turned his attention to ecclesiastical matters.

Aethelbald, in contrast to both of them, effectively controlled Kent, East Anglia, and much of Wessex, and at one time invaded Northumbria. He was undoubtedly the stronger military leader and a very effective ruler, but perhaps not as far-sighted as Offa.

Clearly what sets Offa apart from his two predecessors was his ability to take a broader view of his kingdom's position and act on it. He had the foresight to set a precedent by establishing diplomatic relations with Charlemagne, and conducted these effectively. He was therefore able to enhance learning within the country by introducing tutors from Europe and also had trading connections that stretched as far as Arabia. It is perhaps for his truly innovative and forward-looking rule that he should be remembered above all else.

CHAPTER 8
Offa's Dyke

Because of the sharp change in landscape, the Marches have always been a boundary area, even before the Anglo-Saxon push west which created the Wales of today. Before the Roman invasion of A.D.43, Celtic tribes occupied most of Britain and their most visible memorial is the hill fort. The Welsh Marches are particularly well endowed with these, many being large and elaborate with several tiers of enclosing banks and narrow defendable entrances.[1] For the most part these forts are evenly spaced, between about about $3^{1}/_{2}$ to 6 miles apart,[2] but there are concentrations of them along the Wye valley, the southern Shropshire hills, and around the confluence of the rivers Vyrnwy and Severn.[3] These concentrations are thought to mark the edge of territory for four different Celtic tribes. In the north is the territorial division between the Deceangli of north-east Wales and the Cornovii centred on the upper Severn valley. To the south along the Wye the Cornovii faced the Silures of south-east Wales and the Ordovices to the west. In addition, the boundary with the Dobunii of Gloucestershire and the south-west midlands must also have run near the lower Wye. These Latinized names were given to the native tribes of Britain by the Roman conquerors as they encountered them in the 1st century A.D.; history does not record their Celtic names.

Once the Romans had subdued the British, they established a number marching camps along the edge of what became Wales, and then pushed westwards. As they took over new territory some of these camps in the rear were abandoned, some became forts, and some became towns or civilian settlements associated with forts, called *vici*.[4] Those that remained attracted some local civilian traders and camp followers, but Wales itself remained a military zone throughout the time of the Roman occupation.[5] During the 2nd century the Romans began to abandon some of their forts and the native population also started to withdraw from civilized life, leaving the river valleys near the forts for upland enclosures once again and giving up on trade for a more self-sufficient lifestyle.[6] As Wales was a military zone, when the Roman troops were finally withdrawn, even the reasons for the existence of the garrison towns disappeared.[7] The troop withdrawal also brought invasions of Wales and the Marches by barbarians from other parts of the British Isles. Starting in the late 4th century the Picts from beyond Hadrian's Wall in Scotland began to arrive, along with Irish settlers. Although the Picts were driven out in the 5th century,[8] there is evidence that the Irish stayed and added their influence to the developing Welsh kingdoms.

The process by which the Romanized Celtic tribes transformed themselves into the many small kingdoms of the period known as the Dark Ages is not clear. It is thought that at the end of Roman rule, posts were taken over by local officers known as *praefecti* who were to rule their districts as petty kings and pass the office on to their sons. This may be the basis for the origin of the Welsh kingdoms.[9] One tradition, according to early histories, is that a late Roman governor or the remnant of such an authority, sent for help to the Celts of northern Britain. In response the leader of the Votadini, Cunedda, came south to Wales to drive out the invaders. The story continues that Cunedda brought eight of his nine sons and when the job was completed, they stayed on to become the ancestors of the kings of many of the Dark Age Welsh kingdoms. The names of his sons were Tybion, Ysfal, Rhufon, Dunod, Ceredig, Afloeg, Einion, Yrth, Dogfael, and Edem; the grandson who followed the family to north Wales was Meirion. Several of these names can be recognized in the early kingdoms and in the names of the districts of mid- and north Wales today. However, the story sounds rather too much like other founding father myths from other parts of Britain to be taken at face value.[10]

By whatever route, there emerged four main post-Roman kingdoms in Wales: Gwynedd in the north-west, Powys in the north-east, Dyfed in the south-west, and Gwent in the south-east. Other kingdoms rose later in the 7th, 8th, and 9th centuries, separating off from the larger units, such as Ceredigion along the west coast and Brycheiniog in south central Wales. In the south-eastern region of Wales several small kingdoms rose in the 6th century, including the kingdom of Ergyng in the southern Marches.[11]

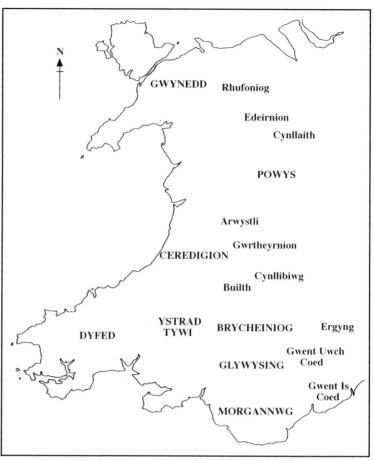

Fig. 1 Map showing the Welsh kingdoms around the time that Offa's Dyke was constructed

The mountainous and difficult landscape of Wales as well as a low population contributed to territorial divisiveness. Fertile coasts and valleys are separated from each other by highlands. Another divisive factor was the Welsh practice of dividing an inheritance equally among all the sons, rather than passing it all on to the eldest. This tended to dissipate power and led to infighting and political weakness.[12]

The kingdoms adjacent to the English border were Powys, Ergyng and Gwent, Powys being by far the largest. In its heyday Powys rivalled Gwynedd in size and strength, reaching from the west coast to cover most of north central Wales as far as Cheshire and north Shropshire and reaching down to the upper Wye valley.[13] According to legend, Brittu, a son of Vortigern, was installed as its first king.[14] But Powys, like the other Welsh kingdoms was not a clearly defined territorial unit. It was a loose alliance of chiefs and petty kings under the distant leadership of the king. This network of allied states covered a variety of landscapes including the highlands of north Wales and the less dramatic lowlands along the adjacent coast. Eventually its territory included the area east of the mountains: the Cheshire plain and the upper Severn valley of north Shropshire. This had been the heartland of the Celtic tribe, the Cornovii before the Roman settlement. The Romans had built two important forts in their territory around which towns developed: Wroxeter on the upper Severn and Chester on the Dee estuary. By the year 90 the conquest of Wales was complete and the legion left Wroxeter, which became a civil town,[15] whilst Chester retained its military component until the troops were withdrawn for good. Left on their own, the Romanized Cornovii of the towns and surrounding area lived independently in their own small, isolated territory.

While many of the boundaries of the kingdom of the Cornovii were imprecise, a recent discovery by archaeologists suggests that their western boundary was very definite indeed. In 1997 an industrial development at Maes y Clawdd near Oswestry was planned on the line of Wat's Dyke, the companion work to Offa's Dyke in the northern Marches. An excavation confirmed the line of the Dyke and, excitingly, a section through the remnants of the bank revealed the remains of a hearth underneath which had last been used just before it was buried. It had generally been reasoned that because Wat's Dyke was so much like Offa's Dyke, only shorter, it had been built in the same century, the 8th, by Offa's predecessor Aethelbald (716-757),[16] though a rival theory suggests that, because it is better constructed and positioned to the east of Offa's Dyke, it was built subsequent to Offa's Dyke when the Mercians had learned better construction techniques but had lost some territory.[17] The radiocarbon date of the charcoal in the hearth confounded both theories. The most likely date of the fire was sometime between A.D.411-561 centring on 446, with the widest possible range being 268-630. A date of 630 would bring the Dyke into the era when Penda was annexing this territory, making it possible that the loss by Powys of its eastern province was physically marked by a dyke. However, the central date and more probable range means that it is more likely to have been the post-Roman Cornovii who built the Dyke to mark their own frontier[18] with their neighbour to the west, the developing kingdom of Powys, formerly the home territory of the Decangli. The first tangible dividing line on the March had been drawn. A possible early post-Roman date for Wat's Dyke could have some interesting implications for Offa's Dyke.

By the 7th century Powys had leap-frogged Wat's Dyke and the kingdom of the Cornovii, or most of it, formed the eastern part of Powys, just when the eastern Welsh kingdoms were themselves beginning to come under pressure from Anglo-Saxon settlers. The battle of Chester in 616 and the subsequent Northumbrian invasion of north Wales brought these kingdoms into an alliance with Mercia and the pagan king Penda.[19] This Northumbrian invasion for the first time cut off land contact between the Celts of the west and those of the north and Scotland; the subsequent expansion of Mercia broke it for good.

In chapter 3 the story of Cynddylan, prince of Powys, and his alliance with Mercia against Northumbria has been told. Perhaps Cynddylan's death led to a Mercian usurpation of eastern Powys, or even that Powys voluntarily gave up its province in the east as a price for its alliance with Mercia. By the end of the 7th century, eastern Powys was firmly under Mercian control and its people were known as the *Wreocensaete*.[20]

Gwent, the southernmost Welsh kingdom of the Marches was also the smallest of the four main kingdoms. This part of Wales, notably that along the south coast, has a more gentle landscape and is more fertile than most of the rest of Wales. It also lies closer to the south-western counties of Gloucestershire and Wiltshire which were favoured for Roman settlement. There were more Roman towns and villas in the south-east of Wales than anywhere else in the country. Its two principal Roman towns were Caerleon, the legionary headquarters of the southern Marches and Wales on the lower tidal part of the river Usk, and Caerwent or *Venta Silurum*, the market town of the Silures 8 miles west of the mouth of the Wye, and from where Gwent gains its name.

In 293 the legions were withdrawn from Caerleon never to return,[21] and as a result the town was slowly abandoned. Caerwent had dwindled into insignificance by the late 6th century and inland hill forts were re-occupied. An archaeological excavation at Dinas Powys, a hill fort near Cardiff, in the early 1960s revealed the remains of several Dark Age buildings surrounded by rubbish pits containing the debris of a rather wealthy household: Mediterranean and Continental pottery, German glass, scrap bronze, and the remains of Celtic metalworking. This was clearly the home of an important family in the 5th and 6th centuries, one able to obtain foreign trade items. Traffic with the late Roman empire, at least among the aristocracy, continued until the 8th century, when the trade in pottery from the Mediterranean ceased.[22]

Gwent, like Powys, had a fragmented political structure with many minor kings establishing small territories.[23] The only source of information about the history of this area during the early post-Roman period is the Llandaff Charters, a collection of land grants relating to monastic and church property in south-east Wales dating mostly to the period before the Norman Conquest. The charters were altered in the 12th century by Bishop Urban who was trying to claim property for the new diocese of Llandaff, but careful study and reading between the lines of the later Medieval formulae reveals much. Most of them are undated but analysis of the witness lists both indicates the dates of the charters and the reigns of the kings. Grants refer to the many small kingdoms—Ergyng is mentioned as a kingdom in the 6th century. Sometimes there appear to be more kings than kingdoms, but perhaps in accordance with the Welsh system of shared inheritance brothers may have shared a throne. The boundaries within which some kings

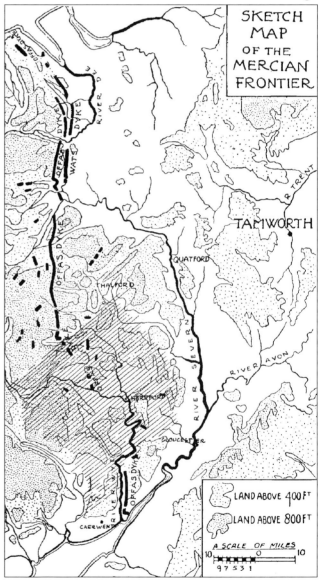

operate are not clearly defined, whilst their responsibilities are somewhat ambiguous.[24] However, in the 7th century, external pressure is clearly having an effect on internal structure. In 577 the Saxons had won the battle of Dyrham which opened up much of the lower Severn to Saxon settlement and the charters start to mention Saxon raids. The pressure of their advance encouraged the kingdom to coalesce under the dynasty of Meurig ap Tewdig.

Meurig married into the family of Glywys. His grandson Morgan, who succeeded him, was called *Rex Glywysing*; it is uncertain what territory Glywysing encompassed. The name Glywysing in time gave way to *Morganwg*, Morgan's land, a reference to a king Morgan ap Owain in the 10th century who appeared to control all of south-east Wales, and hence the name Glamorgan. Morganwg specifically referred to the land between the rivers Tywy and Wye in the late 10th century,[25] Gwent forming only the easternmost part of this territory.[26] Further east, across the lower Wye was the territory of Cantref Coch, the iron-rich Forest of Dean[27] which was part of Ergyng. By the 7th century it had become part of the territory of the *Magonsaete*,[28] Ergyng's territory being reduced to a swathe of land between the Wye and the Black Mountains. The kingdom of Ergyng or Archenfield, its English name, also fell under the domination if not political control of Mercia. Unlike other parts of the Marches that had been absorbed into Mercia, Archenfield had little Anglo-Saxon settlement by Offa's time, though it had become subject to Mercia at least since his reign.[29] Welsh laws were retained and it still had its own bishop in the 10th century (see also p.66).

Fig. 2 Map, based on Frank Noble's work, showing the line of Offa's and Wat's dykes, and of the various short dykes

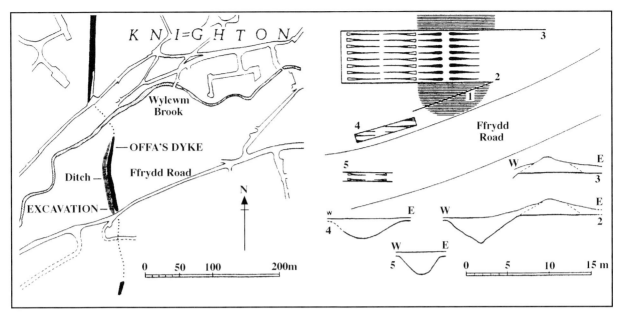

Fig. 3 A section through Offa's Dyke just south of Knighton, indicating the original profile

In the 8th century the kingdoms of south-east Wales came under renewed pressure from the Saxons. In 722 the *Welsh Annals* note that a battle took place in Deheubarth in south-west Wales in which the Britons prevailed. The *Anglo-Saxon Chronicle* for the year 743 records that Aethelbald of Mercia and Cuthred of Wessex fought the Welsh. One of the Llandaff charters dated to about 740 lists, among other valuable objects used to buy land, a Saxon woman who must have been a captive. Another charter of *c*.745 mentions devastation in the Hereford area. The *Welsh Annals* for 760 states that Hereford was devastated by the Welsh, this may have been the work of the king of Glywysing,[30] and then in 777 that King Offa harried the men of Deheubarth. In 783 Offa was again ravaging the Britons but the *Annals* do not specify where in Wales.

With the reign of Offa the period of the Dyke is reached. The first written reference to this structure occurs in Asser's *Life of King Alfred* written in 893, nearly a hundred years after its construction: 'There was in Mercia in fairly recent times a certain vigorous king called Offa, who terrified all the neighbouring kings and provinces around him, and who had a great dyke built between Wales and Mercia from sea to sea'.[31] The 'from sea to sea' comment has caused much debate ever since, as this chapter will show.

The main section of Offa's Dyke (that which runs north from Kington in north-west Herefordshire to Tredduyn in the north) consists of a bank with a ditch on its western side which shows no evidence of having been cleaned out during its lifetime.[32] The Dyke can vary considerably in size depending on how well it was constructed, the type of soil and the pitch of the terrain. Originally the ditch was about 2m (6½ft) deep from ground level, while the bank towered above its bottom to a height of nearly 8m (26ft).[33] The bank is made up of the earth dug from the ditch, usually with some stones and turves incorporated inside to reinforce it and give it extra height. The turves were both stripped from the line of the Dyke and sometimes from the ground behind the bank which can leave the appearance of there having been a ditch to the Dyke's rear. Turves were also sometimes placed along the face of the bank above the ditch as a kind of reinforcing wall or revetment. For much of the Dyke's length the ditch has completely filled in over the centuries but when revealed by excavation it is seen to have been V-shaped, with a smooth 45° angle up the combined face of the ditch and bank making climbing difficult and driving livestock across nearly impossible.[34] There is often a small bank, a counterscarp, on the outer edge of the ditch which is usually less than half the height of the main bank. It is generally made up of material dug from the ditch and its purpose is thought to have been to increase the impression of depth to the ditch. The width of the bank and ditch together can reach to up to 20m (65ft).[35] No evidence of a palisade or wall has ever been found on the top of the bank. In several places a small marking out trench has been noted running under the bank, presumably made by those planning the course of the Dyke. When Cyril Fox excavated the Dyke at Ffrith in the 1920s, he found a small post-hole under the bank which he took to be part of a line of marking out posts, performing the same function as the small ditch.[36] On some excavations of Wat's Dyke a line of stones found under the bank may also be marking it out.[37] No evidence for the long distance sighting and laying out of the Dyke such as beacons, has ever been found.[38]

Historical References to Offa's Dyke

In 1129 Simeon of Durham in his *Historia Regum* continued the history of Britain from where Bede left off. Among his sources was Asser from whom he obtained much information about Offa, but he makes a curious statement—that Offa built the Dyke between England and north Wales. He then seems to contradict himself and uses Asser's quote that the Dyke goes 'from sea to sea' to protect his border from the Welsh.

The learned cleric John of Salisbury wrote *Policraticus*, a political and philosophical work which he completed in 1159. As part of his description of the exploits of Duke Harold Godwinson in pacifying the Welsh he is the first to quote the warning that any Welshman found beyond Offa's Dyke will have his hand cut off.[39]

Giraldus Cambrensis mentions Offa's Dyke in his *Description of Wales* in 1194. His Welsh origins make him more sympathetic towards the Welsh than the other historians quoted, and he includes the Dyke in a list of atrocities that English kings and warriors have committed against his countrymen.

Walter Map's *De Nugis Curialium* was written about 1200. In these 'Courtier's Trifles' the hero Gado encounters Offa as a young teenage king. Offa was identified as the king who had 'shut up the Welshmen in a small corner of their Wales and had surrounded them with a ditch which is called from his name'. The tale records that if they crossed the ditch any Welshman would lose a foot.

Ranulph Higden, in his *Polychronicon*, a history written in 1352, gives a more detailed description of the Dyke than earlier historians. He was writing at Chester, just a short distance from the Dyke and may have had first hand knowledge of it.[40] Even so, he has the Dyke running from the Bristol area to the sea between Colehill and Basingwerk monastery thereby confusing the course of Offa's Dyke with that of Wat's Dyke in north Wales—not the last person to so do. Higden does add that Englishmen and Welshmen are living on both sides of the Dyke.

The *Brut y Saeson* or *Brenhinedd y Saeson*—'the Kings of the Saxons'—is a history of the Saxon kings combined with that of the Princes of Wales, a composite work consisting of some of the Welsh history contained in the *Welsh Annals*, the *Bryt y Tywysogion* and various other histories of Britain written during the Middle Ages among which was probably Higden's *Polychronicon*.[41] The last entry is dated 1461 and so the work was obviously compiled no earlier. Its origin is not clear. In the entry for 783-784 it states '... in the summer the Welsh ravaged Offa's territory. And then Offa had a dyke made as a limit between him and Wales, so that it might be easier for him to resist the attack of his enemies, and that was called Offa's Dyke from that day to this'. None of the earlier Welsh histories mentions Offa's Dyke.

John Leland travelled around the country in the reign of Henry VIII recording what he saw. Concerning a castle called Whittington owned by Lord Fitz Warin he writes it was 'vi miles from Shrewsbiri upward almost on Severn, and by this goith Offa's diche'.[42] He mentions it almost casually, as if there was no need to explain to his readers what Offa's Dyke was.

David Powell writing in 1584 gives a Welsh version of the border in his *History of Cambria*. He says that in the old time the border ran along the rivers Dee and Severn before the Saxons forced the Welsh off

Early Maps of the northern end of Offa's Dyke

The first map to depict the northern part of Offa's Dyke would seem to be that of John Speed in 1676 (Fig. 5 top left). It shows the Dyke starting at Basingwerk in the north and disappearing in the vicinity of Wrexham in Denbighshire. The map maker clearly never saw his subject and was working from inaccurate sources. A map of Flintshire and Denbighshire dated 1754 by Will Williams (Fig. 6 above) shows Wat's Dyke starting at Flint and Offa's Dyke starting at Basingwerk. Although also inaccurate, at least both dykes are being depicted. A 1751 map by E. Bowen of Shropshire still only shows Offa's Dyke. The first accurate depiction of the northern limits of both dykes is that of Jonathan Evans in 1795 (Fig. 7 left) which shows Wat's Dyke running south from Basingwerk and Offa's Dyke arising in the neighbourhood of Treuddyn. Some maps of the period show Offa's Dyke but call it the Devil's Ditch, such as J. Rocque's of 1752 and Cary's of 1787

the plain, notably Offa who built his Dyke. He describes the Dyke as going from Basingwerk in north Wales all the way to Bristol, similar to the description given in *Polychronicon*. Edward Llwyd's *Parochialia* of 1703 also confuses Wat's and Offa's dykes.

Thomas Pennant's *Tours in Wales,* written in 1778 and published in 1810, gives the first accurate account of both dykes noting that they are often confused. He attributes knowledge of Wat's Dyke to an old story recounted by Thomas Churchyard, a 16th-century poet who had the idea that the narrow area between the dykes was a free ground where both Britons and Saxons could meet safely and trade with each other. Pennant also accurately puts the northern end of Offa's Dyke in a marsh near the north Wales town of Treuddyn, nearly 10 miles short of the sea.

Jonathan Williams in his *History of Radnorshire*, written in 1820, puts Offa's Dyke back on its old erroneous course from Basingwerk to Chepstow. He also hints at the existence of the various short dykes that also exist close to the current border by saying that the Welsh obstructed the work and made the builders take a direction inclining more towards the east than they had intended.

In 1831 in the *Gentleman's Magazine* T.D. Fosbroke first suggested that the earthworks on the tops of the cliffs in the lower Wye valley were part of Offa's Dyke. Not even the first edition Ordinance Survey Maps of 1830 show these banks except for the southernmost dyke at Sedbury which is called an 'Ancient Intrenchment'.

George Ormerod appears to have made the earliest map of the Dyke in the lower Wye valley. He shows it from its southern end as far north as Tintern Abbey.[43] In 1856 in *Archaeologia Cambrensis* he identifies the Sedbury Dyke as being named in a charter of 956, known as the Tidenham Charter, granted by King Edwy. In another article in *Archaeologia Cambrensis* the following year, J. Earle complains that the Dyke is being damaged by farmers who obtained their land through enclosure. This article also first mentions the possible connection between a boundary such as Offa's Dyke and the 'Ordinances concerning the Dunsaete', which sets down a code for dealing with disputes between people crossing such a frontier.

In an article of 1875 in *Archaeologia Cambrensis*, W.T. Parkins put forward the idea that the Saxons may have built the Dyke piecemeal over a long period of time, and that Offa may only be responsible for a portion of it but has been given credit for the whole. In a note at the end of the article, however, the author considers Asser's quote about Offa building the dyke to be absolute proof that he so did.

It was not until the later 1884 edition of the Ordnance Survey map that the Dyke was shown accurately and completely.

In *Archaeologia,* 1893, T. McKenny Hughes states that Offa's Dyke is known as the Devil's Ditch in south Shropshire, indeed several maps of the 18th and early 19th centuries call it the Devil's Ditch all the way through Shropshire. Hughes also says that Offa's Dyke is called *trefyn* or terminus in Wales. This author is a strong proponent for the idea that the Dyke was built in sections during Roman times and strung together by Offa.

Explanation of the Course of the Dyke

At its southern end, what is now called 'Offa's Dyke' certainly does go to the edge of the sea—on the Sedbury Cliffs overlooking the broad mouth of the Severn, where it cuts off the end of the peninsula of Beachley Point on the eastern side of the mouth of the river Wye. For its southernmost quarter of a mile, the Dyke is a 3m (9¾ft) high bank and a 2m (6½ft) deep ditch running along the southern edge of Sedbury Park, an old estate boundary. The Dyke continues west of the probably unconnected Buttington Tump on a much reduced scale, being little more than a terrace marking off the higher ground to the north from the lower ground to the south, which on the western side of the peninsula by the river Wye becomes Tallard's Marsh. On the cliff top above the river overlooking modern Chepstow where the Dyke might be expected to terminate is an eroded ringwork about 40m (130ft) wide which has been interpreted as a Mercian fort by both Fox and David Hill of the Offa's Dyke Project.

This mile long southernmost section is completely cut off from the next four sections of the Dyke. These total 9.5 miles (15.2km), each section being separated from the next by a gap of between 20m (65ft) and half a mile. These sections largely run along the edge of the cliffs which rise almost vertically from the edge of the river in some places on the eastern side of the Wye valley up to 210m (700ft.) in height. These sections are built with a high, steep scarp on their western side, and with a lower or almost non-existent slope on the eastern, so emphasizing the ditch. They often have a berm or counterscarp on the western side of the ditch to separate them from the cliff edge, and quarry pits on their eastern side. Where the bank runs on to more level ground, or where the break in slope becomes less pronounced such as in several of the small valleys which interrupt the cliff line, the bank is built more evenly with both faces about the same height, like sections of the Dyke built in other parts of the Marches. This type of bank is found on St. Briavel's Common, built for some reason about ⅓ mile away from the valley's edge along the river. Where streams flow down to the Wye and break the line of limestone cliffs, the dykes follow the slope around to face these tributary valleys, as though they are marking these hill tops and not just the eastern shore of the Wye.

The Dyke builders in the lower Wye valley were not the first people to make use of the singular geography of the area. Several Iron Age hill forts built on either side of the valley use the steep edge for defensive purposes, of which the largest example is the hill fort at Symonds Yat. This is formed of a series of concentric banks which cuts across a promontory. One of these banks was subsequently incorporated into Offa's Dyke.

These main sections of Offa's Dyke in the lower Wye valley come to an end on a hill just south of the village of Redbrook. There is then a 1½ mile gap along the course of the Wye until the banks at Symonds Yat appear. About 1km east of the hill fort is another length of earthwork which runs along the edge of the break in slope where the top of a terrace slopes down to the river at English Bicknor. The development of Lower Lydbrook in the early years of the Industrial Revolution has probably destroyed a length of this section of the Dyke.

Beyond Lydbrook a 50m (160ft) long bank stands some 3 to 4m (9¾ft to 13ft) high on a wooded slope leading down to the Wye from a small valley called Ragman's Slade, now partly damaged by lime-

Fig. 8 Offa's Dyke on steep hillside in the lower Wye valley

171

stone quarrying which has taken place just uphill from it to the east. It was reported as a section of Offa's Dyke by J. Maclean in 1893 but its status is debatable. Why build a bit of a bank here? Where is the rest of it?

There is then a 20 mile gap until the next section of what is believed to be Offa's Dyke is reached, about 5 miles west of the city of Hereford, just west of the village of Bridge Sollars. If the primary aim of the Dyke was to demarcate a fixed frontier, the reason there is no Dyke in much of Herefordshire is that the Wye itself may have formed the boundary, but with the buffer state of Archenfield on the far bank. The main support for this theory lies in a 10th-century document. In 926 King Athelstan held a meeting with a number of Welsh princes in Hereford, one result of which was the drafting of the 'Ordinances Concerning the Dunsaete'. This is a set of rules governing the conduct between the English and the Welsh living on either side of an unnamed river. Given the location of the meeting, the Wye is presumed to be that river and the *Dunsaete* perhaps a forgotten name for the people of Archenfield. These laws, which mainly concern the retrieval of lost cattle, existed in an unwritten oral form by Offa's time. However, they must have been abandoned shortly after they were written down as the laws of Archenfield as set out in the Herefordshire Domesday of 1086 are quite different.[44]

The rules (see opposite) were established to mediate disputes between two neighbouring peoples each of whom had their own system of law. An item of interest among the Ordinances is the first mention of trial by jury—'twelve men, six of them English, six Welsh'. Ordinance nine mentions the *Wensaete* who were once clients of the *Dunsaete*. Just as it is supposition that the *Dunsaete* are the people of Archenfield, the *Wensaete* are considered to be the people of Gwent, or a territory adjacent to Gwent.[45]

The greatest difficulty with accepting the idea that the river Wye was the border with the Welsh in southern Herefordshire, was the position of Hereford with its bishop's see on its eastern bank. It is a curious place to position such an important centre, right on the edge of a potentially dangerous border. It was the westernmost Mercian town in the southern Marches. It may be that Hereford was founded in its marginal position in order to control this part of the border. Archenfield, to the west and south of the river was still under the power of Welsh kings when Hereford was founded, but by Offa's time it had lost its independence. Indeed, the co-operative nature of their relations with Mercia indicates that they may have been in a weak position before that. The presence of a major Mercian settlement must have exerted some influence on the process of Saxon immigration to the area, which perhaps weakened the Welsh position still further, although Welsh was still widely spoken in the city in the 17th century.[46]

If the whole border was to be fortified, it would seem peculiar that Hereford was left so exposed on the frontier. It fell victim to raids from Wales at least twice, once in 760 and again in 1055.[47] There are in fact two lengths of dyke in Hereford, both called Rowe Ditch and both built much later. The first is south of the river and runs roughly east to west across Bishop's Meadow. Excavations revealed an associated ditch in which the earliest pottery found was 13th century, and it was probably cut to protect the southern suburbs.[48] The other, fragmentary, dyke runs along the backs of the gardens of the houses on the south side of Park St. and may have been built by the Scots army which besieged Hereford in 1645 during the Civil War.

At Bridge Sollars a ditch can be seen on the banks of the river Wye leading off in a north-westerly direction. North of the A438 it fades into a field but reappears strongly north of a road which follows the old course of a Roman road heading west from the site of *Magnis*. As it starts to climb the south-eastern side of Garnon's Hill the ditch and bank become deeper and higher respectively until, at the crest of the hill, the bank falls to less than 1m high and the ditch disappears. The bank is lost on the top of the hill due to marl quarrying but the line of the Dyke continues down the north-western side of the hill as a hedge-line. Thereafter the bank reappears intermittently and forms the west side of a deep road or holloway that goes from Upperton Farm to Claypits near the hamlet of Yazor. The total length of this discontinuous line is nearly 3 miles.

ORDINANCES CONCERNING THE DUNSAETE *c*.926 AD

This is the agreement which the English Witan and the counsellors of the Welsh people have established among the Dunsaete:

1) That is: if anyone follow the track of stolen cattle from one river bank to the other, then he must hand over the tracking to the men of that land, or show by some mark that the track is rightfully pursued.

1.1) The man who owns that land must take up the search himself and within nine days he must compensate for the cattle, or deposit on that day a pledge worth half as much again as the cattle. Within nine days from then he must redeem that pledge with the right compensation.

1.2) If it is said that the track is being wrongfully followed then the man who owns the cattle must trace the track to the bank, and there six unselected man of good repute, himself being one, must swear that he claims with folk-right against that land because his cattle went across there.

2) Always, after nine days, right ought to be done by one to another between the (dwellers on) the two banks, both in clearing oneself of charges or of any other dispute between them.

2.1) There is no other way, between Welsh and English, of clearing oneself of a charge, except by ordeal, unless his opponent will allow it.

2.2) A pledge can be siezed from the other bank if justice cannot be obtained in any other way.

3) If a pledge from one man's cattle is siezed on another man's account, let the one on whose account it was taken get the pledge back, or let him satisfy from his own possessions the man whose cattle have been taken.

3.1) Then he will have to do right who would not do it before.

3.2) Twelve lawmen shall declare what is just to Welsh and English: six of them English, six Welsh.

3.3) Let them forfeit all they possess if they give a wrong judgement, unless they clear.themselves as knowing no better.

4) If an Englishman or a Welshman fail to clear himself of a charge of theft, let him pay the simple compensation laid upon him, and no other payment or penalty.

5) If a Welshman kills an Englishman he need not pay over to this side more than half the man-price; no more than an Englishman for a Welshman to the other side, whether he be thane-born or churl-born; half the wergild falls away.

6) Neither is a Welshman to cross over into English land, nor an Englishman to Welsh, without the appointed man from that land, who shall meet him at the bank and bring him back there again without any offence.

6.1) If the man of that land connive at any crime, he shall be liable to the penalty unless he can clear himself of having witnessed it.

6.2) So also, everyone who knows or is involved when a foreigner does harm to a native, must clear himself of being an accessory according to the value of the property: that must be done by a select oath, and the accuser must begin his suit with a preliminary oath.

6.3) If this defence fails he must pay a double fine and the penalty to the lord.

7) 30 shillings shall be paid for a horse, or exculpated at that rate; 20 shillings for a mare, or at that rate; and a 'winter-steal' (one-year-old stallion) the same; 'wilde weorf' (wild cattle?) 12 shillings, or at that rate; an ox with 30 pence; a sow with 24 pence; a pig with 8 pence; a man with a pound; a sheep with one shilling, a goat with 2 pence.

7.1) Other things not seen may be valued on oath and paid for accordingly.

8) If anything is siezed and the possessor wishes to vouch as warrantor someone over the river, let him give security or a pledge so that the case can be concluded.

8.1) Let anyone who claims it make an oath, himself one of six, that he claims it because it was stolen from him.

8.2) And let the one who claims the right to it give his oath alone, saying that he claims it by the warranty of the man who sold it to him.

8.3) If any beyond the river wants to make a claim, that must be by ordeal.

8.4) In the same way English shall do justice to Welsh.

9) Formerly the 'Wentsaete' (people of Gwent) belonged to the Dunsaete, but more correctly they belong to the West Saxons: and they have to send tribute and hostages there.

9.1) But the Dunsaete also need, if the King will grant it to them, that at least they should be allowed hostages for peace.

Nearly 10 km north-west of Yazor bank is another small, detached 500m long low bank and ditch now marking a field boundary at Holme's Marsh in Lyonshall parish, about 1½ miles east of Kington. About 230m (750ft) further north-west and on a direct line with the previous section is another 200m (650ft) length of bank. A third section, near Lynhales, lies almost 100m (325ft) north-west and though eroded by a stream is still large, standing about 5m high from ground level and with an associated ditch 2m (6½ft) deep and 8m (26ft) wide. This section, with a break where the bank has been washed away by a stream, is about 200m (650ft) long. This is the most massive section of bank and ditch of all the length of Dyke south of the 'main' section and rivals that 'main' section in scale.

On the southern bank of the river Arrow about 1km north-east of Kington and a similar distance north from the last Lyonshall section of Dyke is a small 60m (200ft) long, ½m (1ft 7ins) high length of bank which curves slightly towards the west. Directly across the river a hedgeline starts which, at its northern end just south of Berry's Hill in Titley parish, shows signs of a small bank on its western side. The hedge runs into the woods on Berry's Hill and a small bank can be seen along the western edge of this wood at the bottom of the hill, though it disappears towards its northern end.

From the northern end of Berry's Hill a small bank about 70m (240ft) long and 1m (3¾ft) high runs directly out from the northern end of the hill in a similar manner to Garnon's Hill's does to the south, as if the hill itself is being used as part of a boundary marker. This fragile looking bank is ditched to the west.

Fig. 9 (top) The Dyke at Holme's Marsh, Lyonshall
Fig. 10 (lower) The Dyke at Berry's Hill, Titley

Just over ½ mile west-north-west of this bank, in an area where the hills, instead of having a north-south orientation, start to run eastwards over north-west Herefordshire, the 'main' section of Offa's Dyke—the long run of bank and ditch—begins near the top of the ridge of Rushock Hill. It starts its life oriented east-west, ditched to the south and follows the line of the ridge. It then loops around the narrow crest of Herrock Hill, the next hill to the west, before darting down its steep northern side and continuing its long 69 mile journey north across the hills and valleys of the Welsh Marches. The Dyke builders evidently wanted to keep at least the first line of hills along this highland edge in their own territory; the task of building it in this complex and hilly landscape was much harder than if they had done so in the plains to the east.

The Dyke is half-erased from the first valley it crosses, the Hindwell, though a photograph from the 1930s shows it plainly.[49] It then climbs the hills on the north side of the valley, always looping around the west face of the hills. A very monumental, well preserved section of the Dyke descends the hill

174

Fig. 11 The Dyke on Herrock Hill

Fig. 12 Aerial view of Offa's Dyke as it heads north from Herrock Hill

above Yew Tree Farm about 2½ miles west of Presteigne. Here it is possible to gain an idea of the original scale of the Dyke. When it reaches the bottom of the Lugg Valley it disappears. In general it survives best in the highlands where pasture predominates and the plough has not been at work.

Once over the next set of hills it descends into the Teme Valley and Knighton or *Tref-y-Clawdd*—'the town on the Dyke'. A 50m (160ft) long section of Dyke survives at the north-western end of the town near the Offa's Dyke Heritage Centre, were the Dyke once doubled as part of the medieval town wall. After vanishing again by the river Teme, it reappears on the hilltop north of the town and runs continuously in a north-westerly direction all the way to the valley of the river Clun where it again disappears in the valley bottom. As it climbs the hills to the north-west of Clun in Shropshire it is at its best preserved, the bank being at almost its original full height.

It continues north over the highest hills on its route as it crosses the Kerry Ridgeway. From here it descends into the broader valleys of the countryside east of Montgomery, briefly halting at the river Camlad. North of this the Dyke heads more to the north-east, running parallel with the base of the Long Mountain and then turns due north until it reaches the banks of the river Severn at Buttington where it once again disappears, though this time for nearly 8 miles. In this gap the river obligingly flows in a north-easterly direction and it was assumed by Cyril Fox, who carried out extensive research into the Dyke in the 1920s and 30s, and others, that the river itself became the frontier, but recently a dig at Trederwen on the western bank of the river, nearly 5 miles north-west of

Welshpool, located a bank and ditch under the riverside silt on the alignment of Offa's Dyke. This area is badly affected by flooding. The bank may have been washed away and the ditch filled in by water-borne debris and silt. A geological study of the Severn valley a few miles upstream by Welshpool shows that it has changed its course many times in the past 300 years.[50] There is no reason to doubt that the same process has been going on for at least that long in the area of the dig at Trederwen, for there are flood barrier banks on both sides of the river of which this bank could have been an early remnant. The buried dyke could also have been part of a field boundary, for no certain proof was found for its date of origin or purpose.

The Dyke re-emerges for certain in Llandrinio parish on the north bank of the river where the river bends to the east, whence the Dyke continues much more due north than it did in the hillier country farther south. There is a gap of nearly 1¼ miles as it encounters the valley of the river Vyrnwy, reappearing just north of the town of Llanymynech only to be interrupted by quarrying at the southern end of Llanymynech Hill. It

Figs. 13 & 14 Offa's Dyke at Yew Tree Farm, west of Presteigne

resumes around the western side of the hill as the defensive bank of a hillfort similar to that at Symonds Yat. When it reaches Porth y Waen it is again wiped out by extensive quarrying on the southern side of Whitehaven Hill but reappears on its western side. North of here it is intermittent through Treflac and disappears through the town of Trefonen. It reappears to the north and winds around the hills west of Oswestry, characteristically keeping on the western side of the first row of hills in the Marches as it passes west of Selattyn. It carries on in a relatively straight course, interrupted only by small stream valleys until it stops at the edge of the valley of the river Ceiriog. Its line is straight but interrupted as it crosses the grounds of Chirk Castle, then carries on north until it reaches the valley of the river Dee and the town of Newbridge where it stops. North of Newbridge and west of the town of Ruabon the Dyke is badly affected by the quarrying and urban development of Rhosllanerchrugog, where it survives in some places only as a street name. Its course continues through Bersham and the blasted, mined-out countryside west of Wrexham. It becomes more intact as it leaves this area, interrupted again by roads and quarrying in the area of Brymbo. It is absent from the valley of the river Cegidog and the town of Ffrith. North of here it is partly blotted out by road development, but the last three-quarters of a mile can be seen as part of a road embankment as it enters the parish of Treuddyn where it ends in a marsh, 10 miles short of the sea.

There is another dyke, now known as Whitford Dyke, north of Treuddyn on the same alignment as Offa's Dyke and which aims towards Prestatyn on the north Wales coast. The 4½ mile long Whitford

Figs. 15 & 16 Offa's Dyke to the east of Montgomery, looking south (above) and north (above right)

Fig. 17 (lower right) The line of the Dyke is marked by the field boundary on the right as it joins the ramparts of Beacon Ring, east of Welshpool

Fig. 18 (below) To the west of Oswestry the Dyke runs along the far end of the field in the foreground. This photograph gives an impression of the commanding views that the Dyke often has to its west

Dyke, 2½ miles to the north-west of Offa's Dyke, is made up of three sections separated by gaps of 1 mile and 1⅓ miles. Cyril Fox surveyed and dug on this dyke in the 1920s thinking it was part of Offa's Dyke but members of the Offa's Dyke Project from Manchester excavated in several places between Treuddyn and Holywell and failed to find any trace of what should have been a connecting dyke if it was to join Offa's. Moreover, the excavation that Fox undertook on the Whitford Dyke revealed that it has ditches on both sides, indeed the bank being barely higher than the ground surface it is essentially defined by these ditches. When the Manchester group dug on it they gained the same results. Since Fox's days, further excavations have revealed that Offa's Dyke is only ditched on one side and the bank is on average nearly 2m (6½ft) higher than the original ground surface.[51] The Whitford Dyke is, therefore, now thought to be a local boundary marker and not part of Offa's Dyke.[52]

In the north there is also Wat's Dyke, which reaches the sea at Basingwerk on the Dee Estuary $7^{1/2}$ miles north of the end of Offa's Dyke. As mentioned earlier, there is now evidence that the building of Wat's Dyke preceded that of Offa's Dyke by several hundred years. King Offa died in 796 at Rhuddlan, $2^{1/2}$ miles west of his Dyke, the same year that a battle was fought here between the north Welsh and the Mercians. It is possible that Offa's death and the sudden outbreak of warfare delayed the completion of Offa's Dyke in the north.

Mistaking Wat's Dyke for Offa's Dyke is easily done, as the earthworks are of similar size and construction technique. The bank of Wat's Dyke is an average of 10m ($32^{1/2}$ft) wide and 4m (13ft) high from the bottom of the ditch. The ditch is always west-facing and is about 5m (16ft) wide and 2m ($6^{1/2}$ft) deep, making the whole structure about 15m (48ft 9ins) wide. It runs south from the site of Basingwerk monastery and ends about $2^{1/2}$ miles south of the Shropshire town of Maesbury, a distance of 40 miles. It lies east of Offa's Dyke at a distance which varies between $^{1/2}$ mile and $3^{3/4}$ miles, being built on ground which is more level than that on which Offa's Dyke is constructed, lying just east of the highlands for most of its length. Because of this location Wat's Dyke has been subject to more destruction by ploughing and development than Offa's Dyke. There are several large gaps in its length but several excavations on the course of the Dyke in these gaps suggest that it was originally built as a continuous structure over its entire length.[53]

Wat's, like Offa's Dyke is thought to be a defensive structure built along a territorial boundary. Place-name evidence indicates that Wat's Dyke was the boundary between Anglo-Saxon and Welsh territory for some time—many of the place-names between the dykes are Welsh or have Welsh elements. In addition, the boundary between Anglo-Saxon hidated land and Welsh land under Anglo-Norman control as set out in the Shropshire *Domesday Book* lay almost entirely along Wat's Dyke.[54] A boundary would have to be accepted over a long period for abrupt differences in land organization to be so well established. If the presence of Wat's Dyke had enabled an orderly and stable relationship to exist between the Welsh and the Anglo-Saxons then perhaps Offa was trying to both imitate it and strengthen the position of Mercia by building another dyke a short distance farther west. At some later stage, the boundary must have crept back to Wat's Dyke, for most of the place-names between the dykes are Welsh and some of them—such as Selattyn and Brogyntyn—are names with English origins modified by Welsh speakers who must have resettled the area.[55]

The Short Dykes

Apart from Offa's Dyke and Wat's Dyke there are a number of much shorter dykes in the Marches. Indeed there are probably more dykes in the Welsh border area than in any other part of the country. At least 23 short dykes survive, ranging in length from the less than 100m long Sheperds Well Dyke in Radnor Forest to the nearly 2 mile long Rowe Ditch just west of Pembridge in north-west Herefordshire. They range in height from the less than 1m ($3^{1/4}$ft) high Cefn-y-Crug Dyke, to the 2.5m (8ft) high Lower Short Ditch which crosses the Kerry Ridgeway on the Montgomeryshire-Shropshire border. Naturally over time all of these dykes have been shortened or fragmented by natural forces and man's activities. Most cross a road or ridgeway travelling along the top of a mountain ridge. Some control traffic passing over ridges between valleys.[56] Four are cross valley dykes, cutting across a valley which, as well as a road, also contained more valuable, accessible land. Short dykes often occur in pairs such as Cefn-y-Crug Dyke and Sheperds Well, or even systems, with several located near each other, either to control traffic or delimit territory. In highland areas they may have been used to emphasize a boundary crossing which may be obscured by bad weather such as fog.

The short dykes are hard to date for very little archaeological work has been done on them. Fox thought that they were precursers of Offa's Dyke, built by the early Mercians setting out territorial claims.[57] But it is now accepted that dykes are always ditched toward the enemy's side, and the short dykes show a variety of ditching: some are ditched to the west, at least one—Cefn-y-Crug—is ditched to the east and Birtley Dyke, a cross valley dyke in northern Herefordshire, is oriented east to west and is ditched to the south. It is difficult to tell who was building these dykes against whom and when—some, such as the Whitford Dyke, are even ditched on both sides. These are perhaps more passive, serving as boundary banks. The highland ridgeways have been used from Neolithic times (3000-2000BC) through to the time of the cattle drovers in the 19th century. Dykes were used as ranch boundaries in the Iron Age (700BC-48AD), whilst many were built as territorial boundary markers in early post-Roman times, a practice that continued into the medieval era. Circular bank and ditched enclosures were known to surround monastic and park land. One of the short dykes, Ditch Bank, a cross valley ditch just west of New Radnor could even be a siege fortification dating from the late 12th century used in a battle near New Radnor Castle.[58]

The only short dyke which is mentioned in pre-Norman times is the longest—the Rowe Ditch near Pembridge. This dyke is just under 2 miles long and runs north from gentle slopes south-west of Pembridge to the southern edge of Shobdon Hill on the northern side of the valley of the river Arrow. The northernmost 100m (325ft) or so of this dyke has been ploughed out, but is known to have existed as a result of excavation.[59] The dyke sits just west of the crossing of two possible Roman roads whose tracks would still have been in use in Anglo-Saxon times. The eastern boundary of Staunton-on-Arrow parish follows these tracks and not the Rowe Ditch, indicating that the dyke was built some time between the establishment of Staunton as a manor in the post-Roman period and the dyke's first mention in a perambulation or description of the boundaries of the manor in 958. This post-Roman date was supported by an excavation which found Roman remains in and underneath the bank.[60]

The short dykes, which tend to be clustered around the mid-Wales border highlands all became associated with the Mercian period because of their proximity to and resemblance with Offa's Dyke, but there is no evidence to support any connection between them. Yet, the probable presence of at least some of these short dykes by the 8th century does mean that the people of the Marches were familiar with the building and function of these structures. The impression given is that the dykes indicate boundaries between neighbours in a complex landscape, and also the attempt by certain local groups of people to control access to long distance overland routes such as the Kerry Ridgeway.

Offa's Dyke: Its Purpose

Absolute belief in Asser's 'from sea to sea' statement hindered early studies of the Dyke as scholars tried to find connections between all the sections of earthwork scattered along the frontier. Even when all the standing banks and ditches were mapped, more questions were raised than could be answered.

The first man to carry out a systematic and complete survey of all the then known dykes in the Welsh Marches was Sir Cyril Fox. It took him over ten years, carrying out field work in the summer months during the 1920s and 30s, finally publishing his great work, *Offa's Dyke,* in 1955. His study, though very consistent and carefully carried out, is dogged by the assumption of sea to sea completeness. He believed that the Dyke was an agreed boundary between the English and Welsh. His explanation for the short dykes in north-west Herefordshire and the absence of any earthwork in the south of the county is that a great damp oak wood growing on the old red sandstone of the area rendered the building of a dyke difficult and unnecessary since the forest would be impenetrable to invaders. He believed that only clearings were dyked, and hence the short isolated sections of Dyke north of the river Wye. Another of his ideas which is now considered erroneous is that when the Dyke deviates from its straight course and starts curving and weaving slightly, it was going around trees in forested areas which have since been cleared.[61] It is now thought that any forest obstruction would have been eliminated by fire.

Fox recounts four excavations in his book on Offa's Dyke. One was at Brynbella on the northernmost Whitford section of dyke, now known not to be part of Offa's Dyke. This dig revealed ditches on both sides of the rather low bank, the significance of which he failed to grasp, but it was his first excavation and he had nothing with which to compare it. He did, however, comment that the Dyke in Flintshire had 'a weak boundary bank character and was remarkably incomplete',[62] as though the builders had lost heart in their job just before finishing it.

Fox carried out another excavation at Ffrith in southern Flintshire. Here, on the longest section of the main Dyke, he found a single west-facing ditch, only much later to be recognized as the Dyke's distinctive hallmark. The Dyke was built on top of an area of Roman settlement and Fox was able to prove that as Roman pottery and artefacts were found in the bank, it could only be a post-Roman structure. He conducted a third excavation at Bridge Sollars, at the southern end of one of the short sections of Dyke in Herefordshire, in an attempt to find the Roman road that theoretically crossed the Dyke at this point. In this he was unsuccessful. His fourth dig was on the ditch of the fort-like enclosure at Tallard's Marsh on the detached section of Dyke at Sedbury near Chepstow. The results of this trench were inconclusive.

Despite what now seem like obvious weaknesses in Fox's ideas as to the purpose and course of the Dyke, his survey is an invaluable record and an accurate map of the extent and state of all the border earthworks in the early 20th century. Because of his thoroughness and consistency, his conclusions on the Dyke went unchallenged for 20 years. Then, in the 1960s and 70s Frank Noble, a Knighton-based scholar, conducted his own study of the Dyke which led him to question some of Fox's conclusions and the traditional belief in Asser's statement. He disagreed with the idea that the dense forest in southern Herefordshire rendered a Dyke unnecessary or impossible. Noble was the first to put forward the theory that the river Wye itself was the boundary for the stretch of the border between Bridge Sollars and English Bicknor because of the special status of the people of Archenfield. He unearthed the Ordinances of the Dunsaete (see p.173) in order to prove his point. He also argued, less convincingly, that the Dyke was a line of refuge behind which Saxon settlers could escape during times of need, the real frontier being two or three miles beyond Offa's Dyke. This, he argued, explained the clusters of settlements with old English names west of the Dyke and that it splits some parishes. Unfortunately this theory relies on the existence of a number of gates in the Dyke contemporary with its building, but no such gates have been found. Sadly, Frank Noble's health failed and he died before he could finish writing up his survey; his *Offa's Dyke Reviewed* was published posthumously.

Noble's work has been continued by the Offa's Dyke Project carried out by the University of Manchester Extra-Mural Archaeological Society led by David Hill and Margaret Worthington. This group has pursued the study of Offa's Dyke, Wat's Dyke and many other earthworks in the Marches region using modern archaeological techniques such as geophysical survey and aerial photography as well as the more traditional methods of field survey and excavation. They have conducted more than 178 digs to date on the various dykes,[63] and have made several important discoveries. The excavations confirm that both Offa's and Wat's dykes always have a west-facing ditch, and that the long portions of both dykes were originally continuous throughout their course—wherever their banks are now absent, excavation reveals their ditches, and so disproves Noble's theory of gates.[64] The nearly 8 mile gap along the Severn near Welshpool has never been excavated by this group, but a private archaeological contractor digging in this area has found evidence of a ditch by the river but it is not certain if this is part of Offa's Dyke as mentioned on pp.175-6. Wat's Dyke is also proven to be $2^{1}/_{2}$ miles longer in the south than it appears to be on the surface. Excavation has also revealed some of the methods used to plan the Dyke such as a small marking out trench which is occasionally found under the bank.

The Offa's Dyke Project has concluded that the reason why the long continuous 'main' section of Offa's Dyke starts and ends where it does with no strong landmark such as a river or sea coast associated with it, is because the Dyke separates the kingdoms of Mercia and Powys, not England and Wales, whose national identities did not exist in Offa's time. They believe that the events which caused Offa to resort to this extreme measure of demarcation were recorded on the Pillar of Eliseg in the Vale of Crucis near Llangollen. The original inscription on the Pillar has been worn away and is illegible but it was still mostly legible when it was recorded in 1696 by Edward Lhuyd. It says, (translated from its Latin) 'Concenn being great-grandson of Eliseg erected this stone to his great-grandfather Eliseg. It was Eliseg who annexed [the inheritance of Powys] throughout nine [years?] from the power of the English, which he made into a sword-land by fire, [or partly by the sword and by fire]'.[65]

Eliseg, king of Powys, may have been able to take advantage of the political chaos which probably followed the murder of Aethelbald in Mercia in 757 (see pp.132-134), by recovering lost territory in the mid and north Marches. This would have meant that the early years of Offa's reign were taken up with warfare against Powys. Once peace had been established and Mercia had recovered her lost territory, the building of the Dyke may have been a measure taken to make the fluid boundary of the Marches more definite. This, however, does not explain the short sections of Offa's Dyke on the north Herefordshire plain or the sections in the lower Wye valley, nor does it take into consideration the often fragmented nature of the early Welsh kingdoms.

The Dyke is ideally situated on high ground overlooking the west towards Wales, but with higher ground behind it on the English side, presumably for those wishing to see over the Dyke. In some places the Dyke deviates from a straight path and turns and winds across the ground. Whilst Fox took this as evidence that the Dyke was avoiding trees in woodland which has since been cut down, researchers from the Offa's Dyke Project believe the builders were using small elevations in the landscape to help strengthen the Dyke.[66]

Sources of Inspiration for Offa's Dyke

Earthwork dykes had been used in Europe since prehistory, becoming a common type of boundary marker in the post-Roman period. In Anglo-Saxon charters of Worcestershire they are frequently mentioned in boundary perambulations of the 8th, 9th, and 10th centuries, such dykes could be just 1m wide and deep. Sometimes even the agger or raised paved portion at the centre of an old Roman road was sufficiently high and prominent in the landscape to be called a dyke.[67] Some of these dykes are still visible in the landscape today as the bottoms of hedgebanks. Larger boundary dykes, though unrecorded historically, are often assumed to be the frontiers of more important states or kingdoms or to mark the territorial edge of different ethnic or national groups. Wat's Dyke could be such an example.

Wan's Dyke in Wiltshire, which may be two separate dykes—an eastern and a western section, was also studied by Sir Cyril Fox. If they are part of one system then Wan's Dyke is the second longest linear earthwork in Britain after Offa's Dyke, its western section being 12 miles (19.4km) long and its eastern section 10 miles (16.2km) long, with a gap of 16 miles (26km) between them. The eastern section was possibly built by the Saxons of Wessex as a boundary between them and the Saxons of the Thames valley.[68]

In the north of England a concentration of boundary earthworks near the West Yorkshire town of Aberford east of Leeds on the Great North road, an old Roman road, are remnants of old kingdom boundaries, physical reminders of the changing fortunes of early post-Roman politics. The north-facing South Dyke could be a boundary of the kingdom of Elmet. The Reedgate Dyke, an east-facing earthwork built across the Roman road west of nearby Tadcaster may also be part of Elmet's boundary.[69] The south-facing 1½ mile long combined earthworks of the Ridge and Becca Banks to the west of the Great North road, were probably built by the Northumbrians against Mercia.

Farther south near Sheffield, the Roman Ridge Dykes are thought to be more boundary works built by Northumbria against Mercia. These defences are over 6¼ miles long with a visible ditch up to 10m (32½ft) wide.[70] An earthwork with probably a related purpose is the Bar Dyke on Broomhead Moor. Towards the west, in the suburbs of Manchester is the Nico Ditch, a 5 mile-long ditch which curves around the south-eastern side of the city. It crosses the Roman road between the Roman forts of Manchester and Melandra nearly 12½ miles to the east. Though of unknown date, as are all of these northern earthworks, its position makes it likely that it is another Northumbrian boundary against Mercia.

Wat's Dyke apart, there is nothing in Britain to compare with Offa's Dyke at the time of its construction, though the earlier Hadrian's Wall and its mysterious Vallum exceeded it in scale. To look for a comparable system of long distance boundary works it is necessary to look to the Continent, where the most extensive system of long distance linear boundaries in Europe are the *fossa* or *limes*, from which derives the word 'limit'. These mark the boundaries of the Roman empire. It is thought that the earliest boundaries were formed in Germany in the early 2nd century during the reign of Hadrian, who's unnamed biographer writes: 'at this time and on frequent other occasions in many places where the barbarians were divided off not by rivers but by limites, he separated them from us with large stakes sunk deep into the ground and fastened together in the manner of a palisade'.[71] It was Hadrian's policy, and that of all the emperors who came after him, to consolidate an empire which had grown to an almost unmanageable size, and secure her borders with some manner of fortifications and guards.[72]

The *limes* started as pathways or roads between wooden watchtowers situated regularly along the way. These were lined up with each other so that signal lights could be seen between them and messages sent. Later, a wooden palisade with a large v-shaped ditch running in front of it was built to protect the watchtowers and the road. In northern Germany the final phase of the *limes* consisted of a palisade ditch and raised bank or earthwork. The wooden towers were re-built in stone. In southern Germany the frontier consisted of a stone-built 3m (9¾ft) high wall with the watchtowers incorporated into it. Four or five men manned each tower,[73] and roads connected with forts situated near the border. Where the border followed a river such as the Rhine, the Danube, or the Main no *limes* were built (a pointer to the Wye's use).[74]

In the dry, open landscapes of the borders on the east and south of the empire, a landscape populated mainly by a relatively small number of nomads and their flocks, a more open border was thought sufficient. In North Africa, a discontinuous wall and ditch frontier was created, with forts very widely spaced, sometimes up to 66 miles apart.

The area where the Roman *limes* most resemble the Anglo-Saxon earthworks of later centuries is in the north-eastern sector of the frontier, which were built during the later empire after the province of Dacia, approximately what is now Romania, was abandoned, an area that was to come under tremendous pressure during the era of barbarian invasions in the 4th and 5th centuries. The Devil's Dykes are a series of discontinuous multiple rows of dykes that run eastwards across the Hungarian plain for about 112 miles. They then bend toward the south stopping near the Danube east of present-day Belgrade, making a further 200 miles of multiple dykes sometimes four rows deep. Placed end to end in a single row, this mass of bank and ditch would be 2,310 miles long, dwarfing all the other linear earthwork systems in Europe put together! An excavation of one of the dykes revealed a composite of five ditches and intervening banks, each ditch averaging 5.5m (nearly 18ft) wide and 2m (6½ft) deep; combined they have an overall width of over 50 metres. It is thought that this system was built to help protect the Sarmatians, a group loyal to Rome, from the invading Goths.[77]

Another system of 4th century or late empire fortification can be found in the eastern Alps between Italy and what is now Slovenia. These are the *claustra*, or barricades, which consist of a small fort with walls reaching right across small valleys or passes in the eastern or Julian Alps, so blocking them. They are thought to be an attempt to prevent a barbarian invasion of Italy from the north-east after the German *limes* had been breached by repeated attacks. The *claustra* are short, usually less than 1¼ miles in length although one is nearly 6 miles long. Thirteen lengths of wall have been identified positively and 11 more sites are possible, and cover an area of land 46 by 23 miles. Despite being built of stone, they resemble the cross valley short dykes of the mid-Wales Marches.[78]

By their extensive use of frontier earthworks and walls, the Romans were the greatest employers of long distance boundary works ever in Europe. Although the *limes* could not stand up to a concentrated attack by an enemy, their presence could be detected and reported quickly and acted on by the system of

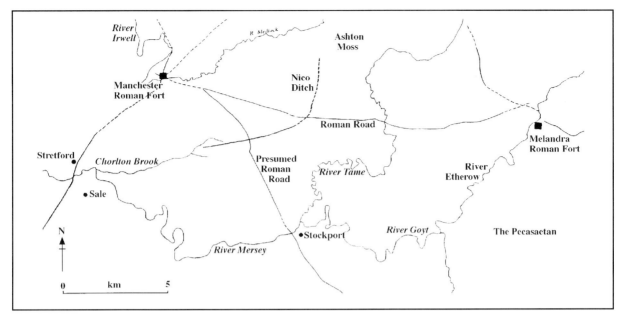

*Fig. 19 Map showing the location of the Nico Ditch,
possibly a Northumbrian delineation of the border with Mercia*

surveillance and signal towers. The *limes* were effective for a time at stopping incursions by migrating or fleeing groups of barbarians during the beginning of the age of migration toward the end of the Roman period. This idea of marking one's territory with earthworks was carried on by those who came after the Romans. Offa's Dyke, perhaps based on the earlier built Wat's Dyke, was the longest and perhaps the last of these to be built in Europe.

The Building of Offa's Dyke

The prototype for such a dyke would have therefore been known to Offa from the nearby Wat's Dyke, from dykes in his northern borders with Northumbria and possibly through information received from the court of Charlemagne. Indeed, Charlemagne may have played an indirect role in instigating the Dyke. One of Charlemagne's pet projects which, for technical reasons, was never completed was a canal link between the Rhine and the Danube in the highlands of southern Germany.[79] When Offa's and Charlemagne's relations soured in the aftermath of Offa's suggestion that his son married Charlemagne's daughter (see p.158), one could speculate that, in fury, Offa had the Dyke built to prove that he could marshall his people and complete a huge civil construction project while his erstwhile friend, supposedly the greatest king in Europe, could not.

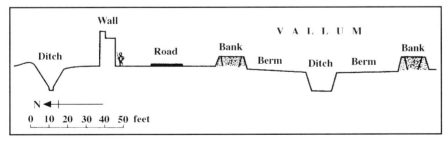

Fig. 20 In Britain Hadrian's Wall and the Vallum were conceived and built as a single project probably by Hadrian himself who visited the Northumbrian frontier in A.D.122.[75] The Vallum is a very large earthwork which follows the southern side of Hadrian's Wall and was built at the same time. Its function is unknown as it does not appear to support the Wall in any practical way[76]

The reason behind the 'main' section of Dyke would seem clear—that it was built against the Welsh kingdom of Powys. The Offa's Dyke Project argues for this theory on the inscription written on the Pillar of Eliseg in the Vale of Crucis noted earlier. Concenn, who died in 854, was king of Powys. He set up the Pillar to commemorate his great-grandfather Eliseg, whom it is calculated, was king of Powys between 765 and 773, during the early years of Offa's reign. It has been argued in chapter 7 that Offa initially had to consolidate his kingdom after the murder of Aethelbald and the short reign of Beornred. It is quite possible that during this period the Welsh of Powys were able to re-establish their territory in the north-eastern Marches which they had previously lost to the Anglo-Saxons. These lands probably included the Vale of Llangollen, Vale Crucis, parts of the Vale of Powys and the area around Montgomery—good flat fertile areas which were no doubt desired by both sides. According to this theory Offa's Dyke was a way of ensuring peace on Mercia's border with Powys, and no other Welsh kingdoms would have been involved.[80] Mercia would have had to recapture all her lost territory and then impose the Dyke on Powys during a period of relative calm between the two kingdoms when Powys must have been in a weakened position. On this basis the Dyke is a military boundary constructed to give all the advantage to the English, a frontier imposed on the Welsh, not built with their necessary agreement as advocated by Fox.[81]

The intermittent and variable nature of Offa's Dyke has led to the suggestion that it was built piece-meal over a number of years, even that it is a collection of smaller dykes built by local groups of people over some length of time to delineate the border. Even considering the 'main' Dyke there are many gaps and variations in the structure. South of Llanfair Hill in south-western Shropshire the Dyke has a weak and variable quality,[82] though this variation could be caused by differences in the geology of the landscape in which the Dyke is built. Sandy or gravelly ground does not hold its shape very well over time and this type of soil occurs in patches in the mountains in the southern part of the 'main' Dyke.[83]

The differences within the main Dyke could also be caused by differences in construction technique. In some parts of the southernmost section it appears to also be ditched on the eastern side but, as mentioned previously, this appearance may be caused by turves having been stripped from the ground to the rear of the Dyke either to face the Dyke or provide stability within its core. One of the celebrated contrasts in building techniques on adjacent sections occurs on Rushock Hill in Herefordshire, where two sections of Dyke, one with a western ditch and one with a so-called eastern ditch meet. It looks like the meeting of two different building gangs. There is also a place at Hergan, west of Clun in Shropshire, where two sections of the Dyke are connected by a weak bank which seems to be the miscalculated meeting of two construction gangs.[84]

The Dyke is absent from almost all the bottoms of narrow valleys in the highlands, both in the mountain zone south of Montgomery and in the highlands of the north above the Severn. The Dyke is also either absent or lies buried under silt for nearly 8 miles as its route runs along the river Severn. But the fact that all of these sections align to one another and that the Dyke keeps its view over the west as much as is possible, is more than different, disparate groups of builders could be capable of over such a long distance. Nor is it likely that the Dyke builders incorporated already existing earthworks. If they did, then why was Wat's Dyke by-passed and another Dyke built at great effort and expense only $1/2$ mile to $3^3/4$ miles to the west? Importantly, on excavation, the dimensions of the bank and ditch and the crucial west-facing ditch all point to a co-ordinated effort managed by a single authority.[85] Only a strongly led organization could overcome the difficulties of supervising and supporting groups of builders in remote and sometimes mountainous terrain. The only strong single power in the region and the only one to hold political sway over the whole of the eastern side of the Marches in the 8th century was Mercia. The work may have been started by Aethelbald and finished by Offa but, as Asser suggests by referring to Offa as a 'vigorous king', it has his will in its name.

There are two accepted alternatives as to how the Dyke was built, either the builders came from the local communities through which the Dyke passed, organized by local thegns under orders from the Mercian king, or else crews of people were called up from throughout the kingdom to help build a certain length of Dyke or to support those who were with supplies of food and other necessities.[86] Fox inclines toward the first view; David Hill from the Offa's Dyke Project favours the latter.

In either case the method of building the 'main' Dyke was the same. The general course of the Dyke was planned by one master engineer, perhaps Offa himself.[87] The long distance route the Dyke was to take was set out perhaps using signals or beacons. On the ground the exact course the Dyke was to take was marked out by methods already described—by a marking-out trench, stakes or stones. Any woodland in the path of the Dyke was probably cleared by fire. There is archaeological evidence for all of these building processes when Offa's and Wat's dykes have been excavated.[88]

The main question is how the gangs of builders were organized. Fox's reason for thinking that the builders came from manors on the route of the Dyke was its variable nature, especially at its southern end. In his view this reflected the different resources of the locality and how able and willing the locals who made up the gangs were to work, for he believed that the income the state normally collected as taxes form these border manors was instead being paid by supplying labour for the Dyke. Fox also held the almost contradictory view that large parts of the border were sparsely populated.[89]

North of Llanfair Hill in southern Shropshire the character of the Dyke becomes much more regular, larger and straighter, with less variation in its scale. Perhaps the builders became more experienced or those that were supervising them became better at utilizing the labourers' skills. If the construction of the Dyke was from south to north, perhaps a regular, experienced group of workers was gradually assembled as the project passed through each area so that the character of the Dyke improved as it went farther north.

An idea suggested by the Offa's Dyke Project is that the method of organizing labour to build the Dyke was based on people throughout Mercia contributing to the construction of the earthwork, either through direct labour or else supporting them by making tools or providing food, the amount depending upon the hidage assessed to tax. On this basis, when Offa ordered his Dyke to be built, in lieu of tax a certain number of men from a hide unit with tools and food under the command of their ealdormen would assemble to build a section of the Dyke. This method of generating labour for large projects was used by the Carolingian empire in northern France, indeed it was used in general in northern Europe.[90]

Even if they provided for themselves, the logistics of moving such a large number of people into and out of a remote area like the Welsh Marches should have left some evidence such as camps for the workers, garrisons, support roads, or beacons. No evidence of these support structures has ever been found,[91] though admittedly the remains they would have left, since they were temporary, would be slight.

No one knows how long the Dyke took to build, but it had to be while Mercia was at peace with the Welsh; the last 12 years of Offa's reign were peaceful.

There is no direct evidence for the Dyke having been guarded, unlike Hadrian's Wall, indeed there is no evidence of a palisade or contemporary wall on top of the bank. It was possible for men to cross the Dyke but it was impossible for them to have done so unknowingly. Despite the lack of evidence for a palisade it was designed to withstand attack from the west and planned to keep visual control over the west as much as possible.

The Dyke would have restricted the ability of Welsh raiders from attacking Mercian frontier settlements, but it would have also controlled legitimate traffic and trade across the border. Unfortunately, it is not known how this worked.[92] The only places along the Dyke which are open are the river valleys: the Hindwell, the Lugg, the Teme, the Clun, the Camlad, the Severn, the Vyrnwy, the Tanat, the Ceiriog, and the Dee. As nearly every valley on the eastern edge of Wales now contains a town, add to that the action of flooding, it would be very difficult to tell whether the Dyke had ever existed in these valleys. Portions of the

Dyke do exist in the Hindwell and in the Teme valley at Knighton, and archaeological excavation has shown that the Dyke came quite close to the water's edge in the valley of the Camlad near Montgomery, but the Dyke could never have cut off these valleys completely, especially when the water level was low.[93]

There is, however, negative evidence that Offa's Dyke operated as a trade barrier—no Mercian coinage has been found west of the Dyke. There is also an intriguing idea that the Dyke could have been built as an economic barrier to keep Welsh wool out and maintain a Mercian a monopoly on the trade with the Continent,[94] but the theory has its problems. The continuous length of 'main' Dyke only runs alongside the north central part of Wales. Wool was and still is produced in most of the rest of Wales as well indeed in most of Britain. Why would only one part of Wales have been singled out by this barrier? In any event, the Welsh themselves lived in small scattered self-sufficient communities where there is little evidence of trade with the outside world. There were no markets or even much local exchange in the countryside of Wales at this period.[95] Their wool production could not have been a major threat. Indeed wool from highland breeds of sheep is generally of a lower quality than from those raised in the lowlands.

However, the 'main' Dyke does block routes out of Wales, especially at its southern end. The Dyke starts on Rushock Hill where the high land that generally runs north to south along the Welsh border breaks this pattern and reaches eastwards across northern Herefordshire and southern Shropshire. This part of the border must have been the most difficult but equally the most necessary to police, as many of the valleys direct traffic from Wales into the midlands. This is the area where the short dykes proliferate and where the unity of one large boundary dyke makes the most sense. The continuation of the Dyke north of the Severn especially where a boundary earthwork, Wat's Dyke, already existed, could have been a demonstration of Mercian leadership, with Offa imposing his will on people living on both sides of the border and perhaps further cementing his control of the newly re-conquered valuable lowlands of the northern Marches.

Assuming that all the parishes crossed by the Dyke were established by the 8th century, then the fact that the Dyke divides these parishes can be taken to mean that its course was imposed—Fox found that only 18.6% of the length of Offa's Dyke coincided with parish boundaries. On Wat's Dyke it is slightly higher at 24.4%. Those that hold this view point to the fact that parish boundaries often follow ancient features in the landscape such as Roman roads, and that some may even shadow ancient prehistoric territorial divisions. Thus, the argument goes, when parish boundaries ignore features in the landscape, the features must be later impositions.[96] If this is the case with Offa's and Wat's dykes, then it raises questions as to how the inhabitants of these divided parishes coped. Was all the land to the west of the Dyke relinquished to the Welsh? Were those who lost land on the other side compensated? In this view the layout of the Dyke was clearly strategic and took no account of communities in the Dyke's path.

But there is another school of thought that argues that parishes are a later invention, that they were being developed as local ecclesiastical units of administration throughout the early medieval period, reaching their final form only towards the end of the Saxon era. Offa's Dyke, as shall be shown later on, probably lost its political significance within a century of its construction as the balance of power along the border and in Mercia shifted. In this event, the parishes formed around it and appear to be divided by it.

Certainly one consequence of the building of the Dyke was the cutting off of whole English speaking communities on its western side. There are two main areas where this occurs, one is in the area of Welshpool, the other in the three fertile valleys of the Hindwell west of Kington, the Lugg west of Presteigne and the Teme west of Knighton. Place-name evidence indicates that the names of English settlements here, especially the ones in the Hindwell valley are of very early Saxon settlements from before the time of Offa. These places, such as Evenjobb, Cascob, Waterdine, and Buttington have always kept their English spellings and presumably their English speaking inhabitants.[97]

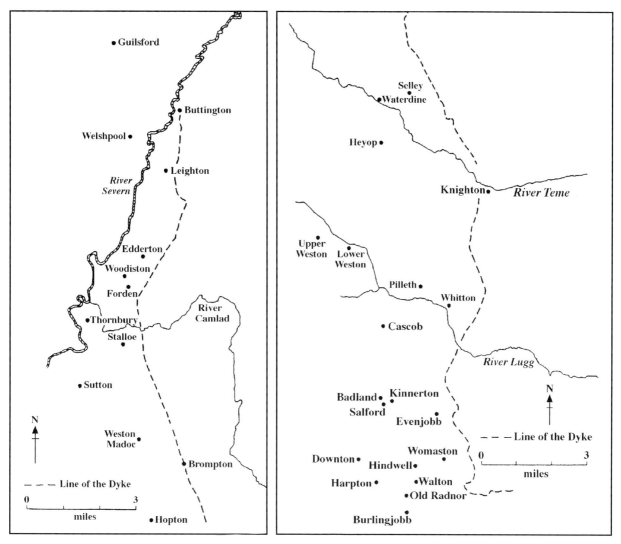

Figs. 21 & 22 Areas of English settlement left to the west of Offa's Dyke include a string of villages near Welshpool (left) and Kington (right)

It was clearly more important for the Dyke to be elevated, looking over the Welsh land to the west than it was to take in all the English settlements. The Welsh still held the western half of the Hindwell valley and there was no way of building the Dyke right across the valley without losing sight of their wider territory. To take in the English settlements in the upper Lugg and Teme valleys would have required a long deviation of the Dyke westwards, perhaps over high ground that was not so securely held. The English settlements near Welshpool are harder to rationalize. Extending the border to the Severn farther south would have taken in most of them, but again perhaps it was deemed more important to over-look the valley from the higher ground of the Long Mynd rather than protect it behind the Dyke. If the Dyke was built by those resident on the border, one wonders if the people of the English communities cut off on the western side were also made to participate. But the survival of the ethnic identity of these villages proves that the Dyke was not the absolute ethnic boundary that early scholars believed. If these communities survived being divided by Offa's Dyke then perhaps its impact on the landscape was not as great as was once thought.

187

There is another small area of English village names some distance on the Welsh side of the border, south of the main section of Offa's Dyke where the Wye flows out of the Welsh hills at Hay-on-Wye. There are also a few settlements with English names such as Gladestry in the hills north of the valley. How these English settlements came to be tolerated so far inside Welsh territory is not known, but their neighbours to the east in what is now southern Herefordshire were the Welsh of Archenfield.

If the intention was for the Dyke to perform as a Roman *lime*, or give warning of Welsh attacks, it would need to have been guarded or patrolled. Guards or patrols would require housing in forts at regular intervals along its length, but no direct evidence for such structures has ever been found on either side of the frontier. The only structure that Fox recognized as a possible fort was the enclosure on the cliff above the Wye at its southern extreme. This structure was first investigated by Fox and then by the Offa's Dyke Project. The results were inconclusive, and it is far from certain that it is a fort. A late addition to any border defences was the Mercian *burh* at Rhuddlan, but this lay north of the end of the Dyke. In 1983 an excavation at Cwrt Llechrydd, a large rectangular moated site in central Wales near Builth Wells, led to the idea of a line of forts in the vicinity of the Dyke to house men charged with guarding Offa's Dyke. Charcoal samples taken from beneath Cwrt Llechrydd's fortifications gave a carbon 14 date between the 8th and 11th centuries with the most likely period of deposition being the 9th or 10th centuries, in the period following the construction of the Dyke. Cwrt Llechrydd is in the southernmost Powys cantref or district of Elfael, and being over 10 miles west of Offa's Dyke would have been firmly in Welsh territory. Five other sites have been identified as forts because of their resemblance to Cwrt Llechryd: Mathrafal and Plas-yn-Dinas, also on the Welsh side, and Old Mills, Nantcribba Gaer and Buttington on the English side. All of these defended sites, which have not been excavated, are rectangular or sub-rectangular with either raised earthworks or wet defences, with the exception of Nantcribba Gaer whose banks and ditches are more circular. This fort stands only 110m (350ft) east of Offa's Dyke. Its proximity to the boundary makes its association with it more obvious, though without excavation or historical references to indicate its date of construction, such association is only conjectural. Old Mills and Buttington lie close to the Severn just to the north of Welshpool in the area where, if there is a Dyke, it is not visible above ground. New Radnor could also be included in this group of possible Dark Age English forts because of its good defensive position at the western end of a valley known to be under Mercian occupation west of the Dyke.[98] The pre-Norman fortifications which may have stood there are now obscured by later medieval development.

Until these sites are tested archaeologically this theory will remain unproven, but several problems do arise when considering it. All the fort sites on the Welsh side are some distance from the Dyke, with Cwrt Llechryd being the farthest. They are certainly not close enough to be guarding the Dyke. Perhaps it was the Welsh who were seeking protection from invading Mercians. If, however, these forts were built as part of some plan to protect the Dyke they seem to be concentrated at its middle and southern end and not spaced evenly along its whole length. It is possible that they may have been built in the style of fortified Mercians *burhs* to guard river crossing sites (all but two—Nancribba Gaer and New Radnor—are built near rivers) and to have used the water for their moats. Two forts—Cwrt Llechryd and Buttington—are possible sites of battles after the time of Offa: a Llechryd is mentioned in the *Brut y Tywysogion* as the location of a battle between Rhys ap Tewdr and the sons of Bleddyn ap Cynan of Powys in 1088. At Buttington the now invisible enclosure around the village could be attributed to the report in the *Anglo-Saxon Chronicle* which describes a battle in 893 when a group of Danes were besieged in a stronghold by armies of Welsh and Saxons in an alliance under King Alfred.[99] In 1838, 400 skulls were found in the churchyard within the enclosure, a chilling piece of evidence to support this story.

Whose Dykes are the Southern Sections?

Whilst a good case can be made that the 'main' section deserves the name Offa's Dyke, both in its construction and purpose, that can not necessarily be said for the southern sections. Of all the earthworks in the Welsh Marches, the most difficult to rationalize are the dykes in the lower Wye Valley. A 50m (162ft) broad river in a valley with very steep, almost sheer sides rising over 210m (700ft) in some places would be, one would think, both an obvious enough and a strong enough natural boundary without the addition of a dyke on their crest. The long gaps between the sections of Dyke in this area has been partly blamed on later limestone quarrying but this cannot explain all the gaps. A number of possible original access points through the Dyke have been recognized through place-name evidence and identifying the courses of known early routes. Where the Dyke coincides with earthworks of earlier Iron Age hill forts, these also may have been access points through the Dyke.[100] Chepstow may have been the site of a Mercian bridgehead on the western side of the Wye obviating the need for a dyke on the opposite river bank.[101]

Fox's explanation for the section of dyke in the lower Wye valley is based on the Tidenham Charter of the 10th century. Tidenham was a large royal manor located between the mouths of the Wye and Severn. The charter states that one hide of land is above (or outside) the Dyke, and that some of this land is let out to *scipwealan*—'Welsh sailors'. Although this place is not named, it is assumed to be the Beachley Peninsula which is cut off from the rest of the eastern bank of the Wye by the section of 'Offa's Dyke' at Sedbury. Fox describes this as a 'little Welsh seaport' which controlled the ferry crossing over the Severn estuary to Aust, and also participated in the river traffic on the lower Wye which was involved in the timber trade. Fox suggests that if this was occurring in the 10th century then it probably was in the 8th century as well. Since the Welsh were navigating the river they would require the right to land on both banks, and since the lower Wye is tidal, they would want the right to land where the highest tide reaches, which is at Redbrook, nearly 10 miles north of the river's mouth and the place where the dykes in the lower Wye valley terminate.[102] This explanation for 'dyking' the course of the river sounds plausible but why would a king with as uncompromising a reputation as Offa's give any concessions to the Welsh? Another explanation for the Dyke in such a monumental position on top of the cliffs of the valley is that Mercia was simply showing off its power to the Welsh on the other side.

To try and understand the purpose of these dykes it might help to look at some local geographical and historical factors. Today the border between England and Wales actually crosses the river at Redbrook and cuts to the north-east, re-joining the river bank just below Symonds Yat, making, for a short distance, both banks of the river Welsh territory. Perhaps the border did this in the 8th century as well. On the lower stretches 'Offa's Dyke' is at its most massive on the cliff above Tintern Abbey which is on the opposite shore of the river. Tintern was a stronghold of the kings of Gwent, and a battle is said to have been fought here in 597 in which the invading Saxons were defeated.[103]

If the Dyke's origin and purpose is obscure, it certainly marked off some territory as 'English'. The dyke system not only defines its western boundary, but is to the west of the ports of Chester and Gloucester which lie close to, respectively, the northern and southern ends of this boundary. To the largely land-locked kingdom of Mercia, control of these ports from neighbouring encroachment in an era just before the threat to its few ports came from the sea itself, must have been an important consideration.

Alternatively the dykes may have been built for economic reasons. As stated before, some of the dykes loop round the sides of the cliff tops and along the valley tops above streams feeding into the Wye, suggesting that the dykes are meant to restrict access to the tops of the hills and not to the whole eastern side of the river. Though wide, the river Wye is fordable in many places, even at its deepest southern end. Perhaps the dykes were built to prevent people coming across the river and taking the resources of the Forest of Dean, known to be an important industrial source of iron and wood since Roman times. The dyke on the cliff could more effectively prevent entry into the forest from the river than any obstacle along the water's edge. The dyke could also have been built here to control access to the exposed hilltops where the wind would help to fire the many iron smelters which may once have been worked in this area.

Though seemingly incongruous, the dykes in the lower Wye valley should not be written off entirely as part of Offa's Dyke or at least works from the Mercian period. Apart from the southernmost Sedbury Park sections, no dyke in this area has ever been properly excavated. There is also evidence from the Welsh and other Annals that there was indeed trouble between the Mercians and southern Welsh in the 8th century.

The section of 'Offa's Dyke' in the lower Wye valley that is the oddest of all is the half mile long section that runs between English Bicknor and Lower Lydbrook. It is separated from the rest of the Wye valley dykes by 2½ miles and is usually not associated with them, partly due to this gap and partly due to the different nature of the Wye valley at this point, where it becomes gentler and more terraced. The author has walked a field directly behind this English Bicknor Dyke and found a number of pieces of Roman pottery and many lumps of slag and iron from iron smelting which was a frequent activity in this area. Perhaps the dykes here were built to control access to woodland that may have covered the valley slopes then, as it does in the steeper parts of the Wye valley below Redbrook now. Wood was necessary to make charcoal for the production and forging of iron, before the local coal was utilized.

What therefore of the short sections of 'Offa's Dyke' in north-western Herefordshire? Fox's explanation is that they marked the boundary that went through a few clearings in an otherwise great forest which covered the whole of western Herefordshire. An accepted theory in Fox's time was that after the departure of the Romans many parts of Britain were neglected and reverted back to woodland.[104] Indeed, evidence from one site in Britain indicates a resurgence of woodland in about A.D.700, but thereafter clearance resumed.[105] As one of the Offa's Dyke Project's digs on Wat's Dyke found, forest can be quickly cleared by fire.[106] Western Herefordshire, especially the broad Wye valley is rich farmland above the flood plain. Surely Saxon settlers would not have allowed this area to remain woodland. By Domesday in 1086, records show that Herefordshire had less woodland than any other English border county. Place-name analysis indicates that there were several Saxon settlements in wooded areas of the north-western Herefordshire plain. Indeed if lined up, the dykes run just north-east of a region of these village names signifying settlements in clearings such as Kinnersley, Eardisley, and Whitney.[107] The exception is Weobley which lies east of the line.

Banks in woods were used to mark separate sections of woodland ownership, and ditches dug through woodland sometimes mark parish boundaries. Pales or hedges were also used to enclose deer within woodland. It is possible, therefore, that the short Herefordshire sections of 'Offa's Dyke' are wood-banks that have lost their woodland. Earthworks within woodland where visibility is poor makes sense but marking small sections of cleared land does not. One of the chief characteristics of the 'main' section of Offa's Dyke is that it is built to gain the best views of the west. If there was any woodland in the way, it would have been eliminated. It is this author's view that the short dykes in north-west Herefordshire have nothing to do with Offa's Dyke. They were built individually to suit local needs.

Fig. 23 Woodland dyke in north Herefordshire

The dyke at Bridge Sollars and over Garnon's Hill may have been built to block a Roman road that runs parallel to the Wye and, as such, is similar to other earthworks in Britain that block earlier routes. The roads were the Romans' way of quickly unifying a once disconnected landscape, and the later dykes can be seen as an equally quick way to reassert local independence and disunity. The bank could be marking a property or jurisdictional boundary starting from the banks of the Wye, centred on *Magnis*, similar but on a much smaller scale to the supposed boundary marked by Wat's Dyke on the edge of the sub-Roman kingdom centred on Chester-Wroxeter. There could have been another right of way through the valley between Garnon's Hill and Burton Hill, the next hill to the north, where the fragments of the Upperton and Claypits banks seem to heading. On the rolling plain of western Herefordshire these hills stand out on the horizon like monuments. It is not surprising if they were used to mark the boundaries of territories in the past.

The dykes at Holme's Marsh and Lyonshall are oriented at right angles to a postulated Roman road which runs from Mortimer's Cross to Clyro a road also blocked by the Rowe Ditch at Pembridge.[108] The dykes at Lyonshall may have been linked up at one time to form a boundary which also blocked the road in the valley of the Curl Brook, for these dykes look like the remnants of a single cross valley dyke with its middle taken out.

The last sections of 'Offa's Dyke' in north-west Herefordshire are the small sections of bank pointing north from the edge of Lyonshall Park Wood and connected by hedgerows or low earthworks to the bank which comes out of the northern end of Berry's Hill. Despite intensive survey by the Offa's Dyke Project, no connection between the end of this bank and the beginning of the main part of Offa's Dyke 1½ miles to the west has ever been found. The proximity of parkland in this area does suggest that these sections of bank might be remnants of a park boundary or even wood-banks which have lost their woods.

All these dykes vary greatly in size and scale. Only the dyke at Lynhales, as pointed out, has anything approaching the dimensions of the main part of Offa's Dyke. Most of them are much smaller. No dating evidence besides what has been said about Rowe Ditch has ever been found in association with these or any of the other short dykes in the Marches region.

After Offa, the Fall of Powys

Powys was to pay a high price for its long and ultimately vulnerable border with Mercia. In the year that Offa died in 796, there was a battle at Rhuddlan, the site of a future Anglo-Saxon *burh* which was supposedly built west of the line that Offa's Dyke would have taken if it had continued on its course to the sea near Prestatyn. It would seem that the Mercians were already by-passing their own boundary. The *Welsh Annals* tell that in 798 the Saxons slew Caradog, king of Gwynedd. In 816 the Saxons took Rhufoniog, a small sub-kingdom in north Wales.[109] In 823 Deganwy, a Welsh fortress at the mouth of the Conwy river on the north coast of Wales was taken and in the same year Powys fell to Saxon rule,[110] a mere 26 years after the death of Offa. The Mercians probably did not try to hold the Welsh kingdom,[111] for their power was already being stretched and the Danish threat was on the horizon. Powys was subsequently absorbed by her western neighbour Gwynedd whose power rose from the 9th century onwards.

In just one generation the Mercians had by-passed Offa's Dyke and subdued the kingdom it was built against. Why? Was it because the Welsh of Powys had been weakened by the Dyke or had they been infuriated by it and attacked and harassed Mercia until she was driven to eradicating her troublesome neighbour. The notations in the *Welsh Annals* and the *Anglo-Saxon Chronicle* for the 9th and 10th centuries always refer to the Saxons attacking Wales, not the other way around. Historically it is impossible to tell if the Dyke was at all effective in helping to maintain peace on the border or if constant conflict led to the building of putative border forts. The impression given by the historical references is that the Welsh were relatively quiescent by the late 9th century, perhaps after the fall of Powys, that the Dyke was doing its job and keeping the peace in the Marches. As the 9th century wore on, Mercia was increasingly on her knees to the invading Danes and the rising power of Wessex, whilst the Welsh were having their own problems with the Norsemen.

In the early 10th century Aethelflaed, 'the lady of the Mercians' fortified Chirbury near the border in Shropshire but whether this was against the Scandinavians or the Welsh is not clear. In 922 the kings of Wales gave their allegiance to King Edward;[112] in 926 King Athelstan and the Welsh kings agreed to the Ordinances of the Dunsaete which suggests that though relations were friendly, border misunderstandings were still an issue.

Conclusion

Offa's Dyke was perhaps the most ambitious attempt to deal with the conflict between the eastern Welsh kingdoms and Mercia. The construction of the Dyke is attributed to Offa because of Asser's comment: that Offa built a dyke 'from sea to sea'. Nearly 100 years separate Offa from Asser, long enough for the legend of a ruthless and powerful leader to obscure the truth in such a remote and fragmented area and in an era of poor education and communication. In effect, Offa's Dyke probably should only refer to the 'main' section running from Rushock Hill north of Kington in Herefordshire, to its northern end near Treuddyn in Flintshire. At the southern end of this 'main' section the Dyke controlled the lines of communication between the highlands of central Wales and those of northern Herefordshire and southern Shropshire. This may be the reason why the main dyke starts just south of these highlands. The continuation of the Dyke north of the Severn, especially when a boundary earthwork already existed in the shape of Wat's Dyke was a demonstration of Mercian power, further cementing control over the valuable lowlands of the northern Marches, which because of political strife in the mid-8th century, may have been newly re-conquered from the Welsh of Powys.

There are many other shorter lengths of dyke or earthwork in the Marches, some of which run along the course that the main Dyke would have taken had it indeed 'run from sea to sea', notably the short dykes in north-western Herefordshire and the discontinuous Whitford Dyke north of the main Dyke in north Wales. The Whitford Dyke has been eliminated from the Offa's Dyke system, not by dating evidence but because its construction, when excavated, was shown to be inconsistent with the rest of Offa's Dyke. With the exception of Rowe Ditch, the dykes in north-west Herefordshire await similar testing and study.

In the southern Marches the lack of a dyke in southern Herefordshire has led to the supposition that the river Wye was the boundary here despite the location of the important commercial and ecclesiastical centre of Hereford on its banks. In the steep lower Wye valley, further historical and archaeological study is also required to prove or disprove the belief that the anomalous, sometimes massive but discontinuous clifftop banks here are part of the Offa's Dyke system.

The idea of a long distance boundary earthwork such as Offa's Dyke may have come from the Roman *limes* of Europe, though if so the design came indirectly, through its imitation of Wat's Dyke, for which there is radio-carbon evidence of early post-Roman construction.[113]

The only indication as to what was happening to the Dyke archaeologically during the late Saxon period is that whenever excavated, the ditch shows no sign of having been re-cut or cleaned out, implying neglect once built. It seems to have gained in symbolic importance long after it was built, helping to define Welsh identity. The Dyke, despite its later reputation as a great ethnic divide, militarily appears to have had a short-lived use. In the Welsh Marches, the landscape itself for the most part forms the true boundary.

CHAPTER 9
The Development of Towns in Mercia

In many Roman towns across England excavation has revealed a clear break in occupation lasting for about 150 years starting from the early 5th century.[1] Such a hiatus in occupation is testified by a layer of dark earth (formed from a build up of organic matter) which overlies the last Roman layers. As Clarke and Ambrosiani observe 'It is difficult to see how settlements where such a deep layer of soil was accumulating could have contained a population of any appreciable size'.[2] As the dark earth layer may have been formed either as a result of the town's abandonment or as a result of land within the former town being cultivated, at best the place may have been occupied by a few people. Whether these people were simply squatters getting by, or an élite perhaps involved with the administration of a nascent kingdom, the settlement—quite possibly 'a useful ruin ... an enclave for an old or new aristocracy, spaciously arranged like a walled park'[3]—could no longer be rightly classified as a 'town'. Only in the early 7th century were there the first traces of an urban renewal.

Most people's understanding of a town would be a settlement of such size and density of population that it drew in its surrounding population both to trade goods and also in search of certain trades, services, businesses and specializations that were unable to exist or thrive in a sparsely populated rural area. But it appears that in the early Anglo-Saxon period there was something of a 'fragmentation of functions in different centres'. Even in a small area one settlement might possess a market, another an ecclesiastical centre and a third a centre for defence and it was only towards the end of the pre-Norman period that these functions became increasingly clustered in the larger centres.[4] At the time of the Norman Conquest it is estimated that only between 7-10% of the population of England lived in towns and this can be 'attributed almost entirely' to the developments of the late 9th to 11th centuries.[5]

Some settlements, with the benefit of hindsight, can be seen as proto-urban. For example the presence of a royal or thegnly residence, of an important monastic settlement or the location on the hub of a road network may prove to have been the trigger for later urban development. Oundle in Lindsey, for instance, was an important monastic centre established in the 7th century by St. Wilfrid, bishop of York and friend of King Aethelred of Mercia which was also the administrative centre for eight hundreds, and subsequently grew into a town.[6] But many such settlements never reached an urban status, ending up as villages, or even disappearing all together, as did Yeavering, Foxley near Malmesbury and Cheddar.

Royal courts and important monasteries were centres for the gift economy—the exchange of gifts between kings, leaders and churchmen, and the parcelling of gains won as a result of warfare. In turn they attracted a number of traders and merchants but this was on quite a different scale to the urbanized market where there was a permanent and large sector of the population involved in specialized crafts and trading.[7]

Much of the general trade within in the early Anglo-Saxon period was carried out at temporary markets or fairs, often on beaches or river banks where goods could be brought in by water. The population of early and middle Anglo-Saxon England usually manufactured what they needed close to hand; pottery was hand-made and produced for domestic use as and when it was required and clothes were manufactured on the ubiquitous loom, evidence of which, in the form of loom weights, are often found when dwellings are excavated. Communities were essentially self-sufficient and only produced what was needed, with any surplus being bartered among one's neighbours. Chapter 1 has already shown how Roman towns were largely abandoned or given over to the occasional household once the Roman empire had cut its links with Britain. It is only in the later 9th century that trade once more began between regions and internationally, and crafts, such as pottery, took on an industrial scale. In Mercia the seeds for this were laid in Offa's reign in the 8th century when textiles were exported to the Continent. Part of the reason for the increase in the 9th century was due to the influence of the new Scandinavian settlements.

What evidence, then, exists for pre-9th-century towns in Mercia? London is one supreme example of an early town, and one which fell under Mercian domination from at least the early 8th century. In addition there are at most three other sites in pre-Viking England which could be classed as having urban status: Southampton (*Hamwic*, to the south-east of the modern town), Ipswich and possibly York. Scull observes that all four of these 'towns' share certain common features: they are all on coastal or riverine locations; in the case of London, Southampton and Ipswich, in their developed phases, they were substantially larger than contemporary rural settlements; and they were permanently occupied by a relatively large population, although they may have had a seasonal influx of extra inhabitants engaged in trade—in addition they all have consistent and plentiful evidence for trade with the Continent and for a range of craft activities within the settlement. Environmental archaeological evidence also suggests these sites were 'net consumers of agri-cultural produce', although there is some evidence that marginal semi-agricultural sites at London and Ipswich may have been supplying some food. The earliest elements of the Anglo-Saxon settlement at *Hamwic* dates to about A.D. 700, and the size of the site, the amount of control shown in its street layout and the presence of a boundary ditch indicates 'a planned settlement, established by royal initiative', possibly by the West Saxon king, Ine.[8] It is London that provides a case study of an early town in the wider Mercian kingdom. London was vital to Mercia as it was a point of entry into Continental Europe and its enormous economic and political opportunities. For early kings, such as Aethelbald and Offa, control of this international emporium was vital to an otherwise largely land-locked kingdom. Both *Hamwic* and Ipswich were established on virgin sites, whereas London's antecedents were in the Roman era.[9]

London—the earliest Mercian example

It is probable that the first Germanic settlers in the London area arrived in the late 4th to early 5th centuries and that they 'may have been mercenaries recruited by Romano-British authorities to defend the region against seaborne raiders'. Indeed, it is related that the early settlements of Mucking and Mitcham, respec-tively south of Basildon on the north bank of the Thames and north-west of Croydon south of the river, may have been inhabited by such mercenaries. It appears that these early Anglo-Saxons concentrated their settlements in the river valleys of the London region, often in areas which had been farmed in Roman times, but whether this denotes a level of continuity or simply that these settlers took over the best places for farming and settlement is debatable.[10] The fact that there is virtually no evidence for continued British pres-ence in the region, excepting a few place-names, raises the question of the fate of the Britons in this area— did they abandon the region, or adopt the ways and material culture of the new Anglo-Saxon immigrants? No evidence of sub-Roman occupation has been found within what is now called the City and it is thought likely that Roman *Londinium* was abandoned not long after Roman administration ceased in Britain, and that it stayed largely uninhabited until about the start of the 7th century.[11]

There is written evidence that Pope Gregory chose London as the primary see for England in 601 and the first cathedral church (St. Paul's) was founded by King Aethelberht of Kent in, or shortly after, 604 to serve the East Saxon diocese; its remains are thought to lie under the present St. Paul's Cathedral or its immediate environs. This is the earliest evidence for Anglo-Saxon activity within the former walled Roman city and the fact it subsequently acquired the name *Paulesbyri* suggests this early church was surrounded by an enclosure, the *byri* element referring to an enclosed, possibly even defended, site. Whereas a possible reason for establishing St. Paul's in this spot may have been that the site was next to two Roman roads 'in an area less encumbered by [Roman] building debris'; it is thought unlikely that the remains of the Roman city had much influence over subsequent Anglo-Saxon development.[12] Nor does the presence of a cathedral imply that London had continued as a settlement for it was papal policy to establish sees in former Roman towns, thought befitting for cathedral status regardless of their current population levels.[13]

However, from the mid-7th century there was clearly an Anglo-Saxon settlement at London, possibly around the time when King Wulfhere of Mercia took control of the port. This port is first mentioned in a charter of 672-4 given by Wulfhere's sub-king Frithuwold,[14] and again demonstrates that London was then a trading centre. In 731 Bede describes London as a city 'which stands on the banks of the Thames, and is a trading centre for many nations who visit it by land and sea'[15] although whether he is referring to 604, the year to which the text relates, or to the year in which he is writing is unclear.

From the available written and archaeological evidence it is thought that during the middle Anglo-Saxon era London consisted of two distinct parts: a trading settlement which was centred on the area of the Strand, just over half a mile (1km) to the west of Roman walled city, and a settlement within the walls of the latter which may have housed a royal hall and churches.[16] London was therefore similar to Canterbury, Winchester and York in having royal and ecclesiastical structures within the former Roman walled city and a complementary trading settlement nearby, a pattern also found in 'equivalent contemporary continental sites'.[17]

In London's case it was the trading settlement that appears to have kick-started its status as a town after the decline of *Londinium* following the end of Roman rule in Britain. The name *Lundenwic* was used in 7th- and 8th-century documents and is thought to refer to this trading settlement since it disappears from use when the focus moved to the walled city in the 9th century.[18] In the mid-1980s Martin Biddle and Alan Vince suggested independently of each other that the area around Aldwych (which significantly

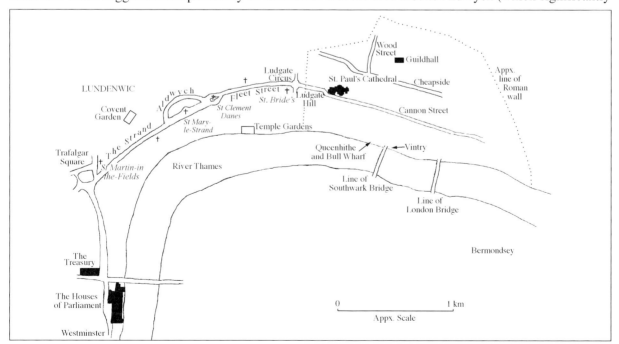

Fig. 1 Map of London showing places mentioned in the text

means the 'old *wic*') and the Strand constituted the site of *Lundenwic*. Subsequent archaeological evidence indicates that *Lundenwic* covered about 60 hectares (150 acres) and stretched from a 7th-century waterfront at York Buildings (north of Victoria Embankment Gardens) northwards to Shorts Gardens, 'and from Trafalgar Square eastwards to Aldwych'.[19] It is from the area around the Strand that small numbers of late 6th- and early 7th-century finds have been made which have led archaeologists to posit that *Lundenwic* was established by *c*.600.[20] Finds of possible 6th to early 7th century date have also been 'reported from the central, Convent Garden area',[21] north of the Strand. At first *Lundenwic* was a rather small settlement but by the early 8th century it had grown into a significant trading port, a development which Cowie and Harding consider 'marked the rebirth of London as a town'.[22] Indeed, the waterfront excavated at York Buildings has had its revetment dendrochronologically dated which suggests it was built in 679 or shortly afterwards. Another 7th-century waterfront may have existed at Buckingham Street, immediately to the west of York Buildings. Other contemporary settlements along the Thames, for example Barking to the north-east, may have also possessed 'beach markets' for trade brought along the river.[23]

The routes of several major Roman roads which radiated out of London were still in use in the medieval period and were, by implication, used in pre-Conquest times. The Strand was probably a major thoroughfare and focus for the *Lundenwic* settlement, being a projected continuation of the Roman road running from Ludgate Hill to Fleet Street; the presence of a 'Saxo-Norman abutment for a bridge' crossing the river Fleet at Ludgate Circus is considered to provide strong evidence for continued use of a road on this proposed alignment.[24] Indeed, it would make perfect sense to have a road linking the trading centre of *Lundenwic* to the possible royal/administrative centre within the walled city, and for Mercian commercial interests as a whole the presence of Watling Street connecting the centre of their kingdom with a major sea port was critical.

It is contended that *Lundenwic* may have had a gridded street pattern similar to those found in the contemporary towns of Ipswich and Southampton, although the evidence is very limited. And yet large quarries were found dating to the middle Anglo-Saxon period at the National Gallery extension which suggests large-scale gravel extraction was occurring, perhaps used for metalling roads and yards.[25]

It may seem strange that the incoming Anglo-Saxons chose to build a trading settlement outside what would have been a protected walled site of the Roman city. The reason may lie in a change in the river's water level and differences in the type of boats used, resulting in difficulty in using the stretch of river bank alongside the Roman wall, Anglo-Saxon boatmen instead using the unencumbered land the west.[26]

No archaeological evidence for any pre-Conquest palace sites has been found within London, although documentary evidence suggests the existence of several royal vills in Greater London where food-rents would be gathered and stored in readiness for one of the regular visits by the king and his household.[27] Tradition has it that the 7th-century King Aethelberht of Kent had a palace within the walled city at Aldermanbury, near to the Guildhall. However, archaeological evidence suggests pre-Conquest settlement only began in this part of the City in the 10th or even the 11th centuries, much later than that around Queenhithe to the south. Similarly, the idea that there was a Mercian palace inside the Cripplegate fort has largely been abandoned, and a theory that St. Alban's church in Wood Street was once a chapel in Offa's palace has been severely challenged.[28]

A royal hall is mentioned in the late 7th-century laws of the Kentish kings, Hlothere and Eadric; again its location is unknown but it may have lain within *Lundenwic* as reference is made to the port or town-reeve, which suggests a commercial location. Royal residences are also implied at Chelsea, approximately 3 miles south-south-west of *Lundenwic*, and at Brentford over 8½ miles south-west, as royal councils and ecclesiastical synods were held there in the 8th century. Indeed, middle Anglo-Saxon occupation at Chelsea has recently been discovered.[29] In 787 the *Anglo-Saxon Chronicle* records 'In this year there was a contentious synod at Chelsea, and Archbishop Jaenberht lost a certain part of his province

[Canterbury], and Hygeberht was chosen [as archbishop of Lichfield] by King Offa'.[30] Attending the synod were Offa, 'two archbishops, nine bishops, six abbots and eight ealdormen' who were likely to have been accompanied by a large retinue and several ships.[31] There were ten or so other synods at Chelsea between 785 and 816. However, in 801, during the reign of Coenwulf in Mercia, in an endorsement to a charter of 767 the synodial assembly is said only to have been 'near the place which is called Chelsea'.[32] The meaning of the place-name Chelsea, formed from the Old English words *cealc* and *hyth*, has been interpreted to mean 'landing place for chalk or lime'. But the endorsement of 801 uses the spelling *Caelichyth* which may indicate the first element is derived from *caelic*—'cup' or 'chalice',[33] giving the meaning of 'landing place for a cup or chalice' which, considering the synods, seems wholly apposite.

It is thought probable that *Lundenwic* was served by several churches. A charter of 959 describes the church at St. Andrew Holborn as an 'old wooden church' and it is contended that it 'was possibly contemporaneous with the settlement'. It is also suggested that the five medieval churches which stand along the Strand and Fleet Street—St. Martin-in-the-Fields, St. Bride, St. Mary-le-Strand, St. Clement Danes and St. Dunstan in the West—may have Anglo-Saxon foundations. An early rubble foundation has been located at St. Bride's, and possible early Christian burials have been discovered at St. Martin-in-the-Fields[34] along with a late 6th- or 7th-century cemetery site. Another such site has been found in the Covent Garden area. Both of these cemeteries would have been on the 'outskirts of the early nucelus of Middle Saxon London'.[35] However, in the main phase of *Lundenwic*'s settlement only one burial of apparent 8th century date has been found, and that at Bedfordbury, north-east of Trafalgar Square, when it would be expected that more would have been found given the size of the settlement. The reason may be that *Lundenwic*'s 8th century population was Christian, in which case many would have been buried in churchyards, most of which would have still been in use in the late Anglo-Saxon and medieval periods. As the graves would not have been 'richly furnished with goods', Cowie and Harding comment that this makes any mid- and late Anglo-Saxon graves hard to distinguish from subsequent burials.[36]

It is possible that early 8th-century monastic sites existed at Westminster and Bermondsey. The latter lies roughly 2 miles south-east and across the river from *Lundenwic*, and for where there exists a 12th-century copy of a privilege in the *libra nigra* of Peterborough 'in which Pope Constantine (708-15) addresses *Headda* as abbot of *Vermundesei* (Bermondsey) and *Wocchingas* (Woking)'. Residual artefacts from the middle Anglo-Saxon period have been found at Bermondsey, and also at Westminster where it is postulated that the 10th-century monastery could have been preceded by a minster church which may have been founded in the early 8th century in the reign of Offa of Essex, or possibly by Aethelberht of Kent (died between 616-8) although this is considered less likely.[37] A double monastery was established in about 666 at Barking by a Bishop Eorcenwald who founded a sister house at Chertsey contemporaneously. Barking Abbey went on to have a significant commercial importance—indeed it is the only other site in the London region in the mid-Anglo-Saxon period 'to have produced significant evidence of trade', the breadth of Continental finds from Barking rivalling that of *Lundenwic*.[38] It is possible that Barking started life as a 'beach market' trading site whose sophistication grew with the development of the monastery.

Excavations in the *Lundenwic* area have revealed evidence of a riverside settlement containing buildings, pits, ditches, lanes and environmental evidence that included large amounts of butchered bones, suggesting that livestock was being processed. In recent excavations at the Royal Opera House at Covent Garden an Anglo-Saxon street containing up to 60 buildings was found.[39] Here the buildings, made of timber, measured nearly 12m (about 39ft) long by just over 5.5m (about 18ft) wide, with a door in each of their longer sides. In their size and shape, they are comparable to many found at the trading settlements of *Hamwic* and York.[40] As more buildings were added in the late 7th and early 8th centuries, so 'the arrangement of building plots became more formalised within a network of roads and alleys'.[41] At

Chelsea, Barn Elms (between Fulham and Barnes) and the Thames foreshore at Isleworth middle Anglo-Saxon fish traps, comprising posts set in V-shaped configurations, have recently been discovered and it seems that *Lundenwic*'s inhabitants ate great amounts of fish, oysters and eels.[42]

The abundance of Ipswich Ware (a competently made type of pottery produced between the 7th and 9th centuries in Ipswich) implies that the settlement was thriving by the 720s.[43] In addition pottery was imported from the Surrey border, from the Charnwood Forest area in the eastern midlands and from the Chilterns or North Downs. It also appears that *Lundenwic* was receiving goods from the Continent, with lava quernstones, for example, coming in from the Mayer Niedermendig area in Germany (near modern Koblenz) and pottery from the Rhineland, Low Countries and northern France.[44] There may have also been some imports of wine. *Lundenwic*'s exports may have included slaves and clothing to the Continent.[45] That King Aethelbald of Mercia was granting exemptions to several bishops and Abbess Mildthryth (of Minster-in-Thanet) for paying tolls on ships using London's port in the first half of the 8th century also testifies to *Lundenwic*'s commercial vigour. These and later 9th century documents 'imply that maritime trade in London was under royal control and subject to taxation'.[46]

With such evidence for trade it is no surprise to learn that late 7th-century ('primary phase') *sceattas* (silver pennies) were minted in London—in fact Vince states that 'coins possibly minted in London account for just over a third of the total known in the later seventh century and form 11 per cent of the total in the early to mid-eighth century'.[47] By about 730, during the second phase of *sceatta* production, coins appear with the legend D[E] LVNDONIA, and by Offa's time (mid- to late 8th century) there is enough numismatic evidence to suggest London had become an important mint for this Mercian king, with coins also being issued at London during his successors' reigns up to and including the first of Wiglaf's two reigns (827-9). After a lull, coins were again issued from London from about 843 during Beorthwulf's reign, faltered in 851 probably because of a Viking raid, but output increased again from the mid-860s when London once more became an important mint.[48]

Oddly, for all its implied trading prowess, archaeology has found evidence for only small-scale, 'cottage' industry style manufacture, with no evidence, as yet, of the specialized industry/craft zones found in other contemporary trading settlements, such as the pottery-making area found in Ipswich and *Hamwic*'s possible bone-working zones. At *Lundenwic* there is a widespread distribution of small amounts of waste from bone- and antler-working, metalworking, and with possible tanning and smithing at the Royal Opera House site, along with fairly ubiquitous cloth production.[49]

For most of its existence it appears that *Lundenwic* was not defended. However, among the last features of the settlement were 2m (6½ft) deep ditches, apparently defensive, found at the Royal Opera House site and at Maiden Lane, close to the south-west, dating to the 9th century but which were well inside the settlement site. These may represent the last attempt to defend a small part of the original *Lundenwic* site, or have been part of an encampment that was built when the settlement had been abandoned.[50]

Precisely why and when *Lundenwic* was abandoned is not certain. It seems that the settlement was in decline in the early 9th century, possibly through the disruption of trade.[51] From the late 8th century onwards England was subject to seaborne raids from the Scandinavians and in 842 the *Anglo-Saxon Chronicle* reports 'a great slaughter in London' with further attacks recorded in 851 by 350 ships, and the Danes taking up winter quarters in 872. These may not have been the only incursions on London, but may have been the most memorable. Not surprisingly, there had been a decline in overseas trade which affected towns both in Britain and on the Continent—notably Quentovic in north-western France and Dorestad in the Netherlands, through which much English trade was conducted. It is speculated by Vince that if London had been 'absorbed into the Viking world' at this time, as Ipswich had been, then it may have flourished, rather than declined.[52]

As well as probably precipitating the abandonment of *Lundenwic*, the Viking raids are likely to have prompted the desertion of other riverside settlements, such as Battersea, the Treasury site and Barking.[53] The Viking threat may also have led to the creation of a *burh* within the old Roman city, for references start to appear to *Lundenburh*, as opposed to *Lundenwic*. The *Suthringa geweorche* ('the southern work' or 'the work of the southern people') listed in the Burghal Hidage is assumed to be another new *burh* at Southwark, although it is possible that the site referred to may have been at Kingston-on-Thames, approximately 10 miles to the south-west, where some evidence for late Anglo-Saxon occupation has been discovered. A royal palace and/or minster probably did exist at Kingston at this time because in 838 it was here that King Ecgberht of Wessex presided over a council, and several 10th-century West Saxon kings were crowned there. (The 'coronation stone', which stands outside the Guildhall in Kingston's High Street, is reputedly the stone on which the kings were crowned.[54]) The site at Southwark may have encouraged the construction of London Bridge in the late 9th or early 10th century to link the *burhs* on the opposing sides of the Thames, at the same time creating 'a barrier to prevent Viking raiders from sailing upstream'.[55]

In 886 the *Anglo-Saxon Chronicle* records that 'King Alfred *gesette lundenburg*; and all the English people that were not under subjection to the Danes submitted to him. And he then entrusted the borough to the control of Ealdorman [A]Ethelred'.[56] The phrase '*gesette lundenburg*' could mean that the area of the old Roman town was 'founded', not just 'occupied'.[57]

Lundenburh was enclosed by the walls first built by the Romans, which it appears from historical sources King Alfred repaired shortly after retaking the town.[58] From the paucity of archaeological evidence from this time it seems that this defended settlement was initially rather small, although research 'has identified an area between the Thames and the Cheapside/Eastcheap road axis as a possible site for the Alfredian *burh*' which would have left much space within the walls for horticultural, stock-rearing and/or industrial activities. By the late 10th century this walled settlement had become a major town.[59]

As London was left in control of the Mercian ealdorman, Aethelred, it is no surprise that a Mercian presence was still felt. Even as early as 857 a grant is made by King Burgred of Mercia to Ealhhun, bishop of Worcester, of a house and commercial rights in London. Indeed Burgred granted to Ealhhun 'a certain small portion of a liberty, of a profitable little estate in the town of London, *i.e.* at a place called *Ceolmundinghaga*, which is situated not far from the west gate'.[60] The location is tantalizing for, as John Clark observes, was this estate 'inside the Roman walls or in the "old" *Lundenwic* area', and was it to replace property which had perhaps been lost in the Viking raid of 851?[61] The grant states that the bishop is 'to have in his own liberty, or belonging to the city of Worcester' free use of 'the scale and weights and measures as is customary in the port. The liberty of this estate was brought from the king with 60 shillings of silver, and had been purchased before with the same amount of money—one pound—from Ceolmund the '"prefect"'.[62] Whitelock notes that Ceolmund presumably gave his name to *Ceolmundinghaga*, and that in the context of this grant 'prefect' may mean 'reeve'.[63] The grant notes a yearly rent of 12 pence was to be paid to the king 'from that little estate'.[64] The fact that the estate was profitable only six years or so after a major Viking raid may suggest the resilience of the trading base in London.

One of the more interesting references to the trading activities of late 9th century *Lundenburh* is in a charter of 889 where an estate called *Hwaetmundes stan(e)* is granted to Bishop Waerferth of Worcester by Alfred and Aethelred:

> To Werefrith, the distinguished bishop of the Hwicci, for the church at Worcester, one court in London, which by the citizens is called Hwaetmundes stane, meaning 'the old stone building', from the public street right to the wall of the said city ... we set it down for church ownership, and grant and give it, to be possessed in full freedom in every respect for evermore: and let it have an urn (for measuring) and scales within, for the purpose of weighing in buying or selling, or for proper and free necessary

use of all lands; and let it continue absolved, and pass every debt or fiscal penalty or public charge, except what pertains within to the ownership of the bishop of the Church of Worcester. Now if anyone of his (folk) buys anything outside, whether in the public street or in the river-bank market, let him pay toll to the hand of the aforementioned bishop.[65]

It is clear from these charters that the bishops and their men were involved in trade and profited from the tolls, regulating trade on the public street or in a riverside market. 'The old stone building', *Hwaetmundes stane*, may refer to a Roman structure—before the 10th century stone was only used in the most important secular and ecclesiastical buildings. The estate in this charter and one mentioned in a record of a council meeting at Chelsea in 898/9 are believed to have been the same. In the 898/9 record Bishop Waerferth is granted the right to moor ships along the width of his property and it is thought that such extra rights were probably given to boost London's economy, especially as the council at Chelsea, in which this grant was given, was concerned with the renewal of London.[67]

Queenhithe (of about late 9th century date) and Billingsgate appear to have been among the earliest waterfront developments in *Lundenburh*. At the latter a late Roman quay was deliberately removed and at Queenhithe it appears this site was free of the 'remains of late Roman revetments'.[68] In the 889 charter already referred to reference is made to the 'trading shore' (*ripa emptoralis*) at Queenhithe and archaeological evidence suggests that at first 'parts of the foreshore may have been used as an open marketplace, with transactions being carried out from beached boats', an activity that would leave little trace as few permanent facilities would have been needed. At Bull Wharf (immediately to the east of Queenhithe) the earliest evidence of pre-Conquest activity comprised only 'a few mooring posts and timber structures' interpreted as gangplank trestles.[69] By the late 10th to the early 11th century 'embankments with stepped profiles' were constructed and

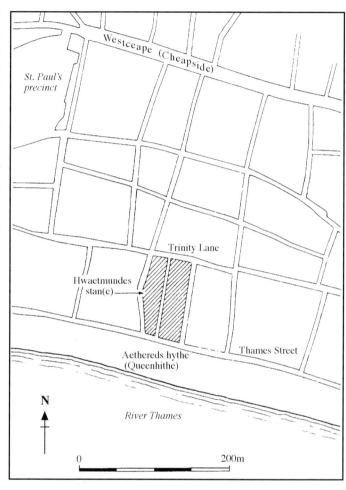

Fig.2 The Hwaetmundes stane *estate has been located close to Queenhithe and would have been in an excellent trading position, especially as a market and harbour had been established at Queenhithe at about that time or earlier. In the ten years between the documents dated 889 and 898/9 several roads were set out in the vicinity, indicating a degree of town planning. Significantly, Queenhithe was originally known as* Aetheredes hid, *almost certainly named after the Mercian Aethelred. He was the joint grantor in the 888/9 grant in which he styles himself* subregulus et patricus Merciorum[66] *and the charter is witnessed by Aethelflaed, his wife, 'the Lady of the Mercians', which is testimony to the strength of the Mercian presence in 9th century London*

have been found at Billingsgate Lorry Park, New Fresh Wharf (immediately east of London Bridge) and Swan Lane (just west of London Bridge by Fishmongers' Hall), with the lower step perhaps being 'used for berthing boats and the upper for unloading cargoes'.[70] Schofield remarks that finds from the late 9th-century Bull Wharf and the vicinity suggest there was once a buoyant trade with ports in Frisian and Viking territories and include the best collection of Carolingian and Scandinavian 9th- and 10th-century metalwork found in the country (excluding hoards).[71] The remains of late pre-Conquest boats have been found at New Fresh Wharf, Malvern House and 'part of a Scandinavian-type vessel' at Vintry. Late Anglo-Saxon boat timbers have also been found at Fennings Wharf at Southwark, but the most complete vessel—a late 10th-century logboat—to have been discovered in London was found on the banks of the river Lea at Clapton (about 4 miles north-north-east of the City) which provides 'direct evidence for the use of lesser rivers in the London area'.[72]

By the first millennium it seems that London was a buoyant place with much economic vigour. Not only was it engaged in a wide variety of crafts but it is likely it had established a reputation for luxuries and high class goods. It was also an internationally important port in a trading network that extended around the North Sea into the Baltic and was the biggest and most important city in England.[73] Although it was not to become of the capital until two centuries later, it managed to retain its eminent place above all other towns and, in its time, was essential to the land-locked kingdom of Mercia.

Northampton—a Proto-urban Site

From archaeological evidence it appears that the area in and around present day Northampton was attractive to the earliest prehistoric settlers, lying as it does in the fertile upper Nene basin. Whereas the river itself provided a ready westward access into the midlands from the Wash, it would have been an obstacle to north-south routes in the eastern half of England. But at Northampton there was a crossing point and it became a natural centre of communications.[74] A causewayed enclosure, utilized possibly from the 5th millennium to the end of the 2nd millennium B.C., lay at Briar Hill, approximately 1 mile from the present day town centre, and is now under modern housing. Half that distance again to the south of Briar Hill is a small hill fort at Hunsbury, built in about 500 B.C., which was possibly the home of a local chiefdom. Pottery finds suggest the site was re-used some time between A.D. 400-850.[75]

At Duston, roughly 1½ miles west of Northampton's town centre, a small Romano-British 'town' appears to have developed in the 1st century A.D. It covered at least 20 acres and may have developed from an Iron Age settlement, evidence for which has been found on the

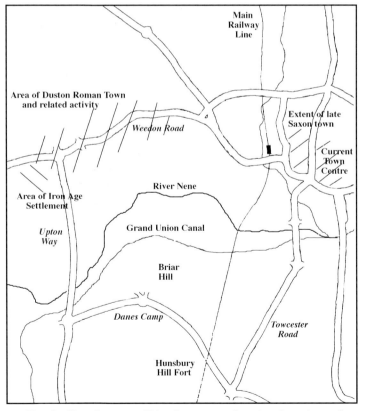

Fig.3 Sketch map of Northampton showing location of outlying sites referred to in the text

201

western fringes of the Roman town. Finds of late Roman coins and two similarly dated buckles indicate the Roman town was used into the 5th century.[76]

Archaeological evidence suggests that early Anglo-Saxon settlements, indicated by the presence of cemeteries, were often sited along the spring lines of the river valleys in this region with a noted concentration around Northampton itself. The largest early Anglo-Saxon cemetery lies along the western edge of the Romano-British 'town' at Duston, grave goods suggesting the cemetery was used mainly in the mid-5th to mid-6th centuries. A Roman lead coffin found in about 1903 in the middle of the cemetery even suggests some continuity between the Roman and early Anglo-Saxon periods from the date range of the grave goods it contained. Further cemeteries have been found south of the river Nene between Hardingstone and Hunsbury, and to the east of the town centre at St. Andrew's Hospital. Early Anglo-Saxon settlement has been found at Upton and Briar Hill, which is in the area formerly favoured by prehistoric and Roman settlement. In addition, four *Grubenhäuser* (early Anglo-Saxon sunken-floored buildings) were found at Briar Hill, and a large one at Upton—probably just parts of larger settlements, reflecting continuing occupation from the fall of Roman Britain.[77]

A recently excavated cemetery (about 2 miles south-east of the town centre) between Brackmills and Great Houghton raises the possibility of a particularly exciting continuity of occupation from the Iron Age to the 7th century. Down the hillside from an Iron Age settlement, 23 inhumation burials were found which probably formed the western edge of a cemetery of unknown size sited beyond an, as yet, unrecognized settlement. As the bodies were aligned west to east, a Christian origin is suggested, and a radiocarbon date on one of the male skeletons pointed to a 7th century date. Intriguingly, an Iron Age female skeleton, from the hill settlement above, had a particular wrist abnormality which only occurs in 1.4% of the modern population, yet the same peculiarity was found in the 7th-century male skeleton.[78] It would be a surprising, although possible, coincidence if two unconnected individuals from completely different periods, and both representing small populations, possessed this unusual abnormality—a genetic link is therefore a possibility,[79] suggesting that perhaps the descendants of the Iron Age community inhabited the hillside for over a thousand years, surviving both the coming of the Romans and the Anglo-Saxons. The implications of this are remarkable, for it implies communities could be extraordinarily static and inward-looking for immense periods of time.

Early Anglo-Saxon settlement in Northampton

It appears that the south-western part of Northampton was the original Anglo-Saxon settlement. Five possible buildings have been found in Chalk Lane and at a site at St. Peter's church. Where sufficient of these structures remained, they have been interpreted as simple rectangular hollows cut into the ground with a post at either end. Two in Chalk Lane gave radiocarbon dates of 570 + or - 70 while one in St. Peter's Gardens gave a date of 470 + or - 70. Several features were also observed which may have been the foundation trenches of an early Anglo-Saxon timber building predating the timber hall (see below). Two disc brooches, 25 decorated pottery sherds and over 2,000 sherds of plain black gritty ware were recovered from the vicinity. dating to between the 5th and 8th centuries, but nothing to indicate that it was a centre of importance before the 8th century or, indeed, any different from a small 'typical rural site of the period'.[80]

However, in the 8th century all this changed. In the St. Peter's church area (see Fig.4) there is evidence of a large timber hall whose scale and precision of craftsmanship and layout indicate that it was either the hall of an aristocrat, perhaps even a king, or a very important monastic site. A mid-8th century date has been suggested for the building which, in size and plan, most nearly resembles Edwin's royal hall at Yeavering and the later one at Milfield in Northumberland, Sprouston in the Scottish Borders, the possible palace site at Atcham in Shropshire (close to Wroxeter), a structure within a complex at

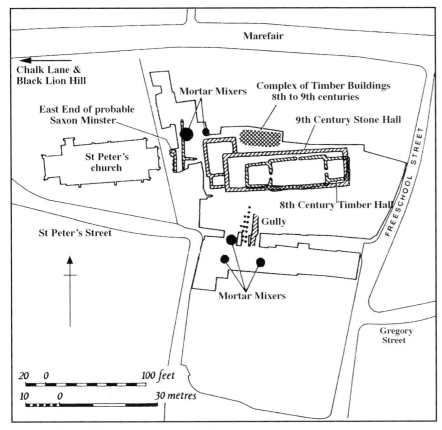

Fig.4 Map showing the St. Peter's church site, Northampton

Map labels:

Marefair

Chalk Lane & Black Lion Hill

Mortar Mixers

Complex of Timber Buildings 8th to 9th centuries

East End of probable Saxon Minster

9th Century Stone Hall

St Peter's church

FREESCHOOL STREET

8th Century Timber Hall

Gully

St Peter's Street

Mortar Mixers

Gregory Street

20 0 100 feet

10 0 30 metres

Malmesbury in Wiltshire and a building/hall near Leamington Spa. The timber hall measured about 29.7m by 8.6m overall (approximately 97½ft by 28ft) and was positioned to the east of the present church (and its probable minster predecessor) close to the top of the hill which Northampton occupies. The main hall comprised a large rectangular central section and an annexe at each end, both about 21ft square, and was built with posts set into a continuous foundation trench 1m (39in) deep and wide. Smaller timber structures located to the north-west, west and south-west of the main hall, thought to be of the same date, may well be part of the overall complex. A timber building on Black Lion Hill and some of the structures found on Chalk Lane perhaps also belong to this 8th-century period.[81] It is likely that a king/aristocrat or an abbot dwelt in the largest building, with several of the smaller dwellings providing for his retainers/servants as well as supplying accommodation for visitors. Such complexes have been found at Yeavering in Northumbria and Cheddar in Somerset.

There is evidence that Northampton's main timber hall had structural problems as a number of post-holes flanked the building, possibly indicating some form of shoring due, perhaps, to a failure at roof level.[82] The roof may have covered the hall in a single span and as a result may have 'spread' or twisted. Nonetheless this was a massive and sophisticated building.

It appears that the timber hall was replaced by a much larger stone hall, possibly early in the 9th century. This was a rectangular structure about 37.6m long, later extended to 43.3m, and about 11.4 metres wide (approx. 123ft-142ft by 37ft), which is enormous for an Anglo-Saxon building. The foundations were between 1.2m (c.4ft) and 1.3 metres (4½ft) wide and 0.6 m (nearly 2ft) deep and 'were well coursed and tightly packed in an earth matrix', although the walls themselves appear to have been mortared together. It is not known how thick the walls were, but it is thought unlikely they were much less than 1m (3¼ft) thick. To give some idea of how substantial this is, of the 186 naves of Anglo-Saxon churches that the eminent Anglo-Saxon architectural historian Harold Taylor examined, only 13 were recorded with walls greater than 1m thick, underlining the substantial nature of the Northampton stone hall. There is evidence that the hall's inside walls were plastered and white lime-washed, although the treatment of its exterior is unknown. The stone was locally derived and may have been obtained through robbing existing stone structures, for nearly 200 fragments of Roman tile were found on the site, some of

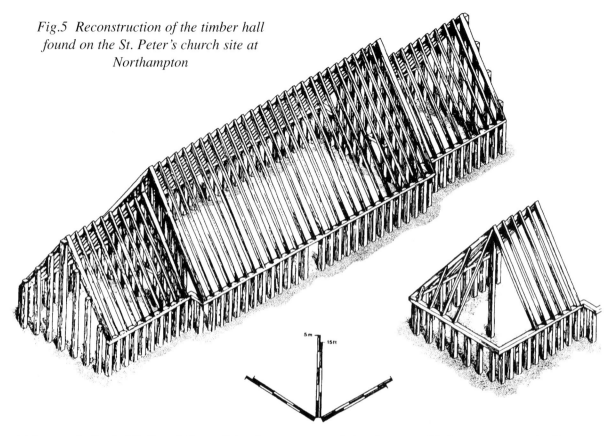

which were in the hall's foundations. It has been suggested that the most likely source was the Romano-British settlement at Duston over 1 mile to the west. As no roofing materials were found in the excavations, the building was probably roofed with thatch or shingles. The span of the hall was wider than its timber predecessor and may have presented similar structural problems; however the span is similar to that of the nave at Brixworth church (Fig.6) which may be its contemporary. Clearly the skill was available to build such impressive structures.[83]

Splendid stone structures apparently existed in Alfred the Great's day (mid-late 9th century) as his contemporary biographer, Asser, comments: 'And what of the royal halls and chambers marvellously constructed of stone and wood at his [Alfred's] command? And what of the royal residences of masonry, moved from their old position and splendidly reconstructed at more appropriate places by his royal command?'[84] It is a pity that Asser does not give any idea of the dimensions of these halls. Similarities in scale for the Northampton hall can be found on the Continent, for example at Zurich (Switzerland), Frankfurt and Paderborn (Germany).[85] It is suggested that the width of the walls of Northampton's stone hall indicates a two-storey structure containing a *triclinium*—a dining hall;[85] a raised floor level is suggested for a 6th/7th-century hall at Cowdery's Down in Hampshire (Fig.7) and for the 9th-century hall at Cheddar. In nearly all of the Continental sites the hall was an important part of the whole palace complex, and Northampton's hall was at the heart of one which probably included a minster church, a graveyard and even a chapel at the hall's eastern end. Whereas Anglo-Saxon timber halls are generally thought to have had a largely domestic use, albeit in some cases on a great scale, the Continental halls may have had a more ritual function where homage to the ruler was performed. A ceremonial use has been suggested for the 10th-century west hall at Cheddar, and the scale of the stone hall at Northampton indicates a similar possibility.[87] Indeed, the parallels indicate that this hall was typical of a palace of the Continental Carolingian age; as Hodges observes the technology and the form of the building are alien to middle Anglo-Saxon England and asserts: 'the Mercian architect was striving to emulate a Carolingian model'.[88] Secular stone buildings were exceptionally uncommon in England before the 10th century but their magnificence was not lost on the Anglo-Saxons as can be judged from the poem *The Ruin* where the once glorious town, probably Bath, is described by the Anglo-Saxon poet as the 'work of giants' and its decay is mourned and its past splendours imagined.[89]

It is difficult from the archaeological record to determine whether its use was primarily secular or religious,[90] and the historical record is silent. Built for whichever purpose, the status of the building must have been one reason why Northampton became a town in the late Anglo-Saxon period. The site would have attracted a certain amount of specialization in terms of crafts and presumably had a resident, permanent population not involved in agriculture but in service or administration.

One of the signs of a high status secular site is the possession of a minster church, and to the west of the stone hall the extreme eastern end of a stone building was found. Its foundations were similar to those of the extensions of the stone hall, which may suggest they were contemporary. As this building extends westwards under the present St. Peter's church, and the excavated walls lay immediately east of the present church and respected the latter's alignment, they could relate to the original old minster, the ancestor of the present church. (In Edward the Confessor's reign the priest who was in charge of St. Peter's presided over many churches in the area, suggestive of a minster system that had survived the Danish invasions.)

Fig.6 The interior of Brixworth church showing the span of the nave which is considered to be similar to that for Northampton's stone hall and gives an idea of the size of the latter. Brixworth's church and Northampton's stone hall may, indeed, have been contemporary

The weight of archaeological evidence suggests very strongly that Northampton was a royal or ecclesiastical estate of considerable importance from the 8th century, and its place-name, which was originally just *Hamtun* —'the village proper' or 'the chief manor of a large estate',[91] indicates it was a central residence surrounded by outlying and dependent holdings. In the estimation of Gover, Mawer and Stenton 'it may be surmised that the original Northampton was a royal residence and estate at which were rendered the dues payable by the men of the folk ... settled around it'.[92] However, there is still no sign of it having reached the status of a town before the 10th century, and the arrival of the Danes.

The stone hall appears to have been abandoned during the early to mid-10th century, coinciding with a fundamental change in the settlement's character, evidenced by a metal-working complex immediately south-west of the hall. With this new use were associated two St. Edmund memorial pennies, indicating Danish occupation[93]—for these pennies were Danish coins minted in the southern Danelaw before 910 which remained in circulation until 930, although Williams suggests it is unlikely that they 'were deposited in Northampton after 917'.[94] This change to an activity so markedly different from the high-status royal/religious function that preceded it, makes it unlikely that the stone hall was still in existence. It is widely thought that the stone hall was abandoned at the time of the Danish occupation, the Danes having no use for it. Northampton was incorporated within the Danelaw between 877 and 917, an area which comprised the eastern half of England using Watling Street as a boundary, where Danish legal and social customs prevailed. As the settlement was effectively on the border between the Danes to the north and east, and the Anglo-Saxons to the south and west, it probably had an influx of soldiery which would have helped boost its economy. Indeed, border settlements often witness the most activity for their size. Recent excavations have determined that Northampton's defences were built in the 10th century, although whether during the period of the Danelaw or after its reconquest is as yet unclear. They initially consisted of a timber revetment, later rebuilt in stone.[95]

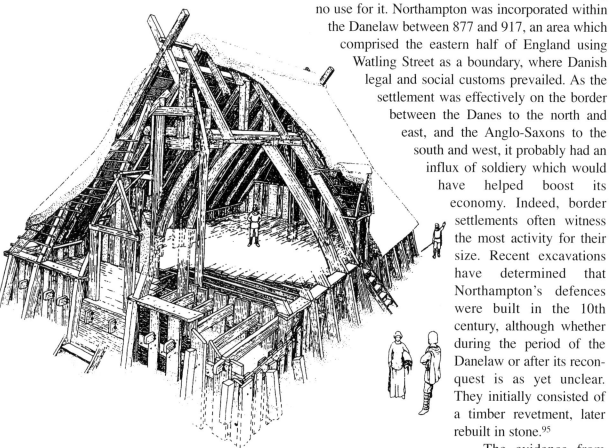

Fig.7 Reconstruction of one of the early 7th-century timber halls at Cowdery's Down, Hampshire by Simon James. Only the ground floor plan was revealed through excavation, but the foundations were massive and carried implications for the shape of the structure above, as hypothesized in the drawing

The evidence from Northampton and its environs suggests that it had an administrative function as early as the Romano-British period which was

Fig.8 Northampton is remarkable in having in situ *remains of five mortar mixers. Two were found just north of the present church and stone hall, while three others were found approximately 20m (65¹/₂ feet) south of the hall and were almost certainly used in the construction of the stone hall and/or minster. A bowl, 2-3m (6¹/₂-c.10ft) in diameter in which the mortar was mixed, was either cut into the ground or, in one example, constructed above ground level by means of a circular bank. The walls of the bowl were then lined with wattle and daub. In the centre of the bowl was erected a central post on which was a placed a rotating horizontal beam from which were suspended six paddles. It probably took four men or two animals to work the mixer by rotating the horizontal beam. Only one other example of a mixer is known in England, at Monkwearmouth in Northumbria where it was associated with the important monastery. An early 9th century date has been ascribed to the Northampton mixers, whereas the example from Monkwearmouth is dated to the late 7th or 8th century.⁹⁶ Other examples have been found in Poland, Belgium, Switzerland and Germany and, like their English counterparts, are invariably associated with high status sites. Again a Carolingian influence is suggested at Northampton because these types of mixers are well-known from that period. According to Hodges, that building technology of this kind was present in Northampton is considered to be perhaps 'the clearest illustration of the exchange of information and science during this time' between England and the Continent.⁹⁷ The Carolingian influence can be seen working further afield in Mercia, for example archaeological work at Repton in Derbyshire and Worcester Cathedral has shown some of the great minsters were also receptive to Continental architectural styles*

carried on into the Mercian era. But it was the arrival of the Danes who turned Northampton into a major centre with urban characteristics, its first historical reference coming in the *Anglo-Saxon Chronicle* in 913 in the fighting between Saxon and Dane in the reign of Edward the Elder. This process of urban development was consolidated in the 10th and 11th centuries with the gaining of a mint and reference to it being a 'port'—meaning either a market town or a walled town.⁹⁸

Planned and fortified towns: the precedence for Alfredian and Aethelflaedan *burhs*
The conventional wisdom is that the move towards planned towns began with Alfred the Great's construction of *burhs* in the late 9th century, a scheme that was carried into Mercia by his daughter, Aethelflaed,

and his Mercian son-in-law, Aethelred, and by Edward, Alfred's eldest son. However, there is strong evidence that Mercia played an earlier and major role in the creation of the planned Anglo-Saxon town. The kingdom predates Wessex by nearly 100 years in its mention of borough (*burh*) work (the building and maintenance of fortifications), the earliest mention of which is in one of Aethelbald's charters of 749. As Bassett observes, the Mercian kings had been 'vigorously pursuing a sustained, coherent policy of what we may call national defence' since at least the middle of the 8th century. Charters from this time show that these kings insisted that all land under their jurisdiction, unless it was specifically excepted, had to provide men for army service, *burh* maintenance and the building and repair of bridges, the latter being a vital part of military communications. As well as the Mercian fortifications of Hereford, Tamworth and Winchcombe being 'on a scale not far surpassed' by Alfred and his successors, Bassett also points out that they were on a much greater scale than the defences needed merely to fortify an episcopal centre or royal residence. Indeed he suggests that, with the exception of the former Roman walled towns, middle Anglo-Saxon centres of comparable significance in Mercia, for example Shrewsbury, Derby, Worcester and, possibly, Stafford and Warwick, should also be considered 'candidates for the possession of similarly early fortifications'.[99]

The possible antecedents for Alfred the Great's *burghal* towns that can best be described as fortified settlements with a planned street layout, are Hereford in western Mercia and *Hamwic* in Wessex. Hereford provides the clearest example and was possibly built by Offa during his campaign against the Welsh. Indeed, the claims for Hereford are particularly impressive, 'combining administrative, ecclesiastical and commercial functions within a defensive circuit by the eight or early ninth century [it] may be considered to have been the most sophisticated purely Anglo-Saxon settlement to have grown up in England by that time'.[100]

In 1968 excavations on the western part of the Anglo-Saxon defences in Victoria Street, less than 500m (1,640ft) north-west of the cathedral, revealed at least two, possibly three, phases of pre-Conquest defences. The first was found above two L-shaped grain-drying ovens which yielded a radiocarbon date

Fig.9 A part of the Anglo-Saxon defences of Hereford reconstructed at the rear of St. Owen's Court

centring on 761.[101] However, a date range of the mid-7th to 8th century has been ascribed to these ovens and gives an idea of the date after which the first defences were constructed. The ovens may suggest more than simply rural activity was taking place at the site, even though it was agriculturally-based. Fragments of re-used Roman altars and other Roman masonry were used in their construction[102] which is more likely to have originated from Hereford than from the nearby Roman town of *Magnis*. Indeed there is recent archaeological evidence for Roman occupation in the Broad Street area of Hereford.

A timber building was built over the destroyed remains of the grain-drying ovens and may have been associated with a small bank and ditch on its western side, a possible property boundary,[103] although it may have been the first phase of a defensive system. Indeed, this north-south orientated bank and ditch was seen on other sites north and south of Victoria Street and seems to have subsequently determined the line of the western defences. Although there was no dating evidence associated with this building or the bank and ditch, the first stage of a gravel rampart (the next phase of defence) sealed it and this has been tentatively dated to the mid-9th century, although an earlier date is possible. This raises the possibility that the gravel rampart predates the reign of Alfred the Great, and the faint possibility that 'it could be as early as the reign of Offa' (757-796). The gravel rampart was built from loose pink gravel mixed in with layers of clay and enclosed about 32 acres (13 hectares). The cathedral precinct and the possible later 8th century grid pattern of streets, thought to have been superimposed over an original cross-roads settlement, were included within this fortification.[104] This crossroads lay at the heart of the enclosure, being the junction of a north-south route from the ford on the Wye—a route partly surviving in the present Broad Street—and an east-west route that survives in part in St. Nicholas Street, King Street and the extreme western end of Castle Street. Biddle suggests that the 'sub-rectangular pattern' of Hereford's streets at this period may reflect nothing more 'than an efficient approach to the division of land and the provision of easy communication from point to point', an observation which can also be applied to many later planned Anglo-Saxon towns. Biddle adds that this organization of space would not have been a novelty for these people 'whose fields had for generations been tilled in a regular fashion and whose administrators could think in the orderly patterns recorded, for example, in the Tribal Hidage'.[105]

In conclusion it may be said that the rectilinear outline of Hereford's defences, the regularity of its street plan and the inclusion of the cathedral within the defences suggest that this was 'a deliberately planned foundation', probably pre-dating the 9th century. In a turbulent border area, it is not surprising that an important settlement and episcopal centre would be defended from a relatively early date. The idea of a defended settlement is clearly not a late Anglo-Saxon invention—people had been building banks and ditches around their settlements from time immemorial—and

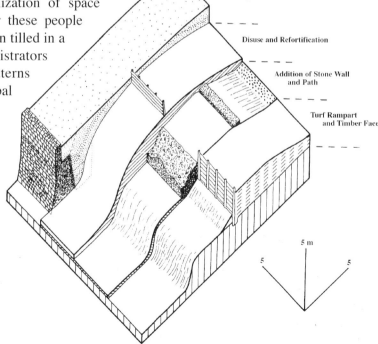

Medieval Wall and
Gravel Upcast

Disuse and Refortification

Addition of Stone Wall
and Path

Turf Rampart
and Timber Face

5 m

*Fig.10 Diagram showing the development
of the walls around Hereford*

in this extreme western Mercian area there is a surfeit of Iron Age hill forts. Offa's Dyke, built between 784-796, would have been a more recent example.[106]

A late 9th- or early 10th-century turf and clay timber-faced rampart succeeded the gravel predecessor, increasing the enclosed area to just under 52 acres (21 hectares).[107] The defences were later revetted and strengthened with stone.

The real impetus for fortified and planned settlements came with the Scandinavian invasions of the 9th century. The Norwegians had only a limited effect on western Mercia, but by contrast the Danes took over and settled extensive areas of eastern Mercia and even imposed their own law and customs. The first Danish raids began in the late 8th century and occurred sporadically until the mid-9th. Many places were attacked and pillaged, some even wasted and the second phase, beginning in 865, saw the Danes on a campaign of organized invasion.[108] Lack of land in Denmark and southern Sweden seems to have been the primary cause, although the invasion of England should be seen as part of a larger scale movement which took the Scandinavians to the eastern coasts of America and through Eastern Europe into Russia and the Middle East.

By 871 the Danes threatened to take over all of England, but were halted by Alfred the Great's campaign which culminated in the victory at Edington in Wiltshire (north-east of Warminster) in 878 from which the Treaty of Wedmore was secured and the Danes withdrew from Wessex and western Mercia. Alfred followed up his success by starting the planned building of *burhs*.

The Alfredian *Burhs* and their influence on Mercia

Although the origins of this type of planned town may well have developed within Mercia itself, as suggested for example by Hereford's earliest defences, the Alfredian *burhs* in Wessex perhaps provided the immediate prototypes for their Mercian counterparts in the early 10th century in English Mercia and for Edward the Elder's *burhs* in the Danelaw.[109] Alfred built several *burhs* in Wessex between *c*.878 and *c*.892 in a scheme of defence which ensured that no place was further than 20 miles from a fortified settlement—the *burh*. The most northerly of these *burhs* included places that had at one time been, or still were, part of Mercia, for example Bath, Wallingford, Oxford and Buckingham.

It is important to make the distinction between *burghal* towns and *burghal* forts which made up the 30 Wessex *burhs*. Biddle states that the former were relatively large and the streets of their modern successors often show traces of an original planned layout, whereas *burghal* forts were, by comparison, small and never seem to have been organized within their defences on regular lines for permanent settlement. *Burghal* towns sometimes re-used existing Roman walled towns, as with Bath; some were built on new sites with a rectilinear perimeter as at Oxford and Wallingford; while others were built as new settlements on promontory sites and had an irregular perimeter such as Malmesbury and Shaftesbury. Although they were built for reasons of defence, the *burghal* towns were also founded on sound economic principles, for it was only by securing a resident and growing population and a thriving economy that the large *burghal* towns could be properly protected and the defences maintained. It is possible that, initially, financial or other economic incentives were given to entice people to settle in the *burh* but, once established, people would be attracted to live there, especially in a period of perceived danger from bands of marauders.[110] For a craftsman such as a potter or metalworker, a defended settlement offering protection against marauders would have been a far more attractive proposition than sticking it out in an unprotected agricultural community. In turn, the *burhs* would also become increasingly dependent on a rural hinterland to supply agricultural goods which the residents would be unable to grow in sufficient quantity to support themselves. Thus the settlement would become dependent on trade, with its associated administrative structure, and so a true town emerged.

The defences of these late 9th- to early 10th-century Wessex *burhs* comprised earthern ramparts, which could be strengthened with turf and wooden strapping and were 'presumably crowned with timber palisades, and fronted by a ditch system'. The internal layout of the *burhs* intended to become towns appear to have been planned from the start with regularly arranged streets which divided the area enclosed by the defences into blocks which could be subdivided later for permanent settlement; these streets also gave ready access to and from each part of the town and facilitated 'an easy and rapid approach to any point of the defences in time of need'.[111] In Wareham and Winchester there appear to have been both small and large plot sizes which suggest different functions. It has been suggested by Aston and Bond that the small plots may have been the 'original permanent building sites' and the larger plots were open areas serving as 'camping-sites' where the people from the surrounding rural settlements could seek refuge in times of danger.[112]

The open market-place, which is such a feature of many towns these days, was not found in these late Anglo-Saxon grid-plan *burhs*, markets simply being held in the widest streets.[113] Biddle notes that the street which ran on the inside of the defences, called the wall- or intra-mural street, is a recurrent feature of the large rectangular *burh* street plans. This is not a feature found in Romano-British town plans, although they did occur in Roman forts or fortresses, and emphasizes the original military purpose of the Alfredian *burhs*,[114] where the ability to rapidly reinforce a section of the defences was crucial.

These planned West Saxon *burhs* show a remarkable consistency in their layout, whatever the physical drawbacks of the site which suggests a standard blue-print was envisaged from the start. There is apparently no known contemporary European parallel for such a 'deliberate scheme of town foundation on such a scale'.[115]

Prior to 860 Mercia appears to have remained relatively unaffected by Scandinavian attack, which is evidenced in the eastern midlands at least by the continued artistic and architectural output from these monasteries. In fact the Mercians appear to have been more concerned with campaigns against the Welsh in western Mercia. In 865 this apparent calm changed when a Dane by the name of Ivarr the Boneless, together with his brother, Halfdan, brought over a great Viking army from the Continent. After the capture of York in 866/7, they turned their attention on Mercia and in 867 Nottingham was taken under their control. A second army then arrived under the Danish leader Guthrum. Halfdan took command of the first army on Ivarr's departure for Ireland where he had been ruling as king, and in 872 the two armies over-wintered at Torksey, 10 miles north-west of Lincoln. By the autumn of 873 Repton was threatened and there the Danes duly overwintered. This appears to have triggered a political crisis within Mercia in 874 and the king, Burgred, was driven out and a rival claimant, Ceolwulf II, was installed in his place with Danish backing in return for tribute. In the area around and including Repton monastery the Danes built a 3½ acre (8.65 hectares) fortress which used the monastery church as a stronghold or gatehouse. The earliest mausoleum, west of the church, was re-used by the Danes for a high-status, probable pagan burial, in all likelihood for one of their leaders, around which the remains of some 250 people were stacked. The final insult, if any more was needed, was the construction within this defended site of a large dock in the banks of the Trent for the repair of the Danish longboats. The irony is strong. What had been a symbolic royal burial place for several 8th and 9th century Mercian kings was now turned into a Viking stronghold from which they could launch attacks, attacks which led to the end of Mercia as a separate kingdom. Stafford also suggests that the camp at Repton was very likely to have been a deliberate act of defiance and strategy on the part of the Danes, showing the 'incapacity of Burgred's defence' and 'may have been designed to bring [him] to tribute'[116]—by occupying such a high profile site that was close to Tamworth and Lichfield, it broke the political heart of Mercia. In 877, when the Danes partitioned Mercia, Ceolwulf II was given a portion as a reward for his loyalty; after Guthrum was defeated by Alfred the Great, Ceolwulf—perhaps surprisingly—kept a part of Mercia around Worcester which he ruled subject to Alfred. Ceolwulf II might appear something of a traitor, but, by coming to terms with the Danes, he did in effect protect Mercia from total invasion.[117]

As Stafford relates, in the early 870s the Viking leaders in England seem to have been 'uncertain whether settlement or tribute through alliance and domination was their aim'. After 875 a campaign of 'direct tribute-taking through settlement was adopted' and in 877 part of the Viking army settled in Mercia, probably north and east of Watling Street. By about 910 this area (along with other parts of eastern England) was under the control of Danish jarls, or leaders, such as Jarl Thurferth at Northampton, Jarl Thurcytel at Bedford and Jarl Toli at Huntingdon, who each ruled the armies based on these towns. It is suggested by Stafford that rather than being the 'pattern of the settlement of the 870s and 880s', this control of towns could well have been a 'deliberate military regrouping' by the Danish armies against the military advances made by Aethelflaed and her brother Edward the Elder in the early 10th century. By 911, Tamworth, the former 'capital' of the Mercian kingdom was merely a border town and Aethelred and Aethelflaed, who ruled English Mercia, had chosen Gloucester and the Severn Valley as their new political centre.[118] They set about securing this western half of the kingdom and it appears that they fortified several western Mercian towns before Aethelred's death in 911. There is evidence that Gloucester, Shrewsbury, Chester (907) and, of course, Hereford and Worcester had been (re)fortified by 910.

After Aethelred's death a renewed Viking campaign began. In 913 the Danish armies from Northampton and Leicester raided English Mercia reaching Hook Norton, about 7 miles south-west of Banbury in Oxfordshire on the old *Hwiccian* borders. These raids apparently made Aethelflaed more determined than ever to regain the lost Mercian areas,[119] but under West Saxon and not Mercian overlordship. In this context the construction of the post-910 *burhs* may possibly be viewed as a way of destroying any residual Mercian independence. This was in advance of the shire system which politically wiped Mercia off the map.

The construction of *burhs* followed apace. The first was at Bridgnorth, a settlement first mentioned in the *Anglo-Saxon Chronicle* in 895 when the Danes '... went overland till they reached Bridgnorth on the Severn and built that fortress ... Then they stayed the winter.' The place-name *Cwatbrycg(e)* is used in one version of the original.[120] *Cwat*, from which the present place-names Quatt and Quatford, close to Bridgnorth, are derived, is considered by Gelling to be a district name but its etymology is obscure. In the following year the Danes dispersed. Gelling also observes that in 910 *Aethelweard's Chronicle** notes that a group of 'Northumbrian Danes crossed the Severn at *Cwatbrycg*' before they were defeated at Tettenhall near Wolverhampton in southern Staffordshire. The *Mercian Register* states that in 912 '... Aethelflaed, lady of the Mercians, came on the holy eve of the Invention of the Cross [2nd May] to *Scergeat,* and built the borough there, and in the same year that at Bridgnorth'.[121] *Scergeat* has not been identified. However, in this chronicle Bridgnorth is recorded as *Bricge*,[122] as it was generally known in the Anglo-Saxon period. It does not appear that a town developed and Bridgnorth may be an example of a *burghal* fort, used to protect the important river-crossing on the Severn.

In 912 Aethelflaed's brother, Edward, constructed *burhs* at Hertford and Witham in Essex. In 913 the *Mercian Register* records that Aethelflaed 'went with all the Mercians to Tamworth, and built the borough there in the early summer'. Florence states that Aethelflaed rebuilt the town which suggests it had been devastated, possibly during the time when the Danes had been based at Repton. From Tamworth, Florence of Worcester records that Aethelflaed 'went to Stafford, and built or threw up a fort on the north bank of the river Sowe'.[123]

In 914 the *Mercian Register* then records that Aethelflaed built a fortification '... at Eddisbury in the early summer, and ... in the early autumn, that at Warwick'.[124] There are two Eddisburys in Cheshire and both have traces of fortifications. One is near Delamere, a village about 10 miles west of Chester, and the other in Rainow, a village 3 miles north-east of Macclesfield. While either could have been the 10th-century *burh*, the Iron Age hill fort of Castle Ditch near Delamare in central Cheshire is usually identified with Aethelflaed's *burh* on what is, admittedly, rather thin archaeological evidence. If this is indeed the

---

*Aethelweard was a descendant of the West Saxon King Athelred I (865/6 - 871), brother of Alfred the Great, and was ealdorman between 973 and *c*.998. He translated a version of the *Anglo-Saxon Chronicle* (now lost) into Latin verse.

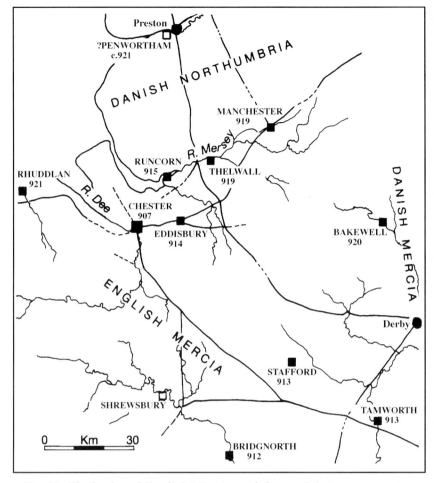

Fig.11 The burhs *of English Mercia and dates of their construction,*
(based on N.J. Higham, The Origins of Cheshire, *1993)*

site, then it is suggested by Higham that Aethelflaed must have wanted some control over the Roman roads which ran from the Mersey crossings at Warrington and Stretford (Manchester), by which route the Danes could have invaded in 910. From the uncertainty of the position of Aethelflaed's Eddisbury *burh*, it is clear that this is an example of a fortification which did not develop into a town; indeed, it is probable that this site was never intended to be held on a permanent basis.[125]

In 914 Aethelflaed fortified Warwick. Warwick is recorded as *Waerincgwican* between 723-37 and in 914 as *(aet) Waeringwicum, Waerincwic* in the C and D versions of the *Anglo-Saxon Chronicle*[126] and has been interpreted by Gelling as 'dwellings by a weir'. This rather modest meaning argues against it being a settlement of note before the *burh* was constructed. Unlike Tamworth and Stafford, Warwick saw a period of relative prosperity between the creation of the *burh* in 914 to the Norman Conquest. A population of between 1,000-1,500 has been estimated from the Domesday account which records 248 houses, 22 burgesses and 100 'bordars'[127] (a bordar was a smallholder, a tenant with a few acres of farmland or just a cottage garden—the Anglo-Saxon term 'cottar' was synonymous). In 914 Edward also constructed *burhs* on either side of the Ouse at Buckingham.

In 915 Edward took the *burh* at Bedford where he built a second on the south side of the Ouse. The *Mercian Register* records that Aethelflaed built a fortress at 'Cyricbyrig and that at *Weardbyrig*; and in the same year before Christmas, that at Runcorn'. Florence of Worcester records these events under 916. *Weardbyrig* has not been identified although coins were being struck here in Athelstan's reign (924-39).[128] *Cyricbyrig* is believed to be the Chirbury on the Shropshire/Welsh border, about 6 miles south-east of Montgomery. Chirbury Castle is the name given to a rectangular enclosure in the north-west corner of the village which may have been the site of the *burh*, although Stanford reports that excavations have not uncovered any evidence of a defensive ditch, palisade or any internal occupation.[129] The place-name Chirbury means 'burg or fort with a church',[130] which does lend support to this being one of Aethelflaed's *burhs*.

Higham suggests that the probable site of the 10th-century *burh* at Runcorn was on Castle Rock, 'a promontory jutting into the Mersey valley from the south side which was removed in 1862 to improve navigation'. Promontory sites were often utilized and if Castle Rock was used, it was probably intended mainly 'to guard a major river crossing against Danish forces'. It appears that efforts were made to develop Runcorn as a town through changes in local land tenure and administrative units. Higham considers that the dedication of an apparently new church to Bertelin, an obscure Mercian saint, suggests Aethelflaed's involvement as she was an advocate of this saint. Runcorn and Eddisbury were very likely designed to deter the Northumbrian Danes from any further attack from the north—they had already caused great damage in Cheshire. With the protection of these new fortresses, Chester was made much more secure and shielded 'from the front line of a volatile war'.[131]

In 916 Edward ordered the construction of a *burh* at Maldon in Essex, and in 917 those at Towcester and at an unidentified *Wigingamere*. The latter two *burhs*, along with that of Bedford, were all subject to Danish attack during the year, but on each occasion the Danes were defeated. In 917 Edward was again active in East Anglia, and the following year took Stamford, where he built a *burh*.

Aethelflaed died on 12 June 918, aged about 50, at Tamworth[132] and was buried at St. Oswald's in Gloucester. Her brother Edward took control after ousting Aethelflaed's daughter. The Irish Norse seized York in 919 and one of Edward's first tasks was to further reinforce the Mersey frontier. In 919 the *Chronicle* records 'In this year after autumn King Edward went with the army to Thelwall and ordered the borough to be built, occupied and manned; and while he stayed there he ordered another army, also from the people of Mercia, to occupy Manchester in Northumbria, and repair and man it'. Thelwall is 3 miles east of Warrington but no fortifications of Edward's *burh* have ever been identified, although it is thought the *burh* may have been built 'to control the important fords between Wilderspool/Latchford and Warrington'.[133] The *burh* at Manchester would have controlled a significant Roman road junction between York and the river Mersey, a confrontational gesture to the Viking kings.[134] With this north-western boundary fortified, Edward, before mid-summer of 920, 'went with the army to Nottingham, and ordered to be built the borough on the south side of the river, opposite the other, and the bridge over the Trent between the two boroughs. Then he went from there into the Peak district to Bakewell, and ordered a borough to be built in the neighbourhood and manned'.[135] The *burh* at Bakewell has not been securely identified, but it may lie under the town, possibly on the steep hillside around All Saints Church.[136]

In the following year, 921, the *Mercian Register* records that Edward built a *burh* at *Cledemutha*, which is identified with Rhuddlan and was the only *burh* to be built in Wales. After this, the construction of *burhs* ceased as, by 922, Edward was overlord of Britain, with the exception of the Norse settlements of York, Orkney and the Western Isles.[137]

Stafford

Stafford lies on a terrace in a bend of the river Sow near the Sow's junction with the river Penk. In Anglo-Saxon times the surrounding area was marshy and the terrace was, in effect, a peninsula of dry land. Stafford, 'one of the settlements on the frontier of the Danelaw', was fortified by Aethelflaed in 913.[138] The *Mercian Register* relates that Aethelflaed had gone 'with all the Mercians to Tamworth, and built the borough there early in the summer' of the same year 'and afterwards, before Lammas, [1st August] that at Stafford', which implies that Stafford's defences were built swiftly.[139] This indicates a pressing need for protection from the Danes, as well as the determination of this remarkable warrior queen.

Place-name etymology suggests Stafford 'is one of the earliest settlements in the region to acquire its English name'. The 'Staf' element derives from the Old English word *staeth*—'landing-place',[140] implying that access to the settlement was primarily along the river Sow.

One theory holds that there was an Anglo-Saxon settlement at Stafford in the 7th or 8th century prior to the foundation of the *burh,* which may have comprised a religious community, whereas an alternative suggests that, if the manufacture of Stafford Ware turns out to be as early as suspected, then the origins of Stafford might be sought in an 8th- or 9th-century royal manor or *villa regalis*.[141] Unfortunately, no pre-*burh* settlement has been identified. In either event, the marsh-bound peninsula might have been chosen as a *burh* simply because it was deemed especially defensible against Scandinavian attack.[142]

In 1994 Moffett noted that 'no definite evidence of Saxon defences has so far been recognised in any of the excavations in the town'. In 1999 the Oxford Archaeological Unit found a ditch at Tipping Street which pre-dated the line of the walls depicted by Speed in 1610. However, the earliest fills contained 12th- and 13th-century pottery, and any part of the boundary line of the *burh* defences has yet to be found.[143] Carver speculates that such defences would have comprised a turf bank, topped by a palisade or have been revetted with a stone wall, and enclosed a large area, possibly even the whole peninsula. Certainly, sherds of 10th-century pottery have been found from all over the peninsula, suggesting settlement of the whole area.[144] In 1983 a central area around St. Mary's church (the probable site of the Anglo-Saxon minster), and possibly that demarcated by Crabbery Street, Greengate Street, Mill Street and Earl Street (see Fig.12) was tentatively suggested by Cane *et al* as being the area of the *burh*, an area now fossilized as the reserved enclave called the College Quarter. The northern half of this area was apparently given over to the storage of grain and bread-making as no evidence of domestic occupation has been found in this area, but whether this activity 'was a purely commercial concern or part of the services of the 10th-century Aethelflaedan garrison is less clear'.[145] It is speculated that this central, possible *burh* area 'was characterised by dispersed and/or ephemeral settlement clustered around centralised services, such as baking' with a more stable nucleus, possibly a religious building, in the area of St. Bertelin's chapel immediately south of the present St. Mary's church.[146] With archaeological excavation showing that the 'storage and processing of grain' was one of Stafford's main activities, it has led to the theory that the *burh* was a collection point for tax paid in the form of grain, as well as being 'assigned responsibility for producing a supply of pottery'.[147]

Radiocarbon dates from charcoal found in four sites, including that from the last firing of the pottery kilns used in Tipping Street (see below), produced a calibrated date of the early to mid-9th century, indicating the likelihood of a settlement before the construction of the *burh*. The tentative picture that emerges is of a 'possible high-status establishment or perhaps a community which dedicated this area of the settlement to the essential household tasks of drying grain for milling and baking bread' and that the 'local arable landscape may have been fairly well-developed' a theory supported by pollen analysis from the locality. Experimental archaeology demonstrated that the potential for

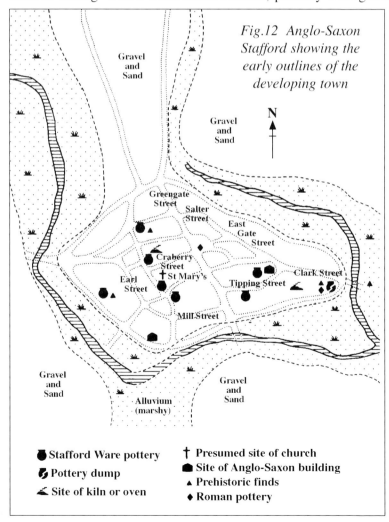

Fig.12 Anglo-Saxon Stafford showing the early outlines of the developing town

N

Gravel and Sand

Gravel and Sand

Greengate Street
Salter Street
East Gate Street
Crabbery Street
St Mary's
Earl Street
Tipping Street
Clark Street
Mill Street

Gravel and Sand

Gravel and Sand

Alluvium (marshy)

● Stafford Ware pottery
⚡ Pottery dump
◿ Site of kiln or oven
✝ Presumed site of church
⬟ Site of Anglo-Saxon building
▲ Prehistoric finds
◆ Roman pottery

Fig.13 Examples of early Stafford Ware

baking bread and/or drying grain in the ovens ready for milling was substantial and the implication is that this activity would have met the needs of a high ranking household (religious or secular) with retainers, or of a military establishment, or even of the whole community.[148]

To the east of St. Mary's, around Tipping Street and Clarke Street, was another late Anglo-Saxon site which specialized in the production of 10th-century pottery, called Stafford Ware. Four pottery kilns have been identified with the latest found in 1993 in Salter Street when an extension to Marks and Spencer was being constructed. The kilns appear to both pre-date and post-date the *burh*, but were no longer in production after the Conquest.[149] Little pottery was produced in the mid-9th century in England, but a century later its use was widespread at all levels of society. Stafford became a centre for pottery manufacture in the late Anglo-Saxon period, producing a wide variety of wares including cooking pots, deep bowls, spouted pitchers and lamps. Stafford Ware-type vessels have been found throughout the Severn Valley but it is not certain whether these came from Stafford or were copies; indeed, Stafford Ware is similar to the pottery imported into the town from East Anglian kilns, especially those at Thetford. The clay at Stafford was tempered with river sand and was generally fired to an orange colour. It was well-finished, often having a band of routletting—a decoration applied by a roller on the rim or shoulders of the vessel. Kiln waste has been found in Tipping Street, at Clarke Street beyond the *burh* defences, and was also dumped by the cart-load in the marshland which was clearly used as a rubbish tip. Indeed, the waste at Clarke Street may have been used as infilling in this marshy area.[150]

There was no evidence for any other industry apart from butchery, which was likewise centralized in a specific area. A mint existed at Stafford in the late Anglo-Saxon period from which some of its silver pennies survive. Otherwise the settlement seems to have had largely agricultural functions—the *Domesday Survey* records six plough-teams, a mill, meadowland and a wood. Its population at this time has been calculated as at least 750 people, though nearly a third of its 162 houses for burgesses were unoccupied.[151]

Tamworth, the royal centre of Mercia

Tamworth stands on a spur of land overlooking the confluence of the rivers Tame and Anker. One of three trackways, of probable prehistoric origin, crossed the Tame by a ford to the west of the confluence continuing along a holloway across the spur on which Tamworth town centre stands, and has been incorporated into the present-day Holloway, Silver Street and Aldergate (see Fig.14). Today's Bolebridge Street, Colehill and Gungate probably represent the route of a second prehistoric track which approached the Tamworth site from the south-east, using a ford across the river Anker.[152]

The main Romano-British settlement in the area was *Letocetum* (Wall), some 7 miles west of Tamworth. Part of a double-ditched enclosure, possibly a Romano-British fortlet, has been found about 1 mile to the west of Tamworth's town centre, guarding the third route, which passed north of the site, connecting the territories of the Coritani and Cornovii, and a ford over the Tame. North and south of Tamworth there is a good deal of evidence for Romano-British rural settlement along the Tame valley, indicating a healthy rural economy. Roman tile and painted plaster found in a residual context in Bolebridge Street, close to the site of an Anglo-Saxon watermill, indicates a Romano-British structure existed here, but its function is uncertain.[153]

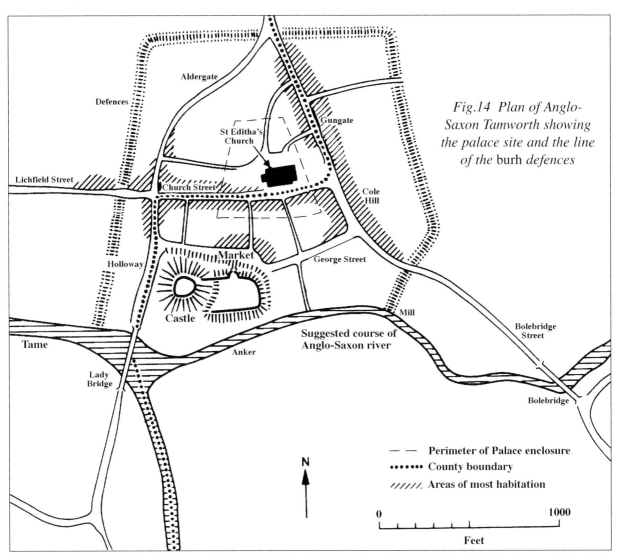

Fig.14 Plan of Anglo-Saxon Tamworth showing the palace site and the line of the burh *defences*

Tamworth takes its name from the river Tame which, as with many river names, has a British origin, but Meeson suggests that place-name evidence in the vicinity of Tamworth indicates 'an indigenous British population may have survived the Anglo-Saxon migration'. Indeed, Tamworth was situated in the border zone of two Iron Age tribes—the Cornovii and the Coritani—and it is thought that a distinct tribal unit may have been centred on the Tamworth/Lichfield region,[154] which survived into the post-Roman period.

Tamworth in the Anglo-Saxon period

Tamworth was the principal royal and adminsitrative centre of the Mercian kings up to the middle of the 9th century, if not later. It is not known why Tamworth was chosen or, indeed, whether this arrangement dated back to Penda's time in the first half of the 7th century,[155] when Outer Mercia was established.

The earliest historical reference to Tamworth may occur in a memorandum written at Peterborough between 675-92 (probably in 691), which records the sale of an estate by Aethelred, king of Mercia, to the newly founded monastery at Breedon-on-the-Hill in Leicestershire: 'When this was done, King Ædilred in his chamber in his own *vicus* called *Tomtun*, joining hands with the queen and bishop Saxwulf, placed a turf from the land on a gospel-book before many witnesses in confirmation.'[156] Although it is generally accepted that *Tomtun* refers to Tamworth, this identification is not proven. If it does, then there is the possibility that *Tomtun* lay at the centre of an estate whose boundary could reflect the later ecclesiastical parish boundary. The place-name *Tomtun* belongs, with only five others in the country, to the earliest stratum of *tun* names recorded before 730, when the *tun* element may have had a much more limited meaning and may have denoted a 'royal vill'. If this interpretation is correct, it follows that gatherings involving Mercian royalty occurred at Tamworth from the late 7th century, Rahtz and Meeson suggesting that there may have been a monastery or palace present by that time.[157]

Although there is no archaeological evidence to support any suggestion of settlement on the site before the 7th century,[158] by the 780s it had become 'a favourite residence of the Mercian royal household', for they appear to have regularly stayed at Tamworth at Easter and Christmas between at least 781 and 857.[159] For example, in a charter issued by King Burgred on 18 April 857 concerning a grant to the bishop of Worcester of a house and commercial rights in London, 22 years before Bishop Waerferth's acquisition of the *Hwaetmundes stan(e)* estate, it is stated that the charter was witnessed 'in the famous place called Tamworth, on the holy Easter of the Lord'.[160]

Date	Issued by	Reference to Tamworth
Christmas 781	Offa	in sede regali sedens ... In Tamouurdie
Christmas 781	Offa	in regali palatio in Tamouuorthige (This charter may be spurious, although with an authentic basis)
799	Coenwulf	in vicu regio aet Tomepordige
Easter 808	Coenwulf	in loco ... vulgo vocatur Tomepordig
Christmas 814	Coenwulf	in vico celeberrimo qui vocatur Tompordig
Easter 840	Beorhtwulf	in pascha ad Tomepordie
Christmas 841	Beorhtwulf	in natali domini aet Tomanpordie
Christmas 841	Beorhtwulf	in celebri vico Tomeuuorthie (probably a spurious charter)
Christmas 841	Beorhtwulf	in celebre vico on Tomepordie
841	Beorhtwulf	in loco qui dicitur Tomanpordie
Christmas 845	Beorhtwulf	in loco regali qui dicitur Tomeuuordig
849	Beorhtwulf	In famosae loco qui dicitur Tomepeording
855	Burgred	in vico qui Tompeordin
855	Burgred	in vico celebre qui a multis vocitatur Tomanpordigne
857	Burgred	['in the famous place called Tamworth']

Fig.15 Anglo-Saxon charters witnessed at Tamworth (based on the work of P. Rahtz and R. Meeson)

The change in name from *Tomtun* to *Tamouurdie* or *Tamouuorthige*—the latter two are both recorded in Offa's charters of 781—must have occurred in the intervening 100 years. Gelling suggests the change from *tun* to *worthig(n)* occurred 'probably for a specific reason which had to do with a change in the nature of the settlement'. *Worthig* is a derivative of *worth*, the Old English for a settlement, probably an 'enclosed settlement', and in the midlands *worthig* may originally have had the early meaning 'akin to that of *burh*, and was used for sites of considerable importance'. Gelling therefore speculates that if this change in name 'signifies an enlargement of the enclosed settlement-area' in the 8th century, 'this could indicate ... the population grew to include people' not directly involved with the upkeep of the royal household. However, she stresses that this does not imply that Tamworth became a trading centre as well as a palace site at this time and adds that there is no evidence to suggest Tamworth developed commercially to any significant degree until after the Danish wars of the 10th century.[161] Tamworth was probably akin to the high status site at Northampton, a proto-urban site which, unlike Northampton, did not develop into a sizeable town in pre-Conquest times.

Altogether 15 charters were witnessed at Tamworth, the majority, particularly from Beorhtwulf's reign (840-52), deal with land in the *Hwiccian* kingdom. This is probably because such charter material has survived in the cathedral of Worcester which, unlike other ecclesiastical centres, survived attacks from the Scandinavians. An outline of these grants with references to Tamworth is shown in Fig.15.[162]

The Mercian palace and the two phases of Anglo-Saxon defences

The exact location of the Mercian royal palace in Tamworth has yet to be found, but Meeson proposes that the palace enclosure was situated on the summit of the spur of land between the rivers Anker and Tame, and within the triangle between these rivers and the two early tracks (see Fig.14). This palace enclosure lay at the centre of a much larger enclosure which may have been delineated by an insubstantial bank and ditch of possible 8th century date. In the early summer of 913 Aethelflaed replaced this with a ditch that fronted a berm, 'a substantial turf and timber rampart' and a road which ran inside the rampart. No evidence has yet been found for a southern rampart, so it is assumed that the rivers Anker and Tame formed a suitable boundary.[163]

The smaller enclosure that possibly surrounded the palace has been identified from a study of the property boundaries and a detailed contour study. Here, excavations in 1969 revealed part of a structure which had massive post-pits but, unfortunately, it was not dated reliably, although it is likely to be pre-Norman. Several Anglo-Saxon structures were also located near the eastern boundary of this enclosure, and St. Editha's church, which is near the centre, may also contain remains of two pre-Conquest buildings.[164]

Traditionally, Offa's palace was thought to have been beneath the Norman castle site. This tradition probably stems from the belief that the herringbone masonry in the wall on the north side of the castle bailey

Fig.16 Engraving Tamworth Castle and church in 1780

was of Anglo-Saxon origin. However, it has now been shown to be of Norman origin. Nor does the wall indicate the perimeter of the pre-Conquest palace because in other areas of the bailey the stone wall has been shown to replace an earlier rampart with a timber frame—a rampart believed to have been part of the Norman motte and bailey castle. Indeed, in three excavations in the area of the castle bailey no evidence was found for Anglo-Saxon structures. It is conceded, however, that the castle area might have had some earlier settlement because of its situation—it comprises a 'broad, flat, elevated terrace' which overlooks the confluence of the Tame and Anker rivers and an important ford, and had a supply of fresh springwater. Meeson relates that 'half of the castle bailey was levelled down in the 17th century', whilst 'a Norman ditch between the motte and the bailey has cut away any possible Anglo-Saxon occupation layers'. Any putative pre-Conquest remains can only have survived in 'a very small area of the bailey' and 'the ground sealed beneath the motte'.[165]

As the royal Mercian household celebrated both Easter and Christmas at Tamworth on a number of occasions, at least from Offa's reign (757-796), it is suggested by Meeson that there may have been a church associated with the palace, even that an Anglo-Saxon *monasterium* existed on the site. The 'palace' enclosure might then be that which actually defined the inner territory of a monastery, for it is known that monasteries often provided the facilities for meetings held by secular rulers and officials. The same problem is faced as at Northampton: was Tamworth an important monastic site with a palace attached, or was it a royal centre with a minster church? As there is no documentary evidence for a monastery but there is charter evidence for a palace, it is safer to assume that the smaller 'palace' enclosure housed a palace complex with a minster church. St. Editha's church stands almost at the centre of the smaller enclosure and is the only church site known to be of pre-Conquest origin in the *burh*, suggesting it is built on the site of an Anglo-Saxon minster. However, the palace complex may also have had a proprietory church or chapel, as with many Anglo-Saxon sites.[166]

It is not known how long the palace survived at Tamworth but the latter's position just over a mile north of Watling Street and, therefore, inside the fringe of the Danelaw made it a border town in the early 10th century. Indeed, once the Danes had overwintered at Repton in 873/4, about 16 miles north-east, it is likely that the palace at Tamworth was not considered a safe enough place for the Mercian royal household to meet. Aethelflaed's fortification of Tamworth should not been seen as particularly significant in this context, as the creation of a defended *burh* here was part of a scheme aimed at bringing the Danelaw back into English control. As such, Tamworth was just one of a number of sites which were fortified to create bases from which to launch a concerted attack on the Danes. Significantly there is no archaeological evidence of Danish settlement of the *burh*, although the street names of *Gumpegate* (Gungate) and *Ellergate* (Aldergate) are at least partly Danish, implying Danish occupation.[167] Quite what happened to the palace remains a mystery. Meeson comments that neither the Danes who sacked Tamworth nor the West Saxons who regained it would wish to leave any trace of a Mercian royal palace.[168]

The Anglo-Saxon watermill

One of the most exciting Anglo-Saxon finds at Tamworth was that of a watermill. Between 1971-8, excavations in the south-east corner of Tamworth revealed the remains of a horizontal-wheeled watermill just outside the Anglo-Saxon defences which dated to the mid-9th century or earlier. It had a timber wheel-race and a clay-built dam, and was powered by a leat fed by the river Anker. This mill was abandoned either because it was destroyed or, more likely, because of water leakage. A second mill was built on the remains on the first and was dated by dendrochronology to around the mid-9th century—this too was of a horizontal-wheeled design and was served by a millpool positioned at a higher level which was fed by a new leat. The second Tamworth mill shows considerable skill and competence in its construction, which is not surprising as this type had been well-developed in Britain for at least 200 years.[169]

The excavation report notes that among the finds 'were the sole-tree of the mill [a device which was involved in the raising or lowering of the wheel assembly which varied the gap between the millstones in the millhouse above], with its steel bearing; one of the wheel paddles; many fragments of millstones, of local stone and imported lava; fragments of the clay bed in which the lower millstone was set; and the residues of lead window cames. Grain and grain impressions include oats and possibly barley'. The imported lava millstones may have come from the Rhineland. Even though Tamworth was near to local supplies of suitable stone which would have made large scale imports unnecessary, lavas were probably favoured as wear simply exposed another rough edge. Lava querns are often found on mid- to late Anglo-Saxon sites.[170] In a letter of 796 from Charlemagne to Offa there is an apparent reference to the Mayen grey lava which was used in the 'black stones': 'As for the black stones which your Reverence begged to be sent to you, let a messenger come and consider what kind you have in mind, and we will willingly order them to be given, wherever they are to be found, and will help with their transport'.[171]

The second mill was destroyed by fire during the late Anglo-Saxon period and, after a period of abandonment, during which many of the mill's timbers were robbed, the site was sealed by metalling and roads.[172]

It is important to note that Tamworth's was a horizontal-wheeled mill and not the vertical-wheeled type. Gelling states that the former is characteristic of the outer regions of the British Isles and is considered less technologically advanced than the vertical-wheeled type, which one would think would have been more suitable for a high-status site such as the 'capital' of Mercia. Indeed, Holt suggests that after the Norman Conquest vertical-wheeled mills were built for the lords of a manor, whereas the horizontal-wheeled watermill was 'associated with peasants'. The answer may lie in that, whereas most horizontal-wheeled mills were formerly believed to lack gears unlike their vertical counterparts, evidence for gears in the former has now been found in a few sites. Indeed, a horizontal-wheeled mill has recently been found at Orphir in Orkney associated with a high-status Norse settlement.[173] The building of the Tamworth mill could have been a form of royal investment in new construction, and to be associated with its ingenuity may well have been seen as adding prestige to the royal family.[174]

Oats and possibly barley were recovered from what is presumed to be the last use of the mill, indicating that it was used for animal feed rather than for human consumption—the use of oats has been identified as the likely fodder for horses at Stafford's Anglo-Saxon oven site, although the general population would also have eaten them, even if those of a higher status were more likely to have consumed wheat. There might have been a substantial number of horses present when the palace was in use, and subsequently when Tamworth was fortified by Aethelflaed with a possible garrison in residence. However, if the last use of the mill was for the production of livestock feed, then this indicates Tamworth had lost an appreciable degree of status. The destruction of the second mill might be associated with the wars of the late 9th and early 10th centuries, but it could just have easily met a more mundane end in an accidental fire. Even in wartime accidents can and still do happen. After this the site was abandoned and the 'next phase of activity cannot safely be dated before the middle of the 11th century'.[175]

Did Anglo-Saxon Tamworth have urban characteristics?

With reference to Fig.14, it is possible that the alignments of Hollow Way/Silver Street/Aldergate, and Bolebridge Street/Colehill/Gungate reflect the course of two of the pre-Anglo-Saxon trackways. It is thought by Rahtz and Meeson that Lichfield Street and Church Street were probably set out at some time in the development of the *burh*, and therefore two separate stages in the development of the settlement's layout are immediately discernable. The other two main streets in the town plan, Market Street and George Street, are of likely post-Conquest date.[176]

It has been suggested that the larger 8th-century enclosure, which contained the palace enclosure, might have been set aside for the general populace, an occasion which possibly caused the change from *tun* to *worthig*. While a cluster of buildings probably formed outside the limits of the 'palace' enclosure, the settlement had few definable urban characteristics in the pre-913 era. Although the pre-Athelflaedan settlement may have had a residential function, no hard evidence that it was defended in a military sense or that the place was systematically manned as a fortress has been found.[177]

As previously noted, the earliest Anglo-Saxon towns were on coastal or riverine locations where there was a natural incentive for trade. Tamworth's rivers are shallow and unnavigable, which was not conducive for its emergence as a trading centre in the pre-Conquest period, even though it may have been an early focal point for several tracks. A marketplace has been located outside the walls near the gate of the *burh* in Lichfield Street, but it is thought unlikely that it existed in the 8th or 9th centuries.[178]

Rahtz and Meeson remark that the charters make reference to the 'celebrated or famous place' of Tamworth which may implies it was something more than a palace complex which, in itself, was usually referred to as a *villa regalis* or *villa regis*. In spite of the presence of a palace making Tamworth politically and administratively important, it appears that no 'significant administrative function devolved upon the overall settlement'. Neither is there any evidence that Tamworth was important as a commercial or urban centre in the 8th and 9th centuries. Excavation has not revealed evidence of a large population or the 'numerous regulated plots and houses of urban type', and there is no evidence of a mint before the reign of Edward the Elder's son Athelstan (924/5-939). Indeed, Gelling notes that 'the number of surviving pre-Conquest coins with [the Tamworth] mint signature is not large' and the quantity of surviving coins minted at Tamworth in Aethelred II's ('the Unready') reign, 978-1013, is also 'consistently low' when compared with other boroughs. Only one pre-Conquest coin was found in the 1960-71 excavations at Tamworth, a silver cut half penny of Edmund the Martyr which was minted at Torksey in Lincolnshire and dates to 975-9. Although a coin minted at Torksey is very rare, it is stated by Gelling that this find cannot 'do much to relieve the general impression of [Tamworth's] failure to thrive as a commercial centre which emerges from archaeology and records'.[179]

After Mercia became a subordinate kingdom, Tamworth clearly lacked the royal support that had been so significant in its early development. From the 10th to the 14th centuries there is a sense of 'consistent poverty' in Tamworth,[180] with the town facing competition from more than 20 others in the general area.[181]

While the settlement had a proto-urban character which should have logically made it the most suitable candidate for the shire town or, at least a commercial and administrative centre, this clearly did not happen. When the shire system was imposed, Stafford was chosen as the county town and Tamworth was split between Staffordshire and Warwickshire. This makes sense if it is thought that Edward the Elder's, and the subsequent West Saxons' kings' reasons for shiring Mercia was to undermine Mercian identity and, with it, its power. While it has been suggested that in the 10th century Stafford and Warwick together may have been 'more important militarily' than Tamworth,[182] which led to the latter's demotion, what better than to split the old Mercian 'capital' literally in two by putting the boundary of Staffordshire and Warwickshire through the *burh*. Surely this was a symbolic emasculation?

Tamworth's decline as a centre may be gauged from the *Domesday Book* where it receives only passing mention and where there is 'no entry relating specifically to the borough', although a space was left for such an entry.[183] What was its magic for the 8th and 9th century Mercian royal household? We may never know.

Anglo-Saxon Church Architecture in Mercia

All Saints', Brixworth, Northamptonshire (SP 747713)
All Saints Church may have an 8th century origin, elements of which remain in the nave and lower parts of the tower. The stair turret (top left) is dated to c.1000 and is probably the latest Anglo-Saxon feature in the church. The ring crypt (bottom left) at the eastern end of the church is tentatively dated to about 850 and would have originally been roofed over. The remains of two blocked doorways and of stairs suggest pilgrims entered by one door to view relics, held in a small chamber, and left by the other. The ring crypt is thought to have been modelled on that at St. Peter's in Rome, built in about 600. Michael Wood suggests the church may have been built in the late 8th century to house one of St. Boniface's relics, who was martyred in 754, as Boniface was particularly revered at Brixworth. Wood also postulates it was a Mercian royal church 'and that the likeliest patron was the great builder Offa himself'.

Below: All Saints' Earls Barton, Northamptonshire (SP 852638). Doorway in the west face of the tower; note its robust but dignified effect

Above and top right: St. Peter's, Stanton Lacy, Shropshire (SO 495788)
There are two remaining Anglo-Saxon parts to this church which date to between the mid-10th to the 11th century: the north and west walls of the nave and most of the north transept. The picture above shows the west wall of the nave with its five pilaster strips. The blocked doorway (top right) is in the north nave wall. Above it is an equal-armed cross, perhaps a consecration cross

Above: All Saints, Wittering, Lincolnshire (TF 056020)
All Saints was built between 950-981 and originally comprised a chancel and a nave. The stone used came from Barnack quarry 2½ miles to the north-east. Each corner of the nave has long and short work. The chancel arch has been described by H.M. and J. Taylor as 'of a massive grandeur unequalled in any other of the smaller Anglo-Saxon churches', and the whole church as an 'unusually complete example of a small parish church of the two-cell type'

Above: St. John the Baptist, Barnack, Northamptonshire (TF 079050)
Barnack was a monastic estate in the 7th century, the present church dating from the 10th century. Pilaster strips, a quintesstial Anglo-Saxon device, are seen on the tower

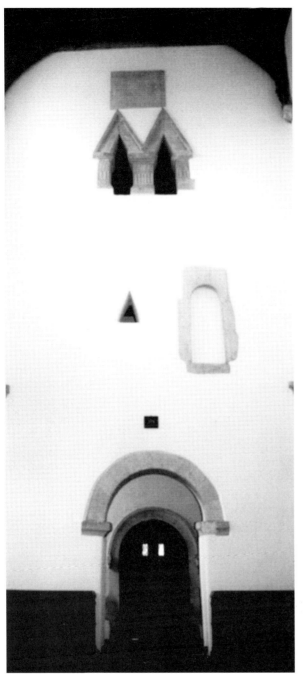

*Above: St. Mary's, Stow-in-Lindsey, Lincolnshire (SK 882819)
The original church was allegedly founded by Ecgfrith, king of
Northumbria, in 674 and destroyed by the Danes in 870. In
c.975 Bishop Aelfnoth of Dorchester-on-Thames, Oxfordshire,
built a new church as head minster for the Lincolnshire part of
his diocese. This church was destroyed by fire and rebuilt in the
mid-11th century when it was richly endowed by Earl Leofric of
Mercia and his wife, Lady Godiva. The tower belongs to the 15th
century, but the walls shown here belong mainly to this later pre-
Conquest phase. The doorway (above right) is in the north
transept and dates to the 10th century. Single stones span the
thickness of the wall, and the left-hand side includes 'long and
short' work*

*Above: St. Matthew's, Langford, Oxfordshire (SP 249025)
This church has been described by John Blair as 'a superb monument to the Anglo-Saxon fusion'. It
combines Anglo-Saxon features, such as pilaster strips and windows splayed both internally and exter-
nally, with Norman Romanesque styles. The arch (left) is one of two that leads from the tower and,
although of probable late 11th century date, it uses a traditional Anglo-Saxon style with its tall,
narrow shape and rounded head*

CHAPTER 10
Decline

Offa's son Ecgfrith ruled Mercia for 141 days between July and December 796. His accession to the throne was the most secure of any succession between the beginning of the 8th century and the effective end of Mercia as a separate state. He was possibly the only Mercian, or even Anglo-Saxon king, who was anointed as king in the lifetime of his predecessor. Not only did Ecgfrith inherit a stable political position, but also a strong means of government and the experience, through his anointment nine years earlier, of acting as sub-king to his father.

Alcuin describes Ecgfrith posthumously in a letter of 797 to the Mercian ealdorman, Osbert, as a 'most noble young man' and adds significantly that he did not die 'for his own sins; but the vengeance for the blood shed by the father has reached the son. For you know very well how much blood his father shed to secure the kingdom on his son. This was not a strengthening of his kingdom, but its ruin'.[1]

Alcuin's words suggest strongly that Offa killed all rival contenders to the throne. Indeed, his letters seem to indicate there was actually some opposition to Ecgfrith's accession during Offa's lifetime, presumably from other princes who felt they had a claim. But Offa's culling of any close rivals effectively left his line without a male heir once Ecgfrith was dead. Ecgfrith's successor, Coenwulf, was a distant relative from a widely separated branch of the Mercian royal family, possibly a very distant cousin. It is not certain how or why Ecgfrith died; it may have been through natural causes, but there is a suspicion that Coenwulf may have engineered his own succession, for he proved an ambitious and ruthless man.[2]

On succeeding to the throne, Ecgfrith did not hesitate to use his authority, as demonstrated through charter evidence. During the five months of his reign he granted land in four charters in Gloucestershire, Wiltshire and Hertfordshire.[3] Only one (Sawyer's no.151) has been generally regarded as openly spurious. Yet the rate at which he produced charters is rapid compared to other Mercian monarchs, albeit subject to the vagaries of their survival down the centuries.

Although he appears quite active, Mercian power began to crumble in his short reign. In both Kent and East Anglia, Mercian rule was overthrown. Eadberht Prean, the ordained pretender to the throne of Kent and exile of necessity who had obtained the protection of Charlemagne from the enmity of Offa, returned to England and, it is believed, seized the throne and ruled between 796-8. He began minting coins in his own name at Canterbury by moneyers who had previously worked for Offa. Similarly Eadwald, king of East Anglia, also began to issue his own coinage.[4]

Mercian influence in the Church waned too. Aethelheard, archbishop of Canterbury, was symbolic of Mercian rule in Kent, particularly as he had worked with Offa to decrease Canterbury's authority with the establishment of the Lichfield archbishopric. He was now advised by his monastic community at Christ Church to flee—'The good shepherd' quoted Alcuin, pointedly against Aethelheard 'giveth his life for his sheep, but the hireling fleeth'—and found shelter with Ecgfrith who had granted him a monastery and land, possibly at Patney, Wiltshire. There is some indication that Christ Church had been attacked around this time, as its charters, books and records from the 7th and 8th centuries have not survived,[5] although whether on Eadbhert Praen's orders is unclear. The bishops of Lindsey and London left their sees and the country in 796, never to return, and it is believed that the sees of Hereford and Sherbourne also fell vacant. Whether all these events were connected is uncertain, but it indicates an ecclesiastical crisis at this juncture.

After the death of Ecgfrith in December 796 the situation in Mercia began to resemble that of 8th-century Northumbria, with rival dynasties continually trying to install one of their own as king.

Coenwulf - reigned 796-821

'... gloriously received the crown of the kingdom of the Mercians, and held it with unconquered strength by the strong vigour of his government'. Simeon of Durham *c*.1129[6]

Coenwulf claimed descent from the younger brother of Penda and Eowa, Cenwalh, but his claim was viewed with suspicion even in his own day. It is possible that Coenwulf's father had been an ealdorman, and Coenwulf himself appears to have had a power base at Winchcombe where he was closely associated with the abbey. Bassett considers that Coenwulf was possibly closely related by blood to one or more of the 'last members of the Hwiccian royal family' to have held authority in the sub-kingdom, a group that would have included the brothers Eanberht, Uhtred and Ealdred (see chapter 6, p.106). This relationship could have been through either Coenwulf's mother or father. Interestingly, his name, together with those of his brothers, Cuthred and Ceolwulf, and of his own children, Cynhelm and Cwoenthryth, resemble the names of several 7th- and 8th-century aristocrats in the *Hwiccian* kingdom, some of whom may have been 'lesser members of the Hwiccian royal family'.[7]

Steven Bassett has identified the area around Winchcombe as being the possible heartland of the original *Hwicce*. A short-lived county, Winchcombeshire, was created in the later 10th century as part of the shire system and survived until about 1017, after which it was absorbed into Gloucestershire. Winchcombeshire's territorial boundaries can be reconstructed and there is some evidence that the area had long had a separate identity as its own kingdom. In a charter of 897, concerning an estate at Blockley, north-east of Winchcombe, there is a reference made by Coenwulf to his 'hereditary land belonging to Winchcombe'. Coenwulf's personal links with Winchcombe are well known: his daughter was the abbess of Winchcombe's monastic church and his son Cynhelm was buried in the church. Later he himself was buried at the abbey, probably in a 'freestanding stone mausoleum' of the type found at Repton, beside his son. Both Coenwulf and Offa were major patrons of the church at Winchcombe, and the place had been a royal *tun* for the *Hwiccian* and then the Mercian kings.[8]

Bassett has shown that reliable land grants made

*Fig.1 Winchcombe looking towards the church,
itself built very close to the site of the original abbey*

by Mercian kings before 727 include no territory from the future county of Winchcombeshire, whereas those made by Mercian kings between 727 and *c*.821, show a significant concentration in the future short-lived county. This strongly suggests that by the later 720s the *Hwiccian* kings had lost sole control of this heartland, and that which is identified by Coenwulf as his 'hereditary land belonging to Winchcombe' is the land which stayed in the private ownership of the *Hwiccian* royal family the longest. The absence of reliable charters for this area before the 720s also supports the idea that this land was the *Hwiccian* kings' 'most prized and anciently held land, their patrimony' which would have been kept intact against all odds[9]—until a branch of the family took over the larger Mercian kingdom. By the 10th century, however, most of this land had been given to the church of Worcester and in due course became part of Worcestershire. (The land not granted to the church subsequently formed Winchcombeshire, later to be incorporated into Gloucestershire, which thus surrounded pockets of church lands that long formed isolated parts of Worcestershire.) The Winchcombe heartland has been identified by Bassett as being the type of land-unit that is described in Latin sources of the 7th and 8th century as a *regio,* or occasionally as a *provincia*: a large, discrete area that had some administrative independence and often formed a major part of the big kingdoms such as Mercia and Northumbria.[10] Several other *regiones* or *provincia* are known to have existed in the *Hwiccian* kingdom, of which the *provincia* of the *Husmerae* and the *regio* of the *Stoppingas* are mentioned elsewhere.

Whether Coenwulf was of *Hwiccian* stock or not, it is with his accession that the *Hwicce* disappear as an independent kingdom.

Alcuin in his letter to the Mercian ealdorman, Osbert, of 797 suggests that he should:

> admonish the more diligently your king [Coenwulf], and also the king of my country, [the Northumbrian king, Eadwulf] that they hold themselves in godliness, avoiding adulteries; and do not despise their former wives in order to commit adultery with women of the nobility; but under the fear of God either keep their own wives or with their consent hold themselves in chastity.[11]

Even Offa, whom Alcuin had criticized earlier in the letter for his apparent purge of contenders for his son's throne, is held up as an example of propriety, which must say much about Coenwulf's character.

This character, whatever its faults, included skills which enabled Coenwulf to reign for 25 years, a reign that has been described as 'just as successful and as powerful as Offa'.[12] But it was not an easy reign.

His first concern was the situation in Kent. The loss of control of the see at Canterbury was an unsatisfactory political position, but his hands were tied. He could not attack Kent because of the possibility that Eadberht Praen was ordained, and to do so would have meant his own instant excommunication, but if it could be proven that Eadberht *was* ordained, he would have to relinquish the crown.

Coenwulf worked on building up his relationship with Rome, showing his acumen as a politician by using the past decrees of Pope Gregory the Great to his advantage. In a letter of 798 to Pope Leo III, he questions Offa's action in establishing an archbishopric at Lichfield, and requests that the sees of both Lichfield and Canterbury be abolished and the metropolitan see moved to London in accordance with the canons of Gregory, which decreed that the Church should be ruled from London and York. (Canterbury had replaced London as that was where Augustine had died and been buried).[13] Brooks observes that the plan would fulfill St. Gregory's wish, which memory had been kept alive by holding provincial synods in the diocese of London: at Brentford, Hatfield, Chelsea and Hertford, as well as London itself, and enable the Canterbury problem to be swept aside and a new archbishopric created in a Mercian controlled town. The elevation of London to a metropolitan see would also offer 'a basis for negotiation and coexistence with Eadberht Praen, or with the Kentish nobility'. Pope Leo, however, decided not to move the see of Canterbury, even though London was the natural ecclesiastical centre for the south of England for geographical, economic and political reasons.[14] Lichfield was also left as an archbishopric. However, the pope did pass judgement on Eadberht Praen:

... we, accounting him like Julian the Apostate, excommunicate and reject him, having regard to the safety of his soul. For if he still should persist in that wicked behaviour, be sure to inform us quickly, that we may send the apostolic reminder to all in general, both to princes and to all people dwelling in the island of Britain, exhorting them to expel him from his most wicked rule and procure the safety of his soul. For on account of a king of this kind, we have very greatly blessed and praised our brother the aforesaid archbishop, [Aethelheard] because he endangered his life for the orthodox faith'.[15]

The pope's judgement gave Coenwulf the chance to impose his authority on Kent. Simeon of Durham gives a vivid account for the year 798:

... Cenwulf, king of the Mercians, invaded the province of the people of Kent with the whole strength of his army, and mightily devastated it with a grievous pillaging almost to its utter destruction. At the same time Eadberht, king of the people of Kent, was captured, and the king of the Mercians ordered his eyes to be torn out and his hands ruthlessly cut off, because of the pride and the deceit of those people. Then, having obtained it with the Lord's help, he added the dominion of that kingdom to his own dominions ....[16]

A tradition relates that Eadberht was brought back to Coenwulf's estates at Winchcombe and held in custody as a mutilated prisoner at Coenwulf's newly founded Winchcombe Abbey, some records stating that Eadberht was released on the day of the dedication of the new church, which was probably in 811, to find no support in his old kingdom of Kent.[17] William of Malmesbury's account of Eadberht's release provides a colourful picture of such an occasion and the splendour of an early 9th-century church dedication. Coenwulf

moved with sentiments of pity ... released him. For at Winchelcombe, where he had built a church to God, which yet remains, [William was writing in the 12th century] on the day of its dedication he freed the captive king at the altar, and consoled him with liberty; thereby giving a memorable instance of his clemency. Cuthred, whom he made king over the Kentish people, was present to applaud this act of royal munificence. The church resounded with acclamations, the street shook with crowds of people, for in an assembly of thirteen bishops and ten dukes, no one was refused largesse, all departed with full purses. Moreover, in addition to those presents of inestimable price and number in utensils, clothes, and select horses, which the chief nobility received, he gave to all who did not possess landed property a pound of silver, to each presbyter a marca of gold, to every monk a shilling, and lastly he made many presents to the people at large. After he had endowed the monastery with such ample revenues as would seem incredible to the present time, he honoured it by his sepulture, in the twenty-fourth year of his reign.[18]

It must be borne in mind that William of Malmesbury admired Coenwulf, for he writes that he 'was a truly great man, and surpassed his fame by his virtues, doing nothing that malice could justly find fault with. Religious at home, victorious abroad, his praises will be deservedly extolled so long as an impartial judge can be found in England'.[19] Clearly Eadberht Praen would not have shared William's opinion for as a blind and hand-less man his future, if he did indeed survive the effects of his injuries and incarceration, would have been bleak.

According to both William and the *Melrose Chronicle*, Coenwulf installed his own brother, Cuthred, as king of Kent. Cuthred apparently had great delegated powers which included the right to mint coins in his own name;[20] however, on his death in 807, Coenwulf took direct control of the kingdom and by so doing had Canterbury under his personal jurisdiction too.

Aethelheard returned to Canterbury in *c*.798/9 as archbishop and strove to re-establish its authority over the churches south of the river Humber as well as recovering from Coenwulf the property Offa had taken from the Church. Within the year he had received professions of faith and obedience from the bishops of Lindsey and Dunwich and within three years those of the bishops of Worcester and Hereford.[21] In mid-801, at Alcuin's instigation, Aethelheard travelled to Rome with the bishop of Winchester via the court of Charlemagne to obtain Pope Leo's approval for the ending of Lichfield's status as an archbishopric. This was ratified at a synod held at *Clofesho* on 12 October 803, the proceedings stating: '... that never shall kings or bishops or ealdormen or men of any tyrannical power presume to diminish the honour of St. Augustine and his holy see, or to divide it in the slightest extent', and so it has stayed until the present day.[22]

Aethelheard died on 12 May 805 and was succeeded as archbishop by Wulfred (805-832). Alcuin had written to Aethelheard eight years earlier to suggest that he made arrangements to select a successor, and Wulfred was his archdeacon. That Wulfred was chosen from the *familia* of Christ Church is significant, as the last certain such selection had occurred in 667-8, and this would have shown respect to local sensibilities. However, Coenwulf would almost certainly have tried to prevent the selection of a successor from the Kentish nobility, so that another archbishop like Jaenberht would be avoided—indeed the fact that Wulfred seems to have had family connections in Middlesex, making him probably of Middle Anglian or Mercian origin, would have made him acceptable to the Mercian king.[23]

Wulfred was given the freedom to mint coins without naming the Mercian king on the reverse, something never granted to his predecessor, which has generally been interpreted as as a sign of Coenwulf's goodwill—but Kirby suggests it could also be interpreted that Mercian influence was weakening at Canterbury. Whatever the goodwill at the start of Wulfred's episcopate, Coenwulf's relationship with Wulfred soon soured. By 808 a rift, of which the cause is unknown, between the two men had become common knowledge, even on the Continent the pope reported to Charlemagne that Coenwulf had still not made peace with the archbishop. The dispute was, however, apparently settled, as between 809 and 815 Coenwulf made generous gifts of land to Wulfred at Barham, Rainham, Graveney near Faversham, Romney Marsh, Elmstead and elsewhere in Kent. In 816 they soured again when, at a synod held in Chelsea, Wulfred and his bishops attacked the lay and royal control of religious houses and, in Kirby's words 'the secularization of ecclesiastical land'. The crux of the problem was that Coenwulf claimed to be the heir of the Kentish kings and, as such, was in control of the royal monasteries of Minster-in-Thanet and Reculver. Indeed Coenwulf's own daughter, Cwoenthryth, had recently been appointed abbess of the latter, which happened to be one of the most affluent royal nunneries in Kent. The synod directly challenged the right of Coenwulf to appoint people to vacant livings at monastic centres, although earlier papal privileges had allowed Offa, and more recently Coenwulf, to do so. Yorke remarks that as Wulfred 'was anxious to reform his diocese on Carolingian lines', he took a stand against lay ownership and stated that they should come under his authority instead. The matter was referred to the new pope, Paschal I, who confirmed Coenwulf's rights in 817. Even so, Wulfred and Coenwulf continued to argue about each other's rights to the Kentish church's estates and their revenues.[24]

Coenwulf lodged serious complaints against the archbishop and Wulfred was suspended from office, for possibly up to six years. In turn, Wulfred lodged complaints about Coenwulf, the bishops supporting his cause by apparently taking the rather drastic step of withholding the right to baptism from the people for an equivalent period. In 821, the stand off continuing, Coenwulf summoned Wulfred to a council at London and told him that unless he gave up the estates in dispute and pay a fine of £120, he would strip the archbishop of his possessions and exile him. Coenwulf made it clear that, if exiled, Wulfred would not be allowed to re-enter the country, even if the pope or Frankish authorities interceded on his behalf, suggesting that Coenwulf was increasingly estranged from Frankish Europe. Wulfred unwillingly accepted Coenwulf's terms. Nevertheless, it was only a year after Coenwulf's death that Wulfred was restored as archbishop in September 822 when Ceolwulf, the next Mercian king, had to reconcile himself with the archbishop so that he could be anointed as king.[25] Indeed it was on 17 September 822 that

Ceolwulf and Wulfred 'presided' over a council of Mercian bishops and nobles at the royal vill of *Bydictun* where Ceolwulf was consecrated as king.

Coenwulf's control over central Mercia and its sub-kingdoms had been quickly established after the initial problems, ruling through *dux* or ealdormen. His authority was recognized in Kent (post-rebellion), Sussex, Essex and East Anglia. There is only a small amount of charter evidence for this widespread authority however, and includes a grant of land given by Coenwulf in Denton, Sussex in 801 which is considered questionable.[26] The vast majority of Coenwulf's grants deal with land in Kent (21 out of 38 recorded charters) while there are 11 dealing with land in the *Hwiccian* kingdom, although this may reflect the survival of charters and not his actual activity. Coenwulf's authority in the disputed or marginal territory north of the Thames was quickly established, however, and it appears that Middlesex and the area around London was under Coenwulf's control at the outset of his reign. As early as 797 he was able to confirm the grant of Glastonbury Abbey made by King Ecgfrith and Pope Leo to his son Cynehelm and his successors.[27] Cynehelm is the Kenelm of legend who was allegedly murdered as a seven year old under the auspices of his wicked sister (see p.234); however, the existence of this grant undermines the legend. Indeed, Cynehelm had been appointed by his father as an ealdorman, along with one of Coenwulf's brothers.[28] In 798 Pope Leo III confirmed Cynehelm's ownership of Glastonbury Abbey and Cynehelm also signed a number of charters from 803 to 811. But Cynhelm died in 812, nine years before his father, possibly in conflict against the Welsh, and was buried in the newly-founded Winchcombe Abbey.[29]

In 799 Coenwulf concluded a new peace treaty with Wessex which seems to have ended a period of estrangement between the two.[30] It is possible that Ecgberht of Wessex, whom Beorhtric had exiled, with or without Offa of Mercia's assistance, may have returned to claim back the West Saxon crown in the badly documented period between 796-99. If he did, his bid was unsuccessful and it is likely that he retired to Kent, staying there until Eadberht Praen was deposed by Coenwulf in 798, when he returned to the Frankish court. It is probable that Ecgberht was welcome on the Continent as his Kentish ancestry gave him strong Frankish connections. Indeed, it is thought likely that Eadberht Praen had had Carolingian support for his takeover bid in Kent, and there is even a suggestion that Ecgberht, who was Eadberht's cousin, may have been involved in this uprising. Ecgberht finally succeeded to the West Saxon throne when Beorhtric died in 802. The *Anglo-Saxon Chronicle* reports that on the same day ealdorman Aethelmund rode 'from the province of the Hwiccians across the border at Kempsford' and was met by the troops of Ealdorman Weohstan. Both were killed, but it was the Mercian force who were defeated. It is not known whether Aethelmund's was the spearhead of a larger force, or just an ill-conceived impulsive reaction, for Ecgberht's return must have seemed ominous to the authorities in Mercia. At the time of his expulsion Ecgberht had been a very able but extremely young man, and during his time in exile he may have campaigned with Charlemagne and learned about military tactics as well as the art of kingship.[31] Whatever the degree of foreboding sensed on the part of the Mercians, Ecgberht was fairly quiet in his dealings with Mercia for the first 20 years of his reign and left Coenwulf, obviously a powerful king, relatively undisturbed.

Problems with Northumbria arose early in Coenwulf's reign. Following the murder of Aethelred of Northumbria in March 796, the province was in disarray. Aethelred's opponent Eardwulf took the throne and a few years later ordered the execution of a son of a previous king whom, it transpired, had been plotting to seize the throne with Mercian support. Incensed, Eardwulf led an army against Mercia in 801. Simeon of Durham records that Coenwulf:

> ... collected an army and led many forces from other provinces with him. When there had been a long campaign between them, they finally made peace by the advice of the English bishops and nobles on both sides ... And an agreement of most firm peace was made between them, which both kings confirmed with an oath on the gospel of Christ, calling God as witness and surety that in their life-

time, as long as they should possess this present life and be invested with the insignia of the kingdom,
a firm peace and a true friendship should persist between them, unbroken and inviolate ...[32]

It would seem that the fighting proved inconclusive, and perhaps engendered mutual respect, for the treaty appears to have lasted for the rest of Coenwulf's reign.

In spite of being ruled directly by Offa after the murder of their young king, Aethelberht, in 794, East Anglia had shown an inclination towards autonomy since the death of Aethelbald in 757, whose close connection with this kingdom was never emulated by the Mercian monarchs who succeeded him. After Aethelberht's murder and Offa's death, one Eadwold or Eadwald seems to have taken control and was minting coins in his own name in 798. What happened to him after this time is uncertain. However, Coenwulf was presumably able to re-establish his authority in the province for he was minting coins in his own name by about 805.[33]

Kirby states that when the Welsh confronted Mercian forces at Rhuddlan in 796 or 797 they were not to know that Coenwulf would so swiftly reassert Mercian power in England or that he would be able to invade Wales in 798 and kill the king of Gwynedd, Caradog ap Meirion. In 816 or 817, when the next king of Gwynedd, Cynan ap Rhodri, died, the Mercians under Coenwulf ravaged north-west Wales and took the inland principality of Rhufoniog, which probably lay between the rivers Conway and Clwyd. The Mercian forces may also have been involved in a battle in Anglesey in 817 or 818, and in 818 or 819 Coenwulf even devastated Dyfed to the south, thereby taking his army into the most south-westerly of the Welsh kingdoms. It seems that from 817 until his death in 821, he was engaged upon a fairly constant offensive campaign against the Welsh, and indeed was killed in action at Basingwerk in Flintshire at the northern end of Wat's Dyke. It is considered by Stenton that he may have been organizing another major offensive against the Welsh, as a campaign only a few months later, in 822 or 823 succeeded in destroying the fortress of Degannwy in Gwynedd and in conquering Powys.[34]

Mercia lost a very powerful and effective king when Coenwulf was killed in 821. His forcefulness and energy had, on the whole, resulted in a general period of peace within the territories he ruled as over-lord. He lacked Offa's international influence, but in his efficiency of government and military control at home he was just as effective as Offa, arguably even more so.

The years 821-827

The 820s was a period of change and a lack of continuity of government seeing three different kings whose combined reigns totalled less than six years. It was also the period where the power of Wessex grew rapidly, and incursions by Danish forces grew more numerous. It was a time of a reduction in Mercia's power, when Kent, Surrey, Sussex and Essex were detached from Mercian control, never to be regained.

Ceolwulf, reigned 821-823

On Coenwulf's death, his brother, Ceolwulf, succeeded to the Mercian crown. His reign only lasted two years before he was deposed by Beornwulf, probably one of his 'less distinguished ealdormen' whose name appears low down the list of those attesting charters of 812 and 823 for both Coenwulf and Ceolwulf.[38]

It was during the years 821-823 that the fortress of Degannwy near Conway was taken and Powys overrun and conquered by Mercian forces. The *Annales Cambriae* record for 822 (some consider the date should be 823) 'Degannwy is destroyed by the Saxons [Mercians], and they took the region of Powys into their own power'. Stenton considers this action to have been the last great achievement of Mercia. Within a generation the last male descendant of the kings of Powys had left for Rome, 'worn out by age and misery'.[39] There is some debate concerning which of the two Mercian kings, Ceolwulf or Beornwulf, led the successful forces. Most opinion favours Ceolwulf, but Kirby describes Beornwulf as a 'vigorous ruler' and a 'man of action', and the more likely of the two to have led such an attack in the first few months of

The Legend of Kenelm

The version below is that given by William of Malmesbury:

Kenulf, king of the Mercians, his father, had consigned him, when seven years old, to his sister Quendrida, for the purpose of education. But she, falsely entertaining hopes of the kingdom for herself, gave her little brother in charge to a servant of her household, with an order to despatch him. Taking out the innocent, under pretence of hunting for his amusement or recreation, he murdered and hid him in a thicket. But strange to tell, the crime which had been so secretly committed in England, gained publicity in Rome, by God's agency: for a dove, from heaven, bore a parchment scroll to the altar of St. Peter, containing an exact account both of his death and place of burial ... [the letter was written in English and had to be translated to the pope] who wrote a letter to the kings of England, acquainting them with the martyrdom of their countryman. In consequence of this the body of the innocent was taken up in the presence of a numerous assembly, and removed to Winchcomb. The murderous woman was so indignant at the vocal chaunt of the priests and loud applause of the laity, that she thrust out her head from the window of the chamber where she was standing, and, by chance, having in her hands a psalter, she came in course of reading to the psalm "O God my praise," which, for I know not what charm, reading backwards, she endeavoured to drown the joy of the choristers. At that moment, her eyes, torn by divine vengeance from their hollow sockets, scattered blood upon the verse which runs, "This is the work of them who defame me to the Lord, and who speak evil against my soul." The marks of her blood are still extant, proving the cruelty of the woman, and the vengeance of God. The body of the little saint is very generally adored, and there is hardly any place in England more venerated, or where greater numbers of persons attend at the festival; and this arising from the long-continued belief of his sanctity, and the constant exhibition of miracles.[35]

Florence of Worcester gives a similar account and there are at least eight manuscripts which contain the story of Kenelm. A lengthy version is printed by William Caxton in his *Golden Legend* which adds much local detail. In this Kenelm is said to have been taken hunting in the Clent Hills (near Birmingham) and is killed in a wood and his body 'cast into a deep pit in a valley between two hills'. His burial place was eventually discovered by a poor widow and her white cow through a miracle and the place was then called 'Cowbage'. When the body was exhumed in a solemn gathering attended by the archbishop and the other bishops 'forthwith there welled up on that spot a fair spring, which is called St. Kenelms Well unto this day, where much people have been healed of divers maladies'. Indeed a well dedicated to St. Kenelm still exists in an undercroft below the east end of a chapel built at the spot and dedicated to this saint. Another spring that rises close by is known as a clouty well, being dressed with small pieces of material as offerings.

In a charter of 1175 from Pope Alexander III, Winchcombe Abbey's possession of St. Kenelm's chapel was confirmed. A small town called Kenelmstowe was said to have developed around the building and holy well, but after pilgrimages to it ceased the town gradually decayed and in the late 19th century it was said by Brassington that 'nothing remains ... but an almost forgotten name'.

As Kenelm's body was being taken back to Winchcombe for burial by the men of Gloucestershire 'an armed band of the people

Fig.2 c.12th-century figure popularly believed to be that of St. Kenelm carved on a stone built into the exterior south wall of St. Kenelm's church, north-west of Romsley, near Clent

of Worcestershire came up, and a dispute arose' as to who should have Kenelm's body. Both groups decided to sleep on it at a place called *Pyriford*, possibly Pershore. However the abbot of Winchcombe awoke first the next morning and he and his men were five miles away before the others came to. What follows was a chase with the abbot and his men 'calling on Kenelm, [as they] rushed along a narrow path into a wood'. Close to collapse from exhaustion and thirst the abbot thrust his cross into the ground and 'a fair well of water sprang up, whereof they drank and refreshed them much'. Mick Sharp records that the monks had been aided by the 'miraculous appearance of a series of wells' along their route which spawned a series of chapels afterwards visited by pilgrims. The monks eventually reached Winchcombe and when they carried Kenelm's body into the abbey 'the bells rang without man's hand'. Kenelm's shrine was housed in the abbey alongside which is St. Peter's parish church which succeeded the Anglo-Saxon minster. Sharp observes that 'a low mound in the churchyard's northern corner may mark the Hwiccian royal mausoleum where Kenelm and his father were first buried'.[36]

As it appears that Cynehelm/Kenelm was an adult when he died (see p.232), how did the legend of the boy-king martyr come about? It seems that anyone who was of royal blood and had been murdered was in line for the status of a martyr, and the murder of a child, and therefore of innocence, would have even more resonance, even if it was fiction. It is possible that after his son's death, Coenwulf was keen to elevate his son to saintly status. Winchcombe Abbey was revived in the second half of the 10th century by bishop Oswald of Worcester at a time when Cynehelm was certainly regarded as a martyr. The development of the legend was the next stage and this occurred in the 11th century. As Farmer puts it so succinctly 'The Legend of Kenelm is a good example of how a writer with a vivid imagination and some half-understood historical data produced a completely fictitious account of a prince who certainly existed but of whom virtually nothing is known'. A saint's relics were a useful way of bringing in revenue to a monastery.[37]

This is very similar to the origins of the cult of the Anglo-Saxon prince, Wystan, who was murdered by his mother's prospective husband as Wystan objected to the match. He too was subsequently revered as a martyr and was buried in the mausoleum at Repton which soon became a place of pilgrimage.

Why Cwoenthryth, the Quendrida of Malmesbury's account and the Quyndre/Quendreda in Caxton's publication, was portrayed from the 11th century as the wicked instigator of her brother's crime is more difficult to fathom. Perhaps there is an element of revenge by the Church for her having been installed as the abbess of Minster-in-Thanet, the richest nunnery in Kent, at a time when Archbishop Wulfred was trying to reform central church appointments.

his reign than Ceolwulf, who is held to be an obscure monarch whose reign was a time of general disorder and ended in deposition. Kirby argues that if Ceolwulf had led a successful military campaign into Wales it is unlikely he would have been deposed as he would have enjoyed the backing of his army.[40] However, if Ceolwulf had not led the campaign, his brother's earlier campaigns would have been partially wasted, Beornwulf would have to start from scratch after his coup, take an army into Wales, conquer Degannwy, then consolidate the position in north Wales, before heading south to subdue the whole of Powys from Flintshire to Brecknock all within a space of about six months if the date of 823 for the Degannwy action is accepted.

Upon balance, one would support Stenton's view that on his accession, Ceolwulf swiftly restarted and led the successful campaign against Wales,[41] but perhaps neglected affairs in central Mercia. For a document issued at *Clofesho* in 825 states that after Coenwulf's death and therefore, by implication, during Ceolwulf's reign, 'much discord and innumerable disagreements arose between various kings, nobles, bishops and ministers of the Church of God on very many matters of secular business',[42] although charter evidence suggests Ceolwulf restored relations with Archbishop Wulfred, a policy continued by Beornwulf. Perhaps the discord led to him being deposed.

Beornwulf, reigned 823-826

At first Beornwulf appears to have been a more effective administrator, as demonstrated by a charter of 30 October 824 for the settlement of an argument between the church of Worcester and Berkeley Abbey concerning the future descent of a monastery at Westbury in Gloucestershire. He seems to have worked closely with Archbishop Wulfred, assisting him in the settlement of claims over property, particularly the monastery at Minster-in-Thanet, which had been the subject of such controversy in Coenwulf's reign.[43]

Stenton notes that Beornwulf's authority was recognized in Essex, Middlesex and Kent and that 'he was the

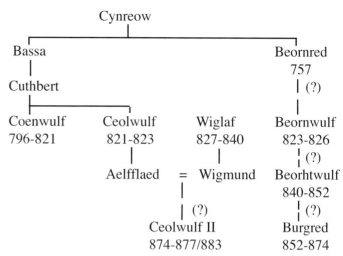

Fig.3 *The later family tree of the kings of Mercia as proposed by Cyril Hart (1977)*

dominant figure in southern England as late as the summer of 825'. He does not seem to have personally exercised royal power in Kent, as a king named Baldred (or Bealdred) was issuing coins in his own name, but it is possible that Baldred was Beornwulf's kinsman and the latter had appointed him sub-king. Kirby suggests that under Beornwulf's predecessor the south-east had been showing signs of further unrest and that Beornwulf appears to have contained it by adopting Coenwulf's policy of imposing a Mercian client king on Kent.[44]

Turning to ill-advised aggression, Beornwulf attacked the most powerful monarch in the south of England—Ecgberht of Wessex. It is possible that Beornwulf was trying to take advantage of recent fighting between Ecgberht and the forces of Devon and Cornwall (Dumnonia).[45] The two armies met at *Ellendun* (Wroughton) near Swindon in 825 in the old disputed territory by the Thames and an immense battle ensued, which saw the Mercian force badly defeated. The *Anglo-Saxon Chronicle* states that: 'Egbert had the victory and a great slaughter was made there'. Ecgberht quickly followed up his success and sent his son Aethelwulf at the head of a large force into Kent where 'they drove King Bealdred [Baldred] north across the Thames; and the people of Kent and of Surrey and the South Saxons and the East Saxons submitted to him ...'.[46] Ecgberht began to mint coins in his own name at Canterbury and Rochester, then at Winchester and Southampton, indicating he had authority in these areas.

The East Anglians appear to have used the opportunity created by this Mercian reverse to revolt and appealed to Ecgberht for protection. Beornwulf assembled new forces and marched east, but was killed in the campaign in 826.[47]

Ludeca, reigned 826-827

Ludeca, an ealdorman and a probable kinsman of Beornwulf, succeeded to the Mercian throne. It appears that the dynastic line of the Mercian monarchy had ended with Coenwulf and Ceolwulf, and now ealdormen took the opportunity of establishing themselves as kings. In trying to redress the balance of his predecessor's disastrous defeats, he launched another fateful attack upon the East Angles, probably only a few months later. Under 827 the *Anglo-Saxon Chronicle* records: 'In this year Ludeca, king of the Mercians, was killed, and his five ealdormen with him; and Wiglaf succeeded to the kingdom'.

Within six years Mercia had lost three kings and control of southern and eastern England. The area under its authority had been reduced to Central Mercia, Lindsey and the sub-kingdoms of the *Magonsaete* and the *Hwicce*.[48]

Wiglaf, reigned 827-842

It appears that Wiglaf's line was distantly connected with the old dynasty, for Wiglaf's grandson, Wigstan, was remembered at Evesham Abbey as being a descendent of Coenred, the grandson of Penda and the founder of the abbey. But whether this means Wiglaf was of Penda's line is not known, for the connection may have been through Wiglaf's wife Cynethryth. As Wiglaf and Wigstan were buried at Repton's monastery, Kirby suggests this may imply kinship with Aethelbald's line,[49] and thus to Penda's brother, Eowa. But any distant dynastic connection may have been welcomed, for the recent Mercian defeats are believed to have had an enormously destabilizing influence on the area remaining to the kingdom, and a period of stability was indeed required.

Fig.4 Coin of Ludeca's reign, showing a bust and his and the moneyer's name (1.5 times actual size)

There is little information about the first three years of Wiglaf's reign. He probably tried to consolidate the territory remaining in Mercian hands, but in 829 Ecgberht attacked Mercia, drove out Wiglaf, over-ran the kingdom, took the title of '*Rex Mercorium*' (King of the Mercians) and advanced towards Northumbria, which submitted to him at Dore, now a south-western district of Sheffield. Northumbria remained independent, but the campaign established Ecgberht as overlord of all of England south of the Humber. The submission of Mercia appears to have been complete, for coins in Ecgberht's name as king of Mercia were struck in the former Mercian port of London. In 830 the *Anglo-Saxon Chronicle* reports: 'King Egbert led an army among the Welsh, and he reduced them all to humble submission to him'.[50]

Perhaps somewhat surprisingly, this supremacy was short lived. Within a year Wiglaf was once more established as king of Mercia. Possibly Ecgberht overstretched himself, or incurred the displeasure of the Frankish court, his erstwhile supporter, for at the time of his invasion of Mercia and Northumbria, the Frankish commercial network, on which it seems he was partly dependant for financial gain, collapsed. In 830 internal strife broke out which intermittently split the Frankish kingdom and almost certainly halted any support which Ecgberht may have had from that quarter.[51] The Franks may also not have approved of Ecgberht's invasion of Mercia, with whom they had had diplomatic relations for 50 years and which would have blocked the established trading link between Mercia and the Franks, disrupting the established power structure.

The *Anglo-Saxon Chronicle* simply says that: '... Wiglaf again obtained the kingdom of the Mercians'. As Stenton remarks, if Ecgberht had restored Mercia to him, it is likely this would have been emphasized in the *Chronicle* in order to magnify Ecgberht's greatness, for the *Chronicle* was largely a West Saxon creation. A revolt against Ecgberht (in the manner of that which brought Wulfhere to power in Mercia in *c*.657) may have been a factor in Wiglaf's reinstatement, but the true circumstances of the restoration are never likely to be known.[52] Whilst Wiglaf regained control of Central and Outer Mercia, Kent, Surrey and Sussex were never under Mercian control thereafter, although he once more held the disputed area north of the Thames, an area which probably included Berkshire.

In East Anglia King Aethelstan had begun to mint his own coins at some stage between 827-30, which implies some degree of independence from both Wessex and Mercia. But any influence over Anglian territory exerted by Ecgberht probably began to fade following Wiglaf's return to Mercia after 830.[53]

Essex may have been re-established as a Mercian satellite by Wiglaf under the East Saxon king Sigeric II as Ecgberht appears to have lost control of the London mint by 830, with Wiglaf driving a wedge between Essex and Kent. Certainly, a charter of 831 by Wiglaf to Archbishop Wulfred concerning land at Botwell in Middlesex, strongly suggests that this county, and therefore London, was under his control again. However Stenton states that after 825 Essex, along with Kent, Surrey and Sussex stayed under the control of the West Saxons until Essex was detached from Wessex by Danish conquest.[54]

Wiglaf seems to have enjoyed fairly good relations with the Church, although he made very few grants of land. Brooks notes that the only acquisition of land made by Archbishop Wulfred after 825 was the 5 hides at Botwell in Middlesex which adjoined his property at Hayes, and which was probably given to him as a gift by Wiglaf.[55] If the two men had been on friendly terms some Mercian influence would have remained at Canterbury, even though Kent was now ruled by Ecgberht's son, Aethelwulf, as sub-king to his father.

At the end of his reign Wiglaf had improved the status of Mercia considerably from that immediately following Ecgberht's invasion. In 836, for example, he was able to hold an assembly at Croft in Leicestershire which was attended by the archbishop of Canterbury and all the bishops of the southern province of the Church. Wiglaf refers to those attending as 'my bishops, *duces*, and magistrates', and such an assembly would normally have been held in the diocese of London. Stenton claims that such an assembly not only proves Wiglaf's independence, 'but also the revival of Mercian authority over the southern episcopate'. It was at this assembly that the monastery at Hanbury, near Droitwich in Worcestershire, was granted land, salt pits and lead furnaces. Mercia was clearly once again an independent state with authority over most of its traditional territory, but with the significant exception of the lands in the south and south-east, though probably retaining Essex. By the end of the 830s Mercia was of virtually equal standing to Wessex[56] in terms of military strength and political power.

Wigmund - ?ruled 839-40?

Local tradition at Evesham Abbey holds that Wigmund, Wiglaf's son, ruled Mercia. It is possible that Wiglaf had made him sub-king of the *Hwiccian* territory, but if he did succeed as king of Mercia, he could not have survived his father for long because Beorthwulf, the next king, wanted his son, Beorthfrith, to marry Wigmund's widow, Aelfflaed. As Aelfflaed was Ceolwulf's only surviving heir and also heiress to much of the family's wealth, she was obviously a highly desirable wife to 'any upwardly mobile male of the royal house' which sparked yet another dynastic feud. Apparently Aelfflaed's son, Wigstan, objected to the match, ostensibly because Beorhtfrith was his father's kinsman and Wigstan's own godfather.[57] Wigmund was buried at Repton.

Beorhtwulf, 840-852

Beorhtwulf's reign and the years that it covers tends to be overlooked. However his reign, being longer than Wiglaf's, should be recognized, not for any great military or political achievements, but rather for the period of stability that it represents. It was, in effect, the lull before the storm, as events across the North Sea would come into full focus just before the end of his reign. Mercia did not loose its independence because of the the increasing power of Wessex, but because of the invasion of the Danes.

There is only incidental charter evidence for the date of both his, and his successor's, accession to the Mercian throne. In an Evesham tradition, Beorthwulf's son is claimed to be a kinsman of Wigstan, Wigmund's son, whereas his own name suggests he may have been related to Beornwulf who had deposed Ceolwulf in 823. The kings with the 'B' prefix may well represent another rival Mercian part of the royal family, as has been mentioned earlier, for after Beorthwulf came Burgred, and it is even possible that the ill-fated Beornred who reigned in 757 between Aethelbald and Offa may have belonged to the same family. However, a familial connection cannot be proven but it is noted that they assiduously promoted kinsmen whose names also started with 'B' during their reigns.[58] Beorhtwulf's position upon succession seems fairly secure.

The closeness of Beorthwulf's relationship with the Church is apparent throughout his reign. He consolidated his political influence with the bishops by granting numerous charters, particularly involving land in the *Hwiccian* kingdom. Nevertheless, the synod of the province of Canterbury held at Croft in Leicestershire in 836 (mentioned above) and presided over by Wiglaf, was the last time such a 'full synod of the southern English province' is known to have been held under the auspices of a Mercian king. From 838 Archbishop Ceolnoth established friendly relations between his church and the rulers of Wessex, and from then on the shift of influence over Canterbury to Wessex was confirmed.[59]

King Ecgberht of Wessex's son, Aethelwulf, had succeeded to the throne upon his father's death, handing the rule of the provinces of Sussex, Kent, Surrey and Essex to his eldest son Athelstan.[60] At some stage after 844 Berkshire passed to Wessex, by agreement it seems, for its Mercian ealdorman, another Aethelwulf, retained his status. Asser's *Life of King Alfred* states that Aethelwulf's son, Alfred the future great West Saxon king, was born in 849 'at the royal estate called Wantage, in the district known as Berkshire'. However, in the earliest surviving version of the West Saxon regnal table, Alfred is said to have been 21 when he succeeded to the West Saxon crown shortly after Easter 871, which suggests he was born between the Easters of 847 and 848. Whichever was the year of his birth, the Mercian ealdorman still ruled the area. Kirby states that a coin minted with Beorhtwulf's portrait on the reverse and Aethelwulf's name on the obverse has been seen as evidence of an alliance between the two kings, even a commemoration of 'a peaceful surrender of Berkshire by Be(o)rthwulf in return for minting rights in Kent', although it is conceded that the coin might be 'an irregular and imitative issue'. However, although dies from Rochester in Kent were used by Beorthwulf, it is likely his coins were minted at London rather than Rochester, for Beorthwulf had revived Mercian coinage at the London mint by about 842.[61]

Beorhtwulf's system of rule via ealdormen and *dux* is implied by the attestations in his early charter of 840 where eight ealdormen and six untitled individuals act as witnesses alongside the bishops of Lichfield, Worcester, Hereford and Lindsey.[62] Several of Beorthwulf's charters are secular in nature and suggest rewards to some of the ealdormen.

In 841 the *Anglo-Saxon Chronicle* records '... and later in the same year [many men] in Lindsey, East Anglia and Kent, were killed by the enemy [the Scandinavian invaders]'. In 842 the Frankish port of Quentovic, which had been so important to Mercian trade, was attacked as well as London and Rochester and 'great slaughter' was reported. In 851 the Danes invaded Kent and overwintered in Thanet for the first time. According to Florence of Worcester, the Danes, with a large force of 350 ships, ravaged Canterbury, then sailed up the Thames to London, still a Mercian port. Beorhtwulf came to London's defence and counter-attacked. It is the only recorded large military venture of his reign, but unfortunately he was defeated and put to flight. The Danish force was eventually defeated—it is said they were all killed at *Aclea*—Ockley, 'Field of Oaks'—6 miles north of Horsham in Surrey after travelling south, where they were attacked by Aethelwulf of Wessex and his son Aethelbald. It was undoubtedly a relief for Mercia that the Danes moved into Surrey rather than into their own territory.[63]

These Danish incursions mark the start of a very different era for Mercia. The relatively peaceful period that the kingdom had enjoyed drew to a close with Beorhtwulf's death in 852.

Burgred 852-874 and the arrival of the Danes and Norwegians

It has already been mentioned that Beorhtwulf had a son, Beorhtfrith, whom he wanted to marry Wiglaf's widowed daughter-in-law Aelfflaed, to secure his position to the throne. Wiglaf's grandson, Wigstan, had been supported by the people as the successor to his father, but he preferred a life in the Church, and declared that Aelfflaed should become regent. Wigstan objected to the proposed marriage between Beorthfrith and his mother because, it is said, he considered the union would have been incestuous. Beorhtfrith was enraged by his opposition and killed him, his own godson, in 849 during a council meeting at *Wistanstowe*, probably Wiston, 6 miles south-east of Leicester. Three of Wigstan's followers died with him. Just as Coenwulf had promoted the cult of his son, Cynehelm at Winchcombe, so

Wigstan's family made the most of the circumstances of his death to claim him as a family saint, thus enhancing their own prestige. Wigstan was buried at Repton and soon a cult developed. Indeed, the remains of his shrine can still be seen in the crypt at St. Wystan's church—Wystan being an alternative form of Wigstan. What happened to Beorthfrith is unclear, but he then disappears from view, perhaps disposed of because of his crime. The *Life of St. Wigstan* claims that what Yorke refers to as the 'B' and 'Wig' families were related, and Yorke notes that it would not be surprising to find several royal lines existing in the 9th century, bearing in mind Penda and his sons' 7th-century policy of placing royal kinsmen in charge of newly-conquered provinces.[64] Unfortunately, dynastic rivalries were the almost certain consequence. On Beorthwulf's death, Burgred ascended to the throne as the last truly independent Mercian king.

The earliest Scandinavian raiders almost certainly came from Norway comprising small groups seeking their fortune.[65] Many of these earliest Norwegians by-passed England altogether, sailing round the north of Scotland and founding colonies in the Shetlands, Orkneys, Caithness, Sutherland and the Hebrides on their way to Ireland where more settlements were founded. By 838 these settlements had become powerful enough to land a force in Cornwall and, with the aid of the 'West Welsh' (the Cornish) they attacked Ecgberht of Wessex at Hingston Down. They were defeated, giving Ecgberht control of Cornwall.

The events which led to a sustained Scandinavian invasion of England were inadvertently partly brought about by Charlemagne. Stenton records that from about the late 7th century to the time of Alfred the Great (i.e. pre-871) the Frisians had dominated the North Sea, and the Saxons in Germany who were still independent had acted as a barrier to anything but occasional communication between the people of the Baltic and the Frankish kingdom. However Charlemagne completed what had been a 'long process of Frankish encroachment on Frisia' and also ended Saxon independence. Charlemagne's new frontier was now with a Danish king who regarded himself as Charlemagne's equal and who claimed authority over Saxony and Frisia. In gaining control over Frisia Charlemagne restricted its sea power, opening the North Sea to the Danes. The Frankish kingdom, according to Stenton, had never been powerful enough at sea to protect its coastline which by the 8th century stretched from the mouth of the river Elbe to the Rhine delta. Likewise English kings from the later 7th century to Alfred the Great's time (871-899) had no fleet worthy of the name. Both kingdoms were thus vulnerable to sea-borne attack. However, Frankish territory would be safe as long as the good diplomatic relations Charlemagne had developed with the Danes were continued by his successors. Although Charlemagne's successor, Louis the Pious, maintained relations with the Danes for 20 years, the Frankish Empire became disjointed because of the friction between his sons, and the Danish encroachments began. From 834 incessant Danish raids were made on Frankish territory, and in 835 England felt their force at Sheppey.[66]

From 825 the Danes had been ruled by Horik who had been embarrassed by the unofficial raids by groups of his men on Frankish territory. Indeed, Horik was keen to curtail piracy and unofficial adventures in his own people—it was of no advantage to him that his nobles and fighting-men should escape his control, become rich on booty and ally themselves with any member of the royal household who could attract them to his side, but his efforts were not wholly successful and raids were often carried out by his enemies among the Danes. In due course, in 854, his nephew Guthrum, who may have been residing abroad as a pirate, led a coup in which virtually all the royal household were killed.[67] Consequently chaos ruled within Denmark and the kingdom collapsed. With no central control and the sea at their command, the Danes were free to attack England.

The first recorded raid on England had in fact occurred many years before Horik's reign, in 789. The *Anglo-Saxon Chronicle* records: '... there came for the first time three ships of Northmen and then the reeve [a man called Beaduheard of Dorchester] rode to them and wished to force them to the king's residence, for he did not know what they were; and they slew him. Those were the first ships of Danish men which came to the land of the English'. Lindisfarne was sacked in 793 and Northumbria raided. There followed a long interval of apparent inactivity until 835 when Sheppey in Kent was attacked, coinciding with the loss of Frankish influence with Denmark. But the period of seeming inactivity saw the country nevertheless beset by unease, as indicated in charters for the period. As early as 804 the Mercian king, Ceolwulf, with Cuthred, king of Kent, conceded 'a small parcel of land [6 acres] in the city of Canterbury as a refuge in necessity' to Abbess Selethryth and the monastic community of Lyminge in Kent. Whitelock suggests this charter shows concern for the safety of monasteries on the coast exposed to potential raiders. Brooks suggests that St. Mildred's in Canterbury may have had a similar origin as a refuge for the community of Minster-in-Thanet. Groups of Vikings appear to have been building fortresses in Kent before 811 and on his coronation on 17 September 822 Ceolwulf had given land near Kemsing, about 3 miles northeast of Sevenoaks in Kent, free from burdens except 'military service against pagan enemies, and the construction of bridges and the fortification or destruction of fortresses among the same people'; the 'pagan enemies' are taken to be the Vikings. In his charter of 836 concerning Hanbury in Worcestershire, Wiglaf had freed the monastery and its dependencies 'from small and from great causes ... except the construction of ramparts and bridges'. Even in the heart of England there was a perceptible need for defence. Indeed, it was in 836 that a Danish force comprising 35 ships landed and defeated Ecgberht of Wessex and his army at Carhampton, 1 mile south-east of Dunster in Somerset, where 'a great slaughter was made'. It was the only recorded defeat of his reign.[68]

In 839 Ecgberht died after reigning for 37 years and 7 months, probably aged around 69, and his son Aethelwulf succeeded to the West Saxon kingdom.

In 840 the Danish crews of 33 or 34 ships fought with the ealdorman of Southampton and the same year the Danes attacked Portland in Dorset and killed the ealdorman. In 841, Lindsey, East Anglia and Kent were attacked; in 842 London and Rochester; in 843 the Danes defeated King Aethelwulf of Wessex at Carhampton, but in 845 the forces of Somerset and Dorset gained revenge at the mouth of the river Parrett. In 851 an ealdorman, Ceorl, with a 'contingent of the men of Devon', defeated a force at an unidentified location called *Wicganbeorg*, the same year that the Danes overwintered in England at Thanet, on the eve of Burgred's accession to the throne of Mercia. That year also saw an attack by 350 ships on London and Canterbury. The combination of events in 851 are felt by Kirby to have shaken both the Mercians and West Saxons.[69] Thereafter the Danish armies became even larger.

Burgred may have been a kinsman to his predecessor but this cannot be proven. From the start it appears that Burgred ruled as an ally, perhaps even as a client king, to the West Saxon king, Aethelwulf, whose daughter he had married at Easter in 853 at Chippenham in Wiltshire. Certainly co-operation between Mercia and Wessex is illustrated near the beginning of Burgred's reign in 853. Asser states that Burgred requested help from Aethelwulf 'so that he could subject to his authority the inland Welsh, who live between Mercia and the western sea and who were struggling against him with unusual effort. As soon as King Aethelwulf had received his embassy, he assembled an army and went with King Burgred to Wales, where immediately on entry he devastated that race and reduced it to Burgred's authority. When he had done this, he returned home'.[70] They had defeated the forces of Powys and Kirby remarks that it may have been this campaign that led to their king Cyngen ap Cadell leaving the country for Rome, where he died two years later. The Pillar of Eliseg near Valle Crucis Abbey, which was raised by Cyngen to the memory of his own great-grandfather's reconquest of the territory of Powys, is also a testament to his own military success, and it is possibly this latter which may have sparked the Mercian/West Saxon attack. Indeed it is said by Ashley that Beorthwulf, Burgred's predecessor, was preoccupied with conflict with Powys as Cyngen ap Cadell fought to regain land in what became Herefordshire and Shropshire.[71] Problems between Mercia and the Welsh had clearly been occurring for over a decade.

Burgred appears as a strong monarch with full control over Central and Outer Mercia. Although Mercia was now a reduced kingdom, in 865 he moved deep into Gwynedd and reached Anglesey. However, without the important kingdom of Kent, the wealth available to him was less than that to his predecessors, although the kingdom no longer had the ear of the archbishop of Canterbury and consequently its influence was less.

Fewer land grants were made than in previous reigns, but those that survive give some feel for his rule. The first charter for which there is a record, although the original is now missing, is dated tentatively to 853, and thus at the beginning of his reign, and is to one Aethelred who Finberg suggests may have been of Wessex and his brother-in-law, for land at Lydney, Gloucestershire.[72] Another early charter of 855 concerns a monastery at Blockley, in Gloucestershire. In spite of the *Hwicce* not having their own ruler for many years, a distinction is still drawn between this area and the Central Mercian areas when it is stated that Burgred 'will free it from the feeding and maintenance of all hawks and falcons in the land of the Mercians, and of all huntsmen of the king or ealdorman except only those who are in the province of the *Hwicce*'. The degree to which the regional distinction is emphasized in this charter is notable. As Blockley is 3 miles north-west of Moreton-in-the-Marsh, and therefore some considerable distance from the Welsh border, it is perhaps surprising to find the next clause: '... likewise even from the feeding and maintenance of those men whom we call in Saxon *Walhfaereld* [literally 'Welsh expedition' a term which Whitelock suggests could mean 'the messengers who passed between England and Wales, or possibly an English patrol of the borders'] and from lodging them and from lodging all mounted men of the English race and foreigners, whether of noble or humble birth'.[73]

The regional distinction is also shown in a charter of 855 by Bishop Alhwine (Ealhhun) who calls himself 'bishop of the *Hwicce*' in a lease to an ealdorman, Aethewulf, and his wife.[74] The degree to which these regions continue to attract recognition, in spite of having become obsolete in administrative terms, is noteworthy, and indeed continues to the end of the Anglo-Saxon period.

A charter dated 18 April 857 granting a 'profitable little estate' and commercial rights in London to Bishop Ealhhun, demonstrates Burgred's continued control of London, as well as the king and the Church having close connections with trade (for more on this charter see p.199).[75]

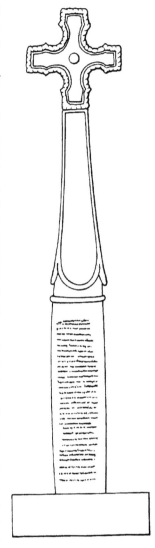

Fig.5 The Pillar of Eliseg drawn to show how it would have appeared

A charter of 855 concerns a grant of a privilege for lands in Gloucestershire in return for 'two gold armlets of skilled workmanship, which weigh 45 mancuses' by Burgred and Ealhhun, who this time styles himself as 'bishop of Worcester'. The transaction occurred at *Oswaldesdun* and the charter adds ominously 'when the pagans were in the province of the Wrekin-dwellers'. This is the only record that shows that the Danes had penetrated into the area of the *Wreconsaete* in the mid-9th century, and thus into western Mercia; the *Anglo-Saxon Chronicle* makes no mention of it.[76] Burgred's last charter is dated 869, the inference being that warfare with the Danes prevented any further transactions.

In 865 a Danish force once again encamped at Thanet, Kent agreeing to buy them off in order to keep the peace. Extortion was the Danes' usual practice and the probable understanding was that a huge sum of money was paid or else the area would be wrecked and the people massacred. The Danes accepted the offer, but 'under cover of that peace and promise of money the army stole away inland by night and ravaged all eastern Kent'. Asser refers to them as being 'like crafty foxes' and that they spurned the promised money knowing they could exact more 'from stolen booty than from peace'.[77]

This period of warfare with the Danes is inextricably linked with the name of Alfred the Great. Aethelwulf had been on the throne of Wessex since his father's death in 838, and Alfred was his youngest son. It is reported by Asser that Aethelwulf sent Alfred to Pope Leo IV in Rome in 853, the pope anointing 'the child Alfred as king, ordaining him properly, received him as an adoptive son and confirmed him'. Alfred would have only been four or five years old at the time. The date of this visit has been questioned but Kirby remarks that what is beyond doubt is that Alfred 'received consecration at papal hands' although it cannot have feasibly been a royal anointing for Alfred had three surviving brothers who were older than himself. Instead Kirby suggests the 'confirmation-anointing' was probably later interpreted by Alfred's court, including Asser, as a royal anointing. It is more likely that Aethelwulf was considering a life in holy orders for Alfred, and indeed Asser reports that Aethelwulf took his son to Rome again in 855/6. Aethelwulf stayed on the Continent for about a year, staying the summer and early autumn of 856 at the court of Charles the Bald, king of the west Franks, where he married Charles' 13 or 14 year-old daughter Judith. Before leaving for the Continent, Aethelwulf had established his eldest surviving son, Aethelbald as ruler Wessex and his next eldest, Aethelberht over the south-eastern provinces. On his return, according to Asser, Aethelbald 'with all his councillors - or rather co-conspirators' attempted to expel Aethelwulf from his own kingdom. In order to avert a civil war, Aethelwulf surrendered the western districts to Aethelbald but kept his authority in the eastern districts. Asser closes the chapter by observing 'So that iniquitous and grasping son ruled where by rightful judgement the father should have done; for the western part of the Saxon land has always been more important than the eastern.' However, Kirby considers that if there was indeed a division, other evidence suggests it was within the West Saxon terri-tory itself with Aethelbald ruling in western Wessex and Aethelwulf ruling eastern and central Wessex. This left Aethelberht still in control of Kent and meant that a territory and suitable position had been carved out for Aethelbald, the older of the two brothers.[78]

After Aethelwulf had died in 858 and Aethelbald in 860, Aethelberht brought the whole territory back under one rule. Aethelberht himself died in 865, apparently childless, as had Aethelbald, and thus the whole kingdom passed to the third son, Aethelred. His reign began at the time that Danish activity was increasing greatly, and he and his remaining brother, Alfred, acted in unison. From the outset Alfred appears to have been the most adept of the two at warfare.

The same year that Aethelberht died, the Danes changed their tactics. Instead of raiding parties, a whole army arrived, not to extort protection money but to try to take over the area. They landed first in East Anglia and over-wintered there, then in 866 taking advantage of the civil war raging in Northumbria between King Aella and his brother Osberht, who had recently been deposed, they crossed the Humber estuary and captured York on 1 November. The two Northumbrian brothers joined forces to try to recapture the city, but were both killed on 21 March 867 and, although having broken through the city wall, 'eight leading noblemen' were killed with them. Indeed Asser records that 'Virtually the entire force of Northumbrians was annihilated there, ... but the remainder, who escaped, made peace with the Vikings'. The Scandinavians secured York and took control of Deira. Asser then notes that in 868 'the Viking army left Northumbria, came to Mercia and reached Nottingham ... and they spent the winter that year in the same place ...'.[79]

Burgred, fresh from campaigning in Wales, had a considerable force of men with which to attack the Danes. However, he still called for assistance from Wessex, and in the company of Aethelred and Alfred they attacked Nottingham with an immense army. Even the combined forces failed to drive out the Danes, who probably used Nottingham's ancient cave defences (which still exist underneath the city centre) to consolidate their defensive position, but peace was established between the Mercians and the Vikings.[80]

In the autumn of 869 the Vikings were back on the defensive, travelling to East Anglia and Thetford where they overwintered. King Edmund, the last independent king of East Anglia, had succeeded to the throne in 854 at the age of 13 or 14. In the winter of 865/6 he had given the Danes quarter and thereafter they used East Anglia as a base from which to raid the west and north. Returning in 869 the Danes, under Ivarr the Boneless, found that Edmund was intent on expelling them. Battle ensued at Hellesdon, about 2 miles north-west of Norwich, in Norfolk. It turned into a disastrous defeat for Edmund who was captured, tortured and then slain on 20 November. East Anglia was over-run by the Danes, and Kirby suggests that several coins in the name of two kings, Aethelred and Oswald, which appear to be East Anglian and post-date Edmund's death, may imply they ruled as 'pliant dependants' of Ivarr's.[81]

In the autumn of 870, 'the Pagan army, of hateful memory, quitting East-Anglia and entering the kingdom of Wessex, came to the vill of Reading, situated ... in the district called Berkshire. And there, on the third day after their arrival, two of their chiefs, with great part of their forces, rode out to plunder the country, while the rest were throwing up a rampart between the rivers Thames and Kennet on the right of the said royal vill'. A huge battle was then fought between the Danes and Aethelwulf, the ealdorman appointed by Beorhtwulf of Mercia who was kept on by the West Saxons when Berkshire had been passed to them, at a place called Englefield, which Florence of Worcester interprets as 'The Field of the Angles'. Aethelwulf was victorious, and four days later joined forces with Aethelred and Alfred to storm Reading. This time victory went to the Danes, and Aethelwulf was killed. A further four days later a battle between the West Saxons and the Danes was fought at Ashdown, with Alfred leading the troops; Aethelred was apparently hearing Mass when the battle started and refused to break off to fight until the service had finished. It was a West Saxon victory. The armies fought again two weeks later at Basing, 2 miles east of Basingstoke in Hampshire, and two months later at *Meretun* (Merton). The West Saxons were defeated in both of these last encounters.[82]

In April 871 Aethelred died, possibly as a result of injuries sustained in battle, and Alfred succeeded to the whole of Wessex. However, in May he was defeated at Wilton, and later that year made peace with the Danes, probably by paying tribute. In the autumn of 871 the problem came nearer home for the Mercians as the Danish king, Halfdan, and his army took winter-quarters in London and Halfdan began minting coins in his own name. The effect on Central Mercia was extremely serious as the port of London was vital for trade. In 872 there is a record of the bishop of Worcester selling property in Warwickshire to a thegn to raise funds to pay off the Danish tribute that was being exacted in London (see p.127).[83]

In 872 a revolt broke out in Deira. It seems that a Northumbrian nobleman, Ricsige, who may have been of royal descent, rebelled against the Vikings' control of Deira and their puppet king, Ecgberht, whom they had set up in 867. The upshot was that Ricsige established himself as king and Ecgberht and Wulfhere, the archbishop of York, fled and sought refuge with Burgred in Mercia. The rebellion brought the Danes north to intervene in Northumbria and away from their London stronghold, but although they contained the rebellion it appears that they did not go any further as Ricsige kept his independence until 876, after which he disappears from the record. After 876 the Danes settled in Deira and established their kingdom of Jorvik under Haldan, the brother of Ivarr the Boneless.

After quelling the rebellion in Northumbria, the Danes only appear to have stayed for a few weeks before moving south to establish winter quarters at Torksey, north-west of Lincoln in Lindsey—Mercian territory. Stenton records that, after the Danes had occupied Torksey for a year, the 'Mercians bought peace from them for themselves and the men of their province of Lindsey'. However, the Danes broke this understanding and overwhelmed Repton. Although Burgred had been able to form alliances with Wessex earlier on in his reign, it appears that once the Danes had established themselves in London in 871, both Mercia and Wessex were impelled to act on their own. Each kingdom was fighting for its own life. Indeed, the fact that the Scandinavian armies were able to overwinter at Nottingham as early as 868, and then subsequently in London and Lindsey and had to be repeatedly bought off implies Burgred was struggling to contain an increasingly impossible situation.[84] In the end he failed and his fate is recorded in the *Anglo-Saxon Chronicle* for 874, in which year the Danish army:

> went from Lindsey to Repton and took up winter quarters there, and drove King Burgred across the sea, after he had held the kingdom 22 years. And they conquered all that land. And he went to Rome and settled there; and his body is buried in the church of St. Mary in the English quarter. And the same year they gave the kingdom of the Mercians to be held by Ceolwulf, a foolish king's thegn; and he swore oaths to them and gave hostages, that it should be ready for them on whatever day they wished to have it, and he would be ready, himself and all who would follow him, at the enemy's service.[85]

Under Danish Rule: Ceolwulf II and Ealdorman Aethelred of Mercia

From the above quote it is inferred that Ceolwulf II was a mere puppet of the Danes, even a turn-coat, but as Stenton points out, between 874 and 877 Ceolwulf was recognized as the legitimate king of Mercia by the Church and was served by some of Burgred's own ealdormen.[86]

In the summer of 875 there is the first mention of Alfred's naval force. It attacked seven enemy ships, captured one and put the others to flight. But the Danes' determination to conquer Wessex was reinvigorated. In 876 they captured Wareham and moved on to Exeter. In 877 a Danish supporting naval force was hit by a storm off Swanage and 120 ships were lost. Then in the August 'in the harvest season the army went away into Mercia and shared out some of it, and gave some to Ceolwulf.'[87] The matter-of-fact way in which the *Anglo Saxon Chronicle* reports this event belies its immense significance for Mercia. Stenton records that after leaving Exeter the Danish army moved into Gloucester which was almost immediately followed by the 'dismemberment of the Mercian kingdom'. Indeed by the end of 877 Mercia and its dependent provinces had been divided into two enormous regions with one being left under Ceolwulf's control and the other 'partitioned among those in the [Danish] army who wished for a share in it.'[88] This partitioning was the beginning of the process which created English Mercia and Danish Mercia, the latter becoming part of the Danelaw.

A cursory look at a map of the distribution of Scandinavian place-names might suggest there was a mass settlement of Danes in the eastern half of England. However, Stafford observes that in the east midlands only in the Wreake valley, which lies between Melton Mowbray and Leicester, and in small areas of Lincolnshire do Scandinavian place-names comprise half or more of the total; in the rest of the east midlands most are English place-names. The vast majority of the Scandinavian place-names probably represent the re-naming of existing settlements and there is little to suggest that the Vikings made any real impression on settlement patterns.[89] It seems that they were absorbed into an existing Anglo-Saxon agricultural and settlement framework.

A treaty between Alfred the Great and Guthrum, dated between 886 and 890, defined the boundary between Wessex and the southern Danelaw and, according to Keynes and Lapidge, this 'presumably represents a modification of the boundary established when the Vikings divided Mercia with Ceolwulf in 877'. One of the primary concerns of the treaty was to regulate the behaviour between the Danish settlers and the native population. In spite of the treaty, it appears that conflict occurred along the boundary of the Danelaw.

Within the Danelaw the Danes set down their own distinctive legal customs. Within this broad band Stenton observes that there were four main regions—the shires dependent on the Five Boroughs of Stamford, Lincoln, Nottingham, Leicester and Derby; the south-east midlands; Northumbria; and East Anglia. However, Stafford observes that the earliest of the 11th-century writings which refer to the Danelaw, such as the *Laws of Edward the Confessor*, suggest 'a more restricted "true" Danelaw' which encompassed Nottinghamshire, Derbyshire, Leicestershire, Lincolnshire, part of Northamptonshire, as well as Yorkshire. In early post-Conquest documents three spheres of law are referred to based on the differences of legal custom: the Danelaw, West Saxon law and Mercian law, with the latter covering Cheshire, Shropshire, Staffordshire, Warwickshire, Worcestershire, Herefordshire, Gloucestershire and Oxfordshire.[90] That such regional differences were still thus defined in the early Norman period demonstrates that the division of Mercia, so laconically recorded in the *Anglo-Saxon Chronicle*, went on to have very real and lasting repercussions.

In 878 the *Anglo-Saxon Chronicle* records 'In this year in midwinter after twelfth night the enemy army came stealthily to Chippenham, [which Asser records as a royal residence] and occupied the land of the West Saxons and settled there, and drove a great part of the people across the sea, and conquered most of the others ...'. Guthrum led the army from Gloucester which they had held since late 877. Stenton ascribes their success to a change in tactics,[91] using the winter as a time of campaigning rather than settling down in winter quarters and so giving them the advantage of surprise. However, earlier in 878 there had been one English success at Countisbury Hill, west of Porlock in Somerset. A Danish force with 23 ships had crossed from south Wales to Devon, but their leader and more than 800 of his men (Asser has 1,200) were killed. That Alfred had been pushed this far west implies how desperate the situation had become. Alfred, Asser records, 'with his small band of nobles and also with certain soldiers and thegns, was leading a restless life in great distress amid the woody and marshy places of Somerset. He had nothing to live on except what he could forage by frequent raids, either secretly or even openly, from the Vikings as well as from the Christians who had submitted to the Vikings' authority'.[92] Indeed, Stenton remarks that there was every likelihood that before 878 was over Wessex would have been divided out between the Danish army.[93]

However, Alfred brought about the most startling turn-around in events. Asser takes up the story:

> In the same year, after Easter [23 March], King Alfred, with a few men, made a fortress at a place called Athelney, and from it with the thegns of Somerset he struck out relentlessly and tirelessly against the Vikings. Presently in the seventh week after Easter [4-10 May], he rode to Egbert's Stone, which is in the eastern part of Selwood Forest; and there all the inhabitants of Somerset and Wiltshire and all the inhabitants of Hampshire - those who had not sailed overseas for fear of the Vikings - joined up with him. When they saw the king, receiving him (not surprisingly) as if one restored to life after suffering such great tribulations, they were filled with immense joy.

A few days later there followed the most decisive battle of the whole Danish war, for the Danes were defeated and, after holding out at their Chippenham camp for a further 14 days, they eventually had to come to terms with Alfred. Under these terms the Danes were to leave Wessex and their king, Guthrum, was to be baptised. Three weeks later the baptisim took place at Wedmore, south of Axbridge, with Alfred standing as his godfather, and Guthrum received the English name of Athelstan, under which name he went on to rule the Scandinavians of East Anglia.

There are only two extant charters for Ceolwulf II's reign and both of these are issued in the *Hwiccian* kingdom with the same authority as earlier Mercian kings.[94] The Worcestershire charter for 875 is deemed authentic and frees 'the whole diocese of the Hwicce' from the charge of 'feeding the king's horses and those who lead them' in return for a lease of four lives of land at Daylesford, Gloucestershire, as well as spiritual benefits. This charter is attested by the bishops of (probably) Lichfield and also Hereford and Worcester, and two ealdormen in the same way that they would be for any other king.[95] Whitelock argues that this charter shows Ceolwulf was regarded or accepted as 'the true king of Mercia', otherwise it would not have been attested by bishops and ealdormen. However, the list of witnesses is comparatively much smaller than for previous monarchs' charters. In the other charter Ceolwulf grants land at Overbury, Conderton and Pendock in Worcestershire to St. Mary's minster at Worcester, but this is considered untrustworthy, or at least interpolated as St. Mary's was not built until the later 10th century.[96]

It is likely that many people chose to act in a way that would guard their own safety by recognizing Ceolwulf II as king, whatever their own personal resentment of his link with the Danes, rather than to expose themselves to danger by resisting him. The fact is that his authority and power as king were real and effective, if not autonomous. Indeed, it might be argued that by working with the Danes he did at least 'save' the western half of Mercia from Danish overall rule.

Ashley records that later chronicles state that Ceolwulf II was of royal descent and that it has been speculated that he was perhaps the son of Wigmund and Aelfflaed and, therefore, the grandson of Ceolwulf I who had ruled Mercia between 821-3. Indeed, Yorke remarks that his very name suggests he might have been a member of the Coenwulf and Ceolwulf I lineage.[97] He issued a joint coinage with Alfred the Great, and shared moneyers with Alfred, as well as helping in Alfred's restoration of a high quality silver coinage which is thought unlikely to date before 878. Indeed it is possible that Ceolwulf was ruling into the early 880s as *rex Merciorum*—'king of Mercia'—as there is no evidence to suggest he was superseded by an ealdorman of the Mercians called Aethelred before 883. But conflicting theories do exist concerning Ceolwulf's duration of rule. On one hand, it is suggested that Ceolwulf retained English Mercia until his death which Florence of Worcester implies was in 886, just before Alfred retook London from the Danes. This theory is supported by the coin evidence discussed above. However, charter evidence suggests his absence after 875 and Stenton observes that he disappears from history in 877, with nothing known of Mercian government for the next six years until 883, when Aethelred, the ealdorman, appears suddenly as Mercia's ruler. This is the Aethelred who became Alfred the Great's son-in-law. Ashley suggests that if Ceolwulf had been the younger brother of the murdered Wigstan (whose father was Wigmund) then by 883 he may well have been in his sixties—a ripe old age for the times. This old age and possible royal descent may have made him particularly attractive to the Danes as a client ruler—his years would have encouraged inactivity, whereas his royal lineage would have made him acceptable to the Mercians.[98]

Aethelred's origins are unknown, indeed his name indicates he could have been of either Mercian or West Saxon descent. His authority developed at a time when the Danes were still in effective control of Mercia, although they were struggling in the wars with Alfred. The wording used in a charter of 883 states that Aethelred 'ealdorman of the Mercians' issued the grant with 'the consent of King Alfred and of the whole Mercian council', which might indicate that he was elected by the Mercian council, or assumed power with their approval as the most able among them. The reference to Alfred suggests that the West Saxon king had gained control over Mercia by 883 and was regarded by Aethelred as his overlord. Indeed Keynes and Lapidge state that by the early 880s Alfred was recognized as overlord of Mercia, but how he achieved this is not clear. Another charter for 887 describes Aethelred as *'dux et patricius'* of Mercia.[99]

In 886 or 887 Aethelred married Aethelflaed, Alfred's eldest child, and from then on their names are inextricably linked with the history of Mercia; indeed they became one of the strongest and most effective ruling husband and wife partnerships in English history. Even if Aethelred was ruler of Mercia subject to Wessex, he was hardly treated as an inferior, for it appears that Alfred held his son-in-law in great respect as evidenced by his entrusting London to Aethelred's care in 886 after he had seized it from the Danes. Asser records that in 886 Alfred

> restored the city of London splendidly - after so many towns had been burned and so many people slaughtered - and made it habitable again; he entrusted it to the care of Aethelred, ealdorman of the Mercians. All the Angles and Saxons - those who had formerly been scattered everywhere and were not in captivity with the Vikings - turned willingly to King Alfred and submitted themselves to his lordship.[100]

Keynes and Lapidge consider this submission was clearly a great political event and may have been marked by taking a general oath of loyalty to Alfred, a sort of 'ceremonial commitment' in which he was

The King's Council

The king's council was called the Witan in Old English and meant literally 'wise men'. It comprised members of the royal household, the archbishops of Canterbury and York, the bishops and prominent abbots. Among lay people included were ealdormen and other men of major military or administrative standing, such as the king's thegns. The queen or queen-mother 'might be occasionally included' and more rarely abbesses, otherwise it was a male preserve. Membership depended on rank and position. In the 10th and 11th centuries the Witan met regularly and it could approve and elect a new king and also de-select one that was felt unsatisfactory. As early as the 7th century the Witan was consulted before laws were promulgated, and by the 10th and 11th centuries it not only dealt with laws and the authorization of land grants but also with 'judicial judgements, the settlement of disputes, the election of archbishops and bishops' and major matters of Church and State.[103]

given support in all his endeavours and recognized as leader and ruler by all Englishmen who were beyond the Danelaw.[101]

Alfred's capture of London from the Danes was in the interests of both Mercia and Wessex and, according to Keynes and Lapidge, probably 'set the seal on their relations'.[102] By entrusting London to Aethelred Alfred respected London's former status as a Mercian town.

Mercia as a Sub-Kingdom

Mercia's status was clearly now that of a sub-kingdom to Wessex. Alfred was a capable and wise ruler and his treatment of Mercia is comparable with that of Aethelbald's (716-757) relations with Kent in that he allowed it some degree of autonomy, accepting Aethelred in effect as a sub-king and allowing London to remain in Mercian control. Wessex and Mercia had learnt that they needed to work together in the face of the continued Danish threat.

The Danelaw was a wealthy area, strongly held, and it was not until the first decades of the 10th century that any of its major towns (apart from London) came back into English control.

After a few quieter years, in 892 a Danish army landed in Kent. In 893 it received support from Scandinavians in Northumbria and East Anglia. Fighting seems to have occurred in several places in England, the Danes eventually being heavily defeated at Buttington, almost certainly that 2 miles north-east and across the Severn from Welshpool.[104]

Further raids were made in 895 but, as Stenton observes, by the end of the 9th century much of the impetus had gone from the Scandinavian attack on western Europe and the possibility of a Danish conquest of the whole of England became increasingly remote as Alfred's defensive policy of *burhs* came into force and was expanded,[105] closing off any more English territory to them.

At the time of Alfred's death in 899 the area of England under English rule included the area north of the river Tees and west of the Pennines (the remnants of the Northumbrian kingdom) which was ruled by several English ealdormen. Aethelred, ealdorman of Mercia, ruled over what is now Cheshire with the river Mersey as the northern boundary, down a border with the Welsh to Gloucestershire and a swathe of territory across the midland plain and into central and southern Buckinghamshire and London. Watling Street, which divided the Mercian Warwickshire from Danish Leicestershire, probably continued as Aethelred's Mercian frontier into the southern midlands up to about 30 miles north-west of London where it entered the region controlled by that city, and which it appears Aethelred controlled until his death in 911.[106] Much energy was still expended in keeping destructive Danish raids in check but, as life and wealth became increasingly centred on fortified *burhs*, this became easier to do.

Charter evidence for the period is quite numerous, many charters containing the names of both Aethelred and Aethelflaed, and indicate considerable activity. In *c*.900 Aethelflaed, termed 'lady of the

Mercians', in return for 30 *solidi* and 60 swine granted land 'to her faithful friend Alchelm' probably, in Stanton-in-the-Peak 'with its berewick at Birchover, north-west of Matlock in Derbyshire, which shows this area of the county was still under Mercian control.[107] It is known from Irish sources that by 902 Aethelred was suffering ill-health which prevented him from active participation in government, and this may explain why charters, even in 900, start to appear in Aethelflaed's name alone. However, that they were still acting jointly is demonstrated in a charter for 901 concerning an exchange of land between Aethelred and Aethelflaed and the monastic community at Much Wenlock, and in a lease of 904 to them by the bishop of Worcester for land and property in Worcester.[108]

Together with his wife, Aethelred had driven forward the *burh* system into Mercia. Worcester, as has been mentioned, may have been fortified as early as the 890s under their auspices, and, as Stenton points out, Shrewsbury, which had been described as a city in a charter of 901, was unlikely to have been left as an open, undefended town. Chester's walls had been repaired in 907 probably in order to protect the Cheshire plain against attack by Norwegians who had recently founded a colony on the Wirral.[109]

In 911 Aethelflaed took over Mercian governance after Aethelred's death; indeed, because of his long-term infirmity she had probably been in effective control of Mercia since 900, although Aethelred appears to have taken part in negotiations with the Danes as late as 906. Meanwhile, King Alfred of Wessex had died on 26 May 899 to be succeeded by his son Edward the Elder, Aethelflaed's brother. Edward was a proficient soldier from childhood but was not of a scholarly nature like his father or indeed his own son, Athelstan. Edward had been born in about 871, and in 892 and 893 had commanded part of the army that caught the Danish raiders. In 902 Edward was able to enter into a peace treaty with the Danes in eastern England but the Danes in the north, ruling York (Jorvik) defied Edward's sovereignty. In 909, after much provocation from Danish border raids, Edward raised an immense army of Mercians and West Saxons and invaded Northumbria 'compelling their kings, however reluctantly, to renew with king Edward the peace they had broken'.[110] However, in the following year, 910, another crisis occurred. The army in Northumrbria broke the peace with Edward and ravaged Mercia. Edward had at this time collected about 100 ships and was in Kent waiting for reinforcements from the central and western coastlands of Wessex. The Danes, believing that most of Edward's fighting men were on these ships, thought 'that they could go unopposed wherever they wished' but Edward gathered a force of men from Mercia and Wessex and set off in pursuit. Aethelweard the Chronicler adds greater detail to the event, which he places in 909.

> The fields of the Mercians are wasted on all sides by the aforesaid disturbance, right up to the River Avon, where begins the boundary of the West Angles [i.e. Saxons] and the Mercians ... But when, exulting in their rich spoils, they withdrew homewards ... the troops of the Mercians and the West Saxons suddenly went against them. A battle ensued and the English without delay obtained the victory at Wednesfield [near Tettanhall], and the army of the Danes was put to flight, overcome by weapons. These things are said to have been done on the fifth day of the month of August.[111]

The Northumbrian Danes never recovered their strength after this crushing defeat, which allowed Norse invaders in from Ireland who, by 919, had founded a new Scandinavian kingdom based at York. However, in spite of the defeat of their Northumbrian counterparts, the power of the east midland and East Anglian Danish armies remained strong.

Following Aethelred's death in 911, Edward took possession of London and Oxford and 'all the lands which belonged to them'. In 912 he 'ordered the northern borough [*burh*] at Hertford to be built' and in the summer the *burh* at Witham, between Colchester and London, was constructed, possibly with a view to suppressing the East Anglian Danes. During this time many people who had been under Danish rule submitted to Edward.[112]

After Easter in 913 the Danish army from Northampton and Leicester rode out and 'killed many men at Hook Norton and round about there' and another raiding band rode out against Luton. 'And then the people of the district became aware of it and fought against them and reduced them to full flight and rescued all that they [the Danes] had captured and also a great part of their horses and their weapons'.[113]

In 914 an attack came from a different quarter. A Scandinavian army landed in the Severn estuary from Brittany and attacked Wales, ravaging 'everywhere along the coast where it suited them'.[114] After taking the bishop of Archenfield, Cyfeiliog, hostage, whom Edward ransomed for £40 (an enormous amount of money), Henry of Huntingdon records 'Afterwards, the [Danish] army landed in a body, intending to pillage the neighbourhood of Archenfield, but they were met by the men of Carleon [the *Anglo-Saxon Chronicle* has Gloucester here] and Hereford, and other neighbouring burgs, who fought and defeated them'. The Danes were driven into a 'certain fortified camp', where Edward's army 'besieged them till they gave hostages and solemnly swore to depart the king's territories. Then the king caused the shores of the Severn to be guarded, from the south coast of Wales round to the Avon; so that the Danes durst nowhere attempt an irruption in that quarter'.[115]

Florence of Worcester notes for the year 917 (a year in advance of the date given in the *Mercian Register*) that in July '... Ethelfleda, the lady of the Mercians, sent an army into the territory of the Britons to take the castle at Brycenamere [Brecknock]; and having stormed it, they carried the wife of the British king captive to Mercia, and thirty-four men with her'. The reason for this is not clear.[116]

In 917 Wessex and Mercia went on the offensive. Aethelflaed attacked Derby and captured it and the surrounding region. Henry of Huntingdon records 'there was a numerous [enemy] garrison in the town of Derby, but they durst not sally forth against her. Whereupon she commanded a vigorous assault to be made on the fortress, and a desperate conflict took place at the very entrance of the gate, where four of Ethelfled's bravest thanes were slain, but, notwithstanding, the assailants forced the gate, and made a breach in the walls.' Thereafter Derby and the region for which it was the military centre was annexed to English Mercia. Stenton considers it likely that Aethelflaed was acting in concert with Edward in this campaign and that the fighting around Derby kept a large enemy force engaged which may otherwise have joined the Danes in the Ouse valley.[117]

Then, in the summer of 917 at Tempsford, in Bedfordshire, the English army stormed a rebuilt Danish fortress and killed all the defenders including the Danish king of East Anglia.[118] The years 917 and 918 were to see the subjugation East Anglia and the confederation of the Five Boroughs — the towns of the latter often by use of overwhelming force.

After her peaceful capture of Leicester, one of the Five Boroughs, Aethelflaed died at Tamworth on 12 June 918, probably aged about 50. Possibly concerned that, without his sister in control, Mercia might try to form a breakaway state at a time when he needed to retain a united front in the war against the Danes, Edward broke off his campaign in Lincolnshire after the fall of Stamford, marched into Mercia and occupied the borough of Tamworth, indicating that it was still perceived as a Mercian royal centre and a possible focus for Mercian sympathisers. The Mercian Council swore allegiance to him, but they still wished to retain some independence by keeping Aethelflaed's daughter, Aelfwynn, as their own *subregulus* or *dux*. Initially Edward, her uncle, appeared to allow this, but never being one to show respect to Mercian feelings, he kidnapped her in the winter of 919 and subjected Mercia to his rule. It is possible that he felt that Aelfwynn, then aged about 20, was unable to control Mercia at such a critical time, although it is more likely that he wanted to leave Mercia as an administrative unit to his eldest son, Athelstan, upon his death. Indeed, it is likely that Aethelflaed had expected Athelstan to succeed in Mercia for she had fostered and raised her nephew in her own court. Nothing more is heard of Aelfwynn after her kidnapping and it is likely she lived out her days in a nunnery.[119]

Mercian autonomy as an independent state was over.

Anglo-Saxon Carving in Mercia

Above: St. Michael & All Angels', Edenham, Lincolnshire (TF 062218)
This decorative roundel is unusual in that it is one of two that survive in their original position, above a plain, square-sectioned string-course. It would have probably formed part of a design that was carried on around the church and been brightly painted. Each roundel is c.0.6m (2ft) in diameter

Left: St. Mary's, Deerhurst, Gloucestershire (SO 870299)
This panel is probably in its original position above the inner doorway from the tower into the nave. Unusually the Christ child is depicted as being in the womb rather than a babe-in-arms. Slight traces of colour remain, indicating the carving ws once painted

Above: Font at St. Mary's, Deerhurst, Gloucestershire (SO 870299)
This font is dated to the mid- to late 9th century and is acknowledged as one of the finest Anglo-Saxon fonts in existence. It stands 51cm (20ins) high and 73cm (29ins) across the rim. The outer surface is decorated with a broad band of spiral decoration within a frame of vine scroll ornamentation. Spiral patterns died out in manuscript art by the latter half of the 8th century, but were fairly widely used in Mercian sculpture. The font sits on a stem which may originally have been part of a cross shaft

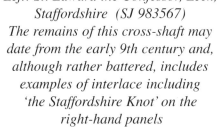

Cross-shafts

Left: St. Edward the Confessor, Leek, Staffordshire (SJ 983567)
The remains of this cross-shaft may date from the early 9th century and, although rather battered, includes examples of interlace including 'the Staffordshire Knot' on the right-hand panels

Centre: St Michael and all Angels', Edenham, Lincolnshire (TF 062218)
This partial cross-shaft dates to the 9th century, before the Danish invasions of this area. The figure is thought to be a seated representation of the Virgin Mary

Above right: St Mary's and All Saints, Nassington, Northamptonshire (TL 063962)
This shaft is c.0.93m (3ft) high and may date to the 10th century. Again there is an emphasis on interlace and circles

Lower right: All Saints, Bradbourne, Derbyshire (SK 209528)
This dates to c.800 and, among its scrolling and circular designs, it also has figural representations. The wear on the top panel is partially explained by its use as a stile into the churchyard until its provenance was recognized!

Left and above: Eyam Cross, St. Lawrence's, Eyam, Derbyshire (SK 218765)
The cross-head survives on a truncated shaft, which date to the late 8th or early 9th century. This fine example of an early high cross retains interlace (detail on right), figural and plant decoration (detail in centre) and, being on the borders of Mercia and Northumbria, is probably a mix of styles from the two kingdoms. The cross may originally have been plastered, painted and decorated with glass, giving a highly colourful appearance

Right: The Cropthorne Cross, St. Michael's, Cropthorne, Worcestershire (SO 001452)
The illustration shows the rear of this early 9th-century equal-armed cross-head, 0.84m (2³/₄ ft) high. Animated birds and dog-like animals are depicted, linked with vine-scroll. Pevsner dates the cross to 825-50. Webster and Backhouse suggest the cross-head may have come from the same workshop that carved the cross-shaft now re-used as a lintel to the south doorway of St. Giles', Acton Beauchamp, and is similar in style and subject to the cross-shaft now re-set in the eaves of the south wall of St. Andrew's at Wroxeter in Shropshire

St Mary and St. Hardulph's, Breedon-on-the-Hill,
Leicestershire (SK 406233)
*This church is renowned for its collection of Anglo-Saxon
sculptural remains, of which a selection is shown on the
this and the opposite page*

Left: The Breedon Angel
*This panel is reset in the bell-ringing chamber of the
tower. At 91cm (c.36ins) high, this figure dates to around
the early 9th century and is accepted as one of the finest
examples of Anglo-Saxon figural sculpture. Eastern inspiration can be seen, with flowing robes, two flowering
plants arising from the base and a Byzantine-style
blessing*

*Right: This figure (53cm,
c.21ins high) is found on the
wall behind the altar in the
Lady Chapel. The figure's hair
is covered, so a woman is
depicted, possibly the Virgin
Mary. She gives a Byzantine-
style blessing with her right
hand, which helps date the work
to the early 9th century. The
'drilled hole' effect of the eyes
and formal robes are typical of
the figurework found in contemporary illuminated manuscripts*

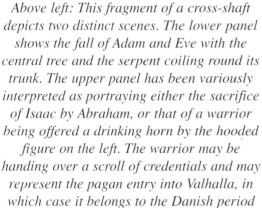

Above left: This fragment of a cross-shaft depicts two distinct scenes. The lower panel shows the fall of Adam and Eve with the central tree and the serpent coiling round its trunk. The upper panel has been variously interpreted as portraying either the sacrifice of Isaac by Abraham, or that of a warrior being offered a drinking horn by the hooded figure on the left. The warrior may be handing over a scroll of credentials and may represent the pagan entry into Valhalla, in which case it belongs to the Danish period

Above right: This strange lion-like creature is believed to be a midland creation, derived from both Celtic and Mediterranean influences

Right: This panel in the Lady Chapel is considered by David Wilson to show a liveliness not found in Northumbrian monuments. The figures are reminiscent of the two bishops in a panel at Peterborough Cathedral (see p.40)

The Wirksworth Stone, St. Mary the Virgin, Wirksworth, Derbyshire (SK 288539)
This dates to 9th-century pre-Viking Mercia and was discovered in 1820 below the floor in front of the altar with ts carved face pointing downwards and covering a stone-built vault which contained a large human skeleton. The stone is divided into two and portrays eight religious scenes. The top row shows (from the left): Christ washing his disciples' feet; a slain lamb on a cross; the body of Mary being carried for burial; and the Christ child held in the arms of Simeon. The bottom layer shows the Harrowing of Hell with Christ leaning forward to save a swaddled figure, possibly representing Man; three figures (bottom left), Cain, Herod and Judas Iscariot, burn in a brazier; then follows Christ's Ascension helped by four angels; a seated Mary visited by the Angel of the Annunciation; and, far right, the probable figure of St. Peter standing in a boat symbolizing the Church

Left: The Newent Stone, St. Mary the Virgin's, Newent, Gloucestershire (SO 723259)
This stone measures only 8 inches by 6½ inches (c.20 x 16½ cm) and may be either a funerary tablet or portable altar, possibly dating from the 11th century. It was discovered on the north side of the church in 1912 under a skull of one of two skeletons. If it was a funerary tablet, then it was probably of the Edred carved in the top left-hand corner; if it was a portable altar, the name may have been added later when it was subsequently used for such a funerary purpose. The central figure has been interpreted either as an ecclesiastic wearing a pectoral cross and perhaps holding a crozier, or as a Harrowing of Hell scene with Christ holding a key and figures falling about in misery

CHAPTER 11
The Twilight Years

Between the 6th and the 9th centuries Mercia had been fiercely independent, often at war with the other major kingdoms to preserve its own identity or to expand its area of control. Arguably, the last true king of Mercia was the West Saxon, Athelstan, who was willingly chosen by the Mercians in 924. Edgar too was apparently 'chosen' in 957, as shall be seen below, but it is not clear how enthusiastically. Thereafter, the kings of the English used the title of 'king of Mercia' as an additional, and, arguably, an outmoded, appellation, useful on occasion as when Edmund Ironside came to terms with Cnut in 1016 in defining the territory over which he was to rule. Mercia had become the equivalent of Wales before devolution—a recognized territorial area with its own distinctive history but, in terms of government, firmly under the government of a power based elsewhere.

The old kingdoms of this new, centralized England were governed on the part of the king by ealdormen, who, by the 10th century, acted as local representatives of the English king. The ealdorman's role included leading the men of his area in war, presiding over shire and other courts and levying taxes from the area for which he was responsible. As Stafford observes there was 'no fixed number nor geographical pattern of ealdormanries'—sometimes the old kingdoms were governed by one ealdorman, Mercia included, at other times, for example during the reigns of Eadwig and Edward the Martyr, new ealdormanries could be carved out of existing ones, or older ones revived, for reasons of reward or gaining loyalty.[1]

From the early 10th century control over Mercia was not the pressing aim of any king: control over the whole of England was the real goal and from the time of Edward the Elder's removal of his niece, Aelfwynn, in early December 919 Mercia was increasingly subject to the will of Wessex. The most significant alteration, administratively, was the introduction of the shire system, an innovation that had begun in Wessex, perhaps as early as the 7th or 8th century, and was gradually implemented in Mercia, receiving considerable momentum in the early 10th century. By the late 10th century the shire, 'a unit in the national administrative system',[2] divided into hundreds—or wapentakes in the case of Leicestershire, Nottinghamshire, Lincolnshire and Derbyshire—was the standard administrative unit used in Mercia, apparently over-riding traditional provincial areas. Each hundred in the shire had its own court—the hundred court—which in the mid-10th century was supposed to meet every four weeks and deal with such criminal concerns as theft and violence, and also with land transactions.[3] In the midlands these units were often assessed at about 100 hides (nominally a hide was 120 acres but this could vary); however, in southern England the term 'a hundred' was given to varying acreages, suggesting that some other local measure may have been in earlier use. A borough (*burh*)-meeting was also held thrice yearly and a shire-meeting held twice a year in the presence of the diocesan bishop and the ealdorman, which, among other things, dealt with land litigation and the dissemination of directives from the king or his councillors.[4]

By the mid-9th century the area south of the Thames appears to have possessed a shire system. Berkshire, for example, may have been created when control of this area passed from Mercian into West Saxon hands. (Unusually it owes its name to a natural feature not to a fortified centre: Asser informs us Berkshire 'is so called from Berroc Wood, where the box-tree grows very abundantly'.)[5] The shire system was subsequently extended into Central Mercian territory, but quite when or by which king it is not clear. Three possibilities are proposed by Keynes: during the time of, and in connection with, the Danish wars fought by Aethelred, Aethelflaed and Edward the Elder; during Athelstan's reign as 'king of the English' (927-39) when it would have formed a part of a 'larger process of political consolidation'; or even as late as the early 11th century, for example under the auspices of Eadric Streona ('the grasping/acquisitor'),[6] who was appointed Mercian ealdorman in 1007. However, one is inclined to agree with Stenton who suggests Edward the Elder as the most likely king to have at least started to impose what is regarded by many as an artificial administrative system over the old kingdom of Mercia. Stenton argues that such a division of the western midlands must have been the work of a king who was powerful enough to ignore resentments and local traditions and who had 'no respect for the ancient divisions of Mercia';[7] subdividing the kingdom into many new and smaller units would certainly have been a potent way of destroying any former identity. However, Bassett has shown that on closer inspection only the former provincial boundaries in Shropshire and Warwickshire are 'comprehensively ignored' in the pre-Conquest layout. In these, the future shire towns of Shrewsbury and Warwick lay next to the old provincial boundaries which meant the latter had to be ignored in order to create a 'coherent territory' for both new shires. In the case of Staffordshire, Worcestershire, Herefordshire, Gloucestershire and, until about 1017, Winchcombeshire, Bassett has shown that their layout generally conforms well with that of the provinces which predated them,[8] based around the settlements of Stafford, Worcester, Hereford and Gloucester (and Winchcombe before 1017), all important settlements, as has been shown, within Mercia. Indeed, it seems far more probable, on practical grounds alone, that the West Saxon kings adapted what was already there to their advantage rather than imposing a completely new system, and only radically altered the layout of administrative units when necessary.[9]

The east midland shires probably evolved in a similar fashion to their west midland counterparts in that the territories that were created by the Danish armies were adopted and adapted as necessary by the new English kings of the 10th and 11th centuries.

In the event the shiring of Mercia was almost certainly not the result of the work of a single monarch. There was undoubtedly an element of suppression on the part of the West Saxon kings, but it is possible that, as the shires were adopted by the Mercians—there certainly seems to be no recorded rebellion against the arrangements—it may have been a change that was seen as necessary in the broader economic and political development of the country, even though the old provincial names were still occasionally used within Mercia. A people's identity does not disappear because it is demanded of them, only in time and with their acceptance might it fade. The same might be said for Mercia as a whole. It could be argued that Mercia ceased to exist at this time and that Wessex succeeded it, however Mercia does have a definite and important presence in the history of the next 90 or so years, in the run up to the invasion of England by Cnut.

Mercia under Edward the Elder 919-924

Edward the Elder's activity in constructing *burhs* in south-eastern Outer Mercia up to and including 918 has been mentioned in chapter 9. Following the death of his sister Aethelflaed in June 918, he exercised authority over Mercia, not that the Mercians were always content or compliant with his rule. Stenton suggests that following Aethelflaed's death it could not be taken for granted that Mercia would continue being subordinate to Wessex; indeed, for the first time for a generation the Mercian aristocracy would have been technically free to give their allegiance to whomsoever they chose. Edward's immediate seizure of Tamworth was almost certainly intended to forestall that eventuality and the likely concomitant that Mercia might break away from Wessex.[10] His campaign in the east midlands was one of conquest, not of liberation, yet Mercia may not have chosen to rebel against Edward as perceptions of the benefits of co-operation against common enemies may have been gaining ground.

By the end of 918 the Danish armies based at Nottingham and, possibly, Lincoln were forced to capitulate to Edward. The main roads to the south and west were controlled by English garrisons, whereas a hostile Norse army was closing in on York and the Danes' natural allies.[11] After Nottingham's surrender Edward established a new garrison comprising both Danes and Englishmen. However, there is a question mark over Lincoln (and Lindsey's) fate as the area may have been under the control of York's Vikings and only submitted to West Saxon authority when Northumbria fell in 927 to Athelstan, Edward's successor— it appears that Lincoln and Lindsey had been under the rule of York's Vikings in the 890s and that Lincoln was minting coins which were based on those from York as late as the 920s.[12] Nevertheless, in 919, with the possible exception of Lindsey, Edward was in control of Wales and England as far north as the river Humber.

However, further trouble was never far away and Norsemen from Ireland were making inroads from the north-west of England. In the very early 900s they had set up a colony on the Wirral peninsula. The danger posed by these raiders from Ireland appears to have drawn the English of northern Northumbria into an alliance with the kings of the Scots against their common enemy, Ragnall, a grandson of Ivarr the Boneless. Ragnall mounted an all out attack on the Scots, the two armies meeting on the Northumbrian borders on the banks of the river Tyne, probably at Corbridge, south of Hadrian's Wall. Ragnall was victorious, overwintered in Northumbria and then pushed southwards on to York where he established himself as king in 919.[13] This exposed Aethelflaed's *burh* at Runcorn on the Mersey, separated as it was from other English garrisons at Chester and Eddisbury by the deep Weaver valley. In the autumn of 919 Edward acted to strengthen this part of the Mercian border by constructing a *burh* at Thelwall, about 10 miles north-east of Runcorn, and repairing the Roman defences at Manchester, to the north-east of Thelwall.[14] But even these improved defences did not stop Ragnall's brother, Sigtrygg *Caech* ('Squinty'), also known as Sihtric, from invading north-western Mercia with an army from Dublin in 920; all that is recorded however is that 'King Sihtric destroyed Davonport', near Manchester.[15] Edward's reaction in the early summer of 920 was to move to Nottingham, where he built a new *burh* on the south bank of the Trent and a bridge to connect it with the fortress he had taken from the Danes a few years earlier. By so doing he created a defended crossing over the river Trent where local midland forces could be gathered prior to an advance on Northumbria.[16] Edward then moved on to Bakewell in Derbyshire near the junction of two valleys which offered routes to the north and north-west, where he built another *burh*,[17] before advancing further north. Whether there was any fighting and, if so, on what scale is unrecorded. Suffice to say that 'the kings of the Scots and all the people of the Scots, and Ragnald, and the sons of Eadwulf and all who live in Northumbria, both English and Danish, Norsemen and others, and also the king of the Strathclyde Welsh and all the Strathclyde Welsh, chose him as father and lord'.[18]

Early the following year, 921, Ragnall died and Sigtrygg *Caech* succeeded him in York and refused to recognize Edward as his overlord. Edward was unable to embark on another campaign in the north for government in the south were causing him problems, not least the English and Danish Mercians from whom Stenton suggests Edward received only grudging obedience.[19]

By 924 Edward's apparent lack of empathy with Mercian opinion appears finally to have led to trouble. William of Malmesbury records that Edward 'subdued the contumacy of the city of Chester, which was rebelling in confederacy with the Britons'. Edward suppressed the rebellion quickly and placed a new garrison at Chester, but died a few days later at Farndon-on-Dee, near Wrexham, on 17 July. Interestingly neither the *Anglo-Saxon Chronicle* nor the *Mercian Register* mention this rebellion. It is highly probable that the Mercians expected Aelfwynn, Aethelred's and Aethelflaed's daughter, to have taken over the kingdom on the death of her mother. Simmering resentment over her removal by Edward may have led to such a rebellion,[20] and could well have been one of the reasons that prevented Edward from embarking on a campaign in the north in 921.

There are only about 37 extant charters for Edward's reign, almost all deal mainly with the Church and land in southern England, notably around Winchester, the new administrative centre. His charter activity in Mercia is surprising by its absence, with the exception of a couple of grants in Berkshire.

Athelstan - king of Mercia and Wessex 924-39

William of Malmesbury records that 'Concerning this king a strong persuasion is prevalent among the English, that one more just or learned never governed the kingdom ... Extremely beloved by his subjects from admiration of his fortitude and humility, he was terrible to those who rebelled against him, through his invincible courage'.[21] If it were not for William of Malmesbury, who used parts of a lost life of Athelstan in his account, very little would now be known about his military successes or his reputation in Europe.[22]

Athelstan—'noble stone'—was the eldest son of Edward the Elder and, as a leader of the Mercian people, was a completely different proposition to his father. He was born in about 895 and it is likely that he was illegitimate or that his mother, Ecgwynn, who was possibly a noble Mercian woman, was Edward's concubine, rather than his legal wife. What is certain is that Athelstan was born before Edward was king. Edward subsequently married twice and both these wives were 'successively acknowledged as queen', a title denied to Athelstan's mother.[23] It is likely that because of his probable illegitimacy that, Alfred the Great, Athelstan's grandfather, arranged for Aethelflaed and Aethelred, his aunt and uncle, to raise him at their court in Gloucester.[24] From an early age Athelstan was groomed to rule Mercia as 'Lord of the Mercians'.

Being raised by Aethelflaed and Aethelred he was known to the Mercian nobility and was familiar with their opinions. He was very popular within Mercia, evidenced by the fact that after Edward's death, he was almost immediately elected king in that kingdom at a great meeting held at Tamworth and attended by Mercian bishops and magnates; indeed he received a degree of loyalty from his Mercian subjects that his forebears had never enjoyed.[25] By contrast, the West Saxon councillors deliberated for some time as to whether Athelstan should become king of Wessex. It is likely that Edward had suggested Athelstan should succeed him in Mercia, while one of his legitimate sons should take the West Saxon crown[26] and so avert a succession crisis. However, Edward's eldest legitimate son, Aelfweard, whom Winchester sources record had been made king by Edward in his own lifetime, outlived his father by a mere 16 days,[27] and they were both buried at Winchester. If Aelfweard had been created king, it was a peculiar choice even though he was the eldest legitimate son, as he was reputedly a hermit at Bridgnorth. The third son, Edwin, was either dead—it is unclear whether he died in 923 or 933—or was the probable cause of the delay in the acceptance of Athelstan as king of Wessex (see below).[28] The other children by Edward's first wife were daughters. Through his second wife, there were two sons: Edmund, born in about 921, and Eadred, born in about 923, who were too young to be considered for kingship, being only about three years' and one year old respectively.

Protracted argument in Wessex as to whether the crown should be offered to Athelstan is only likely if Edwin was still alive: Athelstan was not finally accepted as king of England until the summer of 925 and then had to wait until 4 September 925 for his coronation at Kingston-on-Thames in Surrey, by which time he was about 30 years old.[29] Miller suggests the West Saxons may have pushed Edwin's title to the throne to such an extent that it conceivably led to civil war between Wessex and Mercia,[30] although there is no record of this. If Edwin did survive this trial of strength, then the 'disturbances in the kingdom' recorded for the year 933 related to further fighting over the crown—this is one of the years given for Edwin's death when he drowned at sea (see p.265).

Athelstan followed his father's expansionist principles as a leader, but had a different approach to the people and kingdoms he ruled. He is known to have been an intellectual, and comparable with Alfred in his ability, energy, devotional prowess and also in his enquiring nature. Like his grandfather, Athelstan was also an avid reader and is described in a poem quoted by William of Malmesbury as 'avidly drinking the honey of learning, he passed not childishly the years of childhood'.[31] He received a Mercian education, possibly at the school attached to the monastery at Worcester, and is the first king of his line who is known to have been literate as a child.[32] Athelstan was also renowned as being a collector of relics on a scale that no other English monarch touched. He gave gifts of books, relics and other treasure, as well as large amounts of land. He entertained scholars from abroad at his court, as well as maintaining communications with foreign monasteries.[33] In so doing, he played an important role on the European stage, not unlike Offa of Mercia.

Athelstan's strong position in Mercia undoubtedly encouraged Sigtrygg *Caech* to propose an alliance with him, with Sigtrygg duly marrying Athelstan's sister at Tamworth on 30 January 926, and converting to Christianity. Alas, it was not a happy arrangement for, as Roger of Wendover records, 'not long afterwards he [Sigtrygg] cast off the blessed maiden and, deserting his Christianity, restored the worship of idols, and after a short while ended his life miserably as an apostate'.[34]

Sigtrygg was dead by March 927, leaving as heir, by a former wife, a son, Olafr Sigtryggson (also known as Anlaf) who was accepted as Sigtrygg's successor by the Northumbrian Vikings. Olafr's uncle, Gothfrith, king of Dublin, arrived in Northumbria from Dublin either in support of the youth or to claim York's throne for himself. Whatever Gothfrith's real motive, it is clear that Athelstan would not countenance the continuation of 'an independent Viking Northumbria'.[35] He made a pre-emptive strike with Mercian assistance and drove Gothfrith and Olafr out of the country, Gothfrith seeking 'refuge with the king of Scots', Constantine, and Olafr moving back to Ireland.[36]

Athelstan sent ambassadors to the northern British kings, Owain, king of the Cumbrians, Constantine, king of the Scots and, probably, Donald, king of the Strathclyde Welsh, who, under the threat of war, submitted to Athelstan. On 12 July 927 at Eamont Bridge (1 mile south-east of Penrith in Cumbria), at what Wood terms 'the first great "imperial" council of the tenth century', these British kings and the English Bamburgh dynasty under Ealdred Ealdulfing became tributaries to Athelstan.[37] Constantine had promised to give Gothfrith up to Athelstan but Gothfrith escaped on the way to Eamont Bridge and, gathering a war-band, briefly laid siege to York. William of Malmesbury records that Athelstan 'levelled with the ground the castle which the Danes had formerly fortified in York, that there might be no place for disloyalty to shelter in; and the booty which had been found there, which was very considerable, he generously divided, man by man, to the whole army'.[38] This was an historic moment: a southern (Saxon) king had never ruled directly in York before.[39] Athelstan was also the first king of Mercia to take control of any part of Northumbria since at least the 7th century.

Soon after his defeat at York, Gothfrith, whom William of Malmesbury describes as an 'incorrigible pirate, [more] accustomed to live in the water like a fish', sought peace. It is a measure of Athelstan's magnanimity that Gothfrith was 'amicably received by the king, and sumptuously entertained for four days' before being allowed to return to Ireland.[40]

Athelstan's humane treatment of Gothfrith is notable and unusual, and it is likely that his apparent unwillingness to use oppression unless absolutely necessary was the key to his success in obtaining co-operation within Mercia and elsewhere. Indeed, William comments:

For he had prescribed himself this rule of conduct, never to hoard up riches; but liberally to expend all his acquisition either on monasteries or on his faithful followers. On these, during the whole of his life, he expended his paternal treasures, as well as the produce of his victories. To the clergy he was humble and affable; to the laity mild and pleasant; to the nobility rather reserved, from respect to his dignity; to the lower classes, laying aside the stateliness of power, he was kind and condescending.[41]

William of Malmesbury also gives a rare physical description of Athelstan: 'He was, as we have heard, of becoming stature, thin in person, his hair flaxen, as I have seen by his remains, and beautifully wreathed with golden threads'.[42]

Although tough penalties existed in his law codes, Athelstan is recorded as stating 'no man younger than fifteen should be killed unless he tried to defend himself or fled' and took a more lenient view on the very young and on petty criminals.[43] Clearly such humanity is relative in our modern terms, but it was certainly an advance on the 'eye-for-an-eye' brand of legislation created by Alfred, his grandfather.[44]

In July 927 on returning south from Cumbria, Athelstan attacked the northern Welsh kings who, although they had grudgingly given submission to Edward, were now apparently openly hostile to Athelstan. For a while, led by the king of Gwynedd, Idwal *Foel* ('the bald'), they resisted his attacks, but once brought to battle in the field were put to flight. Athelstan subsequently summoned a meeting with the then five Welsh kings at Hereford in the old *Magonsaetan* territory and 'after some opposition' he compelled them 'to surrender to his power'.[45] Among these Welsh rulers was Hywel Dda, the powerful king of Dyfed. He, more than any other Welsh leader of the time, or, indeed, in the following decades, was influenced by English methods of government and ways, even to the extent of minting silver coins in the English fashion and giving one of his sons an English name,[46] Edwin.

At this Hereford meeting Athelstan actually 'brought to pass what no king before him had even presumed to think of: which was, that they [Welsh kings] should pay annually by way of tribute, twenty pounds of gold, three hundred of silver, twenty-five thousand oxen, besides as many dogs as he might choose, which from their sagacious scent could discover the retreats and hiding places of wild beasts; and birds, trained to make prey of others in the air'.[47] As Stenton comments these figures 'verge on but perhaps do not quite reach the incredible'; certainly by anyone's estimation it was a punitive tribute, indicating that Athelstan's victory over the Welsh must have been crushing.[48] The meeting also established the river Wye as the boundary between the English and Welsh in the locality of Hereford. It was also around this time that the set of laws called the *Ordinance of the Dunsaete*, which aimed for a 'peaceful settlement of disputes', was set down between the English and Welsh settlers on either side of the border (see p.173).[49]

After his successful conclusion of matters with the Welsh, William of Malmesbury records that Athelstan attacked the Britons of Cornwall and established the river Tamar as the boundary between England and Cornwall. If the chronology in William of Malmesbury is correct, it appears that Athelstan achieved this startling list of accomplishments between July 927 and April 928, that is, within 10 months.[50]

During Easter 928 a great court was held at Exeter which Wood observes 'probably signifies the successful conclusion to Athelstan's conquest of Britain'.[51] Exactly 50 years previously Alfred, his grandfather, was fighting for his life at Athelney with his authority reduced to an area of a few square miles of Somerset marshland; yet Athelstan was now rejoicing in the title of 'Emperor of the world of Britain' — the first king to rule the whole island of Britain.[52]

As a result it is perhaps not surprising that Athelstan held an impressive reputation among the leaders of Europe, many of whom were keen to marry his (half)sisters and sent incredible treasures to help 'persuade' him. Athelstan soon enjoyed a series of alliances through his sisters and the marriages of his aunts with the courts of Flanders, Saxony, and France, and possibly even Norway. Such was his Continental reputation that a German cleric reworked a 9th-century poem on Charlemagne in praise of

Athelstan; a Frankish cleric wrote to him as 'excelling in fame and honour all earthly kings of modern times' and, perhaps surprisingly, he was remembered in Ireland as the west's most honoured figure. In Norway he was termed 'Athelstan the Victorious' and described as the 'greatest king in the northern world'.[53] Matthew of Westminster records that 'so great a friendship arose between king Athelstan and Robert, duke of Normandy, that each of them had influence in the affairs of the other, and that, in all their wars, they were benefitted by their reciprocal co-operation'.[54] He is also the first English king known to have sent a fleet to help an ally on the Continent: Louis d'Outremer of France.[55]

With King Harald (Fairhair or Finehair) of Norway, who had himself established a unified kingdom, Athelstan shared a common aim: to prevent raids by uncontrolled Viking raiders from fleets still at large in the seas to the west. Harald dispatched a mission to Athelstan at York where the latter was presented with a highly ornate ship with a purple sail and gilded shields as a gift.[56] Norse tradition also has it that Harold's youngest son, 7 year-old Hakon, was sent to England to learn about English government. Athelstan apparently fostered him, a not uncommon practice at the time, and he and his court clearly made such a good job that, after Hakon returned to Norway, a general uprising deposed his half-brother, the appositely named Erikir Bloodaxe, in favour of the milder-natured Hakon.[57] Other foreign kings are also said to have sent their sons to be fostered in his court,[58] a further testimony to Athelstan's reputation.

Such wide-ranging alliances throughout Europe and Scandinavia also helped improve trading and cultural links and it is probably no coincidence that town development is much in evidence in Athelstan's time. In a set of his laws issued at Gratel(e)y (now a village 6 miles south-west of Andover in Hampshire) it is stated '... we have pronounced that no goods over 20 pence are to be bought outside a town, but they are to be bought there in the witness of the town-reeve or of another trustworthy man, or, again, in the witness of the reeves in a public meeting'.[59] The restriction imposed on the buying (and by implication the selling) of goods to towns (*burhs*) is regarded by Wood as 'an important stage in developing urban life in places which had often begun life simply as strongholds'. It is possible that Athelstan decided that some of the *burghal* forts should not to be encouraged to develop into towns, for example the forts of Pilton, Halwell and Eashing disappear or were closed down to be replaced as boroughs by the more favourably-sited Barnstaple, Totnes and Guildford. In the wider Mercian region it appears that the *burhs* of Oxford, Wallingford, and possibly Hereford, were given new ditch systems and/or stone walls.[60] Such long-term and well-planned policies can only have encouraged trade and the growing wealth of England. It is little wonder that in the 980s an English writer remarks 'From this period [Athelstan's reign] there was peace and abundance of all things'.[61]

The 'Grat(e)ley' laws also state 'that there is to be one coinage over all the king's dominion, and no one is to mint money except in a town'.[62] The laws also describe the penalties for those moneyers who broke the law—a convicted moneyer would have the hand 'with which he committed the crime' cut off and 'put up on the mint'. They then go on to state how many moneyers should be in each town: for example London was prescribed eight, Canterbury seven, and Shaftesbury two while the majority of other boroughs were allowed one.[63] These were the first coinage laws in English history.

However, Athelstan was not without military problems in the latter half of his reign. In 934 Constantine, king of the Scots, broke the Eamont treaty with Athelstan by marrying his daughter to Olafr Gothfrithson, king of Dublin, which courted a swift response.[64] Athelstan gathered a huge army at Winchester, which included four subordinate Welsh kings and their own contingents. Then, moving northwards, they gathered additional forces at Nottingham, including those of 'Scandinavian earls from the Danelaw'.[65] (The Danelaw had, since its reconquest, largely by Edward the Elder, owed allegiance to the English king. Some of its Viking leaders and followers had left, but most remained, retaining their lands and customs, a mixture of both pre-Danish and Danish in origin and often distinct between adjoining areas.)[66] A supporting Mercian and West Saxon fleet sailed up the coast. Cumbria, Pictland and Scotland were ravaged by Athelstan's forces and the northern kings capitulated, their kingdoms once again becoming tributary to Athelstan.[67]

Yet the north was not subdued. Just three years' later a new coalition formed, instigated by Constantine and Olafr Gothfrithson. The poem *Armes Prydein* shows that the Welsh were also hopeful that they would rid themselves of the West Saxons and their allies the 'Mercian incendiaries' and drive them away as far as Sandwich where they had supposedly first landed.[68] Florence of Worcester records that Olafr and Constantine 'entered the mouth of the Humber with a powerful fleet'.[69] The Northumbrians submitted and York was used as a campaign headquarters from which the invaders unsettled Danish settlers in the east midlands by attacking south of the Humber.[70] Wood speculates that the North Welsh under Idwal *Foel* may have attacked Athelstan's western flank.[71] If so, the coalition would have certainly bitten deep into Mercia from the north and the west. A lost poem used by William of Malmesbury lets vent to the poet's feelings:

> ... there returned that plague and hateful ruin of Europe. Now the fierce savagery of the North couches on our land, now the pirate Olaf, deserting the sea, camps in the field, breathing forbidden and savage threats. At the will of the king of the Scots, the northern land lends a quiet assent to the raving fury; and now they swell with pride, now frighten the air with words. The natives give way, the whole region yields to the proud.[72]

The next statement is astounding in suggesting that Athelstan did nothing in the face of such a threat:

> For since our king, confident and eager in youth, deeming his service done, had long spent slow leisure hours, they despoiled everything with continuous ravages, driving out the people, setting fire to the fields. The green crops withered in the fields, the blighted cornfield mocked at the husbandman's prayers. So great was the force of foot-troops, so fierce that of horsemen, a host of countless coursers. At length the complaining rumour roused the king, not to let himself thus be branded that his arms gave way before the barbarian axe.[73]

Wood suggests that Athelstan was playing 'a waiting game' and speculates that this account may have been written 'as an exemplar for one of Athelstan's less effective successors' — a warning against hesitation or idleness perhaps. Wood also conjectures that any actual delay by Athelstan in moving north might be explained by the time it would have taken to raise as many Mercian and West Saxon levies as possible; other sources comment on how hard it was to muster a large army unless a king personally travelled through the shires.[74]

The poem quoted in William of Malmesbury then suddenly changes tack, announcing:

> There is no delay; he [Athelstan] fiercely unfolds in the wind standards, leading victorious cohorts, a hundred banners. A vigorous force of men, a hundred thousand strong, follow their standards to the scene of battle. The mighty report of their approach terrified the raiders, the din so shook the legions of the plunderers, that, dropping their spoils, they sought their own lands.[75]

The culminating battle was fought late in 937 at a fort called *Brunanburh* in several sources, and *Wendun/Weondun* by Simeon of Durham.[76] The location of *Brunanburh/We(o)ndun* is not known, although Bromborough, just south of Port Sunlight on the Wirral, Cheshire, is thought a likely candidate.[77]

A poem recorded in the *Anglo-Saxon Chronicle* under the year 937, and which was probably written by a cleric not long after, gives a rather fuller account of the battle and the Mercians role in it: 'In this year King Athelstan, lord of nobles, dispenser of treasure to men, and his brother also, Edmund atheling, won by the sword's edge undying glory in battle round *Brunanburh*. Edward's sons clove the shield-wall, hewed the linden-wood shields with hammered swords ... Their enemies perished; the people of the Scots and the pirates fell doomed. The field grew dark(?) with the blood of men'[78] from sun-rise to sun-set.

Wood states that English fought in separate armies, with the Mercians fighting against the Scandinavians and the West Saxons the Celts.[79] The poem continues:

> The whole day long the West Saxons with mounted companies kept in pursuit of the hostile peoples, grievously they cut down the fugitives from behind with their whetted swords. The Mercians refused not hard conflict to any men who with Olaf had sought this land in the bosom of a ship over the tumult of waters, coming doomed to the fight. Five young kings lay on that field of battle, slain by the swords, and also seven of Olaf's earls, and a countless host of seamen and Scots.[80]

Among the slain kings was Owain, king of Cumbria. The instigator, Constantine — 'the old and wily one' — fled back to his own land 'shorn of his kinsmen and deprived of his friends' and 'left his young son on the field of slaughter'.[81] The 'Norsemen, the sorry survivors from the spears, put out in their studded ships on to Ding's mere, to make for Dublin across the deep water, back to Ireland humbled at heart'.[82] It was another crushing victory by Athelstan, one which over 40 years later Aethelweard the Chronicler notes was still referred to as 'the great battle' by ordinary folk.[83]

For the next two years Athelstan ruled his kingdom in peace and died on 27 October 939 at Gloucester at the age of 44, probably of the hereditary illness which appears to have afflicted his family, including his grandfather, Alfred. He never married and is not recorded as having any children. His childlessness may, indeed, have been a deliberate act of policy, a view held by a German ambassador to the Court in 929 who suggests that Athelstan was, in effect, a 'caretaker king' who was raising the legitimate sons of Edward and his queens.[84] If this is true, it would say much about the selflessness of Athelstan. Yet there is one potential blemish. Both William of Malmesbury and Matthew of Westminster relate that Edward's eldest legitimate surviving son, Edwin, was exiled by Athelstan for some alleged treachery and was deliberately put out to sea in a small, oarless and age-worn boat with only one attendant. After drifting about for a long time, Edwin threw himself overboard in despair and drowned.[85] Matthew states that, knowing himself to be illegitimate, Athelstan feared Edwin might seize the throne, then, horrified at what he had done, he underwent seven years' penance and subsequently founded two monasteries at Middleton and 'Michelena' 'for the soul of his brother Edwin', richly endowing them with land and possessions.[86] On this whole incident the last word perhaps belongs with William of Malmesbury: 'The circumstances of Edwin's death, though extremely probable, I the less venture to affirm for truth, on account of the extraordinary affection he manifested towards the rest of his brothers; for, as his father had left them very young, he cherished them whilst children with much kindness, and, when grown up, made them partakers of his kingdom ...'.[87]

Athelstan was buried at his own request in Malmesbury Abbey in Wiltshire, on the border of Mercia and Wessex, wholly symbolic one feels of his success in drawing together these once disparate kingdoms.

During his reign an apparent change of the system of government occurred in England. Until the end of the 9th century Stenton observes that the people who attended the king and acted as witnesses to his official acts were generally the ealdormen, together with his bishops and retainers (men with whom the king 'was in constant, if not familiar, association').[88] Previous 8th- and 9th-century Mercian kings had occasionally presided over bigger and more general assemblies, although these largely concerned themselves with ecclesiastical matters. Under Athelstan's rule a new type of assembly appears, but it is just possible that larger and more centralized assemblies were forming in Edward the Elder's reign as a consequence of the huge enlargement of his kingdom. In Athelstan's reign, the West Saxon bishops, ealdormen and thegns were combined with the lay and ecclesiastical magnates from every part of the country for national assemblies which dealt even with the most ordinary business and where local interests were represented.[89] The fact that Athelstan is not known to have travelled far out of Wessex in the normal course of government suggests he expected officials to travel to him and by so doing administration must have become more centralized. North of the Thames, the only places at which Athelstan is known to have held court in peace-time were at Tamworth, London, Whittlebury (3 miles south of Towcester in Northamptonshire), and Buckingham in the wider Mercian territory, as well as Colchester and York.[90]

These courts were often very large. For example in March 931, at least 68 dignatories met with him in Colchester, which would have given rise to a temporary population of several hundred people allowing for the accompanying retinues. Such national assemblies undoubtedly went a long way towards breaking down the earlier 'provincial separatism'.[91] A charter drawn up at Nottingham in June 934 for land in northern Lancashire is also attested by nearly 60 bishops, ealdormen and thegns from all over the country.[92]

Athelstan's charters are numerous, although the relative absence of royal charters in Alfred's reign and their cessation before Edward the Elder's death may be a consequence of the Danish wars interrupting the ordinary business of the kingdoms and/or the charters themselves may have been destroyed in the wars. A large proportion of Athelstan's charters are concerned with land in Wessex, but the remainder cover the whole country and demonstrate his system of ruling by proxy even at the start of the reign, by using ealdormen for local government. A charter of 926, for example, concerning land at Chalgrove and Tebworth, respectively 4 miles north and north-west of Dunstable in Bedfordshire, is given to Ealdred his *minister*,[93] and another dated 925 is to Eadric, *minister*, confirming land at Whittington in Staffordshire.[94] *Ministers* are also mentioned in 931 in relation to grants of land in Berkshire.[95]

It is not surprising that Athelstan's reign has been remembered as something of a golden age by later chroniclers, such as William of Malmesbury, for it appears he ruled wisely and justly. It might be argued that although of undeniably West Saxon lineage, Athelstan was the last of the true Mercian kings in that he was raised and educated in Mercia, by implication understanding the intimate workings of the kingdom, and was chosen freely by the Mercians as their king. In this sense he was truly Mercia's man. His sure-footed rule stands in sharp contrast to the chaos which followed, notably after Edmund's reign.

Edmund, reigned 939-46

Edmund, born in about 921, was Edward the Elder's first child of his third marriage. He was raised in Athelstan's household and it is conjectured that the prominence given to Edmund in the *Anglo-Saxon Chronicle*'s poem concerning *Brunanburh* may indicate he was Athelstan's chosen heir.[96] He was only 18 at his accession in October 939, the first king to succeed to the whole of England. Yet, Olafr Gothfrithson, now king of Dublin, although defeated by Athelstan and Edmund at *Brunanburh*, had not been deprived of his power or resources in Ireland and still harboured the intention of taking back York. He promptly took advantage of Edmund's newness as king by invading and occupying the city a month or so after Edmund's succession, meeting with no effective resistance.[97]

Olafr's invading force poured south into Mercia early in 940 devastating towns and countryside in their wake. Simeon of Durham states that Olafr 'besieged Northampton. But accomplishing nothing there, he turned his army to Tamworth and ravaged everything round about it'.[98] Manuscript D of the *Anglo-Saxon Chronicle* records that Olafr 'took Tamworth by storm, and the losses were heavy on both sides, and the Danes were victorious and took away much booty with them'.[99] In due course Edmund besieged Olafr at Leicester, according to Chronicle D, but the latter managed to escape.[100]

A peace deal was eventually brokered by Oda, archbishop of Canterbury, and Wulfstan, archbishop of York, by which England was once again split by Watling Street, with the Norsemen controlling the north. But this reversal in fortune did not last long. Olafr Gothfrithson died late in 941, and Edmund in turn used the opportunity to win back the lost part of Mercia including the territory of the Five Boroughs, seemingly to the relief of the Danes settled there.

The *Anglo-Saxon Chronicle* records the liberation in a contemporary poem which Stenton regards as significant in that it is the first political poem known in the English language and 'contains the earliest known reference to the confederation of the Five Boroughs' which later appears as a distinctive part of the east midlands. The poem also indicates that the Danes of eastern Mercia, after 15 years of government under Athelstan, now regarded themselves as the 'rightful subjects of the English king'. It also highlights the hostility between the Danes and Norwegians.[101]

> In this year [942] King Edmund, lord of the English, protector of men, the beloved performer of mighty deeds, overran Mercia, as bounded by Dore, Whitwell gate and the broad stream, the River Humber; and five boroughs, Leicester and Lincoln, Nottingham and likewise Stamford, and also Derby. The Danes were previously subjected by force under the Norsemen, for a long time in bonds of captivity to the heathens, until the defender of warriors, the son of Edward, King Edmund, redeemed them, to his glory.[102]

In 944 Edmund also won back Northumbria.

Outside the arena of militarism, Edmund was generous with the Church. William of Malmesbury asserts that among many donations to churches, Edmund 'exalted ... Glastonbury, through his singular affection towards it, with great estates and honours ...'.[103] It was this association with Glastonbury and, particularly with Dunstan, whom he made abbot in 939/40 and who brought the Benedictine rule to the abbey, that was to have important religious connotations in 10th-century Mercia and elsewhere.

On 26 May 946, the feast of St. Augustine, Edmund 'was stabbed to death at the royal vill called Pucklechurch, [north-east of Bristol and in the territory of the *Hwicce*] by Leof, a ruffianly thief, while attempting to defend his steward from being murdered by the robber'.[104] Edmund had reigned for just five years and seven months.

Charter evidence shows that Edmund was an extremely energetic and capable young man, following in the footsteps of Athelstan. His short reign produced many charters, giving land throughout England not just to the Church, but also to many ealdormen upon whom he was dependant. In Mercia, grants to ealdormen, *ministers* and thegns are very apparent.

Eadred, reigned 946-955

As Edmund left two very young sons, Eadwig and Edgar, his younger brother Eadred succeeded him and was crowned at Kingston-on-Thames in Surrey on 15 August 947. Eadred's reign lasted nine years, during which the main political problem remained with the north, where the Norwegians attempted to regain control of Northumbria. By 954, however, after several changes in fortune, Northumbria was once more firmly part of England, a position that was to hold thereafter.

Eadred had a very close relationship with Dunstan, supporting the monastic reform movement of which Dunstan was the prime mover, and even 'entrusted all his treasures to his guardianship'.[105] Dunstan, it seems, was on hand to give him good counsel, as he had been with Edmund.

There is little direct comment on the political position or events relating to Mercia during Eadred's reign. Charter evidence shows that his rule in Mercia was largely conducted through ealdormen. Many of the 'Mercian' charters relate to Berkshire, the traditionally disputed area between Mercia and Wessex, although there are also examples from western and eastern Mercia. It is possible that in the latter part of his reign Eadred delegated some of his authority to Dunstan and others due to a prolonged illness, as between 953-5 less than one-third of the charters are actually witnessed by the king.[106] Indeed it was Dunstan who comforted the ailing king by urging him to endure 'with patience his frequent bodily pains'.[107] Eadred is reported as being constantly afflicted with sickness and 'of so weak a digestion, as to be unable to swallow more than the juices of the food he had masticated, to the great annoyance of his guests'.[108] He died on 23 November at Frome in Somerset, aged about 32, and was buried at Winchester Cathedral.

Eadwig, reigned 955-9

As Eadred died unmarried and childless, Eadwig, his nephew and Edmund's eldest son succeeded. He was only 14 or 15 years old at his accession and his extreme youth may partly explain the chaos that appears to be the mark of his reign. As with Penda centuries before, Eadwig may be a victim of 'bad press'—as most of the chroniclers who mention Eadwig were clerics, often monks, and Eadwig was at least indifferent to monasticism unlike Eadred or his successor Edgar, our view of him may be coloured by their prejudice. For example, William of Malmesbury adjudges him '... a wanton youth, who abused the beauty of his person in illicit intercourse ...'.[109] The *Anglo-Saxon Chronicle* barely mentions Eadwig, only outlining his accession, the subsequent division of the kingdom between his brother Edgar and himself, his divorce and the date of his death, and so one is left to the later medieval chronicles and the accretions of legend.

From these the picture emerges of an extremely rash young man, far too irresponsible for the task in hand at so young an age, and far too headstrong to be controlled by more mature council. He swiftly acquired a poor reputation among the nobility. Matthew of Westminster records that even on the day of his consecration as king 'the prince, immediately after he had received the royal unction, suddenly he leapt down from the table and left the pleasant banquet, while wanton and full of wine, to satisfy himself with lascivious pleasures'.[110] Dunstan and the bishop of Lichfield went to retrieve him, but on entering the king's bedchamber 'they found the kingly crown, splendid and beautiful as it was, thrown carelessly off his head down on the ground, and the king lying between ... two women [and] wallowing in the mire of impurity'.[111] Dunstan dragged Eadwig back to the banquet to avoid further offence to those attending.

According to William of Malmesbury, 'on the archbishop's compelling him to repudiate the strumpet, made him his enemy for ever'.[112] The ladies in question appear to have been Aethelgifu and her daughter, Aelfgifu, the latter in fact becoming Eadwig's wife. Their marriage was subsequently dissolved, in 958, apparently on grounds of consanguinity but probably for political rather than religious reasons. Indeed, Aelfgifu was remembered at New Minster, Winchester, in a list of 'illustrious women, choosing this holy place for the love of God, who have commended themselves to the prayers of the community by the gifts of alms'.[113]

Shortly after the fracas at the coronation, Dunstan was driven into exile in Flanders. The break with Dunstan appears to have been personal, rather than with the Church as a whole as, for example, highly esteemed ecclesiastics were prepared to come to Eadwig's court when both Aelfgifu and Aethelgifu were present, including Bishop Coenwald of Worcester who owed nothing to Eadwig concerning his position.[114]

However, evidence of Eadwig's impulsive behaviour may be seen from the astonishing number of charters he granted in his four year reign. Ninety survive and a staggering 60 or so date from the year 956, the number possibly indicating a desperate attempt to secure a core of loyal retainers.[115] About thirty-two are to his *ministers* or *princeps*, 17 are to his family, *filelis*, *comes*—'familiars' or associates; four are to 'noble ladies' or 'faithful women' and one is to his hunstman. Nevertheless, some do relate to the Church—ranging from the archbishop of Canterbury to the 'priests in charge of Bampton church in Oxfordshire'.[116] And it was Eadwig who granted the land on which Southwell minster, near Nottingham, was founded, indeed Stenton suggests that Eadwig's gifts to monasteries are sufficient to show that neither he, nor those who influenced him, were antagonistic to the monastic institution.[117]

It was during Eadwig's reign that changes were made in those who governed Mercia as ealdormen, by promoting those of his own kin. Until his retirement in 956, one Athelstan, who had been appointed in 932 as ealdorman by King Athelstan, had administered the 'newly-reconquered Danish settlements' of eastern England, not only in Norfolk and Suffolk, but also the east midlands and Essex, the extent of his power earning him the nickname 'Half-King'. He was a close friend of Dunstan and he and his wife, Aelfwynn, a wealthy east midlands' noblewoman, were foster parents to Eadwig's younger brother, Edgar.

During the reigns of Athelstan, Edmund and Eadred, Athelstan 'Half-King' had been the premier ealdorman.[118] However, after 956 he retired, whether by force or on his own volition is unclear, and became a monk at Glastonbury. Eadwig then appointed a kinsman, Aelfhere, as ealdorman of Mercia, and his brother, Aelfheah, was promoted to the ealdordom of Hampshire in 959.[119] Two more of their brothers were also ranked high among Eadwig's thegns. Not surprisingly, this was one of the most powerful families in the kingdom.[120] That Athelstan 'Half-King' and his family lost ground to Eadwig's kinsmen would have undoubtedly caused bad feeling. Yet it is notable that Aelfhere and Aelfheah, and the ealdorman of Essex, Byrhtnoth, and that of East Anglia, Aethelwold, who were all apparently promoted by Eadwig, were retained by the subsequent king, Edgar, to govern England. In Stenton's words 'It can at least be said for King Eadwig that he agreed to the promotion of good servants'[121] and this is from a king who was barely 20 years old when he died.

In 955 Eadwig had been chosen as king separately by the Mercians, the West Saxons and, probably, by the Northumbrians, but between May and December 957 the kingdom was split between his younger brother Edgar, who took control of Mercia and Northumbria, and Eadwig who retained Wessex,[122] for reasons about which one can only speculate. In some quarters the division has been seen as a result of a northern revolt against Eadwig's rule. Matthew of Westminster hints at this possibility in a colourful and 'popular' later account:

> A.D. 957. King Edwy [Eadwig] was wholly abandoned by the people of Mercia and Northumberland, because he acted foolishly in the government committed to his charge, through hatred and folly; destroying all the wise men of the kingdom, and all the nobles, and cherishing the ignorant and wicked with love and affection. And when he had been deposed by the unanimous conspiracy of all men, they, prompted by God, elected his brother Edgar king, and, with the approbation of the people, the whole government of the kingdom was divided between the two brothers, so that the river Thames separated their several dominions.[123]

The same sentiment is also found in Florence of Worcester's chronicle.[124] If the division was caused because of an insurrection of the Mercians and Northumbrians, it shows that both kingdoms, although allegedly subordinate to Wessex, were still capable of significant independent action through effectively sacking their overlord. Yet if a revolt was the reason for the division, it seems that it was the person not the system who offended, for the latter was left largely unaltered.

Yet it is as possible that the division was agreed upon before 957; it was in that year that Edgar became of age (14) and, therefore, might have assumed a preordained role as sub-king and Eadwig's designated heir.[125] Contemporary sources are too scant to be sure. But whether the result of an insurrection, or by agreement, the division appears to have taken place peacefully, with the ealdormen and bishops north of the Thames going to Edgar's court, while those south of the river stayed on at Eadwig's.[126]

The picture remains complicated, for there is some evidence that Eadwig kept overall power. Coins apparently struck on each side of the Thames were in his name until his death in 959, and in his charters he is still styled *rex Anglorum*—'king of the English', whereas Edgar is termed only 'king of the Mercians'.[127] Yet Edgar, a youth of only 14 or 15, was able to recall Dunstan from exile which implies a certain autonomy on his part, especially considering Eadwig's enmity towards this ecclesiastic. On the death of Coenwald, bishop of Worcester, Edgar promoted Dunstan to the vacancy before raising him to the bishopric of London in 958/9.

Eadwig died childless on 1 October 959, probably of the inherited family illness, although some complicity in his death on the part of his enemies cannot be discounted.

As a last word on Eadwig the opinion of Aethelweard the Chronicler should be mentioned. It is believed Aethelweard was either his brother-in-law or distant cousin and was thus in a good position to comment because, unlike the later chroniclers, he almost certainly knew Eadwig first-hand. Aethelweard remarks that ordinary people called Eadwig the 'all-fair' (*eall-faeger*) because of his personal beauty and states that he 'deserved to be loved'.[128]

Edgar, king of Mercia 957-959, king of England, 959-75

'Beloved both by God and man, his great concern was to promote peace among all the nations of his realm, nor did any of his predecessors hold the reins of power so quietly and so happily'.[129]

Edgar's elevation to the kingship of Mercia had undoubtedly been helped by his having been raised by Athelstan 'Half-King', ealdorman not only of East Anglia but also of Danish Mercia.[130] In four charters dating to 958 he is described as 'king of Mercia',[131] the last monarch to be so accorded.

On Eadwig's death the *Anglo-Saxon Chronicle* (manuscripts B and C) declare that Edgar succeeded 'both in Wessex and in Mercia and in Northumbria, and he was then 16 years old'.[132] Florence of Worcester adds that Edgar was chosen to succeed Eadwig 'by the unanimous voice of the Anglo-Britons ... and the divided kingdoms were thus re-united'.[133]

On becoming king of England Edgar promoted Dunstan to the archbishopric of Canterbury. Edgar's foster family had been 'closely associated with the monastic reform movement', Edgar himself being educated by Aethelwold, abbot of Abingdon, a prime participant in the re-endowment and reform of the Benedictine monasteries in England. Edgar made him bishop of Winchester in 963.[134] A charter of 974 quoted by William of Malmesbury purportedly gives Edgar's explanation for his support of the movement:

> In aid of my pious devotion, heavenly love suddenly insinuated to my watchful solicitude, that I should rebuild all the holy monasteries throughout my kingdom, which, as they were outwardly ruinous, with mouldering shingles and worm-eaten boards, even to the rafters, so, what was still worse, they had become internally neglected, and almost destitute of the service of God; wherefore, ejecting those illiterate clerks, subject to the discipline of no regular order, in many places I have appointed pastors of an holier race, that is, of the monastic order, supplying them with ample means out of my royal revenues to repair their churches wherever ruinated.[135]

A significant part of the neglect was almost certainly a consequence of the Danish wars which destroyed some monasteries and badly affected others. However, one gains the feeling from the medieval chroniclers that the heart had gone out of the institution and those in charge were demoralized, perhaps even freeloading in some instances. Dunstan had spent his exile on the Continent where he had experienced the running of Benedictine monasteries, and it was his and the other reformers' aim to bring Anglo-Saxon England in line with the Continent and to reinvigorate monastic life.

This reform took off with Aethelwold ejecting the secular canons at the Old Minster at Winchester and replacing them with monks whom he had trained; as such this monastery became the first English cathedral possessing a monastic chapter.[136] He was also involved with similar expulsions from other religious houses in Wessex.

In 969 Florence of Worcester noted:

> Edgar the Pacific, king of England, commanded St. Dunstan, archbishop of Canterbury, and St. Oswald and St. Ethelwold, [Aethelwold] bishops of Worcester and Winchester, to expel the clerks and settle monks in the larger monasteries of Mercia. Thereupon St. Oswald, in compliance with the king's wishes, expelled from the monastery the clergy of the church of Worcester who refused to become monks: but on their complying, as he tells us, in the present year, he accepted their monastic vows, and appointed Wynsin, a monk of Rumsey, [Ramsey] a man of deep piety, their abbot, instead of a dean.[137]

William of Malmesbury observes that Oswald, 'treading the same paths' as Dunstan and Aethelwold in the reforms 'extended the monastic profession by his authority ... he filled the cathedral of Worcester with monks, the canons not being driven out by force, but circumvented by pious fraud'.[138] Giles explains the latter by noting that Oswald built another church at Worcester to house the monks and the canons 'finding the people desert them in order to obtain the favour of the new comers, by degrees took the monastic habit'.[139]

It was undoubtedly the period of peace under Edgar that allowed for the success of this monastic reform and, indeed, there is no record of internal strife or of renewed Viking attack during his reign, the second wave of which only began again in 980. From the available charter evidence it does appear that a proportionately larger amount of land was granted by Edgar to the Church than by his predecessors. But Ashley notes the reforms also gave church officials greater freedom from the Crown, which saw its most extreme expression in the creation of the Soke of Peterborough where the abbot of St. Peter's was given virtually complete independence. It is noted that the extensive 'transference of land from lay to ecclesiastical control' and the arbitrary way it was given out caused great resentment, which broke out into bitter reaction after Edgar's death in 975.[140]

Although Edgar may appear a pious and almost saintly king, there is evidence, particularly in William of Malmesbury's chronicle, that he was no chaste saint. William records 'There are some persons, indeed, who endeavour to dim his exceeding glory by saying, that in his earlier years he was cruel to his subjects, and libidinous in respect of virgins'.[141] William then goes on to relate Edgar's alleged dalliances, including the story that he carried off 'a certain virgin, who was dedicated to God' by force from her monastery and 'ravished her, and repeatedly made her the partner of his bed'. Dunstan, appalled by this, 'vehemently reproved' Edgar who was forced to do seven years' penance, which consisted of fasting and foregoing the wearing of his crown.[142] William also notes that 'it is reported that he [Edgar] was extremely small both in stature and in bulk' and was grossly offended when it reached his ears that the king of the Scots had commented, albeit in jest, 'that it seemed extraordinary to him how so many provinces should be subject to such a sorry little fellow'.[143] Edgar sought and obtained an apology which he immediately accepted, which says something about his character.

Indeed this fairness may be seen in his possible tolerance and respect for local customs and traditions, examples of which occur in charters relating to old Mercian territory. One concerns an estate at Staunton-on-Arrow, about 10 miles west of Leominster in Herefordshire, where in 958, in spite of the shire system, the land is recorded as being 'in the province of the *Magonsaete*'. Although Whitelock remarks that the use of 'an ancient regional name' in the west midlands instead of the shire name (Herefordshire) 'suggests that the organization into shires was not yet complete',[144] it is feasible that Edgar was perhaps respecting former territories; indeed a dogmatic ruler with no respect for local sensibilities, would not have allowed the use of old tribal names when the shires were being created or had, indeed, been completed. Similarly, in a grant for 969 by Edgar concerning Kineton in Warwickshire, 10 miles north-west of Banbury, the shire boundary is ignored and 'the original distinction between the Mercians proper and the Hwicce was still felt; for the boundary of the Mercians mentioned is not that of the great kingdom ruled by the kings of Mercia from the eighth century, but the line of demarcation separating the original Mercians from the settlers in the Severn valley'; it is still the diocesan division.[145]

Edgar's wisdom as a ruler is further evidenced by Stenton's observation that he was the first king to recognize through law that the Danish eastern side of England was a component part of the country and 'no longer a conquered province'.[146] This recognition is found in a law code issued at the unidentified place of *Wihtbordesstan* between 962-3 where the following clauses exist:

2.I. And it is my will that secular rights be in force among the Danes according to as good laws as they can best decide on.

2.Ia. Among the English, however, that is to be in force which I and my councillors have added to the decrees of my ancestors, for the benefit of all the nation.

Later on in the code is the clause which explains Edgar's decision:

12. ... and I have ever allowed them this and will allow it as long as my life lasts, because of your loyalty, which you have always shown me.[147]

The penultimate clause shows the arrangements made for the code's circulation in Mercia, Northumbria and East Anglia:

15.1. And many documents are to be written concerning this, and sent both to Ealdorman Aelfhere [of Mercia] and Ealdorman Aethelwine [of East Anglia], and they are to send them in all directions, that this measure may be known to both the poor and the rich.[148]

Florence records that in winter and spring Edgar used to travel throughout the provinces of England and 'enquire diligently' whether his own ordinances and the laws of the land were being obeyed 'so that the poor might not suffer wrong and be oppressed by the powerful'.[149] Thus, with an apparently tolerant style of rule but within a rigorous legal framework which was annually checked, a great deal of security was provided for all Edgar's subjects.

As Stenton remarks, unlike Alfred and Athelstan, Edgar was never forced into the position of having to defend his kingdom from overseas raids or to deal with internal strife.[150] This may have resulted from his policy of regular and powerful military display both on land and at sea, coupled with tact towards settlers within England, a policy built on the security that Alfred, Edward and Athelstan had established.

Such power was also displayed in other ways. On 11 May 973, some 14 years after his succession he held a consecration ceremony at Bath. That Bath, on the borders of Mercia and Wessex, was chosen indicates his consideration for both parts of the kingdom and it is significant that Edgar was the first king to be crowned 'king of the English' although other kings had previously used the title an occasion[151] but had never been consecrated as such. Following the ceremony, Edgar's army marched up the Welsh border to Chester while his fleet sailed up the Irish sea to meet them. Between six to eight subordinate kings from throughout Britain came to Chester to give Edgar pledges of support, and Edgar had them row him on the Dee while he took the helm—a symbolic demonstration of his power.

Edgar died suddenly on 8 July 975 aged about 32 and was buried at Glastonbury Abbey. It is in the D and E versions of the Anglo-Saxon Chronicle that one gets closest to Edgar's real political and military achievement:

In this year [975] died Edgar, ruler of the Angles, friend of the West Saxons and protector of the Mercians. It was widely known throughout many nations across the gannet's bath, that kings honoured Edmund's son far and wide, and paid homage to this king as was his due by birth. Nor was there fleet so proud nor host so strong that it got itself prey in England as long as the noble king held the throne.[152]

Unfortunately this golden age was not to last.

Edward the Martyr, reigned 975-8

The D and E versions of the *Anglo-Saxon Chronicle* set the scene for Edward's short and troubled reign:

In this year [975] Edgar's son Edward succeeded to the kingdom. And soon in the same year in harvest time there appeared the star 'comet', and in the next year there came a very great famine and very manifold disturbances throughout England.[153]

One of the problems encountered on Edgar's death was that of succession—the fact was that Edgar had two surviving sons by two different mothers. Edward was probably the son from Edgar's first marriage to a lady called Aethelflaed Eneda ('the white duck') who was the daughter of a Hertfordshire magnate.[154] By another wife, Aelfthryth, there were two sons, Edmund and Aethelred, who is later known to history as Aethelred the *Unraed* ('the ill-advised, lacking counsel') or more commonly (and erroneously) as 'the Unready'. In 975 Edward was about 13 years old and Aethelred perhaps as young as seven. Edgar had apparently made efforts to avert a crisis over the succession for in 966 the refoundation charter of New Minster, Winchester, gave Aelfthryth's eldest son, Edmund, primacy over Edward[155] — but Edmund had died in 971. Edmund's mother had been crowned queen (unlike Edward's mother),[156] and Aethelred may have, therefore, been the logical heir. However, Edward was supported in his claim to the throne by Dunstan, Oswald (by then archbishop of York as well as bishop of Worcester) and the ealdorman of East Anglia, Aethelwine, with whom Edgar had been raised; whereas Aethelred was backed (not surprisingly!) by his mother Aelfthryth, and also by Aelfhere, ealdorman of Mercia and, possibly, Bishop Aethelwold of Winchester.[157] However, Florence of Worcester records that as a consequence of these disputes '... the archbishops Dunstan and Oswald, with their suffragans, and many abbots and ealdormen, met in a body and chose Edward, as his father had directed'.[158] Edward was crowned at Kingston-on-Thames later in 975 but dissension stained his reign.

Ealdormen Aelfhere of Mercia and Aethelwine of East Anglia were at loggerheads not only over the matter of succession but also over religious matters. Aelfhere objected to Edgar's earlier creation of the liberty of Oswaldslow in central Worcestershire which comprised 300 hides and belonged to the bishopric of Worcester, and from which Aelfhere's powers as ealdorman were excluded.[159] To complicate matters, Oswald, bishop of Worcester and archbishop of York, was a close friend of Aethelwine, and Aelfhere soon became cast as the enemy of the monastic reforms. Version D of the *Anglo-Saxon Chronicle* declares: 'In his [Edward's] days because of his youth, the adversaries of God, Ealdorman Aelfhere and many others, broke God's law and hindered the monastic life',[160] while versions A, B and C state 'Then in Mercia ... widely, almost everywhere, the praise of the Ruler was cast down to the ground; many of the wise servants of God were dispersed'.[161] Versions E and F observe 'And Ealdorman Aelfhere caused to be destroyed many monastic foundations which King Edgar had ordered the holy Bishop Aethelwold to institute'.[162] These statements have a retrospective feel even though they are entered under 975, the year of Edward's succession. Matthew of Westminster notes that one Aelferius (undoubtedly Aelfhere) 'overthrew nearly all the monasteries which the most reverend Ethelwold [Aethelwold] had built in the province of Mercia, and had behaved with great insolence'.[163] From reading Florence of Worcester it appears that Aelfhere was wreaking havoc with the monasteries at the same time as the succession crisis was taking place.[164]

In an anonymous *Life* of Oswald, written at some time between 995-1005 by a monk of Ramsey Abbey,[165] a far more vivid account is given:

> ... by his [Edgar's] death the state of the whole kingdom was thrown into confusion, the bishops were agitated, the noblemen stirred up, the monks shaken with fear, the people terrified; the clerics were made glad, for their time had come. Abbots, with their monks, were expelled; clerics, with their wives, were introduced ... Abbot Germanus [of Winchcombe Abbey, formerly Prior of Ramsey] also was expelled along with the others ... Thus also the ealdorman of the Mercian people, Aelfhere by name, appropriating enormous revenues, which blind the eyes of many, ejected, as we have said, with the advice of the people and the outcry of the crowd, not only the sheep but the shepherds also ... In those days, if the common crowd discried a man of our habit, [in monks' clothes] an outcry was raised as if it saw a wolf among the sheep, for they put their trust in the above-mentioned ealdorman ... It came to pass after the course of a few years that those who were then especially violent against the monks had neither their own nor others' goods. Indeed, it is a scandal how the common folk and many - one cannot say nobles, but ignobles, since they can more rightly be called thus - perished, defiling themselves with filth. When the fickle opinion and hostile madness of the enemy wished to reach with its pollution the eastern peoples of the Mercians, and to root out the glory of the people and the monasteries, God-fearing men stood firm against the blast of the mad wind which came from the western territories, [Aelfhere] driven from its proper course by the pleasures which withdraw the hearts of

many from the right way and incite their minds to evil desires. The warlike thegn Aelfwold [Ealdorman Aethelwine of East Anglia's brother] opposed the iniquity which the will of Aelfhere, prospering according to the world's grandeur, was supporting, along with the people gathered to him. The wicked said among themselves, not rightly considering: 'Let us encompass the monks and oppress them, "and the inheritance shall be ours". May there be none to pity them, but let them be expelled, hurled down, derided, suppressed, bound, beaten, that not one may remain in all the land of the Mercians'.[166]

Even given that some prejudice and exaggeration is likely, it is clear that Mercia was in crisis. The root of the problem was the backlash against the accrual of huge amounts of land by the Church, often indiscriminately given, particularly so in Mercia where donations and religious foundations had been so numerous. The resulting power imbalance made the work of secular administration difficult because of underfunding in favour of the Church.

Opposition to this 'anti-monastic movement' was headed by Aethelwine and Aelfwold who, according to Florence of Worcester, with 'the religious ealdorman Brihtnoth ... declared that they could not permit the monks who possessed all the religion of the kingdom to be driven out of it; they therefore assembled troops and defended the monasteries of the Eastern-Angles with great spirit'.[167] Division and discontent took hold and, if civil war did not actually occur in 975 or 976, it must have been imminent. Two synods were held to try to resolve matters peacefully, the first at Winchester, the second at Calne in 978, which ended in disaster. The debate turned into a very heated argument directed against Dunstan, in the middle of which the flooring of the upper chamber, in which the meeting was being held, collapsed, leaving Dunstan standing on the only beam that remained intact, and his aggressors either dead or injured on the ground below.[168] Not surprisingly, this was seen as a miracle.

Given all this strife, it is notable that of the five charters listed in Sawyer which were granted by Edward, two are of a religious nature: one is to a bishop Aelfstan for land at Kingston Bagpuize in Berkshire and the other for land in the same place to St. Mary's at Abingdon[169]—unfortunately they can only be dated to sometime within his three year reign and not to a specific year. More significantly, however, considering Aelfhere's animosity towards Oswald is the existence of a clutch of charters between the years 977 and 978 in which Oswald was able to grant a number of leases 'with the consent of King Edward, (and) of Aelfhere, ealdorman of Mercia',[170] suggesting that relations between these three were not quite as hostile as the sources would have us believe.

During this period of trouble, Matthew of Westminster appears to suggest that Edward concentrated on religious affairs and 'allowed his brother Ethelred, and his [Aethelred's] mother, to manage all the affairs of his kingdom'.[171] This is also recounted in William of Malmesbury's chronicle, who stresses Edward's affectionate conduct to his brother and stepmother.[172] Clearly if this was so, Aelfthryth would have been ruling as a regent as Aethelred would have still been too young to rule.

However, a rather different account is given of Edward's character in the anonymous *Life* of St. Oswald where it is stated that in the initial disagreements over succession, some of the nobles wanted to elect Aethelred 'because he appeared to all gentler in speech and deeds. The elder, [Edward] in fact, inspired in all not only fear but even terror, for (he scourged them) not only with words but truly with dire blows, and especially his own men dwelling with him'.[173] It is suggested that it may partly have been this aspect of his temperament that provoked his murder at Corfe in Dorset on the evening of 18 March 978.[174] Later chroniclers try to implicate Aelfthryth in the murder of her step-son but no contemporary source apportions such blame to her. Even so it was very likely a politically motivated killing.

Aethelred succeeded his brother and his reign, although of some 28 years duration, was blighted by troubles, not least by the renewed Viking attacks which eventually led to the take-over of England by Cnut of Denmark. Aelfhere continued as premier ealdorman until his death in 983, but arguably this is all Mercia had become, an area with ealdormen, who, during the strife of Aethelred's reign, too often appear on opposing sides. By the late 10th and early 11th centuries Mercia existed, finally, only in name.

References

Abbreviations used:

TWAS   *Transactions of the Worcestershire Archaeology Society*
TWNFC   *Transactions of the Woolhope Naturalists' Field Club*

Andere	Andere, Mary, *Arthurian Links with Herefordshire*, Logaston Press, 1995
Anderson	Anderson, M.D., *History and Imagery in British Churches*, John Murray, 1971
Ang. Sax. Ency.	Lapidge, Michael; Blair, John; Keynes, Simon & Scragg, Donald (eds.), *The Blackwell Encyclopaedia of Anglo-Saxon England*, Blackwell, 2001
ASC	*Anglo-Saxon Chronicle*
Ashley	Ashley, Mike, *British Monarchs — The Complete Genealogy, Gazetteer and Biographical Encyclopedia of the Kings and Queens of Britian*, Robinson, 1998
Asser	Keynes, S. and Lapidge, M. (trans.) Asser's *Life of King Alfred*, Penguin, 1983
Aston & Bond	Aston, Michael & Bond, James, *The Landscape of Towns*, Archaeology in the Field Series, Dent, 1977
Austerberry	Austerberry, Jennie, *Chad - Bishop and Saint*, English Life Publications Ltd., 1984
Baring-Gould	Baring-Gould, Sabine, *Lives of the English Saints*, Llanerch, 1990
Bassett	Bassett, Steven, 'In search of the origins of Anglo-Saxon kingdoms; in Bassett, Steven (ed.), *The Origins of Anglo-Saxon Kingdoms*, Leicester University Press, 1989
Bede	Sherley-Price, Leo (trans.) revised by R.E. Latham: Bede, *A History of the English Church and People*, Penguin, 1968
Berresford Ellis	Berresford Ellis, Peter, *Celt and Saxon — The Struggle for Britain AD 410-937*, Constable, 1993
Biddle (1975)	Biddle, M., 'Evolution of Towns Before 1066' in *The Plans and Topography of Medieval Towns in England and Wales*, ed. M.W. Barley, CBA Research Report, No.14, Council of British Archaeology
Biddle (1976)	Biddle, M., *The Archaeology of Anglo-Saxon England*, Cambridge University Press, 1976
Blackmore *et al.*	Blackmore, L., Bowsher, D., Cowie, R., & Malcolm, Gordon, 'Royal Opera House' in *Current Archaeology*, 158, Vol.XIV, No.2, July 1998, pp.60-3
Blair	Blair, John, *Anglo-Saxon Oxfordshire*, Sutton/Oxfordshire Books, 1994
Bradley	Bradley, S.A.J. (trans.), *Anglo-Saxon Poetry*, Everyman, 1991
Branston	Branston, Brian, *The Lost Gods of England*, Thames and Hudson BCA, 1974 edition
Brooks (1984)	Brooks, Nicholas, *The Early History of the Church of Canterbury*, Studies in the Early History of Britain, Leicester University Press, 1996 edition
Brooks (1989)	Brooks, Nicholas, 'The formation of the Mercian kingdom', in Bassett, Steven, *The Origins of Anglo-Saxon Kingdoms*, Leicester University Press, 1989
Brooks (1996)	Brooks, Rev Dr. E.C., *The Life of St. Ethelbert, King and Martyr 779 AD - 794 AD*, Bury Clerical Society, 1996
Brooks &Cubitt	Brooks, Nicholas and Cubitt, Catherine (eds.), *St. Oswald of Worcester: Life and Influence*, Leicester University Press, 1996
Buteux & Hurst	Buteux, Victoria & Hurst, Derek, *Archaeological Assessment of Droitwich*, Hereford and Worcester County Council, Dec. 1996
Cameron	Cameron, Kenneth, *English Place-Names*, Batsford, 1961
Campbell (1982)	Campbell, James (ed.), 'The First Christian Kings' in *The Anglo-Saxons*. Phaidon, 1982, Penguin Reprint, 1991
Campbell (1986)	Campbell, James, *Essays in Anglo-Saxon History*, The Hambledon Press, 1986
Carver (1981)	Carver, M.O.H., *Underneath Stafford Town*, Birm. Univ. Field Arch. Unit, 1981
Cane *et al.*	Cane, C.B.K., Cane, J. & Carver, M.O.H., *Saxon and Medieval Stafford, new results and theories 1983*, Birm. Univ. Field Arch. Unit, 1983
Chapman	Chapman, A., 'Brackmills, Northampton - An early Iron Age torc' in *Current Archaeology*, 159, Sept. 1998
Charles-Edwards	Charles-Edwards, Thomas, 'Early medieval kingships in the British Isles', in Bassett, Steven (ed.), *The Origins of Anglo-Saxon Kingdoms*, Leicester University Press, 1989
Clarke & Ambosiani	Clarke, Helen & Ambrosiani, Björn, *Towns in the Viking Age*, Leicester University Press, 2nd revised ed., 1995
Cleary	Cleary, Esmonde A.S., *The Ending of Roman Britain*, Batsford, 1989
Colgrave	Colgrave, Bertram, *Felix's Life of St. Guthlac*, Cambridge University Press, 1956
Coplestone-Crow	Coplestone-Crow, Bruce, *Herefordshire Place-Names*, B.A.R. Bristish Series, 214, 1989

Cowie & Harding	Cowie, Robert, with Harding, Charlotte, 'Saxon Settlement and Economy from the Dark Ages to Domesday' in *The Archaeology of Greater London - An assessment of archaeological evidence for human presence in the area now covered by Greater London*, Museum of London, 2000
Cubitt	Cubitt, Catherine, *Anglo-Saxon Church Councils c.650-c.850*, Leicester University Press, 1995
Dark Age Dict.	Williams, A., Smyth, A.P. & Kirby, D.P., *A biographical dictionary of Dark Age Britain - England, Scotland and Wales, c.500-c.1050*, Seaby, 1991
Davies	Davies, Wendy, 'Annals and the origins of Mercia' in *Mercian Studies*, ed. Ann Dornier Leicester University Press, 1977
Doble	Doble, G.H., (ed. by D. Simon Evans), *Lives of the Welsh Saints*, University of Wales Press, 1971
Dornier	Dornier, A. (ed.), *Mercian Studies*, Leicester University Press, 1977
Dumville	Dumville, David, 'Essex, Middle Anglia, and the expansion of Mercia in the South-East Midlands' in Bassett, 1989
Eddius	'Eddius Stephanus: Life of St. Wilfrid' in *Lives of the Saints*, trans. J.F. Webb, Penguin, 1965
Ekwall	Ekwall, Eilert *The Concise Oxford Dictionary of English Place-Names*, Oxford University Press, 1960
Farmer	Farmer, David Hugh, *The Oxford Dictionary of Saints*, Oxford University Press, 1978
Finberg (1964)	Finberg, H.P.R., *The Early Charters of Wessex*, Leicester University Press, 1964
Finberg (1972)	Finberg, H.P.R., *The Early Charters of the West Midlands*, Leicester University Press, 1972 (2nd edition)
Finberg (1976)	Finberg, H.P.R., *The Formation of England 550-1042*, Paladin, 1976
Fletcher	Fletcher, Richard, *Who's Who in Roman Britain and Anglo-Saxon England*, Shepheard-Walwyn, 1989
Florence	Forester, T. (trans.), *The Chronicle of Florence of Worcester*, AMS Press, 1968
Foot	Foot, Sarah, 'What was an Early Anglo-Saxon Monastery?' in *Monastic Studies - the Continuity of Tradition*, ed. Judith Loades, Headstart History, 1990
Garmonsway	Garmonsway, G.N., *The Anglo-Saxon Chronicle*, Dent, 1972
Gelling (1978)	Gelling, M., *Signposts to the Past*, Dent, 1978
Gelling (1984)	Gelling, M., *Place-Names in the Landscape — The Geographical roots of Britain's place-names*, Dent, 1984
Gelling (1992)	Gelling, M., *The West Midlands in the Early Middle Ages*, Leicester University Press, 1992
Gelling (2000)	Gelling, M., 'Place-Names' in *The Gale of Life - Two Thousand Years in South-West Shropshire*, ed. Leonard J. *et al*, Logaston Press, 2000
Gildas	(see under Nennius)
Geoffrey	Thorpe, Lewis (trans.), *Geoffrey of Monmouth — The History of the Kings of Britain*, Penguin, 1966
Greenslade	Greenslade, Michael W., *Saint Chad of Lichfield and Birmingham*, Archdiocese of Birmingham Historical Commission Publication no.10, 1996
Gregory	Gregory, Donald, *Yesterday in Village Church and Churchyard*, Gomer, 1989
Hart (1966)	Hart, C.R., *The Early Charters of Eastern England*, Leicester University Press, 1966
Hart (1971)	Hart, C.R., 'The Tribal Hidage' in the *Transactions of the Royal Historical Society*, Fifth Series, Vol.21, Royal Historical Society
Hart (1975)	Hart, C.R., *The Early Charters of Northern England and the North Midlands*, Leicester University Press, 1975
Hart (1979)	Hart, C.R., 'The kingdom of Mercia' in Mercian Studies, ed. Ann Dornier, Leicester University Press, 1977
Henry	Forester, T. (trans.), *The Chronicle of Henry of Huntingdon*, AMS Press, 1968
Higham (1992)	Higham, N.J., 'King Cearl, the Battle of Chester and the Origins of the Mercian "Overkingship"' in *Midland History*, Vol. XVII
Higham (1993)	Higham, N.J., *The Kingdom of Northumbria, AD 350 -1100*, Sutton, 1993
Hillaby (1976)	Hillaby, J., 'The Origins of the Diocese of Hereford' in *TWNFC*, Vol. XLII, Part I, 1976
Hillaby (1987)	Hillaby, J., 'Early Christian and Pre-Conquest Leominster: An Exploration of the Sources' in *TWNFC*, Vol. XLV, Part III, 1987
Hodges	Hodges, Richard, *The Anglo-Saxon Achievement*, Cornell University Press, 1989
Hooke (1985)	Hooke, Della, *The Anglo-Saxon landscape—the Kingdom of the Hwicce*, Manchester University Press, 1985
Hooke (1981)	'The Droitwich Salt Industry: An examination of the West Midland Charter Evidence' in *Anglo-Saxon Studies in Archaeology and History*, ed. David Brown, James Campbell and Sonia Chadwick Hawkes, BAR British Series 92, 1981
Hurst	Hurst, J.D., *A multi-period salt production site at Droitwich: excavations at Upwich*, CBA Report 107, 1997
Kirby	Kirby, D.P. *The Earliest English Kings*, Unwin Hyman, 1991
Kohn	Kohn, George C., *The Wordsworth Encyclopedia of Plague and Pestilence*, Wordsworth, 1998

Leland Toulmin Smith, Lucy (ed.), *The Itinerary of John Leland*, Southern Illinois University Press, 1964

Lias Lias, Anthony, *Place-Names of the Welsh Borderlands*, Palmers Press, 1991

Loyn Loyn, H.R., *Anglo-Saxon England and the Norman Conquest*, Longmans, 1962

Marsden Marsden, J., *Northanhymbre saga—The History of the Anglo-Saxon Kings of Northumbria*, Kyle Cathie, 1992

Matthew Yonge, C.D. (trans.), *Matthew of Westminster 'The Flowers of History - especially such as relate to the affairs of Britain—from the beginning of the world to the year 1307 - collected by Matthew of Wetsminster'*, Vol.1, AMS Press, 1968 edition

Mawer *et al.* Mawer, A., Stenton, F.M. & Houghton, F.T.S., *The Place-Names of Worcestershire*, English Place-Name Society, Vol.IV, 1993 edition

Mayr-Harting Mayr-Harting, H., *The Coming of Christianity to Anglo-Saxon England*, Batsford, 1991

McCarthy & Brooks McCarthy, Michael R. & Brooks, Catherine M., *Medieval Pottery in Britian A.D. 900-1600*, Leicester University Press, 1988

Meeson Meeson, R.A., 'The Formation of Tamworth', Unpub.MA Thesis, Univ. of Birmingham, Diss A3.B79, 1979

Moffett Moffett, Lisa 'Charred cereals from some ovens/kilns in late Saxon Stafford and the botannical evidence for the pre-burh economy' in *Environment and Economy in Anglo-Saxon England*, ed. James Rackham, CBA Research Report 89, CBA, 1994

Morris (1973) Morris, John, *The Age of Arthur — A History of the British Isles from 350 to 650*, Weidenfeld & Nicholson, 1973 (Phoenix p/b 1995)

Morris (1989) Morris, Richard, *Churches in the Landscape*, Dent, 1989

Morris (1995) Morris, John, Arthurian Sources—Vol.4, *Places and Peoples, and Saxon Archaeology*, Phillimore, 1995; Vol.3 *Persons*, 1995

Nennius Wade-Evans, A.W., *Nennius's 'History of the Britains' together with 'The Annals of the Britains' and 'Court Pedigrees of Hywel the Good' also 'The Story of the Loss of Britain'*, SPCK, 1938

Northampton (1) Williams, J.H., Shaw, M. & Denham, V., *Middle Saxon Palaces at Northampton*, Northampton Development Corporation Archaeological Monograph, No.4, 1985

Northampton (2) Shaw, M., Chapman, A. & Soden, I., 'Northampton' in *Current Archaeology*, No.155, Vol.XIII, No.11, Dec.1997

Owen Owen, Gail, R. *Rites and Religions of the Anglo-Saxons*, Barnes & Noble, 1996

Peters Peters, R., *Ancient Bassetlaw*, The North Trent Local History Society Series

Pretty Pretty, Kate, 'Defining the Magonsaete' in Bassett, Steven, *The Origins of Anglo-Saxon Kingdoms*, Leicester University Press, 1989

Rackham Rackham, Oliver, *The History of the Countryside*, Dent, 1986

Rahtz Rahtz, P. 'The Archaeology of West Mercian Towns' in Dornier, A., *Mercian Studies*, Leicester University Press, 1977

Rahtz & Meeson Rahtz, P. & Meeson, R., *An Anglo-Saxon Watermill at Tamworth*, CBA report No.83, 1992

RCHM(V) Royal Commission on Historical Monuments, *An Inventory of the Historical Monuments in the County of Northampton*, Vol V, HMSO, 1985

Revill Revill, S.,'King Edwin and the Battle of Heathfield', *Transactions of the Thoroton Society*, Vol. LXXIX, 1975

Rollason Rollason, David, *Saints and Relics in Anglo-Saxon England*, Blackwell, 1989

Sant Sant, Jonathan, *Healing Wells of Herefordshire*, Moondial, 1994

Sawyer Sawyer, P.H., *Anglo-Saxon Charters—An Annotated List and Bibliography*, Royal Historical Society No.86

Scarfe West, S.E. & Scarfe, Norman with contrib. by Cramp, Rosemary, 'The Historical Evidence Revealed' in 'Iken, St. Botolph and the Coming of East Anglian Christianity', *Transactions of the Suffolk Institute of Archaeology and History*, Vol.35, 1984

Schofield Schofield, John, 'Saxon London in a tale of two cities' in *British Archaeology, No.44,* May 1999

Scull Scull, Christopher, 'Urban Centres in Pre-Viking England?' in *The Anglo-Saxons from the Migration Period to the Eighth Century: An Ethnographic Perspective*, ed. John Hines, Boydell Press, 1997

Shoesmith (1980) Shoesmith, R., *Excavations at Castle Green*, Hereford City Excavations Vol. 1, CBA Research Report 36, CBA, 1980

Shoesmith (1982) Shoesmith, R., *Excavations on and close to the defences*, Hereford City Excavations Vol. 1, CBA Research Report 46, CBA, 1982

Sims-Williams Sims-Williams, Patrick, *Religion and Literature in Western England 600-800*, Cambridge University Press, 1990

Stafford Stafford, Pauline, *The East Midlands in the Early Middle Ages*, Leicester University Press, 1985

Stanford   Stanford, S.C., *The Archaeology of the Welsh Marches*, 2nd revised edition, 1991

Stenton   Stenton, Sir Frank, *Anglo-Saxon England*, Oxford University Press, 1971

Swanton   Swanton, Michael (trans.) *Anglo-Saxon Prose*, Everyman, 1993

Taylor & Taylor Taylor, H.M. & Taylor, J., *Anglo-Saxon Architecture*, Vols. 1 & 2, Cambridge University Press, 1980 (p/b edition)

Vince   Vince, Alan, *Saxon London: An Archaeological Investigation*, Seaby, 1990

Webster & Backhouse   Webster, L. & Backhouse, J. (eds.), *The Making of England—Anglo-Saxon Art and Culture, A.D. 600-900*, British Museum Press, 1991

White & Barker   White, Roger & Barker, Philip, *Wroxeter - Life and Death of a Roman City*, Tempus, 1998

Whitehead   Whitehead, David, in Shoesmith (1980)

Whitelock   Whitelock, Dorothy, *English Historical Documents, Vol. 1, c.500-1042*, Eyre & Spottiswoode, 1968

William   Giles, J.A. (ed), *William of Malmesbury's Chronicle of the Kings of England*, AMS Press, 1968

Williams   Williams, John. 'The Early Development of the Town of Northampton' in Dornier, A., *Mercian Studies*, Leicester University Press, 1977

Wilson   Wilson, D., Anglo-Saxon Art, *Thames & Hudson*, 1984

Wood   Wood, Michael, *In Search of the Dark Ages*, BBC, 1981

Woods   Woods, Rev. John, *Through the Needle's Eye: Cornovian Place-Names in Shropshire*

Yorke   Yorke, B., *Kings and Kingdoms of Early Anglo-Saxon England*, Seaby, 1990

The Written Sources

1. Brooks (1989), p.159, who refers to Sawyer, nos.67-226, pp.87-127
2. Dumville, p.140
3. Esmonde Cleary, pp.165, 170. Re. Germanus, Esmonde Cleary refers to E.A. Thompson, *Saint Germanus of Auxerre and the End of Roman Britain*, Woodbridge, 1984
4. Bede, II.14, p.129
5. White & Barker, p.131
6. Berresford Ellis, pp.92, 97
7. Wade-Evans, p.7
8. Morris (1973), p.37
9. Wade-Evans, pp.10-1
10. Morris (1973), p.37
11. Garmonsway, p.Xl
12. Whitelock, p.109
13. Garmonsway, p.xxxiv
14. *Ibid.*, p.xxxv
15. Whitelock, pp.111-2
16. Garmonsway, p.xxxix
17. *Ibid.*, p.xxxvii-xxxix
18. Davies, p.17
19. *Ibid.*, p.18
20. *Ibid.*, p.19
21. Brooks (1989), p.163
22. *Ibid.*, p.159
23. *Ang. Sax. Ency.*, p.188
24. Tyerman, Christopher, *Who's Who in Early Medieval England*, Shepheard-Walwyn, 1996, p.110
25. *Ibid.*, p.110-3; *Ang. Sax. Ency.*, p.477
26. *Ang. Sax. Ency.*, p.232
27. Tyerman, Christopher, *op.cit.*, p.118-9
28. *Ibid.*
29. *The Compact Edition of the Dictionary of National Biography*, Oxford University Press, 1975, p.2237

Chapter 1

1. Esmonde Cleary, p.42
2. *Ibid.*, p.64, 66, 75, 78, referring to his own paper 'The quick and the dead: suburbs, cemeteries and the town' in F. Grew & B. Hobley (eds.), *Roman Urban Topography in Britain and the Western Empire*, CBA Research report 59, London, 1985, pp.74-7; reference is also made to B.C. Burnham 'The Morphology of Romano-British "Small Towns"' in *Archaeological Journal*, CXLIV, 1987, pp.156-90; on characteristic artisan strip buildings, D. Perring 'Domestic buildings in Romano-British towns', in J. Schofield, R. Leech (eds.), *Urban Archaeology in Britain*, CBA Research Report 61, London, 1987, pp.147-55
3. *Ibid.*, pp.64, 78, 80
4. *Ibid.*, p.80
5. *Ibid.*, pp.8-9, 72-3, referring to A.H.M. Jones *The Later Roman Empire, 284-602*, Oxford, 1964, Chapter XIII; M. Hendy, *Studies in the Byzantine Monetary Economy: c.300-1450*, Cambridge, 1986
6. *Ibid.*, p.1, who refers to A.H. M. Jones, *op.cit*, pp.23-4 in relation to the 20 emperors and other rulers
7. Morris, (1973), p.3
8. Esmonde Cleary, pp.1, 4
9. Morris, (1973), pp.4-5
10. Esmonde Cleary, p.9
11. Morris, (1973), pp.6, 8
12. Esmonde Cleary, pp.71-2
13. *Ibid.*, p.43, referring to J.S. Johnson, *The Roman Forts of the Saxon Shore*, London, 1976
14. *Ibid.*, p.45, referring to Ammianus Marcellinus, XXVIII, 3 for the year 367; Morris (1973), p.15
15. *Ibid.*, p.138
16. *Ibid.*, p.165
17. Bede, I.15, p.56
18. Morris (1973), pp.55-6
19. *Ibid.*, p.55
20. Pretty, p.174
21. Berresford Ellis, p.32
22. Fletcher, p.11
23. Morris (1973), p.56
24. Wade-Evans, p.34
25. Berresford Ellis, p.32

26. Morris, (1995), p.172
27. Bede, I.14, p.55
28. Bede, I.15, p.56
29. Nennius, *History of the Britons*, 37, p.58
30. *Ibid.*, 37, p.59
31. Morris (1973), p.74
32. Nennius, *op.cit.*, 31, p.53
33. Morris (1973), p.71
34. *Ibid.*, p.73
35. Nennius, *op.cit.*, 38, p.61
36. Berresford Ellis, pp.34-36
37. Gildas, *The Story of the Loss of Britain*, translated in Wade-Evans, (x 'Of the overthrow of cities'), pp.148-9
38. Bede, I.15, p.57
39. Berresford Ellis, p.36; Morris (1973), p.75
40. Morris (1973), pp.76-7
41. Bede, I.13, p.54
42. Morris (1973), p.82
43. *Ibid.*, p.84
44. Morris (1973), p.84
45. *Ibid.*, p.90
46. Berresford Ellis, p.100
47. *Ibid.*, pp. 92, 103
48. Gildas, Section (Y) 'Of the Remnants' in *The Story of the Loss of Britain*, in Wade-Evans, pp.150-1
49. Esmonde Cleary, pp.172-3, 186
50. *Ibid.*, pp.6-7
51. *Ibid.*, p.34, referring to A.H.M. Jones, *The Later Roman Empire, 284-602*, Oxford, 1964, p.566 on the phrases *cingulum sumere* and *cingulum ponere* ('to put on' and 'take off the belt') as being symbolic of entering or leaving the civil service
52. White & Barker, pp.118-21
53. *Ibid.*, p.106; Morris (1995), p.164
54. White & Barker, p.132
55. *Ibid*, p.125
56. Dr. Margaret Gelling, pers. comm., July 2000
57. White & Barker, pp.121-3
58. *Ibid.*, p.118
59. *Ibid.*, p.125
60. *Ibid.*, pp.123, 126
61. *Ibid.*, p.127
62. Esmonde Cleary, p.174, who refers to J. Turner, 'The Vegetation' in M. Jones & G. Dimbleby (eds.), *The Environment of Man: the Iron Age to the Anglo-Saxon Period*, BAR British 87, 1981, Oxford, pp.67-73
63. Hodges, R., *Wall-to-Wall History - The story of Roystone Grange*, Duckworth, 1991, pp.76-7
64. *Ibid.*, pp.87, 90
65. Esmonde Cleary, p.179, who refers to Leslie Alcock, *By South Cadbury that is Camelot ... Excavations at Cadbury Castle 1966-70*, London, 1972 & Alcock's, 'Cadbury Camelot: A Fifteen-Year Perspective', in *Proceedings of the British Academy*, LVIII, 1982, pp.355-88
66. *Ibid.*, p.200
67. Berresford Ellis, pp.91-107, on language pp.98-9
68. *Ibid.*, p.99
69. *Ibid.*, p.100
70. *Ibid.*, p.103
71. John Morris' theory discussed in Berresford Ellis, p.101-2
72. Esmonde Cleary, pp.186-7, who refers to M. Lapidge, 'Gildas's education and the Latin culture of sub-Roman Britain', in M. Lapidge, D.N. Dumville (eds.), *Gildas: New Approaches*, Woodbridge, 1984, pp.27-50; on Llandaff charters reference is made to Wendy Davies, *An Early Welsh Microcosm*, London, 1978

Chapter 2

1. Stenton, p.40
2. Stafford, p.96, who refers to P. Hunter Blair, 'The Northumbrians and their southern frontier' in *Archaeologia Aeliana*, 4th Series, XXVI, (1948), pp.98-126
3. Yorke, p.102
4. Davies, pp.22-3 (referring to and quoting from *Flores*)
5. *Ibid.*, p.23
6. *Ibid.*, p.22, after H.M. Chadwick, *The Origin of the English Nations*, 1907, p.118
7. Brooks, (1989), p.162

8. Sims-Williams, p.19
9. White, R. (ed.), *West Midlands Archaeology Journal*, Report (ref.no.)
   HWCM 15305, Vol. 36, CBA West Midlands, 1993, p.46
10. Stanford, S.C., *The Archaeology of the Welsh Marches*, 2nd, revised edition,
   1991, p.113 and p.115
11. *Ibid.*, p.115
12. Gelling, pers. comm.
13. Gelling, 2000, pp.43, 45
14. Nicholaisen, W.F.H., Gelling, M. & Richards, M., *The Names of Towns and
   Cities in Britain*, Batsford, 1970, pp.187-8 (for meaning of *walh* see
   under Wallasey entry p.187)
15. *Ibid.*, p.187
16. Gelling, (1992), p.59, who refers to J. Gould on observations concerning
   records of the tumulus at Rowley Hill Farm
17. Sawyer, no.94, p.95; Bassett, pp.18-20 & note 48, p.242. Bassett notes that
   Stoppingas may mean 'the people of the hollow' after the Old English
   word *stoppa* (meaning 'bucket') being used in a topographical sense,
   and refers to M. Gelling, 'The placename volume for Worcestershire
   and Warwickshire: A new look' in *Field and Forest: An Historical
   Geography of Warwickshire and Worcestershire*, ed. T.R. Slater and
   P.J. Jarvis, Norwich, 1982, p.69
18. Dumville, David, 'Essex, Middle Anglia and the expansion of Mercia in the
   south-east Midlands' in Bassett, p.133
19. Hart, Cyril, 'The Kingdom of Mercia' in *Mercian Studies*, ed. A. Dornier,
   p.44
20. Brooks, (1989), p.159
21. Higham, (1992), pp.7, 9 & note 57, p.15; Bede, II.9, p.114
22. Dumville, *op.cit*, p.130
23. Davies, p.20
24. *ASC* in Whitelock, p.146
25. In a charter dated 26 December 731 Offa of Mercia granted freedom from
   all royal tribute on land at Hampton Lucy, north-east of Stratford-on-
   Avon and at *Faehha leage* to the Church of St. Peter, Worcester, also
   being spelt *Fachanleah* in 966 and *Faccanlea* in 969. Hart considers
   this to be the most plausible site for the battle and gives the
   Warwickshire Avon as representing 'the limit of West Saxon advance
   against the Britons at this date'. (Hart, Cyril, *The Early Charters of
   Northern England and the North Midlands*, Leics. Univ. Press, 1975,
   p.76, no.48 & p.81, no.61, & notes to both.) However, Gelling
   considers these Warwickshire examples 'philologically unsound' as the
   sound described by the elements -hh-, -ch- and -cc- does not 'inter
   change with that represented by -th- in the Old English period'. Thus
   the Warwickshire spellings could never have developed from the
   Fethan leag of the 584 entry. Gelling observes that the wood in the
   Stoke Lyne identification, spelt *Fethelee* in 1198, is a natural
   development of the pre-Conquest *Fethan leag* spelling but warns that,
   as there is only one mention of it, more than one spelling would be
   preferred 'to support such an important identification'. (Gelling,
   (1978), p.14)
26. Henry, p.53
27. Brooks, (1989), p.163. For reference to the *Iclingas* Brooks refers to *Felix's
   Life of Saint Guthlac*, ed. B. Colgrave, 1956, c.2, who refers to D.N.
   Dumville, The Anglian collection of royal genealogies and regnal lists'
   in Anglo-Saxon England, V, 1976, pp.23-50 esp. p.33; for pre-Icel part
   of the genealogy reference is made to 'Kingship, genealogies and
   regnal lists' in *Early Medieval Kingship*, ed. P. Sawyer and I. Wood,
   1977, pp.72-104, esp. p.93; H.M. Chadwick, *The Origin of the English
   Nation*, 1907, pp.111-43; Davies, p.23 (who quotes H.M. Chadwick,
   op.cit., p.15f; Morris (1973), p.272
28. Stenton, p.39
29. Brooks, (1989), p.163
30. Stenton, pp.39-40
31. see Brooks, (1989), p.163
32. *Ibid.*, p.163 & p.164. Reference to Stenton is to *The Place-Names of
   Worcestershire*, ed. A. Mawer and F.M. Stenton, Eng. Place-Name Soc.
   iv, 1927, p.xxii
33. *Ibid.*, p.164
34. Ekwall, p.129 for Credenhill, p.136 for Curbridge & Curdworth, p.273 for
   Kersoe, p.535 for *worp*
35. *Ibid.*, p.360
36. Mawer *et al.*, p.245
37. *Ibid.*, p.277
38. *Ibid.*, p.216
39. Ekwall, p.361

40. Mawer *et al.*, p.223
41. Brooks, (1989), p.164
42. Whitelock, *Laws of Ine* no.32, p.371, 70.1
43. Finberg, (1976), pp.63, 79

Chapter 3
1. Higham (1992), p.1
2. *Ibid.*, pp.4, 10
3. *Ibid.*, p.4
4. *Ibid.*, p.10
5. *Ibid.*, pp.11-2
6. *Ibid.*, p.11
7. *Ibid.*, pp.4, 5, 10, 11
8. *Ibid.*, p.12
9. *Ibid.*, p.7
10. Bede, II.2, pp.103-4
11. ASC in Whitelock, p.148
12. Higham (1992), p.6
13. *Ibid.*, p.7
14. *Ibid.* who refers to Bede, II.12
15. Bede, I.34, p.92
16. Nennius, 'History of the Britons', 63, p.81, also 'Anglian Genealogies' in
   Wade-Evans, 57, p.76
17. Marsden, p.74
18. Higham (1992), p.5, who refers to Bede, II.12
19. Henry, p.56
20. Higham (1993), p.113
21. Marsden, p.73
22. ASC in Whitelock, p.150
23. Henry, p.57
24. Ashley, pp.250-1
25. William, p.70
26. Bede, II.20, p.138; Stenton, p.45
27. Ashley, p.251
28. Higham (1992), note 29, p.13
29. Bede, II.20, p.138
30. Ashley, p.251
31. Bede, II.20, p.138
32. ASC in Whitelock, p.150
33. Revill, p.41
34. Leland, Vol.1, p.36
35. Higham (1993), p.89
36. *Ibid.*, p.124
37. Revill, p.48
38. Revill, p.45, on Edwinstowe place-name ref. made to J.E.B. Glover et al.,
   The place-names of Nottinghamshire, 1940, p.75
39. *Ibid.*, pp.45-6 who refers to M.J. Jackson, *Edwinstowe - the story of a forest
   village*, 1975, esp. p.4
40. Peters, p.47
41. *Ibid.*
42. Revill, pp.46-8
43. Bede, II.20, p.138
44. Peter Hunter Blair quoted in Marsden, p.102
45. Ashley, p.280
46. Kirby, p.85, for text and translation of the poem see J. Rowland, *Early
   Welsh Saga Poetry: A Study and Edition of the Englynion*,
   Woodbridge, 1990
47. Gelling (1992), p.74
48. *Ibid.;* Higham (1992) note 52, p.14 who refers to D. Kenyon, *The Origins
   of Lancashire,* Manchester, 1991, p.77
49. Brooks (1989) p.168 who quotes Dr. Jenny Rowland in *Early Welsh Saga ·
   Poetry* (see ref.46 above)
50. Matthew of Westminster suggests that Penda was actually a subordinate
   ally of Cadwallon. According to Matthew, this came about when
   Penda was besieging Cadwallon's nephew in Exeter, Cadwallon
   having fled to Brittany, only to return with a large army and lift the
   siege, defeating Penda and taking him prisoner in the process. To
   regain his liberty, this version records, Penda swore fealty to
   Cadwallon and became his ally in the wars against Northumbria. Yet
   Matthew suggests that Cadwallon lived and fought on after his
   generally accepted death at Heavenfield in 635, which raises doubts
   as to the accuracy of this record, although it derives perhaps from an
   unknown and now lost British source. (Matthew, see pp.295-6, 298,
   301, 309, 317)

51. Bede, III.9, pp.156-7
52. Brooks (1989) discussed in Kirby, p.91
53. Brooks (1989), p.166
54. Kirby, p.91
55. Brooks (1989), p.166; Bede, II.20, p.138
56. Brooks (1989), p.166
57. Bede, III.18, p.171
58. Scarfe, p.294
59. *Ibid*, pp.294-5
60. *Ibid*, p.295
61. Henry, p.59
62. Bede, II.5, pp.107-8
63. Bede, III.16,p.167
64. Kirby, p.93, following Bede III.21
65. Kirby, pp.93-4, following Bede III.13
66. Bede, III.24,p.182
67. *Ibid*, p.183
68. *Ibid*.
69. Bede III,24, p.183
70. Kirby, pp.90, 95 who refers to K.H. Jackson, 'Bede's *Urbs Giudi*: Stirling or Cramond? in *Cambridge Medieval Celtic Studies*, Vol.2, 1981, pp.1-7
71. Henry, p.103
72. Kirby, p.95
73. Nennius, 'History of the Britons' in Wade-Evans, 64, p.83 & 64, p.82
74. Brooks (1989), p.170
75. Bede, III.24, p.185
76. *Ibid*.
77. Marsden, pp.156-7
78. Bede, III.24, p.185
79. Stenton, p.84
80. *Ibid*.
81. Kirby, p.114, who refers to his 'Bede and Northumbrian Chronology' in *Eng. Hist. Review*, Vol.78, 1963, p.514-27, esp. p.520
82. *Ibid*.
83. Ashley, p.253
84. *Ibid*.
85. Kirby, p.115, reference is made to J. Blair 'Frithuwald's kingdom and the origins of Surrey' in Bassett, pp.99-107
86. Ashley, p.254
87. Garmonsway, *The Laud Chronicle* (E) under the year 656, p.29
88. Garmonsway, p.xxxvii
89. Florence, p.22
90. Kirby, p.116
91. Webb, J.F. (trans.) 'Eddius Stephanus: Life of Wilfrid' in *Lives of the Saints*, Penguin Classics, 1965, Chapter 20, p.153
92. Henry, pp.61-2
93. Matthew, p.314
94. Bede, III.30, p.201
95. Florence, p.24
96. Ashley, p.254
97. William, p.71
98. Bede, IV.6, p.217; Mellows, Charles & Mellows, W.T. (trans.), 'The Peterborough Chronicle of Hugh Candidus', Peterborough Museum Society, 1997, p.3
99. D.F. Mackreth, pers. comm. June 2001
100. *Ibid*.
101. Matthew, p.311
102. Ashley, p.254
103. Campbell (1982), pp.54-5

Chapter 4
1. Mayr-Harting, p.33 who refers to W.H.C. Frend, 'Religion in Roman Britain in the Fourth Century', *Journal of the British Archaeological Association*, Vol.18 (1955), pp.1-17
2. *Ibid.*, p.29
3. Morris (1989), pp.60-2. Re.Palmers of Ludlow guild regs. Morris refers to T. Smith, *English Gilds*, Early English Text Society, old series, 40, 1870, p.194
4. Morris (1989), p.62
5. *Ibid.*, pp.62, 71
6. Anderson, pp.21-2
7. Morris (1989). p.65

8. Bede, II. 13, p.128
9. Mayr-Harting, p.23
10. Owen, p.43 who refers to B. Hope-Taylor, *Yeavering*, London.1977
11. Owen, pp.43-5
12. From Bede's *De Temporum Ratione*, XV in Owen, p.46 who qoutes C.W. Jones (ed.), *Bedae Opera de Temporibus*, Cambridge, Mass., 1943, pp.211, 213
13. Owen, pp.45-6. On 1,000 ox-skulls found at Harrow Hill Owen refers to G.J. Copley, *An Archaeology of South-East England*, London, 1958, p.162: to the ox-heads found at St.Paul's Cathedral Owen refers to A.W. Smith, 'The luck in the head: a problem in English folklore', *Folklore*, LXXII, 1962, p.23
14. Mayr-Harting, p.24 who lists the work of F.M. Stenton, 'The Historical Bearing of Place-Name Studies: Anglo-Saxon Heathenism', *Trans. Royal Hist. Soc.*, 4th Series, Vol.23, (1941), pp.1-24; J.E.B. Glover, A. Mawer, F.M. Stenton (eds.), 'The Place-Names of Surrey', *English Place-Name Society*, (1934), pp.xii-xiv, p.207; M. Gelling, 'Place-Names and Anglo-Saxon Paganism', *Univ. of Birmingham Hist. Journ.*, Vol.VIII (1961), pp.7-25
15. Morris (1989),pp.65-6
16. Gelling (1978), pp.110, 159 who refers to Gelling 1961, *op.cit.*
17. Ekwall,p.221
18. Morris (1989), p.68. Morris refers to the RCHME *Northamptonshire*, 2, pp.80-1 re. Great Harrowden; the votive offering quote comes from P. Liddle, *Leicester Archaeology - the Present State of Knowledge. Volume 2, Anglo-Saxon and Medieval Periods*, Leic's. Museum Pub., 38, 1982, p.6
19. Morris (1989), pp.68-9 who refers to Gelling, 1961 *op.cit.* (in ref.14), p.10; Blair, p.18 who refers to M. Gelling 'The Place-Names of Oxfordshire', Vol.(i), *English Place-Name Society*, p.195
20. Mawer *et al.*, p.333
21. Branston, p.55
22. Church guide, *St. Michael's Church, Stowe-Nine-Churches, Northamptonshire*, 1988
23. Dark Age Dict., p.235
24. Morris (1989), p.67
25. *Ibid.*, p.68
26. Church guide, *op.cit.*
27. Morris (1989),p.68
28. Taylor & Taylor, p.596 - 3rd of the references re: Stowe-Nine-Churches concerning note made by Sir Henry Dryden
29. Morris (1989), p.67
30. Ekwall, p.503
31. *Ibid.*, p541
32. Gelling (1984), p.326
33. Ekwall, p.541
34. Gelling (1984), p.326
35. Ekwall, p.540
36. Lias, p.63
37. Coplestone-Crow, p.199
38. Branston, p.94
39. *Ibid.*; Whitlock, Ralph, *In Search of Lost Gods - A guide to British Folklore*, Phaidon, 1979, pp.60-1, 132
40. Branston, p.96
41. Owen, pp.12-3 who refers to Hilda Ellis Davidson, *Gods and Myths of Northern Europe*, Harmondsworth, 1964, pp.50-1
42. Owen, p.20
43. Ekwall, p.503
44. Owen, p.9
45. Morris (1989), p.66 who refers to Gelling, 1961, *op.cit.*, pp.10-11
46. Gelling (1961), quoted in Morris (1989), p.66
47. Gelling (1978), p.159
48. Owen, p.9
49. Gelling, (1978), p.161
50. Owen, pp.9-10
51. *Ibid.*, p.10
52. Gelling (1978), pp.149, 150
53. Branston, pp.112-3
54. Mayr-Harting, p.26
55. Owen, p.24
56. Mayr-Harting, p.27
57. *Ibid.*, p.26
58. *Ibid.*, pp.26, 27

59. Blair, p.18 & note 60, p.187 who refers to the Place-Names of Oxfordshire, *English Place-Name Society.*, (i), pp.xix-xx
60. Owen, pp.23-4; Branston, p.42
61. Owen, p.28
62. Branston, pp.74, 93
63. Owen, pp.28-9
64. Gelling (1992), p.92
65. Owen, p.28
66. Mayr-Harting, p.28
67. Gelling (1992), p.92 who refers to the *VCH Warwickshire*, Vol.V, p.175 on 'near Sunrising Inn' loc.
68. Branston, p.127
69. Owen, p.22
70. *Ibid.*, p.23
71. *Ibid.*, p.33
72. *Ibid.*, pp.23, 33-4. On the worship of Nerthus by 1st century Germanic tribes see S.A. Handford (trans.), Tacitus - *The Agricola and the Germania*, Penguin, 1970, Chap. 39, p.134
73. Owen, p.22; Branston, p.42; Ekwall, p.189
74. Owen, p.56 who refers to R.W.V. Elliott, 'Runes, yews and magic', *Speculum*, XX XII, 1957, pp.250-61
75. Owen, p.56
76. Gregory, p.38
77. Rackham, p.229 who refers to T. Willliamson and L. Bellamy, *Ley lines in question*, World's Work, Kingswood, Tadworth, 1983
78. Mabey, Richard, *Flora Britannica*, Sinclair Stevenson, p.28, who refers to the work of Allen Meredith, e.g.*Touchwood*, Milner, 1992; Morris (1989), p.79
79. Sant, pp.9, 10, 12
80. Morris (1989), pp.86-7 who refers to F. Jones *The Holy Wells of Wales*, 1954, Cardiff, pp.24-5, 28
81. *Ibid.*, p.85
82. *Ibid.*; Ekwall, pp.188, 247
83. Gelling (1984), pp.31-2
84. Ekwall, p.413
85. Morris (1989), p.81
86. Williams, Howard, 'Ancient Landscapes and the Dead: The Reuse of Prehistoric and Roman Monuments as Early Anglo-Saxon Burial Sites', *Medieval Archaeology*, Vol.XLI, 1997, pp.1-32
87. Morris (1989), pp.81, 83-4
88. Ekwall, p.379
89. Williams, Howard, *op.cit.*, p.1
90. *Ibid.*, Table 1, p.21, also Fig.14, p.20
91. Stanford, p.115
92. Owen, p.65; Ekwall, p.421; Lias, p.63
93. Lias, p.63
94. Owen, p.65
95. *Ibid.*
96. Cameron, p.124
97. Owen, p.65
98. *Ibid.*, p.64
99. *Ibid.*, p.65
100. Gelling (1978), p.150
101. Cameron, p.125
102. Lias, p.63
103. Ekwall, p.375
104. Gelling (1978), p.150
105. Mawer *et al.*, p.252
106. Gelling (1978), p.150
107. Cameron, p.125; Ekwall, p.224 (see also his entry under Hassall, same page, for *haeste* element)
108. Wright, David (trans. & intro.) *Beowulf*, Penguin, 1957, lines 2272-2276, p.80
109. Owen, pp.65-6; Gelling (1978), p.142□
110. Gelling (1978), pp.141-2
111. *Ibid.*, p.142; Owen, p.65
112. Gelling (1978), p.142
113. *Ibid.*
114. Coplestone-Crow, pp.141, 215
115. Gelling (1978), p.142
116. Ekwall, p.250
117. Gelling (1978), p.142
118. *Ibid.*

Chapter 5

1. Farmer, David, 'St. Augustine's life and legacy' in *St. Augustine's Abbey, Canterbury*, edited by Richard Gem, Batsford/English Heritage, 1997, pp.16-7
2. Bede, I.28, p.66
3. Campbell (1986), pp.69-73 & note 4, p.70 who, among others, refers to J.N.L. Myres, *Anglo-Saxon Pottery & the Settlement of England*, 1969 on movement of Germanic settlers in 5th century; K. Cameron, 'Eccles in English Place-Names' in *Christianity in Britain, 300-700*, ed. M.W. Barley and R.P.C. Hanson, 1968, pp.87-92; *Adomnan's Life of Columba*, ed. A.O. & M.O. Anderson, 1961, pp.486 & 512 on names of Pilu and Genereus at Iona
4. Mayr-Harting, pp.32-3 - who refers to K. Cameron, 'Eccles in English Place-Names', *op.cit.*
5. Gelling (1984), p.278
6. Cameron, p.34
7. Gelling (1984), p.109 who refers to Professor C. Thomas, *Christianity in Roman Britain to AD 500*, 1980, pp.262-5
8. Gelling (1978), p.98
9. Coplestone-Crow, pp.130, 152
10. Ekwall, p.159 (under the Eccles entry for Lancashire and Norfolk)
11. Coplestone-Crow, p.25\
12. Farmer, David, 'St. Augustine's life and legacy', in Gem, *op.cit.*, p19
13. Bede, II.14, p.128
14. Bede, II.13, p.127
15. Campbell (1986), p.73
16. *Ibid..*, p.74. Bishop Daniel's letter to St. Boniface can be found in translation in C.H. Talbot's *The Anglo-Saxon Missionaries in Germany*, 1954
17. Campbell (1986), p.77
18. Mayr-Harting, Henry, 'Two Conversions to Christianity: the Bulgarians and the Anglo-Saxons' in *Stenton's 'Anglo-Saxon England'- fifty Years on*, Regional Historical Studies I, Papers given at a colloquium held at Reading 11-12 November 1993, ed. Donald Matthew, University of Reading, 1994, pp.10-11
19. Kohn, George C., *Wordsworth Encyclopedia of Plague & Pestilence*, Wordsworth, 1998. (First published by Facts on File, 1995), p.357
20. Bede, III.30, p.201
21. Mayr-Harting, 'Two Conversions to Christianity...', *op.cit.*, p.11; Mayr-Harting, pp.6-7 who refers to Raymond Firth's *Rank and Religion in Tikopia: a Study in Polynesian paganism and Conversion to Christianity*, London, 1970. In the latter study the conversion of the Tikopian people (who live in an island north of New Zealand) gives a fascinating modern day comparison of conversion and the associated anxieties of letting go of paganism
22. Campbell (1986), p.75
23. Dark Age Dict., p.44
24. *Ibid.*, p.198
25. Attwater, Donald & John, Catherine Rachel, *Dictionary of Saints*, 1995 (3rd edition), pp.44-5; Aston, Michael, *Know the Landscape-Monasteries*, Batsford, 1993, p.34
26. Morris (1989), pp.98-100
27. *Ibid..*, p.97
28. *Ibid..*, pp.97-8. Morris refers to I.N. Wood, 'A prelude to Columbanus: the monastic achievement in the Burgundian territories', in H.B. Clarke and M. Brennan (eds.) *Columbanus and Merovingian Monasticism*, BAR A 113, pp.3-32, esp. p.4
29. Morris (1989), p.100. (On the Romano-British villa at Llanwit Major, Morris refers to RCAHMW *Glamorgan*, 1.2, pp.110-14, for Llancarfen *ibid.*, p.114, for Llandough monastery ref. made to W. Davies, *The Llandaff Charters*, 1979, no.101)
30. Taylor & Taylor, p.695
31. *Ibid..*, p.32
32. Morris (1989).p.105
33. Coplestone-Crow, pp.2-5
34. Doble, p.86
35. Fenn, R.W.D., 'Early Christianity in Herefordshire', *TWNFC*, Vol.XXXIX, Part II, 1968, p.338
36. Doble, p.86 who refers to R.W.D. Fenn, 'St. Dyfig and Christianity in South East Wales', *Province*, xi, pp.22-5, 60-67 on *Ariconium* being the source of 5th-6th century Welsh Christian movement; Farmer, p.114
37. Andere, p.33

38. Coplestone-Crow, p.100
39. Duncumb; Herefordshire Archaelogy Unit, Leominster, File number 6436
40. Andere, p.41
41. Bede, II.2, p.103
42. Morris (1989), p.112
43. Doble, p.67
44. Sims-Williams, p.121 who refers to D.B. Schneider, 'Anglo-Saxon Women in the Religious Life: A Study of the Status and Position of Women in an Early Medieval Society', Unpubl. PhD dissertation, Cambridge University, 1985, esp. p.272-3; also refers to Stafford, p.101 & Thacker, 'Pre-Viking Mercia' (see ref.47 for full listing)
45. Rollason, pp.126-7 who cites, for example, W.A. Chaney, *The Cult of Kingship in Anglo-Saxon England: The Transition from Paganism to Christianity*, Manchester University Press, 1970, esp. chapter 3
46. Rollason, pp.127-9 who refers to Janet Nelson, 'Royal Saints and Early Medieval Kingship' in Studies in Church History, Vol.10, 1973, pp.39-44, and also Rollason 'The cults of murdered royal saints in Anglo-Saxon England', *Anglo-Saxon England*, ed. Peter Clemoes, Vol.11, Cambridge University Press, 1983, pp.1-22 esp. p.17
47. Thacker, Alan, 'Kings, Saints and Monasteries in Pre-Viking Mercia', *Midland History*, Vol.X, 1985, p.1; Rollason, p.117, who quotes Thacker's paper, *ibid.*, pp.1-25
48. Stafford, p.101
49. Foot, pp.50-1 who refers to Aldhelm's prose work *On Virginity*, XIX & Theodore's *Penitential*, II, xii, 8, 11, 13; on physicians at Ely see Bede, IV.19, p.240 where mention is made of a physician, Cynifrid, who attended the abbess of Ely at her last illness
50. Bede, III.11, pp.158-9
51. Rollason, p.121
52. Sims-Williams, pp.118,119,120. Among others Sims-Williams refers to D.B. Schneider's paper 'Anglo-Saxon Women in the Religious Life...', *op.cit.*, pp.25-6 where Schneider can find no positive evidence for nunneries in early Anglo-Saxon England but does not discount their possible existence
53. Morris (1989), pp.125-6. Bede's quote is taken from Morris p.126. The letter from Bede to Archbishop Egbert of York, dated 5 November 734, can be found in Whitelock, no.170., pp.735-45
54. Morris (1989), pp.126-7 who quotes from Bede via Whitelock *ibid*
55. Sims-Williams, p.135
56. Foot, p.50
57. Sims-Williams, p.115
58. Morris (1989), p.128
59. Stenton, F.M., 'Medeshamstede and its Colonies' dated 1933, in *Preparatory to Anglo-Saxon England - being the collected papers of Frank Merry Stenton*, ed. D.M. Stenton, 1970, section 2, p.182; Stafford, p.182; Foot, p.50
60. Stenton, 'Medeshamstede', *ibid.*, sections 3 & 4
61. Foot, p.50
62. Bede, III.23, p.182
63. Magnusson, Magnus, *Lindisfarne - the Cradle Island*, Oriel Press, 1984, pp.45-6
64. Austerberry, p.4
65. *Ibid.*; Baring-Gould, p.24
66. Greenslade, p.3
67. Austerberry, p.6
68. Greenslade, p.4, Dark Age Dictionary, p.237
69. Mayr-Harting, p.97
70. Austerberry, p.8
71. Pevsner, Nikolaus, *The Buildings of England - Staffordshire*, Penguin, p.125
72. Baring-Gould, p.29
73. Greenslade, p.5; Ang. Sax. Ency., p.287 on quote of gift of Lichfield to Wilfrid from King Wulfhere
74. Gallyon, Margaret, *The Early Church in Wessex and Mercia*, Terence Dalton Ltd., 1980, p.89
75. Gould, in Gelling (1992), p.96
76. Gelling, *ibid*.
77. Brooks (1989), p.169
78. Gelling (1992), p.73 who refers to Dr. Jenny Rowland's *Early Welsh Saga Poetry: Study and Edition of the Englynion*, Woodbridge, 1990, on the interpretation of the *Marwnad Cynddylan*, esp. p.133
79. *Ibid.*; Dr. Jenny Rowland, *op.cit.*, p.134
80. Brooks (1989), p.162
81. *Ibid.*, p.169; Gelling (1992), p.96
82. *Ibid.*; Bede, IV.3, p.212
83. Leland, Vol.II, p.99
84. Baring-Gould, pp.34-5; Greenslade, pp.6-7
85. Greenslade, pp.7-8
86. Austerberry, pp.9-10
87. Bede, IV.3, p.211
88. Greenslade, p.8
89. Webster & Backhouse, no.90, p.127; Farmer, pp.75, 368
90. Bede, IV.3, p.212
91. Greenslade, p.9
92. Austerberry, p.12
93. Gelling (1992), pp.152-3
94. Greenslade, pp.10, 11, 13
95. *Ibid.*, pp.14-8
96. *Ibid.*, pp.25-6
97. Hart (1966), no.142, p.98
98. Walsh, Michael (ed.), *Butler's Lives of the Saints*, Burnes and Oates, concise ed.,1985, p.65
99. Austerberry, p.14
100.Rollason, pp.76-7
101. Colgrave, p.15: Swanton, introd. notes to *The Life of St. Guthlac*, p.88
102. Colgrave, p.16
103. *Ibid.*, pp.73, 75, I & II
104. *Ibid.*, p.176
105. *Ibid.*, p.81, XVI & XVII
106. *Ibid.*, p.3; Kirby, p.126
107. Colgrave, p.3 & fn 5 where Whitelock's theory on Guthlac's exile is discussed
108. *Ibid.*, p.87, XXIV
109. *Ibid.*, p.89, XXV
110. Phillips, C.W. (ed.) 'The Fenland in Roman Times' maps to accompany text, The Royal Geographical Society, R.G.S. Research Series: No.5, Sheet K
111. Colgrave, p.1
112. Loyn, p.21
113. Colgrave, pp.91, 93, 95, XXVI, XXVII & XXVIII
114. *Ibid.*, pp.183
115. *Ibid.*, pp.183, 184
116. Rollason, pp.84-5
117. Mayr-Harting, p.234 who quotes pp.80-1 of Dorothy Whitelock's *The Audience of Beowulf*, 1951
118. Mayr-Harting, p.235
119. Colgrave, pp.165, 167, LII
120. *Ibid.*, p.163, LI; Rollason, p.42
121. Colgrave, p.161, LI
122. Thacker, Alan, 'Kings, Saints and Monasteries in pre-Viking Mercia', *op.cit.*, pp.5-6 who refers to CBA Res. Report, XXXVI, 1, 5; *History of the King's Works*, H.M. Colvin (ed.), II (1963), p.676
123. Information from The Society of the Precious Blood
124. Thacker, *ibid.*, p.6 who refers to *The Life of St. Guthlac*
125. *Ibid.* refers to *The Life of St. Guthlac*
126. Whitehead, in Shoesmith (1980), p.1 (see also p.5) who refers to Colvin, *op.cit.*, p.676
127. Mayr-Harting, p.20
128. Loyn, p.180
129. Cannon, John (ed.), *The Oxford Companion to British History*, Oxford Univ. Press, 1997, p.918
130. Charles-Edwards, p.37 who refers to *The Life of St. Guthlac*, Colgrave, pp.73, 81 and Bede, II.20 & IV.15
131. Rollason, p.84
132. *Ibid.*, p.98

Chapter 6
Magonsaete

1. Nennius, 'Hostory of the Britons', 63, p.81
2. Stafford, p.97. Stafford refers to the paper 'Barton-upon-Humber, Castledyke South', *Med. Arch.*, XXVII (1983), p.184
3. Gelling (1992), p82
4. *Ibid.*, p.83; Florence, pp.422, 448
5. Hart (1971), pp.140-1 quoted in Pretty, p.181. On the two separate sees see 'Pre-Conquest Herefordshire' in *Preparatory to Anglo-Saxon England*, Stenton, 1970, p.194, note 5. On land grants which mention the

Magonsaete, reference is made to Sawyer no,1264, p.367, no. 1782, p.470 and no.677, p.226

6. Pretty, pp.181-2. Re. pagan Anglo-Saxon burials Pretty refers to her paper *The Severn Basin in the 5th and 6th centuries AD,* and notes Stanford's discovery of a possible Anglo-Saxon cemetery at Bromfield
7. Gelling (1992), pp.83-4
8. Gelling (1978), p.102
9. *Ibid.*, p.105
10. Leland, iii, p.103
11. Gelling (1992), p.140
12. Brooks (1989) in Bassett, pp.168-9. On lack of record to Mercian/Welsh hostilities until the Welsh victories of early 8th century, Brooks refers to F.M. Stenton's *Preparatory to Anglo-Saxon England: Collected Papers,* ed. D.M.Stenton (1970), pp.357-63
13. *Ibid.*, p.169
14. Gelling (1992), p.86
15. Pretty, pp.171-83
16. Sheppard, June A., *The Origins and Evolution of Field and Settlement Patterns in the Herefordshire Manor of Marden*, Occasional Paper No.15, Department of Geography, Queen Mary College, University of London, 1979, pp.30, 36. Sheppard quotes Lord Rennel of Rodd 'The land of the Lene', in Foster, I.L.I. and Alcock, L. (eds.) *Culture and Environment, Essays in Honour of Sir Cyril Fox*, London, 1963, p.304 on the idea that *Magene/Magana* was a district name; also F.M. Stenton, *op.cit.*, pp.193-202; H.P.R.Finberg, *Lucerna*, 1964, pp.66-82 on *Magonsaete*
17. Coplestone-Crow, pp.11,13
18. Hillaby (1987), pp.604-5
19. Garmonsway, p.29 - The Laud Chronicle 'E'
20. Hillaby (1987), p.571 (see also his note 65 on p.670); Sawyer, no.91, pp.94-5□
21. Gelling (1992), p.82
22. Finberg, H.P.R. 'Princes of the Magonsaete' in Finberg (1972), p.219
23. Quoted in Hillaby (1987), p.568. Hillaby refers to N.K. Chadwick, 'The Celtic Background of Early Anglo-Saxon England' in *Celt and Saxon: Studies in the Early British Border*, ed. K. Jackson *et al.*, 1963, pp.336-7
24. Gelling (1992), p.81
25. Leland, ii, p.74
26. Leland, ii, pp.74-5
27. Reeves, Norman, *The Town in the Marches*, 1972, p.26
28. Leland, ii, p.75
29. Reeves, *op.cit.*, p.26
30. Coplestone-Crow, p.113
31. Shoesmith, Ron, *Castles & Moated Sites of Herefordshire*, Logaston Press, 1996, p.153
32. Hillaby (1987), p.561
33. *Ibid.*, p.564. Although the Wenlock original of Goscelin's *Life* of St. Mildburg is now lost, Hillaby remarks that it has come down in both a shortened and a longer version, with only the latter containing the story of Merewalh's conversion. There are two extant versions of this longer form: one held in the British Library Additional MS 34,633, which 'is a composite manuscript of the 13th century, written in several hands' (and appears to have originally belonged to St. Mary's Augustinian Priory at Beddgelert, Gwynedd), and a version in a library at Gotha in Germany, which 'is an English manuscript of 14th-century date'. As these two manuscripts have only slight textual differences, it is believed they were ultimately dependent on the Wenlock original. Hillaby further observes that another manuscript, the British Library Harley MS 2253, is a collection of English, Latin and English texts and the handwriting suggests 'it was drawn up in the 1340s'. It contains three saints' *Lives* including the *Legend of St. Etfrid, Priest of Leominster* which describes Merewalh's conversion.(Hillaby (1987), p.564)
34. Hillaby (1987),pp. 609 & table 4 on p.610
35. *Ibid.*, p.604. For more on St. David's connection with Leominster see A.W. Wade-Evans' *Life of St. David*, S.P.C.K.,1923
36. *Dark Age Dict.*, p.222
37. Brooke, Christopher N.L., 'The Diocese of Hereford, 676-1200' in *TWNFC*, 1994 (5), p.25
38. Hillaby (1987), p.610
39. Whitehead, in Shoesmith (1980), p.3
40. Quoted in Hillaby (1976), p.28, who refers to William of Malmesbury's *Gesta Pontificum* IV, p.163
41. Leland, ii, pp.65-6

42. Whitehead, in Shoesmith (1982), p.1
43. Shoesmith, Ron, *The Story of Castle House, Hereford: The Beginnings*, 1999
44. Whitehead, in Shoesmith (1980), p.4, & Shoesmith in *ibid.*, p.25, 55
45. Shoesmith (1980), p.55
46. *Ibid.*, pp.53, 56
47. Shoesmith, Ron, *The Story of Castle House, Hereford: The Beginnings*, 1999
48. Finberg, H.P.R. 'St. Mildburg's Testament' in Finberg (1972), pp.199, 207
49. ASC in Whitelock, p.152; Scarfe, pp.293, 295, who refers to R.L.S. Bruce-Mitford, *The Sutton -Hoo Ship-Burial* I, British Museum, London, 1975, p.707,n.
50. Cameron, p.30; Ekwall, p.28; Taylor & Taylor, p.49 + fig.25
51. Rev. J. Woods, pp.59, 62 and pers. comm. June 2001
52. see Whitehead in Shoesmith (1980), pp.3-4
53. Hillaby (1976), p.28
54. Quoted in Sims-Wiliams, p.342, note 58
55. Sims-Williams, pp.50-1, 342
56. Hillaby (1976), pp.31, 33, 34, 36
57. *Ibid..*, pp.43-4
58. *Ibid..*, p.43
59. *Ibid..*, pp.43-4
60. *Ibid.*, p.43
61. Whitehead, in Shoesmith,(1980),p.4. Re: 1st mention of Aethelberht dedication, Whitehead refers to D. Whitelock (ed.) *Anglo-Saxon Wills*, pp.54-6
62. *Ibid.*, p.1 Re: Wulfgeat's will & the early 11th century legal document, reference made to Whitelock, *Anglo-Saxon Wills*, pp.54-5, 163-7 & A.J. Robertson's *Anglo-Saxon Charters*, 1939, p.186
63. Whitehead, in Shoesmith (1980), pp.2,4-5
64. Hillaby (1976), pp.33-4 who refers to version 'D' of the *Anglo-Saxon Chronicle*
65. *Ibid.*, p.45
66. ASC in Whitelock, p.227 — versions 'C' , 'D', 'E'
67. Garmonsway, p.152, version 'D' of the *Anglo-Saxon Chronicle*

Hwicce

1. Sims-Williams, p.29
2. Gelling quoted in Hooke (1985), p.11. Hooke refers to Gelling, 'The place name volumes for Worcestershire and Warwickshire; a new look' in T.R. Slater and P.J. Jarvis (eds.) *Field and Forest, an Historical Geography of Warwickshire and Worcestershire*, Norwich, 1982, p.69
3. Hooke (1985), p.13
4. Whitelock, no.113, p.519 intro. notes, p.520, note 5
5. Ekwall, p.512; Hooke (1985), p.13. Charters referred to are Sawyer, no.116, p.101 & no.731, p.237; Hooke also refers to her paper 'Early Cotswold Woodland', *Journal of Historical Geography*, 1978, pp.334-5
6. Hooke (1985), p.13. Charters refred to are Sawyer, no.167, p.113 & no.109, p.99
7. Hooke (1985), p.14. Reference is made to Asser's *Life of King Alfred*; Sawyer, no,139, pp.106-7 which charter dates to between 793-796
8. Hooke (1985), pp.12-13. The 11th-century manuscript desribes Bishop Athelstan's diocese of Hereford and is found in 'Bishop Athelstan's Boundary' in Finberg (1972), pp.225-7
9. Hooke (1985), p.16
10. *Ibid.*, pp.85. 86. See also Sawyer, no.1272, p.369, charter dated 849; Hooke refers to her work *The Landscape of Anglo-Saxon Staffordshire: the Charter Evidence*, Keele, 1983, pp.10-28
11. Mawer *et al.*, p.xv
12. *Ibid.*; Hooke (1985), p.14. Hooke refers to A.H. Smith's paper 'The Hwicce' in J.B. Bessinger and R.P. Creed (eds.) *Franciplegius, Medieval and Linguistic Studies of Francis Peabody Magoun Jr.,* New York, 1965, pp.56-65, esp. p.64; Ekwall, p.516
13. Hooke (1985), pp.14-5. Reference to the 862 charter may be found in Sawyer, no.209, pp.123-4 and also in Finberg (1972), p.163, footnote 2. The 841 charter is Sawyer, no.196, p.121
14. Summarized from Wilson, Margaret, 'The Hwicce' in the *TWAS* Third Series, Vol. 2,1968-69, pp21-22. She refers to Collingwood & Myres, *Roman Britain and the English Settlements* 1937; A. Mawer & F.M. Stenton, *The Place-names of Worcestershire*, 1927; A.H. Smith, 'The Hwicce' in *Franciplegius: Medieval and Linguistic Studies in Honour of Francis Peabody Magoun Jr.* Bew York U.P. 1965; E.T. Leeds, 'The distribution of the Angles and Saxons, Archaeologically Considered' in *Arch.* 91, 1945; W. Stubbs, 'The Cathedral, Dioceses and Monasteries

of Worcester in the Eighth Century' in *Arch. J.*XIX 1962; H.P.R. Finberg, *The Early Charters of the West Midlands*; J.C. Russell, 'The Tribal Hidage' *Traditio* Vols. 5-6, 1947-8; S.C. Hawkes & G.C. Dunning, 'Soldiers and settlers in Britain, fourth to fifth century' in *Med. Arch.*V. 1961

15. *Ibid.*, p.22 para 6 *EPNS Glos*, Smith (1965 (b) theory
16. Hooke (1985), p.5 and fig.1, p.6; Cannon, J. (ed.) *The Oxford Companion to British History*, 1997, p.299 (entry by Keith Branigan)
17. Pretty, Kate, 'The Welsh Border and the Severn and Avon valleys in the 5th and 6th centuries', 1975, p.74 quoted in Hooke (1985), p.26; see also p.24
18. Sims-Williams, pp.31-2
19. *Ibid.*, p.32; Mawer *et al*, pp.115-6
20. Mawer *et al*, pp.137-8
21. Sims-Williams, p.32
22. Bassett, pp.6-17
23. Bede, IV, 13, p.227
24. Finberg,H.P.R., 'The Princes of the Hwicce' in Finberg (1972), p.171
25. see Finberg (1972), no.1, p.31
26. as 24, p.174
27. Finberg (1972), no.1, p.86
28. Sims-Williams, p.124
29. Finberg,H.P.R., 'The Early History of Gloucester Abbey' in Finberg (1972), p.161
30. Sawyer, no.51, p.83; Finberg,H.P.R., 'The Princes of the Hwicce' in Finberg (1972), p.173
31. Finberg, *ibid.*, p.172
32. *Ibid., p.175*
33. Florence of Worcester discussed in *ibid.*, p.175
34. *Ibid.*, p.177
35. Sims-Williams, p.36, refers to Sawyer, no.89, p.94
36. Whitelock, no.67, p.454
37. Sims-Williams, p.36, f.n.101, refers to Sawyer no.54, p.84 & no.79, p.91
38. Sawyer, no.94, p.95; quotes are from Sims-Williams, p.36
39. Sims-Williams, p.36, Finberg (1972), no.23, pp.35-6; Sawyer, no.99, pp.96-7
40. Finberg, H.P.R., 'The Princes of the Hwicce' in Finberg (1972), p.178 & family tree on p.179
41. Heighway, Carolyn, *Deerhurst St. Mary & Gloucester St. Oswald: Two Saxon Minsters*, the 6th Deerhurst lecture, repr.1994, p4
42. Hare, Michael, *The Two Anglo-Saxon minsters of Gloucester*, Deerhurst Lecture, 1992, pp.6-7. On Chester translation of relics Hare refers to A.T. Thacker 'Chester and Gloucester: Early Ecclesiastical Organization in two Midland burhs', *Northern History*, 18 (1982), pp.199-211 at p.211
43. Hare, *op.cit.*, p.6; Heighway, *op cit*, p.4
44. Heighway, *op.cit.*, pp.4-5
45. *Ibid.*, p.5
46. Sims-Williams, pp.36-7
47. Finberg (1972), no.26, p.36; Sawyer, no.56, pp.84-5
48. Finberg, *ibid.*, no.214, p.92
49. Sims-Williams, pp.37 (fn.106 & 107), 124
50. Sawyer, nos.57-61, pp.85-6
51. Finberg,H.P.R., 'The Princes of the Hwicce' in Finberg (1972), p.179
52. Hooke (1985), p.19; Sawyer, no.113, p.100
53. Finberg,H.P.R., 'The Princes of the Hwicce' in Finberg (1972), p 180; Sawyer, no.126, p.103
54. Sims-Williams, p.38; Sawyer, nos.58 & 59, p.85 & no.139, p.106
55. Hooke (1985), p.240. Hooke refers to Sawyer, no.1297, p.375 charter dated 963 & no.786, p.250 charter dated 972
56. Hooke (1985), pp.230, 234, 235, 250
57. *Ibid.*, p.190
58. *Ibid.*, pp.220-1
59. *Ibid,.* p.215
60. *Ibid.*, p.191
61. *Ibid.*, pp.194, 196, 197
62. Finberg (1976), p.56
63. Swanton, 'Two Estate Memoranda—I Duties and Perquisites', p.29
64. Finberg (1976), pp.56-7
65. *Ibid.*, pp.57, 60
66. *Ibid.*, p.57
67. Whitelock, no.29, p.358, fn.6
68. Finberg (1976), p.68
69. *Ibid.*, p.58

70. *Ibid.*, p.64
71. *Ibid.*, p.67
72. *Ibid.*, p.64
73. *Ibid.*, p.73
74. *Ibid.*, p.58
75. Stenton quoted in Whitelock, no.32, p.365, fn.2
76. *Ibid.*
77. Swanton, *op.cit.*, p.27
78. *Ibid.*, & fn.2
79. Whitelock, no.32, p.366, fn.3
80. Finberg (1976), p.63
81. Whitelock, as 79 & also no.31, p.362, fn.3
82. Finberg (1976), pp.66-8
83. Swanton, 'Aelfric's Colloquy', introductory notes p.169
84. *Ibid.*, pp.169-70
85. *Ibid.*, p.170
86. *Ibid.*
87. Finberg (1976), p.73
88. Quoted in Hooke (1981), p.123
89. Nennius, Sect.67, p.116
90. Swanton, 'Aelfric's Colloquy', p.173
91. Hooke (1981) p.123
92. Hurst pp.151-2
93. *Ibid.*, p.135
94. *Ibid.*, pp.17-19, 23, 24
95. *Ibid.*, pp.23-4, 112
96. *Ibid.*, p.110
97. Hooke (1981), p.144
98. Leland, ii, pp.92-4
99. Hurst pp.27-8
100. *Ibid.*, pp.27, 30
101. Finberg (1972), no.195, p.86. The charter has not survived in complete form but was in Worcester Cathedral in 1622 when James I's librarian, Patrick Young, took detailed notes from it; William Dugdale noted it in briefer form in 1643. Finberg (1972), pp.11-2; *ibid.*, no.197, p.86
102. Hurst, p.30 who refers to the charters in Finberg *op.cit.*
103. Whitelock, no.64, p.450
104. Finberg (1972), no.206, p.90
105. Hurst, D., Worcestershire Archaeological Service, pers.comm. Feb. 2000
106. Leland, Vol. V, p.93
107. Mawer *et al.*, p.287
108. Hooke (1981), p.144
109. Hooke (1985), p.123; see also Sawyer, no.97, p.96; Finberg (1972), no.207, p.90 & no,212, p.91
110. Mawer *et al.*, pp.285-6
111. Thorn & Thorn, F. & C. (eds.) *Domesday Book* Vol. 16 Worcestershire, 1982, Folio 172 b:1,1a; Hooke (1981), p.129
112. Finberg (1972), no.265, p.106
113. *Ibid.*, no.268 pp.106-7
114. Harmer, F.E. (ed.), *Select English Historical Documents of the Ninth and Tenth Centuries*, Cambridge, 1914, pp.55, 107
115. Buteux & Hurst, pp.3-4. On tax yield ref. to Palliser 1987, p.66
116. *Ibid.*, p.3
117. *Ibid.* Buteux, & Hurst note, however, via pers.comm. with S. Bassett, that the documentary evidence which indicates Droitwich was a *wic* in the late 7th century is 'not very reliable'
118. *Ibid.*, p.129; Sawyer no.220, p.126 who records that Stenton comments the charter is 'not completely reliable' (in Stenton, p.257, n.3)
119. Harmer, F.E, *op.cit.*, pp.58, 110
120. Hooke (1981), p.129; Sawyer no.178, p.116 & no.188, p.119
121. Hooke (1981), p.129
122. Derek Hurst, Worcestershire Archaeological Service, pers.comm., February, 2000
123. Mawer *et al*, p.285
124. Hooke (1981), p.127
125. Hooke (1981), pp.133-4
126. *Ibid.*, p.140; Sawyer, no.190, pp.119-20; Whitelock, no.85, p.478
127. Hamer, F.E. *op cit*, no.XII, p.54; Hooke (1981), p.140, see also Sawyer, no.218, pp.125-6; Finberg (1972), no.83, pp.49-50
128. Hart, C.R. *The Early Charters of Northern England and the North Midlands*, Leicester University Press, 1975, p.102, no.99
129. Bridges, Tim, *Churches of Worcestershire*, Logaston Press, 2000, p.233
130. Barker, P.A. & Cubberley, A.L. 'Two burials under the refectory of

Worcester Cathedral' in *Medieval Archaeology*, Vol.XVIII, 1974, p.146
131. *Ibid.*, pp.146, 149. Elisabeth Crowfoot's analysis of spun gold thread
132. Chris Guy, pers.comm.
133. Radford, C.A. Raleigh, in Barker & Cubberley, *op.cit.*, p.150
134. Webb, J.F. (trans.) *Lives of the Saints* incl. 'Eddius Stephanus:Life of Wilfrid', Penguin, 1965, ch.17, p.150
135. Baker, Nigel, 'Churches, Parishes & Early Medieval Topography' in *TWAS*, 3rd Series, Vol.7 *Medieval Worcester* edition, p.33; Martin Carver, 'Catalogue of archaeological data relating to Worcester city' in same volume, cat.no.12/1, p.298
136. Dalwood, Hal, Worcestershire Archaeology Service, pers.comm.
137. Farmer, p.188
138. Baker, Nigel, *op.cit.*, p.33 who refers to J. Magilton, 'Excavations of Ebor Brewery, York' in *The Archaeology of York*, York Archaeological Trust; W. Rodwell, *Historic Churches—a wasting asset*, CBA Research Report, no.19, 1977
139. Bridges, *op.cit.*, p.233
140. Dark Age Dict., p.99; Ang. Sax. Ency., p.134
141. Bradley, pp.164, 217
142. *Ibid.*, p.218
143. *Ibid.*, p.165
144. *Ibid.*, Verse XII, p.190
145. Baker, *op.cit.*, p.34 referring to Buchanan-Dunlop, 1939, p.14
146. Hooke (1985), p.110
147. Baker, *op.cit.*, p.34
148. Bassett, S. quoted in Baker, N., Dalwood, H., Holt, R., Mundy, C., Taylor, G. 'From Roman to medieval Worcester: development and planning in the Anglo-Saxon city' in *Antiquity*, Vol.66, No.250, March 1992, p.72
149. Baker, *op.cit.*, p.116. Synod translated and discussed in Atkins, 1940; part II, *TWAS* pp.204-207; on St. Helen's 960 date *ibid.*,p.205 & Buchanan-Dunlop, 1939, p.15
150. Baker, Dalwood, Holt, Mundy & Taylor *op.cit.*, p.72. Reference is made to Darlington, R.R. (ed.) *The Vita Wulfstani of William of Malmesbury*, London: Camden, 3rd Series 40, 1928
151. Finberg (1972), no.207, p.90. Reference is made to W.D. Macray (ed.) *Chronicon Abbatiae de Evesham*, Rolls series, 29, 1863, p.73
152. Baker, Dalwood, Holt, Mundy & Taylor, *op.cit.*, p.72. Reference is made to Clarke, H.B. & C.C. Dyer 'Anglo-Saxon and Early Norman Worcester: The Documentary Evidence' in *TWAS*, 3rd Series, Vol.2, 1968-9, pp.27-33
153. Carver, Martin 'Catalogue of archaeological data relating to Worcester city' in *TWAS*, 3rd Series, Vol.7, 1980, p.308, cat.no.61/11. Reference is made to the *Victoria County History, Worcestershire*, Vol.II, p.250
154. Carver, Martin, 'The Sites and Settlements at Worcester' in *TWAS*, 3rd Series, Vol.7, 1980, p.19. Reference is made to Richardson 'Iron Smelting by the Romans in Worcester' (part 2), *TWNC*, 11.2, 1956-7, p.96
155. Ekwall, p.534
156. Dalwood, Hal, pers.comm., Feb.2000
157. see Dalwood, C.H., Buteux, V.A. and Dallington, J., 'Excavations at Farrier Street and Other Sites North of the City Wall, Worcester 1988-1992',*TWAS*, third series, Vol,14, 1994, pp.82, 84
158. see Dalwood, C.H., Buteux, V.A. and Jackson, R.A., 'Interim Report on Excavations at Deansway, Worcester, 1988-1989', *TWAS*, third series, Vol.13, 1992, p.124
159. Bede, IV.23, p.248
160. Green, Bertram, *Bishops and Deans of Worcester*, *c*.1960, p.5
161. Sims-Williams, p.88
162. Bede, IV.23, p.247
163. Green, Bertram, *op.cit.*, p5
164. Farmer, p.127
165. Green, Bertram, *op.cit.*, p.5
166. Farmer, p.127
167. Sims-Williams, p.144
168. *Ibid.*, pp.147-8 (containing quotation from Bede)
169. *Ibid.*, p148; Whitelock, no.67, pp.453-4; for the theory on the Anglo-Saxon minster at Kidderminster on or near present parish church of St. Mary's see P.W. King, 'The Minster *Aet Stur* in Husmere and the Northern Boundary of the Hwicce', *TWAS*, 3rd Series, Vol.15, 1996
170. Whitelock, no.67, p.453
171. Sims-Williams, pp.328-9
172. *Ibid.*, p.151. On Acton Beauchamp being held by a Worcestershire religious house reference made to F.T.S. Houghton, 'Salt-Ways',

Transactions of the Birmingham Archaeological Society, 54, (1929-30), pp.1-2; *Worcestershire*, 3rd ed., rev. M. Moore, The Little Guides (London, 1952)
173. Sims-Williams, p.152
174. Taylor & Taylor, p.63
175. *Ibid.*, Vol.1, p.65 (& fig.30 for tentative reconstruction of the east wall of the nave
176. Sims-Williams, p.152
177. McKitterick, Rosamond, *Anglo-Saxon Missionaries in Germany*, Vaughan Paper no.36: University of Leicester, Eighth Brixworth Lecture,1990, pp.23,27
178. Sims-Williams, pp.332, 345, 346, 347
179. *Ibid.*, p.359
180. Dark Age Dict., p.235
181. Fletcher, p.142
182. Whitelock, no.99, p.498
183. *Ibid.*, no.94, p.490
184. *Ibid.*, introductory notes
185. Fletcher, p.142
186. This section (which incorporates ref.187) is a summary of discussions with Mr. Christopher Guy, Cathedral Archaeologist at Worcester and Dr. Sally Crawford of the University of Birmingham, who were co-directors of the excavations
187. Barker, P. & Guy, C. 'Archaealogy at Worcester Cathedral', *Report of the Seventh Annual Symposium*, 1997, p.5
188. Green, Bertram, *op.cit.*, p.7
189. Wilson, Margaret, 'The Hwicce', *TWAS*, 3rd Series, Vol.2, 1968-9, p.24 who refers to Hearne, T. (ed.) *Hemingi Chartularium Ecclesiae Wigorniensis*, Oxford, 1723
190. Barrow, Julia, 'The Community of Worcester, 961-*c*.1160' in Brooks & Cubitt, pp.91, 98. Reference is made to Hearne, T., *ibid.*, pp.232-3 & also Sawyer, no.1308, p.337 concerning St. Peter's holding episcopal throne

Chapter 7

1. Bede, V.23, p.331
2. Kirby, p.130
3. William, p.72
4. Ashley, p.254
5. Bede, IV.12, p.226
6. Yorke, p.30 following Bede *Ibid*
7. Dutton, Leonard, *The Anglo-Saxon Kingdoms — The Power Struggles from Hengist to Ecgberht*, SPA, 1993, p.203
8. Yorke, p.30
9. Ashley, p.235-6
10. Kirby, pp.122-3
11. Bede, IV.26, p.259; Stenton, p.62; Yorke, p.30; Sawyer, no.17, p.75
12. Kirby, pp.123-4
13. Bede, IV.21, p.243; Henry, p.62
14. Stenton, p.85
15. Stenton, p.68-9
16. Stenton, p.143; Eddius, ch.45, p.178; Bede, IV.23, p.248
17. Kirby, p.127
18. Stenton, p.144; Eddius ch.47, pp.179-80, chs.64-66, pp.201-4
19. Finberg, H.P.R., 'The Princes of the Hwicce', in Finberg (1972), pp.176-7; Kirby, p.127
20. Bede, V.24, p.335; Henry, p.117
21. Ashley, p.255
22. Ang. Sax. Ency. pp.144-145
23. Yorke, p.110. On saints' cults see Thacker, A. 'Kings, saints and monasteries in pre-Viking Mercia' in *Midland History*, 10, pp.1-25
24. William, p.72
25. Bede, V.13, p.295
26. Stenton, p.203, note p.214
27. Sawyer, nos.78-80, p.91
28. *Ibid*, no,1786, p.471
29. *Ibid*.no.1801, p.473, Finberg, no.405, p.139
30. Rev. J. Woods, his thesis & pers.comm. June 2001
31. Whitelock, no.62, p.449, no.61, p.448; Sawyer, no.65, p.87
32. Bede, V.19, p.305; Yorke, p.111
33. Bede, V.19, p.305
34. Henry, p.118
35. William, p.75

36. Ashley, p.255; Whitelock, no.177, p.755
37. Kirby, p.128; Henry, p.119 and notes
38. Sawyer, no.54, p.84
39. *Ibid*, no.65, p.87
40. *Ibid*, no.1800, p.473
41. Rev. J. Woods, his thesis & pers.comm. June 2001
42. Whitelock, no.177, p.755
43. Ashley, p.255; Yorke, pp.111-2
44. Ashley, p.255; Yorke, pp.111, 119
45. Florence, p.37
46. Henry, p.119
47. Stenton, p.205; Bede, V.23, p.331; Whitelock, no.67, pp.453, 454, notes on p.453 to no.67
48. ASC in Whitelock, p.159; Henry, p.120; Kirby, p.131
49. Kirby, p.131
50. Dark Age Dict., p.20; Kirby, pp.131, 133; ASC in Whitelock, p.159; Stenton p.204; Henry, p.123
51. ASC in Whitelock, p.161; Henry, p.128
52. Henry, pp.128-9
53. Sawyer, nos.1410 & 1679; Finberg, H.P.R., *The Early Charters of Wessex*, Leics. Univ. Press, 1964, no.384, p.116, no.634, p.179; Whitelock, no.79, pp.468-9 and notes
54. Henry, pp.129-31
55. Florence, p.42
56. Yorke, p.140; Ashley, p.311; Stenton, p.204, Finberg, *Wessex Charters*, *op.cit.*, no.189, pp.70-1; Kirby, p.134
57. Yorke, p.113
58. Stenton, p.204
59. Ashley, p.256
60. Sawyer, no.88, p.93
61. *Ibid*, nos.86-7, p.93
62. *Ibid*, no.91, pp.94-5
63. Whitelock, no.66, p.451, ref. to this grant made in preliminary notes
64. Kirby, pp.131-2
65. Sawyer, no.90, pp.94-5
66. Kirby, p.150; Whitelock, no.5, p.259; Henry, p.128; Stenton, p.92
67. Kirby, pp.129, 131-2
68. *Ibid*, p.134
69. Sawyer, nos.83-103, pp.92-7
70. Stenton, p.205
71. William, p.74; Whitelock, no.177, pp.751-6 & notes
72. William, p.74; Whitelock no.177, pp.752-4
73. Whitelock no,177, pp.754-5
74. Kirby, p.136
75. Metcalfe, D.M. in *Mercian Studies*, 1977, p.88; Yorke, p.115; Ashley, p.256
76. Metcalf, D.M. in *Mercian Studies*, 1977, pp.87, 90, 91; Kirby, p.136
77. Stenton, p.205, Henry, p.131
78. Yorke, p.112
79. William, p.77
80. Henry, p.133
81. Nennius, sect.60, p.78; Yorke, p.112
82. Sims-Williams, pp.152-3, note 52; Bassett, in Bassett, p.241, note 35; Scharer advances the theory of Offa's power base being in the *Hwiccian* kingdom in *Die Angelsächsische Königsurkunde*
83. Fox, Cyril *Offa's Dyke*, British Academy, 1955, p.289 and note 4; Scharer referred to in note 52 in Sims-Williams, p.153
84. Yorke, p.112; Whitelock, no.77. p.466; Kirby, p.163
85. Yorke, p.112; Florence, p.43; 'Continuation' of Bede, in Whitelock, no.5, p.260; Scharer, *op.cit.*, p.215, referred to in Kirby, p.163, & note 4, p.180; ASC in Whitelock, p.163
86. Matthew, p.363
87. Matthew, p.366
88. Stenton, p.206, & note 1
89. Stenton p.206; Yorke, p.31
90. Sawyer, no.33, pp.79-80; Kirby, p.165
91. Stenton, p.206; Kirby, p.165; Sawyer, no.105, p.98
92. Kirby, p.165
93. Sawyer, no.34, p.80
94. *Ibid*, no.110 & 111, p.99
95. Brooks (1984), pp.319-20
96. Brooks (1984), p.319
97. ASC in Whitelock, p.165; Henry, pp.134-5
98. Stenton, p.207; Kirby, pp.165-6
99. Kirby, p.166; Ashley, p.224; Stenton, p.207
100. Kirby, p.167
101. Sawyer, no.123, p.102
102. *Ibid*., no.125, p.103
103. *Ibid*., no.128, p.104
104. *Ibid*., no.140, p.107
105. *Ibid*., no,127, pp.103-4
106. *Ibid*., nos.129-131, p.104
107. *Ibid*., no.132, pp.104-5
108. *Ibid*., no.123, p.102
109. *Ibid*., no.1614, p.445
110. *Ibid*., no.134, p.105
111. *Ibid*., no.96, p.96; Stenton, p.204
112. ASC in Whitelock, p.165
113. Finberg (1964), no.192, p.71 and also p.218; Sawyer, no.104, p.98
114. Sawyer, no.145, p.108; Finberg (1964), p.23, & no.193, p.71
115. Sawyer, no.1692, p.459; Finberg (1964), no.397, p.118
116. Finberg (1964), no.195, pp.71-2, also pp.218, 236; Sawyer, no.229, p.128
117. Finberg (1964), no.196, p.72; for doubts see notes/comments in Sawyer, no.149, p.109
118. Finberg (1964), no.338, p.116
119. Sawyer, nos.260-4, pp.136-7, no.1256, p.365, nos.1681-90, pp.458-9; Whitelock, p.23
120. Stenton, p.209
121. Whitelock, p.23; Florence, p.45
122. Stenton, p.209; William, pp.94-5
123. Dr. K. Ray, pers.comm. June 2001
124. Stenton, p.204
125. Sawyer, no.106, p.98
126. *Ibid*., no.119, p.102
127. *Ibid*., no.132, pp.104-5
128. *Ibid*., no.144, p.108
129. Stenton, p.210
130. *Ibid*., p.208
131. Kirby, p.167; Sawyer, no.49, p.83
132. Sawyer, no.46, pp.82-3
133. *Ibid*., no.108, pp.98-9
134. *Ibid*., no.133, p.105
135. Kirby, p.167; Sawyer no.1178, p.347
136. Sawyer no.1183, p.348
137. *Ibid*., no.1184. p.348
138. Stenton, p.208
139. Simeon of Durham, in Whitelock, p.243
140. Kirby, pp.167-8, note 34 p.181; Stenton, p.208, note 6; concerning Aldwulf, Sawyer, no.50, p.83, no.1178, p.347, no.1183, p.348; re: Bexhill lease, Sawyer no,108, pp.98-9
141. Kirby, p.166
142. Brooks (1996), pp.7, 12, 13
143. Brooks (1996), p.13
144. *Ibid*., p.18
145. Matthew, p.374
146. Brooks (1996), p.21; Farmer, p.137
147. Brooks (1996), p.17. (In footnote: Friar, S. *A Companion to the English Parish Church*, Bramley Books, p.341)
148. Wood, p.98
149. Brooks (1996), p.22
150. Stenton, p.212
151. Ashley, p.291; Dark Age Dict., p.26
152. Sawyer, nos.104-147, pp.98-108
153. Whitelock, no.204, p.792
154. Brooks (1984), p.117
155. Stenton, p.215-6; Brooks (1984), p.118; Whitelock, no.191, p.770
156. William, p.78
157. Stenton, pp.218-9; Matthew, p.371
158. Whitelock, no.80, p.471
159. *Ibid*., no.79, p.469
160. *Ibid*., pp.469-70
161. Brooks (1984), p.129
162. William, p.78. An extensive account of Offa's finding of the sepulchre of St. Alban and his involvement with the establishment of the monastery of St. Alban's can be found in Matthew of Westminster's *The Flowers of History* (see bibliography) pp.375-80. It is a very favourable account concerning Offa

163. Whitelock, no.195, p.779
164. Stenton, p.219; Matthew, p.368
165. Kirby, p.175 although in his ref.83 Kirby does point out that as far as
Alcuin in 790 was concerned, the two kings had been 'former friends'
and no estrangment is hinted at
166. Whitelock, no.192, p.775
167. Stenton, p.221
168. *Ibid.*
169. Loyn, pp.83-5; Clarke and Ambrosiani, pp.16-18
170. Loyn, p.84
171. Stenton, p.221
172. Whitelock, no.197, p.781
173. Loyn, p85
174. *Ibid.*, p.86; Hinton, David A., *Southampton Finds Volume Two — The
Gold, Silver and other non-ferrous alloy objects from Hamwic*,
Southampton Archaeology Monographs, 6, Alan Sutton/Southampton
City Council, 1996, p.101
175. Loyn, p.86
176. Whitelock, no.197, p.782
177. Stenton, p.223
178. Whitelock, no.197, p.781
179. Whitelock, no.198, p.782
180. Wood, pp.102-3
181. Matthew, p.383
182. Stenton, p.219

Chapter 8 Offa's Dyke

1. Stanford (1991), p.43
2. Stanford 'Native and Roman in the Central Welsh Borderland' in *Roman
Frontier Studies*, ed. Eric Birley, Brian Dobson and Michael Jarrett,
1974, p.44
3. *Ibid.*, p.44
4. *Ibid.*, p.41
5. Thomas, Ruth, *South Wales*, 1977, p.16
6. *Archaeology of Montgomeryshire*, 1990, p.68
7. Stanford (1991), p.110
8. Laing, Lloyd and Jenny, *The Picts and the Scots*, Sutton, 1993, p.15
9. Rowley, Trevor., *The Landscape of the Welsh Marches*, 1986, p.67
10. Cummins, W.A., *The Age of the Picts*, Sutton, 1995, p.72
11. Davies, Wendy, *Wales in the Early Middle Ages*, Leicester University Press,
1982, p.91
12. *Ibid.*, pp.76-78
13. Millward Roy and Robinson, Adrian, *The Welsh Borders*, 1978, p.87
14. Rowley, *op.cit*, p.67
15. White & Baker, pp.50
16. Fox, Offa's Dyke, 1955, p.285
17. Lecture given by David Hill, 13/3/97
18. Hannaford, *Transactions of the Shropshire Arch. and Historical Soc.
Vol.LXXIII*, 1998, p.6
19. Sylvester, Dorothy, *The Rural Landscape of the Welsh Borderland*, 1969,
p.93
20. White & Baker, pp.134-5
21. Stanford (1991), p.82
22. Alcock, Leslie, *Dinas Powys*, 1963, p.vii
23. Davies, *op.cit*, p.91
24. Davies, Wendy, *Early Welsh Microcosm*, 1978, pp.92-5
25. *Ibid.*, p.97
26. Davies, Wendy, *Wales in the Early Middle Ages*, 1982, p.103
27. Stanford (1991), p.101
28. Walters, Brian, *The Archaeology of Ancient Dean and the Wye Valley*,
Thornhill Press, 1992, p.125
29. Gelling (1992), pp.116
30. Davies, *op.cit*, pp.103, 113
31. Asser, p.71
32. Allen, David, 'Excavations on Offa's Dyke at Ffrydd Rd., Knighton, Powys
1976', *TRS*, 1988
33. Hill, David, *An Atlas of Ango-Saxon England*, Blackwell, 1981, p.75
34. Fox, *op.cit*, p.170
35. Gelling (1992), p.105
36. Hill, David, 'The Construction of Offa's Dyke', *Antiquaries Journal*
(1985b), p.141
37. Worthington, p.181
38. Hill, David, 'A Frontier in Flames' in *The Gale of Life*, Logaston Press,
2000, p.72

39. John of Salisbury (ed.) C.J. Nederman, *Policraticus*, p.114
40. Worthington, *Bulletin of the John Rylands University Library of
Manchester Vol.79*, no.3, autumn 1998p.179
41. *Tywysogion*, p.xxix
42. Leland, *v.*13
43. *Archaeologia*, 1842, Plate II between pp.16 & 17
44. Gelling & Noble, *British Arch. Report*, 1983, p.16
45. Gelling (1992) p.118
46. Shoesmith, Ron, *The Civil War in Hereford*, Logaston Press, 1995, p.39
47. Stenton, p.565
48. Shoesmith (1982), p.69
49. Fox, *op.cit*, plate XXIX
50. Taylor, Mark P. & John Lewin, 'River Behaviour and Holocene Alluviation:
The River Severn at Welshpool, Mid-Wales' in *Earth Surafce
Processes and Landforms*, Vol.21, 1996
51. Hill, David, 'Offa's and Wat's Dykes - Some Explanatory Work on the
Frontier Between Celt and Saxon' from Rowley, T. *Anglo-Saxon
Settlement and Landscape*, BAR, 1974, p.104
52. Letter from Don Butler 22/3/97
53. Worthington, *op.cit*, p.186
54. *Ibid.*, pp.188-9
55. Stanford (1991) p.120
56. Fox, pp.160-2
57. *Ibid.* p.164
58. Remfry, Paul, *Radnor Castle 1066 to 1282 A Short Guide*, 1995, p.8
59. Young, Susan M., John Clark & Terry Barry, *Medieval Archaeology*, 30,
1986, p.152
60. Lewis, Beryl, 'Boundary Landscapes' MS, p.172
61. Fox, *op.cit*, p.122
62. *Ibid.*, p.263
63. David Hill lecture, 8/5/98
64. Hill, David, 'A Frontier in Flames' in *The Gale of Life*, Logaston Press,
2000
65. Hill, David, 'Offa versus the Welsh' in *British Archaeology*, 2000, p.20-1
66. Hill, David, 'A Frontier in Flames' in *The Gale of Life*, Logaston Press,
2000, p.72
67. Hooke, Della, *The Anglo-Saxon Chareters of Worcestershire*, 1990, p.174
68. *VCH History of Wiltshire* Vol.1, pt 2, p.478
69. Higham, 1993, pp.87, 88
70. *Ibid.*, pp.142-4
71. Maxfield, V., 'Mainland Europe' in *The Roman World*, John Wacher (ed.),
Routledge and Keegan; *Historia Augusta, vita Hadriana*, p.157
72. Williams, D., *The Reach of Rome*, Constable, 1996, p.83
73. Schultz, H., *The Romans in Central Europe*, 1985, p.31
74. Maxfield, V., 'Mainland Europe' in *The Roman World*, John Wacher (ed.),
1987, p.157
75. Williams, D., *op.cit*, pp.96-7
76. *Ibid.*, pp.103-6
77. *Ibid.*, pp. 254, 256
78. *Ibid.*, pp.273-4
79. Collins, Roger, *Charlemagne*, Macmillan, 1998, pp.127-8
80. Hill, David, *op.cit*, pp.67-9
81. Fox, *op.cit*, p.279
82. Gelling & Noble, *op.cit*, pp.48-9
83. Fox, *op.cit*, p.67
84. *Ibid.*, pp.80, 153
85. *Ibid.*, p.160
86. Gelling (1992), p.105
87. Fox, *op.cit*, p.80
88. Webster, Leslie E. & John Cherry, *Medieval Archaeology Vol.XXI*, 1977,
pp.219-21
89. Fox, *op.cit*, pp.80-1, 121
90. Hill, David, *An Atlas of Ango-Saxon England*, 1981, p.75
91. Hill, David, 'A Frontier in Flames', *op.cit*, p.72
92. *Ibid.*, p.72
93. Young, Susan M., John Clark & Terry Barry, *Medieval Archaeology*, 30,
1986, p.151
94. *The Archaeology of Montgomeryshire*, 1990, pp.72-3
95. Davies, *Wales in the Early Middle Ages, op.cit.*, p.57
96. Gelling (1992), p.104
97. *Ibid.*, pp.106, 108-110
98. Musson, C.A. & Spurgeon T.J., 'Cwrt Llechrhyd, Llanelwedd; an unusual
moated site in Central Wales' in *Med. Arch.*, 1988, p.107
99. *Anglo-Saxon Chronicle, The Parker Chronicle*, 894 [893], p.87

100. Hoyle, John. 'Offa's Dyke Management Survey' in *Glevensis* 29, 1996, p.30
101. *Ibid.*, p.30
102. Fox, *op.cit*, pp.216-7
103. Gelling & Noble, *op.cit*, p.6
104. Fox, *op.cit*, p.207
105. Young, Susan M., John Clark & Terry Barry, *Medieval Archaeology*, Vol. XXV, 1981, pp.168-9
106. Webster, Leslie E. & John Cherry, *Medieval Archaeology*, 21, 1976, p.219
107. Gelling (1992), pp.16-7
108. Lewis, Beryl, 'Boundary Landscapes', MS, p.172
109. *Twysogion*, p.7
110. *Ibid.*
111. Gelling (1992), p.126
112. *Anglo-Saxon Chronicle, Parker Chronicle*, 922, pp.103-4
113. Crawford, O.G.S., *Archaeology in the Field*, Phoenix House, 1953, makes a similar suggestion, of which the author only became aware in 2002

Chapter 9
1. Clarke & Ambrosiani, p.9
2. *Ibid.*
3. Martin Carver *Underneath English Towns*, London, 1987, p.46 quoted in *Ibid.*, p.11
4. Aston & Bond, pp.58-9
5. Scull, pp.272-3; the statistic comes from Biddle & Dyer
6. Stafford, p.43
7. *Ibid.*, pp.42-3
8. Scull, pp.274, 276, 280
9. Clarke and Ambrosiani, p.15
10. Cowie & Harding, p.198
11. *Ibid.*, p.197
12. Schofield, p.12; Cowie & Harding, p.183, reference is made to Biddle 1989 re: *Paulesbyri*
13. Schofield, p.12
14. Blackmore *et al.*, p.62
15. Bede, II.3, p.104
16. Cowie & Harding, p.182
17. Clarke & Ambrosiani, p.15
18. Cowie & Harding, p.182, who refer to Cowie & Whytehead, 1989; Vince, 1990, fig.43
19. *Ibid.*, pp.182-3, on the extent of *Lundenwic* reference is made to Cowie, 1988; Cowie & Whytehead, 1989; Mills, 1991
20. *Ibid.*, p.182
21. John Clark, Curator (Medieval), Museum of London, pers. comm., Dec. 2000
22. Cowie & Harding, p.182
23. *Ibid.*, p.184, ref. made to Cowie 1992; Tyres *et. al* on waterfront
24. *Ibid.*, reference is made to PWB88, & McCann & Orton 1989 for Roman road located in excavations at Ludgate Hill; Margary, 1955, p.51
25. *Ibid.*, reference to Vince, 1990, p.124, on possible gridded street pattern
26. Clarke & Ambrosiani, pp.13-4
27. Cowie & Harding, p.185
28. John Clark, pers. comm. Dec. 2000
29. Cowie & Harding, p.185
30. ASC in Whitelock, p.166
31. Denison, Simon, 'Waterfront "used at the Synod of Chelsea"' in *British Archaeology*, no.27, Sept.1997, p.5
32. Whitelock, no.73, p.461
33. Cubitt, p.308 acknowledging etymology from Ekwall, p.99; Gelling (1970), p.203; Gelling (1984), p.78
34. Cowie & Harding, p.188
35. *Ibid.*, p.189
36. *Ibid.*, pp.189-90, 198
37. *Ibid.*, p.189, on *liber nigra* evidence reference is made to John Blair 1991; on theory of early minster at Westminster, reference to Rosser, 1989
38. *Ibid.*, p.188, on date of foundation of monastery at Barking reference to John Blair 1991
39. Schofield, p.12
40. Cowie & Harding, p.185, on dimension of *Ludenwic*'s buildings reference made to Blackmore *et al.*; at *Hamwic*, Morton,1992 & Andrews, 1997; York (*Eorfwic*) Kemp, 1996
41. Blackmore *et al.*, p.62
42. Cowie & Harding, p.186
43. Blackmore *et al.* p.62

44. Cowie & Harding, p.188
45. *Ibid.*
46. *Ibid.*, p.187
47. Vince, p.112
48. Cowie & Harding, p.187—who refer to Pagan, 1986; Stewart, 1986; Vince, 1990
49. *Ibid.*, p.188
50. *Ibid.*, p.183
51. John Clark, pers. comm. Dec. 2000
52. Vince, pp.17-19
53. Cowie & Harding, pp.190, 198
54. *Ibid.*, pp.191, 192, 194—on usual identification of *Suthringa geweorche* with Southwark reference made to Sheldon, 1978; Vince 1990
55. *Ibid.*, p.191
56. ASC in Whitelock, p.183
57. John Clark, pers. comm. Dec. 2000
58. Cowie & Harding, p.192
59. *Ibid.*, p.191. On site of Alfredian *burh* they refer to Milne & Goodburn, 1990, p.631
60. Whitelock, no.92, p.487
61. John Clark, pers. comm. Dec. 2000
62. Whitelock, no.92, pp.487-8
63. *Ibid.*, note 7, p.487 & note 1, p.488
64. *Ibid.*, p.488
65. Translation found in Jones, A.E.E., *Anglo-Saxon Worcester*, 1958, p.92; also noted in Sawyer, no.346, p.156
66. Vince, pp.20-2. Vince acknowledges the work of T. Dyson, esp. 'Two Saxon land grants at Queenhithe' in Bird, J., Chapman, H. and Clark J. (eds.) *Collectanea Londiniensis: studies ... presented to R. Merrifield* LAMAS Special Paper 2, 1978, pp.200-15; Schofield, p.13
67. Vince, *ibid.* on detail on refs, see above
68. Cowie & Harding, p.193, reference made to Brigham 1990a p.142 concerning the deliberate removal of the Roman quay at Billingsgate
69. *Ibid.*, ref. made to Ayre & Wroe-Brown 1996, pp.19-20 re. Bull Wharf
70. *Ibid.*, ref. made to Steedman *et al.*,1992, p.134
71. Schofield, p.13
72. Cowie & Harding, p.194, ref. made to Vince 1990, pp.33-4; Marsden 1994
73. Schofield, p.13
74. Williams, p.134
75. A. Chapman, pers. comm. Dec. 2000; Northampton (1), p.37; RCHM (V), p.40
76. A. Chapman, pers. comm. Dec. 2000; Northampton (1), p.37 referring to RCHM and Hawkes & Dunning, 1961, on coins and buckles
77. Williams, p.134; Northampton (1), p.38; RCHM(V), pp.40 & 41
78. Chapman, pp.94-5;
79. A. Chapman, pers. comm. March 2000
80. Northampton (1), pp.9, 38
81. *Ibid.*, pp.9, 30, 39; RCHM(V), p.41
82. Northampton (1), p.30
83. *Ibid.*, pp.31, 39; RCHM(V), p.41; Taylor & Taylor, p.359
84. Asser, p.101
85. Northampton (1), p.31
86. Hodges, p.131
87. Northampton (1), pp.31, 35. (Cowdery's Down is covered by Millett & James, 1983; Cheddar by Rahtz, 1979)
88. Hodges, p.131
89. *Ibid.*, p.132; Bradley, p.402
90. Northampton (2), p.408
91. Northampton (1), pp.21, 39, 40
92. *Ibid.*, pp.39-40 quoting Gover, Mawer & Stenton, 1933, xvii-xviii
93. Northampton (1), p.43
94. Williams, John H. *Saxon and Medieval Northampton*, 1982, pp.25 & 27
95. A. Chapman, pers. comm. Dec. 2000
96. Northampton (1), Table 1, p.37
97. *Ibid.*; Hodges, p.132
98. ASC in Whitelock, pp.194 & 197; RCHM(V), pp.43, 46, 47; Williams, p.131
99. Bassett, Steven, 'The administrative landscape of the diocese of Worcester in the tenth century' in Brooks & Cubitt, p.156. Brooks notes that the setting up of a burghal system in Mercia in the late 8th century was first noted by Haslam in J. Haslam, 'market and Fortress in England in the reign of Offa', *World Archaeology*, 19, (1987), pp.76-93, and in pp.79 & 89 suggests Mercia was first shired in the late 8th century
100. Clarke & Ambrosiani, p.37

101. Rahtz, p.111
102. *Ibid.*; Shoesmith (1982), p.30
103. Rahtz, p.111; Shoesmith (1982), p.31
104. Shoesmith (1982), pp.31, 34, 76, 77, 92
105. Biddle (1976), pp.120-122, who acknowledges the use of the phrase 'sub-rectangular' rather than rectilinear to describe the 'characteristic slightly irregular layout' of planned Anglo-Saxon towns to Prof. M.R.G. Conzen
106. *Ibid.*, pp.121-2
107. Shoesmith (1982), Table 10 p.74
108. Aston & Bond, pp.64-5
109. Biddle (1976), p.134
110. *Ibid.*, pp.125, 126, 133. On *burghal* towns after Biddle and Hill, 'Late Saxon Planned Towns' in *Antiq. Journal*, li, 1971, pp.70-85. On layout of *burghal* forts Biddle expresses caution here as only Porchester has been excavated on any appreciable scale and he states 'work in the other forts may yet reveal elements of deliberate military planning', p.148, n.208
111. *Ibid.*, p.129.
112. Aston & Bond, p.69
113. *Ibid.*
114. Biddle (1976), p.130. Reference is made to Biddle & Hill, *op.cit.*, p.76, figs.2-4
115. Biddle (1975), p.29 & Biddle (1976), p.125
116. Stafford, pp.109-111
117. Ashley, pp.262-3
118. Stafford, pp.110-2
119. *Ibid.*, p.112
120. *ASC* in Whitelock, p.188 & note 6
121. Gelling (1992), pp.135, 204 and chapter 8 note 1; *Mercian Register* in Whitelock, p.193-4
122. Gelling (1992) p.135
123. *Mercian Register* in Whitelock, p.194; Florence, p.90
124. Whitelock, p.194
125. Higham, N.J. *The Origins of Chester*, Manchester University Press, 1993, p.111. Reference to archaeological work in W.J. Varley, 'Excavations of the Castle Ditch, Eddisbury, 1935-38' in *Trans. of the Historical Society of Lancashire and Cheshire*, 1950, 102, pp.1-68
126. Ekwall, p.499
127. Gelling (1992), pp.156, 158, who on Warwickshire's population size in Domesday quotes Darby and Terret 1954; Dyer, 1985, pp.96, 102
128. Whitelock, p.195; Florence, p.92; Stenton, p.536
129. Stanford, S. *The Archaeology of the Welsh Marches*, 1991, p.131
130. Ekwall, p.105
131. Higham, N.J. *Chester op.cit.*, p.111, who refers to Thacker, 1985, and his own work, 1988 on 'The Cheshire *Burhs* and the Mercian Frontier to 924' in *Trans. Antiq. Soc. of Lancs. & Cheshire*, Vol.85, pp.193-221
132. Ashley, p.263
133. Higham, N.J. *Chester op.cit.*, p.113; *ASC* in Whitelock, p.198
134. Higham, N.J. *Chester op.cit.*, p.113
135. *ASC* in Whitelock, p.199
136. Barnatt, John & Smith, Ken, *Peak District*, English Heritage, 1997, p.56
137. Ashley, p.472
138. Moffett, p.55
139. *Mercian Register* in Whitelock, p.194
140. Gelling (1992), p.153
141. Carver (1981); Cane *et al.*, p.51
142. Moffett, p.55; Carver (1981)
143. Moffett, p.55; David Wilkinson, Borough Archaeologist,Stafford Borough Council, pers. comm. Dec. 2000
144. Carver (1981)
145. Cane *et al.*, pp.51 & 57
146. *Ibid.*, p.61
147. Gelling (1992), p.153, quoting Martin Carver's theory as expressed in a lecture of Dec. 1984
148. Moffett, pp.56, 62, 63
149. David Wilkinson, *op.cit.* & Pers.comm., Dec.2000
150. Carver (1981) incl. figs. 8, 24 & 25; McCarthy, M.R & Brooks, C.M., *Medieval Pottery in Britain AD 900-1600*, Leicester University Press, 1988, pp.67, 204-5
151. Cane *et al* , p.51; Carver (1981); Gelling (1992), p.153 who quotes Darby & Terrett, 1954, on poulation size
152. Rahtz & Meeson, p.5

153. *Ibid.*, p.1; Bob Meeson, pers. comm. Dec. 2000 who refers to his article 'An early thoroughfare crossing Staffordshire and Shropshire?', *West Midlands Archaeological News Sheet*, 19, (1976), pp.8-9
154. Meeson, p.96; Rahtz & Meeson, p.1
155. Gelling (1992), p.146
156. Stenton's translation quoted in Gelling, p.147
157. Meeson, 97; Gelling (1992), p.147 discussing James Campbell's work on the words *tun* and *vicus*; Rahtz & Meeson, p.1
158. Meeson, p.97
159. Rahtz & Meeson, p.1
160. Whitelock no.92, pp.487-8
161. Gelling (1992), pp.147-8; Gelling (1984), p.326
162. Rahtz & Meeson, Table 1, p.2
163. *Ibid.*, p.5; Meeson, p.25, fig.10 p.32
164. *I*Rahtz & Meeson, p.5
165. Meeson, pp.22, 23, 29
166. *Ibid.*, pp.22, 29
167. *Ibid.*, p.98; Meeson, pers. comm. Dec. 2000 who refes to D.M. Palliser, *The Staffordshire Landscape*, 1976, pp.144-5, on Danish influence on street names
168. Meeson, pers. comm. Dec. 2000
169. Rahtz & Meeson, pp.xi, 158; Hinton, D.A., *Archaeology, Economy and Society - England from the fifth to the fifteenth century*, Seaby, 1993, p.44
170. Rahtz & Meeson, pp.xi, 72-3, who quote the information on lava wear from David Williams pers. comm.
171. Whitelock, No.197, p.782
172. Rahtz & Meeson, p.xi
173. Gelling (1992), p.149; Holt quoted in Rahtz & Meeson, p.156
174. Hinton, *op.cit*, p.44
175. Rahtz & Meeson, p.158
176. Meeson, p.99; Rahtz & Meeson, p.5
177. Meeson, pp.33, 98
178. Meeson, pp.20-1; Rahtz & Meeson, p.3
179. Rahtz & Meeson, pp.1, 3, 5; Gelling (1992), p.151. On low figures for Tamworth mint coins Gelling quotes Dr. D.M. Metcalfe's work
180. Gelling (1992), p.151, who refers to Gould, 1969, pp.38-41
181. Meeson, pers. comm. Dec. 2000
182. Gould referred to in Rahtz & Meeson, p.5
183. Gelling (1992), p.151; Meeson, pers. comm. Dec. 2000

Chapter 10
1. Whitelock, no.202, p.787
2. Kirby, p.173; Yorke, p.118; Ashley, p.259
3. Sawyer, nos.148-151, p.109
4. Brooks (1984), p.121; Kirby, p.178. On the minting of coins by Eadberht and Eadwald both Brooks and Kirby refer to C.E. Blunt *Coinage of Offa* pp.50, 54, 55
5. Whitelock, no.203, p.789; Brooks (1984), pp.121-2
6. Whitelock, no.3, p.249
7. Yorke, p.118; Ashley,p.259; Bassett, Steven 'In search of the origins of Anglo-Saxon kingdoms' in Bassett, note 29, pp.239-40
8. Basssett, *op.cit.* pp.6-8. For further information see S.R. Bassett 'A probable Mercian royal mausoleum at Winchcombe, Gloucestershire' in *Antiquaries Journal*, vol.1xv (1985), p.84. On Winchcombeshire see C.S. Taylor 'The Origin of the Mercian Shires' in *Gloucestershire Studies* ed. H.P.R. Finberg (1957), pp.17-45 & also H.P.R. Finberg 'The ancient shire of Winchcombe' in Finberg (1971) pp.228-35 and also Julian Whybra *A Lost English County - Winchcombeshire in the Tenth and Eleventh Centuries*, Boydell & Brewer. On the 897 Blockley charter see Sawyer, no.1442, p.405 & also Finberg (1971), no.86, p.51 who considers it authentic and states that 'King Coenwulf had enjoined that his heirs should not grant leases of his lands in the territory of Winchcombe for more than one lifetime'.
9. Bassett, *op.cit.*, p.8, fig,1.7; p.14, fig.1.8; p.15, p.17
10. *Ibid*, p.17 - Bassett refers to Stenton, pp.292-7 & James Campbell's *Bede's Reges & Principes*, Jarrow Lecture for 1979, pp.3-4
11. Whitelock, no.202, pp.787-8
12. Yorke, p.121
13. Brooks (1984), p.123; letter found in Whitelock, no.204, pp.791-3
14. Brooks (1984), p.124
15. Whitelock, no.205, p.794
16. Simeon of Durham in Whitelock, p.249 & note 4.

17. Brooks (1984), p.125
18. William, p.87
19. William, p.86
20. Yorke, p.118
21. Brooks (1984), p.125
22. Stenton,p.227; Whitelock, no.210, p.799
23. Brooks (1984), p.132
24. Kirby, pp.186-7; Sawyer, nos.164,168-170, pp.113-4; Yorke, p.118, p.121
25. Stenton, p.229 & note 5; Brooks (1984), pp.134-5; Kirby, p.187; Yorke, p.121
26. Sawyer, no.158, p.111
27. Sawyer, no.152, p.110
28. Yorke, p.167
29. Farmer, p.231
30. Kirby, p.179; see note in Finberg (1972), no.233, p.97 on peace treaty
31. Ashley, p.314; Kirby, p.185; ASC in Whitelock, p.169
32. Ashley, p.283; Simeon of Durham in Whitelock, p.250
33. Ashley, p.244; Kirby, p.179. Kirby refers to Grierson and Blackburn, *Medieval European Coinage*, Vol.I, p.293 and also Blunt, Loyn and Stewart, *The Coinage of Southern England*, pp.26, 40
34. Kirby, pp.187-8; Stenton, p.230
35. William, pp.238-9
36. W. Salt Brassington, *Historic Worcestershire - Worcestershire Historical, Biographical, Traditional, Legendary and Romantic*, Midland Educational Company, nd (late 19th century), pp.73-80; Pevsner, N., *The Buildings of England - Worcestershire*, Penguin, 1968, p.254; Sharp, Mick, *The Way and the Light - An Ilustrated Guide to the Saints and Holy Places of Britain*, Aurum Press, 2000, pp.172-3
37. Farmer, p.231
38. Stenton, p.231 and fn. 1
39. *Ibid.*, p.230; The *Annals Cambriae* in Wade Evans, p.96
40. Kirby, p.188
41. Stenton, p.230
42. Quoted in Kirby, p.188 who refers to Sawyer, no.1435, p.403
43. Whitelock, no.84, p.476; Brooks (1984), p.136
44. Stenton, p.231; Brooks (1984), p.136; Kirby, p.189
45. Kirby, p.189
46. ASC in Whitelock, p.171
47. Kirby, p.191
48. ASC in Whitelock, p.171; Stenton p.231
49. Kirby, p.191. For Evesham Abbey Kirby refers to *Chronicon Abbatia de Evesham*, ed. W.D. Macray, Rolls Series, London, 1863, pp.325-6
50. Stenton, pp.232; ASC in Whitelock, p.171
51. Kirby, pp.192-3
52. Whitelock, p.171; Stenton, p.233
53. Kirby, p.192
54. Sawyer, no.188, p.119; Kirby, p.191 referring to Barbara Yorke's article 'The Kingdom of the East' in *Anglo-Saxon England*, Vol.14, 1985, pp.1-36 when discussing Essex as a possible Mercian satellite; Stenton, p.233
55. Brooks (1984), p.137
56. Stenton, p.234-5. For the Hanbury charter see Whitelock, no.85, pp.477-9 and Brooks (1984) p.145
57. Ashley, p.261; Yorke, p.120
58. Yorke, p.119
59. Brooks (1984), p.145
60. Stenton, p.236
61. Kirby, p.195 referring to C.S. Loyn, 'Historical problems of Anglo-Saxon coinage - (2) The ninth century - Offa to Alfred', British Numismatic Journal, Vol.37 (1968), pp.216-38, p.229 and n.2 along with H.E. Pagan, *Coinage in England, 796-874*, pp.55-6 and P. Grigson and M. Blackburn, Medieval European Coinage, Vol.I, p.293; Asser, Ch.1, p.67 and note 2, p.228
62. Whitelock, no.86, p.480
63. ASC in Whitelock, p.173; Florence, pp.54-5; Kirby, p.211
64. Ashley, p.262; Farmer, p.410; Kirby, p.194; Yorke, p.120
65. Stenton, p.239
66. *Ibid.*, pp.240-1
67. *Ibid.*, pp.241-2
68. ASC in Whitelock, p.166; Whitelock, p.172, no.82, p.474, no.83, p.475, no.85, p.478; Brooks (1984), p.201; Ashley, p.315
69. ASC in Whitelock, pp.172-3; Kirby, p.211
70. Ashley, p.262; Asser, p.69

71. Kirby, p.195, on the Pillar of Eliseg testifying to Cyngen ap Cadell's military success referring to *Early Genealogical Tracts*, ed. P.C. Bartrum, Cardiff, 1966, pp.1-3; Ashley, p.262
72. Finberg (1972), no.72, p.47
73. Whitelock, no.91, p.486 & fn. 5
74. Finberg (1972), no.75, p.47
75. Whitelock, no.92, p.487-8
76. *Ibid.*, no.90, pp.485-6; Finberg (1972), no.77, p.48
77. ASC in Whitelock, p.176; Asser, ch.20, p.74
78. Stenton, p.245; Kirby, pp.199-201; Asser, ch.8 and ch.12, pp.69-70
79. Kirby, p.212; Florence, p.60; Asser, ch.27, p.76 and ch.30, p.77
80. Kirby, p.212
81. Ashley, p.245; Kirby, p.213. On coins of Aethelred and Oswald Kirby refers to Grierson and Blackburn, *Medieval European Coinage*, Vol.I, p.294
82. Florence, p.62; ASC in Whitelock, pp.177-8
83. Stenton, pp.250-1
84. Ashely, p.295; Stenton, p.251; Kirby, p.213; Yorke, pp.122-3
85. ASC in Whitelock, p.178
86. Stenton, p.252
87. ASC in Whitelock, p.179
88. Stenton, p.254
89. Stafford, p.117, 120, 121
90. Stenton, pp.505, 508; Stafford p.115
91. ASC in Whitelock, p.179; Stenton, p.255
92. Asser, ch.53, p.83
93. Stenton, p.255
94. Sawyer, nos.215-6, p.125
95. *Ibid.*, no.215, p.125; Whitelock pp.491-2 and intro. notes to p.491
96. Sawyer, no.216, p.125; Finberg (1972), no.264, pp.105-6; Whitelock, no.95, p.491 (intro. notes)
97. Ashley, p.262; Yorke, p.123
98. Kirby, p.215; Whitelock, p.32; Stenton, p.259; Ashley, p.263
99. Ashley, p.263; Finberg (1972), no.83, p.49; Sawyer, no.217, p.125; Keynes and Lapidge intro in Asser, p.37
100. Asser, pp.97-8
101. Keynes and Lapidge in Asser, pp.38, 266
102. Intro in Asser, pp.37-8
103. Yorke, Barbara, Ang. Sax Ency., p.124
104. Stenton, p.267, n.1
105. *Ibid.*, p.319
106. *Ibid.*, pp.320-1
107. Hart, C.R., *The Early Charters of Northern England and the North Midlands*, Leics. Univ. Press, 1975, no.100, pp.102-3
108. *Ibid.*, notes to no.100, p.103
109. Stenton, p.326
110. Ashley, pp.470-1; Florence, pp.88-9
111. Aethelweard the Chronicler, in Whitelock, p.193, fn.1
112. ASC in Whitelock, p.193
113. ASC in Whitelock, p.194
114. *Ibid.*
115. Henry, pp.164-5
116. Florence, p.92
117. Henry, p.167; Stenton, p.328
118. ASC in Whitelock, p.197
119. *Mercian Register* in Whitelock, p.198; Ashley, p.264

Chapter 11
1. Pauline Stafford, in *Ang. Sax. Ency.*, p.152
2. Stenton, p.292
3. Stafford, p.142; Sean Miller, in *Ang. Sax. Ency.*, p.243
4. *Ang. Sax. Ency.*, pp.243, 421
5. Asser, ch.1, p.67; Simon Keynes in *Ang. Sax. Ency*; p.421
6. *Ibid.*
7. Stenton, p.337
8. Basssett, in Brooks & Cubitt, p.155
9. see *Ibid.*, pp.155-7
10. Stenton, pp.329-30
11. *Ibid.*, p.330
12. Stafford, p.114, who refers to I. Stewart, 'The St. Martin coins of Lincoln', *B.Num.J.*, XXXVI (1967), pp.49-54; A Smyth, *Scandinavian York and Dublin, II*, New Jersey and Dublin, 1979, p.7
13. Stenton, pp.332-3
14. *Ibid.*, p.333-4

15. *Ibid.*, p.334; Simeon of Durham, in Whitelock, p.252
16. Stenton, p.334
17. *Ibid.*
18. ASC, version A, in Whitelock, p.199
19. Stenton, pp.338-9
20. William, p.131; Sean Miller in *Ang. Sax. Ency.*, p.162
21. *Ibid.*, p.130, 133
22. Wood, p.126
23. *Ibid.*, pp.129-130
24. William, p.131; Ashley, p.472
25. Wood, p.130; Ashley, p.472
26. Ahley, p.472
27. Wood, p.130
28. Ashley, p.472; Matthew, p.469
29. Wood, pp.130-1
30. Sean Miller, in *Ang. Sax. Ency.*, p.16
31. William of Malmesbury, in Whitelock, no.8, p.279
32. Wood, p.130
33. Stenton, p.356; William of Malmesbury, in Whitelock, no.8, p.279
34. Roger of Wendover, in Whitelock, p.257. Roger of Wendover names Athelstan's sister as Eadgyth who 'having preserved her chastity, remained strong in good works to the end of her life, at Polesworth...' (Roger of Wendover in Whitelock, p.257) Polesworth is about 3.5 miles south-east of Tamworth. The same story is related in Matthew of Westminster. (Matthew, p.466) In the Old English list of saints' resting places a St. Edith is mentioned as resting at Polesworth by the river Anker and, although the temptation is strong to identify Eadgyth with this saint, Gould observes that the Anglo-Saxon Chronicle does not name the sister who marries Sigtrygg or her eventual fate. Although it is known that Athelstan did have a sister called Edith, she married Otto, the future emperor of Germany, and lived on the Continent, and also lived too late to be the Edith of the saints' resting place list. Gould also notes that a nunnery under this St. Edith and others has been claimed in Tamworth by historians as far back as Leland's time, but there is actually 'not a shred of evidence' for this foundation; in fact, Gould suggests that the Edith of Polesworth is possibly the sister of the mid-9th century King Aethelwulf of Wessex who ruled between 839-58) (Gould, Jim, 'Saint Edith of Polesworth and Tamworth' in *South Staffs. Arch. & Hist. Soc. Trans.*, 1985-86, Vol.XXVII, pp.35-38
35. Stenton, p.340; Wood, p.133
36. Stenton, p.340
37. Wood, p.134
38. Stenton, p.340 William, p.133
39. Wood, p.133
40. William, p.133
41. *Ibid.*
42. *Ibid.*
43. Quoted in Wood, p.138
44. Wood, p.137
45. Wood, p.134; William, p.134
46. Stenton, p.341. Hywel Dda is also said to have issued a set of laws, still named after him; however as they survive in a 13th-century collection, it is not certain how many of the laws ascribed to him are actually his. However, it was probably 'the English conception of the king as legislator' which first inspired him to start this codification of Welsh customary law—*Dark Age Dict.*, p.156; Stenton, p.341
47. William, p.134
48. Stenton, p.340. Outraged 'Welsh reaction to it appears in the contemporary poem "Armes Prydein"'. (Wood, p.135) This poem, also known as *The Prophecy of Britain*, appears to have been composed in Dyfed in the 930s or 940s and calls for a war in which all the British (Celtic) peoples and the Scandinavians of Dublin, were to drive the Saxons out of 'the Isle of Britain'. (*Dark Age Dict.*, p.156; MacKillop, James, *Dictionary of Celtic Mythology*, Oxford, 1998, p.22); Wood, p.135
49. Stenton, p.341
50. Wood, p.135
51. *Ibid.*
52. *Ibid.*, p.136
53. *Ibid.*, p.136-7
54. Matthew, p.466
55. Stenton, p.347
56. *Ibid.*, p.348-9
57. *Ibid.*, p.349, 360
58. Wood, p.136
59. Whitelock, 12, no.35, p.384
60. Wood, p.138
61. Quote in Wood, p.139
62. Whitelock, 14, no.35, p.384
63. *Ibid.*, 14, 14.1 & 14.2, no.35, p.384; Wood, p.139
64. Ashley, p.475
65. Wood, p.140
66. See Higham, in *Ang. Sax. Ency.* p.137
67. Wood, p.140
68. *Ibid.*, p.143
69. Florence, p.97
70. Wood, p.144
71. *Ibid.*, p.144-5
72. William of Malmesbury, in Whitelock, no.8, pp.282-3
73. *Ibid.*, p.283
74. Wood, p.145
75. William of Malmesbury, in Whitelock, no.8, p.283
76. Simeon of Durham, in Whitelock, no.3, p.253 & footnote
77. *Ang. Sax. Ency.*, p.55. Ashley (p.475) suggests a site near Nottingham and Wood (p.145) suggests it may have been among the frontier forts in the Don valley in Yorkshire
78. ASC in Whitelock, p.200. The poem occurs in manuscripts A, B, C and D of the *Anglo Saxon Chronicle*, and is in the form of praise-song or panegyric, which is acclaimed by most critics as the best poem recorded in the *Chronicle*
79. Wood, p.146
80. ASC in Whitelock, p.201
81. *Ibid.*
82. *Ibid.*
83. Wood, p.147
84. *Ibid.*, p.131
85. William, p.140
86. Matthew, pp.469-70
87. William, p.140
88. Stenton, p.351-2
89. *Ibid.*, p.352
90. *Ibid.*, pp.349, 351
91. *Ibid.*, p.352
92. Whitelock, no.104, pp.505-8
93. Sawyer, no.396, p.168
94. *Ibid.*, no.395, p.167
95. *Ibid.*, nos.411 & 413, p.171
96. *Dark Age Dict.*, p.126
97. Sean Miller, in *Ang. Sax. Ency.*, p.159; Ashley, p.476; Stenton, pp.356-7
98. Simeon of Durham, in Whitelock, p.253
99. ASC in Whitelock, p.202
100. *Ibid.*
101. Stenton, pp.358-9
102. ASC, versions A, B, C & D in Whitelock, p.202
103. William, p.141
104. Florence, p.99
105. Matthew, p.475
106. Sean Miller, in *Ang. Sax. Ency.*, p.150
107. William, p.145
108. From the *Life of St. Dunstan*, signed only 'B', quoted in William, footnote, p.145
109. William, p.145
110. Matthew, p.478
111. *Ibid.*
112. William, p.146
113. Stenton, p.366
114. *Ibid.* & footnote 2
115. Sean Miller, in *Ang. Sax. Ency.*, p.151
116. Stenton, p.365
117. *Ibid.*
118. *Dark Age Dict.*, p.51
119. *Ibid.*, p.8-9
120. *Ibid.*, p.9
121. Stenton, pp.364-5
122. *Ibid.*, p.366
123. Matthew, p.479
124. Florence, p.101

125. *Dark Age Dict.*,p.115
126. Sean Miller, in *Ang. Sax. Ency.*, p.151
127. *Ibid.*
128. Stenton, p.364 & footnote 1; *Dark Age Dict.*, p.115
129. Henry, p.174
130. Ashley, p.478
131. Sawyer, nos.675-8, pp.225-6
132. ASC in Whitelock, p.205
133. Florence, p.101
134. *Dark Age Dict.*, pp.34, 123-4
135. William, p.155
136. *Dark Age Dict.*, p.34
137. Florence, pp.103-4
138. William,p.149
139. J.A.Giles, footnote in William, p.149
140. Ashley, p.478; *Dark Age Dict.*,p.124
141. William, p.159
142. *Ibid.*, p160
143. *Ibid.*, p.158
144. Whitelock, introductory notes to no.109, p.514
145. *Ibid.*, introductory notes to no.113, p.519
146. Stenton, p.371
147. Whitelock, no.41, Edgar's code issued at 'Wihtbordesstan' (IV Edgar, 962-963), pp.399-400
148. *Ibid.*, introductory notes, p.398 & pp.400-1
149. Florence, p.106

150. Stenton, p.368
151. *Dark Age Dict.*, p.124
152. ASC in Whitelock, p.208
153. *Ibid.*
154. *Dark Age Dict.*, p.22
155. Sean Miller, in *Ang. Sax. Ency.*, p.159
156. *Dark Age Dict.*, p.128
157. *Ibid.*
158. Florence, p.106
159. *Dark Age Dict.*, p.10
160. ASC in Whitelock, p.209
161. *Ibid.*
162. *Ibid.*
163. Matthew, p.486
164. Florence, p.106
165. Whitelock, introductory notes to no.236, p.839
166. *Ibid.*, p.839-40
167. Florence, p.106
168. William, p.163; ASC, versions D & E, in Whitelock, p.210
169. Sawyer, nos.828-9, p.261
170. Finberg, (1972), nos.305-312, pp.118-20
171. Matthew, p.487
172. William, p.163
173. Whitelock, no.236, p.841
174. *Dark Age Dict.*, p.129

Index